Steck-Vaughn

GED

MATHEMATICS

P9-DGT-577

PROGRAM CONSULTANTS

Liz Anderson, Director of Adult Education/Skills Training
Northwest Shoals Community College
Muscle Shoals, Alabama

Mary Ann Corley, Ph.D., Director
Lindy Boggs National Center for Community Literacy
Loyola University New Orleans
New Orleans, Louisiana

Nancy Dunlap, Adult Education Coordinator
Northside Independent School District
San Antonio, Texas

Roger M. Hansard, Director of Adult Education
CCARE Learning Center
Tazewell, Tennessee

Nancy Lawrence, M.A.
Education and Curriculum Consultant
Butler, Pennsylvania

Pat L. Taylor, STARS Consultant for GEDTS
Adult Education/GED Programs
Mesa, Arizona

STECK-VAUGHN
ELEMENTARY · SECONDARY · ADULT · LIBRARY

A Harcourt Company

www.steck-vaughn.com

Acknowledgments

Executive Editor: Ellen Northcutt

Supervising Editor: Julie Higgins

Associate Director of Design: Cynthia Ellis

Designers: Rusty Kaim
                    Katie Nott

Media Researcher: Sarah Fraser

Editorial Development: Learning Unlimited, Oak Park, Illinois

Production Development: LaurelTech

Photography: Cover: (building) ©Superstock; (scale) ©Gary Hush/Stone; (graph/pie chart) ©VCG/FPG International; p.32 ©CORBIS; p.162 ©Superstock; p.208 ©CORBIS; p.272 ©David Young-Wolff/PhotoEdit.

ISBN 0-7398-2835-5

Contents

To the Learner 1
What Are the GED Tests? 1
Why Should You Take the GED Tests? 4
How to Prepare for the GED Tests 4
What You Need to Know to Pass Test Five:
   Mathematics 5
The Mathematics Test Items 7
Test-Taking Skills 9
Study Skills 10
Taking the Test 12
Using this Book 12

Pretest 13
Pretest Performance Analysis Charts 30
Study Planner 31

**Unit 1: Numbers and
Operations** 32
Lesson 1 34
Number and Operation Sense 34
Choosing the Operation 38

Lesson 2 42
Operations with Whole Numbers 42
Step-by-Step Problem-Solving 46
Basic Calculator Functions 48
GED Mini-Test Lessons 1 and 2 50

Lesson 3 52
Steps for Solving Word Problems 52
Writing in Answers in a Standard Grid . . . 56

Lesson 4 58
Steps for Solving Multi-Step Problems 58
Setting-Up Problems 62
Order of Operations 64
GED Mini-Test Lessons 3 and 4 66

Lesson 5 70
Introduction to Fractions 70
Choosing the Operation 74

Lesson 6 78
Fractions, Ratios, and Proportions 78
Writing Fractions in a Standard Grid 86

Lesson 7 88
Operations with Fractions 88
Estimating with Fractions 96
Writing Fractions in a Standard Grid 98
GED Mini-Test Lessons 5–7 100

Lesson 8 104
Introduction to Decimals 104
Estimation and Money 108

Lesson 9 112
Operations with Decimals 112
Solving Multi-Step Problems 116
Writing Decimals in a Standard Grid 118

Lesson 10 120
Decimals and Fractions 120
Using Decimals & Fractions in a
   Standard Grid 124
Fractions and Decimals 126
GED Mini-Test Lessons 8–10 128

Lesson 11 132
The Meaning of Percent 132
Using Proportions with Percents 136

Lesson 12 138
Solving Percent Problems (Part 1) 138
Using Mental Math 142

Lesson 13 144
Solving Percent Problems (Part 2) 144
Solving Multi-Step Problems 148
Calculators and Percents 150
GED Mini-Test Lessons 11–13 152

Unit 1 Cumulative Review 156
Unit 1: Performance Analysis 161

**Unit 2: Measurement and
Data Analysis** 162
Lesson 14 164
Measurement Systems 164

Lesson 15 170
Measuring Common Figures 170
Choosing Perimeter, Area, or Volume 176
Drawing a Picture 178
GED Mini-Test Lessons 14 and 15 180

Lesson 16 184
Measures of Central Tendency and
    Probability 184
Mean and Median 190

Lesson 17 192
Tables, Charts, and Graphs 192
GED Mini-Test Lessons 16 and 17 198

Unit 2 Cumulative Review 202
Unit 2 Performance Analysis 207

Unit 3: Algebra 208
Lesson 18 210
Integers and Algebraic Expressions 210
Using Number Lines 218

Lesson 19 220
Equations 220
Translating Problems into Equations 224
Using Distance and Cost Formulas 228
GED Mini-Test Lessons 18 and 19 230

Lesson 20 234
Exponents and Roots 234
Working Backwards 238
Applying Patterns and Functions 240

Lesson 21 242
Factoring and Inequalities 242
Solving Quadratic Equations 246

Lesson 22 250
The Coordinate Plane 250
Plotting Ordered Pairs 252
Finding the Equation of a Line 260
GED Mini-Test Lessons 20–22 262

Unit 3 Cumulative Review 266
Unit 3 Performance Analysis 271

Unit 4: Geometry 272
Lesson 23 274
Applying Formulas 274
Converting Measurements 282
Solving for Variables in Formulas 284

Lesson 24 286
Lines and Angles 286
Using Logical Reasoning 292
GED Mini-Test Lessons 23 and 24 294

Lesson 25 298
Triangles and Quadrilaterals 298
Using Proportion in Geometry 306

Lesson 26 308
Irregular Figures 308

Lesson 27 312
Working with Right Triangles 312
Recognizing Applications of the
    Pythagorean Relationship 314
GED Mini-Test Lessons 25–27 320

Unit 4 Cumulative Review 324
Unit 4 Performance Analysis 331

Posttest 332
Posttest Performance Analysis Charts 349

Simulated Test 350
Simulated Test Performance
    Analysis Charts 367

Answers and Explanations 368

Glossary 460

Index 466

Calculator Handbook 469

Answer Sheets 473

What Are the GED Tests?

You have taken a big step in your life by deciding to take the GED Tests. By the time that you have opened this book, you have made a second important decision: to put in the time and effort to prepare for the tests. You may feel nervous about what is ahead, which is only natural. Relax and read the following pages to find out more about the GED Tests in general and the Mathematics Test in particular.

The GED Tests are the five tests of General Educational Development. The GED Testing Service of the American Council on Education makes them available to adults who did not graduate from high school. When you pass the GED Tests, you will receive a certificate that is regarded as equivalent to a high school diploma. Employers in private industry and government, as well as admissions officers in colleges and universities, accept the GED certificate as they would a high school diploma.

The GED Tests cover the same subjects that people study in high school. The five subject areas include: Language Arts, Writing and Language Arts, Reading (which, together, are equivalent to high school English), Social Studies, Science, and Mathematics. You will not be required to know all the information that is usually taught in high school. However, across the five tests you will be tested on your ability to read and process information, solve problems, and communicate effectively. Some of the states in the U.S. also require a test on the U.S. Constitution or on state government. Check with your local adult education center to see if your state requires such a test.

Each year more than 800,000 people take the GED Tests. Of those completing the test battery, 70 percent earn their GED certificates. The *Steck-Vaughn GED Series* will help you pass the GED Tests by providing instruction and practice in the skill areas needed to pass, practice with test items like those found on the GED Test, test-taking tips, timed-test practice, and evaluation charts to help track your progress.

There are five separate GED Tests. The chart on page 2 gives you information on the content, number of items, and time limit for each test. Because states have different requirements for how many tests you take in a day or testing period, you need to check with your local adult education center for the requirements in your state, province, or territory.

The Tests of General Educational Development

Test	Content Areas	Items	Time Limit
Language Arts, Writing, Part I	Organization 15% Sentence Structure 30% Usage 30% Mechanics 25%	50 questions	75 minutes
Language Arts, Writing, Part II	Essay	about 250 words	45 minutes
Social Studies	U.S. History 25% World History 15% Civics and Government 25% Geography 15% Economics 20%	50 questions	80 minutes
Science	Life Science 45% Earth and Space Science 20% Physical Science 35%	50 questions	80 minutes
Language Arts, Reading	Nonfiction Texts 25% Literary Texts 75% • Prose Fiction • Poetry • Drama	40 questions	65 minutes

Mathematics	Number Operations
	  and Number Sense 25%
	Measurement and
	  Geometry 25%
	Data Analysis, Statistics,
	  and Probability 25%
	Algebra 25%
		Part I: 25 questions with optional use of a calculator
		Part II: 25 questions without a calculator
			90 minutes

In addition to these content areas, you will be asked to answer items based on business- and consumer-related texts across all five tests. These do not require any specialized knowledge, but will ask you to draw upon your own observations and life experiences.

The Language Arts, Reading, Social Studies, and Science Tests will ask you to answer questions by interpreting reading passages, diagrams, charts and graphs, maps, cartoons, and practical and historical documents.

The Language Arts, Writing Test will ask you to detect and correct common errors in Edited American English as well as decide on the most effective organization of text. The Essay portion of the Writing Test will ask you to write an essay offering your opinion or an explanation on a single topic of general knowledge.

The Mathematics Test will ask you to solve a variety of word problems, many with graphics, using basic computation, analytical, and reasoning skills.

GED Scores

After you complete each GED Test, you will receive a score for that test. Once you have completed all five GED Tests, you will receive a total score. The total score is an average of all the other scores. The highest score possible on a single test is 800. The scores needed to pass the GED vary depending on where you live. Contact your local adult education center for the minimum passing scores for your state, province, or territory.

Where Can You Go to Take the GED Tests?

The GED Tests are offered year-round throughout the United States and its possessions, on U.S. military bases worldwide, and in Canada. To find out when and where tests are held near you, contact the GED Hot Line at 1-800-62-MY-GED (1-800-626-9433) or one of these institutions in your area:

- An adult education center
- A continuing education center
- A local community college
- A public library
- A private business school or technical school
- The public board of education

In addition, the GED Hot Line and the institutions can give you information regarding necessary identification, testing fees, writing implements, and on the scientific calculator to be used on the GED Mathematics Test. Also, check on the testing schedule at each institution; some testing centers are open several days a week, and others are open only on weekends.

Other GED Resources

- www.acenet.edu This is the official site for the GED Testing Service. Just follow the GED links throughout the site for information on the test.

- www.steckvaughn.com Follow the Adult Learners link to learn more about available GED preparation materials and gedpractice.com. This site also provides other resources for adult learners.

- www.nifl.gov/nifl/ The National Institute for Literacy's site provides information on instruction, federal policies, and national initiatives that affect adult education.

- www.doleta.gov U.S. Department of Labor's Employment and Training Administration site offers information on adult training programs.

Why Should You Take the GED Tests?

A GED certificate is widely recognized as the equivalent of a high school diploma and can help you in the following ways:

Employment

People with GED certificates have proven their determination to succeed by following through with their education. They generally have less difficulty changing jobs or moving up in their present companies. In many cases, employers will not hire someone who does not have a high school diploma or the equivalent.

Education

Many technical schools, vocational schools, or other training programs may require a high school diploma or the equivalent in order to enroll in their programs. However, to enter a college or university, you must have a high school diploma or the equivalent.

Personal Development

The most important thing is how you feel about yourself. You now have the unique opportunity to accomplish an important goal. With some effort, you can attain a GED certificate that will help you in the future and make you feel proud of yourself now.

How to Prepare for the GED Tests

Classes for GED preparation are available to anyone who wants to prepare to take the GED Tests. Most GED preparation programs offer individualized instruction and tutors who can help you identify areas in which you may need help. Many adult education centers offer free day or night classes. The classes are usually informal and allow you to work at your own pace and with other adults who also are studying for the GED Tests.

If you prefer to study by yourself, the *Steck-Vaughn GED Series* has been developed to guide your study through skill instruction and practice exercises. *Steck-Vaughn GED Exercise* books and www.gedpractice.com are also available to provide you with additional practice for each test. In addition to working on specific skills, you will be able to take practice GED Tests (like those in this book) in order to check your progress. For information about classes available near you, contact one of the resources in the list on page 3.

What You Need to Know to Pass
Test Five: Mathematics

The GED Mathematics Test focuses on the practical use of number operations and number sense; measurement and data analysis, statistics, and probability; algebra, functions, and patterns; and geometry. Each content area will account for approximately 25 percent of the items on the test. You will be tested on your understanding of how to solve a problem and on your ability to do the mathematical computations to find a solution.

The test takes 90 minutes and has 50 problems divided into two parts of 25 problems each. Both parts contain problems addressing all four content areas. For Part I you will be allowed to use a calculator that will be issued to you at the test site for your use. When you complete Part I, you will turn in the calculator and continue the test, answering items in Part II without its use.

Approximately 20 percent of the test will entail entering your answer on one of the two alternate answer formats—a standard grid and a coordinate grid. Each part of the test contains directions on the use of these "bubble-in" formats.

In addition to items that require you to solve the problem, other items ask you to show *how* you would solve (set up) the problem. These set-up items test how well you can find the correct approach to solving a problem.

Some items will test your ability to do the basic mathematics operations: addition, subtraction, multiplication, and division. Others will test mathematical concepts such as ratio and proportion, estimation, and formulas. You will be provided a formulas page for each part of the test. The formulas page includes all the formulas you will need to take the test.

The GED Mathematics Test requires you to use and apply your knowledge of mathematics in both mathematical problems and real world situations reflecting practical, everyday tasks. You will also be expected to demonstrate analytical and reasoning skills and be able to read and interpret mathematical context in both written and graphic forms. Approximately 50 percent of the test items on both parts will involve graphics in the form of drawings, diagrams, charts, and graphs.

The following information summarizes the content areas and concepts tested on the GED Mathematics Test.

Number Operations and Number Sense

Items from this content area will test your ability to work problems involving whole numbers, fractions, decimals, and percents and the use of ratios and proportions. You must to be able to represent and use numbers in a variety of equivalent forms, compare numbers and draw conclusions, and relate the basic arithmetic operations to each other, use them in the proper order of operations, and perform computations both with and without a calculator.

Measurement and Data Analysis, Statistics, and Probability

Measurement items test your ability to use basic math skills in items about length, perimeter and circumference, area, volume, and time. You will need to understand both the customary U.S. measurement system and the metric system and be able to make conversions in each system. Some measurement items test less commonly used concepts such as square roots, exponents, and scientific notation.

Data analysis items test your ability to use information presented in tables, charts, and bar, line, and circle graphs. You will be asked to decide which pieces of information you need to solve the problem, locate the information, and work the problem. You may also be asked to find the mean (average), median, mode, or range of a set of data and the probability that a given event will occur.

Algebra, Functions, and Patterns

Algebra items will test your understanding of variables in tables, equations, and written descriptions and your ability to use algebraic symbols and expressions and to write and solve algebraic equations.

Some items will require the use of the formulas page. You will be asked to show how to solve for any variable within a formula. Percent, ratio, and proportion will also be applied to algebra items. A few items may include powers and roots, factoring, solving inequalities, graphing equations, and finding the slope of a line.

Algebra items also test your understanding of the coordinate grid and ordered pairs. The new coordinate grid alternative answer format requires that you indicate your answer by bubbling in the location of the ordered pair.

Geometry

Geometry items test your understanding of lines and angles, triangles and quadrilaterals, and indirect measurement. You will use the basic arithmetic operations to find values of angles and line segments in both common and irregular figures. Indirect measurement items require an understanding of congruence, similarity, and the Pythagorean Relationship and may involve the concepts of perimeter, circumference, area, and volume.

The Mathematics Test Items

1. Which of the following expressions can be used to find the area of a rectangle that is 8 feet long and 5 feet wide?

   (1) $A = 2(8) - 2(5)$
   (2) $A = 2(8) + 2(5)$
   (3) $A = 8^2$
   (4) $A = \frac{1}{2}(8)(5)$
   (5) $A = (8)(5)$

Answer: **(5) $A = (8)(5)$**

Explanation: This is an example of an item that tests the topic of measurement. To solve this item, you must know which formula to select from the formulas page that accompanies the test. Then you must select the one option that uses tho information from the problem correctly in the formula. Since the formula for finding the area of a rectangle is $A = lw$, where l = length and w = width, option (5) $A = (8)(5)$ is the correct answer.

2. The square root of 150 is between which of the following pairs of numbers?

   (1) 10 and 11
   (2) 11 and 12
   (3) 12 and 13
   (4) 13 and 14
   (5) 14 and 15

Answer: **(3) 12 and 13**

Explanation: This item is an example of an item that tests the topic of number relationships. This item tests your understanding of square roots. Note that the item is not asking you to find the exact square root of 150, but rather is testing your ability to estimate the square root.

3. Approximately how many times more money does the Cortez family spend on entertainment than it spends on utilities?

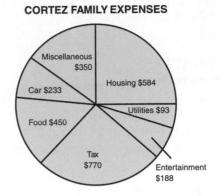

CORTEZ FAMILY EXPENSES

   (1) 2
   (2) 3
   (3) 5
   (4) 6
   (5) 8

Answer: **(1) 2**

Explanation: This is an example of an item that tests the topic of data analysis. To find the information you need to solve the item, you must be able to read the circle graph. Then you can compare either the amounts from the graph or sectors on the graph. The entertainment sector is approximately twice as large as the utilities sector: $188 is approximately twice $93.

4. If cartons of strawberries are priced at 3 for $1.00, how much would 60 cartons of strawberries cost?

    (1) $15
    (2) $18
    (3) $20
    (4) $40
    (5) $60

Answer: **(3) $20**

Explanation: This is an example of an algebra item. The item tests your ability to apply the concept of ratio and proportion. To find the correct answer, you must set up and solve an equation.

$$\frac{3}{\$1} = \frac{60}{x}$$
$$3x = \$60$$
$$x = \frac{\$60}{3}$$
$$x = \$20$$

5. An insurance company estimates that 75 out of every 100 renters do not have any insurance on their personal belongings. What fraction is this?

Mark your answer in the circles in the grid on your answer sheet.

Answer: Remember to reduce your answer to the lowest terms. $\frac{75}{100} = \frac{3}{4}$

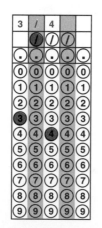

6. If angles 1 and 2 in triangle *ABC* are each 60 degree angles, what is the measure of angle 3?

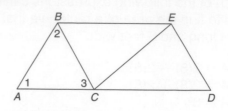

    (1) 180 degrees
    (2) 120 degrees
    (3) 90 degrees
    (4) 60 degrees
    (5) 45 degrees

Answer: **(4) 60 degrees**

Explanation: This is an example of a geometry item. To answer this item, you need to know that the measures of the angles of a triangle sum to 180 degrees. Add the two known angles (60 + 60 = 120) and subtract from 180: 180 − 120 = 60 degrees.

7. Show the location of the point whose coordinates are (5,3).

Mark your answer on the coordinate plane grid on your answer sheet.

Answer: Remember that the ordered pair is always written with the *x*-coordinate first and the *y*-coordinate second. Start at the origin (0,0). Move 5 units to the right along the *x*-axis, and move up 3 units along the *y*-axis.

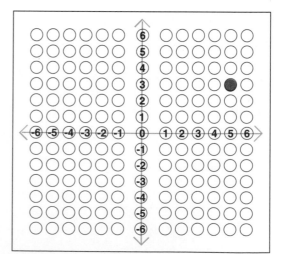

Test-Taking Skills

The GED *Mathematics Test* will test your ability to apply your conceptual and computational mathematics skills. This book will help you prepare for this test. In addition, there are some specific ways that you can improve your performance on the test.

Answering the Test Items

- Never skim the directions. Read them carefully so that you know exactly what to do. If you are unsure, ask the test-giver if the directions can be explained.

- Read each question carefully to make sure that you know what it is asking.

- Read all of the answer options carefully, even if you think you know the right answer. Some of the answers may not seem wrong at first glance, but one answer will be the correct one.

- Before you answer a question, be sure that there is evidence in the problem to support your choice. Don't rely on what you know outside the context of the problem.

- Answer all the items. If you cannot find the correct answer, reduce the number of possible answers by eliminating all the answers you know are wrong. Then go back to the passage to figure out the correct answer. If you still cannot decide, make your best guess.

- Fill in your answer sheet carefully. To record your answers, mark one numbered space on the answer sheet beside the number that corresponds to the item. Mark only one answer space for each item; multiple answers will be scored as incorrect.

- Remember that the GED is a timed test. When the test begins, write down the time you have to finish. Then keep an eye on the time. Do not take a long time on any one item. Answer each item as best you can and go on. If you are spending a lot of time on one item, skip it, making a very light mark next to the item number on the sheet. If you finish before time is up, go back to the items you skipped or were unsure of and give them more thought. (Be sure to erase any extraneous marks you have made.)

- Don't change an answer unless you are certain your answer was wrong. Usually the first answer you choose is the correct one.

- If you feel that you are getting nervous, stop working for a moment. Take a few deep breaths and relax. Then begin working again.

Study Skills

Study Regularly

- If you can, set aside an hour to study every day. If you do not have time every day, set up a schedule of the days you can study. Be sure to pick times when you will be the most relaxed and least likely to be bothered by outside distractions.

- Let others know your study time. Ask them to leave you alone for that period. It helps if you explain to others why this is important.

- You should be relaxed when you study, so find an area that is comfortable for you. If you cannot study at home, go to the library. Most public libraries have areas for reading and studying. If there is a college or university near you, find out if you can use its library. All libraries have dictionaries, encyclopedias, and other resources you can use if you need more information while you're studying.

Organize Your Study Materials

- Be sure to have pens, sharp pencils, and paper for any notes you might want to take.

- Keep all of your books together. If you are taking an adult education class, you probably will be able to borrow some books or other study material.

- Make a notebook or folder for each subject you are studying. Folders with pockets are useful for storing loose papers.

- Keep all of your materials in one place so you do not waste time looking for them each time you study.

Take Notes

- Take notes on things that interest you or things that you think might be useful.

- When you take notes, do not copy the words directly from the book. Restate the information in your own words.

- Take notes any way you want. You do not have to write in full sentences as long as you can understand your notes later.

- Use outlines, charts, or diagrams to help you organize information and make it easier to learn.

- You may want to take notes in a question-and-answer form, such as: *What is the main idea? The main idea is . . .*

ISD # 347
Community Education & Recreation
325 Willmar Ave. SW
Willmar, MN 56201
ADDRESS SERVICE REQUESTED

Improve Your Vocabulary

- As you read, do not skip a word you do not know. Instead, try to figure out what the word means. First, omit it from the sentence. Read the sentence without the word and try to put another word in its place. Is the meaning of the sentence the same?

- Make a list of unfamiliar words, look them up in the dictionary, and write down the meanings.

- Since a word may have several meanings, it is best to look up the word while you have the passage with you. Then you can try out the different meanings in the context.

- When you read the definition of a word, restate it in your own words. Use the word in a sentence or two.

- Use the Glossary at the end of this book to review the meanings of the key terms. All of the words you see in **boldface** type are defined in the Glossary. In addition, definitions of other important words are included. Use this list to review important vocabulary for the content areas you are studying.

Make a List of Areas that Give You Trouble

As you go through this book, make a note whenever you do not understand something. Then ask your teacher or another person for help. Later go back and review the topic.

Taking the Test

Before the Test

- If you have never been to the test center, go there the day before you take the test. If you drive, find out where to park.

- Prepare the things you need for the test: your admission ticket (if necessary), acceptable identification, some sharpened No. 2 pencils with erasers, a watch, glasses, a jacket or sweater (in case the room is cold), and a snack to eat during breaks.

- Get a good night's sleep. If the test is early in the morning, set the alarm.

The Day of the Test

- Eat a good breakfast. Wear comfortable clothing. Make sure that you have all of the materials you need.

- Try to arrive at the test center about twenty minutes early. This allows time if, for example, there is a last-minute change of room.

- If you are going to be at the test center all day, you might pack a lunch. If you have to find a restaurant or if you wait a long time to be served, you may be late for the rest of the test.

Using this Book

- Start with the Pretest. It is identical to the real test in format and length. It will give you an idea of what the GED Mathematics Test is like. Then use the Pretest Performance Analysis Chart at the end of the test to figure out your areas of strength and the areas you need to review. The chart will refer you to units and page numbers to study. You also can use the Study Planner on page 31 to plan your work after you take the Pretest and, again, after the Posttest.

- As you study, use the Cumulative Review and the Performance Analysis Chart at the end of each unit to find out if you need to review any lessons before continuing.

- After you complete your review, use the Posttest to decide if you are ready for the real GED Test. The Performance Analysis Chart will tell you if you need additional review. Then use the Simulated Test and its Performance Analysis Chart as a final check of your test readiness.

MATHEMATICS
Part I

Directions

The Mathematics Pretest consists of multiple-choice and alternate format questions intended to measure your general mathematical skills and problem-solving ability. The questions are based on short readings that often include a graph, chart, or diagram.

You will have 90 minutes to complete the 50 questions on Parts I and II. Work carefully, but do not spend too much time on any one question. Be sure to answer every question. You will not be penalized for incorrect answers. When time is up, mark the last item you finished. This will tell you whether you can finish the real GED Test in the time allowed. Then complete the test.

Formulas you may need are given on page 16. Only some of the questions will require you to use a formula. Not all the formulas given will be needed.

Some questions contain more information than you will need to solve the problem; other questions do not give enough information. If the question does not give enough information to solve the problem, the correct answer choice is "Not enough information is given."

You may use a calculator on Part I. Calculator directions for the CASIO *fx-260SOLAR* scientific calculator can be found on page 15.

Record your answers on a copy of the separate answer sheet provided on page 473. Be sure all required information is properly recorded on the answer sheet.

To record your answers, mark the numbered space on the answer sheet that corresponds to the answer you select for each question on the test.

Example: If a grocery bill totaling $15.75 is paid with a $20.00 bill, how much change should be returned?

(1) $5.25
(2) $4.75
(3) $4.25
(4) $3.75
(5) $3.25   ① ② ● ④ ⑤

The correct answer is $4.25; therefore, answer space 3 would be marked on the answer sheet.

Do not rest the point of your pencil on the answer sheet while you are considering your answer. Make no stray or unnecessary marks. If you change an answer, erase your first mark completely. Mark only one answer for each question; multiple answers will be scored as incorrect. Do not fold or crease your answer sheet.

When you finish the test, use the Performance Analysis Chart on page 30 to determine whether you are ready to take the real GED Test, and, if not, which skill areas need additional review.

Adapted with permission of the American Council on Education.

MATHEMATICS

Mixed numbers, such as $3\frac{1}{2}$, cannot be entered in the alternate format grid. Instead, represent them as decimal numbers (in this case, 3.5) or fractions (in this case, 7/2). No answer can be a negative number, such as -8.

To record your answer for an alternate format question

- begin in any column that will allow your answer to be entered;
- write your answer in the boxes on the top row;
- in the column beneath a fraction bar or decimal point (if any) and each number in your answer, fill in the bubble representing that character;
- leave blank any unused column.

Example:

The scale on a map indicates that $\frac{1}{2}$ inch represents an actual distance of 120 miles. In inches, how far apart on the map will two towns be if the actual distance between them is 180 miles?

The answer to the above example is 3/4, or 0.75, inches. The answer could be gridded using any of the methods below.

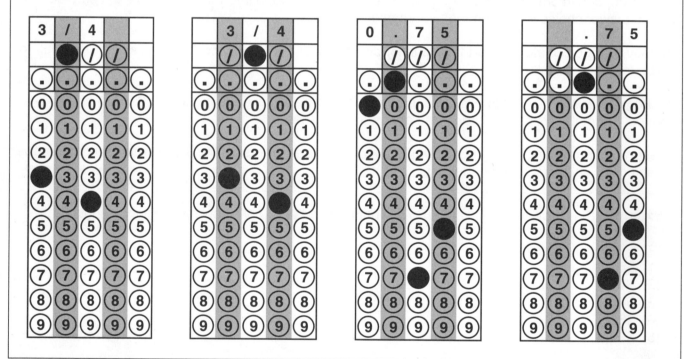

Points to remember:

- The answer sheet will be machine scored. **The circles must be filled in correctly.**
- Mark no more than one circle in any column.
- Grid only one answer even if there is more than one correct answer.
- Mixed numbers, such as $3\frac{1}{2}$, must be gridded as a decimal (3.5) or fraction (7/2).
- No answer can be a negative number.

Adapted with permission of the American Council on Education.

CALCULATOR DIRECTIONS

To prepare the calculator for use the ***first*** time, press the ⒪Ⓝ (upper-rightmost) key. "DEG" will appear at the top-center of the screen and "0." at the right. This indicates the calculator is in the proper format for all your calculations.

To prepare the calculator for ***another*** question, press the ⒪Ⓝ or the red ⒶⒸ key. This clears any entries made previously.

To do any arithmetic, enter the expression as it is written. Press ⑥ (equals sign) when finished.

EXAMPLE A: $8 - 3 + 9$

>First press ⒪Ⓝ or ⒶⒸ.
>Enter the following:
>>$8 \ominus 3 \oplus 9 \ominus$
>
>The correct answer is 14.

If an expression in parentheses is to be multiplied by a number, press ⓧ (multiplication sign) between the number and the parenthesis sign.

EXAMPLE B: $6(8 + 5)$

>First press ⒪Ⓝ or ⒶⒸ.
>Enter the following:
>>$6 \ (×) \ ([(\cdots) \ 8 \ (+) \ 5 \ (\cdots)]) \ (=)$
>
>The correct answer is 78.

To find the square root of a number

>- enter the number;
>- press ⓈⒽⒾⒻⓉ (upper-leftmost) key ("SHIFT" appears at the top-left of the screen);
>- press (x^2) (third from the left on top row) to access its second function: square root.
> **DO NOT** press ⓈⒽⒾⒻⓉ and (x^2) at the same time.

EXAMPLE C: $\sqrt{64}$

>First press ⒪Ⓝ or ⒶⒸ.
>Enter the following:
>>$64 \ (SHIFT) \ (x^2)$
>
>The correct answer is 8.

To enter a negative number such as –8,

>- enter the number without the negative sign (enter 8);
>- press the "change sign" ($(+/-)$) key which is directly above the 7 key.

All arithmetic can be done with positive and/or negative numbers.

EXAMPLE D: $-8 - -5$

>First press ⒪Ⓝ or ⒶⒸ.
>Enter the following:
>>$8 \ (+/-) \ (-) \ 5 \ (+/-) \ (=)$
>
>The correct answer is –3.

FORMULAS

AREA of a:

square	Area = side^2
rectangle	Area = length × width
parallelogram	Area = base × height
triangle	Area = $\frac{1}{2}$ × base × height
trapezoid	Area = $\frac{1}{2}$ × (base$_1$ + base$_2$) × height
circle	Area = π × radius^2; π is approximately equal to 3.14

PERIMETER of a:

square	Perimeter = 4 × side
rectangle	Perimeter = 2 × length + 2 × width
triangle	Perimeter = side$_1$ + side$_2$ + side$_3$

CIRCUMFERENCE of a circle — Circumference = π × diameter; π is approximately equal to 3.14

VOLUME of a:

cube	Volume = edge^3
rectangular container	Volume = length × width × height
square pyramid	Volume = $\frac{1}{3}$ × (base edge)^2 × height
cylinder	Volume = π × radius^2 × height; π is approximately equal to 3.14
cone	Volume = $\frac{1}{3}$ × π × radius^2 × height; π is approximately equal to 3.14

COORDINATE GEOMETRY

distance between points = $\sqrt{(x_2 - x_1)^2 + (y_2 - y_1)^2}$; (x_1, y_1) and (x_2, y_2) are two points in a plane.

slope of a line = $\frac{y_2 - y_1}{x_2 - x_1}$; (x_1, y_1) and (x_2, y_2) are two points on a line.

PYTHAGOREAN RELATIONSHIP

$a^2 + b^2 = c^2$; a and b are legs and c the hypotenuse of a right triangle.

MEASURES OF CENTRAL TENDENCY

mean = $\frac{x_1 + x_2 + \ldots + x_n}{n}$; where the x's are the values for which a mean is desired, and n is the total number of values for x.

median = the middle value of an odd number of _ordered_ scores, and halfway between the two middle values of an even number of _ordered_ scores.

SIMPLE INTEREST — interest = principal × rate × time

DISTANCE — distance = rate × time

TOTAL COST — total cost = (number of units) × (price per unit)

Adapted with permission of the American Council on Education.

Part I

Directions: Choose the one best answer to each question. You MAY use your calculator.

Questions 1 and 2 refer to the following information.

AVERAGE DAILY PARK ATTENDANCE

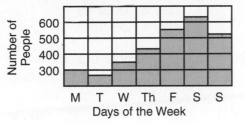

1. Approximately how many more people visit the park on Saturdays than on Mondays?

   (1) 210

   (2) 320

   (3) 410

   (4) 620

   (5) 920

2. The park rules require that one security guard be on duty for every 50 people who visit the park. How many guards should be on duty each Friday?

   (1) 5

   (2) 11

   (3) 15

   (4) 18

   (5) Not enough information is given.

3. The Baskins pay 9.4 cents for each kilowatt-hour of electricity they use. Their electric bill for one month is $42.30. About how many kilowatt-hours of electricity did the Baskins use during the month?

   (1) fewer than 360

   (2) between 360 and 420

   (3) between 420 and 480

   (4) between 480 and 540

   (5) more than 540

Question 4 refers to the following diagram.

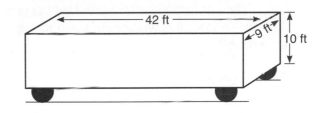

4. The freight inside the freight car takes up 3000 cubic feet. In cubic feet, what volume of the freight car is empty space?

   Mark your answer in the circles in the grid on your answer sheet.

5. What is the value of the expression below?

   $6 + 27 \div (5 - 2)$

   Mark your answer in the circles in the grid on your answer sheet.

Questions 6 and 7 refer to the following information.

A furniture store sells five styles of table lamps. The chart below shows the wholesale price (the cost to the store) and the retail price (the cost to the consumer).

Style	Wholesale Price	Retail Price
A	$32.00	$45.00
B	$16.80	$24.90
C	$34.00	$41.80
D	$23.00	$28.90
E	$56.50	$74.50

6. Which style of lamp has the greatest percent of increase from the wholesale price to the retail price?

   (1) A
   (2) B
   (3) C
   (4) D
   (5) E

7. The store's profit (P) can be found by using the function $P = n(r - w)$, where n = the number of items, r = the retail price of the item, and w = the wholesale price of the item.

   A hotel buys eight lamps of Style D. What is the store's profit on the sale?

   (1) $231.20
   (2) $184.00
   (3) $ 51.90
   (4) $ 47.20
   (5) $ 5.90

8. At an appliance store, employees who average at least 20 sales per day for five days earn a bonus. Joel has the following numbers of sales during a four-day period.

   Day 1–15 sales
   Day 2–22 sales
   Day 3–18 sales
   Day 4–26 sales

   What is the least number of sales that Joel needs on Day 5 in order to earn a bonus?

   (1) 31
   (2) 24
   (3) 19
   (4) 17
   (5) Not enough information is given.

9. A baseball team won 22 of the first 40 games it played. If the team's wins and losses continue at the same rate, how many games will the team win during a 162-game season?

   (1) 55
   (2) 68
   (3) 81
   (4) 89
   (5) 111

10. Vanya needs $3\frac{3}{8}$ yards of fabric to make a vest. What is the greatest number of vests she can make from $17\frac{1}{2}$ yards of fabric?

    (1) 4
    (2) 5
    (3) 6
    (4) 7
    (5) Not enough information is given.

Question 11 refers to the following figure.

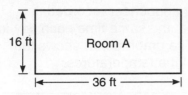

16 ft | Room A
36 ft

11. Room B has the same area as Room A, shown above. If Room B is square, what is the length in feet of each of its sides?

(1) 16
(2) 23
(3) 24
(4) 26
(5) 36

12. The repairs to Barbara's car will cost $875 for labor and $1400 for new parts. Used parts cost 60 percent less than new parts. If Barbara asks for used parts, what will be the total cost of her repairs?

Mark your answer in the circles in the grid on your answer sheet.

Question 13 refers to the following drawing.

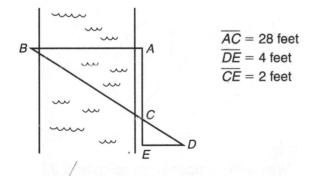

$\overline{AC}$ = 28 feet
$\overline{DE}$ = 4 feet
$\overline{CE}$ = 2 feet

13. To find the width of the river, a surveyor made the measurements shown in the drawing. Lines *AB* and *DE* are parallel. What is the width in feet of $\overline{AB}$, the shortest distance across the river?

Mark your answer in the circles in the grid on your answer sheet.

14. The 48 employees of Young Construction Company were given a choice of three different retirement plans. If twice as many employees chose Plan A as chose Plan B, how many employees chose Plan B?

(1) 12
(2) 16
(3) 24
(4) 32
(5) Not enough information is given.

15. Specialty Graphics uses 3 cartons of copier paper every 5 days. Which equation could be used to find out how many days (*d*) it will take the company to use 18 cartons of paper?

(1) $\dfrac{5(18)}{3} = d$

(2) $\dfrac{3(5)}{18} = d$

(3) $5(3d) = 18$

(4) $\dfrac{3(18)}{d} = 5$

(5) $5(18)(3) = d$

16. Max's company requires him to record the exact time that he starts and ends each repair job. On one job, he worked from 10:50 A.M. to 11:26 A.M. What fraction of an hour did he spend on the repair?

(1) $\dfrac{1}{36}$

(2) $\dfrac{1}{10}$

(3) $\dfrac{3}{5}$

(4) $\dfrac{5}{8}$

(5) $\dfrac{2}{3}$

17. Two lines intersect at a point with coordinates of (−4,2). Show the location of the point.

Mark your answer on the coordinate plane grid on your answer sheet.

18. Boxes A and B are cubes. Each side of Box A measures 2 feet. The sides of Box B are twice the length of the sides of Box A. Which of the following is a true statement about the volume of the boxes?

(1) The volume of Box A is $\frac{1}{6}$ the volume of Box B.

(2) The volume of Box A is $\frac{1}{2}$ the volume of Box B.

(3) The volumes of the boxes are equal.

(4) The volume of Box B is four times the volume of Box A.

(5) The volume of Box B is eight times the volume of Box A.

19. Stuart is planning a trip from San Francisco to Kansas City, a distance of 1860 miles. What is the average (mean) number of miles Stuart must drive each day to complete the trip in 5 days?

(1) 304

(2) 310

(3) 372

(4) 426

(5) 460

20. Which of the following inequalities is represented by the graph shown below?

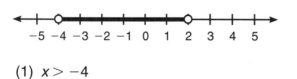

(1) $x > -4$

(2) $x < 2$

(3) $-4 < x < 2$

(4) $-4 < x > 2$

(5) $-4 > x > 2$

Question 21 refers to the following information.

A weather announcer recorded the temperature at the same time each day for two weeks. The graph below shows the distribution of the temperatures.

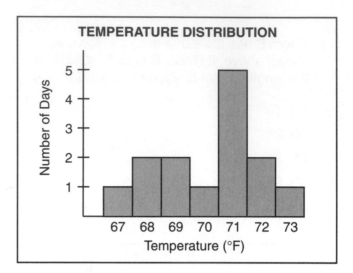

TEMPERATURE DISTRIBUTION

21. What is the median temperature in degrees for the 14-day period?

Mark your answer in the circles in the grid on your answer sheet.

_____

22. The spinner below contains eight equal sections.

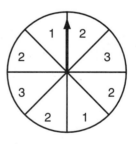

What is the probability of spinning a 2?

Mark your answer in the circles in the grid on your answer sheet.

Questions 23 and 24 refer to the following figure.

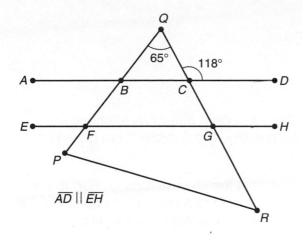

$\overline{AD} \parallel \overline{EH}$

23. What is the measure of ∠QBC?

    (1)   53°
    (2)   62°
    (3)   65°
    (4) 127°
    (5) Not enough information is given.

24. Which of the following angles is supplementary to ∠QGH?

    (1) ∠GRP
    (2) ∠QCD
    (3) ∠DCG
    (4) ∠BFG
    (5) ∠QBA

25. The area of Australia is approximately 2,940,000 square miles. How would this number be written in scientific notation?

    (1) 2.94×10^5
    (2) 2.94×10^6
    (3) 2.94×10^7
    (4) 29.4×10^5
    (5) 29.4×10^6

Answers start on page 368.

MATHEMATICS
Part II

Directions

The Mathematics Pretest consists of multiple-choice and alternate format questions intended to measure your general mathematical skills and problem-solving ability. The questions are based on short readings that often include a graph, chart, or diagram.

You will have the time remaining of the total 90 minutes to complete the 25 questions on Part II. Work carefully, but do not spend too much time on any one question. Be sure to answer every question. You will not be penalized for incorrect answers. When time is up, mark the last item you finished. This will tell you whether you can finish the real GED Test in the time allowed. Then complete the test.

Formulas you may need are given on page 24. Only some of the questions will require you to use a formula. Not all the formulas given will be needed.

Some questions contain more information than you will need to solve the problem; other questions do not give enough information. If the question does not give enough information to solve the problem, the correct answer choice is "Not enough information is given."

The use of calculators is not allowed on Part II.

Record your answers on a copy of the separate answer sheet provided on page 474. Be sure all required information is properly recorded on the answer sheet.

To record your answers, mark the numbered space on the answer sheet that corresponds to the answer you select for each question on the test.

Example: If a grocery bill totaling $15.75 is paid with a $20.00 bill, how much change should be returned?

(1) $5.25
(2) $4.75
(3) $4.25
(4) $3.75
(5) $3.25   ① ② ● ④ ⑤

The correct answer is $4.25; therefore, answer space 3 would be marked on the answer sheet.

Do not rest the point of your pencil on the answer sheet while you are considering your answer. Make no stray or unnecessary marks. If you change an answer, erase your first mark completely. Mark only one answer for each question; multiple answers will be scored as incorrect. Do not fold or crease your answer sheet.

When you finish the test, use the Performance Analysis Chart on page 30 to determine whether you are ready to take the real GED Test, and, if not, which skill areas need additional review.

Adapted with permission of the American Council on Education.

MATHEMATICS

Mixed numbers, such as $3\frac{1}{2}$, cannot be entered in the alternate format grid. Instead, represent them as decimal numbers (in this case, 3.5) or fractions (in this case, 7/2). No answer can be a negative number, such as -8.

To record your answer for an alternate format question

- begin in any column that will allow your answer to be entered;
- write your answer in the boxes on the top row;
- in the column beneath a fraction bar or decimal point (if any) and each number in your answer, fill in the bubble representing that character;
- leave blank any unused column.

Example:

The scale on a map indicates that $\frac{1}{2}$ inch represents an actual distance of 120 miles. In inches, how far apart on the map will two towns be if the actual distance between them is 180 miles?

The answer to the above example is 3/4, or 0.75, inches. The answer could be gridded using any of the methods below.

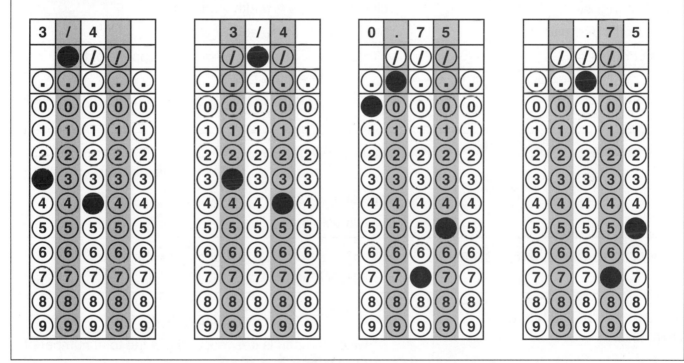

Points to remember:

- The answer sheet will be machine scored. **The circles must be filled in correctly.**
- Mark no more than one circle in any column.
- Grid only one answer even if there is more than one correct answer.
- Mixed numbers, such as $3\frac{1}{2}$, must be gridded as a decimal (3.5) or fraction (7/2).
- No answer can be a negative number.

Adapted with permission of the American Council on Education.

FORMULAS

AREA of a:

square	Area = side²
rectangle	Area = length × width
parallelogram	Area = base × height
triangle	Area = $\frac{1}{2}$ × base × height
trapezoid	Area = $\frac{1}{2}$ × (base$_1$ + base$_2$) × height
circle	Area = π × radius²; π is approximately equal to 3.14

PERIMETER of a:

square	Perimeter = 4 × side
rectangle	Perimeter = 2 × length + 2 × width
triangle	Perimeter = side$_1$ + side$_2$ + side$_3$

CIRCUMFERENCE of a circle   Circumference = π × diameter; π is approximately equal to 3.14

VOLUME of a:

cube	Volume = edge³
rectangular container	Volume = length × width × height
square pyramid	Volume = $\frac{1}{3}$ × (base edge)² × height
cylinder	Volume = π × radius² × height; π is approximately equal to 3.14
cone	Volume = $\frac{1}{3}$ × π × radius² × height; π is approximately equal to 3.14

COORDINATE GEOMETRY   distance between points = $\sqrt{(x_2 - x_1)^2 + (y_2 - y_1)^2}$; (x_1, y_1) and (x_2, y_2) are two points in a plane.

slope of a line = $\frac{y_2 - y_1}{x_2 - x_1}$; (x_1, y_1) and (x_2, y_2) are two points on a line.

PYTHAGOREAN RELATIONSHIP $a^2 + b^2 = c^2$; a and b are legs and c the hypotenuse of a right triangle.

MEASURES OF CENTRAL TENDENCY   **mean** = $\frac{x_1 + x_2 + \ldots + x_n}{n}$; where the x's are the values for which a mean is desired, and n is the total number of values for x.

median = the middle value of an odd number of _ordered_ scores, and halfway between the two middle values of an even number of _ordered_ scores.

SIMPLE INTEREST   interest = principal × rate × time

DISTANCE   distance = rate × time

TOTAL COST   total cost = (number of units) × (price per unit)

Adapted with permission of the American Council on Education.

PART II

Directions: Choose the <u>one best answer</u> to each question. You may <u>NOT</u> use your calculator.

1. The numbers 6 and 15 are factors of which of the following numbers?

    (1) 3
    (2) 15
    (3) 24
    (4) 45
    (5) 60

Question 2 refers to the following figure.

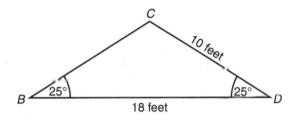

2. What is the length in feet of side *BC*?

    (1) 10
    (2) 18
    (3) 25
    (4) 28
    (5) 130

_____

3. Of the employees at Dower Industries, 75% responded to a company survey. If 120 employees answered the survey, how many employees does the company have?

    (1) 90
    (2) 150
    (3) 160
    (4) 175
    (5) 210

4. What is the perimeter of the figure?

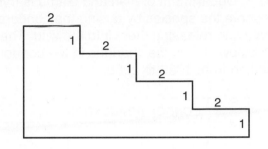

    (1) 10
    (2) 12
    (3) 20
    (4) 24
    (5) 30

5. Which point on the number line below represents the value $\frac{19}{8}$?

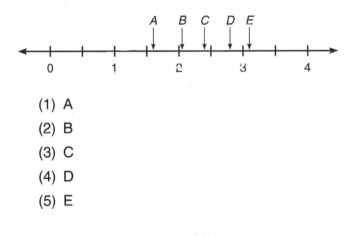

    (1) A
    (2) B
    (3) C
    (4) D
    (5) E

6. Karen has a picture that is 2 feet wide and 3 feet long. She wants to reduce the picture so that the width will be 16 inches. Find the new length, in inches, of the reduced picture.

   Mark your answer in the circles in the grid on your answer sheet.

Questions 7 and 8 are based on the following information.

The condor is an endangered species of bird. The U.S. Department of Fish and Game is trying to preserve the species by raising the condors in captivity and releasing them into the wild. The graph below shows the changes in the condor population from 1990 to 2000.

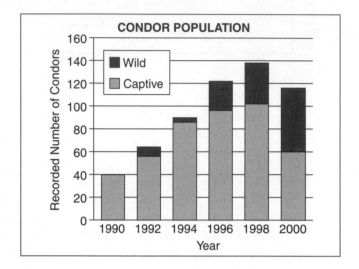

7. In which year shown was the number of condors in captivity between 90 and 100?

(1) 1994

(2) 1996

(3) 1998

(4) 2000

(5) Not enough information is given.

8. Which of the following conclusions can you draw from the information in the graph?

(1) The number of wild condors declined between 1998 and 2000.

(2) The number of wild condors increased between 1994 and 2000.

(3) The number of captive condors nearly doubled between 1996 and 1998.

(4) The number of captive condors doubled between 1990 and 2000.

(5) The number of wild condors doubled between 1992 and 1994.

9. Out of every 400 radios produced at a factory, 8 are defective. What is the probability that a radio made at this factory will be defective?

(1) $\frac{1}{8}$

(2) $\frac{1}{40}$

(3) $\frac{1}{50}$

(4) $\frac{1}{80}$

(5) $\frac{1}{150}$

Question 10 refers to the following diagram.

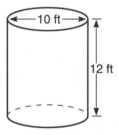

10. The water tank shown in the diagram has the shape of a cylinder. Which of the following expressions could be used to find the approximate volume of the tank in cubic feet?

(1) $3.14 \times 5^2 \times 12$

(2) $3.14 \times 10^2 \times 12$

(3) $3.14 \times 5 \times 12$

(4) $3.14 \times 12 \div 5^2$

(5) 3.14×10

11. The expression $x - (2y - 3z)$ is equal to which of the following expressions?

(1) $x - 2y - 3z$

(2) $x - 2y + 3z$

(3) $x + 2y - 3z$

(4) $x + yz$

(5) $-2xy - 3xz$

12. What are the coordinates of the *y*-intercept of the equation $y = 3x + 4$?

Mark your answer on the coordinate plane grid on your answer sheet.

Questions 13 and 14 refer to the following graph.

HOW TAKE-HOME PAY IS SPENT

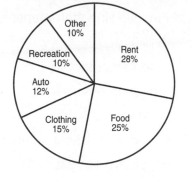

Other 10%
Rent 28%
Recreation 10%
Auto 12%
Clothing 15%
Food 25%

13. The graph above shows the Enriquez family budget. According to the graph, on which two items combined does the family spend over half of its take-home income?

    (1) auto and rent
    (2) clothing and rent
    (3) auto and food
    (4) clothing and food
    (5) food and rent

14. If the family's monthly take-home pay is $1680, how much do they spend on food and clothing per month?

    (1) $ 252
    (2) $ 420
    (3) $ 672
    (4) $1260
    (5) Not enough information is given.

15. If the area (*A*) and the base (*b*) of a triangle are known, which of the following expressions can be used to solve for height?

    (1) $\dfrac{2A}{b}$

    (2) $\dfrac{2b}{A}$

    (3) $\dfrac{b}{2A}$

    (4) $\dfrac{Ab}{2}$

    (5) $\dfrac{A}{2b}$

16. The Pizza Factory opens at 10 A.M. and serves an average of 120 customers per hour. At this rate, how many customers will the restaurant serve by 3:30 P.M.?

    (1) 396
    (2) 540
    (3) 600
    (4) 660
    (5) 780

17. Alicia borrowed $900 for two years. She paid $252 in simple interest. Which expression could be used to find the annual rate of interest she was charged?

    (1) $\dfrac{252(2)}{900}$

    (2) $\dfrac{252}{900(2)}$

    (3) $\dfrac{252(900)}{2}$

    (4) $252(900)(2)$

    (5) $\dfrac{(900)(2)}{252}$

18. Stan bought two CDs for $12.98 each. He paid $2.14 in sales tax. If he paid for the purchase with two twenty-dollar bills, how much money should he have received in change?

Mark your answer in the circles in the grid on your answer sheet.

Question 19 refers to the following drawing.

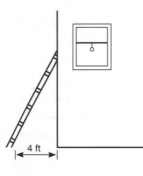

4 ft

19. Approximately how high up on the wall does the 12-foot ladder in the drawing reach if the bottom of the ladder is 4 feet from the wall?

(1) between 8 and 9 feet

(2) between 9 and 10 feet

(3) between 10 and 11 feet

(4) between 11 and 12 feet

(5) Not enough information is given.

20. The sum of 3 and twice a number is equal to the negative of the number. Let x = the unknown number. Which of the following equations could be used to solve for x?

(1) $2x = 3 + (-x)$

(2) $2(3 + x) = -x$

(3) $2(3) + x = -x$

(4) $3 + 2x = -3$

(5) $2x + 3 = -x$

21. In the figure below, line a is parallel to line b.

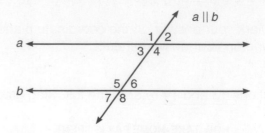

a || b

Which of the following statements about the figure is true?

(1) $\angle 6$ is supplementary to $\angle 7$.

(2) $\angle 1$ is complementary to $\angle 2$.

(3) $m\angle 2 + m\angle 5 = 180°$

(4) $\angle 2$ and $\angle 6$ are vertical angles.

(5) $\angle 1$ and $\angle 6$ are corresponding angles.

22. The ordered pair $(-1,1)$ is a solution of which of the following equations?

(1) $2x - 3y = 1$

(2) $3x - 2y = -5$

(3) $4x + 2y = 6$

(4) $-2x - 3y = 1$

(5) $-3x + 2y = -1$

23. The perimeter of a rectangle is 48 feet. The length of the rectangle is 3 times the width. What is the width in feet of the rectangle?

(1) 4

(2) 6

(3) 8

(4) 12

(5) 16

Questions 24 and 25 refer to the following information.

Design Central has two stores in the same city. The owner of the company keeps track of the number of sales for each store for an 8-week period. The information is shown on the graph below.

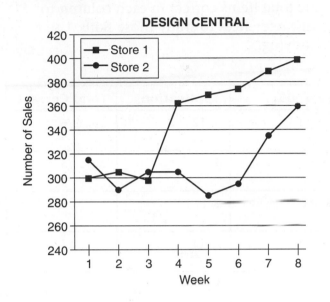

DESIGN CENTRAL

25. Based on the data for weeks 5 through 8, which of the following conclusions can you draw?

(1) Sales at both stores increased the most between weeks 7 and 8.

(2) Sales are increasing at a faster rate at Store 1 than at Store 2.

(3) Sales are increasing at a faster rate at Store 2 than at Store 1.

(4) During week 5, Store 1 had more than twice as many sales as Store 2.

(5) The gap between the number of sales at each store is widening.

24. During week 8, what was the ratio of sales at Store 1 to sales at Store 2?

(1) 3:2

(2) 5:4

(3) 7:6

(4) 9:8

(5) 10:9

Answers start on page 368.

Pretest Performance Analysis Charts
Mathematics

The following charts can help you determine your strengths and weaknesses on the content and skill areas of the GED Mathematics Test. Use the Answers and Explanations starting on page 368 to check your answers to the test. Then circle on the charts for Part I and Part II the numbers of the test items you answered correctly. Put the total number correct for each content area and skill area in each row and column. Look at the total items correct in each column to determine which areas are difficult for you. Use the page references to study those skills. Use a copy of the Study Planner on page 31 to guide your studying.

Part I

Content Area/Thinking Skill	Concept	Procedure	Application	Total Correct
Number Sense and Operations *(Pages 32–161)*	5	3, 9, 10	**6**, 12	____/6
Measurement *(Pages 162–183)*	18	16	**4**	____/3
Data Analysis *(Pages 184–207)*	**22**	**1, 21**	2, 8, 19	____/6
Algebra *(Pages 208–271)*	17, **20**, 25	**11**, 15	7, 14	____/7
Geometry *(Pages 272–331)*	**24**		**13, 23**	____/3
Total Correct	____/7	____/8	____/10	____/25

Part II

Content Area/Thinking Skill	Concept	Procedure	Application	Total Correct
Number Sense and Operations *(Pages 32–161)*	1, **5**		3, 6, 18	____/5
Measurement *(Pages 162–183)*		16	**4**	____/2
Data Analysis *(Pages 184–207)*	**7, 8**		9, **13, 14, 24, 25**	____/7
Algebra *(Pages 208–271)*	11, 12, 15, 20	17	22, 23	____/7
Geometry *(Pages 272–331)*	**2, 21**	**10**	**19**	____/4
Total Correct	____/10	____/3	____/12	____/25

The item numbers in **bold** are based on graphics.

© 2002 Steck-Vaughn Company. *GED Mathematics.* Permission granted to reproduce for classroom use.

Mathematics Study Planner

These charts will help you organize your study after you take the Mathematics Pretest and Posttest. After each test, use your results from the corresponding Performance Analysis Chart to complete the study planner. Place a check mark next to the areas in which you need more practice and plan your studies accordingly. Review your study habits by keeping track of the start and finish dates for each practice. These charts will help you to see your progress as you practice to improve your skills and prepare for the GED Test.

Pretest (pages 13–29): Use results from your **Performance Analysis Chart** (page 30).

Content	Correct/Total	✓	Page Numbers	Date Started	Date Finished
Number Sense and Operations	____/11		32–161		
Measurement	____/5		162–183		
Data Analysis	____/13		184–207		
Algebra	____/14		208–271		
Geometry	____/7		272–331		

Posttest (pages 332–348): Use results from your **Performance Analysis Chart** (page 349).

Content	Correct/Total	✓	Page Numbers	Date Started	Date Finished
Number Sense and Operations	____/10		32–161		
Measurement	____/4		162–183		
Data Analysis	____/11		184–207		
Algebra	____/16		208–271		
Geometry	____/9		272–331		

Numbers and Operations

Numbers are an important part of your daily life. Have you ever calculated the number of miles between where you are and where you want to go? When was the last time that you estimated whether or not you had enough cash to purchase items in a store? Have you ever paid part of a bill and then figured out how much you had left to pay?

All of these everyday actions rely on your understanding of numbers, number sense, and basic math operations. This unit covers basic number sense and operations with whole numbers, fractions, decimals, and percents. Keep in mind that you will use the skills in this unit on 20 to 30 percent of the questions on the GED Mathematics Test.

Whether you realize it or not, you use many math skills every day.

The lessons in this unit include:

Lesson 1: **Number and Operation Sense** and
Lesson 2: **Operations with Whole Numbers**
Understand the relationship between numbers and learn to add, subtract, multiply, and divide.

Lesson 3: **Steps for Solving Word Problems** and
Lesson 4: **Steps for Solving Multi-Step Problems**
Learn strategies for solving both simple and multi-step word problems.

Lesson 5: **Introduction to Fractions** and
Lesson 6: **Fractions, Ratios, and Proportions**
Understand the forms and sizes of fractions and the relationships among them.

Lesson 7: **Operations with Fractions**
Learn how to add, subtract, multiply, and divide with fractions.

Lesson 8: **Introduction to Decimals** and
Lesson 9: **Operations with Decimals**
Learn to write, compare, and calculate with decimals.

Lesson 10: Decimals and Fractions
Fractions and decimals are both ways to express part of a whole. Learn ways to convert between them and to use them together in problems.

Lesson 11: The Meaning of Percent
Percents are used to find a part or a whole when several numbers are given. Learn to use percents with or interchanged with fractions or decimals.

Lesson 12: Solving Percent Problems—Part 1
Lesson 13: Solving Percent Problems—Part 2
Learn everyday applications of percents including finding the percent by which a value increases or decreases and finding interest on money.

PROBLEM-SOLVING SKILLS

- Choosing the Operation
- Step-by-Step Problem Solving
- Setting Up Problems
- Estimating
- Using Your Calculator
- Writing Answers in a Standard Grid
- Order of Operations
- Solving Proportions
- Using Mental Math
- Solving Multi-Step Problems

GED SKILL Number and Operation Sense

Place Value

Whole numbers are made up of these ten **digits:** 0, 1, 2, 3, 4, 5, 6, 7, 8, and 9. The number 3820 has four digits; 1,000,000 is a seven-digit number, although six of the digits are the same.

Our number system is based on place value. **Place value** means that the value of a digit depends on its position, or place, in a number. This chart shows the names of the first 12 whole number places.

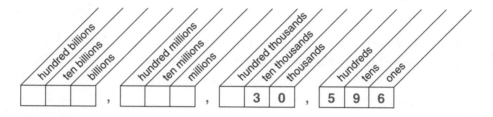

The total value of a number is the sum of the values of the digits in each place.

Example   What is the value of each digit in 30,596?
3 is in the ten thousands place. $3 \times 10,000 =$ **30,000**
0 is in the thousands place. $0 \times 1,000 =$ **0,000**
5 is in the hundreds place. $5 \times 100 =$ **500**
9 is in the tens place. $9 \times 10 =$ **90**
6 is in the ones place. $6 \times 1 =$ **6**

Reading and Writing Numbers

TIP

Four-digit numbers can be written with or without a comma. The number four thousand five hundred twenty can be written as 4520 or 4,520. Both are correct.

When writing a number, place commas every three digits counting from the right. Each group of three digits is called a **period** and is named for the number place to the left of the comma. Always read a number from left to right. Read each group of digits before a comma; then say the name of the period the comma represents.

Write a number in words exactly as you read it aloud. Do not say or write the word *and* or *ones* when reading or writing whole numbers.

Example   Read the number 12,950,068, and write it in words.

12, 950, 068
millions thousands [ones]

The number is read and written in words as **twelve million, nine hundred fifty thousand, sixty-eight.**

Rounding Whole Numbers

Use **rounding** to make difficult calculations easier to perform. Round the numbers you are working with when you do not need an exact answer.

Example   Round the number 24,902 to the thousands place.

Step 1	Find the digit you want to round to. Circle it.	2④,902
Step 2	Look at the digit to the right of the circled digit.	2④,9̲02
Step 3	If the digit to the right is 5 or more, add 1 to the circled digit. If the digit is less than 5, do not change the circled digit. Change all digits to the right of the circled digit to zeros.	2⑤,000

Examples   Round to the nearest thousand.   ③,499 rounds to **3,000**
1⑨,9̲30 rounds to **20,000**

GED SKILL FOCUS

A. Write the value of the underlined digit in words. Refer to the chart on page 28.

Example: 6̲27   <u>six hundred</u>

1. 5,5̲17 _____

2. 3̲,742,691 _____

3. 26̲,154 _____

4. 4,7̲00,510 _____

5. 964,2̲51 _____

6. 3,400̲,500 _____

B. Match each number in Column A with its word form in Column B.

Column A

_____ 7. 8,416

_____ 8. 8,420,106

_____ 9. 84,200,160

_____ 10. 842,016

_____ 11. 84,216

Column B

a. eighty-four million, two hundred thousand, one hundred sixty

b. eighty-four thousand, two hundred sixteen

c. eight hundred forty-two thousand, sixteen

d. eight million, four hundred twenty thousand, one hundred six

e. eight thousand, four hundred sixteen

C. Round each number as directed. Refer to the chart on page 28.

12. Round 8,621 to the hundreds place. _____

13. Round 5,099,620 to the nearest million. _____

14. Round 46,055 to the nearest ten thousand. _____

15. Round 10,562 to the nearest thousand. _____

Answers start on page 372.

Comparing, Ordering, and Grouping

When shopping, you often compare prices to find the best buy. You can use the following rules when **comparing** whole numbers.

RULE 1   The whole number with the most digits is always greater.

Example   Compare 7235 and 848. The number 7235 (4 digits) is greater than 848 (3 digits).

RULE 2   When two numbers have the same number of digits, compare the digits from left to right.

Example   6<u>4</u>6 is less than 6<u>9</u>0 because 40 is less than 90.

To write number comparisons, use the following symbols:

=	means *equals*	140 = 140	140 equals 140
>	means *is greater than*	25 > 23	25 is greater than 23
<	means *is less than*	4 < 5	4 is less than 5

TIP

Think of the "greater than" and "less than" symbols as arrows that always point to the smaller number.

Using the same rules, you can put several numbers in order of value.

Example 1   An Internet company sells books, toys, and videos. Yesterday, the company recorded these sales in each category: books, 1247; toys, 1271; and videos, 990. Arrange the sales in order from <u>least to greatest</u>.

Step 1   Count the digits in the sales numbers. Since 990 has only 3 digits and the other numbers have 4 digits, 990 is less than the other two sales numbers.

Step 2   Compare the digits in 1247 and 1271, working from left to right. The digits in the thousands place and the hundreds place are the same in both numbers. So, look at the tens place in each. Since 40 is less than 70, the number 1247 is less than 1271.

From least to greatest, the sales are **990, 1247,** and **1271.**

Understanding place value can also help you find the range that contains a certain number.

Example 2   Samuel is looking for a file #13496. A label on the front of each drawer tells the range of file numbers in the drawer. For example, Drawer A contains files numbered from #13090 to #13274. Which drawer contains file #13496?

Drawer A	Drawer B	Drawer C	Drawer D
#13090 to #13274	#13275 to #13490	#13491 to #13598	#13599 to #14701

Compare the number 13496 to the signs. File #13496 will be between the two numbers on the correct drawer. Since 13496 is greater than 13491 and less than 13598, the file is found in **Drawer C.**

A. Compare the following numbers. Write >, <, or = between the numbers.

1. 1,305 _____ 1,503

2. 34,000 _____ 29,989

3. 102,667 _____ 102,657

4. 5,690,185 _____ 5,690,185,100

5. 875,438 _____ 875,438

6. 75,390,000 _____ 75,391,540

7. 9,500,000 _____ 9,500,000,000

8. 45,100 _____ 45,099

9. 7,456,795 _____ 7,500,000

10. 319,002,110 _____ 319,002,011

B. Solve.

Refer to the following chart to answer Questions 11 through 14.

Daily Sales Totals Week Ending March 4	
Monday	$18,756
Tuesday	12,316
Wednesday	13,940
Thursday	13,772
Friday	21,592
Saturday	28,795

12. Which day had the lowest sales?

_____

13. Which day had the highest sales?

_____

14. Arrange the sales on the chart in order from lowest to highest.

_____

_____

11. Which day had higher sales, Wednesday or Thursday?

_____

Refer to the following information to answer Questions 15 through 17.

Bob's Auto Parts stores some of its inventory in bins. Each part is assigned a catalog number and sorted into the bins. A range of numbers indicates the contents of each bin.

Bin A
Parts 1010
–1490

Bin B
Parts 1491
–1720

Bin C
Parts 1721
–2050

Bin D
Parts 2051
–2480

15. In which bin would you find Part Number 1750? _____

16. Gina needs parts 1488 and 1491. In which bins should she look? _____

17. Part numbers higher than 2050 can be found in which bin? _____

Answers start on page 372.

GED STRATEGY Solving Word Problems

Choosing the Operation

To solve math word problems, you must make several decisions. You need to decide what the question is asking and what information you require to solve the problem. You must also choose the operation needed to solve the problem: addition, subtraction, multiplication, or division.

Read the word problem carefully, and think about the information you are given in the problem and how you will solve it. Here are some guidelines that may help you choose an operation.

You	When You Need To
Add (+)	Combine quantities Find a total
Subtract (−)	Find a difference Take away a quantity Compare to find "how many more," "how much less," or "how much is left"
Multiply (×)	Put together a number of equal amounts to find a total Add the same number repeatedly
Divide (÷)	Split a quantity into equal parts

Example 1   Victor has a doctor's bill of $55 and a pharmacy bill of $12. Which operation shows the total of the bills?

    (1) $55 + $12
    (2) $55 − $12
    (3) $12 × $55
    (4) $55 ÷ $12
    (5) $12 − $55

You need to find a total, so you add the amounts. The correct answer is **option (1).**

Example 2   Ahmed, Rita, and Lilia are sharing equally the $126 profit from their yard sale. Which operation shows how much each person will receive?

    (1) 3 + $126
    (2) $126 − 3
    (3) $126 × 3
    (4) $126 ÷ 3
    (5) 3 ÷ $126

To split $126 into equal amounts, divide. The correct answer is **option (4).**

Note that the order in which you write numbers in subtraction and division problems is important. The amount being subtracted from or being divided must come first.

Directions: Choose the <u>one best answer</u> to each question.

1. The Chang family pays a car loan payment of $269 a month. Which of the following operations shows how much they will pay on the loan in a 12-month period?

   (1) 12 + $269
   (2) $269 − 12
   (3) $269 × 12
   (4) $269 ÷ 12
   (5) 12 − $269

2. Last month Teresa paid $137 to heat her home. This month she paid $124. Which of the following operations shows the total cost of heating her home for the 2 months?

   (1) $137 + $124
   (2) $137 − $124
   (3) $124 × $137
   (4) $137 ÷ $124
   (5) $124 ÷ $137

3. Carl filled up the gas tank on his delivery truck. The total cost of the gas is shown on the pump below. If he paid for the gas with a fifty-dollar bill, which of the following operations shows how much money Carl should get back in change?

   (1) $50 + $28
   (2) $28 − $50
   (3) $28 × $50
   (4) $50 ÷ $28
   (5) $50 − $28

4. Kim needs to read a 348-page book for class. She has three weeks to read it, and she plans to read an equal number of pages each week. Which of the following operations shows how many pages Kim must read per week?

   (1) 3 + 348
   (2) 348 − 3
   (3) 348 × 3
   (4) 348 ÷ 3
   (5) 3 ÷ 348

5. Mark starts with $327 in his checking account. If he writes a check for $189, which of the following operations shows how much will be left in his account?

   (1) $189 + $327
   (2) $327 − $189
   (3) $189 × $327
   (4) $327 ÷ $189
   (5) $189 ÷ $327

6. Four friends carpool to work together Monday through Friday. Each week they pay a total of $62 for gas, parking, and tolls. Which of the following operations shows how they could split the cost evenly?

   (1) 4 + $62
   (2) $62 − 4
   (3) 4 × $62
   (4) 4 ÷ $62
   (5) $62 ÷ 4

TIP You may need to read a problem carefully to find all of the numbers. Sometimes a number appears as a word, such as "four" friends.

Answers start on page 372.

GED SKILL Using Number Lines

A **number line** can help you compare the value of numbers. Number lines show numbers at equally spaced **intervals.**

On the number line below, the equally-spaced intervals increase by one whole number. Thus, as you move to the right on a number line, the values increase. The arrows at each end of a number line show that the line doesn't end but extends in both directions.

You may see a number line on the GED Mathematics Test, or you may want to draw one to help you see the relationship between different numbers.

Example 1   Place a dot on the number line below to show a whole number that is greater than 2 and less than 4.

For problems like the example above, there is only one possible correct whole number answer. The number 3 would be correct.

For some number lines, you will need to determine the value of unlabeled intervals. In the example below, every fifth interval is labeled. By counting the intervals between 5 and 10, you'll find each interval represents an increase of 1 as you move from left to right.

Example 2   Place a dot on the number line below to locate the whole number 8.

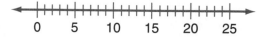

On this number line only every 5th whole number is labeled. You must find an unlabeled whole number by counting the lines between 5 and 10. In this example, you count each line between 5 and 10 and place a dot on the third line, which represents the whole number **8.**

![number line from 0 to 25 with dot at 8]

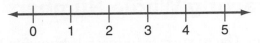
Show your answers by placing one or more dots on the number line below each problem.

1. Show the location of the whole number 4.

```
<———+———+———+———+———+———+———>
     0   1   2   3   4   5
```

2. Show the location of the whole number 38.

```
<—|++|+++|++|+++|++|+++|++|+++|++|+++|++|—>
   0    10    20    30    40    50
```

3. Show the location of each whole number including zero that is less than 3.

```
<———+———+———+———+———+———+———>
     0   1   2   3   4   5
```

4. Show the location of the whole number eighteen.

```
<—|++++|++++|++++|++++|++++|—>
   0    5    10    15   20   25
```

5. Show the location of the whole number that makes this comparison true: 1 < ? < 3.

```
<———+———+———+———+———+———+———>
     0   1   2   3   4   5
```

6. Show the location of the whole number twenty-two.

```
<—|++++|++++|++++|++++|++++|—>
   0    5    10    15   20   25
```

7. Show the location of the whole number that makes this comparison true: 16 > ? > 18.

```
<—|++++|++++|++++|++++|++++|—>
   0    5    10    15   20   25
```

8. Show the location of the whole number forty-three.

```
<—|++|+++|++|+++|++|+++|++|+++|++|+++|++|—>
   0    10    20    30    40    50
```

Answers start on page 372.

Lesson 1

41

Lesson 2 GED SKILL Operations with Whole Numbers

Adding and Subtracting Whole Numbers

One key to success in math is knowing how to perform the basic operations accurately and when to use each operation. Use **addition** to combine quantities, or find a total, or **sum.** Follow these steps to add whole numbers.

Step 1 Line up the numbers being added so digits with the same place value are aligned. Start with the ones column. Working from right to left, add the numbers in each column.

Step 2 When a column of digits has a sum greater than 9, **regroup,** or **carry,** to the next column on the left.

Example 1 EZ Video rented 169 videos on Thursday and 683 videos on Friday. Find the total rentals for the two days.

Step 1 Add the ones column (9 + 3 = 12). Write 2 in the ones column; regroup 1 to the tens column.

Step 2 Continue adding the remaining columns, regrouping when necessary.

$$\begin{array}{r} \overset{1}{1}69 \\ +683 \\ \hline 2 \end{array} \qquad \begin{array}{r} \overset{1\ 1}{1}69 \\ +683 \\ \hline 852 \end{array}$$

On your calculator, enter the numbers to be added.

169 + **683** = **852.**

EZ Video rented a total of **852 videos** on Thursday and Friday.

Use **subtraction** to find the **difference** between two numbers or amounts. Follow these steps to subtract whole numbers.

Step 1 Write the number being subtracted below the other number, making sure to line up the place-value columns. Starting with the ones column, work from right to left, subtracting the numbers in each column.

Step 2 When a digit in the bottom number is greater than the digit above it, you must regroup, or **borrow,** to subtract the column.

Example 2 Jeff's Home Repair charges $5025 to remodel a kitchen and $2438 to paint a two-story house. Find the difference in cost.

Step 1 Arrange the numbers in columns. Regroup 1 ten from the tens column to subtract the ones column (15 − 8 = 7).

$$\begin{array}{r} \overset{\ \ \ 1\ 15}{\$50\cancel{2}\cancel{5}} \\ -\ 2438 \\ \hline 7 \end{array}$$

Step 2 Subtract the tens column. Regroup. Since there are no hundreds, borrow from the thousands. Now there are ten hundreds in the hundreds column.

$$\begin{array}{r} \overset{4\ 10\ 1\ \ 15}{\$\cancel{5}\cancel{0}\cancel{2}\cancel{5}} \\ -\ 2438 \\ \hline 7 \end{array}$$

		9 11
		4 ~~10~~ ~~1~~ 15
		$~~5025~~
Step 3	Finally, regroup from the hundreds column and complete the subtraction.	− 2438
		$2587
		1 1 1
Step 4	Check your answer by adding the result and the number you subtracted. The sum should equal the top number in the problem.	$2587
		+ 2438
		$5025

On your calculator, enter the larger number first.

5025 ⊟ 2438 ⊟ 2587.

The remodeling job costs **$2587** more than the painting job.

GED SKILL FOCUS

A. Solve these problems using paper and pencil.

1. 305
    +463

2. 4172
    +4510

3. 6795
    + 132

4. 193
    +629

5. 86
    −51

6. 494
    −167

7. 680
    −268

8. 5067
    −3795

9. 81,427 + 3,541 + 24,625 =

10. Find the sum of 76 and 58.

11. 10,508 − 3,679 =

12. Combine 176 and 54,095.

13. Subtract 16,567 from 20,000.

14. What is the total of 950, 308, 77, and 50?

B. Use your calculator to solve these problems.

15. 56,439
     + 4,796

16. 35,075
      1,936
     +17,950

17. 19,067
     +35,196

18. 65,196
      6,725
     +27,718

19. 800
     −219

20. 1258
     − 295

21. 51,964
     −20,651

22. 3205
     −2276

23. What is the total of 36, 9, 74, 48, 6, and 15?

24. How much more is 419,003 than 12,018?

25. Find the difference between 37,500 and 18,642.

26. Subtract 75,510 from 100,000.

Answers start on page 373.

Multiplying and Dividing Whole Numbers

Use **multiplication** when you need to add the same number many times. The answer to a multiplication problem is called the **product.** Follow these steps to multiply.

Step 1 Working from right to left, multiply the digits in the top number by the digit in the ones column of the bottom number to find a **partial product.** Then multiply the top number by the tens digit of the bottom number to find a partial product and so on.

Step 2 Line up each partial product under the digit you multiplied by. Then add the partial products together.

Example 1 A company spends $913 per week on advertising. How much will the company spend in 52 weeks?

Step 1 To multiply $913 by 52, first multiply $913 by the ones digit, 2. The partial product 1826 is lined up under the ones column.

Step 2 Multiply $913 by the tens digit, 5. The partial product 4565 is lined up under the tens column. Use zero as a placeholder. Add the partial products to find the product.

$$
\begin{array}{r}
\$913 \\
\times\ 52 \\
\hline
1\,826 \\
45\,650 \\
\hline
\$47{,}476
\end{array}
$$

On your calculator, enter the numbers to be multiplied.

913 ✕ 52 ＝ 47476.

The company will spend **$47,476** on advertising in a 52-week period.

Use **division** when you need to separate a whole (the **dividend**) into equal parts. The answer to a division problem is called a **quotient.** The example will help you understand the steps in long division. Put the dividend inside the bracket. Put the number you are dividing by (the **divisor**) outside the bracket on the left. Work from left to right.

Example 2 Elena is packaging glassware. She packs 18 juice glasses into each carton. If she has 7310 glasses to pack, how many cartons can she completely fill?

Step 1 Divide 7310 by 18. Since 18 does not go into 7, look at the first two digits: divide 18 into 73. Write 4 in the answer above the hundreds place. Multiply 18 by 4, and then subtract that amount from 73. Bring down the next digit.

$$
\begin{array}{r}
4 \\
18\overline{)7310} \\
72 \\
\hline
11
\end{array}
$$

Step 2 18 will not divide into 11. Write 0 above the tens place in the quotient and bring down the next digit (the ones digit). Continue dividing. Use the letter r to show the **remainder.**

$$
\begin{array}{r}
406\ \text{r}2 \\
18\overline{)7310} \\
72 \\
\hline
110 \\
108 \\
\hline
2
\end{array}
$$

		406
		$\times$ 18
Step 3	To check your answer, multiply it by the number you divided by. Then add the remainder. The result should be the number you were dividing.	3248
		4060
		7308
		+ 2
		7310

To divide using a calculator, enter the numbers in the order shown below. On a calculator, the remainder is given as a decimal. You will learn more about decimal remainders in Lesson 9.

7310 ÷ 18 = 406.1111111

This answer tells us Elena can fill **406 cartons** and will have some glasses left over.

GED SKILL FOCUS

A. Solve these problems using paper and pencil.

1. 746
   $\times$ 5

2. 4862
   $\times$ 9

3. 36
   $\times$23

4. 5084
   $\times$ 76

5. $7\overline{)3206}$

6. $4\overline{)23,984}$

7. $12\overline{)76,402}$

8. $24\overline{)219,315}$

9. $2584 \times 2700 =$

10. Multiply 25,097 by 25.

11. Divide 30,321 by 46.

12. $606,450 \div 15 =$

13. $190 \times 2186 =$

14. Divide 139,400 by 205.

15. $130,112 \div 16 =$

16. Find the product of 8050 and 509.

B. Use your calculator to solve these problems. Round to the nearest whole number.

17. 775
    $\times$775

18. 3056
    $\times$2500

19. 885
    $\times$ 62

20. 1247
    $\times$3014

21. $6\overline{)3502}$

22. $18\overline{)254,178}$

23. $13\overline{)100,000}$

24. $35\overline{)38,450}$

25. Find the product of 15,663 and 8.

26. Multiply 1193 by 45.

27. Divide 508,320 by 120.

28. Divide 712,000 by 25.

29. $40,409 \times 9 =$

30. $419,357 \div 163 =$

Answers start on page 374.

GED STRATEGY **Solving Word Problems**

Step-by-Step Problem Solving

TIP

Some questions require only an estimated answer. The word "about" often indicates that only an estimate is needed. But estimating can always help you be sure that your answer makes sense.

The key to solving word problems is to read and understand the problem before doing any calculations. Use the following five steps to organize your problem-solving approach.

Step 1 Read the problem and decide what you are asked to find. Identify what information you need to solve the problem.

Step 2 Choose the operation (addition, subtraction, multiplication, or division) you will use to solve the problem.

Step 3 Estimate to find an approximate answer. This will help you determine whether your actual answer is correct.

Step 4 Solve the problem.

Step 5 Check your answer to make sure it makes sense. Does it answer the question posed by the problem? Does it seem reasonable? Compare your answer to your estimate.

Apply this strategy to the following problem.

Example Roberto drove 357 miles on Monday and 509 miles on Tuesday. How many more miles did he drive on Tuesday than on Monday?

(1) 146
(2) 152
(3) 357
(4) 509
(5) 866

Step 1 You need the number of miles from each day: 357 miles and 509 miles.

Step 2 Since you need to find the *difference* in miles, subtract. Tuesday's mileage is greater than Monday's mileage, so subtract 357 from 509.

Step 3 Estimate an answer. Round 509 to 500 and 357 to 350. Subtract.

Estimate: $500 - 350 = 150$

Step 4 Solve the problem.

Step 5 Check your answer. Is it reasonable? The answer 152 is close to the estimate of 150 so it is reasonable.

$$\begin{array}{r} ^{4\ 10} \\ \cancel{509} \\ -357 \\ \hline 152 \end{array}$$

Option (2) 152 is correct. Roberto drove 152 more miles on Tuesday than on Monday.

Directions: Choose the <u>one best answer</u> to each question. Use your calculator when indicated.

1. Last month the Lees paid $137 to heat their home. This month they paid $124. What is the total cost of heating their home for the two months?

    (1) $ 13
    (2) $130
    (3) $161
    (4) $251
    (5) $261

2. Marcus has $827 in his checking account. He writes a check for $189. How much will be left in the account?

    (1) $1016
    (2) $ 762
    (3) $ 738
    (4) $ 648
    (5) $ 638

Question 3 refers to the following diagram.

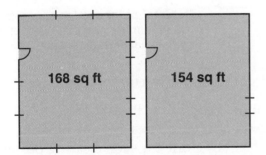

168 sq ft   154 sq ft

3. Alexa is buying carpet for her home. The diagram shows the amount of carpeting needed for each of two rooms. What is the total square feet of carpet that Alexa needs?

    (1) 322
    (2) 320
    (3) 312
    (4) 222
    (5) 214

4. The Valdez family pays $289 a month on a car loan. How much will the family spend on the car loan in a 1-year period?

    (1) $ 289
    (2) $ 360
    (3) $1200
    (4) $2890
    (5) $3468

5. Six friends commute to work together. Each week, the gas, parking, and tolls cost $114. If they split the costs equally, how much does each friend pay per week toward the commuting costs?

    (1) $ 17
    (2) $ 18
    (3) $ 19
    (4) $108
    (5) $120

6. Emily worked 68 hours in 2 weeks. She earns $7 per hour. How much did she earn in the 2 weeks?

    (1) $ 51
    (2) $ 75
    (3) $435
    (4) $476
    (5) $952

TIP On the GED Mathematics Test you will need to know common equivalencies such as:
24 hours = 1 day; 7 days = 1 week
52 weeks = 12 months = 1 year

Answers start on page 374.

GED STRATEGY **Using Your Calculator**

Basic Calculator Functions

On Part One of the GED Mathematics Test, you will be able to use a calculator. Each testing center will provide examinees with a calculator to use on the test. Throughout this book, you will practice solving problems with calculators. Although various calculators may look different, the keys on the calculators function the same way.

Here are some important points to know about basic calculator use.

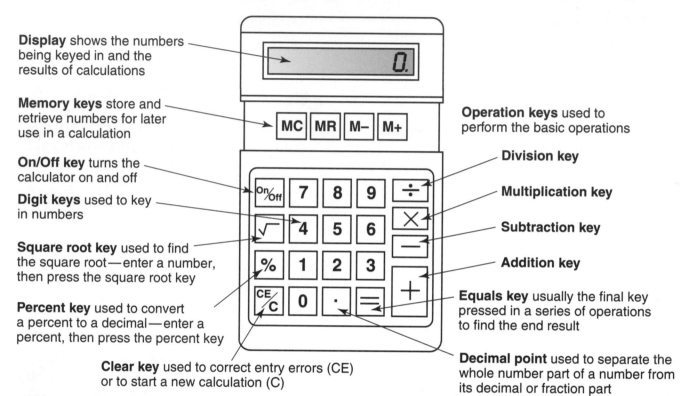

Display shows the numbers being keyed in and the results of calculations

Memory keys store and retrieve numbers for later use in a calculation

On/Off key turns the calculator on and off

Digit keys used to key in numbers

Square root key used to find the square root—enter a number, then press the square root key

Percent key used to convert a percent to a decimal—enter a percent, then press the percent key

Clear key used to correct entry errors (CE) or to start a new calculation (C)

Operation keys used to perform the basic operations

Division key

Multiplication key

Subtraction key

Addition key

Equals key usually the final key pressed in a series of operations to find the end result

Decimal point used to separate the whole number part of a number from its decimal or fraction part

For information about the calculator used on the GED Mathematics Test, review pages 469 – 472. You can practice with this calculator at the testing center before taking the test.

Here are some more important points about calculator use:

- Some calculators have a combined CE/C key. Press it once to clear your last entry; press it twice to clear all entries and calculations. Other calculators have two clear keys, one for each clearing purpose.
- Even though you may be only entering whole numbers, many calculators will automatically display a decimal point at the end of the whole number.
- When adding or multiplying, it doesn't matter in what order the numbers are entered. However, it is very important to enter the numbers in the correct order when subtracting or dividing.
  - **Subtraction problems**—the number being taken away must be entered second: $32 - 28$
  - **Division problems**—the number being divided must be entered first: $24 \div 3$

Example 1   Katie drove 236 miles on Friday, 304 miles on Saturday, and 271 miles on Sunday. How many miles did she drive during the three-day period?

Add to find the total number of miles that Katie drove.

$$236 + 304 + 271$$

You can enter these numbers in a calculator in any order. It is very important, however, to make sure that the digits within a number stay in the same order. Any of the following entries will give you the same answer.

236 **+** 304 **+** 271 **=**   or   271 **+** 304 **+** 236 **=**

or   304 **+** 271 **+** 236 **=**

You should see the answer **811** in the display. It is not necessary to press the **=** key until you finish entering all the numbers.

Example 2   Malik's workteam made 1056 widgets in 6 hours. How many widgets did they make per hour?

1056 **÷** 6 **=**   NOT   6 **÷** 1056 **=**

You should see the answer **176** in the calculator display.

GED PRACTICE

Directions: Choose the <u>one best answer</u> to each question. You <u>MAY</u> use your calculator.

1. Scott changed the oil in his car when the odometer read 35,297 miles. The next time he changed the oil the odometer read 38,874 miles. How many miles did he drive between oil changes?

   (1) 3,377
   (2) 3,477
   (3) 3,577
   (4) 3,677
   (5) 3,777

2. Each month Carlos pays $595 in rent. How much does he pay in rent for two years?

   (1) $ 1,190
   (2) $ 5,950
   (3) $ 7,140
   (4) $14,280
   (5) $28,560

3. On Wednesday, J & R Electronics had total sales of $14,688 for its new stereo system. If each system sold for $459 (including tax), how many new stereo systems did J & R sell?

   (1) 31
   (2) 32
   (3) 33
   (4) 34
   (5) 35

4. Kim's bank statement listed a balance of $76 in her checking account. Over the next month, she made deposits of $96, $873, and $98. What is the new balance in her account after all these transactions?

   (1) $ 603
   (2) $1047
   (3) $1067
   (4) $1134
   (5) $1143

Answers start on page 375.

GED Mini-Test • Lessons 1 and 2

Directions: This is a thirty-minute practice test. After thirty minutes, mark the last item you finished. Then complete the test and check your answers. If most of your answers are correct, but you didn't finish, try to work faster next time.

Part 1

Directions: Choose the <u>one best answer</u> to each question. You <u>MAY</u> use a calculator.

1. What is the value of 6000 − 2784?

   (1) 8784
   (2) 4785
   (3) 4784
   (4) 4216
   (5) 3216

2. What is the value of 3024 ÷ 6?

   (1)   54
   (2)   504
   (3)   540
   (4) 5004
   (5) 5040

3. Karin needs $3220 for a used car. If she saves $230 each month, how many months will it take her to save the entire amount?

   (1) 11
   (2) 12
   (3) 13
   (4) 14
   (5) 15

4. Yvonne pays $480 for rent each month. How much rent does she pay in one year?

   (1) $14,400
   (2) $ 5,760
   (3) $ 4,800
   (4) $ 576
   (5) $ 480

Questions 5 through 7 refer to the following table.

Number of Videotapes Rented	
January	4,320
February	5,980
March	4,987
April	6,007
May	7,985

5. What was the total number of videotapes rented in February and March?

   (1) 10,300
   (2) 10,400
   (3) 10,967
   (4) 11,067
   (5) 15,287

6. How many more videotapes were rented in May than in April?

   (1)   993
   (2) 1,070
   (3) 1,978
   (4) 1,988
   (5) 13,992

7. Twice as many videotapes were rented in June as in January. How many videotapes were rented in June?

   (1) 15,970
   (2) 12,014
   (3)   9,974
   (4)   8,640
   (5)   2,160

Directions: Choose the <u>one best answer</u> to each question. You <u>MAY NOT</u> use a calculator.

8. Which of the following represents *two hundred three thousand, forty-nine?*

   (1)   2,349
   (2) 203,049
   (3) 203,490
   (4) 230,049
   (5) 230,490

9. Which of the following is the value of 39,462 rounded to the nearest thousand?

   (1) 39,000
   (2) 39,400
   (3) 39,460
   (4) 39,500
   (5) 40,000

10. Tom pays $387 a month on a school loan. Which of the following operations represents how much he pays in 12 months?

    (1) 12 + $387
    (2) $387 − 12
    (3) $387 × 12
    (4) $387 ÷ 12
    (5) 12 ÷ $387

11. Three friends rent an apartment for a total of $972 per month. If they share the rent equally, which of the following operations represents the amount each one pays per month?

    (1) 3 + $972
    (2) $972 − 3
    (3) $972 × 3
    (4) $972 ÷ 3
    (5) 3 ÷ $972

12. Empire Clothing Company presented a training seminar to 35 employees. If the company paid $12 per person for lunch, how much did the company pay to feed the employees?

    (1) $700
    (2) $420
    (3) $350
    (4) $336
    (5) $ 70

13. Cynthia works 4 hours each day, 6 days a week. How many hours does she work in 3 weeks?

    (1) 12
    (2) 18
    (3) 24
    (4) 48
    (5) 72

14. Alfredo has $1200 in his checking account. If he takes out $140, what is the balance left in his account?

    (1) $1340
    (2) $1160
    (3) $1140
    (4) $1060
    (5) $ 200

15. A computer system costs $1050. If Roberto has $985 saved, how much more does he need to purchase the system?

    (1) $ 65
    (2) $ 75
    (3) $ 165
    (4) $ 985
    (5) $1050

Answers start on page 375.

Lesson 3

GED SKILL Steps for Solving Word Problems

Estimating to Solve Problems

To **estimate** means to find an approximate value. Suppose you stop at the grocery store to buy a few items, but you have only $20. How do you know if you have enough to pay for the items? You could estimate a total by rounding each price up to the nearest whole dollar and adding.

A good way to estimate an answer is to round the numbers in the problem to a convenient place value.

Example 1 The city of Lakewood has 13,968 registered voters. In a recent election, only 4,787 people voted. Approximately how many registered voters did not vote?

(1) 6,500
(2) 7,500
(3) 8,000
(4) 9,000
(5) 10,000

To find the difference between the number of registered voters and the number of people who voted, you need to subtract. The word *approximately* tells you to estimate the answer. To estimate the difference, round the numbers to the nearest thousand and subtract.

Estimate: $14,000 - 5,000 = 9,000$. The correct answer is **option (4).**

You can also use estimation to see if a computed answer makes sense. In the problem below, estimate first to see that your answer should be around 9,000. You subtract and get 9,181 as your answer. Your estimate confirms that this answer makes sense.

Example 2 Lakewood has 13,968 registered voters. In a recent election, only 4,787 people voted. How many voters did not vote?

(1) 2,917
(2) 4,787
(3) 8,221
(4) 9,181
(5) 18,755

Use the estimate from Example 1 to eliminate options (1), (2), and (5) as either too low or too high. Subtract: $13,968 - 4,787 = 9,181$. **Option (4)** is correct. Your estimate tells you it makes sense.

An estimate can help you check whether your answer makes sense. Estimating is also a quick check that you have pressed the correct calculator keys.

Another way to estimate is to work with **compatible numbers.** Numbers that divide exactly and are easy to work with are compatible. To estimate the answer to a division problem, find compatible numbers that are close to the numbers in the problem.

Example 3   Clarissa divides 1935 by 9. She uses her calculator, and the display reads 21.4444444. Is her answer reasonable?

The number 9 is close to 10, and 1935 is close to 2000. You know that $2000 \div 10 = 200$, so the correct answer should be close to 200. Clarissa's answer of a little more than 21 is too low. She may have pressed a wrong key on her calculator. She should rework the problem. The answer is **215.**

GED SKILL FOCUS

Use rounding or compatible numbers to estimate an answer for each problem. Then find the exact answer. Use either pencil and paper or a calculator.

Example:	**Estimate**	**Exact**
$267 + 95 + 308$	700	670

1. $1424 - 989$ _____ _____

2. 18×29 _____ _____

3. $1798 \div 62$ _____ _____

4. Lotte worked 39 hours last week. She earns $9 per hour. How much will she be paid for her work?

5. Meg needs to have her furnace repaired. A new thermostat will cost $38. Cleaning and repair of the heating unit will cost $196. She will also pay $145 in labor. How much will the repairs cost?

6. Last week Lee sold 15 computers, each priced at $1137. What were his total sales for the week?

7. Wrightway Shoes has 1192 employees. If the company has to lay off 315 employees, how many employees will remain?

8. Maya plans to make 12 monthly payments on bedroom furniture. The total cost of the furniture plus interest is $1152. How much will she pay per month?

9. The Bonilla family drove 177 miles on the first day of a three-day trip. If the family drives the same distance every day, how many miles will the Bonilla family drive?

10. This week Selma earned $396 working part-time as a data entry clerk. This amount is $104 more than she earned last week. How much did Selma earn last week?

11. Marshall needs to eat 2400 calories per day to gain weight. So far today he has eaten 685 calories. How many more calories must he consume today to meet his goal?

12. A small town spends $225,125 each year on street maintenance and $18,725 on tree trimming. How much is spent on both items combined?

Answers start on page 375.

Choosing and Organizing Information

Some problems present more information than you need to solve a problem. Your first step is to organize the information, if necessary, and then find the facts you need.

Tables and charts contain many items of data organized in columns and rows. To find the information you need, pay close attention to labels, titles, and headings. Don't be distracted by information that you do not need to solve the problem.

Example 1 The Fairfax Public Library kept the following records on book circulation from January through April.

January	February	March	April
10,356	7,542	7,625	9,436

How many more books were borrowed in April than in February?

(1)   83
(2)   820
(3) 1,811
(4) 1,894
(5) 16,978

You are asked to find the difference between February and April so you need only the numbers of those two months to solve the problem. Subtract to find the difference: 9,436 − 7,542 = 1,894. The correct answer is **option (4) 1,894.**

Some problems may not give all the information you need. Read the problem carefully. What facts do you need to answer the question?

Example 2 A driver must transport 200 cartons of shoes, 150 cartons of clothes, and 75 cartons of bedding from the warehouse to the stockroom. Using a truck, how many trips must the driver make to transport all the cartons?

(1)   3
(2) 17
(3) 25
(4) 75
(5) Not enough information is given.

Do you see that some information is missing? You need to know how many cartons the truck can hold. It is impossible to solve the problem with only the information given in the problem. The correct answer is **option (5) Not enough information is given.**

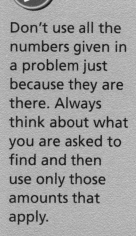

Don't use all the numbers given in a problem just because they are there. Always think about what you are asked to find and then use only those amounts that apply.

A. Circle or underline <u>only</u> the facts needed to solve each problem. <u>You do not need to solve the problem.</u>

1. Arcadia Coliseum seats 26,500. The East-West football game has been held at the coliseum for the past 8 years. This year the tickets for the game sold for $6 each. If the game sold out, how much did the coliseum make in ticket sales?

2. A digital camera is regularly priced at $89. The sale price for this weekend is $59. Ramon buys the camera at the sale price using a $10-off coupon. How much does he pay for the camera?

3. This week, Nita earned $456 as an administrative assistant. Last month, she earned $2112 at the same job. If she is paid $12 per hour, how many hours did she work this week?

4. A public school wants to raise $25,000 to improve its library. The same school raised $18,400 last year for new computers. A local manufacturer has offered to donate $11,450 for the library. How much more does the school need to raise?

B. Solve or state what information is missing.

Refer to the following chart to answer Questions 5 and 6.

SPORTS-WAREHOUSE CLEARANCE		
	Regular Price	Sale Price
T-shirts	$12	$ 8
Sweat Shirts	$18	$14
Sweat Pants	$14	$12
Team Jackets	$59	$35

5. On Friday the store sold 24 pairs of sweat pants at the sale price. How much money did the store take in on sweat pants?

6. The store sold 25 T-shirts at the regular price before the sale began. How many T-shirts did the store have in stock to start the sale?

7. Mr. and Mrs. Pierotti are remodeling their kitchen. They spent $548 for new cabinets and $618 on plumbing. The tiles for the kitchen floor will cost $3 each. If they need 240 tiles, how much will the tiles cost?

8. Wilshire Recreation Center has youth athletic programs. Last fall, 320 children (152 boys and 168 girls) between the ages of 8 and 16 signed up to play basketball. In the spring, 432 boys and girls signed up to play baseball.

   How many more children signed up to play baseball than signed up to play basketball?

Answers start on page 375.

Writing in Answers in a Standard Grid

One type of special format question that appears on the GED Mathematics Test is the **standard grid** shown below. For this type of question, instead of choosing among five multiple-choice options, you write and bubble in your answer on the grid.

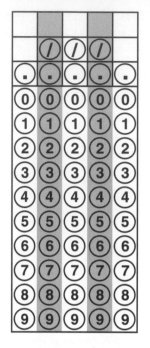

Here are some important points to keep in mind when using the standard grid:

- The grid is used to enter a single numerical answer.
- The row at the top is blank and is intended for you to write in your answer. Although you can actually leave this row blank, it is helpful to fill it in as a guide for marking in the circled numbers in the rows below.
- Your answer can start in any of the five columns, as long as your answer is complete.
- Any unused columns should be left blank.
- For answers that are whole numbers, you will not use the second row of fraction bars, ⊘, or the third row of decimal points, ⊙.

Example   Mark drove 157 miles on Saturday and 189 miles on Sunday. How many miles did he drive in all for the two days?

The total number of miles for the two days is 157 + 189 = 346.

First write the answer 346 in the blank first row. Then darken in the corresponding circled numbers in the standard grid below. Note that since the answer can start in any of the five columns, all three grids shown below are correctly filled in.

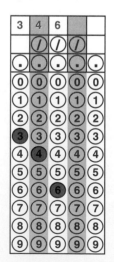 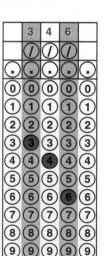 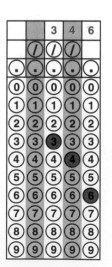

Directions: Solve the following problems and enter your answers on the grids provided.

1. Susan's weekly gross salary is $615. If $172 is taken out for taxes and $35 is taken out for other deductions, what is the amount of Susan's weekly take-home salary?

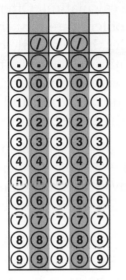

2. Alberto buys a computer and pays for it in 24 equal monthly installments. If each installment is $78, how much will Alberto pay in all for the computer?

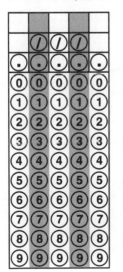

3. Six sisters send their family a total of $720 every month. If the contribution is divided equally among the sisters, how much does each sister contribute?

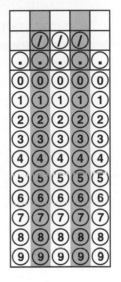

4. This week Lourdes earned $620 in commissions on her sales. If this amount is $54 more than she earned last week, how much did she earn in commissions last week?

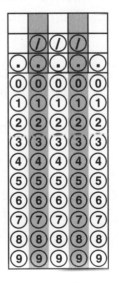

Answers start on page 376.

GED SKILL Steps for Solving Multi-Step Problems

Order of Operations

Multi-step problems require more than one calculation. Often, they involve more than one operation. Read the problem carefully, think about the situation, and do the operations in the order that gives the correct answer. Some questions on the GED Mathematics Test ask you to choose the correct method for solving a problem; others ask you to find the answer. In both situations, you need to know how to write and evaluate mathematical expressions that contain more than one operation.

The order in which you do operations in multi-step problems may affect your answer. Look at the problem $5 \times 3 + 6$. This problem uses both multiplication and addition. There are two ways to work the problem, and they give different results; only one is correct. Do you know which one?

Option 1   Multiply first (5×3), then add: $15 + 6 = 21$
Option 2   Add first $(3 + 6)$, then multiply: $5 \times 9 = 45$

The answer could be 21 or 45 depending on the order in which the operations are performed. Mathematicians have agreed upon an **order of operations.** With these rules everyone gets the same solution to a problem. Following the order of operations, the correct answer is **21.**

Step 1   Do operations in parentheses.
Step 2   Do multiplication and division in order from left to right.
Step 3   Do addition and subtraction in order from left to right.

Example 1 $7 \times 4 + 15 \div 3 - 12 \times 2 = ?$

Step 1   There are no parentheses. Go on to the next step.
Step 2   Multiply and divide: $7 \times 4 + 15 \div 3 - 12 \times 2 = ?$
                                             $28 \quad + \quad 5 \quad - \quad 24 \quad = ?$
Step 3   Add and subtract: $33 \qquad\qquad - \quad 24 \quad = 9$

The correct solution is **9.**

Parentheses are used to change the order of operations. Always do an operation in parentheses first.

Example 2 $(12 + 8) \div 4 - 2 = ?$
                   Without the parentheses, you would begin by dividing 8 by 4, but the parentheses tell you to add first.

Step 1   Do the operation in parentheses: $(12 + 8) \div 4 - 2 = ?$
Step 2   Divide: $20 \quad \div 4 - 2 = ?$
Step 3   Subtract: $5 \quad - 2 = 3$

The correct solution is **3.**

There are other properties of numbers that will help you solve problems. The **commutative property** applies to both addition and multiplication. This property states that you can add or multiply numbers in any order and the result will be the same.

TIP

Group numbers that give results of 10 or multiples of 10.

Examples $a + b = b + a$ $a \times b = b \times a$
  $7 + 5 = 5 + 7$ $6 \times 3 = 3 \times 6$

The **associative property** also applies to both addition and multiplication. When adding or multiplying three or more numbers, the way in which you group the numbers does not affect the final result.

Examples $(a + b) + c = a + (b + c)$ $(a \times b) \times c = a \times (b \times c)$
  $(15 + 2) + 8 = 15 + (2 + 8)$ $(18 \times 5) \times 20 = 18 \times (5 \times 20)$

GED SKILL FOCUS

A. Use the order of operations to find the values of the following expressions.

1. $25 - 20 \div 4 =$

2. $(9 + 5) \times (6 - 3) =$

3. $18 - 6 \times 3 =$

4. $60 \div (30 - 10) =$

5. $20 + 12 \div 4 =$

6. $13 + 7 \times 2 + 10 =$

7. $24 \div 6 \times 4 + 2 =$

8. $12 \div 2 \times (8 - 6) =$

9. $11 \times (4 + 2) \times 2 =$

10. $7 \times (3 + 6) =$

11. $15 + 10 - 9 \times 2 =$

12. $54 \div (4 + 5) =$

B. Translate the words into numbers and symbols. Then use the order of operations to perform the calculations. The first one is started for you.

13. Multiply the sum of 7 and 12 by the sum of 16 and 3. $(7 + 12) \times (16 + 3) =$

14. Add 20 and 25, and then divide by 5.

15. Add the product of 4 and 5 to the sum of 10 and 12. *Hint:* Remember that the *product* is the answer to a multiplication problem.

C. Answer the following.

16. Suppose you need to add the following: $28 + 15 + 2 + 5$. How could you group the calculations to make the addition easier?

_____

17. Suppose you need to multiply the following: $25 \times 7 \times 4$. How could you group the calculations to make the computation easier?

_____

Answers start on page 376.

Solving Multi-Step Problems

TIP

Multi-step problems often contain extra information. Identify the problem you are asked to solve. Then focus on the information that will help you find the answer.

To solve a multi-step problem you perform more than one calculation. The key to solving multi-step problems is to think about the situation, identify the needed information and each step and operation needed *before* you work the problem.

The examples below are based on the following information.

Employee	Hourly Wage	Hours Worked				
		M	T	W	T	F
D. Suddeth	$8	8	7	8	8	6
S. Bartok	$9	7	5	6	5	5

Example 1 How much did Dillon Suddeth earn for the week?

(1) $259
(2) $296
(3) $320
(4) $333
(5) Not enough information is given.

There are two steps needed. Determine how many hours Dillon worked and then multiply the number of hours by the hourly wage.

Step 1 Add the hours worked for each day: $8 + 7 + 8 + 8 + 6 = 37$
Step 2 Multiply by the hourly wage of $8: $37 \times \$8 = \$296$

The correct answer is **option (2) $296.**

There may be different ways to solve a problem. In Example 1 you could find the daily earnings (hours worked each day × the hourly wage). Then add the daily earnings to find the earnings for the week.

Example 2 Sharon Bartok set a goal of earning $342 per week. How many more hours would she have to work this week to reach her goal?

(1) 10
(2) 28
(3) 38
(4) 90
(5) 252

Compare the hours Sharon needs to work to earn $342 to the number of hours she already worked during the week shown in the table.

Step 1 Sharon earns $9 per hour. Divide to find how many hours she needs to work to earn $342. $\$342 \div 9 = 38$
Step 2 Add to find the hours she worked during the week shown. $7 + 5 + 6 + 5 + 5 = 28$
Step 3 Compare by subtracting. $38 - 28 = 10$

The correct answer is **option (1) 10.**

Solve as directed.

Refer to the following information to answer Questions 1 and 2.

South Bay Preschool placed the following online order for disposable diapers:

Quantity	Diaper Size	Number in Box
15 boxes	medium	66
18 boxes	large	42
24 boxes	extra-large	24

1. You need to find how many more medium diapers were ordered than extra-large diapers.

   a. How could you find how many medium diapers were ordered? _____

   b. How could you find how many extra-large diapers were ordered? _____

   c. What operation would you use to compare the numbers? _____

   d. Find the answer. _____

2. Regardless of size, each box of diapers costs the preschool $13. You need to find out how much the entire order will cost.

   a. Find the total number of boxes ordered by the preschool. _____

   b. What operation would you use to find the total cost of the order? _____

   c. Then find the total cost. _____

   d. Think of another way to solve the problem and describe it. _____

3. Appliance City is advertising a 27-inch television set for $650 cash or $58 per month for 12 months on credit.

   a. What operations would you need to perform to find out how much a customer would save

   by paying cash instead of buying on credit? _____

   b. Find the amount of the savings. _____

4. Felicia and Jay Oser buy a new refrigerator. They must make eight payments of $115 each and one final payment of $162.

   a. What operations would you need to perform to find the total amount the Osers will spend

   on the refrigerator? _____

   b. Find the total amount the Osers will spend. _____

Answers start on page 377.

GED STRATEGY **Solving Word Problems**

Setting Up Problems

Some multi-step GED problems ask you only to recognize the setup needed to solve the problem, without computing the final answer. Your understanding of the order of operations is important to your success with this type of question. The key is to think about what steps are needed to solve the problem before you begin to choose from the answer options.

Example 1   Grace charges $15 for a haircut and $45 for a permanent. If she does 10 haircuts and 3 permanents on Tuesday, how much will she earn that day?

   (1) $15 + $45
   (2) $15 × 10
   (3) $45 × 3
   (4) ($15 × 10) + ($45 × 3)
   (5) ($15 + 10) × ($45 + 3)

To solve the problem, find the total amount Grace earned for haircuts ($15 × 10) plus permanents ($45 × 3). This is represented by **option (4).**

- Option (1) shows only the cost of one haircut and one permanent.
- Option (2) shows the cost of haircuts only, and option (3) shows the cost of permanents only.
- Option (5) reverses the operations, showing addition where you should multiply and multiplication where you should add.

The use of parentheses and fraction bars is very important in set-up problems. The fraction bar is used as a way to indicate division.

Example 2   Eli and 3 friends met for lunch. The cost of the meal was $20, plus they left a tip of $4. If they split the cost of the lunch evenly, how much did each friend pay?

   (1) 3 + $20 + $4

   (2) 3 × ($20 + $4)

   (3) 4 × ($20 + $4)

   (4) $\dfrac{(\$20 + \$4)}{3}$

   (5) $\dfrac{(\$20 + \$4)}{4}$

To solve the problem, you would need to find the total amount spent for lunch divided by the total number of people splitting the cost. The total cost of the meal included the tip ($20 + $4). The total number of people would be Eli plus his 3 friends, or 4. **Option (5)** is the only option that shows the total cost of the meal divided by 4.

Directions: Choose the <u>one best answer</u> to each question.

1. West Freight held an awards banquet for its 65 employees. The company paid $350 for the use of a banquet room and $9 per person for food. Which expression shows how much the company paid for the room and the food?

   (1) $65 \times \$350$

   (2) $65 \times \$9$

   (3) $(\$350 + \$9) \times 65$

   (4) $(65 \times \$9) + \$350$

   (5) $\dfrac{(\$350 + \$9)}{65}$

2. David can drive 300 miles on 1 tank of gas. Which expression shows how many tanks of gas he will need to drive 1200 miles?

   (1) $300 + 1200$

   (2) $1200 - 300$

   (3) 300×1200

   (4) $\dfrac{300}{1200}$

   (5) $\dfrac{1200}{300}$

3. A parking garage has spaces for 70 cars and charges each driver $6 per day for parking. If all of the spaces are full, which expression shows how much more the garage owner could make if he charged $8 per day?

   (1) $70 + \$8 + \$6$

   (2) $70 \times \$8 \times \$6$

   (3) $70 \times (\$8 - \$6)$

   (4) $70 \times (\$6 + \$8)$

   (5) $\dfrac{(70 \times \$6)}{(70 \times \$8)}$

TIP
Remember there can be more than one way to write some expressions.
$40 \times (7 - 5)$ is $(40 \times 7) - (40 \times 5)$

4. Janet has worked out a payment schedule to pay off an $1800 debt. The schedule calls for her to pay $300 the first month and $150 per month after that. Which expression shows how many $150 payments it will take for Janet to pay off the debt?

   (1) $\dfrac{(\$1800 - \$300)}{\$150}$

   (2) $\$1800 - \$300 - \$150$

   (3) $\dfrac{(\$1800 - \$150)}{\$300}$

   (4) $\$1800 - (\$300 + \$150)$

   (5) $\$1800 - \$300 \times \$150$

5. Arturo had $150 to spend on his college books. He bought 2 textbooks costing $35 each, and 3 textbooks for $18 each. Which expression shows how much money he had left after his purchase?

   (1) $\$150 - (2 \times \$35) + (3 \times \$18)$

   (2) $\$150 - (2 \times \$35) - (3 \times \$18)$

   (3) $(2 \times \$35) - (3 \times \$18)$

   (4) $\$150 - \$35 - \$18$

   (5) $\$150 \times \$35 \times \$18$

6. Teresa sold 2 cameras for $175 each and 3 cameras for $150 each. If she earns a $35 commission for each sale, which expression shows how much she earned in commissions?

   (1) $(\$175 + \$150) \times \$35$

   (2) $(2 \times \$175) + (3 \times \$150)$

   (3) $\$35 \times 2 \times 3$

   (4) $(2 + 3) \times \$35$

   (5) $\dfrac{(\$175 + \$150)}{\$35}$

Answers start on page 377.

GED STRATEGY **Using Your Calculator**

Order of Operations

The order of operations also applies when using a calculator.

Step 1 Do operations in parentheses.
Step 2 Do multiplication and division in order from left to right.
Step 3 Do addition and subtraction in order from left to right.

You should always check to see if the calculator you are using is programmed with the order of operations. You can perform this simple test. Key in the following expression:

3 **+** **4** **×** **2** **=**

If your calculator is programmed with the order of operations, it will perform the multiplication first (4 × 2 = 8), and then the addition (3 + 8). The correct answer is **11.**

> **TIP**
>
> The calculator that you will use on the GED Mathematics Test is programmed with the order of operations. See pages 469 – 472 for more information.

If your calculator does not have the order of operations programmed into it, it will perform the operations in the order that you enter the numbers, giving 3 + 4 = 7 first, and then 7 × 2 = 14 as the answer. If your calculator does not perform the order of operations, you need to be extra careful when using your calculator to help you solve problems.

Example 1 Constance, an office assistant, is buying 3 printer cartridges that cost $24 each. If she gives the cashier a $100-bill, how much change should she receive?

To solve this problem, you could key in the following expression on your calculator:

100 **−** **3** **×** **24** **=**

Remember, be careful if you are using a calculator that does not have the order of operations programmed into it. The calculator will display the wrong answer of 2328.

In order to get the correct answer with this calculator, follow the order of operations by keying in the multiplication first: 3 × 24 = 72. Then subtract the result from 100: 100 − 72 = 28. The correct answer is **$28.**

Example 2 Anthony has already saved $272. If he saves $2 a day for 1 year, how much will he have saved in all?

First think of 1 year as 365 days. Solve by adding how much Anthony has now to how much he will save. Be sure the multiplication is performed first.

2 **×** **365** **+** **272** **=**

The final answer is **$1002.**

Directions: Choose the <u>one best answer</u> to each item. You <u>MAY</u> use your calculator.

Questions 1 and 2 refer to the following information.

The tenants in two apartment buildings agree to hire a private trash collector to serve their buildings. The total yearly cost of the service will be $3096. There are 18 apartments in one building and 25 apartments in the other.

1. Which combination of operations would you need to perform to find out how much each apartment will pay per year for the service if each apartment pays an equal share of the cost?

    (1) addition and multiplication

    (2) addition and division

    (3) subtraction and division

    (4) multiplication and subtraction

    (5) multiplication and division

2. How much is each apartment's share of the yearly cost?

    (1) $ 7

    (2) $ 43

    (3) $ 72

    (4) $124

    (5) $172

3. What is the value of the expression 2,184 + 1,476 × 408?

    (1)   498,982

    (2)   499,982

    (3)   598,093

    (4)   604,392

    (5) 1,493,280

4. What is the value of the expression (908 + 23 × 48) ÷ 2 + 687?

    (1)   1,092

    (2)   1,693

    (3)   1,963

    (4) 23,031

    (5) 23,301

Questions 5 and 6 refer to the following table.

Stock Purchases	
Stock	**Price per Share**
Ampex	$58
Branton	$87
Comtex	$92

5. Marissa invests money for her clients. She purchased 112 shares of Ampex and 89 shares of Comtex. What was the total cost?

    (1) $ 201

    (2) $ 351

    (3) $ 6,496

    (4) $ 8,188

    (5) $14,684

6. Marissa also bought 68 shares of Branton stock for a different client. If this client had $6,000 to invest, how much money still remains to be invested?

    (1) $ 84

    (2) $ 155

    (3) $ 5,845

    (4) $ 5,916

    (5) $516,084

Answers start on page 377.

GED Mini-Test • Lessons 3 and 4

Directions: This is a thirty-minute practice test. After thirty minutes, mark the last item you finished. Then complete the test and check your answers. If most of your answers are correct, but you didn't finish, try to work faster next time.

Part 1

Directions: Choose the <u>one best answer</u> to each question. You <u>MAY</u> use your calculator.

1. Last month, Delta Computers had net sales of $685,170 for its laptop computers. If each laptop computer cost $1,986, how many were sold?

   (1) 694,700
   (2)   3,500
   (3)   3,450
   (4)   345
   (5)   35

2. Atlas Corp. gave each of its 1,216 employees a $760 year-end bonus. What was the total amount of the year-end bonuses?

   (1) $924,160
   (2) $ 92,416
   (3) $ 9,242
   (4) $ 9,241
   (5) Not enough information is given.

3. What is the value of 50 + 15,000 ÷ 25?

   (1) 650
   (2) 602
   (3) 250
   (4) 200
   (5) 25

4. Last year, a bookstore sold 569,346 novels, 234,908 biographies, and 389,782 travel books. What was the total number of books sold in these three categories?

   (1) 11,940,360
   (2)   1,194,036
   (3)   119,404
   (4)   11,940
   (5) Not enough information is given.

5. What is the value of 40(50 − 5 × 2)?

   (1)   40
   (2)   800
   (3) 1600
   (4) 3600
   (5) 3990

6. In a recent election, the winner received 290,876 more votes than his opponent. If the winner received 3,898,705 votes, how many votes did his opponent receive?

   (1) 4,189,581
   (2) 4,089,581
   (3) 3,707,829
   (4) 3,608,829
   (5) 3,607,829

Action Athletics	
Department	**Net Sales**
Footwear	$20,897
Outerwear	$57,941
Sporting Goods	$31,009
Exercise Equipment	$28,987
Skiing Equipment	$18,883

7. What were the total net sales for the five departments listed?

(1) $137,717

(2) $147,707

(3) $147,717

(4) $157,717

(5) Not enough information is given.

8. Combined net sales for Footwear and Sporting Goods were how much less than the net sales for Outerwear?

(1) $ 6,000

(2) $ 6,035

(3) $20,897

(4) $68,053

(5) Not enough information is given.

9. What was the difference in net sales between the department with the largest net sales and the department with the smallest net sales?

(1) $76,828

(2) $57,941

(3) $39,058

(4) $37,644

(5) $28,954

Advertising Expenses		
Category	**January**	**February**
Network TV	$526,987	$540,987
Magazines	$420,885	$398,702
Radio	$249,342	$266,981
Newspapers	$384,692	$312,908

10. How much more was spent for magazine advertising in January than in February?

(1) $ 4,000

(2) $ 17,639

(3) $ 22,183

(4) $ 71,784

(5) $819,587

11. What was the total amount spent for advertising in the first three months of the year?

(1) $ 134,112

(2) $1,519,578

(3) $1,581,906

(4) $1,653,690

(5) Not enough information is given.

12. If the amount spent for advertising on network TV increased by the same amount from February to March as it did from January to February, what would be the amount spent for advertising on network TV in March?

(1) $ 14,000

(2) $ 16,987

(3) $512,987

(4) $554,987

(5) $604,989

Directions: Choose the one best answer to each question. You may NOT use your calculator.

13. Cooper's Fashions has 2100 employees working at 14 branches. After 200 new employees are hired, what is the total number of employees?

    (1) 214
    (2) 2114
    (3) 2300
    (4) 2314
    (5) 4900

14. R.J. Landscaping buys supplies at wholesale. To do the landscaping for a model home, the company spent $560 for bushes and $638 for river rock. The company also purchased paving blocks at $3 each. If 250 blocks are needed, which expression shows how much the paving blocks will cost?

    (1) $\frac{(\$560 + \$638 + \$3)}{250}$
    (2) ($560 + $638 + $3) × 250
    (3) $560 + $638 + $3 − 250
    (4) 250 × $3
    (5) $\frac{250}{\$3}$

15. Marcus buys a computer on credit. He makes a down payment of $720. He also agrees to pay $85 per month on the remaining balance. What is the total cost of the computer?

    (1) $ 720
    (2) $ 765
    (3) $1020
    (4) $1275
    (5) Not enough information is given.

16. What is the value of $3 + 4 \times 2 - 6 \div 2$?

    (1) 4
    (2) 8
    (3) 10
    (4) 14
    (5) 16

Questions 17 and 18 refer to the following information.

A furniture store advertises a couch for $760 if paid in cash or for $75 per month for the next 12 months if paid in installments.

17. Which operation would you use to find the total cost of the couch if you paid in installments?

    (1) addition
    (2) subtraction
    (3) multiplication
    (4) division
    (5) Not enough information is given.

18. How much money would you save by paying in cash instead of by paying in 12 monthly installments?

    (1) $100
    (2) $140
    (3) $560
    (4) $760
    (5) $900

Questions 19 and 20 refer to the following table.

T-Shirts Ordered		
T-Shirt Size	Quantity	Number in Box
Small	10 boxes	60
Medium	12 boxes	48
Large	20 boxes	20

19. About how many medium sized T-shirts were ordered?

(1) 12
(2) 20
(3) 50
(4) 120
(5) 500

20. How many more small T-shirts were ordered than large T-shirts?

(1) 1000
(2) 600
(3) 400
(4) 200
(5) 30

21. Rizal sold 2 lawn carts for $200 each and 3 push mowers for $130 each. If he earns a $25 commission for each machine sold, which expression shows his commission for these sales?

(1) 25(2 × 200) + 25(3 × 130)
(2) 25(2 × 200) − 25(3 × 130)
(3) 25(200 + 130)
(4) 25(200 + 130)
(5) 25(3 + 2)

Questions 22 through 24 refer to the following table.

Crunch's Rentals	Charge (daily rate)
Wet/Dry Vacuum	$40
Rotary Hammer, electric	$30
Air Compressor	$45
Portable Generator	$35
Chipper/Shredder	$75

22. How much more does it cost per day to rent a chipper/shredder than an air compressor?

(1) $25
(2) $30
(3) $35
(4) $40
(5) $45

23. How much more would it cost to rent the wet/dry vacuum and the air compressor for one day than to rent the chipper/shredder?

(1) $10
(2) $30
(3) $35
(4) $70
(5) $80

24. The Burkes are clearing some property they bought. If they rent the chipper/shredder for 3 days, what is the total cost?

(1) $ 25
(2) $ 75
(3) $150
(4) $225
(5) $300

Answers start on page 377.

Facts About Fractions

To count, you use whole numbers. To show part of something, you use fractions. Fractions show part of a whole object or part of a group.

A **fraction** is two numbers, separated by a fraction bar. The bottom number, or **denominator,** tells the number of equal parts into which the whole object or group is divided. The top number, or **numerator,** tells the number of equal parts in the object or group being considered. The numerator and denominator are the **terms** of the fraction.

To use a fraction to show a part of a whole, imagine that the object is divided into equal parts. For example, the rectangle below is divided into 6 equal parts, or sixths. The entire rectangle represents $\frac{6}{6}$ or 1 whole. Any fraction with the same numerator and denominator is equal to 1.

TIP

When the numerator of a fraction has nearly the same value as the denominator, the value of the fraction is close to 1.

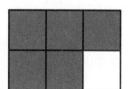

5 of the 6 parts are shaded.
The fraction $\frac{5}{6}$ represents the shaded part.

$\frac{5}{6}$ ← number of shaded parts (numerator)
  ← number of equal parts in the whole
   (denominator)

You can also use a fraction to show part of a group.

Example   Nicco received 18 orders on Wednesday. There were 11 phone orders. What fraction of the orders came by phone?

$\frac{11}{18}$ ← number of phone orders
   ← number of orders received on Wednesday

$\frac{11}{18}$ of Wednesday's orders came by phone.

The fractions $\frac{5}{6}$ and $\frac{11}{18}$ are examples of proper fractions. A **proper fraction** shows a quantity that is less than 1. The numerator of a proper fraction is always less than the denominator.

An **improper fraction** is used to show a quantity equal to or greater than 1. The numerator of an improper fraction is equal to or greater than the denominator.

The figure is divided into three equal parts, and three parts are shaded. The fraction $\frac{3}{3}$ represents the shaded part. $\frac{3}{3}$ is an improper fraction because it is equal to 1 whole.

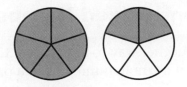

Each circle is divided into 5 equal parts, and 7 parts are shaded. The fraction $\frac{7}{5}$ represents the shaded part. $\frac{7}{5}$ is an improper fraction because the numerator is greater than the denominator. $\frac{7}{5}$ is greater than 1.

GED SKILL FOCUS

A. Write the fraction for the shaded portion.

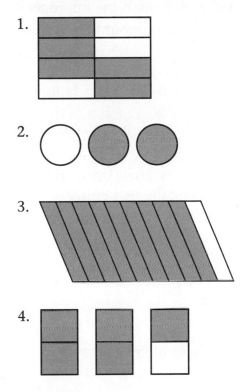

1.

2.

3.

4.

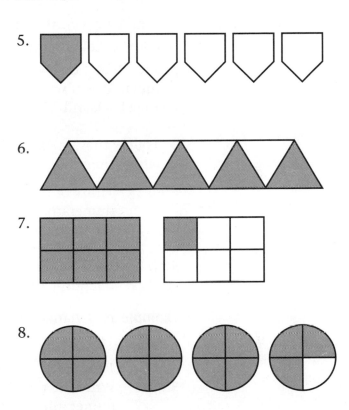

5.

6.

7.

8.

B. Solve.

9. On Tuesday, 9 of Steve's 16 customers paid using credit cards. What fraction of his customers used credit cards?

10. Out of the 10 people in Carla's office, 7 regularly watch the evening news on television. What fraction of the workers watches the evening news?

11. In the election for union representative, Carlos received 19 votes. What fraction of the union's 45 members voted for Carlos?

12. Yuki arrived early for work on 47 of the last 50 workdays. What fraction of the time has she been early for work?

13. Of the 70 orders shipped yesterday by AB Technology, 9 were shipped by air. What fraction of the orders was shipped by air?

14. A video rental store has 500 movies in stock. Only 43 are children's movies. What fraction of the movies in stock is for children?

Answers start on page 378.

Changing Improper Fractions and Mixed Numbers

A **mixed number** is another way to show a fraction greater than 1. A mixed number consists of a whole number and a proper fraction.

Example 1   Write a mixed number for the shaded portion.

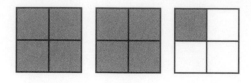

In the figure, each square is divided into 4 equal parts. Two of the squares are completely shaded, and $\frac{1}{4}$ of the last square is shaded. The shaded portion is $2\frac{1}{4}$. The mixed number $2\frac{1}{4}$ means two and one-fourth or $2 + \frac{1}{4}$.

You have seen that the shaded portion above equals the improper fraction $\frac{9}{4}$. So, you can conclude that $\frac{9}{4} = 2\frac{1}{4}$. Any amount equal to or greater than 1 can be expressed as either an improper fraction or a mixed number. As you work with fractions, you will need to know how to change back and forth between improper fractions and mixed numbers.

Follow these steps to change an improper fraction to a mixed number or whole number.

Step 1   Think of the fraction bar as a division symbol. Divide the numerator of the improper fraction by the denominator. The whole number answer becomes the whole number part of the mixed number.

Step 2   Write the remainder over the original denominator. This is the fraction part of the mixed number.

Example 2   Change $\frac{14}{3}$ to a mixed number.

Step 1 $\frac{14}{3}$ means $14 \div 3$. Divide. The whole number is 4.

Step 2   Write the remainder as the numerator over the divisor as the denominator: 2 over 3.

$$\begin{array}{r} 4 \leftarrow \text{whole} \\ \text{denominator} \rightarrow 3\overline{)14} \quad \text{number} \\ \underline{12} \\ 2 \leftarrow \text{numerator} \end{array}$$

The improper fraction $\frac{14}{3}$ equals $4\frac{2}{3}$.

A mixed number can also be changed to an improper fraction.

Step 1   Multiply the whole number part of the mixed number by the denominator of the fraction.

Step 2   Add the numerator of the fraction part.

Step 3   Write the total over the original denominator.

Example 3   Change $2\frac{3}{8}$ to an improper fraction.

whole number   denominator

Step 1   Multiply 2 by 8. $2 \times 8 = 16$

Step 2   Add the numerator, 3. $16 + 3 = 19$

Step 3   Write the total over the denominator, 8. $\frac{19}{8}$

The mixed number $2\frac{3}{8}$ equals $\frac{19}{8}$.

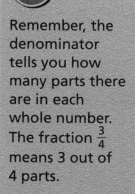

Remember, the denominator tells you how many parts there are in each whole number. The fraction $\frac{3}{4}$ means 3 out of 4 parts.

A. For each shaded portion, write the improper fraction and the mixed number.

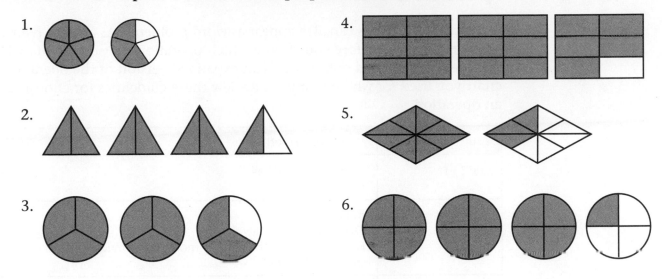

1.

2.

3.

4.

5.

6.

B. Change each improper fraction to a whole or a mixed number.

7. $\frac{7}{2} =$

8. $\frac{8}{3} =$

9. $\frac{57}{10} =$

10. $\frac{15}{3} =$

11. $\frac{10}{3} =$

12. $\frac{77}{9} =$

13. $\frac{19}{4} =$

14. $\frac{31}{8} =$

15. $\frac{42}{6} =$

16. $\frac{9}{2} =$

17. $\frac{17}{6} =$

18. $\frac{41}{12} =$

C. Change each mixed number to an improper fraction.

19. $6\frac{1}{2} =$

20. $8\frac{1}{2} =$

21. $5\frac{3}{8} =$

22. $3\frac{5}{6} =$

23. $2\frac{1}{5} =$

24. $6\frac{4}{7} =$

25. $1\frac{5}{8} =$

26. $11\frac{3}{4} =$

27. $10\frac{1}{2} =$

28. $4\frac{2}{9} =$

29. $5\frac{1}{12} =$

30. $9\frac{2}{5} =$

Answers start on page 379.

GED STRATEGY Solving Word Problems

Choosing the Operation

Fraction problems can also appear as word problems. As always, read a problem carefully before you choose which operation to use. Identify what you are trying to find out. Below is an expanded version of the operations chart you used for whole numbers. Review these guidelines for choosing an operation.

You	When You Need To
Add (+)	Combine quantities Find a total
Subtract (−)	Find a difference Take away a quantity Compare to find "how many more," "how much less," or "how much is left"
Multiply (×)	Put together a number of equal amounts to find a total Add the same number repeatedly Find a "part of" a whole item or group
Divide (÷)	Split a quantity into equal parts Find how many equal parts are in a whole

Example 1   A worker at a coffee shop mixed $10\frac{3}{8}$ pounds of gourmet coffee with $6\frac{3}{4}$ pounds of regular grind coffee. How many more pounds of the gourmet coffee were used than the regular grind coffee?

(1) $10\frac{3}{8} + 6\frac{3}{4}$

(2) $10\frac{3}{8} - 6\frac{3}{4}$

(3) $6\frac{3}{4} \times 10\frac{3}{8}$

(4) $10\frac{3}{8} \div 6\frac{3}{4}$

(5) $6\frac{3}{4} - 10\frac{3}{8}$

The correct answer is **option (2).** You subtract to find "how many more."

Example 2   Of Ed's 128 employees, $\frac{3}{8}$ volunteered to work on Saturday. How many employees volunteered to work on Saturday?

(1) $\frac{3}{8} + 128$

(2) $128 - \frac{3}{8}$

(3) $128 \times \frac{3}{8}$

(4) $128 \div \frac{3}{8}$

(5) $\frac{3}{8} \div 128$

The correct answer is **option (3).** You need to find "part of" a group.

TIP

When solving a fraction problem that asks you to find a "part of" a whole or other fraction, you multiply.

Directions: Choose the <u>one best answer</u> to each question.

1. A recipe calls for $5\frac{3}{4}$ cups of flour. Brian has only $2\frac{3}{8}$ cups left in the bag. How much more does he need?

   (1) $5\frac{3}{4} + 2\frac{3}{8}$

   (2) $5\frac{3}{4} - 2\frac{3}{8}$

   (3) $2\frac{3}{8} \times 5\frac{3}{4}$

   (4) $5\frac{3}{4} \div 2\frac{3}{8}$

   (5) $2\frac{3}{8} \div 5\frac{3}{4}$

Question 2 refers to the following diagram.

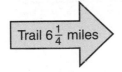

Trail $6\frac{1}{4}$ miles

2. Steve is taking the path shown by the sign above. If he averages $2\frac{1}{2}$ miles per hour, how many hours will it take him to reach the end of the trail?

   (1) $6\frac{1}{4} + 2\frac{1}{2}$

   (2) $6\frac{1}{4} - 2\frac{1}{2}$

   (3) $2\frac{1}{2} \times 6\frac{1}{4}$

   (4) $6\frac{1}{4} \div 2\frac{1}{2}$

   (5) $2\frac{1}{2} \div 6\frac{1}{4}$

3. A restaurant ordered $15\frac{3}{4}$ pounds of almonds. The nut supplier sent only $\frac{1}{2}$ of the order. How many pounds of almonds did the supplier send?

   (1) $\frac{1}{2} + 15\frac{3}{4}$

   (2) $15\frac{3}{4} - \frac{1}{2}$

   (3) $15\frac{3}{4} \times \frac{1}{2}$

   (4) $15\frac{3}{4} \div \frac{1}{2}$

   (5) $\frac{1}{2} \div 15\frac{3}{4}$

4. Kim's driving class lasts $\frac{3}{4}$ of an hour. How many classes can she teach in $4\frac{1}{2}$ hours?

   (1) $4\frac{1}{2} + \frac{3}{4}$

   (2) $4\frac{1}{2} - \frac{3}{4}$

   (3) $\frac{3}{4} \times 4\frac{1}{2}$

   (4) $4\frac{1}{2} \div \frac{3}{4}$

   (5) $\frac{3}{4} \div 4\frac{1}{2}$

5. Phil rode his bike $18\frac{1}{2}$ miles on Friday and $12\frac{2}{5}$ miles on Saturday. How many miles did he ride in the two days?

   (1) $18\frac{1}{2} + 12\frac{2}{5}$

   (2) $18\frac{1}{2} - 12\frac{2}{5}$

   (3) $12\frac{2}{5} \times 18\frac{1}{2}$

   (4) $12\frac{2}{5} \div 18\frac{1}{2}$

   (5) $18\frac{1}{2} \div 12\frac{2}{5}$

6. At Howard Brothers Manufacturing, $\frac{5}{8}$ of the employees takes the bus to work. Of these, $\frac{2}{5}$ takes the express bus. What fraction of the employees takes the express bus?

   (1) $\frac{5}{8} + \frac{2}{5}$

   (2) $\frac{5}{8} - \frac{2}{5}$

   (3) $\frac{2}{5} \times \frac{5}{8}$

   (4) $\frac{5}{8} \div \frac{2}{5}$

   (5) $\frac{2}{5} \div \frac{5}{8}$

TIP To find a fraction of a fraction multiply just like when finding a fraction of a whole. For example, to find $\frac{1}{2}$ of $\frac{1}{4}$, multiply: $\frac{1}{2} \times \frac{1}{4}$.

Answers start on page 379.

GED SKILL Fractions on Number Lines

Earlier in this book you used number lines to locate whole numbers. You can also use number lines to locate and compare fractions. Remember these facts about number lines:

- values are equally spaced
- as you move to the right on a number line, the values increase
- arrows at the ends of the number line mean that the line extends indefinitely in both directions

Also, note that all proper fractions are somewhere between 0 and 1 on the number line, and all improper fractions and mixed numbers are located at 1 or to the right of 1.

Example 1   Place a dot on the number line below to locate a fraction with a numerator less than its denominator.

If the numerator of a fraction is less than its denominator, its value is less than 1. Therefore, a dot placed anywhere between 0 and 1 would be correct. Two possible answers are shown below.

Example 2   Place a dot on the number line below to locate a number that makes this comparison true: 2 < ? < 3.

Remember, the expression, 2 < ? < 3, means a *number greater than 2 and less than 3*. Therefore, a dot placed anywhere between 2 and 3 would be correct. Two possible answers are shown below.

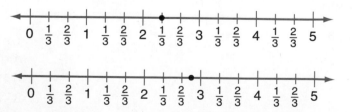

Solve the following problems. Show your answers by placing a dot on the number line below each problem.

1. Place a dot on the number line below to locate the mixed number $3\frac{3}{4}$.

```
  ←|++|++|++|++|++|++|++|++|++|++|→
    0    1    2    3    4    5
```

2. Place a dot on the number line below to show the location of the mixed number $1\frac{3}{5}$.

```
  ←|++|++|++|++|++|++|++|++|++|++|→
    0    1    2    3    4    5
```

3. Place a dot on the number line below to show the mixed number $4\frac{1}{3}$.

```
  ←|++|++|++|++|++|++|++|++|→
    0    1    2    3    4    5
```

4. Polls for the upcoming election predict that candidate Manning can expect to receive $\frac{4}{5}$ of the votes. Place a dot on the number line below to show the fraction of the votes that candidate Manning is predicted to receive.

```
  ←|++|++|++|++|++|++|++|++|++|++|→
    0    1    2    3    4    5
```

5. A ring is made of $\frac{2}{3}$ pure gold and $\frac{1}{3}$ other metals. Place a dot on the number line below to show the fraction of the ring that is pure gold.

```
  ←|++|++|++|++|++|++|++|++|→
    0    1    2    3    4    5
```

6. Jan arrived at work at 8:30 A.M. and went home at 4:15 P.M. Place a dot on the number line below to show the time Jan went home as a mixed number.

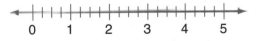

```
  ←|+|+|++|++|++|++|++|++|++|→
    0    1    2    3    4    5
```

7. Amy needs $3\frac{3}{4}$ yards of material for a size 6 dress. Place a dot on the number line below to show how much material she needs.

```
  ←|++|++|++|++|++|++|++|++|→
    0    1    2    3    4    5
```

Answers start on page 379.

GED SKILL Fractions, Ratios, and Proportions

Equal Fractions

You know from experience that different fractions can have the same value.

- Since there are 100 pennies in a dollar, 25 pennies is equal to $\frac{25}{100}$ of a dollar. The same amount also equals a quarter, or $\frac{1}{4}$ of a dollar.
- On a measuring cup, $\frac{1}{2}$ cup is the same amount as $\frac{2}{4}$ cup.
- On an odometer, $\frac{5}{10}$ of a mile is the same as $\frac{1}{2}$ mile.
- Out of a dozen doughnuts, six doughnuts equal $\frac{6}{12}$, or $\frac{1}{2}$ dozen.

Fractions that have the same value are called **equivalent** or **equal fractions.** You can tell if two fractions are equal by finding **cross products.**

Example   Are $\frac{4}{8}$ and $\frac{3}{6}$ equal fractions?

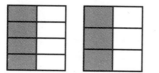 Multiply diagonally as shown by the arrows below. If the cross products are equal, the fractions are equal.

$$\frac{4}{8} \diagdown \frac{3}{6} \qquad \begin{array}{l} 4 \times 6 = 24 \\ 8 \times 3 = 24 \end{array}$$

Since the cross products are equal, $\frac{4}{8} = \frac{3}{6}$.

Reducing Fractions

Reducing a fraction means finding an equal fraction with a smaller numerator and denominator. The fraction is reduced to **lowest terms** when there is no number other than 1 that will divide evenly into both the numerator and the denominator.

To reduce a fraction, divide both the numerator and the denominator by the same number, and write the new fraction.

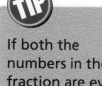

TIP

If both the numbers in the fraction are even numbers, you can always divide by 2.

Example 1   In one hour, 10 customers visited Stuart's newsstand. Of those, 6 bought a magazine. What fraction of the customers purchased a magazine?

Write a fraction: $\frac{6}{10}$. Reduce the fraction to lowest terms by dividing both the numerator and denominator by 2.

$$\frac{6}{10} = \frac{6 \div 2}{10 \div 2} = \frac{3}{5} \qquad \textbf{\frac{3}{5}} \text{ of the customers made a purchase.}$$

You may need to divide more than once to reduce a fraction to lowest terms. Remember, keep dividing until there is no number other than 1 that will divide evenly into both numerator and denominator.

Example 2   Write $\frac{24}{30}$ in lowest terms.

Step 1   First divide the numerator and denominator by 3. However, the fraction $\frac{8}{10}$ is not in lowest terms.

$$\frac{24}{30} = \frac{24 \div 3}{30 \div 3} = \frac{8}{10}$$

Step 2   Divide the numerator and denominator by 2. The fraction $\frac{4}{5}$ is in lowest terms.

$$\frac{8}{10} = \frac{8 \div 2}{10 \div 2} = \frac{4}{5}$$

Note: If you noticed that 6 divides evenly into both 24 and 30, you could reduce the fraction to lowest terms in one step.

GED SKILL FOCUS

A. Reduce each fraction to lowest terms.

1. $\frac{2}{4} =$

2. $\frac{6}{9} -$

3. $\frac{10}{25} =$

4. $\frac{6}{8} =$

5. $\frac{6}{15} =$

6. $\frac{18}{27} =$

7. $\frac{5}{20} =$

8. $\frac{12}{48} =$

9. $\frac{16}{20} =$

10. $\frac{12}{30} =$

11. $\frac{7}{42} =$

12. $\frac{24}{36} =$

B. Circle the two equal fractions in each line. You may find it helpful to reduce each fraction to lowest terms.

13. $\frac{4}{6}$ $\frac{8}{12}$ $\frac{6}{10}$ $\frac{2}{4}$ $\frac{10}{12}$

14. $\frac{8}{16}$ $\frac{2}{3}$ $\frac{5}{12}$ $\frac{3}{6}$ $\frac{3}{4}$

15. $\frac{3}{12}$ $\frac{8}{16}$ $\frac{2}{8}$ $\frac{4}{20}$ $\frac{2}{6}$

16. $\frac{5}{8}$ $\frac{6}{8}$ $\frac{6}{10}$ $\frac{4}{16}$ $\frac{3}{5}$

C. Solve. Express each answer in lowest terms.

17. Sadrac worked 8 hours on Monday. If he worked 40 hours during the week, what fraction of the total time did he work on Monday?

18. Morley's Paint advertised its store sale in the newspaper. On Friday, the store had 50 customers. Of those, 15 saw the advertisement. What fraction of Friday's customers saw the advertisement?

19. Crown Manufacturing completed 1000 assemblies today. Of those, 50 were defective. What fraction of the assemblies was defective?

20. Jean withdrew $40 from her savings account. She spent $24 at the pharmacy. What fraction of the withdrawal did she spend at the pharmacy?

Answers start on page 380.

Raising Fractions to Higher Terms

Sometimes you need to find an equal fraction with higher terms. You raise a fraction to higher terms by multiplying both the numerator and the denominator by the same number (except 0).

$\frac{5}{8}$ and $\frac{20}{32}$ are equal fractions.

Often you will need to find an equal fraction with a specific denominator. To do this, think, "What number multiplied by the original denominator will result in the new denominator?" Then multiply the original numerator by the same number.

Example $\frac{3}{4} = \frac{?}{24}$

Since $4 \times 6 = 24$, multiply the numerator 3 by 6. $\frac{3 \times 6}{4 \times 6} = \frac{18}{24}$

The fractions **$\frac{3}{4}$ and $\frac{18}{24}$ are equal fractions.**

Comparing Fractions

When two fractions have the same number as the denominator, they are said to have a **common denominator,** and the fractions are called **like fractions.** When you compare like fractions, the fraction with the greater numerator is the greater fraction.

Example 1   Which fraction is greater, $\frac{3}{5}$ or $\frac{4}{5}$?

The fractions $\frac{3}{5}$ and $\frac{4}{5}$ are like fractions because they have a common denominator, 5. Compare the numerators.

Since 4 is greater than 3, **$\frac{4}{5}$ is greater than $\frac{3}{5}$.**

Fractions with different denominators are called **unlike fractions.** To compare unlike fractions, you must change them to fractions with a common denominator.

The common denominator will always be a **multiple** of both of the original denominators. The multiples of a number are found by going through the times tables for the number. For instance, the multiples of 3 are 3, 6, 9, 12, 15, 18, and so on.

You can often find a common denominator by using mental math. If not, try these methods:

1. See whether the larger denominator could be a common denominator. In other words, if the smaller denominator can divide into the larger denominator evenly, use the larger denominator as the common denominator.

2. Go through the multiples of the larger denominator. The first one that can be divided evenly by the smaller denominator is the **lowest common denominator.**

TIP

Finding common denominators is important to your success on the GED Mathematics Test. Practice writing the first 12 multiples of the numbers 2 through 12.

Example 2 Which is greater, $\frac{5}{6}$ or $\frac{3}{4}$?

Go through the multiples of the larger denominator: 6, 12, 18, 24, 30 . . .
Since 12 can be divided evenly by both 4 and 6, 12 is the lowest common
denominator.

Build equal fractions, each with the
denominator 12:

$$\frac{5 \times 2}{6 \times 2} = \frac{10}{12} \qquad \frac{3 \times 3}{4 \times 3} = \frac{9}{12}$$

Compare the like fractions. Since $\frac{10}{12} > \frac{9}{12}$, the fraction $\frac{5}{6} > \frac{3}{4}$.

GED SKILL FOCUS

A. Find an equal fraction with the given denominator.

1. $\frac{2}{3} = \frac{?}{12}$

2. $\frac{2}{7} = \frac{?}{21}$

3. $\frac{4}{5} = \frac{?}{25}$

4. $\frac{5}{8} = \frac{?}{32}$

5. $\frac{7}{9} = \frac{?}{63}$

6. $\frac{3}{10} = \frac{?}{120}$

7. $\frac{3}{4} = \frac{?}{36}$

8. $\frac{4}{9} = \frac{?}{81}$

9. $\frac{9}{50} = \frac{?}{150}$

B. Compare the fractions. Write >, < , or = between the fractions.

10. $\frac{1}{3}$ $\frac{1}{4}$

11. $\frac{3}{4}$ $\frac{7}{8}$

12. $\frac{3}{9}$ $\frac{1}{3}$

13. $\frac{2}{3}$ $\frac{1}{2}$

14. $\frac{5}{6}$ $\frac{15}{18}$

15. $\frac{9}{12}$ $\frac{3}{4}$

16. $\frac{7}{10}$ $\frac{2}{3}$

17. $\frac{7}{15}$ $\frac{2}{5}$

18. $\frac{9}{10}$ $\frac{3}{4}$

C. Solve.

Refer to the following information to
answer Questions 19 through 22.

A manufacturing plant has five assembly
lines. The table shows the fraction of
assigned work that each team has
completed.

Team A	$\frac{2}{5}$ of goal
Team B	$\frac{1}{2}$ of goal
Team C	$\frac{1}{4}$ of goal
Team D	$\frac{3}{5}$ of goal
Team E	$\frac{3}{4}$ of goal

19. Which team has completed the
    smallest part of its goal?

20. Which team has completed the
    greatest part of its goal?

21. Which teams have completed more
    than $\frac{1}{2}$ of their goal?

22. Which teams have completed between
    $\frac{3}{8}$ and $\frac{5}{8}$ of their goal?

TIP If you have trouble finding the
lowest common denominator,
multiply the two denominators.
The result will be a common
denominator, although probably
not the lowest one.

Answers start on page 380.

Working with Ratios

A **ratio** is a comparison of two numbers. A ratio can be written with the word *to*, with a colon (:), or as a fraction. Always write the terms of the ratio in the same order as the problem compares them.

Example 1   A painter mixes 4 quarts of white paint and 2 quarts of blue paint. What is the ratio of white paint to blue paint?

The ratio of white paint to blue paint can be written as **4 to 2, 4:2,** or $\frac{4}{2}$.

Just as you can reduce fractions to lowest terms, you can simplify ratios to their lowest terms. The ratio $\frac{4}{2}$ can be simplified to $\frac{2}{1}$, which means for every 2 quarts of white paint, there is 1 quart of blue paint. Ratios are written as a fraction even if the denominator is 1.

Ratios have much in common with fractions, but there is an important difference. A ratio may look like an improper fraction, but it should not be changed to a whole or mixed number because it is a comparison of two items, not just a part of a whole.

Ratios often express rates. A ratio with the denominator 1 is called a **unit rate.** Unit rates are often expressed using the word *per*.

Example 2   If Barbara earns $180 in 15 hours, how much does she earn per hour?

Write the ratio of earnings to hours. Then divide to find the unit rate.

$$\frac{\text{dollars earned}}{\text{hours}} = \frac{\$180}{15} = \frac{180 \div 15}{15 \div 15} = \frac{\$12}{1 \text{ hr}}$$

Barbara earns $12 for every 1 hour she works. In other words, she earns **$12 per hour.**

Some ratio problems require more than one step. You may not be given both of the numbers you need to write a ratio. Instead, you may have to solve for one of the numbers.

Example 3   Kimball Discount has 25 employees. Of those 25 employees, 15 are women. What is the ratio of the number of men to the number of women employees?

You need to write a ratio comparing the number of men to the number of women. You have been given the total number of employees and the number of women employees.

Step 1   Subtract to find the number of men. $25 - 15 = 10$ men

Step 2   Write the ratio of men to women. $\frac{\text{men}}{\text{women}} = \frac{10}{15}$

Step 3   Simplify the ratio. $\frac{10}{15} = \frac{10 \div 5}{15 \div 5} = \frac{2}{3}$

The ratio of men to women employees at Kimball Discount is $\frac{2}{3}$.

TIP

Writing the ratio in words will help you keep the numbers in the correct order. The words will also help you remember the meaning of the numbers. Including labels in your final ratio is also helpful.

A. Write each ratio as a fraction in lowest terms.

1. 18 wins to 6 losses

2. 80 full-time workers to 100 part-time workers

3. 16 fiction books to 12 non-fiction books

4. $21 to $9

5. 69 female employees to 90 total employees

6. 16 minutes to 30 minutes

7. 85 miles to 100 miles

8. 35 customers to 7 sales

9. 10 adults to 120 children

10. 15 wins to 20 games played

B. Find each unit rate.

11. 400 miles in 5 hours

12. $216 in 18 hours

13. 54 calories in 6 grams of fat

14. 432 people for 36 teams

15. $10 for 10 pounds of grass seed

16. 5400 oranges in 60 bags

17. 1024 feet in 16 seconds

18. $150 for 25 yards of fabric

19. 135 pages in 3 hours

20. 460 calories in 2 servings

C. Solve as directed.

21. The Monarchs won 30 games and lost 6 games.

    a. What is the ratio of games won to games lost?
    b. What is the ratio of games lost to games played?
    c. What is the ratio of games won to games played?
    d. What is the ratio of games lost to games won?

22. In a factory, there are 35 union workers and 14 non-union workers.

    a. What is the ratio of non-union to union workers?
    b. What is the ratio of union workers to the total number of workers?
    c. What is the ratio of the number of non-union workers to the total number of workers?
    d. What is the ratio of union workers to non-union workers?

23. On a quiz, Denzel answered 16 questions correctly and 4 questions incorrectly.

    a. What is the ratio of correct to incorrect answers?
    b. What is the ratio of correct answers to total questions?
    c. What is the ratio of incorrect answers to total questions?

24. A manufacturer produced 1000 electric switches. Of these, 50 were found to have defects.

    a. What is the ratio of defective switches to total switches?
    b. What is the ratio of defective to good switches?
    c. What is the ratio of good switches to total switches?

Answers start on page 381.

Solving Proportions

When two ratios are written as equal ratios, the equation is called a **proportion.** Think about the following statement:

Example 1 If Paul earns $8 in 1 hour, then he will earn $56 in 7 hours.

From the information in the sentence, you can write a proportion. Use cross products to make sure the ratios are equal.

$$\frac{\text{dollars earned}}{\text{hours}} \qquad \frac{8}{1} \diagdown\!\!\!\!\diagup \frac{56}{7} \qquad \text{Cross products: } 1 \times 56 = 8 \times 7$$
$$56 = 56$$

As you can see from the example above, every proportion has four terms. In a proportion problem, one of the four terms is missing. The proportion can be solved using this rule:

> **Cross-product Rule:** To find the missing number in a proportion, cross multiply and divide the product by the third number.

TIP

In a proportion, the terms in both ratios must be written in the same order. In this example, both ratios have miles on the top and hours on the bottom. Use labels to keep track of the order.

Example 2 Gayla drove 165 miles in 3 hours. At the same rate, how far can she drive in 5 hours?

In this problem, you are comparing miles to hours. Set up two equal ratios. Write x to stand for the missing term.

$$\frac{\text{miles}}{\text{hours}} = \frac{165}{3} = \frac{x}{5}$$

Step 1 Find the cross product. $165 \times 5 = 825$

Step 2 Divide by 3, the remaining term. $825 \div 3 = 275$

Gayla can drive **275 miles** in 5 hours.

You can easily solve proportion problems using a calculator. Enter the numbers and operations in this order:

165 ✕ 5 ÷ 3 = 275.

Some proportion problems state a ratio using a colon. Read carefully to understand what the numbers in the ratio represent.

Example 3 At a school board meeting, the ratio of parents to teachers is 3:2. If there are 72 parents at the meeting, how many teachers are there?

Step 1 The ratio 3:2 compares parents to teachers. Write the second ratio in the same order. $\frac{\text{parents}}{\text{teachers}} = \frac{3}{2} = \frac{72}{x}$

Step 2 Find the cross product, and divide by the remaining term. $2 \times 72 = 144$
$144 \div 3 = 48$

There are **48 teachers** at the meeting.

A. Solve for the missing term in each proportion.

1. $\dfrac{2}{3} = \dfrac{x}{15}$

2. $\dfrac{28}{12} = \dfrac{14}{x}$

3. $\dfrac{9}{10} = \dfrac{x}{20}$

4. $\dfrac{5}{6} = \dfrac{x}{18}$

5. $\dfrac{3}{4} = \dfrac{9}{x}$

6. $\dfrac{15}{24} = \dfrac{5}{x}$

7. $\dfrac{12}{15} = \dfrac{24}{x}$

8. $\dfrac{14}{6} = \dfrac{7}{x}$

9. $\dfrac{115}{30} = \dfrac{x}{6}$

10. $\dfrac{5}{20} = \dfrac{8}{x}$

11. $\dfrac{49}{7} = \dfrac{x}{10}$

12. $\dfrac{32}{8} = \dfrac{x}{15}$

13. $\dfrac{18}{6} = \dfrac{3}{x}$

14. $\dfrac{6}{120} = \dfrac{5}{x}$

15. $\dfrac{64}{8} = \dfrac{x}{5}$

B. For each situation, the first ratio has been written for you. Write the second ratio to complete the proportion and solve.

16. A recipe that serves 8 people calls for 2 cups of milk. How many cups of milk will be needed for 36 servings?

$\dfrac{\text{servings}}{\text{cups of milk}}$ $\dfrac{8}{2} = \dfrac{?}{?}$

17. Sandra can drive 32 miles on 2 gallons of gasoline. How far can she drive on a full tank of 13 gallons?

$\dfrac{\text{miles}}{\text{gallons}}$ $\dfrac{32}{2} = \dfrac{?}{?}$

18. A person uses about 315 calories to jog 3 miles. How many calories will be used in a 10-mile jog?

$\dfrac{\text{calories}}{\text{miles}}$ $\dfrac{315}{3} = \dfrac{?}{?}$

19. An architect is planning a city parking lot. For every 12 commuters, the parking lot will need 5 parking spaces. How many parking spaces will be needed for 132 commuters?

$\dfrac{\text{commuters}}{\text{parking spaces}}$ $\dfrac{12}{5} = \dfrac{?}{?}$

C. Write a proportion and solve for the missing term.

20. The scale on a map says that 2 inches equal 150 miles. If two cities are actually 750 miles apart, how many inches apart will they be on the map?

21. The ratio of full-time to part-time employees at Kelly Manufacturing is 5:3. If there are 48 part-time employees at the plant, how many full-time workers are there?

22. Ky bought 2 gallons of paint for $27. How much would he spend for 10 gallons?

23. The ratio of wins to losses for the Bulldogs was 7:2. If the team won 21 games, how many did they lose?

Answers start on page 382.

GED STRATEGY Working with Special Formats

Writing Fractions in a Standard Grid

The standard grid that you used earlier in the book to write whole number answers can also be used to write fractional answers.

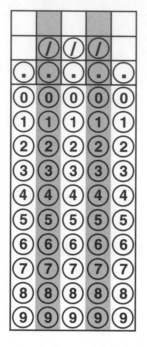

Here are some important points to keep in mind when using the standard grid with fractional answers:

- The grid is used to enter a single fractional answer.
- Your answer can start in any of the five columns, as long as your answer is complete. Any unused columns should be left blank.
- Fill in the corresponding circle in each column to show the numerator of the fraction, then the fraction bar in the second row of the grid, $\oslash$, and then the denominator of the fraction.
- Mixed numbers cannot be entered on the grid. Therefore, change all mixed number answers to improper fractions before entering them on the grid.

Example   On Thursday morning, 7 out of the 15 clients at Maya's Hair Salon paid with a credit card. What fraction paid with a credit card?

The fraction is $\frac{7}{15}$.

Note that since the answer can start in any of the five columns, both grids shown below are filled in correctly.

Directions: Solve the following problems. Write your answer in the top row of each grid, and then fill in the corresponding bubbles to match your answer.

1. In an election for club president, Naomi received 23 out of the 47 votes cast. What fraction of the votes did Naomi receive?

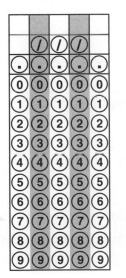

2. At dinner, Neil paid $17 and Sam paid $15. What is the ratio of the amount paid by Sam to the amount paid by Sam and Neil together?

3. Casey fills a carpet cleaner with 3 gallons of water and adds 6 ounces of carpet cleaning solution. What is the ratio of ounces of cleaning solution to gallons of water?

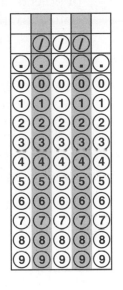

4. Karen typed 7 pages in 21 minutes. What is the simplified ratio of minutes to typed pages?

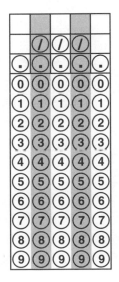

 TIP Be sure to write your answer in the blank row at the top of each grid. This will help you fill in the bubbles in the correct order.

Answers start on page 382.

GED SKILL **Operations with Fractions**

Adding and Subtracting Fractions

Adding and subtracting can only be performed with the same kinds of objects. You can add dollars to dollars and inches to inches, but not dollars to inches. This is also true of fractions. You can add or subtract only **like fractions,** those with the same, or common, denominator.

With like fractions, add or subtract the numerators and write the answer over the common denominator. If necessary, reduce the answer to lowest terms. Rewrite an improper fraction as a whole or mixed number.

Example 1 Add $\frac{3}{8}$ and $\frac{4}{8}$.

Step 1 Add the numerators. $3 + 4 = 7$

Step 2 Write sum of numerators over common denominator. $\frac{7}{8}$

The sum of $\frac{3}{8}$ and $\frac{4}{8}$ is $\frac{7}{8}$.

Example 2 Subtract $\frac{2}{12}$ from $\frac{11}{12}$.

Step 1 Remember the order of the numbers
in subtraction. The fraction being $\frac{11}{12} - \frac{2}{12} = \frac{11-2}{12} = \frac{9}{12}$
subtracted <u>from</u> must be written first.
Then subtract the numerators.

Step 2 Reduce to lowest terms. $\frac{9 \div 3}{12 \div 3} = \frac{3}{4}$

The difference of $\frac{11}{12}$ and $\frac{2}{12}$ is $\frac{3}{4}$.

Unlike fractions have different denominators. Use these steps to add or subtract unlike fractions.

Step 1 Find a common denominator and change one or both of the fractions to make like fractions.

Step 2 Add or subtract the like fractions.

Step 3 Reduce the answer if necessary. If the answer is an improper fraction, rewrite it as a whole or mixed number.

Example 3 Jarod bought $\frac{1}{2}$ pound of dark chocolate and $\frac{3}{4}$ pound of white chocolate. How many pounds of chocolate did he buy?

Step 1 The lowest common denominator for both
fractions is 4. Raise $\frac{1}{2}$ to an equal fraction with $\frac{1}{2} = \frac{1 \times 2}{2 \times 2} = \frac{2}{4}$
a denominator of 4.

Step 2 Add $\frac{2}{4}$ and $\frac{3}{4}$. $\frac{2}{4} + \frac{3}{4} = \frac{5}{4}$

Step 3 Reduce the improper fraction to lowest terms. $\frac{5}{4} = 1\frac{1}{4}$

Jarod bought **$1\frac{1}{4}$ pounds** of chocolate.

TIP

Whenever possible, use the lowest common denominator. The numbers in the problem will be smaller and easier to work with.

A. Add. Reduce answers to lowest terms. Change improper fractions to whole or mixed numbers.

1. $\dfrac{2}{3}$
   $+\dfrac{1}{3}$

2. $\dfrac{1}{9}$
   $+\dfrac{5}{9}$

3. $\dfrac{1}{6}$
   $+\dfrac{3}{6}$

4. $\dfrac{3}{10}$
   $+\dfrac{9}{10}$

5. $\dfrac{3}{4}$
   $+\dfrac{1}{8}$

6. $\dfrac{1}{3}$
   $+\dfrac{3}{4}$

7. $\dfrac{1}{6}$
   $+\dfrac{1}{2}$

8. $\dfrac{5}{8}$
   $+\dfrac{1}{4}$

B. Subtract. Reduce answers to lowest terms.

9. $\dfrac{3}{4}$
   $-\dfrac{1}{4}$

10. $\dfrac{7}{8}$
    $-\dfrac{3}{8}$

11. $\dfrac{13}{15}$
    $-\dfrac{9}{15}$

12. $\dfrac{7}{12}$
    $-\dfrac{5}{12}$

13. $\dfrac{3}{4}$
    $-\dfrac{1}{2}$

14. $\dfrac{2}{3}$
    $-\dfrac{1}{6}$

15. $\dfrac{5}{6}$
    $-\dfrac{1}{2}$

16. $\dfrac{6}{9}$
    $\dfrac{1}{12}$

C. Add or subtract as directed. Simplify your answers.

17. $\dfrac{2}{5} + \dfrac{1}{3} =$

18. $\dfrac{3}{4} - \dfrac{1}{3} =$

19. $\dfrac{9}{10} - \dfrac{1}{2} =$

20. $\dfrac{2}{8} + \dfrac{1}{5} =$

21. $\dfrac{1}{2} + \dfrac{3}{10} + \dfrac{1}{5} =$

22. $\dfrac{7}{16} - \dfrac{1}{4} =$

23. $\dfrac{5}{8} + \dfrac{1}{6} + \dfrac{1}{4} =$

24. $\dfrac{5}{6} - \dfrac{3}{4} =$

25. $\dfrac{1}{2} + \dfrac{5}{8} + \dfrac{1}{4} =$

D. Decide whether to add or subtract. Solve. Simplify your answers.

26. Chris estimates that he spends $\dfrac{1}{4}$ of his income on rent and $\dfrac{1}{6}$ on transportation. What fraction of his income does he spend on these two items?

27. Shedon is making a vest for her daughter. The pattern calls for $\dfrac{3}{8}$ yard of ribbon. If she has $\dfrac{3}{4}$ yard of ribbon, how much will be left over?

28. A walkway will require $\dfrac{2}{3}$ cubic yard of concrete. A worker has already mixed $\dfrac{4}{9}$ cubic yard. How many more cubic yards of concrete will he need?

29. Ariel walked $\dfrac{3}{10}$ mile to the market, $\dfrac{1}{2}$ mile to her child's school, and then $\dfrac{1}{4}$ mile to a friend's house. How many miles did she walk in all?

Answers start on page 382.

Adding and Subtracting Mixed Numbers

A mixed number is a whole number and a proper fraction. To add or subtract mixed numbers, work with each part separately and then combine the results.

TIP

If you can't decide which operation to use in a fraction word problem, think about how you would solve it using only whole numbers. Then use the same operation with the fractions.

Example 1 For a painting job, Leland spent $6\frac{1}{3}$ hours preparing the rooms to be painted and $4\frac{3}{4}$ hours doing the painting and cleanup. How many hours did he spend on the job?

Step 1 Write the fractions with common denominators.

$$6\frac{1}{3} = 6\frac{1 \times 4}{3 \times 4} = 6\frac{4}{12}$$
$$+4\frac{3}{4} = 4\frac{3 \times 3}{4 \times 3} = 4\frac{9}{12}$$

Step 2 Add the fractions first. Add the numerators and put the sum over the common denominator. Then add the whole numbers.

$$6\frac{4}{12}$$
$$+4\frac{9}{12}$$
$$\overline{10\frac{13}{12}}$$

Step 3 Change the improper fraction to a mixed number. Add this to the whole number answer.

$$\frac{13}{12} = 1\frac{1}{12}$$
$$10 + 1\frac{1}{12} = 11\frac{1}{12}$$

Leland spent $\mathbf{11\frac{1}{12}}$ hours on the job.

When subtracting mixed numbers, sometimes the fraction you are subtracting from will be smaller than the fraction you are subtracting. In this situation, you will need to regroup, or borrow, 1 from the whole number and rewrite it as a fraction. Remember, a fraction with the same numerator and denominator equals 1.

Example 2 A pipe is $5\frac{1}{8}$ feet long. If a piece measuring $3\frac{3}{4}$ feet is cut from the pipe, what is the length of the remaining piece? Is the remaining piece long enough to cut a piece that measures $1\frac{1}{8}$ feet long?

Step 1 Write the fractions with common denominators. The lowest common denominator is 8.

Step 2 Because $\frac{1}{8}$ is less than $\frac{6}{8}$, you need to regroup. Regroup 1 from the whole number 5, rewriting 5 as $4\frac{8}{8}$. Then add the fractional parts $\frac{1}{8}$ and $\frac{8}{8}$.

Step 3 Subtract. The fraction is already reduced to lowest terms.

Step 1	Step 2	Step 3
$5\frac{1}{8} = \quad 5\frac{1}{8}$	$= 4\frac{8}{8} + \frac{1}{8} =$	$4\frac{9}{8}$
$-3\frac{3}{4} = -3\frac{6}{8}$		$-3\frac{6}{8}$
		$\overline{1\frac{3}{8}}$

The remaining piece of pipe is $\mathbf{1\frac{3}{8}}$ feet in length. Since $\frac{3}{8}$ is greater than $\frac{1}{8}$, $1\frac{3}{8}$ is greater than $1\frac{1}{8}$. The remaining piece is long enough to cut a piece of pipe $1\frac{1}{8}$ feet long.

A. Add or subtract as directed. Reduce answers to lowest terms.

1. $3\frac{3}{4}$
    $+4\frac{1}{3}$

2. $1\frac{1}{2}$
    $+5\frac{5}{8}$

3. $12\frac{3}{5}$
    $+\ 9\frac{1}{3}$

4. $6\frac{7}{8}$
    $+8\frac{2}{3}$

5. $2\frac{3}{10}$
    $+9\frac{4}{5}$

6. $22\frac{1}{9}$
    $+21\frac{2}{3}$

7. $7\frac{3}{10}$
    $+2\frac{1}{5}$

8. $5\frac{3}{5}$
    $+12\frac{1}{3}$

9. $6\frac{1}{2}$
    $-3\frac{1}{3}$

10. $8\frac{5}{6}$
    $-2\frac{1}{4}$

11. $11\frac{1}{4}$
    $-\ 3\frac{2}{5}$

12. $16\frac{1}{4}$
    $-12\frac{1}{6}$

13. $20\frac{1}{3}$
    $-\ 8\frac{2}{3}$

14. $5\frac{2}{3}$
    $-3\frac{3}{4}$

15. $25\frac{1}{3}$
    $-17\frac{4}{7}$

16. $40\frac{3}{4}$
    $-15\frac{7}{8}$

B. Solve. Reduce your answers.

17. Belinda kept records of her gasoline purchases for one month. She bought $8\frac{1}{2}$ gallons, $9\frac{3}{10}$ gallons, and $8\frac{7}{10}$ gallons. How many gallons of gasoline did she buy that month?

18. Paul earns 10 vacation days per year. He has used $4\frac{1}{2}$ days this year. How many vacation days does he have left?

19. Maria planned to spend $3\frac{1}{2}$ hours organizing the stockroom. She has been working for $1\frac{3}{4}$ hours. How many more hours does she plan to work on this task?

20. Evan needs to shorten this fence post to $5\frac{3}{4}$ feet. How much should he cut off the fence post?

$8\frac{1}{3}$ feet

21. A recipe calls for $1\frac{2}{3}$ cups of milk, $\frac{1}{2}$ cup of cooking oil, and $\frac{3}{4}$ cup of water. What is the total amount of liquid used in the recipe?

22. Ted estimated he would need 35 square yards of carpet to cover his living room floor. The job required $30\frac{3}{4}$ square yards of carpet. By how much did his estimate exceed the actual amount of carpet needed?

23. John exercises by power walking at a local park. This week John walked $2\frac{1}{2}$ miles, $1\frac{3}{4}$ miles, $2\frac{5}{8}$ miles, and $2\frac{3}{4}$ miles. How many miles did John power walk this week?

24. Kyra can work up to 20 hours per week at a part-time job. She has already worked $16\frac{1}{4}$ hours this week. How many more hours can she work this week?

Answers start on page 384.

Multiplying Fractions and Mixed Numbers

To multiply fractions, you do not need to change the fractions to like fractions. Simply multiply the numerators, then the denominators, and reduce your answer.

Example 1   A piece of electric wire is $\frac{1}{6}$ yard long. Max used $\frac{2}{3}$ of the wire for a job. How much wire did he use?

Step 1   Multiply one numerator by the other numerator. Then multiply one denominator by the other denominator.

$$\frac{1}{6} \times \frac{2}{3} = \frac{1 \times 2}{6 \times 3} = \frac{2}{18}$$

Step 2   Reduce the answer to lowest terms.

$$\frac{2 \div 2}{18 \div 2} = \frac{1}{9}$$

Max used $\frac{1}{9}$ **yard of wire.**

> **TIP**
>
> A fraction followed by the word *of* means that you should multiply by that fraction. For example, when you find $\frac{1}{6}$ of $\frac{2}{3}$, you multiply $\frac{1}{6} \times \frac{2}{3}$.

As you know, reducing a fraction means to divide the numerator and the denominator by the same number. You can use this principle to simplify before you work the problem. This process is called **canceling.**

Example 2   Find $\frac{1}{6}$ of $\frac{2}{3}$.

Both the numerator of one fraction and the denominator of the other fraction can be divided by 2. Since $2 \div 2 = 1$, draw a slash through the numerator 2 and write 1. Since $6 \div 2 = 3$, draw a slash through the denominator 6 and write 3. Then multiply the simplified fractions.

$$\frac{1}{6} \times \frac{2}{3} = \frac{1 \times \overset{1}{\cancel{2}}}{\underset{3}{\cancel{6}} \times 3} = \frac{1}{9}$$

Since you used canceling before multiplying, there is no need to reduce the answer: $\frac{1}{6}$ of $\frac{2}{3}$ is $\frac{1}{9}$. Notice that canceling gives the same answer as in Example 1 above.

When you cancel, make sure you divide a numerator and a denominator by the same number. The canceling shown here is incorrect. Although 6 and 3 can both be divided by 3, both numbers are in the denominator.

Incorrect:

$$\frac{1}{6} \times \frac{2}{3} = \frac{1 \times 2}{\underset{2}{\cancel{6}} \times \underset{1}{\cancel{3}}}$$

To multiply with mixed numbers, change the mixed numbers to improper fractions before you multiply.

Example 3   Multiply $1\frac{2}{3}$ by $7\frac{1}{2}$.

Step 1
Change to improper fractions.

$$1\frac{2}{3} \times 7\frac{1}{2} = \frac{5}{3} \times \frac{15}{2}$$

Step 2
Cancel and multiply.

$$\frac{5}{\underset{1}{\cancel{3}}} \times \frac{\overset{5}{\cancel{15}}}{2} =$$

Step 3
Write as a mixed number.

$$\frac{25}{2} = 12\frac{1}{2}$$

The product of $1\frac{2}{3}$ and $7\frac{1}{2}$ is **$12\frac{1}{2}$.**

Example 4 A restaurant had 125 customers during the lunch rush hour on Monday. Two-fifths of the customers ordered the lunch special. How many customers ordered the special?

This problem asks you to find a fractional part of a whole number. You need to find $\frac{2}{5}$ of 125. To write a whole number as an improper fraction, write the whole number over 1.

$$\frac{2}{\cancel{5}_1} \times \frac{\cancel{125}^{25}}{1} = 50$$

Of the 125 customers, **50 customers** ordered the lunch special.

GED SKILL FOCUS

A. Multiply. Use canceling when needed. Make sure your answers are reduced to lowest terms.

1. $\frac{7}{8} \times \frac{4}{5} =$

2. $\frac{3}{4} \times \frac{3}{7} =$

3. Find $\frac{1}{2}$ of 11.

4. What is $\frac{8}{9}$ of $\frac{5}{6}$?

5. Find $\frac{2}{15}$ of $\frac{3}{8}$.

6. $9 \times 5\frac{1}{3} =$

7. $2\frac{2}{5} \times 2\frac{1}{2} =$

8. $3\frac{1}{3} \times 4\frac{1}{8} =$

9. Find $\frac{5}{6}$ of $4\frac{1}{2}$.

10. $\frac{4}{5} \times 1\frac{2}{3} =$

11. $2\frac{3}{4} \times 6 =$

12. What is $\frac{4}{7}$ of $1\frac{2}{5}$?

13. $4 \times 1\frac{7}{8} =$

14. $3\frac{1}{9} \times 2\frac{1}{4} =$

15. What is $\frac{2}{9}$ of 24?

B. Solve. Answers should be in lowest terms. You may use your calculator.

16. A restaurant ordered $55\frac{3}{4}$ pounds of mozzarella cheese. The cook used $\frac{1}{2}$ of the order over the weekend. How many pounds of mozzarella are left for the rest of the week?

17. The measurements of a den are shown in the diagram. Find the area of the den in square feet by multiplying the length by the width.

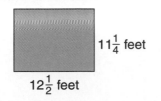

11¼ feet

12½ feet

18. Last year, Elio earned $18,720. His boss gave him a raise equal to $\frac{1}{12}$ of last year's salary. What is the dollar amount of the raise?

19. A furniture factory has a stack of 40 tabletops. If each tabletop is $1\frac{3}{4}$ inches thick, what is the height of the stack?

20. In a survey, $\frac{7}{8}$ of the people said that recycling is important. Of those, only $\frac{1}{2}$ buy products made from recycled goods. What fraction of the people surveyed buy products made from recycled goods?

Answers start on page 386.

Dividing Fractions and Mixed Numbers

Multiplication and division are **inverse** (opposite) operations. You use this relationship to divide fractions.

Example 1 $\frac{6}{8} \div \frac{1}{4} = ?$

To solve this problem, you need to find out how many $\frac{1}{4}$s there are in $\frac{6}{8}$. Follow these steps:

Step 1 Invert, or turn over, the divisor (the fraction you are dividing by) and change the operation to multiplication.

$$\frac{6}{8} \div \frac{1}{4} = \frac{6}{8} \times \frac{4}{1}$$

Step 2 Complete the problem as you would any multiplication problem. Always simplify your answer by reducing to lowest terms and changing improper fractions to mixed or whole numbers.

$$\frac{6}{8} \times \frac{4}{1} = \frac{6}{\underset{2}{8}} \times \frac{\overset{1}{4}}{1} = \frac{6}{2} = 3$$

> **TIP**
>
> When you divide by a proper fraction, the answer will be greater than the number you divided. Knowing this can help you see whether your answer makes sense.

The fraction $\frac{6}{8}$ divided by $\frac{1}{4}$ is **3**. In other words, there are three $\frac{1}{4}$s in $\frac{6}{8}$. This picture shows that this is true.

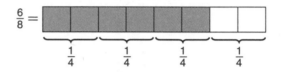

Many real-world situations involve dividing a mixed or whole number by a fraction.

Example 2 A housing subdivision has 24 acres of land available for sale. If this land is divided into home lots that are each $\frac{3}{4}$ of an acre, how many lots are in the housing subdivision?

Step 1 Change the whole number 24 to an improper fraction by writing it over the denominator 1. Invert the number you're dividing by and change the operation to multiplication.

$$24 \div \frac{3}{4} = \frac{24}{1} \times \frac{4}{3}$$

Step 2 Multiply. Write your answer in lowest terms.

$$\frac{24}{1} \times \frac{4}{3} = \frac{\overset{8}{24}}{1} \times \frac{4}{\underset{1}{3}} = \frac{32}{1} = 32$$

> **TIP**
>
> Remember, as in any division problem, the fraction you are dividing must be written first.

The land will be divided into **32** home lots.

Always think about your answer to see whether it makes sense. You can always use multiplication to check a division problem.

Check: $32 \times \frac{3}{4} = \frac{\overset{8}{32}}{1} \times \frac{3}{\underset{1}{4}} = \frac{24}{1} = 24$

A. Divide. Write your answers in lowest terms.

1. $\frac{1}{3} \div \frac{5}{6} =$

2. $\frac{2}{3} \div \frac{2}{5} =$

3. $\frac{7}{10} \div 2 =$

4. $\frac{5}{6} \div \frac{5}{24} =$

5. $\frac{6}{7} \div 3 =$

6. $\frac{4}{9} \div \frac{2}{3} =$

7. $\frac{7}{8} \div \frac{1}{4} =$

8. $4\frac{1}{2} \div \frac{1}{8} =$

9. $12 \div 1\frac{1}{2} =$

10. $3\frac{3}{4} \div 1\frac{2}{3} =$

11. $6\frac{1}{2} \div \frac{1}{4} =$

12. $2\frac{1}{4} \div 1\frac{1}{2} =$

13. $18 \div \frac{2}{3} -$

14. $2\frac{2}{5} \div \frac{6}{25} =$

15. $4\frac{9}{10} \div 1\frac{1}{6} =$

16. $6\frac{1}{9} \div 1\frac{5}{6} =$

17. $2\frac{2}{3} \div \frac{1}{3} =$

18. $4 \div 1\frac{1}{4} =$

19. $9\frac{1}{8} \div 1\frac{2}{3}$

20. $10 \div 1\frac{1}{5} =$

21. $8\frac{3}{4} \div \frac{1}{4} =$

22. $12 \div \frac{4}{9} =$

23. $16 \div \frac{4}{5} =$

24. $4 \div 2\frac{1}{5} =$

B. Solve. Simplify your answers.

25. Hal has a board similar to this one. He needs to cut it into pieces, with each piece measuring $\frac{3}{4}$ foot. How many pieces can he cut from the board?

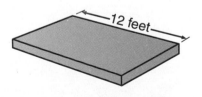
—12 feet—

26. A cook uses $\frac{1}{3}$ pound of hamburger to make the lunch special. How many specials can he make from 15 pounds of hamburger?

27. A stack of books is 24 inches high. Each book in the stack is $\frac{3}{4}$ inch thick. How many books are in the stack?

28. Carina works part-time at a toy store as a bike assembler. She can build a bicycle in $2\frac{1}{2}$ hours. If she works 25 hours in a week, how many bicycles can she assemble?

29. You have 10 cups of sugar. Your cookie recipe calls for $1\frac{1}{4}$ cups of sugar for one batch. What is the greatest number of batches of cookies you could make with the sugar that you have?

Answers start on page 386.

GED STRATEGY Solving Word Problems

Estimating with Fractions

Remember: The words *about* and *approximately* mean you should estimate the answer.

Knowing the approximate value of fractions makes working with these numbers easier. Rounding fractions to the nearest whole number is a good way to estimate answers to problems that involve fractions. To round a fraction to the nearest whole number, compare the fraction to $\frac{1}{2}$.

RULE If a fraction is less than $\frac{1}{2}$, round down the fraction to 0. In a mixed number, the whole number part stays the same.

Example   Round $5\frac{1}{3}$ to the nearest whole number. Compare $\frac{1}{3}$ and $\frac{1}{2}$. Change to like fractions with a common denominator of 6.
$$\frac{1}{3} = \frac{2}{6} \text{ and } \frac{1}{2} = \frac{3}{6}$$

Since $\frac{2}{6}$ is less than $\frac{3}{6}$, $\frac{1}{3}$ is less than $\frac{1}{2}$. Round $5\frac{1}{3}$ down to **5.**

RULE If a fraction is $\frac{1}{2}$ or more, round up the fraction to 1. In a mixed number, add 1 to the whole number part.

Example   Round $8\frac{5}{8}$ to the nearest whole number. Change $\frac{1}{2}$ to a fraction with a denominator of 8 in order to compare $\frac{5}{8}$ and $\frac{1}{2}$.
$$\frac{1}{2} = \frac{4}{8}$$

Since $\frac{5}{8}$ is greater than $\frac{4}{8}$, $\frac{5}{8}$ is greater than $\frac{1}{2}$. Round $8\frac{5}{8}$ up to **9.**

If the numerator of a fraction is more than half its denominator, the fraction is more than $\frac{1}{2}$. If the numerator is less than half the denominator, the fraction is less than $\frac{1}{2}$.

- $\frac{3}{8}$ is less than $\frac{1}{2}$
- $\frac{5}{8}$ is more than $\frac{1}{2}$

Estimation with fractions is more accurate in addition and subtraction than in multiplication and division.

Example   Kiko and Maria each jog twice a week. Kiko jogged $4\frac{3}{4}$ miles and $4\frac{1}{5}$ miles during the week. Maria jogged $3\frac{1}{4}$ miles and $3\frac{7}{8}$ miles during the week. <u>About</u> how many more miles did Kiko jog than Maria?

(1) 0
(2) 1
(3) 2
(4) 3
(5) 4

Step 1   Round the miles that Kiko jogged, then add. $5 + 4 = 9$
$4\frac{3}{4}$ rounds up to 5, and $4\frac{1}{5}$ rounds down to 4.

Step 2   Round the miles that Maria jogged, then add. $3 + 4 = 7$
$3\frac{1}{4}$ rounds down to 3, and $3\frac{7}{8}$ rounds up to 4.

Step 3   Compare the two amounts by subtracting. $9 - 7 = 2$

Option (3) is correct. Kiko jogged about **2 miles** more than Maria.

Directions: Choose the one best answer to each question.

Questions 1 through 3 refer to the table.

Ace Repair: Monday Morning Sales

Paint	$14\frac{1}{3}$ gallons red paint
	$6\frac{3}{4}$ gallons green paint
	$9\frac{1}{4}$ gallons white paint
Hardware	$12\frac{1}{6}$ pounds of nails
Lumber	$9\frac{5}{8}$ feet of 2-by-4 boards
	$27\frac{1}{4}$ feet of 2-by-8 boards
	$4\frac{2}{3}$ feet of 1-by-4 boards
	$36\frac{3}{8}$ feet of 1-by-6 boards

1. What is the best estimate for the number of gallons of paint sold on Monday morning?

   (1) 26
   (2) 28
   (3) 30
   (4) 32
   (5) 34

2. About how many feet of lumber were sold?

   (1) 70
   (2) 74
   (3) 76
   (4) 78
   (5) 82

3. An additional $10\frac{2}{5}$ pounds of nails are sold Monday afternoon. Approximately how many pounds of nails were sold on Monday?

   (1) 20
   (2) 22
   (3) 24
   (4) 26
   (5) 28

Questions 4 through 6 refer to the following information.

Walton Nut Company sells two mixtures.

Mix A: $2\frac{2}{3}$ pounds of cashews

$2\frac{3}{8}$ pounds of peanuts

$3\frac{1}{2}$ pounds of salted walnuts

$2\frac{1}{8}$ pounds of Brazil nuts

Mix B: $6\frac{1}{2}$ pounds of almonds

$3\frac{7}{8}$ pounds of black walnuts

$1\frac{1}{5}$ pounds of peanuts

4. Approximately how many more pounds of peanuts are in Mix B than in Mix A?

   (1) 2
   (2) 4
   (3) 6
   (4) 10
   (5) Not enough information is given.

5. Estimate the number of pounds of cashews and Brazil nuts in Mix A.

   (1) 1
   (2) 2
   (3) 3
   (4) 5
   (5) 15

6. Mix B contains approximately how many more pounds of nuts than Mix A?

   (1) 26
   (2) 15
   (3) 11
   (4) 4
   (5) Not enough information is given.

Answers start on page 387.

GED STRATEGY **Working with Special Formats**

Writing Fractions in a Standard Grid

When using the standard grid to write fractional answers to problems, it is important to remember the following points:

- Write your answer at the top of the grid box.
- In the second row of the grid, the symbol $\oslash$ is the fraction bar.
- Your answer can start in any of the five columns, as long as your answer is complete. Any unused columns should be left blank.
- Mixed numbers cannot be entered on the grid. Therefore, change all mixed number answers to improper fractions.

Example 1   Felipe ran for $1\frac{1}{8}$ hours on Tuesday and for $\frac{1}{2}$ hour on Wednesday. How many more hours did he run on Tuesday than on Wednesday?

$$1\frac{1}{8} - \frac{1}{2} =$$
$$\frac{9}{8} - \frac{4}{8} = \frac{5}{8}$$

TIP

When answering in the grid, remember to write your answer in the top row, fill the correct bubble below, and leave unused columns blank.

The difference between the number of hours Felipe ran on Tuesday and the number of hours he ran on Wednesday is $\frac{5}{8}$ **hour.** All three grids shown at right are filled in correctly.

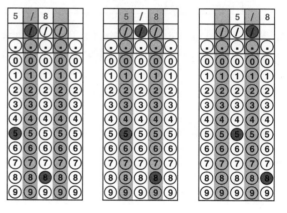

Example 2   Angie worked $5\frac{1}{2}$ hours on Monday and $4\frac{3}{4}$ hours on Tuesday. How many hours did Angie work in all for the two days?

$$5\frac{1}{2} + 4\frac{3}{4} =$$
$$5\frac{2}{4} + 4\frac{3}{4} = 9\frac{5}{4}$$
$$= 10\frac{1}{4}$$

The total number of hours Angie worked is $10\frac{1}{4}$. Since you cannot enter mixed numbers on the standard grid, first change $10\frac{1}{4}$ to the improper fraction $\frac{41}{4}$. Both grids shown at right are correct.

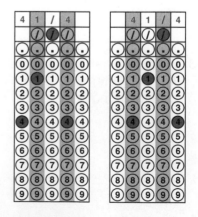

Directions: Solve the following problems and enter your answers on the grids provided.

1. A piece of wood is $2\frac{7}{8}$ feet long. If you cut off $1\frac{3}{4}$ feet, how many feet are left?

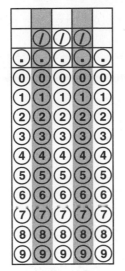

2. Andrea cuts a piece of ribbon that is $2\frac{3}{4}$ yards long into 3 equal pieces. What is the length of each piece?

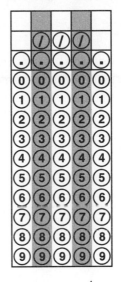

3. Rachel has 4 cups of flour and uses $\frac{2}{3}$ of it for a recipe. How many cups of flour are left?

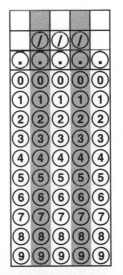

4. A map scale shows that $\frac{1}{3}$ inch on the map equals an actual distance of 3 miles. If a distance on the map is $\frac{3}{4}$ inch, what is the actual distance in miles?

TIP Be sure you are answering the question asked. When asked to find "how much is left," check to see what value you found. Did you find how much was used or how much was left?

TIP There are different approaches to problem solving. For example, if a map scale is $\frac{1}{3}$ inch = 3 miles, then 1 inch equals 9 miles. Thus, $\frac{1}{9} = \frac{\frac{3}{4}}{x}$ or $\frac{3}{4} \times 9 = x$.

Answers start on page 387.

GED Mini-Test • Lessons 5–7

Directions: This is a thirty-minute practice test. After thirty minutes, mark the last item you finished. Then complete the test and check your answers. If most of your answers are correct, but you didn't finish, try to work faster next time.

Part 1

Directions: Choose the <u>one best answer</u> to each question. You <u>MAY</u> use your calculator.

1. Of the 24,000 cellular phones inspected in the last production run, 50 were defective. What fraction of the cellular phones inspected was defective?

   (1) $\frac{1}{4,800}$

   (2) $\frac{1}{960}$

   (3) $\frac{1}{480}$

   (4) $\frac{1}{96}$

   (5) $\frac{1}{48}$

2. Keisha can drive her car 354 miles on 15 gallons of gasoline. At the same rate, how many miles can she drive her car on 20 gallons of gasoline?

   (1) 472

   (2) 359

   (3) $265\frac{1}{2}$

   (4) 236

   (5) Not enough information is given.

3. What is the value of $7\frac{3}{4} + 1\frac{7}{8}$?

   (1) $8\frac{5}{8}$

   (2) $8\frac{5}{6}$

   (3) $8\frac{7}{8}$

   (4) $9\frac{5}{8}$

   (5) $10\frac{5}{6}$

4. Usually, Ramon drives $\frac{3}{5}$ mile to pick up Joe. They then drive another $\frac{4}{5}$ mile to work. Today Joe is sick, so Ramon drives 1 mile directly to the office. How much shorter is the direct route?

   (1) $\frac{2}{5}$ mile

   (2) $\frac{3}{5}$ mile

   (3) $\frac{4}{5}$ mile

   (4) $1\frac{2}{5}$ miles

   (5) $2\frac{2}{5}$ miles

5. Kathy can type 74 words per minute. At this rate, which expression shows how many words she can type over a period of 7 hours?

   (1) 74×7

   (2) $74 \times 60 \times 7$

   (3) $74 \times \frac{7}{60}$

   (4) $74 \times \frac{60}{7}$

   (5) $\frac{74}{60} \times 7$

6. A tank holds 5075 gallons of water. How many containers of water can be filled from the tank if each container holds $6\frac{1}{4}$ gallons?

   (1) 813

   (2) 812

   (3) 811

   (4) 810

   (5) Not enough information is given.

7. Which expression could be used to find the number of feet in $\frac{1}{4}$ mile (1 mile = 5280 ft)?

   (1) $\frac{1}{4} + 5280$

   (2) $5280 - \frac{1}{4}$

   (3) $5280 \times \frac{1}{4}$

   (4) $5280 \div \frac{1}{4}$

   (5) $\frac{1}{4} \div 5280$

8. Charles has an annual salary of $39,000. If he receives a bonus of $\frac{1}{20}$ of his annual salary, what is the <u>approximate</u> amount of his bonus?

   (1) $ 20

   (2) $ 200

   (3) $ 2,000

   (4) $20,000

   (5) Not enough information is given.

9. Carolyn worked $7\frac{2}{3}$ hours yesterday and $6\frac{3}{5}$ hours today. How many hours did she work in the two days?

   (1) $13\frac{4}{15}$

   (2) $13\frac{5}{8}$

   (3) $14\frac{4}{15}$

   (4) $14\frac{5}{8}$

   (5) Not enough information is given.

10. The scale on the plans for a new highway is $2\frac{1}{2}$ inches equal 2200 feet. If the actual distance between two exits on the highway is 5500 feet, how many inches apart are the two exits on the plans?

    (1) $5\frac{3}{4}$

    (2) 6

    (3) $6\frac{1}{4}$

    (4) $6\frac{1}{2}$

    (5) $6\frac{3}{4}$

Questions 11 through 13 refer to the following table.

Company Profit	
Region	**Fraction of Profit**
Northeast	$\frac{1}{8}$
Southeast	$\frac{1}{4}$
Northwest	$\frac{1}{8}$
Southwest	$\frac{1}{5}$
Central	$\frac{3}{10}$

11. Which region had the highest fraction of the company's profit?

    (1) Northeast

    (2) Southeast

    (3) Northwest

    (4) Southwest

    (5) Central

12. The fraction of combined profit from the Northeast and Northwest regions is how much greater than the fraction of profit from the Southwest region?

    (1) $\frac{1}{20}$

    (2) $\frac{3}{20}$

    (3) $\frac{1}{5}$

    (4) $\frac{1}{4}$

    (5) $\frac{2}{5}$

13. If the total company profit last year was $1,987,865, how much profit came from the Southwest region?

    (1) $ 248,483

    (2) $ 397,573

    (3) $ 496,966

    (4) $ 596,966

    (5) $9,939,325

Part 2

Directions: Choose the <u>one best answer</u> to each item. You may <u>NOT</u> use your calculator.

14. On Monday, 4 of the 32 students in the class were absent. What fraction of the class was absent?

    (1) $\frac{1}{32}$

    (2) $\frac{1}{8}$

    (3) $\frac{1}{4}$

    (4) $\frac{4}{7}$

    (5) $\frac{7}{8}$

15. A flight from New York City to Chicago took $2\frac{4}{5}$ hours. The return flight took $3\frac{1}{8}$ hours. Which of the following expressions represents how much longer the return flight was?

    (1) $2\frac{4}{5} + 3\frac{1}{8}$

    (2) $3\frac{1}{8} - 2\frac{4}{5}$

    (3) $3\frac{1}{8} \times 2\frac{4}{5}$

    (4) $3\frac{1}{8} \div 2\frac{4}{5}$

    (5) $2\frac{4}{5} \div 3\frac{1}{8}$

16. If you cut $3\frac{7}{16}$ inches off this art paper, how many inches do you have left?

    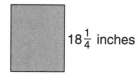 $18\frac{1}{4}$ inches

    (1) $12\frac{9}{16}$

    (2) $13\frac{1}{4}$

    (3) $13\frac{3}{4}$

    (4) $14\frac{13}{16}$

    (5) Not enough information is given.

17. Richard has a piece of rope that is $6\frac{1}{3}$ feet long, and he cuts off a piece $2\frac{7}{8}$ feet long. After he cuts the piece, <u>approximately</u> how many feet of rope does he have left?

    (1) 3

    (2) 4

    (3) 5

    (4) 9

    (5) 10

18. A plant grows at a rate of $5\frac{1}{2}$ inches per week. At this rate, which expression shows how many inches the plant will grow in $2\frac{1}{2}$ weeks?

    (1) $5\frac{1}{2} + 2\frac{1}{2}$

    (2) $5\frac{1}{2} - 2\frac{1}{2}$

    (3) $2\frac{1}{2} \times 5\frac{1}{2}$

    (4) $2\frac{1}{2} \div 5\frac{1}{2}$

    (5) $5\frac{1}{2} \div 2\frac{1}{2}$

19. Kim worked for $5\frac{1}{2}$ hours on Monday, $4\frac{2}{3}$ hours on Tuesday, and $4\frac{3}{5}$ hours on Wednesday. <u>About</u> how much did she earn in the three days?

    (1) 15

    (2) 30

    (3) 40

    (4) 80

    (5) Not enough information is given.

20. Arnie gets 15 vacation days per year. If he has already used $6\frac{1}{4}$ days this year, which expression shows how many vacation days he has left?

(1) $6\frac{1}{4} + 15$

(2) $15 - 6\frac{1}{4}$

(3) $15 \times 6\frac{1}{4}$

(4) $15 \div 6\frac{1}{4}$

(5) $6\frac{1}{4} \div 15$

21. An insurance company estimates that 75 out of every 100 renters do not have insurance on their personal belongings. What fraction of renters do have insurance?

(1) $\frac{1}{25}$

(2) $\frac{2}{3}$

(3) $\frac{1}{10}$

(4) $\frac{1}{4}$

(5) $\frac{2}{5}$

22. At Johan's Cafe the cook uses $\frac{1}{3}$ cup of gravy on each serving of mashed potatoes. How many servings can he make from 12 cups of gravy?

(1) 3

(2) 4

(3) 12

(4) 24

(5) 36

23. Sarah jogs at an average rate of $\frac{2}{15}$ mile per minute. At this rate, how many miles will she jog in 30 minutes?

(1) 2

(2) 4

(3) $4\frac{1}{2}$

(4) $7\frac{1}{2}$

(5) 15

24. A scale on a map shows that $\frac{3}{4}$ inch on the map equals an actual distance of 5 miles. If the actual distance between two cities is 45 miles, how many inches apart are they on the map?

(1) $6\frac{3}{4}$

(2) 9

(3) $9\frac{3}{4}$

(4) 12

(5) $12\frac{3}{4}$

Questions 25 and 26 refer to the following table.

Monthly Budget	
Expense	Fraction Budgeted
Rent	$\frac{3}{8}$
Salaries	$\frac{1}{4}$
Advertising	$\frac{1}{5}$
Supplies	$\frac{1}{8}$
Miscellaneous	$\frac{1}{20}$

25. Which of the expenses received the highest amount of the monthly budget?

(1) Rent

(2) Salaries

(3) Advertising

(4) Supplies

(5) Miscellaneous

26. If the total amount of the budget for March was $16,000, how much was budgeted for Salaries and Supplies combined?

(1) $ 2,000

(2) $ 4,000

(3) $ 6,000

(4) $ 8,000

(5) $10,000

Answers start on page 388.

GED SKILL **Introduction to Decimals**

Understanding Decimals

To show thousandths, imagine dividing each box on a hundredths chart into 10 equal pieces. To show ten-thousandths, imagine dividing each box into 100 equal pieces.

In Lessons 5 through 7, you used fractions to represent quantities less than one. A **decimal number** is another way to express a fractional amount. A decimal is a fraction that uses the place value system. For each diagram below, the shaded portion is expressed as both a fraction and a decimal.

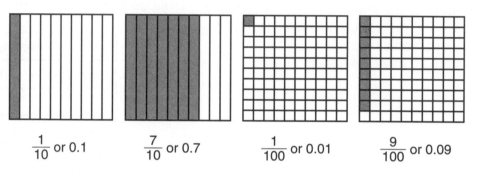

$\frac{1}{10}$ or 0.1 $\frac{7}{10}$ or 0.7 $\frac{1}{100}$ or 0.01 $\frac{9}{100}$ or 0.09

The chart shows the names of the first five decimal place values. Notice that the whole numbers are to the left of the decimal point and the decimals are to the right.

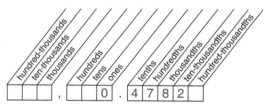

Compare the whole number and decimal place values. Do you see a pattern? Think of the ones column and decimal point as the center of the chart. As you move out from the center, the column names are related.

The zero in the tenths place of 16.034 is a placeholder. Its only purpose is to fill the space between the whole number and the digits farther to the right.

As you move to the left on the chart, each column is 10 times greater than the column to its right. As you move to the right, the value of the columns becomes smaller. Each column is $\frac{1}{10}$ the value of the column to its left.

As with whole numbers, the sum of the values of the digits equals the total value of the number.

Example 1   What is the value of each digit in 0.4782?

4 is in the **tenths** place. 4×0.1 $= \mathbf{0.4}$
7 is in the **hundredths** place. 7×0.01 $= \mathbf{0.07}$
8 is in the **thousandths** place. 8×0.001 $= \mathbf{0.008}$
2 is in the **ten-thousandths** place. $+2 \times 0.0001 = \mathbf{0.0002}$
                                                                              $\overline{\mathbf{0.4782}}$

Note: When a decimal number does not have a whole number part, a zero is often written to the left of the decimal point. The zero has no value.

Example 2   How do you write 16.034 in words?

Read the whole number part of the number. Say *and* to represent the decimal point. Read the digits to the right of the decimal point, and say the place name of the last digit on the right. Note that there are no commas setting off groups of three digits in the decimal part of the number to the right of the decimal point.

The number 16.034 is read ***sixteen and thirty-four thousandths.***

GED SKILL FOCUS

A. Write the value of the underlined digit in words. Refer to the chart on page 98.

Example: 1.5409 _____four hundredths_____

1. 10.9251 _____   4. 36.0029 _____

2. 7.85 _____   5. 4.162 _____

3. 255.07 _____   6. 17.296 _____

B. Match each number in Column A with its word form in Column B.

Column A

_____ 7. 1.35

_____ 8. 1.035

_____ 9. 1.305

_____ 10. 1.0305

Column B

a. one and three hundred five thousandths

b. one and thirty-five thousandths

c. one and thirty-five hundredths

d. one and three hundred five ten-thousandths

_____ 11. 1.2

_____ 12. 0.12

_____ 13. 0.0012

_____ 14. 0.012

a. twelve hundredths

b. twelve thousandths

c. twelve ten-thousandths

d. one and two tenths

C. Write each number in word form.

Example 20.08 _____twenty and eight hundredths_____

15. 5.25 _____   20. 4.05 _____

16. 6.008 _____   21. 3.9 _____

17. 0.37 _____   22. 0.08 _____

18. 1.01 _____   23. 3.004 _____

19. 2.005 _____   24. 12.6 _____

Answers start on page 389.

Rounding, Comparing, and Ordering Decimals

The steps for rounding decimals are similar to those you used for rounding whole numbers. There is one important difference in **Step 3**.

Example 1 Round 5.362 to the nearest tenth.

Step 1 Find the digit you want to round to.
It may help to circle it.   5.③62

Step 2 Look at the digit immediately to the right
of the circled digit.   5.③62

Step 3 If the digit to the right is 5 or more, add 1 to the
circled digit. If the digit to the right is less than 5,
do not change the circled digit. *Drop the remaining digits.*   5.4

Examples Round to the indicated place value.
Round 1.832 to the nearest hundredth. 1.8③2 rounds to **1.83**
Round 16.95 to the nearest tenth.   16.⑨5 rounds to **17.0**
Round 3.972 to the ones place.   ③.972 rounds to **4**

Comparing decimals uses an important mathematical concept. You can add zeros to the right of the last decimal digit without changing the value of the number. Study these examples.

RULE When comparing decimals with the same number of decimal places, compare them as though they were whole numbers.

Example Which is greater, 0.364 or 0.329?
Both numbers have three decimal places. Since 364 is greater than 329, the decimal **0.364 > 0.329.**

The rule for comparing whole numbers in which the number with more digits is greater does not hold true for decimals. The decimal number with more decimal places is not necessarily the greater number.

RULE When decimals have a different number of digits, write zeros to the right of the decimal with fewer digits so the numbers have the same number of decimal places. Then compare.

Example Which is greater, 0.518 or 0.52?
Add a zero to 0.52:   0.518 ? 0.520
Since 520 > 518, the decimal **0.52 > 0.518.**

RULE When numbers have both whole number and decimal parts, compare the whole numbers first.

Example Compare 32.001 and 31.999.
Since 32 is greater than 31, the number **32.001 is greater than 31.999.** It does not matter that 0.999 is greater than 0.001.

Using the same rules, you can put several numbers in order according to value. When you have several numbers to compare, write the numbers in a column and line up the decimal points. Then add zeros to the right until all the decimals have the same number of decimal digits.

Example 2 A digital scale displays weight to thousandths of a pound. Three packages weigh 0.094 pound, 0.91 pound, and 0.1 pound. Arrange the weights in order from greatest to least.

Step 1 Write the weights in a column, aligning the decimal point.

Step 2 Add zeros to fill out the columns.

Step 3 Compare as you would whole numbers.

0.094
0.910
0.100

In order from greatest to least, the weights are **0.91, 0.1,** and **0.094 pound.**

GED SKILL FOCUS

A. Round each number as directed. Refer to the chart on page 98.

1. Round 3.5719 to the tenths place. _____

2. Round 5.132 to the hundredths place. _____

3. Round 0.543 to the ones place. _____

4. Round 7.0813 to the tenths place. _____

5. Round 1.0699 to the thousandths place. _____

B. Compare the following numbers. Write >, <, or = between the numbers.

6. 0.32 _____ 0.3109

7. 0.98 _____ 1.9

8. 0.5 _____ 0.50

9. 0.006 _____ 0.06

10. 1.075 _____ 1.57

11. 0.18 _____ 0.108

12. 2.38 _____ 2.83

13. 3.60 _____ 3.600

C. Solve as directed.

14. Russ inspects transistors. In one test, he measures the masses of four transistors as given below. He needs to report the mass of the transistors in grams (g) rounded to the nearest tenth. What mass should Russ report for each?

Transistor A: 0.3619 g
Transistor B: 0.7082 g
Transistor C: 0.0561 g
Transistor D: 0.9357 g

15. The weights of four packages are given below. Arrange the weights in order from greatest to least.

Package 1: 0.5 pound
Package 2: 0.05 pound
Package 3: 0.15 pound
Package 4: 1.1 pounds

16. A fifth package weighs 0.55 pound. Does it weigh more or less than Package 1?

Answers start on page 389.

GED STRATEGY Solving Word Problems

Estimation and Money

Estimating with money can be a very useful skill. In many everyday situations involving money, you do not need exact amounts. For example, you can estimate when you want to know if you have enough cash to pick up the three things you want at the grocery store or about how much each person should contribute to split the cost of lunch. In such cases, you can use amounts rounded to the nearest dollar (the ones place).

Example 1 Using the price list, <u>about</u> how much would Pat pay for a steering wheel cover, a wide-angle mirror, and an oil drip pan?

(1) between $31 and $33
(2) between $33 and $35
(3) between $35 and $37
(4) between $37 and $39
(5) between $39 and $41

Auto Parts Price List	
Outside Wide-Angle Mirror	$13.45
Steering Wheel Cover	$15.95
Oil Drip Pan	$ 8.73
Windshield Washer Fluid	$ 2.85
Brake Fluid	$ 6.35

Round the cost of each item to the nearest dollar and find the total of the estimates.

Item	Cost	Estimate
Steering wheel cover	$15.95	$16
Wide-angle mirror	13.45	13
Oil drip pan	8.73	+ 9
Total:		$38

The best estimate is **option (4) between $37 and $39.**

You can also use estimation in multiplication and division problems.

Example 2 Use the price list to estimate the number of bottles of brake fluid a customer could buy for $20.

(1) 1
(2) 2
(3) 3
(4) 4
(5) 5

Round the price of one bottle of brake fluid to the nearest dollar: $6.35 rounds to $6. Divide $20 by $6: $20 ÷ $6 = 3 with a remainder of 2. The customer could expect to buy 3 bottles and have some change left over. The correct answer is **option (3) 3.**

TIP

Some remainders must be ignored. Since you cannot buy a partial package of most items you must ignore any remainder—this is your "change." For example, $20 is only enough to buy 3 bottles of $6 brake fluid; you have $2 change.

Directions: Choose the one best answer to each question.

Questions 1 through 3 refer to the chart.

Computer Game	Regular Price	Sale Price
Fast Pitch	$11.79	$8.99
Par 4	8.85	6.29
Dugout Derby	17.25	12.78
Crown of Power	13.72	10.09
Thunderclap Mine	12.99	9.25
Batwing	10.77	7.98

1. Lee wants to buy Fast Pitch, Crown of Power, and Dugout Derby. About how much will the three games cost on sale?

   (1) between $5 and $10
   (2) between $10 and $15
   (3) between $15 and $25
   (4) between $25 and $35
   (5) between $35 and $45

2. Ana has $20 to spend on computer games. If she buys Dugout Derby on sale, which other game can she afford to buy on sale?

   (1) Batwing
   (2) Thunderclap Mine
   (3) Crown of Power
   (4) Fast Pitch
   (5) Par 4

3. Mark wants to buy Dugout Derby and Crown of Power. About how much will he save by buying the games on sale?

   (1) $ 4
   (2) $ 8
   (3) $11
   (4) $12
   (5) Not enough information is given.

4. Hank's Hardware sells carbon monoxide detectors for $38.83 and smoke detectors for $12.39. Choose the best estimate for the cost of 4 smoke detectors.

   (1) $12
   (2) $24
   (3) $40
   (4) $48
   (5) $52

5. Hank's Hardware sells a carton containing 6 boxes of nails. If the carton costs $17.85, about how much does each box of nails cost?

   (1) $ 3
   (2) $ 6
   (3) $18
   (4) $26
   (5) $36

6. Twice a month, $27.50 is deducted from Petra's paycheck for health insurance. About how much does she contribute per year for health insurance?

   (1) $ 30
   (2) $ 60
   (3) $360
   (4) $600
   (5) $700

 It's often helpful to round dollar amounts to the nearest $5 or $10. Although these estimates may not be as accurate as rounding to the nearest dollar, they are easier to work with.

Answers start on page 390.

GED SKILL Decimals on Number Lines

Earlier in the book you used number lines for locating whole numbers and fractions. Number lines can also be used to compare decimals. On the number line below, each of the ten equally spaced intervals represents an increase of $\frac{1}{10}$, or 0.1, as you move to the right.

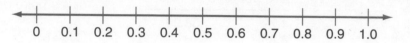

Example 1   Place a dot on the number line below to show the location of the decimal equivalent of $\frac{7}{10}$.

Seven-tenths, or **0.7,** is located at the seventh hash mark to the right of 0.

Example 2   Place a dot on the number line below to locate the decimal equivalent of $\frac{45}{100}$.

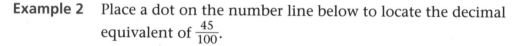

The decimal equivalent of $\frac{45}{100}$ is **0.45,** which is halfway between the hash marks labeled 0.4 and 0.5 on the number line. The dot shown on the number line below is correct.

Example 3   Place a dot on the number line to show 0.453 rounded to the nearest hundredth.

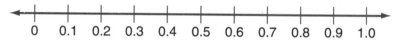

Since 3 in the thousandths place is less than 5, 0.453 rounds down to **0.45.**

Solve the following problems. Show your answers by correctly placing a dot on the number line below each problem.

1. Place a dot on the number line below to show the location of the decimal equivalent of five-tenths.

```
    |   |   |   |   |   |   |   |   |   |   |
    0  0.1 0.2 0.3 0.4 0.5 0.6 0.7 0.8 0.9 1.0
```

2. Place a dot on the number line below to show the location of the decimal halfway between five-tenths and six-tenths.

```
    |   |   |   |   |   |   |   |   |   |   |
    0  0.1 0.2 0.3 0.4 0.5 0.6 0.7 0.8 0.9 1.0
```

3. Place a dot on the number line below that shows 0.825 rounded to the nearest tenth.

```
    |   |   |   |   |   |   |   |   |   |   |
    0  0.1 0.2 0.3 0.4 0.5 0.6 0.7 0.8 0.9 1.0
```

4. Place a dot on the number line below to show the decimal equivalent of $\frac{245}{1000}$ rounded to the nearest hundredth.

```
    |   |   |   |   |   |   |   |   |   |   |
    0  0.1 0.2 0.3 0.4 0.5 0.6 0.7 0.8 0.9 1.0
```

5. Place a dot on the number line below to show the decimal equivalent of one and three-tenths.

```
    |++++++|++++++|++++++|++++++|
    0     0.5    1.0    1.5    2.0
```

6. Place a dot on the number line below that shows the mixed number one and six hundred twenty-five thousandths rounded to the nearest tenth.

```
    |++++++|++++++|++++++|++++++|
    0     0.5    1.0    1.5    2.0
```

7. Place a dot on the number line below that shows the decimal equivalent of $1\frac{1}{4}$ rounded to the nearest tenth.

```
    |++++++|++++++|++++++|++++++|
    0     0.5    1.0    1.5    2.0
```

8. Place a dot on the number line below that shows 1.025 rounded to the nearest tenth.

```
    |++++++|++++++|++++++|++++++|
    0     0.5    1.0    1.5    2.0
```

Answers start on page 390.

Lesson 9 — GED SKILL **Operations with Decimals**

Adding and Subtracting Decimals

Example 1   Anna assembles machine parts. One part comes in two sections with lengths of 4.875 and 3.25 centimeters. Once assembled, what is the total length of the two sections?

Step 1   To add, write the numbers so that the decimal points are aligned. If necessary, write zeros to the right of the last digit so that all the numbers have the same number of decimal places.

$$\begin{array}{r} 4.875 \\ +3.25\mathbf{0} \\ \hline \end{array}$$

Step 2   Add as you would with whole numbers. Regroup as needed.

$$\begin{array}{r} ^{1\ \ 1} \\ 4.875 \\ +3.250 \\ \hline 8\ 125 \end{array}$$

Step 3   Align the decimal point in the answer with the decimal points in the problem.

$$\begin{array}{r} 4.875 \\ +3.250 \\ \hline 8.125 \end{array}$$

 When adding decimals with a calculator, be sure to enter the decimal points where they are needed.

$$4 \;\cdot\; 875 \;+\; 3 \;\cdot\; 25 \;=\; 8.125$$

The total length of the assembled parts is **8.125 centimeters.**

Example 2   Cesar has $213 in a checking account. If he writes a check for $32.60, how much will be left in the account?

Step 1   To subtract, write the numbers so that the decimal points are aligned. Note that a number without a decimal point is understood to have one to the right of the ones place. If necessary, write zeros to the right of the last digit in a number.

$$\begin{array}{r} \$213.\mathbf{00} \\ -\ \ 32.60 \\ \hline \end{array}$$

Step 2   Subtract as you would with whole numbers. Regroup as needed.

$$\begin{array}{r} ^{10\ 12} \\ ^{1\ \cancel{0}} \\ ^{\cancel{2}\ 10} \\ \$\cancel{213}.\cancel{00} \\ -\ \ 32.60 \\ \hline \$180\ 40 \end{array}$$

Step 3   Align the decimal point in the answer with the decimal points in the problem.

$$\begin{array}{r} \$213.00 \\ -\ \ 32.60 \\ \hline \$180.40 \end{array}$$

Cesar will have **$180.40** left in his checking account.

 TIP

When you work with money amounts on a calculator, be careful how you read the results. The sum of $5.55 and $3.75 would appear as 9.3 on the calculator display, but the answer is $9.30.

A. Solve the decimal problems using paper and pencil. Align problems on decimal points.

1.　0.03
　+2.60

9.　1.85
　　0.03
　　19.007
　+62

2.　1.35
　+4.05

10.　12.4
　　11.08
　　16.1
　+ 4.575

3.　6.90
　−1.353

11.　16,004.1
　− 6,972.1

4.　5.075
　−2.15

12.　3.8
　−1.006

5. 7.1 + 8.003

13. 12.87 − 9.923

6. 10.3 − 6.125

14. 23.07 − 5.965

7. 3.61 + 1.2

15. 14.01 + 8.6 + 0.058

8. 16.05 − 4.27

16. 56.8 − 24.95

B. Use your calculator to solve these problems.

17. 0.95 + 1.843 + 3.008 + 0.9

20. 39.05 − 15.7

18. 0.6 − 0.3407

21. 0.125 + 1.4 + 3.76 + 0.01

19. 3.15 + 2.816 + 4.05 + 0.3

22. 25.6 − 12.85

Answers start on page 391.

Multiplying and Dividing Decimals

Example 1   In the deli department at a grocery store, a block of cheese weighs 1.6 pounds and costs $1.79 per pound. To the nearest whole cent, what is the cost of the cheese?

TIP

To multiply by a power of 10 (10, 100, . . .), count the number of zeros and move the decimal point that number of places to the right.

$1.4 \times 100 = 140.$

Step 1   Multiply the weight of the cheese by the cost per pound. Multiply as you would with whole numbers. Note that there is no need to align the decimal points when multiplying.

$$\begin{array}{r} \$1.79 \\ \times\ \ 1.6 \\ \hline 1074 \\ +1790 \\ \hline 2864 \end{array}$$

Step 2   Count the decimal places in the original problem to find how many decimal places are needed in the answer. Place the decimal point in the answer. Starting at the right, count three decimal places.

$\$1.79 \leftarrow 2$ decimal places
$\times\ \ 1.6 \leftarrow 1$ decimal place
$\$2.\mathbf{864} \leftarrow 3$ decimal places

Step 3   The problem says to round your answer to the nearest whole cent. Therefore, round to the hundredths place.

$\$2.864$ rounds to **$2.86**

Enter the numbers to be multiplied. Notice that dollar signs are not entered into a calculator.

     1.6   **×**   1.79   **=**   2.864

The block of cheese costs **$2.86.**

Example 2   Marvin bought a portable CD player for $74.55. He plans to pay for it in 6 equal payments. How much will each payment be? Round your answer to the nearest cent.

TIP

To divide by a power of 10, count the number of zeros and move the decimal point that number of places to the left.

$1.4 \div 100 = .014$

Step 1   Set up the problem. Place the decimal point in the answer directly above the decimal point in the problem.

Step 2   Divide as you would with whole numbers. If there is a remainder, write a zero to the right of the last decimal place in the number you are dividing. Continue this process until either there is no remainder or you reach one place to the right of the desired place value.

$$\begin{array}{r} \$12.425 \\ 6\overline{)\$74.550} \\ \underline{6} \\ 14 \\ \underline{12} \\ 25 \\ \underline{24} \\ 15 \\ \underline{12} \\ 30 \\ \underline{30} \end{array}$$

Step 3   Round your answer to the nearest whole cent.

$12.425 rounds to $12.43

Enter the numbers to be divided. Remember that it's important to enter the number being divided *first*.

     74.55   **÷**   6   **=**   12.425

Each payment is **$12.43.**

Example 3 A pharmacist is preparing capsules with 0.007 gram of aspirin each. How many capsules can be prepared with 14 grams of aspirin?

Step 1 Set up the problem. To divide by a decimal, make the divisor (the number you are dividing by) a whole number. In this problem, move the decimal point three places to the right in the divisor. Write zeros to the right of the number you are dividing so that you can move the decimal point the same number of places: three.

$$0.007\overline{)14.000.}$$

Step 2 Place the decimal point in the answer directly above the decimal point in the number you are dividing. Divide as you would with whole numbers.

$$\begin{array}{r} 2,000. \\ 7\overline{)14,000.} \\ \underline{14} \end{array}$$

Enter the numbers to be divided. Notice that you do not need to move the decimal point when working with a calculator.

14 ÷ 0.007 = 2000.

The pharmacist can prepare **2,000 capsules.**

GED SKILL FOCUS

A. Place the decimal point in each answer. You may need to add zeros.

1. $8.5 \times 0.4 =$ 3 4 0

2. $0.04 \times 0.6 =$ 2 4

3. $5.6 \times 0.002 =$ 1 1 2

4. $12 \times 3.06 =$ 3 6 7 2

5. $21.1 \times 14.7 =$ 3 1 0 1 7

6. $0.008 \times 12 =$ 9 6

B. Solve the decimal problems using paper and pencil.

7. 1.07×12

8. 0.09×6.1

9. $8\overline{)20.48}$

10. $3\overline{)3.2916}$

11. 2.27×1.8

12. 5.04×15

13. $3.6\overline{)7.704}$

14. $1.05\overline{)6.3987}$

15. 0.008×2.5

16. 1.05×0.11

17. $6\overline{)0.021}$

18. $0.07\overline{)4.34}$

 C. Use your calculator to solve these problems. Round answers to the nearest hundredth.

19. 0.012×12

20. $7\overline{)2}$

21. 7.15×0.03

22. $11\overline{)3}$

23. 12.25×1.5

24. $6\overline{)5}$

Answers start on page 391.

GED STRATEGY **Solving Word Problems**

Solving Multi-Step Problems

Example 1 Jeri buys an item that costs $5.24. She also pays $0.31 sales tax. If Jeri pays with a $20 bill, which expression shows how much change Jeri should receive?

(1) $20 + $5.24 + $0.31
(2) $5.24 + $0.31 − $20
(3) $20 − $5.24 + $0.31
(4) $5.24 − ($0.31 + $5.24)
(5) $20 − ($5.24 + $0.31)

TIP

Remember to use the order of operations:

1. First, do all operations in parentheses.
2. Next, do multiplication or division.
3. Then, do addition or subtraction.

Read the problem carefully. What do you need to know to solve the problem? You need to know the total cost (cost of the item plus sales tax). You also need to find the difference between the amount paid and the total cost. In other words, subtract the total cost from $20.

- Option (1) is incorrect because it adds the three amounts.
- In option (2), $20 is subtracted from the total of $5.24 and $0.31. Subtracting $20 from the total is not the same as subtracting the total from $20.
- Option (3) is incorrect because no parentheses means that only $5.24, rather than the sum of $5.24 and $0.31, is subtracted from $20.
- Option (4) is incorrect because the sum is subtracted from $5.24, not from $20.
- **Option (5) is correct.** Because of the parentheses, finding the total cost of the item is the first step ($5.24 + $0.31). Then the total cost is subtracted from $20.

Example 2 Martin is putting weather stripping around the sides and top of his home's doorways. If the weather stripping comes in packages of 15.47 meters, how many meters of weather stripping will be left after Martin lines two doors like the one shown here?

2.25 m

1 m

(1) 4.47
(2) 5.5
(3) 9.97
(4) 11.0
(5) Not enough information is given.

Step 1 Find the total distance around the two sides and top of the doorway. $(2.25 + 1 + 2.25)$

Step 2 Since Martin lined two doorways, find twice the amount found in Step 1. $2(2.25 + 1 + 2.25)$

Step 3 Subtract the amount of weather stripping used for two doorways (see Step 2) from the 15.47 meters that Martin started with.

$15.47 − 2(2.25 + 1 + 2.25)$
$15.47 − 2(5.5)$
$15.47 − 11 = 4.47$

Option (1) is correct. There will be **4.47** meters of weather stripping left.

Directions: Choose the one best answer to each question.

Questions 1 and 2 refer to the following information.

Wanda has $35 in cash. She buys a blouse for $12.98, a belt for $10.67, and a poster for $5.98.

1. Which expression shows how much money Wanda has left to pay for sales tax?

   (1) $35 − $12.98 + ($10.67 − $5.98)
   (2) $35 − ($12.98 + $10.67 + $5.98)
   (3) ($35 + $12.98) − ($10.67 + $5.98)
   (4) $35 + ($12.98 − $10.67 − $5.98)
   (5) $35 − $12.90 + $10.07 + $5.98

2. If Wanda pays $2.37 in sales tax, how much does she have left?

   (1) $ 3.00
   (2) $ 5.37
   (3) $22.02
   (4) $29.63
   (5) $32.00

Question 3 refers to the following information.

The Computer Center sells recordable CDs for $0.89 each. Computer Warehouse sells the same CDs for $1.05 each.

3. Which expression shows how much a customer will save by buying 25 recordable CDs at The Computer Center?

   (1) 25($1.05 − $0.89)
   (2) 25($1.05 + $0.89)
   (3) 25 − ($1.05 + $0.89)
   (4) 25 + ($1.05 − $0.89)
   (5) 25 ÷ ($1.05 − $0.89)

Questions 4 and 5 refer to the following information.

Sam's Garage	
Tire	$45.79
Brakes	$89.99
Oil Change	$18.25

4. Antonio bought two tires and an oil change at Sam's Garage. Which expression shows how much Antonio spent?

   (1) 2($45.79 + $18.25)
   (2) 2($45.79 − $18.25)
   (3) 2($45.79) + $18.25
   (4) 2($45.79) − $18.25
   (5) 2($45.79) + 2($18.25)

5. Another garage had the same tires for sale for $50 each. How much did Antonio save on two tires by going to Sam's?

   (1) $ 4.21
   (2) $ 8.42
   (3) $ 45.79
   (4) $ 91.58
   (5) $100.00

6. Angelo's yearly salary increased from $18,575 to $21,000. What was the monthly increase? Round your answer to the nearest dollar.

   (1) $2,425
   (2) $2,021
   (3) $1,750
   (4) $1,548
   (5) $ 202

Answers start on page 392.

Writing Decimals in a Standard Grid

Earlier in this book you learned how to use the standard grid with whole numbers and fractions. You'll be using the same grid when working with decimals.

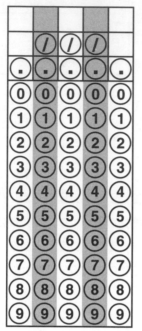

Points to remember:

- Each grid is used to enter a single answer.
- When filling in a grid for a decimal answer, your answer can start in any of the columns as long as the final answer is complete.
- Note that the ⊙ stands for a decimal point.
- Leave any unused columns blank.
- Fill in only one value for each column.

Example Sarah is responsible for tracking her time on a job. She spent 3.75 hours, 4.5 hours, and 1.25 hours getting a customer's computer system running. How many hours did she spend in all on this customer's computer problem?

The problem asks you to find the total number of hours Sarah spent on the customer's computer problem. Add together the hours she worked:

$$3.75 + 4.5 + 1.25 = \mathbf{9.5}$$

Fill in your answer on the grid. Note that all three grids are filled in correctly.

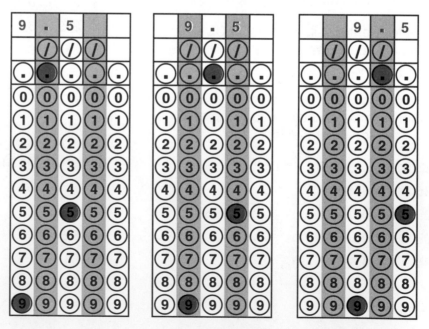

Directions: Solve the following problems. Enter your answers on the grids provided.

1. Marta rides her bike three times a week. She tries to ride a short distance farther each time. This week she rode 4.5 miles, 5.25 miles, and 6 miles. What was her total distance for the week?

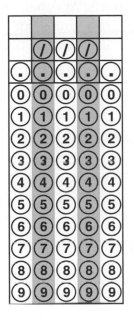

2. Manny's batting average was .275 last year. This year his batting average reached a career high of .340. By how much did his average increase?

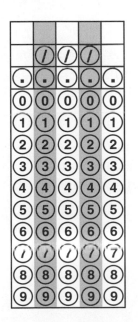

3. A piece of copper tubing is 60 inches long. Assuming there is no waste, how many pieces measuring 1.2 inches in length can be cut from the piece of tubing?

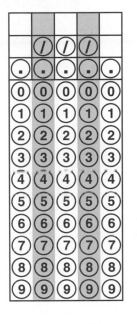

4. Marita ordered 14 parts that cost $2.99 per part. How much was the total order?

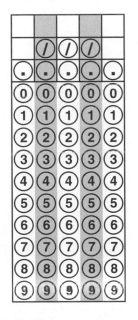

Answers start on page 392.

Changing Decimals to Fractions

Both decimals and fractions can be used to show part of a whole. Sometimes it is easier to calculate using fractions. At other times, decimals are more useful. If you know how to change from one form to the other, you can solve any problem using the form that is best for the situation.

Example 1 Josh is solving a problem using a calculator. The calculator display reads 0.375, but he needs to write the answer in the form of a fraction. Change 0.375 to a fraction.

Step 1 Write the number without the decimal point as the numerator of the fraction. $0.375 = \dfrac{375}{?}$

Step 2 Write the place value for the last decimal digit as the denominator. $0.375 = \dfrac{375}{1000}$

Step 3 Reduce the fraction to lowest terms. $\dfrac{375 \div 125}{1000 \div 125} = \dfrac{3}{8}$

The decimal 0.375 is equal to the fraction $\dfrac{3}{8}$.

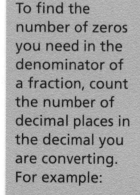

To find the number of zeros you need in the denominator of a fraction, count the number of decimal places in the decimal you are converting. For example:

$0.375 = \dfrac{375}{1000}$

3 decimal places   3 zeros

As you work with money, you will sometimes see decimals with a fraction part. This combination is commonly found as a **unit price,** the cost of one item or unit.

Example 2 On a grocery store shelf, Rita reads that the price per ounce for a brand of shampoo is $0.33\frac{1}{3}$. What fraction of a dollar is the unit price?

Step 1 Write the fraction as you did in the example above. $0.33\frac{1}{3} = \dfrac{33\frac{1}{3}}{100}$

Step 2 In your work with improper fractions, you learned that the fraction bar indicates division.

$\dfrac{33\frac{1}{3}}{100}$ means

$33\frac{1}{3} \div 100$

Step 3 Use the rules for dividing mixed numbers. Change both numbers to improper fractions, invert the number you are dividing by, and multiply.

$$33\frac{1}{3} \div 100 = \dfrac{100}{3} \div \dfrac{100}{1} = \dfrac{\cancel{100}^{1}}{3} \times \dfrac{1}{\cancel{100}_{1}} = \dfrac{1}{3}$$

The unit price is $\dfrac{1}{3}$ **of a dollar.**

A. Change these decimals to fractions. Reduce all fractions to lowest terms.

1. $0.25 =$

2. $0.4 =$

3. $0.35 =$

4. $0.875 =$

5. $0.8 =$

6. $0.76 =$

7. $0.128 =$

8. $0.05 =$

9. $0.31\frac{1}{4} =$

10. $0.08\frac{1}{3} =$

11. $0.46\frac{2}{3} =$

12. $0.93\frac{3}{4} =$

13. $0.26\frac{2}{3} =$

14. $0.06\frac{2}{3} =$

15. $0.23\frac{3}{4} =$

16. $0.08\frac{1}{6} =$

17. $0.10\frac{5}{6} =$

18. $0.12\frac{3}{4} =$

B. For each calculator display, write the decimal in fraction form. Then reduce each fraction to lowest terms if needed.

19. $0.9 = \frac{?}{10}$

20. $0.625 =$

21. $0.28 =$

22. $0.125 =$

23. $0.55 =$

24. $0.3125 =$

C. Solve. Simplify your answers. Remember to change all mixed numbers to improper fractions.

25. A brand of raspberry jam costs $\$0.43\frac{3}{4}$ per ounce. What fraction of a dollar is the unit price?

26. A brand of frozen drink concentrate is $\$0.16\frac{2}{3}$ per ounce of concentrate. Write the unit price as a fraction.

27. The unit price of a bagel is $37\frac{1}{2}$ cents. What fraction of a dollar is the unit price?

28. A company announces a unit price increase of $\$0.02\frac{1}{2}$ per pound. Write the decimal as a fraction.

Answers start on page 393.

Changing Fractions to Decimals

To solve some problems, you may need to change a fraction to a decimal. To do so, you perform the division indicated by the fraction bar.

Example 1   Change $\frac{2}{5}$ to a decimal.

Step 1   Divide the numerator by the denominator:

$$5\overline{)2}$$

Step 2   Set the decimal point in the answer directly above the decimal point in the problem. Add zeros and continue dividing until the remainder is zero, or until you reach the desired number of decimal places.

$$\begin{array}{r} 0.4 \\ 5\overline{)2.0} \\ \underline{2\,0} \end{array}$$

The fraction $\frac{2}{5}$ equals the decimal **0.4.**

A few fractions have decimal equivalents that contain a digit or group of digits that repeats. Round **repeating decimals** to a certain decimal place or express the remainder as a fraction.

Example 2   Change $\frac{2}{9}$ to a decimal. Show the answer to the hundredths place with the remainder expressed as a fraction.

Step 1   Divide the numerator by the denominator:

$$9\overline{)2}$$

Step 2   You can see that the division will continue repeating because the subtraction is the same each time. Write the remainder as a fraction by writing the remainder, 2, over the divisor, 9.

$$\begin{array}{r} 0.22 \\ 9\overline{)2.00} \\ \underline{1\,8} \\ 20 \\ \underline{18} \end{array}$$

The fraction $\frac{2}{9}$ equals the decimal **$0.22\frac{2}{9}$.**

As you may know, a unit price is often stated as a decimal with a fraction. The fraction expresses part of one cent.

Example 3   The unit price of a brand of fruit punch is $8\frac{1}{2}$ cents per ounce. What is the cost of 32 ounces of the punch?

Multiply 32 by $8\frac{1}{2}$ or $\$0.08\frac{1}{2}$ to solve the problem. Change the fraction part of the decimal to a decimal digit. The fraction $\frac{1}{2}$ converts to 0.5 ($1 \div 2 = 0.5$). So $8\frac{1}{2}$ cents can be written as 8.5 cents or $0.085. Multiply.

$$\begin{array}{r} 32 \\ \times 0.085 \\ \hline 160 \\ +2\,560 \\ \hline 2.720 \end{array}$$

The cost of 32 ounces of fruit punch is **$2.72.**

Example 4   What is the cost per pound of a 20-pound bag of dog food that sells for $12.75?

Divide $12.75 by 20 to two decimal places. Write the remainder as a fraction and reduce to lowest terms. $\frac{15}{20} = \frac{3}{4}$

$$\begin{array}{r} 0.63 \\ 20\overline{)12.75} \\ \underline{12\,0} \\ 75 \\ \underline{60} \\ 15 \end{array}$$

The unit price of one pound of dog food is **$63\frac{3}{4}$ cents.**

TIP

If you prefer working with fractions, multiply 32 by $8\frac{1}{2}$. Then express your answer as 2 dollars and 72 cents. Always choose a method for solving a problem that makes the most sense to you.

A. Change these fractions to decimals. Round to three decimal places.

1. $\frac{4}{5} =$

2. $\frac{3}{8} =$

3. $\frac{2}{3} =$

4. $\frac{5}{12} =$

5. $\frac{11}{20} =$

6. $\frac{5}{8} =$

7. $\frac{17}{40} =$

8. $\frac{3}{4} =$

9. $\frac{3}{5} =$

10. $\frac{7}{25} =$

11. $\frac{7}{10} =$

12. $\frac{1}{8} =$

B. Change these fractions to decimals. Divide to two decimal places and write the remainder as a fraction.

13. $\frac{5}{6} =$

14. $\frac{8}{9} =$

15. $\frac{7}{15} =$

16. $\frac{1}{16} =$

17. $\frac{3}{11} -$

18. $\frac{1}{3} =$

C. Solve.

19. An all-purpose cleaner costs $10\frac{3}{4}$ cents per ounce. What is the cost of a 32-ounce bottle?

20. A breakfast cereal costing $4.23 contains 18 servings per box. What is the cost of 1 serving?

21. A store sells two brands of masking tape. Brand A comes in 50-yard rolls and sells for $2.70. Brand B comes in 60-yard rolls and sells for $3.18. Which brand has the best price per yard?

22. A brand of hot cereal costs $6\frac{1}{2}$ cents per serving. What is the price of a box containing 24 servings?

23. A 28-ounce jar of Zesty spaghetti sauce costs $2.59. The store brand comes in a 26-ounce jar and sells for $2.47. Find the price per ounce for each brand. Which is the better buy?

24. A brand of peanut butter costs $13\frac{1}{4}$ cents per ounce. What is the cost of a 16-ounce jar?

Answers start on page 394.

Using Decimals and Fractions with a Standard Grid

When using the standard grid shown below to write decimal or fractional answers, you may choose the form of your answer. You may write your answer either as a decimal or as a fraction. Both forms will be marked correct. For example, if you get the fractional answer $\frac{3}{4}$, you may enter either the fraction or the decimal 0.75 on the grid. The reverse is also true. An answer of 0.5 could be entered as either .5 (without the zero) or $\frac{1}{2}$.

Here are some important points to keep in mind when using the standard grid with decimals or fractions:

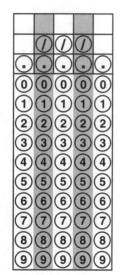

- The grid is used to enter a single answer.
- Your answer can start in any of the five columns, as long as your answer is complete. Any unused columns should be left blank.
- Write your answer in the blank row at the top of the grid. Use this as a guide to filling in the "bubble" rows.
- If you express the answer as a decimal, fill in the whole number part of the answer, then the decimal point in the third row of the grid, then the decimal.
- If you express the answer as a fraction, fill in the numerator of the fraction, then the fraction bar in the second row of the grid, $\varnothing$, and then the denominator of the fraction.
- Mixed fractions cannot be entered on the grid. Therefore, change a mixed fraction to either a decimal or an improper fraction.

Example   In a recent election, Felicia received $\frac{3}{8}$ of the vote, Steve received 0.5 of the vote, and Bill received the rest. What fraction of the votes did Bill receive?

Together, Felicia and Steve received $\frac{3}{8} + 0.5 = \frac{3}{8} + \frac{1}{2} = \frac{7}{8}$ of the vote. Therefore, Bill received $1 - \frac{7}{8} = \frac{1}{8}$ of the vote. Note that since the answer can be entered on the grid either as the fraction $\frac{1}{8}$ or its equivalent decimal 0.125, all the grids shown below are filled in correctly.

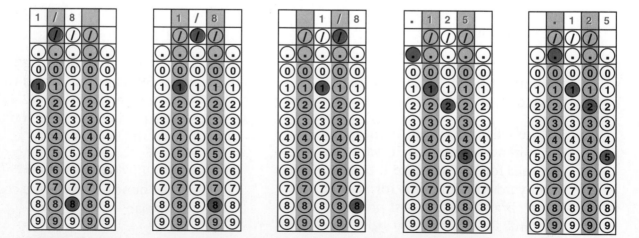

Directions: Solve the following problems and enter your answers on the grids provided.

1. Jim runs $2\frac{1}{4}$ miles on Monday, 1.5 miles on Tuesday, and $3\frac{3}{4}$ miles on Wednesday. How many total miles did Jim run in the 3 days?

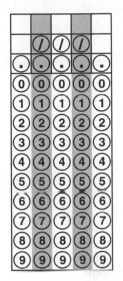

2. If gasoline sells for $1.25 per gallon, how much would $3\frac{3}{5}$ gallons cost?

3. A can of green beans contains $40\frac{1}{2}$ ounces. If one serving is 3.75 ounces, how many servings are in 1 can?

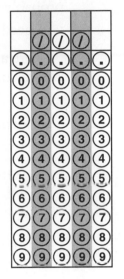

4. Ho Chin has a board that is 9.375 feet long. If Ho Chin cuts off a piece that is $3\frac{1}{8}$ feet long, how many feet are left of the original board?

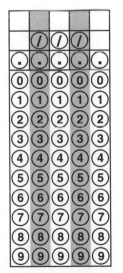

TIP If the answer you need to enter on a grid contains an end zero after the decimal point, you can include it or leave it off. For example, 1.20 could be correctly filled in as 1.20 or 1.2.

TIP Questions involving both fractions and decimals may ask for the answer to be in a certain form. Be sure your answer is in the form asked for, as either a fraction or a decimal.

Answers start on page 395.

GED STRATEGY **Using Your Calculator**

Fractions and Decimals

Most calculators use only decimal numbers and whole numbers. Even whole numbers entered in a calculator usually appear with a decimal point after the ones place. For example, 32 entered on a calculator would probably be displayed as 32. with a decimal point. When using a calculator, you need to change a fraction to a decimal, for example, $\frac{3}{4}$ to 0.75.

Here are some important points to keep in mind when using fractions and decimals on the calculator.

- To change a fraction to a decimal, divide the numerator by the denominator.
  Example Change $\frac{3}{8}$ to a decimal by dividing 3 by 8 = 0.375.

- When working with a mixed number on a calculator, leave the whole number part as it is and change only the fraction to a decimal.
  Example $17\frac{1}{2}$ would become 17.5.

- All decimals that do not contain a whole number part will be displayed with a 0 as the whole number part, even if you do not key in a 0.
  Example The decimal .64, when keyed in, will appear as 0.64.

- When working with decimals, you do not need to key in zeros that are to the right of the last digit in the decimal part of the number.
  Example 24.600 can be keyed in as 24.6.

Example Sam bought a laptop computer for $1620 and made a down payment of $\frac{1}{4}$ of the cost. How much was the down payment?

(1) $ 25.00
(2) $ 40.00
(3) $ 64.80
(4) $ 405.00
(5) $1595.00

Since the problem asks you to find $\frac{1}{4}$ of $1620, you need to multiply. To do this problem on a calculator, you could change $\frac{1}{4}$ to .25. Then you would press the calculator keys in the sequence shown below.

Since $\frac{1}{4}$ also means 1 divided by 4, you could also use either of these sequences:

.25 ⊠ 1620 ▭   or   1 ÷ 4 ⊠ 1620 ▭

You should see the answer 405 in the display. **Option (4) $405** is correct.

Directions: Choose the <u>one best answer</u> to each item. You <u>MAY</u> use your calculator.

1. Carolyn rode her bike 26.8 miles on Thursday, $14\frac{3}{8}$ miles on Friday, and $27\frac{3}{4}$ miles on Saturday. How many miles did she ride in all for the 3 days?

   (1) 26.825
   (2) 67.05
   (3) 67.825
   (4) 68.925
   (5) 80.4

2. During a recent storm, snow fell at the rate of 1.24 inches per hour. At this rate, how many inches of snow would fall in $6\frac{1}{4}$ hours?

   (1) $5\frac{1}{10}$
   (2) $5\frac{2}{5}$
   (3) $7\frac{1}{4}$
   (4) $7\frac{61}{100}$
   (5) $7\frac{3}{4}$

3. Michael is paid at the rate of $9.50 per hour for the first 40 hours worked in a week, and $1\frac{1}{2}$ times that rate for all hours over 40. If he works for $52\frac{1}{4}$ hours in 1 week, what is his gross pay, rounded to the nearest cent?

   (1) $550.56
   (2) $552.56
   (3) $554.56
   (4) $557.56
   (5) $560.56

4. If gasoline sells for $1.39 per gallon, how much would $16\frac{1}{8}$ gallons cost, rounded to the nearest cent?

   (1) $31.12
   (2) $22.49
   (3) $22.41
   (4) $22.24
   (5) $11.60

Questions 5 and 6 refer to the following table.

Miles Jogged	
Alicia	4.875
Brett	$3\frac{3}{5}$
Krystyna	$4\frac{3}{4}$

5. How many more miles did Alicia jog than Brett did?

   (1) 1.275
   (2) 1.375
   (3) 1.400
   (4) 1.500
   (5) 1.575

6. What was the total number of miles jogged by the three people listed?

   (1) 13.525
   (2) 13.425
   (3) 13.325
   (4) 13.225
   (5) 13.125

Answers start on page 395.

Directions: This is a 30-minute practice test. After 30 minutes, mark the last item you finished. Then complete the test and check your answers. If most of your answers are correct, but you didn't finish, try to work faster next time.

Part 1

Directions: Choose the <u>one best answer</u> to each question. You <u>MAY</u> use your calculator.

1. Which of the following decimals has the same value as the fraction $\frac{3}{7}$, rounded to the nearest hundredth?

   (1) 0.04
   (2) 0.42
   (3) 0.43
   (4) 0.44
   (5) 0.45

2. For the first five months of the year Menchu had electric bills of $64.16, $78.92, $63.94, $50.17, and $42.87. What was the total amount of these bills?

   (1) $287.86
   (2) $298.06
   (3) $299.06
   (4) $300.06
   (5) Not enough information is given.

3. Stuart purchased three items at Rite Pharmacy priced at $17.60, $9.25, and $3.68. If the tax was $2.40, and he gave the salesperson a $50 bill, how much change did he receive?

   (1) $17.07
   (2) $17.93
   (3) $18.07
   (4) $18.93
   (5) $19.07

4. Marilyn had a checking account balance of $528.60. If she made deposits of $45.24, $17.50, and $67.45, and wrote checks for $412.72 and $53.19, what was the balance in her account after these transactions?

   (1) $ 67.50
   (2) $192.88
   (3) $406.88
   (4) $492.88
   (5) $558.79

5. Last year Jing drove 28,606.8 miles and used 1,538 gallons of gasoline. How many miles per gallon of gasoline did he average?

   (1) 20.6
   (2) 19.2
   (3) 18.6
   (4) 18.4
   (5) 17.8

6. An insurance policy costs $6.87 for every $1,500 of insurance. At this rate, what would a $25,000 insurance policy cost, rounded to the nearest dollar?

   (1) $ 17
   (2) $ 115
   (3) $ 218
   (4) $1,145
   (5) $3,639

Questions 7 and 8 refer to the following table.

Clarkson's Computer Supplies Sales Receipt

Item	Quantity	Unit Price
Boxes of Computer Disks	65	$7.95
Reams of Paper	25	$3.75
Printer Cartridges	30	$14.85

7. What was the total amount paid for the reams of paper?

   (1) $ 90.75
   (2) $ 93.75
   (3) $ 96.75
   (4) $ 99.75
   (5) $102.75

8. How much more was paid for the boxes of computer disks than for the printer cartridges?

   (1) $75.25
   (2) $74.25
   (3) $73.25
   (4) $72.25
   (5) $71.25

9. Millie went on a $32\frac{1}{2}$ mile hike that took three days. If she hiked 10.6 miles the first day and $11\frac{7}{8}$ miles the second day, how many miles did she hike on the third day?

   (1) 10.025
   (2) 10.250
   (3) 12.025
   (4) 15.275
   (5) Not enough information is given.

10. A plant grows at the rate of $3\frac{1}{4}$ inches per week. At this rate, how many weeks will it take the plant to grow 16.25 inches?

    (1) 4.5
    (2) 5.0
    (3) 5.5
    (4) 6.0
    (5) 6.5

Questions 11 and 12 refer to the following information.

William earns a gross annual salary of $34,000. He budgets $\frac{3}{8}$ of this amount for taxes and 0.25 for food.

11. How much more does William budget for taxes than for food?

    (1) $ 425
    (2) $ 850
    (3) $ 4,250
    (4) $ 8,500
    (5) $12,750

12. After budgeting for taxes and food, what fraction of William's gross annual salary is left to budget for other items?

    (1) $\frac{1}{4}$
    (2) $\frac{3}{8}$
    (3) $\frac{1}{2}$
    (4) $\frac{5}{8}$
    (5) $\frac{7}{8}$

Part 2

Directions: Choose the <u>one best answer</u> to each item. You may <u>NOT</u> use your calculator.

13. Which of the following represents the number written as "23 and 37 thousandths?"

    (1) 23.370
    (2) 23.037
    (3) 2.337
    (4) 0.237
    (5) 0.2337

14. Which of the following is the value of 2.1374 rounded to the nearest hundredth?

    (1) 2.10
    (2) 2.13
    (3) 2.14
    (4) 2.17
    (5) 2.20

15. John paid $1224.96 in 12 equal monthly installments. <u>Estimate</u> the amount of each monthly installment.

    (1) $1200
    (2) $1000
    (3) $ 120
    (4) $ 100
    (5) $ 12

16. Yaffa has $175. She spends $54.25 and $30.50. Which of the following expressions shows how much money Yaffa has left after the two purchases?

    (1) $175 + $54.25 + $30.50
    (2) $175 − ($54.25 + $30.50)
    (3) ($175 + $54.25) − ($175 + $30.50)
    (4) $175 + $54.25 − $30.50
    (5) $175 − $54.25 + $30.50

Questions 17 through 19 refer to the following table.

Paul's Plants Price List	
3-inch Potted Plant	$1.79
4-inch Potted Plant	$2.89
5-inch Potted Plant	$3.69
Bag of Potting Soil	$3.19
Watering Can	$1.89

17. What is the greatest number of 3-inch potted plants that Mohammed can buy with $10?

    (1) 2
    (2) 3
    (3) 5
    (4) 8
    (5) 10

18. Anya buys two 5-inch potted plants and one watering can. What is the greatest number of 4-inch potted plants she can buy so that the total cost is less than $20?

    (1) 2
    (2) 3
    (3) 5
    (4) 8
    (5) 10

19. Roberto buys two bags of potting soil and one 5-inch potted plant. <u>Approximately</u> how much change should he receive from $15?

    (1) $ 2
    (2) $ 3
    (3) $ 5
    (4) $10
    (5) $15

20. Atlas Gas charges $1.25 per gallon of gas and Bradley Gas charges $1.29 per gallon. Which expression shows how much more 14 gallons of gas would cost at Bradley Gas than at Atlas Gas?

(1) 14 + $1.25 + $1.29
(2) 14 − $1.25 − $1.29
(3) 14($1.29 + $1.25)
(4) 14($1.29 − $1.25)
(5) 14($1.29 × $1.25)

21. How much would 2.6 pounds of Swiss cheese cost at $4.85 per pound?

(1) $ 1.26
(2) $ 1.87
(3) $12.61
(4) $13.61
(5) $18.70

22. A package of ground sirloin costs $8.24. If the price per pound is $3.45, how many pounds of ground sirloin are in the package, rounded to the nearest tenth of a pound?

(1) 2.3
(2) 2.4
(3) 2.5
(4) 2.6
(5) 2.7

23. Marcos earns a gross monthly salary of $2383.20. If his monthly mortgage is $\frac{1}{5}$ of this amount, about how much does he pay each month for his mortgage?

(1) $12,000
(2) $ 4,800
(3) $ 1,200
(4) $ 480
(5) $ 120

24. Fabrice is paid $7.90 per hour for the first 35 hours of work in a week, and $1\frac{1}{2}$ times that rate for all hours over 35. What is his gross weekly pay?

(1) $154.05
(2) $276.50
(3) $379.20
(4) $430.55
(5) Not enough information is given.

Questions 25 and 26 refer to the following table.

Price per Share ($) Year to Date		
Stock	High	Low
Ampex	$24\frac{1}{4}$	$18\frac{1}{2}$
Intex	$36\frac{1}{2}$	$29\frac{3}{4}$
Microx	$28\frac{3}{8}$	$24\frac{1}{4}$

25. What was the difference between the high value and the low value of Microx stock?

(1) 4
(2) $4\frac{1}{8}$
(3) $4\frac{1}{4}$
(4) $4\frac{1}{2}$
(5) $4\frac{3}{4}$

26. Which expression shows how much 30 shares of Ampex stock and 40 shares of Intex stock would be worth, if they were both at their high prices?

(1) $30\left(24\frac{1}{4}\right) + 40\left(18\frac{1}{2}\right)$
(2) $40\left(24\frac{1}{4}\right) − 30\left(18\frac{1}{2}\right)$
(3) $30\left(24\frac{1}{4}\right) + 40\left(36\frac{1}{2}\right)$
(4) $40\left(24\frac{1}{4}\right) − 30\left(36\frac{1}{2}\right)$
(5) $30\left(36\frac{1}{2}\right) + 40\left(18\frac{1}{2}\right)$

Answers start on page 396.

Lesson 11   GED SKILL The Meaning of Percent

Percent is another way to show part of a whole. With fractions, the whole can be divided into any number of equal parts. With decimals, the number of parts must be 10, 100, 1000, or another power of 10. With percents, the whole is always divided into 100 equal parts.

A

Drawing A is divided into 100 equal parts. The entire square represents 100%. Fifty parts, or one-half of the whole square, are shaded. The shaded part is 50% of the whole. The percent sign, %, means "out of 100." Fifty out of 100 parts are shaded. The drawing also represents the fraction $\frac{1}{2}$ and the decimal 0.5.

B

Percents can be greater than 100%. Drawing B represents 125%. One whole square and 25 parts of the second square are shaded. Since 100 parts equal 1 and 25 out of 100 parts is $\frac{1}{4}$, 125% equals $1\frac{1}{4}$ or 1.25.

C

Drawing C represents $\frac{1}{2}$%, or 0.5%. Only one-half of one part is shaded. A percent that is less than 1% is less than $\frac{1}{100}$.

$$0.5\% = 0.005 = \frac{5}{1000} = \frac{1}{200}$$

Changing Percents to Decimals

To solve percent problems using pencil and paper, you need to change the percent to either a decimal or a fraction.

TIP

There is always an understood decimal point to the right of the ones digit; 7 is understood to be the same as 7.0.

Example 1   Change 45% to a decimal.
Drop the percent sign, and insert a decimal   45.%
point to the right of the ones digit. Then move   0.45.
the decimal point two places to the left.

The percent 45% is equal to the decimal **0.45.**

Example 2   Change 7.5% to a decimal.
Drop the percent sign, and move the decimal   7.5%
point two places to the left. Write a zero in   0.07.5
the tenths place as a placeholder.

The percent 7.5% is equal to the decimal **0.075.**

To change a percent to a decimal using a calculator, enter the number of the percent and divide by 100.

7.5 $\div$ 100 $=$ 0.075

Changing a Decimal to a Percent

The examples below show how to change a decimal to a percent.

Example   Change 0.15 to a percent.
Move the decimal point two places to the right, and write the percent sign. (Notice that the zero placeholder is no longer needed.)

$0.15. = 15\%$

The decimal 0.15 is equal to **15%**.

Examples   Add a zero in order to move the decimal point two places.

$2.5 = 2.50. = 250\%$

Do not show the decimal point after a whole number or between a whole number and a fraction.

$0.33\frac{1}{3} = 0.33.\frac{1}{3} = 33\frac{1}{3}\%$

 To change a decimal to a percent using a calculator, enter the decimal and multiply by 100.

0.15 ✕ **100** = **15.**

GED SKILL FOCUS

A. Change each percent to a decimal, mixed decimal, or whole number.

1. 60%

2. 38%

3. 10.8%

4. 4%

5. 200%

6. $5\frac{1}{2}\%$

7. 130%

8. $9\frac{1}{4}\%$

9. 325%

B. Change each decimal to a percent.

10. 0.85

11. 0.36

12. 0.144

13. 0.4

14. 4.5

15. $0.16\frac{2}{3}$

16. 8.75

17. 0.375

18. $0.07\frac{1}{3}$

 C. Use a calculator to make the indicated changes.

19. Change 225% to a decimal.

20. Change 1.5 to a percent.

21. Change 80% to a decimal.

22. Change 0.24 to a percent.

23. Change 0.6 to a percent.

24. Change 3% to a decimal.

25. Change 0.125 to a percent.

26. Change 550% to a decimal.

Answers start on page 397.

Changing a Fraction to a Percent

You can convert a fraction to a percent by first changing the fraction to a decimal and then changing the decimal to a percent.

Example 1 Change $\frac{3}{4}$ to a percent.

Step 1 Divide the numerator by the denominator. $\qquad 3 \div 4 = 0.75$

Step 2 Multiply the decimal by 100. Move the decimal $\qquad 0.75 = 75\%$ point two places to the right; write a percent sign.

The fraction $\frac{3}{4}$ is equal to **75%**.

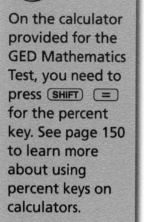

On the calculator provided for the GED Mathematics Test, you need to press SHIFT = for the percent key. See page 150 to learn more about using percent keys on calculators.

You can also change a fraction or a mixed number directly to a percent.

Example 2 Change $\frac{3}{4}$ to a percent.

Step 1 Multiply the fraction by $\frac{100}{1}$.

Step 2 Change to a whole or mixed number and write $\qquad \dfrac{3}{\cancel{4}_1} \times \dfrac{\cancel{100}^{25}}{1} = 75\%$ the percent sign.

The fraction $\frac{3}{4}$ is equal to **75%** by this method as well.

Example 3 Change $3\frac{1}{4}$ to a percent.

Step 1 Change the mixed number to an $\qquad\qquad 3\frac{1}{4} = \dfrac{13}{4}$ improper fraction.

Step 2 Multiply by $\frac{100}{1}$ and add the percent sign. $\qquad \dfrac{13}{\cancel{4}_1} \times \dfrac{\cancel{100}^{25}}{1} = 325\%$

The mixed number $3\frac{1}{4}$ is equal to **325%**.

To change a fraction to a percent using a calculator, divide the numerator by the denominator and press the percent key.

Change $\frac{3}{4}$ to a percent. $\quad$ **3** ÷ **4** SHIFT = **75.** or **75%**

Change $\frac{2}{5}$ to a percent. $\quad$ **2** ÷ **5** SHIFT = **40.** or **40%**

Changing a Percent to a Fraction or Mixed Number

As you know, the word *percent* means "out of 100." To change a percent to a fraction or mixed number, drop the percent sign and write the number as a fraction with a denominator of 100. Then reduce.

Example 1 Change 35% to a fraction.
Write as a fraction with a $\qquad \dfrac{35}{100} = \dfrac{35 \div 5}{100 \div 5} = \dfrac{7}{20}$
denominator of 100 and reduce.

So the percent 35% is equal to the fraction $\frac{7}{20}$.

Example 2 Change 150% to a mixed number.
Write as an improper fraction $\qquad \dfrac{150}{100} = \dfrac{150 \div 50}{100 \div 50} = \dfrac{3}{2} = 1\frac{1}{2}$
(denominator of 100); simplify.

So the percent 150% is equal to the mixed number $1\frac{1}{2}$.

TIP

Your calculator display may look different than the one shown here. Read the instructions that came with your calculator to learn how to use it to solve problems with fractions.

Converting percents with fraction or decimal parts requires extra steps.

Example 3   Change $41\frac{2}{3}\%$ to a fraction.

Write $41\frac{2}{3}$ over 100 and divide.

$$\frac{41\frac{2}{3}}{100} = 41\frac{2}{3} \div 100 = \frac{\overset{5}{\cancel{125}}}{3} \times \frac{1}{\underset{4}{\cancel{100}}} = \frac{5}{12}$$

The percent $41\frac{2}{3}\%$ is equal to the fraction $\frac{5}{12}$.

Example 4   Change 37.5% to a fraction.

Step 1   Change the percent to a decimal: move the decimal point 2 places left.

$37.5\% = .37.5 = 0.375$

Step 2   Change decimal to a fraction; reduce.

$$\frac{375 \div 125}{1000 \div 125} = \frac{3}{8}$$

So the percent 37.5% is equal to the fraction $\frac{3}{8}$.

Some calculators have special keys to change percents to fractions.

To change 150% to a fraction: enter the percent number, press the fraction key, enter 100, then press ▭ .

150 ⬛a b/c **100** ▭ **1 ⌐1 ⌐2.**

This calculator display means $1\frac{1}{2}$.

GED SKILL FOCUS

A. Change each percent to a fraction or mixed number.

1. 65%

2. 84%

3. 140%

4. 275%

5. 39%

6. 450%

B. Use a calculator to make the indicated changes.

7. Change $\frac{3}{8}$ to a percent.

8. Change $\frac{15}{16}$ to a percent.

9. Change 125% to a decimal or mixed number.

10. Change 87.5% to a decimal or mixed number.

C. Fill in the missing numbers.

	Decimal	Fraction	Percent
11.			20%
12.		$\frac{1}{4}$	
13.	0.3		
14.		$\frac{1}{3}$	
15.			40%

	Decimal	Fraction	Percent
16.			60%
17.	$0.66\frac{2}{3}$		
18.		$\frac{3}{4}$	
19.			80%
20.	0.9		

Answers start on page 397.

GED STRATEGY Solving Word Problems

Using Proportions with Percents

There are three basic elements in a percent problem: **base × rate = part.** Think about this statement:

Example   Of 200 applicants, 25% or 50 cannot work weekends.

- The **base** is the whole amount. In this statement, the base is 200.
- The **part** is a piece of the whole or base. In this statement, 50 tells what part of the 200 applicants (the base) cannot work weekends.
- The **rate** is always followed by a percent sign (%). The rate tells the relationship of the part to the base. In this statement, it is 25%.

In a percent problem, one of the three elements is missing. To find the missing element set up a proportion using the base, part, and rate. Substitute the known values, and solve for the missing element.

TIP

The base, or whole, is often an original amount such as an original price, starting balance, or total amount.

$$\frac{\textbf{Part}}{\textbf{Base}} = \frac{\textbf{Rate\%}}{\textbf{100\%}}$$ To find the missing element, cross multiply and divide by the third number.

Example 1   12 is 75% of what number?

    (1)   1200
    (2)   75
    (3)   63
    (4)   16
    (5)   12

Here, you know the part and the rate. You need to solve for the base.

Step 1   Set up the proportion. $\frac{12}{?} = \frac{75}{100}$

Step 2   Cross multiply. $12 \times 100 = 1200$

Step 3   Divide by 75. $1200 \div 75 = 16$

So, 12 is 75% of 16. **Option (4)** is correct.

Example 2   16 is what percent of 80?

    (1)   16
    (2)   20
    (3)   64
    (4)   80
    (5)   100

You know the part and the base. You must find the rate (percent).

Step 1   Set up the proportion. $\frac{16}{80} = \frac{?}{100}$

Step 2   Cross multiply. $16 \times 100 = 1600$

Step 3   Divide by 80. $1600 \div 80 = 20$

Write a percent sign after 20: 16 is 20% of 80. **Option (2)** is correct.

Directions: Choose the <u>one best answer</u> to each question. Use your calculator when indicated.

1. The sweater shown above is on sale for 20% off. If the price tag lists the original price, how much would you save by buying it on sale?

   (1) $ 7
   (2) $ 9
   (3) $12
   (4) $14
   (5) $15

2. Sidney's insurance paid 90% of the cost of getting his car fixed. If the repair bill was $625, how much did the insurance pay?

   (1) $437.50
   (2) $468.75
   (3) $500.00
   (4) $562.50
   (5) $605.15

3. Aldora earns $1344 per month. If 2.5% of her earnings goes to state income tax, how much does she pay per month in state income tax?

   (1) $ 20.16
   (2) $ 26.88
   (3) $ 33.60
   (4) $ 42.20
   (5) $336.00

4. On a test, a student got 80% of the items correct. If the student got 56 items correct, how many items were on the test?

   (1) 64
   (2) 70
   (3) 72
   (4) 84
   (5) 90

5. The Bulldogs won 18 games out of 45. What percent of their games did the Bulldogs win?

   (1) 40%
   (2) 45%
   (3) 50%
   (4) 55%
   (5) 60%

6. Eighty percent of the Usagi Express Company's employees are drivers. If there are 300 drivers in the company, how many employees work for Usagi Express?

   (1) 320
   (2) 335
   (3) 342
   (4) 365
   (5) 375

TIP To solve a percent problem set up a proportion:

$$\frac{\text{Part}}{\text{Base}} = \frac{\text{Rate}\%}{100\%}$$

Determine which element is missing: the base, part, or rate; substitute the numbers into the proportion and solve.

Answers start on page 397.

The Elements of a Percent Problem

You now know that percent problems have three basic elements—the base, the part, and the rate. Think about this statement:

Kina spends $320, or 20%, of her monthly income of $1600 on groceries.

The base, $1600, is the whole amount. The other numbers in the problem are compared to the base. The part, $320, is a portion of the base. The rate, 20%, tells the relationship of the part to the base.

In a percent problem, one of the three elements is missing. You learned earlier how to solve a percent problem by using a proportion. You can also find the missing element using the percent formula:

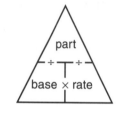

$$\textbf{base} \times \textbf{rate} = \textbf{part}$$

The triangle diagram shows the relationship among the three elements. You will learn how to use the diagram in the examples throughout this lesson.

Finding the Part

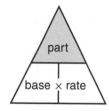

Example   Aretha puts 5% of her weekly paycheck in her savings account. If her weekly paycheck is $326, how much will she put in savings?

Step 1   Identify the elements you know. The base, or whole amount, is $326. Aretha puts a *part* of this amount in savings. The rate is 5%. You need to solve for the part.

Step 2   Use the diagram to find out which operation to perform. Cover the word *part*. The remaining elements are connected by the multiplication symbol. Multiply: **base × rate.**

Step 3   Change the rate to a decimal.   5% = 0.05
Multiply.   326 × 0.05 = $16.30

When you solve any word problem, take a moment to decide whether your answer makes sense. Since 5% is a small part of 100%, you know Aretha's savings should be a small part of her paycheck. The answer $16.30 is a reasonable amount.

TIP

If the rate is greater than 100%, the part will be greater than the base. 150% of 200 is 300.

You need to find 5% of $326. Multiply. Enter the base first.

326 ⊗ **×** **5** ⊗ **SHIFT** ⊗ **=** **16.3**

(Remember: **SHIFT** **=** gives the % key on the GED calculators.)

Aretha will put **$16.30** of her weekly paycheck in savings.

A. Solve using pencil and paper.

1. Find 3% of 500.

2. What is 15% of $950?

3. Find 90% of 72.

4. Find 85% of 140.

5. Find 125% of $220. (*Hint:* Since 125% is greater than 100%, the part is greater than $220.)

6. What is 150% of 184?

7. What is 75% of 80?

8. Find 5% of $200.

9. Find 8% of $1600.

10. What is 55% of $20?

11. Find $5\frac{1}{2}$% of 300.

12. What is $33\frac{1}{3}$% of $600?

B. Use your calculator to solve these problems. Round answers to the nearest hundredth or cent.

13. Find 6% of $84.50.

14. Find 4% of 1278.

15. What is 210% of $158.75?

16. What is 45% of $10.80?

17. Find $8\frac{3}{4}$% of $575.00.

18. What is $1\frac{1}{2}$% of $50.00?

19. What is 7% of 49.5?

20. Find 135% of $17.50.

C. Solve.

21. During the winter, Green Art, a landscaping service, contacted 1200 homeowners. Of these, 15% hired the company to do work at their homes. How many homeowners hired Green Art?

Use the following graph to answer Questions 22 and 23.

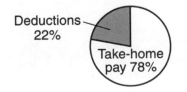

22. Angelo earns $2080 per month. What amount is deducted from his pay each month?

23. Of Angelo's $2080 monthly earnings, how much is his take-home pay?

24. Paul bought a sofa for $690. He paid 8% sales tax on the purchase. What was the total amount of his purchase? (*Hint:* This problem has two steps. Find the amount of the sales tax, and add it to the price of the sofa.)

25. For a party of 8 or more, a restaurant automatically adds a 15% tip to the bill. The bill for a birthday party of 20 diners comes to $186.35. What is the amount of the tip rounded to the nearest cent?

26. Carol's utility bill for April of this year is 150% of her bill for the same month last year. If her April bill last year was $74.22, what is the amount of her bill for April this year?

Answers start on page 398.

Finding the Rate

Example   Joel earns $1700 per month. He decides to take out a loan to buy a used car. His monthly loan payments are $204. What percent of his monthly income is the loan payment?

Step 1   Think about the problem. The whole amount Joel earns each month is the base. Part of these earnings is spent on the loan payment. You need to solve for the percent, or rate.

Step 2   Use the diagram to find out which operation to perform. Cover the word *rate*. The remaining elements are connected by the division symbol: **part ÷ base = rate.**

Step 3   Divide. 204 ÷ 1700 = 0.12.
Convert to a percent. 0.12 = 12%

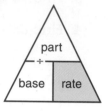

 You can do both calculations in one step using your calculator's percent key or the SHIFT = keys on the GED Test calculator.

204 ÷ 1700 % 12.   or   **204 ÷ 1700 SHIFT = 12.**

Joel spends **12%** of his monthly earnings on the loan payment.

Finding Percent of Increase or Decrease

Some percent problems ask you to find the rate that an amount has changed over time. The change may be either an increase or a decrease. To solve these problems, follow these steps.

Step 1   Subtract to find the difference between the original amount and the new amount.

Step 2   Divide the difference from Step 1 by the <u>original amount.</u>

Step 3   Convert the decimal to a percent.

Example   Brent works as a sales clerk in a clothing store. When he started the job, he was paid $7.50 an hour. Recently, he received a raise. He now earns $8.10 per hour. Find the rate of increase in his hourly pay.

Look for clues in the words of the problem to help you identify the original amount. For example, "what percent of" is usually followed by the base.

Brent's pay started at $7.50 per hour (the original amount) and increased to $8.10, the new amount.

Step 1   Subtract to find the difference. $8.10 − $7.50 = $0.60
Step 2   Divide by the original hourly wage. $0.60 ÷ $7.50 = 0.08
Step 3   Convert the decimal to a percent.   0.08 = 8%

Brent's raise is an **8% increase.**

A. Solve using pencil and paper.

1. What percent is 123 of 820?

2. What percent is $4.50 of $6.00?

3. $18.00 is what percent of $22.50?

4. 350 is what percent of 2000?

5. The number 240 is what percent of 60?

6. What percent of 4000 is 120?

7. $5 is what percent of $160?

8. What percent of $40.00 is $72.00?

B. Use your calculator to solve these problems.

9. $3.50 is what percent of $175.00?

10. What percent is 326 of 1304?

11. What percent of 5000 is 225?

12. $144 is what percent of $150?

13. What percent of $110.00 is $82.50?

14. 40 is what percent of 16?

C. Find the percent of increase or decrease.

15. Original amount: 1500
    New amount: 1725

16. Original amount: $520.00
    New amount: $582.40

17. Original amount: 280
    New amount: 70

18. Original amount: $1200
    New amount: $1140

D. Solve.

19. Rae supervises a loading dock. She needs to have 140 cartons loaded into a truck for delivery. By lunch, 119 cartons have been loaded. What percent of the job is finished?

20. Jorge stocked the store shelves with 25 cases of soft drinks. Of these, 10 are cola drinks, 8 are root beer, and 7 are orange soda. Of the total cases of soft drinks, what percent is cola? (*Hint:* There is extra information.)

21. Stacey was given a raise. Her new monthly pay is $1508. Previously, her monthly pay was $1450. What percent raise did she receive?

22. Ahmad took a test with 50 items. He answered 44 of the items correctly. What percent of the test items did he answer correctly?

Refer to the following information to answer Questions 23 and 24.

ORIGINALLY $790
NOW ONLY $550

23. Smith's Electronics has the camcorder shown above on sale. To the nearest percent, by what percent did the store discount the camcorder?

24. Lucia receives a $44 commission for each camcorder that she sells. What percent of the sale price is her commission?

Answers start on page 398.

GED STRATEGY Solving Word Problems

Using Mental Math

TIP

Remember that a whole number is understood to have a decimal point after the ones place.
$40 = $40.00

You use mental math every day. Whether it's estimating the amount to tip on your restaurant bill or figuring out sale prices, you are calculating in your head. Mental math involving percents is easiest when you use 10%.

Remember, 10% = 0.10 = 0.1. To multiply by 0.1, move the decimal point one place to the left. For example, if a sweater originally cost $40 and is on sale for 10% off, how much would you save? You would save $4.

$4͟0.00

Using this method for finding 10%, you can develop mental math strategies for quickly finding 5%, 15%, and 20% of an amount.

Example 1 Jan's monthly paycheck is $900. If 5% of that amount is deducted for medical and dental insurance, what amount is deducted?

Step 1 To find 5% of an amount, first find 10%, and then divide that amount by 2. In this example, find 10% of $900 by moving the decimal point one place to the left.

$90͟0.00

Step 2 Since 5% is half of 10%, divide $90 by 2.

$90 ÷ 2 = $45

So, 5% of $900 is **$45.**

Example 2 Carlos wants to leave a 15% tip on a $20 restaurant bill. How much money should he leave for the tip?

Step 1 To find 15% of an amount, find 10%, divide that result by 2 to find 5%, and add the 10% and 5% amounts. In this example, find 10% of $20 by moving the decimal point one place to the left.

$2͟0.00

Step 2 Since 5% is half of 10%, divide $2 by 2.

$2 ÷ 2 = $1

Step 3 10% + 5% = 15%, so add $2 + $1.

$2 + $1 = $3

The total tip is **$3.**

Example 3 Sharon received $82 in tips. She gives 20% to her assistant. How much should Sharon give her assistant?

Step 1 To find 20% of an amount, find 10%, then multiply that amount by 2. In this example, find 10% of $82 by moving the decimal point 1 place to the left.

$8͟2.00

Step 2 Multiply by 2 to find 20%.

$8.2 × 2 = $16.40

Sharon should give her assistant **$16.40.**

Directions: Choose the <u>one best answer</u> to each question.

1. The Gardner Public Library records the number of books borrowed each month. Of the 8520 books borrowed in May, 10% were children's books. How many children's books were borrowed in May?

    (1)   85
    (2)   170
    (3)   852
    (4)   1704
    (5)   2000

<u>Question 2</u> refers to the diagram below.

2. Estelle works as a waitress. A customer left a 15% tip based on the total of the check shown above. How much was Estelle's tip?

    (1) $1.30
    (2) $1.60
    (3) $2.75
    (4) $3.90
    (5) $5.00

3. Martin bought some stereo equipment for $150 plus 5% sales tax. How much sales tax did he pay?

    (1) $155.00
    (2) $ 50.00
    (3) $ 30.00
    (4) $ 15.00
    (5) $ 7.50

4. Sara sold a radio/CD player originally priced at $70 and discounted 20%. How much was the discount?

    (1) $20.00
    (2) $14.00
    (3) $ 7.00
    (4) $ 1.40
    (5) $ 0.70

5. Zoila's take-home pay is $1500 a month. Of that amount, 25% goes towards paying rent. How much does she pay each month for rent?

    (1) $ 60
    (2) $150
    (3) $300
    (4) $375
    (5) $500

6. The Johnson Community Center is selling tickets to its fundraising concert. They have sold 30% of the 1800 tickets. How many tickets have they sold?

    (1) 600
    (2) 540
    (3) 60
    (4) 54
    (5)   6

TIP It is sometimes helpful to both estimate and use mental math. For example, in order to leave a 15% tip on an amount of $8.69, round the amount to $9 and then find 15% of $9.

Answers start on page 399.

Finding the Base

Example 1   The employees at Galindo Printing are required to complete a safety course during their first year of work. Of the current employees, 90% have completed the course. If 63 employees have completed the course, how many employees work at Galindo Printing?

Step 1   Think about the problem. The base or whole amount is the total number of employees at Galindo Printing. The number 63 is part of the number of employees. The 63 employees are 90% of the total employees. You need to solve for the base.

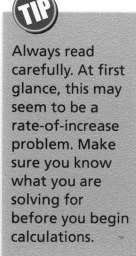

TIP

You can also use a proportion to solve for the base:

$$\frac{63}{x} = \frac{90\%}{100\%}$$

Step 2   Use the diagram to find out what operation to perform. Cover the word *base*. The remaining elements are connected by the division symbol. Divide: **part ÷ rate.**

Step 3   Convert the rate to a decimal.   90% = 0.9
Divide.

$$0.9\overline{)63.0.}$$
$$70.$$
$$63$$
$$\ \ 0\ 0$$

There are **70** employees at Galindo Publishing.

You can perform the calculations in one step using your calculator. Divide.

63 ÷ 90 SHIFT = 70.

Galindo Printing has **70 employees.**

As you know, the part may be greater than the base. You can recognize these situations because the rate is greater than 100%.

TIP

Always read carefully. At first glance, this may seem to be a rate-of-increase problem. Make sure you know what you are solving for before you begin calculations.

Example 2   Regina recently started a better-paying job. Her new weekly salary is 120% of the weekly earnings at her old job. If her new weekly salary is $326.40, how much did she earn per week at her old job?

Step 1   Analyze the situation. Regina's new salary is 120% of her old salary. The new salary, $326.40, is the part even though it is the greater amount. The old salary is the base.

Step 2   Convert the rate to a decimal and divide the part by the rate.

$$120\% = 1.2 \qquad \$326.40 \div 1.2 = \$272.00$$

Regina's old salary is **$272.00.**

A. Solve using pencil and paper.

1. $54 is 60% of what amount?

2. 720 is 9% of what number?

3. 6% of what amount is $1.92?

4. 17% of what number is 85?

5. $495 is 90% of what amount?

6. 270% of what number is 810?

7. 115% of what amount is $207?

8. $1020 is 85% of what amount?

9. $0.21 is 7% of what amount?

10. 125% of what number is 660?

11. $6.30 is 15% of what amount?

12. 6000 is $66\frac{2}{3}$% of what number?

B. Use your calculator to solve these problems.

13. $3.75 is 75% of what amount?

14. 15% of what number is 9.6?

15. 35% of what amount is $157.50?

16. $26.88 is 24% of what amount?

17. $62.40 is 104% of what amount?

18. 3.8% of what amount is $0.76?

19. $679.35 is $5\frac{1}{4}$% of what amount?

20. $1.26 is $3\frac{1}{2}$% of what amount?

C. Solve.

21. Jeff's insurance paid $7500 for his surgery. If the insurance paid 80% of the total bill, what was the amount of the total bill?

22. Last year Florence paid 15% of her annual income in federal income tax. If her tax bill was $3555, what was her annual income?

Refer to the following information to answer Question 23.

89% of CAA Members Vote to Elect Elena Richards

23. If 178 members voted for Elena, how many did <u>not</u> vote for her? (*Hint:* You need to find the base, but the base is not the final answer.)

24. Lori knew that 25% of the store's customers in May made a purchase. If 207 customers made a purchase, how many visited the store?

25. Carmen bought a new jacket for $98. The sale price was 70% of the original price. What was the original price?

Refer to the following table to answer Questions 26 through 28.

Northwest Custom Furniture Catalog Sales for New Items		
Product	**Number of Returns**	**Percent of Total Sales**
Folding Step Chair	8	4%
Art Glass Table	3	20%
Rolling Table	15	$12\frac{1}{2}$%

26. How many art glass tables were sold?

27. How many of the rolling tables that were sold were <u>not</u> returned to the furniture store?

28. What percent of the folding step chairs were not returned?

Answers start on page 399.

Solving Interest Problems

TIP

See page 16 for a copy of the GED formulas page that you will be given for use on the GED Mathematics Test. Be familiar with these formulas and know how to use them before you take the test.

Interest is a fee charged for using someone else's money. When you borrow money for a purchase, you pay interest to the company that loans you the money. When you put your money into a savings account, the bank pays you interest for the use of your money.

If you have had a credit card or have borrowed money, you have had experience with paying interest. There are several different types of interest and ways to calculate it. On the GED Mathematics Test, you will be tested on your understanding of simple interest. **Simple interest** is based on the time of the loan in years.

The formula for finding simple interest is $i = prt.$ This formula is similar to the percent formula you have been using. When the letters, or variables, in a formula are written next to each other, they are to be multiplied. This interest formula can also be written in a triangle.

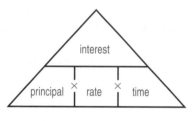

$i =$ **interest**

$p =$ **principal**, the amount borrowed or invested

$r =$ **interest rate**, as a percent

$t =$ **time** of the loan, in years

Example   Lynn Alvarez borrows $2500 for 6 months at a 12% rate of interest. How much interest will Lynn pay on the loan?

The principal (p) is $2500, the amount of the loan. The interest rate (r) is 12%. The time (t) is 6 months, or $\frac{1}{2}$ of a year.

Step 1   Change the interest rate to a decimal. $12\% = 0.12$

Step 2   Write the time in terms of years. $6 \text{ months} = \frac{6}{12} = \frac{1}{2} \text{ year.}$

(If the problem states the time in months, write the time as a fraction of a year. Write the number of months as the numerator and the number 12 as the denominator. Reduce the fraction to lowest terms.)

TIP

To solve interest problems using a calculator, change the fractional part of a year to a decimal. For example, 6 months equals 0.5 year.

Step 3   Multiply: **principal × rate × time.** $\$2500 \times 0.12 \times \frac{1}{2} =$
The result is the interest. $\$300 \times \frac{1}{2} = \$150$

Lynn will owe **$150** in interest.

Some problems ask you to find the **amount paid back.** This includes the principal and any interest owed. In the example above, Lynn borrowed $2500 and must pay $150 in interest. But this does not answer the question. To find the payback amount, add the principal and the interest: $2500 + $150 = $2650.

Lynn must pay back **$2650.**

A. Find the interest on the following loans. Use pencil and paper.

1. A loan of $1250 at 12% for 2 years

2. A loan of $2400 at 9.5% for 1 year

3. A loan of $900 at 8% for 6 months

4. A loan of $4000 at 5% for 3 months

5. A loan of $840 at 9% for 18 months

6. A loan of $1100 at 7.5% for 4 years

B. Find the interest earned on these investments. You may use a calculator.

7. $3200 invested at $5\frac{1}{2}$% interest for 1 year

8. $500 invested at 8% interest for $6\frac{1}{2}$ years

9. $2300 invested at 4% interest for 6 months

10. $800 invested at 7.5% interest for 3 months

11. $600 invested at $3\frac{3}{4}$% interest for 2 years

C. Find the total amount to be paid back on these loans.

12. A loan of $600 at 10% for 6 months

13. A loan of $5400 at 8% for 9 months

14. A loan of $8000 at 12% for 5 years

15. A loan of $300 at 6% for 4 months

D. Solve.

16. Mr. Bradford bought a delivery van. He borrowed $20,000 at $8\frac{1}{4}$% interest for 4 years. How much will he pay in interest on the loan?

17. Ji Sun took out a student loan of $1500 for 18 months at 3% interest. How much will she pay back when the loan is due?

18. To buy a computer, Rene borrowed $900 from her brother for 12 months. She agreed to pay 4% interest on the loan. What is the total amount she will owe her brother in 12 months?

19. Tony borrows $9500 to make repairs to his warehouse. He borrows the money at $9\frac{1}{2}$% for 2 years. How much will he pay in interest on the loan?

20. Sandy borrowed $4500 for 3 years to buy a used car. Interest on the loan is 7.5%. How much will she pay in all for the car?

Refer to the following information to answer Questions 21 and 22.

Capital Investments
Earn 5% interest
6-months required
Minimum principal: $1500

New Vista Accounts
Earn 6% interest
9-months required
Minimum principal: $2500

21. The Grahams plan to invest $2500 for up to 1 year. How much interest would they earn at Capital Investments if they invest their money for 1 year?

22. How much would they earn on an investment of $2500 for 9 months at New Vista Accounts?

Answers start on page 399.

GED STRATEGY **Solving Word Problems**

Solving Multi-Step Problems

TIP

Saving 40% means paying 60% of the original price. The percent you <u>paid</u> is the rate that when multiplied by the base gives you the sale price.

100% − 40% = 60%

$80 × 0.6 = $48

Sometimes percent problems require more than one step to solve. Read the problem carefully, decide what information you need to solve the problem, and break the problem down into steps.

Example 1   Wendy bought an $80 dress on sale for 40% off. How much did she pay for the dress?

(1) $80 × 0.4
(2) $80 − $40
(3) $80 − ($80 × 0.4)
(4) $80 − ($80 × 0.6)
(5) Not enough information is given.

Step 1   You know the base and the rate. You need to find the discount amount. Multiply the base by the rate. This tells how much Wendy saved by buying the dress on sale. $80 × 0.4

Step 2   Find the sale price. Subtract the discount amount from the original price. $80 − ($80 × 0.4)

The sale price is **option (3).**

Example 2   John makes small picture frames to sell at craft shows. Each frame uses $10 worth of materials. If John wants to sell the frames at a 15% profit, how much should he charge for each frame?

(1) $ 1.50
(2) $10.00
(3) $11.50
(4) $25.00
(5) Not enough information is given.

Step 1   Find the amount of profit. Multiply the base by the rate. $10 × 15% = $10 × 0.15 = $1.5 = $1.50

Step 2   Find the price John should charge for a picture frame by adding the amount of profit to the cost of materials. $10.00 + $1.50 = $11.50

John should sell his picture frames for **option (3) $11.50** each.

Example 3   The sale price of a sofa with a 40% discount is $348. What is the original price of the sofa?

Step 1   Find the rate that represents the sale price.   100% − 40% = 60%

Step 2   Find the original price (base). Divide the part by the rate. $348 ÷ 0.6 = $580

The original price of the sofa is **$580.**

Directions: Choose the one best answer to each question.

```
$ $        $ $
$   15% off   $
$
everything
in the store
```

1. Murray's Bargain Basement is having a sale on household goods. What would be the sale price of a twin-size blanket originally priced at $20?

   (1) $ 3.00
   (2) $ 5.00
   (3) $ 7.50
   (4) $17.00
   (5) $18.67

2. Flora received a 6% raise on her hourly wage of $9.00. Choose the expression that shows Flora's new hourly wage.

   (1) $9 + 0.06
   (2) $9 + 0.06 × $9
   (3) $9 − 0.06 × $9
   (4) $9 × 0.06
   (5) $9 × (1 − 0.06)

3. Alfredo bought a used car for $1500. He replaced the engine and repaired the body. He sold the car for $4500. What was the rate of increase in the price of the car?

   (1) 67%
   (2) 133%
   (3) 200%
   (4) 300%
   (5) 400%

4. At a factory, Gloria supervises 30 employees. Next month, her staff will be increased by 40%. Which expression shows the number of employees Gloria will supervise next month?

   (1) 0.4(30) + 0.4
   (2) 0.4(30) + 30
   (3) 0.4(30) − 0.4
   (4) 0.04(30) + 0.4
   (5) 0.4(30) − 30

5. Lavina put on layaway a coat that costs $160. She paid 10% down and will pay the rest in 6 monthly installments. Which expression can be used to find the amount of each monthly payment?

   (1) $\frac{\$160 - (\$160 \times 0.1)}{6}$
   (2) $\frac{\$160}{6}$
   (3) $160 − ($160 × 0.1)
   (4) $160 × 0.1
   (5) $160 + ($160 × 0.1)

6. Grantsville Copper Mines employs 1400 workers. The company must lay off 5% of its workforce immediately and another 20% of the remaining workforce by the end of the year. How many workers will be laid off?

   (1) 350
   (2) 336
   (3) 280
   (4) 210
   (5) 70

Answers start on page 400.

Calculators and Percents

One of the most useful keys on a calculator is the percent key. When using this key, you won't have to change a percent to a decimal or a decimal to a percent—the calculator will do it for you automatically.

Example   Julia paid 32% of her monthly salary of $3540 for taxes. How much did she pay for taxes?

If you don't use the percent key, you would first have to change 32% to decimal form, or 0.32, before multiplying by $3540. This method for using a calculator is shown below.

> **3540**   ✕   **.32**   **=**

You would see the answer 1132.8, or **$1132.80 in taxes,** in the display.

By using the percent key, you would not change the percent to a decimal, but simply key in the numbers as they appear in the problem. This is shown below. (Note that some calculators do not require the equals key at the end.)

> **3540**   ✕   **32**   **%**   **=**

Remember: There is no percent "key" on the calculator used for the GED Mathematics Test. You must press the **SHIFT** **=** keys to work with a percent.

> **3540**   ✕   **32**   **SHIFT**   **=**   **1132.8**

Using the Percent Key

Here are some important points to keep in mind when using the percent key on the calculator.

- **When solving for the base or part, you should key in the percent exactly as it appears in the problem.** Do <u>not</u> move the decimal point. For example, if you want to find 8% of a number, do not change 8% to the decimal 0.08. Simply multiply the number by 8 and press the % key after the 8.
- **When solving for the rate, the answer you see in the display is the percent, not the decimal equivalent.** Do <u>not</u> move the decimal point. For example, divide the part (1) by the base (4) followed by the percent key. (If your calculator display shows 0.04, press the equals key.) The display shows 25, which is 25%. There is no need to move the decimal point.
- **Be careful about the order in which you key in numbers.** When solving for the part, you multiply the base by the percent. When solving for the percent or base, you divide. Be careful to key in the part first.

Directions: Choose the <u>one best answer</u> to each item. You <u>MAY</u> use your calculator.

1. At the end of the first quarter, the *Gazette* had 3450 employees. In the second quarter, 12% more employees were hired. How many new employees did the *Gazette* hire in the second quarter?

   (1)   41
   (2)   404
   (3)   414
   (4)   424
   (5) 4140

2. The Smith family went to dinner at a restaurant and had a total bill of $120. If they left a tip of $21.60, what percent of the total bill did they leave?

   (1) 15%
   (2) 16%
   (3) 17%
   (4) 18%
   (5) 19%

3. The vice president of a bank contributed $8\frac{3}{4}\%$ of her salary to a retirement plan. If she contributed $4,375 to the plan in one year, what was her annual salary that year?

   (1) $42,000
   (2) $43,750
   (3) $49,383
   (4) $50,000
   (5) $50,383

4. The office expenses at Delta Products were reduced from $1400 last month to $1225 this month. What was the percent of reduction in office expenses?

   (1) 12.0%
   (2) 12.5%
   (3) 13.0%
   (4) 13.5%
   (5) 14.0%

5. Axelle bought a microwave oven regularly priced at $394. If the oven was on sale for 40% off the regular price, how much did she pay for the microwave?

   (1) $226.95
   (2) $232.60
   (3) $236.40
   (4) $240.25
   (5) $250.00

Question 6 refers to the following table.

Daly's Pharmacy		
Item	**April Sales**	**May Sales**
Toothpaste	$4200	$4956
Soap	$3980	$4293
Shampoo	$3420	$3290

6. Toothpaste sales in May were what percent higher than the toothpaste sales in April?

   (1) 15%
   (2) 16%
   (3) 17%
   (4) 18%
   (5) 19%

Answers start on page 400.

GED Mini-Test • Lessons 11–13

Directions: This is a 30-minute practice test. After 30 minutes, mark the last item you finished. Then complete the test and check your answers. If most of your answers are correct, but you didn't finish, try to work faster next time.

Part 1

Directions: Choose the <u>one best answer</u> to each item. You <u>MAY</u> use your calculator.

1. Last year, Anne paid $13,600 in taxes, which was 32% of her gross annual salary. What was her gross annual salary?

   (1) $30,000
   (2) $34,500
   (3) $36,000
   (4) $38,500
   (5) $42,500

2. In its current catalog, Sheridan Office Supplies lists an electric stapler for $69.95. If it offers a discount of 35%, what is the price after the discount, rounded to the nearest cent?

   (1) $24.48
   (2) $34.47
   (3) $42.43
   (4) $45.47
   (5) $94.43

3. The value of the inventory at Sam's Sporting Goods store increased from $46,400 to $52,200 during the first quarter of the year. What is the percent of increase in the value of the inventory?

   (1) 10.5%
   (2) 12.0%
   (3) 12.5%
   (4) 58.3%
   (5) Not enough information is given.

4. On Friday, Lambert stock closed at $52.36 per share, a price 23% lower than when it closed on Thursday. What was the closing price on Thursday?

   (1) $40
   (2) $52
   (3) $64
   (4) $68
   (5) $70

5. Daniel bought a couch that listed for $950. If he gave a down payment of $209, what percent of the list price did he give?

   (1) 20%
   (2) 21%
   (3) 22%
   (4) 23%
   (5) 24%

6. John receives a fixed salary of $325 per week and a commission of $7\frac{1}{4}$% on his gross sales. How much does he earn in one week?

   (1) $2800
   (2) $2725
   (3) $2700
   (4) $2525
   (5) Not enough information is given.

Questions 7 and 8 refer to the following table.

Company Sales (Millions of Dollars)	
Month	Sales
Jan.	$ 2
Feb.	$ 6
Mar.	$ 8
Apr.	$ 8
May	$14
June	$18

7. The sales in February were what percent of the total sales for the six months listed? Round to the nearest whole percent.

(1) 10%

(2) 11%

(3) 12%

(4) 13%

(5) 14%

8. Between which two consecutive months was the percent of increase in company sales the greatest?

(1) January to February

(2) February to March

(3) March to April

(4) April to May

(5) May to June

9. Larry borrows $12,500 at 16% simple annual interest for $3\frac{1}{2}$ years. How much interest will he owe on the loan at the end of that period?

(1) $2,000

(2) $3,000

(3) $4,000

(4) $5,000

(5) $7,000

10. Lars has a current annual salary of $38,650. If he gets a raise of $3,280, what percent is the raise of his current annual salary? Round to the nearest whole percent.

(1) 6%

(2) 7%

(3) 8%

(4) 9%

(5) 10%

11. Jim buys a coat for $136 and pays sales tax of $8\frac{1}{4}$%. Which expression shows the amount that Jim paid for the coat, including the sales tax?

(1) $136 + 0.0825

(2) $136 × 0.0825

(3) ($136 × 0.0825) + $136

(4) ($136 + $136) × 0.0825

(5) $\frac{\$136}{0.0825}$

12. Attendance at a craft show dropped from 1420 last year to 1209 this year. What was the percent of decrease in attendance, rounded to the nearest percent?

(1) 15%

(2) 16%

(3) 17%

(4) 18%

(5) 19%

13. In October, the circulation of the local newspaper was 247,624. The circulation of the newspaper in September was 238,100. What is the percent of change in circulation from September to October?

(1) increase of 3%

(2) decrease of 3%

(3) increase of 4%

(4) decrease of 4%

(5) increase of 5%

Part 2

Directions: Choose the <u>one best answer</u> to each item. You may <u>NOT</u> use your calculator.

14. New car sales at a local dealership increased from 150 in July to 180 in August. Which of the following expressions can be used to find the percent of increase in new car sales from July to August?

    (1) $180 \div 150$
    (2) $150 \div 180$
    (3) $180 - (150 \div 180)$
    (4) $(180 - 150) \div 180$
    (5) $(180 - 150) \div 150$

15. A quality control officer finds that 5% of the 2600 telephones inspected are defective. How many inspected telephones are not defective?

    (1)   130
    (2)   247
    (3) 1300
    (4) 2470
    (5) 2500

16. Lana has an annual salary of $26,000. After completing a training program, she receives a raise of $2,080. The raise represents what percent of her current annual salary?

    (1) 5%
    (2) 6%
    (3) 7%
    (4) 8%
    (5) 9%

17. Willa receives a commission of $1,020 for selling a car. If the commission is 5% of the selling price, what is the selling price of the car?

    (1) $20,000
    (2) $20,400
    (3) $20,800
    (4) $21,200
    (5) $21,600

18. Louis pays $420 for a CD\DVD player, including a 5% sales tax. What is the price of the CD\DVD before the sales tax is added?

    (1) $398
    (2) $399
    (3) $400
    (4) $401
    (5) $402

19. Meg borrowed $2500 from her employer for 2 years at $2\frac{1}{2}\%$ interest. What is the total amount she will pay back?

    (1) $2625
    (2) $3137
    (3) $3426
    (4) $5000
    (5) $6150

Unit 1: Numbers and Operations

20. Net sales in August were reported as 120% of net sales in February. If February's net sales were $13,985, what were the net sales in August?

(1) $11,188
(2) $11,654
(3) $14,782
(4) $16,782
(5) $17,481

21. During a sale, an office furniture store marks down the price of a swivel chair by 30%. If the regular price of the chair is $180, what is the price after the markdown?

(1) $ 54
(2) $120
(3) $126
(4) $184
(5) $234

Question 22 refers to the following table.

Expense Budget Total: $60,000	
Category	% of Budget
Advertising	16%
Salaries	35%
Supplies	25%
Rent	24%

22. How much more is budgeted for supplies than for advertising?

(1) $5000
(2) $5400
(3) $6400
(4) $7400
(5) $9000

23. Debra invested $5000 in an account that paid 8% simple annual interest. At the end of 3 years, how much money was in the account, including the interest earned?

(1) $ 400
(2) $1200
(3) $5400
(4) $5800
(5) $6200

24. During the holiday season, the price of a particular toy rose from $1 to $3. What is the percent of increase in the price of the toy?

(1) 100%
(2) 200%
(3) 300%
(4) 400%
(5) 500%

25. Sam bought a new television for $440. If he paid 20% of this amount as a down payment, and paid the rest in 8 equal monthly installments, how much was the amount of each installment?

(1) $43
(2) $44
(3) $45
(4) $46
(5) $47

Answers start on page 401.

Unit 1 Cumulative Review Numbers and Operations

Part 1

Directions: Choose the <u>one best answer</u> to each question. You <u>MAY</u> use your calculator.

1. Sondra buys an insurance policy that costs $7.43 for every $2,500 of insurance. If she buys a policy worth $30,000 of insurance, how much does it cost her?

   (1) $86.08

   (2) $87.16

   (3) $88.08

   (4) $89.16

   (5) $90.08

2. Roberto borrows $14,000 and agrees to pay $9\frac{3}{4}\%$ simple annual interest. Which of the following expressions shows how much interest he will pay if he borrows the amount for $3\frac{1}{2}$ years?

   (1) $\$14,000 + 0.0975 + 3.5$

   (2) $\$14,000 \times 9.75 \times 3.5$

   (3) $\$14,000 \times 0.0975 \times 3.5$

   (4) $\$14,000 \times \frac{0.0975}{3.5}$

   (5) $\frac{\$14,000}{3.5} \times 0.0975$

3. Jocelyn works in a computer store and earns a 7% commission on her sales. If she sold 10 computers to the local school district for a total of $14,000, how much commission did she receive?

   (1) $ 980

   (2) $ 1,302

   (3) $13,020

   (4) $14,980

   (5) Not enough information is given.

4. A business has $15,000 in its checking account. The company deposits checks in the amount of $1,800, $3,000, and $900. It also writes checks for $3,600 and $2,800 to pay bills. How much is in the account after these transactions?

   (1) $27,100

   (2) $16,800

   (3) $14,300

   (4) $ 3,800

   (5) Not enough information is given.

Questions 5 and 6 refer to the following table.

Item	Regular Price	Sale Price
Jackets	$168.99	$135.99
Pants	$ 87.50	$ 62.00
Shirts	$ 38.95	$ 27.95

5. Richard bought 3 pairs of pants and 2 shirts at the sale price. How much did he save on these items by buying them at the sale price instead of at the regular price?

   (1) $11.00

   (2) $22.00

   (3) $25.50

   (4) $76.50

   (5) $98.50

6. What is the percent of discount for shirts from the regular price to the sale price? Round to the nearest percent.

   (1) 26%

   (2) 27%

   (3) 28%

   (4) 29%

   (5) 30%

7. A 16-pound turkey costs $15.92. Which of the following could be used to find how much a 20-pound turkey would cost at the same price per pound?

(1) $\frac{16}{\$15.92} = \frac{20}{?}$

(2) $\frac{\$15.92}{16} = \frac{20}{?}$

(3) $\frac{16}{\$15.92} = \frac{?}{20}$

(4) $\frac{16}{20} = \frac{?}{\$15.92}$

(5) $\frac{20}{16} = \frac{\$15.92}{?}$

8. A lamp regularly priced at $45 is part of an Internet promotion of 15% off all lamps. What is the price of the lamp during the promotion?

(1) $ 6.75

(2) $17.75

(3) $38.25

(4) $44.25

(5) $51.25

9. Mark used $4\frac{1}{2}$ gallons of paint to paint the living room, $2\frac{7}{8}$ gallons to paint the dining room, and $3\frac{1}{8}$ gallons to paint the kitchen. How many gallons did he use in all?

(1) 9

(2) $10\frac{1}{4}$

(3) $10\frac{1}{2}$

(4) $10\frac{3}{4}$

(5) 11

10. From January to February the price of Argon stock rose from $2 per share to $8 per share. What was the percent of increase?

(1) 0%

(2) 40%

(3) 75%

(4) 300%

(5) Not enough information is given.

11. The price of a stereo system on Friday was $272, a discount of 15% from its price on Thursday. What was the price of the stereo system on Thursday?

(1) $231.20

(2) $312.80

(3) $318.20

(4) $320.00

(5) $328.00

12. Mateo jogs 3 times a week. This week he jogged 3 miles on Monday, 3.25 miles on Thursday, and 3.9 miles on Friday. How many more miles did Mateo jog this week than the week before?

(1) 3

(2) 9

(3) 10.15

(4) 30.45

(5) Not enough information is given.

Question 13 refers to the following table.

Miles Driven Last Week	
Anne	1348.6 miles
Barbara	2098.4 miles
Kristen	1984.9 miles

13. Last week, Barbara drove how many more miles than Anne?

(1) 749.8

(2) 730.8

(3) 720.8

(4) 719.8

(5) 709.8

14. Roxanne is buying supplies for a catering job. She bought a piece of salmon for $31.28. If the cost of the salmon was $9.20 per pound, how many pounds did she buy?

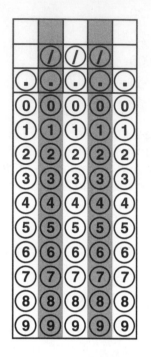

16. Peter went on a diet and lost 5% of his weight by the end of the first month. If Peter weighed 238 pounds when he started his diet, how many pounds did he weigh at the end of the first month?

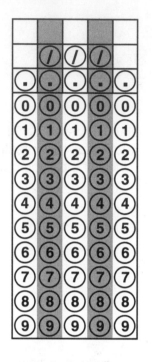

15. Kumiko made a fruit salad for the cafeteria. She used 3 pounds of apples, 2 pounds of oranges, 4 pounds of bananas, 2 pounds of grapes, and 3 pounds of peaches. If she usually uses 20 pounds of fruit, how many fewer pounds of fruit did she use this time?

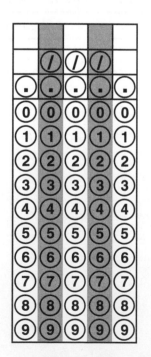

17. Areta borrowed $42.48 from Julia on Monday and another $64.76 on Friday. On Saturday she paid back $\frac{1}{4}$ of the total amount she owed. How much did she still owe?

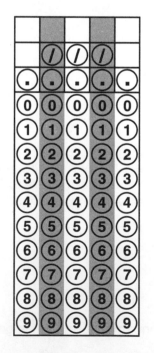

Part 2

Directions: Choose the <u>one best answer</u> to each question. You may <u>NOT</u> use your calculator.

18. Jonathan is saving $80 each month for a vacation that costs $720. If he has already saved $480, how many more months will it take him to save the whole amount?

    (1) 3
    (2) 5
    (3) 7
    (4) 9
    (5) 11

19. Marta worked $2\frac{3}{4}$ hours on Monday, $4\frac{1}{2}$ hours on Tuesday, and $5\frac{7}{8}$ hours on Wednesday. How many hours did she work in all for the three days?

    (1) $11\frac{1}{8}$
    (2) $12\frac{3}{4}$
    (3) $13\frac{1}{8}$
    (4) $14\frac{1}{2}$
    (5) $15\frac{1}{8}$

20. Cheryl drives to work and back five days each week. If her job is 14.82 miles from her home, <u>approximately</u> how many miles does she drive to work and back each week?

    (1) 15
    (2) 30
    (3) 50
    (4) 75
    (5) 150

21. The Jordans borrow $5000 for 3 years at 14% interest. What is the total amount they will pay back to the bank?

    (1) $2100
    (2) $5042
    (3) $6400
    (4) $7100
    (5) $8000

22. A car odometer reads 8,867.3 miles. How many more miles will it take to reach 10,000?

    (1)   832.7
    (2)   982.7
    (3) 1,132.7
    (4) 1,133.3
    (5) 1,133.7

23. A box of cereal costs $1.59. If a case holds 8 boxes, how much would $3\frac{1}{2}$ cases cost?

    (1) $ 5.57
    (2) $12.72
    (3) $28.00
    (4) $38.92
    (5) $44.52

24. Sonia can pick 14.5 baskets of strawberries per hour. At this rate, how many baskets can she pick in $5\frac{1}{2}$ hours?

    (1) 70
    (2) $72\frac{1}{2}$
    (3) $79\frac{3}{4}$
    (4) $82\frac{1}{2}$
    (5) 87

Directions: Solve the following questions and enter your answers on the grids provided.

25. In a recent company survey, $\frac{3}{4}$ of the employees said they drove to work. Of those who drive to work, $\frac{3}{5}$ said they drive in a carpool. What fraction of the employees drives in a carpool?

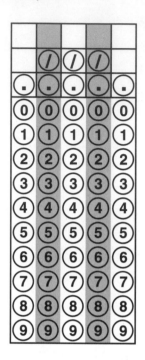

26. Kathy cuts a piece of board 19.6 inches long into 4 equal parts. How many inches long is each piece?

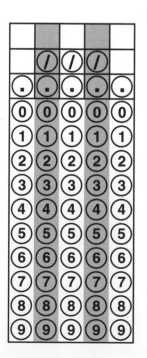

27. Shanti drove 78 miles in $1\frac{1}{2}$ hours. At the same rate, how many miles could she drive in 2.5 hours?

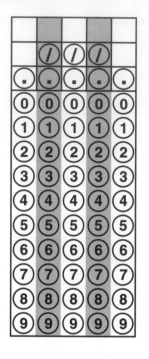

28. Stefan pays $33 per month for the insurance and pays $5 for each visit to the doctor. He went to the Eastside Health Clinic six times in two months. How much did Stefan pay for insurance and treatment for the two months?

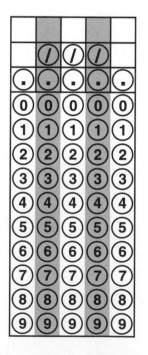

Answers start on page 402.

Cumulative Review Performance Analysis
Unit 1 ● Numbers and Operations

Use the Answers and Explanations starting on page 402 to check your answers to the Unit 1 Cumulative Review. Then use the chart to figure out the skill areas in which you need more practice.

On the chart, circle the questions that you answered correctly. Write the number correct for each skill area. Add to find the total number of questions that you got correct on the Cumulative Review. If you feel that you need more practice, go back and review the lessons for the skill areas that were difficult for you.

Questions	Number Correct	Skill Area	Lessons for Review
4, 12, 15, 18, 20, 28	＿＿/6	Number Sense and Problem Solving	1, 2, 3, 4
1, 7, 9, 19, 24, 25, 27	＿＿/7	Fractions	5, 6, 7
5, 13, 14, 17, 22, 23, 26	＿＿/7	Decimals	8, 9, 10
2, 3, **6,** 8, 10, 11, 16, 21	＿＿/8	Percents	11, 12, 13
TOTAL CORRECT: ＿＿/28			

Question numbers in **boldface** are based on graphics.

Measurement and Data Analysis

Measurement and data analysis are important areas of math that we use every day. We use measurement when we make things. Sometimes we measure items such as gallons of paint or cups of chocolate chips. At other times we measure length or space, such as the perimeter or area of a floor, wall, or garden or the volume of a container. Data analysis is becoming an increasingly important activity in our lives. The increasing use of computers has accelerated the collection, display, and analysis of data, especially information in numerical form. Most often, we see such data presented in the form of tables, charts, and graphs.

Questions related to measurement and data analysis will account for more than 25 percent of the GED Mathematics Test. Additionally, you will find that you can use many of the skills in this unit in your personal life and on the job.

Measuring and analyzing data are becoming important functions in many workplaces.

The lessons in this unit include:

Lesson 14: Measurement Systems
Currently there are two systems of measurement in use. The customary U.S. or English system of measurement is used widely in the United States, and the metric system is used throughout the rest of the world. Measurement problems using either system of measurement require conversion of units as well as addition, subtraction, multiplication, and division.

> ### PROBLEM-SOLVING STRATEGIES
> ○ Choosing Perimeter, Area, or Volume
> ○ Drawing a Picture

Lesson 15: Measuring Common Figures
On the GED Mathematics Test, you will encounter problems that require finding the perimeter, area, or volume of common figures. This includes finding the perimeter and area of squares and rectangles as well as the volume of common rectangular containers.

Lesson 16: Measures of Central Tendency and Probability
Some of the most useful applications of data analysis are finding the mean (average), median (middle number), and mode (most frequent values), as well as the range (the difference between greatest and least values). Analyzing data also includes determining probability, which is used to predict how likely it is that an event will happen.

Lesson 17: Tables, Charts, and Graphs
Tables, charts, and graphs are different ways to present data. Tables and charts organize numbers in columns and rows. Graphs display data visually in a number of ways. For instance, bar graphs present comparisons, line graphs can show comparisons or changes over time, and circle graphs represent parts of a whole.

Lesson 14 GED SKILL Measurement Systems

The Customary U.S. System

Length	Weight
1 foot (ft) = 12 inches (in)	1 pound (lb) = 16 ounces (oz)
1 yard (yd) = 3 ft	1 ton (t) = 2000 lb
1 mile (mi) = 5280 ft	
Volume	**Time**
1 cup (c) = 8 fluid ounces (fl oz)	1 minute (min) = 60 seconds (sec)
1 pint (pt) = 2 c	1 hour (hr) = 60 min
1 quart (qt) = 2 pt	1 day = 24 hr
1 gallon (gal) = 4 qt	1 week = 7 days
	1 year = 12 months = 365 days

Many math problems involve measurement. A measurement is a number labeled with a unit of measure. For instance, you could say that a board is 4 feet long, a bucket holds 2 gallons, or a letter weighs 1 ounce. Feet, gallons, and ounces are units of measure.

The table above shows the units of measure and their equivalencies for the **customary system of measurement** used in the United States. You must know this information.

Converting Measurements

It is often necessary to change from one unit of measure to another. Writing a proportion is one of the simplest methods for converting units.

Example 1 Kiel has 1200 long-distance minutes per month on his phone-calling plan. How many hours of calls does this represent?

Step 1 **Use the appropriate conversion factor.** $1 \text{ hr} = 60 \text{ min}$

Step 2 **Write a proportion.** Write both ratios in the same order (like units on top). $\dfrac{\text{hours}}{\text{minutes}}$ $\dfrac{1}{60} = \dfrac{x}{1200}$

Step 3 **Solve for x.** Find the cross product and divide by the remaining term. $1 \times 1200 \div 60 = 20$

Kiel has **20 hours** per month on his calling plan.

Write the proportion, then do the arithmetic on a calculator.

1 ✕ 1200 ÷ 60 = 20.

Example 2 A board is $5\frac{3}{4}$ feet long. What is its length in inches?

Step 1 Use the appropriate conversion factor. $1 \text{ ft} = 12 \text{ in}$

Step 2 Then write a proportion. $\dfrac{\text{inches}}{\text{feet}}$ $\dfrac{12}{1} = \dfrac{x}{5\frac{3}{4}}$

Step 3 Cross-multiply, divide, and solve. $12 \times 5\frac{3}{4} \div 1 = x$

$$\overset{3}{\cancel{12}} \times \frac{23}{\underset{1}{\cancel{4}}} \div 1 = 69$$

The length of the board is **69 inches.**

Not all conversions come out evenly. When you have a remainder, you can write it as either a smaller unit, a fraction, or a decimal.

Example 3 Convert 56 ounces to pounds.

Step 1 Use the appropriate conversion factor. $1 \text{ lb} = 16 \text{ oz}$

Step 2 Write and solve a proportion.

$$\frac{\text{pounds}}{\text{ounces}} \quad \frac{1}{16} = \frac{x}{56} \qquad 1 \times 56 \div 16 = 3 \text{ r}8 = 3\frac{8}{16} = 3\frac{1}{2} = 3.5$$

A fraction or decimal remainder uses the same unit name as the whole number portion of the answer.

$$1 \boxed{\times} \; 56 \; \boxed{\div} \; 16 \; \boxed{=} \; 3.5$$

The answer is **3 pounds 8 ounces**, $3\frac{1}{2}$ **pounds**, or **3.5 pounds**.

GED SKILL FOCUS

A. Solve. Refer to the chart on page 158. You may use your calculator for Questions 7 through 12. The first problem is started for you.

1. Change 4 minutes to seconds.

   $\dfrac{\text{seconds}}{\text{minutes}} \quad \dfrac{60}{1} = \dfrac{x}{4}; \; 60 \times 4 \div 1 = \underline{}$

2. Change 18 cups to pints.

3. Change $3\frac{1}{2}$ yards to feet and inches.

4. How many minutes are equal to $2\frac{1}{3}$ hours?

5. Change 72 fluid ounces to cups.

6. How many inches are in $1\frac{1}{2}$ yards?

7. Change $4\frac{1}{4}$ pounds to ounces.

8. How many quarts are in $5\frac{3}{4}$ gallons?

9. Change 6 feet 9 inches to yards.

10. Change 74 ounces to pounds.

11. How many feet are equal to 5 miles?

12. How many cups are in 2 gallons?

B. Solve. You may use your calculator.

13. Which is less, $3\frac{1}{4}$ hours or 200 minutes?

14. Which is less, $4\frac{1}{2}$ pounds or 75 ounces?

15. Lauren has a board that measures 30 inches in length. Can she cut a piece 3 feet long from the board?

16. Chase needs $1\frac{1}{2}$ gallons of a neutral latex base paint. He has 13 pints in the storeroom. Does he have enough?

Refer to the following information to answer <u>Questions 17 and 18</u>.

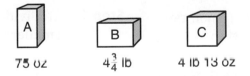

17. What is the weight of Package C in ounces?

18. Which package above (A, B, or C) weighs the least?

Answers start on page 403.

Operations with Measurements

To add, subtract, multiply, or divide measurements, they must be in the same units. You may need to convert one or more measurements.

Example 1 One board is $2\frac{1}{2}$ feet in length. Another board is 2 feet 9 inches. What is the total length of the two pieces?

Step 1 **Convert to like units.** Use the appropriate conversion factor.

$1 \text{ ft} = 12 \text{ in}$
$2\frac{1}{2} \text{ ft} = 2 \text{ ft } 6 \text{ in}$

Step 2 **Set up** the addition problem and add like units.

$\begin{array}{r} 2 \text{ ft} \quad 6 \text{ in} \\ +2 \text{ ft} \quad 9 \text{ in} \end{array}$

Step 3 **Reduce** your answer.

$4 \text{ ft } 15 \text{ in} = 4 \text{ ft} + 12 \text{ in} + 3 \text{ in}$
$= 4 \text{ ft} + 1 \text{ ft} + 3 \text{ in} = 5 \text{ ft } 3 \text{ in}$

The combined length of the boards is **5 feet 3 inches.**

To subtract measurements, you may need to regroup, or borrow, from the column containing the larger measurement unit.

Example 2 John weighed 11 lb 11 oz at 2 months of age. At 4 months he weighed 14 lb 8 oz. How much weight did he gain?

Step 1 **Regroup** as needed—here, borrow 1 lb from the 14 lb and convert it to 16 oz.

Step 2 **Combine** like units—here add 16 oz to 8 oz. Then subtract to find the difference.

$\begin{array}{r} \overset{13}{\cancel{14}} \text{ lb} \ \overset{24}{\cancel{8}} \text{ oz} \\ -11 \text{ lb } 11 \text{ oz} \\ \hline 2 \text{ lb } 13 \text{ oz} \end{array}$

John gained **2 pounds 13 ounces.**

You may also need to convert units and reduce your answer to multiply or divide measurements. To divide, convert to the smaller unit of measure.

Example 3 A plan calls for 4 boards, each 4 ft 3 in long. What is the total length of the boards?

Step 1 Set up the problem and multiply each part of the measure separately. Here, 4 ft × 4 = 16 ft; 3 in × 4 = 12 in

$\begin{array}{r} 4 \text{ ft} \quad 3 \text{ in} \\ \times \qquad 4 \\ \hline 16 \text{ ft } 12 \text{ in} = 16 \text{ ft} + 1 \text{ ft} \end{array}$

Step 2 Convert units and reduce the answer.

$= 17 \text{ ft}$

The total length is **17 feet.**

Example 4 Mel has a pipe that is 14 ft 2 in long. If he cuts the pipe into five equal pieces, what will be the length of each piece?

Step 1 To divide, convert mixed units to the smaller unit. Write a proportion using the appropriate conversion factor. Solve—here, for the inches in 14 feet. Add the remaining smaller unit—here, 2 inches to get the total inches.

$\dfrac{\text{inches}}{\text{feet}} \quad \dfrac{12}{1} = \dfrac{x}{14}$

$12 \times 14 \div 1 = 168 \text{ in}$
$168 \text{ in} + 2 \text{ in} = 170 \text{ in}$

Step 2 Divide—here, by 5 to make 5 equal pieces. $170 \text{ in} \div 5 = 34 \text{ in}$

Step 3 Convert to mixed units—here, feet and inches. $34 \text{ in} = 2 \text{ ft } 10 \text{ in}$

Each piece of pipe will be **34 inches** or **2 feet 10 inches.**

A. Solve. You may <u>not</u> use your calculator.

1. Add 8 ft 8 in, 3 ft 5 in, and 4 ft 9 in.

2. Subtract 20 min 45 sec from $\frac{1}{2}$ hr.

3. Subtract 1 ft 7 in from 2 ft 2 in.

4. Add 3 gal to 5 qt. Write your answer in quarts.

5. Find the total of 3 lb 8 oz, 5 lb 13 oz, and 2 lb 9 oz.

6. Find the difference between 2 ft 6 in and 18 inches.

7. Multiply 3 lb 4 oz by 5.

8. Divide 1 yd 4 in by 5. Write your answer in inches.

9. Multiply 2 yd 1 ft by 8. Write your answer in yards and feet.

10. Divide 3 gallons by 4. Write your answer in quarts.

B. Solve.

11. A piece of plastic tubing is 12 feet long. How many pieces measuring 1 foot 9 inches long can be cut from the length of tubing?

12. Dorie is canning raspberry jam. She makes 2 gallons of jam. If she plans to keep 6 pints for herself, how many pints will she give away?

13. Zola buys $3\frac{1}{4}$ yards of fabric to make a blouse. She uses 2 yards 2 feet 9 inches of fabric. How many inches of fabric are left?

14. Meg needs 15 pieces of wood to make supporting posts for a stairway. If each supporting post is 2 feet 9 inches, what is the total length (in feet) she will need?

15. Marco can assemble one cabinet in 25 minutes. How many cabinets can he assemble in $3\frac{3}{4}$ hours?

Refer to the drawing below to answer Questions 16 through 18.

Tomato Soup Base

Makes 24 fl oz

Serving Size = $1\frac{1}{2}$ cups

16. How many cups of soup will each box of soup base make?

17. How many ounces are in one serving of the soup?

18. A restaurant uses the soup base to prepare its vegetable soup. How many servings will 5 packages of the soup mix make?

Answers start on page 404.

The Metric System

The **metric system** is used throughout most of the world. It uses these basic metric units:

meter (m) unit of length   A meter is a few inches longer than one yard.
gram (g) unit of weight or mass   It takes 28 grams to make one ounce.
liter (L) unit of volume   A liter is slightly more than one quart.

Other units of measure are made by adding the prefixes shown below to the basic units listed above.

milli-	means $\frac{1}{1000}$	A milligram (mg) is $\frac{1}{1000}$ of a gram.	
centi-	means $\frac{1}{100}$	A centimeter (cm) is $\frac{1}{100}$ of a meter.	
deci-	means $\frac{1}{10}$	A deciliter (dL) is $\frac{1}{10}$ of a liter.	
deka-	means 10	A dekagram (dag) is 10 grams.	
hecto-	means 100	A hectoliter (hL) is 100 liters.	
kilo-	means 1000	A kilometer (km) is 1000 meters.	

The metric system is based on the powers of ten. Convert metric units by moving the decimal point. Use this chart to make metric conversions.

To convert to smaller units, move the decimal point right. ----------➤

kilo- 1000	hecto- 100	deka- 10	meter gram liter	deci- $\frac{1}{10}$	centi- $\frac{1}{100}$	milli- $\frac{1}{1000}$

◄-------------- To convert to larger units, move the decimal point left.

Example 1   How many milligrams are in 2 dekagrams?

Step 1   You need to change from a larger unit (dekagrams) to a smaller unit (milligrams). Put your finger on either unit measure in the chart and **count the spaces** to the other measure.

There are 4 spaces.

Step 2   Since you are converting a larger unit to a smaller unit, **move the decimal point** 4 places to the right, adding zeros as needed. $2.0000 = 20,000.$

There are **20,000 milligrams** in 2 dekagrams.

Example 2   A piece of wire is 150 centimeters long. How many meters in length is the wire?

Step 1   You need to change from centimeters to meters. Count the spaces in the chart from one measurement to the other. There are 2 spaces.

TIP

Think about the meaning of the metric prefixes. Since *centi*meter means $\frac{1}{100}$ meter, there are 100 centimeters in 1 meter.

Step 2 Since you are converting a smaller unit to a larger unit, move the decimal point 2 spaces to the left. $1\underset{\smile\smile}{50.} = 1.5$

The wire is **1.5 meters** long.

Since metric measurements use decimals instead of fractions, perform calculations with these measurements as you would in other decimal problems. Remember, you can add and subtract like units only.

Example 3 Ty walked 2.8 kilometers one day and 1575 meters the next day. How many total kilometers did he walk?

Step 1 Change meters to kilometers. Move the decimal point 3 places to the left.

$1\underset{\smile\smile\smile}{575} \text{ m} = 1.575 \text{ km}$

Step 2 Line up the decimal points and add the like units

$$\begin{array}{r} 1 \\ 2.8 \\ +1.575 \\ \hline 4.375 \end{array}$$

Ty walked a total of **4.375 kilometers.**

TIP

Working with metric units uses the same steps as working with decimals. The steps for working with decimals can be found on pages 106–110.

GED SKILL FOCUS

A. Solve using pencil and paper.

1. Change 5000 millimeters to meters.

2. How many milligrams are in 3.4 grams?

3. A CD-player weighs 3 kg. What is its weight in grams?

4. Change 2950 centimeters to meters.

5. How many liters are in 3000 milliliters?

6. A bookcase is 2.4 meters tall. What is the height in centimeters?

B. Solve. You may use your calculator.

7. Hank has three lengths of wire: 75 centimeters, 126 centimeters, and 4.6 meters. What is the total length of the wire in centimeters?

8. Graham Industries makes lamps. Each finished lamp has a mass of 1200 grams. An order of 14 lamps is shipped. What is the total mass in kilograms of the shipment?

Refer to the following diagram to answer Question 9.

```
    3.8 km        1.9 km        4.3 km
●————————————●————————●————————————————————●
Start          ↑      ↑                  Finish
            Checkpoints
```

9. The diagram shows the checkpoints for a 10-kilometer race. What is the distance in meters from the starting point to the second checkpoint?

Answers start on page 405.

Lesson 15 GED SKILL **Measuring Common Figures**

Perimeter

Perimeter is a measure of the distance around the edge of any flat shape. To find the perimeter of any figure, add the lengths of its sides.

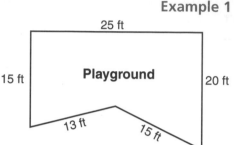

Example 1 The county supervisor plans to fence in the area shown at the left for a playground. How much fencing is needed?

The fence will go around the perimeter of the playground. Find the perimeter by adding the lengths of the sides.

$$15 + 13 + 15 + 20 + 25 = 88$$

It will take **88 feet** of fencing to enclose the playground.

Sometimes not all sides of a figure in a problem are labeled. To find the missing lengths, you will need to apply your knowledge of the properties of that figure.

A **rectangle** has 4 sides, 4 square corners or right angles, and opposite sides of equal length. Opposite sides are directly across from each other.

Example 2 Monica needs to glue yarn around the perimeter of a rectangular piece of poster board that is 18 inches long and 15 inches wide. How much yarn does she need?

Step 1 Fill in the measures of the opposite sides.
Step 2 Add the measurements. $18 + 18 + 15 + 15 = 66$ inches

Another way to approach the problem is to double the length and the width and add the results. $(18 \times 2) + (15 \times 2) = 36 + 30 = 66$ inches

---

If your calculator is programmed with the order of operations (like the one provided on the GED Mathematics Test), you can enter the second method without parentheses. The calculator automatically does the multiplication operations before it adds.

18 ☒ **2** ⊞ **15** ☒ **2** ⊟ **66.**

The perimeter of the poster board is **66 inches.**

TIP

If you use a calculator that is not programmed with the order of operations, you must enter the calculation as an addition problem: $18 + 18 + 15 + 15 = 66$.

A **square** has 4 equal sides and 4 square corners. If you know the length of one side, you can find the perimeter of the square by multiplying by 4.

Example 3   A business owns a square lot of land. If one side of the lot measures 87 feet, what is the perimeter of the lot?

You haven't been given a diagram of the lot, but you know that the figure is a square and that a square has 4 equal sides. Multiply 87 feet by 4 to find the perimeter.

$$87 \text{ ft} \times 4 = 348 \text{ ft}$$

The perimeter of the square lot is **348 feet.**

GED SKILL FOCUS

A. Find the perimeter of each figure. Do not use a calculator.

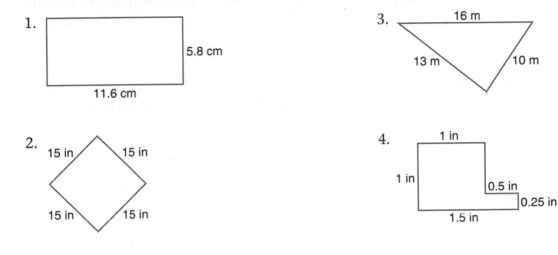

1.   5.8 cm   11.6 cm

2.   15 in   15 in   15 in   15 in

3.   16 m   13 m   10 m

4.   1 in   1 in   0.5 in   0.25 in   1.5 in

   B. Solve. You may use a calculator.

5. A rectangular room is 14 feet by 12 feet. A carpenter plans to install molding along the top of each wall. What is the perimeter of the room in feet?

Refer to the following drawing to answer Question 6.

6. The design for a company logo is shown above. If sides A and C are 14.3 cm long, sides D and E are 13.5 cm long, and side B is 12.4 cm long, what is the perimeter in centimeters of the logo?

Refer to the following drawing to answer Questions 7 and 8.

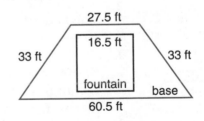

27.5 ft   16.5 ft   33 ft   33 ft   fountain   base   60.5 ft

7. The City Civic Center is planning to install a fountain sculpture. The square fountain will sit on a four-sided concrete base. What is the perimeter of the base in feet?

8. What is the perimeter in feet of the square fountain?

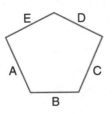

E   D   A   C   B

Answers start on page 405.

Area of Squares and Rectangles

Area is a measure of the surface of a flat figure. Area is measured in **square units.** Area tells how many square units it takes to cover the space inside the figure.

Example 1   A rectangle is 6 inches by 5 inches. What is the area of the rectangle in square inches?

Step 1   The rectangle is 6 inches along the bottom, so 6 squares, each 1 inch by 1 inch, can be lined up on the bottom row. It will take 5 of these rows to fill the rectangle.

Step 2   The area is the number of squares inside the rectangle. A quick way to count the squares is to multiply the number of columns by the number of rows.   6 in × 5 in = 30 square inches

The area of the rectangle is **30 square inches.**

Example 2   Kim's laundry room floor has the shape of a square. He wants to tile the room. If one side of the room measures 11 feet, what is the area of the floor in square feet (sq ft)?

A square is actually a special kind of rectangle. To find the area of a rectangle, you multiply length by width. Use the same method to find the area of a square. The room is 11 ft by 11 ft. To find the area, multiply the length by the width.   11 ft × 11 ft = 121 square feet

---

When you multiply a number by itself, you **square** the number. On a calculator, square a number by multiplying or using the x^2 key. This key multiplies any number, x, by itself. The raised 2 in x^2 (an **exponent**) tells how many times the number should appear in the multiplication problem.

   11 ✕ 11 = 121.   **11 x^2 121.**

The area of the laundry room is **121 square feet.**

TIP

Practice all kinds of problems with and without a calculator. Use the official GED calculator if possible. You will be issued a GED calculator at the test site and will be allowed to use it on the first part of the GED Mathematics Test.

Some complex shapes are actually a combination of squares and rectangles. To find the area of these shapes, break the figure into smaller pieces, find the area of each piece, and add to find the total area.

Example 3   An office suite has the shape shown below. What is the area in square feet of the office suite?

Step 1   Break the shape into squares and rectangles. There may be more than one way to do this. Choose the way that makes sense to you. No matter how the shape is broken up, the area remains the same.

21 ft
21 ft   Office Suite   35 ft
49 ft

Step 2   Find the area of each piece.
Square: The dimensions are 21 ft by 21 ft.
Multiply to find the area.   21 ft × 21 ft = 441 square feet

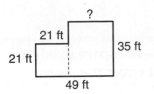

?
21 ft
21 ft
35 ft
49 ft

Rectangle: One side measures 35 ft. The other measurement is not given. However, you know that the side of the square is 21 ft and the length of the entire figure is 49 ft. Subtract to find the missing measurement. $49 \text{ ft} - 21 \text{ ft} = 28 \text{ ft}$

Multiply the rectangle's dimensions. $35 \text{ ft} \times 28 \text{ ft} = 980 \text{ sq ft}$

Step 3 Add the areas of the square and rectangle to find the total area. $441 \text{ ft} + 980 \text{ ft} = 1421 \text{ sq ft}$

Key in the problem in one step using the parentheses keys on a calculator not programmed with the order of operations.

(21 × 21) + (35 × 28) = 1421.

The area of the office suite is **1421 square feet.**

GED SKILL FOCUS

A. Solve. You may <u>not</u> use a calculator.

1. A rectangular room is 4.5 meters by 12 meters. What is the area of the room in square meters?

2. An artist is using a canvas that measures 24 inches by 24 inches. What is the area of the canvas in square inches?

3. A flat section of a roof is 35 feet long and 18 feet wide. The cost to repair the roof is based on the area of the roof. Find the area of this section of the roof in square feet.

4. One side of a square is 4.6 centimeters. What is the square's area to the nearest square centimeter?

5. A rectangular hallway measuring 28 feet by 6 feet needs new carpeting. What is the area of the hallway in square feet?

6. The city wants to preserve a rectangular mural that is 32 feet by 15 feet. One quart of protective coating covers 100 square feet. How many quarts should the city buy to cover the mural?

 B. Solve. You may use a calculator.

Refer to the following diagram to answer Questions 7 and 8.

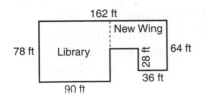

162 ft
New Wing
78 ft Library 28 ft 64 ft
90 ft 36 ft

7. What is the area in square feet of the library before the addition of the new wing?

8. What is the area in square feet of the new wing?

Refer to the following drawing to answer Questions 9 and 10.

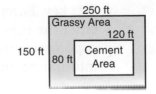

250 ft
Grassy Area
120 ft
150 ft 80 ft Cement Area

9. What is the area in square feet of the cement surface being built?

10. What is the area in square feet of the grassy area? (*Hint:* Total − cement)

Answers start on page 405.

Volume

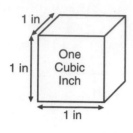

One Cubic Inch

1 in
1 in
1 in

Measures of length can be used to calculate area—the space inside a two-dimensional figure. Area is the square units that cover the space.

Measures of length are also used to calculate volume. **Volume** is a measure of the amount of space inside a three-dimensional object. Volume is measured in three-dimensional units or **cubic units**—cubic inches (cu in), cubic feet (cu ft), cubic yards (cu yd), and cubic centimeters (cu cm) and other metric units. Each of these units is a **cube** with identical square sides.

One of the most common three-dimensional objects is the **rectangular container.** Boxes, crates, and rooms are examples of rectangular containers. To find the volume of these objects, multiply the length times the width times the height.

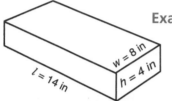

l = 14 in
w = 8 in
h = 4 in

Example 1 What is the volume of a rectangular container that is 14 inches long, 8 inches wide, and 4 inches high?

Multiply: length times width times height.

14 in × 8 in × 4 in = 448 cubic inches

Multiply the numbers as shown.

14 × 8 × 4 = 448.

The volume of the container is **448 cubic inches.** In other words, you could fit 448 one-inch cubes inside the container.

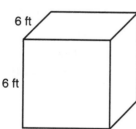

6 ft
6 ft
6 ft

A **cube** is a special rectangular container, so you can find the volume in the same way. However, since each side has the same measure, you are multiplying the same number three times, or "cubing" the number.

Example 2 A shipping crate has the shape of a cube that is 6 feet long on each edge. What is its volume in cubic feet?

Volume = length × width × height
= 6 ft × 6 ft × 6 ft = 216 cubic feet

Using a scientific calculator, you can cube a number using the x^y key. Enter the number you want to multiply, press x^y, enter the exponent 3, and press the = key. Remember, the exponent is the number of times the number is used in the multiplication problem, $x × x × x$. Try both methods to see that you get the same answer.

6 × 6 × 6 = 216.   **6 x^y 3 = 216.**

Note: the GED calculator also has a x^3 key: **6 SHIFT ▶ 216.**
The volume of the shipping crate is **216 cubic feet.**

A. Find the volume of each object shown. Do not use a calculator for these questions.

1.
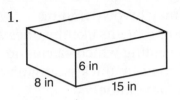
6 in
8 in   15 in

3.
2.5 in
4.2 in   2 in

2.
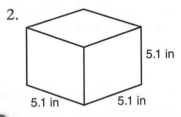
5.1 in
5.1 in   5.1 in

4.
2 cm   6 cm
8 cm

B. Solve. You may use your calculator for these items.

5. What is the volume in cubic inches of a rectangular solid with these measurements: length = 15 inches, width = 24 inches, and height = 4 inches?

6. What is the volume in cubic yards of a cube that measures 3 yards on each side?

Refer to the following drawing to answer Question 7.

EZ Trash Removal, Inc.
6 ft
12 ft   8 ft

7. A contractor has hired a trash hauling service to remove trash from a job site. The trash bins are rectangular containers with the measurements shown in the diagram. How many cubic feet of trash can each container hold?

8. What is the volume in cubic yards of a rectangular container with these measurements: length = 6 feet, width = 3 feet, and height = 9 feet? (*Hint:* 1 cu yd = 27 cu ft)

Refer to the following drawing to answer Question 9.

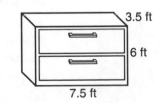

3.5 ft
6 ft
7.5 ft

9. The dimensions of a filing cabinet are shown in the diagram. What is the volume of the cabinet in cubic feet?

Refer to the following drawing to answer Question 10.

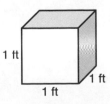

1 ft
1 ft
1 ft

10. How many cubic inches are in 1 cubic foot? (*Hint*: 1 ft = 12 in)

Answers start on page 405.

GED STRATEGY **Solving Word Problems**

Choosing Perimeter, Area, or Volume

Making repairs or improvements at home may involve finding perimeter, area, or volume. Solving math word problems like the ones on the GED Mathematics Test may also involve deciding which calculation is needed. Study the information below so that you can quickly recognize whether you need to solve for perimeter, area, or volume.

Type of Problem	Measurement Unit	Common Situations
perimeter	units of length	putting finishing trim on a room; building a frame; finding the distance around a track; fencing in a yard
area	square units	finding how much paint is needed to cover a wall, or tile or carpet to cover a floor; finding how much space a garden or lawn covers
volume	cubic units	finding how much a container will hold; comparing the space inside (the capacity) of refrigerators; finding the space inside a room to install air conditioning

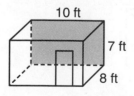

TIP

To remember the definition of perimeter, notice that perimeter contains the word *rim.* The rim is the edge that goes around an object, such as the rim of a glass or the rim of a basketball hoop.

- **Perimeter is a measure of length.** Perimeter is the distance around an object or figure. To find the perimeter, add the lengths of all the sides.
- **Area is the measure of the space that covers a flat object or two-dimensional figure.** Measure area by calculating how many square units it takes to fill the space. To find the area of rectangles or squares, multiply the two dimensions: length × width.
- **Volume is the measure of space inside a three-dimensional object.** Measure volume by calculating how many cubic units it takes to fill the space. To find the volume of a rectangular container, multiply the three dimensions: length × width × height.

Word problems often contain extra information. Read the problem carefully to decide whether to solve for perimeter, area, or volume.

Example The dimensions of a home office are shown in the diagram. How many square feet of wallpaper are needed to cover the wall that is shaded?

(1) 34
(2) 56
(3) 70
(4) 80
(5) 560

10 ft

7 ft

8 ft

The correct answer is **option (3) 70.** You are asked to find square feet—this is the area of the shaded wall. Multiply the length of the wall, 10 ft, by the width, 7 ft: 10 × 7 = 70 square feet. Ignore the 8 ft measurement.

Directions: Choose the one best answer to each question.

Questions 1 and 2 refer to the following diagram.

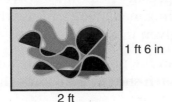

1 ft 6 in

2 ft

1. Cherise wants to frame the painting in the diagram. How many feet of wood will she need to frame the picture?

    (1) 3
    (2) $3\frac{1}{2}$
    (3) 5
    (4) 7
    (5) 9

2. Cherise plans to cover the painting with glass. How many square inches of glass will it take to cover the surface?

    (1)   84
    (2)   168
    (3)   432
    (4) 1008
    (5) Not enough information is given.

3. Cathy wants to install an air conditioner in her office, which measures 10 feet by 8 feet by 7 feet. Which expression could be used to find the measure of the office space in cubic feet?

    (1) 8 + 10 + 8 + 10
    (2) (7 + 8 + 10) × 2
    (3) 8 × 7
    (4) 10 × 8
    (5) 10 × 8 × 7

Questions 4 through 6 refer to the following diagram.

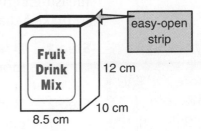

easy-open strip

Fruit Drink Mix

12 cm

10 cm

8.5 cm

4. A new drink mix is packaged in rectangular containers. An easy-open strip goes around the top of the package as shown. What is the length in centimeters of the strip?

    (1)   30.5
    (2)   37
    (3)   61
    (4)   85
    (5) 1020

5. A label completely covers the front of the container. Which of the following expressions could be used to find the area of the label?

    (1) 8.5 + 12 + 8.5 + 12
    (2) (8.5 × 2) + (12 × 2)
    (3) 8.5 × 4
    (4) 8.5 × 12
    (5) 8.5 × 10 × 12

6. The label shows how much the container holds. What is the measure of the space inside the container in cubic centimeters?

    (1)   85
    (2)   102
    (3)   120
    (4)   183
    (5) 1020

Answers start on page 406.

GED STRATEGY Solving Word Problems

Drawing a Picture

Drawing a diagram is a strategy that helps you see how the information in a problem is related. Diagrams are especially helpful for solving measurement and geometry problems. In general, you can use these steps to make a diagram of the information given in a problem.

TIP

The more accurate your drawing is, the easier it is to visualize the answer. Draw the basic shapes and write in the measurements given in the problem. But, if a measurement is about twice another, show that in your drawing.

Step 1 **Draw the shapes** described in the problem. If the problem has more than one shape, your sketch should show how the shapes are placed in relation to each other.

Step 2 **Write the measurements** given in the problem in the correct place on your drawing. This will let you see what information you have, what is missing, and what you can calculate from the information. If possible, calculate any missing dimensions.

Step 3 **Identify** what you are asked to find and **solve** the problem.

Step 4 **Think about your answer** in relation to the diagram. Make sure your answer is reasonable.

Example A rectangular room has a hardwood floor. The room is 15 feet long and 9 feet wide. Part of the floor is covered with a square rug measuring 8 feet per side. In square feet, what is the area of the floor <u>not</u> covered by the rug?

(1) 26
(2) 71
(3) 99
(4) 135
(5) 199

This problem contains a great deal of information. Since you must picture the room and work with numbers at the same time, a drawing would be helpful. Apply the steps above to draw the information in the problem.

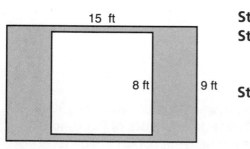

15 ft

8 ft   9 ft

Step 1 Make a sketch showing the square inside the rectangle.

Step 2 Label the drawing with the measurements given in the problem. Your sketch should look something like the drawing on the left.

Step 3 The problem asks you to find the area of the floor <u>not</u> covered by the rug. This is represented by the shaded portion of the drawing. Find the area of the floor and subtract the area of the rug.

Area of the floor: 15 ft × 9 ft = 135 sq ft
Area of the rug: 8 ft × 8 ft = 64 sq ft
Area of the uncovered floor: 135 ft − 64 ft = 71 sq ft

Step 4 Does your answer make sense? Look at the diagram. The rug covers about half the space of the floor. The shaded area should be close to half the entire area of the floor. Since 71 is close to half of 135 sq ft, the answer seems reasonable.

The area of the floor not covered by the rug is **option (2) 71** square feet.

Directions: Choose the <u>one best answer</u> to each question.

1. A rectangular school playground measures 100 meters by 75 meters. There is a square blacktop area in the center of the playground with sides that measure 40 meters. The rest of the playground is seeded with grass. What is the area in square meters of the grassy portion of the playground?

   (1) 9100
   (2) 7660
   (3) 7500
   (4) 5900
   (5) 1000

2. One side of the square base of a milk carton measures 4 inches. If the carton can be filled to a height of 8 inches, how many cubic inches can the carton hold?

   (1) 112
   (2) 128
   (3) 132
   (4) 138
   (5) 146

3. A baby quilt is 4 squares wide and 6 squares long. A tassel is sewn on each point where 4 squares touch. How many tassels are needed to complete the quilt?

   (1) 10
   (2) 15
   (3) 20
   (4) 24
   (5) 35

   TIP Note the unit of measure used in the problem: the volume of a cube with sides of 6 ft (= 2 yd) is both 216 cu ft and 8 cu yd.

4. A 5-kilometer race has three checkpoints between the start and finish line. Checkpoint 1 is 1.8 km from the starting point. Checkpoint 3 is 1.2 km from the finish line. Checkpoint 2 is halfway between checkpoints 1 and 3. How far in kilometers is checkpoint 2 from the finish line?

   (1) 1.2
   (2) 1.5
   (3) 1.8
   (4) 2.0
   (5) 2.2

5. Janice is trying to find her way to a job interview downtown. She starts at a parking garage and walks 4 blocks north, 5 blocks east, 2 blocks south, 2 blocks west, and 2 blocks farther south. How many blocks east of the parking garage does she end up?

   (1) 1
   (2) 2
   (3) 3
   (4) 4
   (5) Not enough information is given.

6. A new game is played on a rectangular field that is 150 feet by 60 feet. A chalk line is drawn on the field exactly 2 feet inside the outer rectangle at all points. What is the total length in feet of the chalk line?

   (1) 112
   (2) 202
   (3) 210
   (4) 292
   (5) 404

Answers start on page 406.

Directions: This is a thirty-minute practice test. After thirty minutes, mark the last question you finished. Then complete the test and check your answers. If most of your answers are correct, but you didn't finish, try to work faster next time.

Part 1

Directions: Choose the one best answer to each question. You MAY use your calculator.

1. The length of a rectangle is 36 centimeters. What is its area in square centimeters?

   (1) 324
   (2) 432
   (3) 504
   (4) 576
   (5) Not enough information is given.

2. What is the perimeter in centimeters of the figure below?

   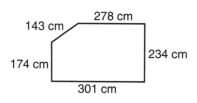

   (1) 829
   (2) 852
   (3) 956
   (4) 987
   (5) 1130

3. In January, Sue's puppy weighed 8 pounds 15 ounces. In April, he weighed 11 pounds 12 ounces. How much weight did the puppy gain?

   (1) 3 pounds 13 ounces
   (2) 3 pounds 3 ounces
   (3) 2 pounds 13 ounces
   (4) 2 pounds 10 ounces
   (5) 2 pounds 3 ounces

Questions 4 and 5 refer to the figure below.

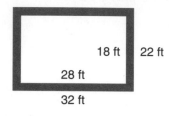

4. The figure is formed by two rectangles. What is the area, in square feet, of the shaded part?

   (1) 100
   (2) 200
   (3) 504
   (4) 704
   (5) 1208

5. How many more feet is the perimeter of the larger rectangle than the perimeter of the smaller rectangle?

   (1) 8
   (2) 16
   (3) 56
   (4) 92
   (5) 108

6. One gallon of paint covers 200 square feet. How many gallons are needed to paint a rectangular floor that is 40 feet by 60 feet?

   (1) 12
   (2) 24
   (3) 40
   (4) 60
   (5) 120

7. Ralph is building a bookcase and uses 4 boards, each 3 yards 2 feet in length. What is the total length of the boards?

(1) 16 yards 2 feet

(2) 15 yards 2 feet

(3) 14 yards 2 feet

(4) 13 yards 2 feet

(5) 12 yards 2 feet

8. The three sides of a triangle measure 16.52 inches, 17.24 inches, and 22.19 inches. What is the perimeter of the triangle, in inches?

(1) 53.95

(2) 51.45

(3) 54.95

(4) 55.45

(5) 55.95

9. Anthony has an odd-shaped plot of grass that he would like to border with a hedge. How many feet long is the border of the plot, rounded to the nearest foot?

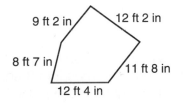

9 ft 2 in   12 ft 2 in
8 ft 7 in   11 ft 8 in
12 ft 4 in

(1) 41 feet

(2) 44 feet

(3) 54 feet

(4) 60 feet

(5) Not enough information is given.

10. What is the volume, in cubic feet, of a cube that measures 3.5 feet on one side?

(1) 12.250

(2) 22.875

(3) 32.875

(4) 42.250

(5) 42.875

11. A swimming pool having the shape of a rectangular solid has a length of 100 feet, a width of 32 feet, and a depth of 8 feet. If the pool is $\frac{3}{4}$ full with water, how many cubic feet of water are in the pool?

(1) 2,400

(2) 6,400

(3) 10,400

(4) 19,200

(5) 25,600

Question 12 refers to the rectangle below.

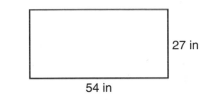

27 in

54 in

12. Anna wants to protect the top of her coffee table with a piece of glass. How many square inches of glass would she need to cover the top of her coffee table?

(1) 81

(2) 100

(3) 162

(4) 200

(5) 1458

Part 2

Directions: Choose the <u>one best answer</u> to each question. You may <u>NOT</u> use your calculator.

13. Which expression can be used to find the perimeter of the figure below?

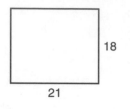

18

21

(1) 21 + 21 + 12 + 12

(2) 21 + 21 + 18 + 18

(3) 2(12 + 18)

(4) 12 + 18

(5) 21 × 18

14. What is the distance in feet around a rectangular flower bed that measures 25 feet by 3 feet?

(1) 56

(2) 60

(3) 65

(4) 66

(5) 75

15. How many square meters is the surface of the rectangle?

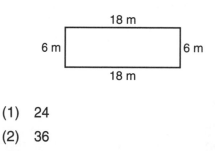

18 m

6 m   6 m

18 m

(1) 24

(2) 36

(3) 72

(4) 108

(5) 144

Question 16 refers to the figure below.

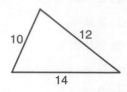

10   12

14

16. What is the perimeter of the figure?

(1) 22

(2) 24

(3) 26

(4) 36

(5) Not enough information is given.

17. Two pieces of wood are 6 feet 8 inches and 4 feet 7 inches in length. What is the total length of the two pieces?

(1) 10 feet 1 inch

(2) 10 feet 3 inches

(3) 11 feet 1 inch

(4) 11 feet 3 inches

(5) 15 feet 10 inches

18. Mark has a piece of rope 7 feet 9 inches long. If he cuts the rope into 3 equal pieces, what is the length of each piece?

(1) 2 feet 3 inches

(2) 2 feet 4 inches

(3) 2 feet 5 inches

(4) 2 feet 6 inches

(5) 2 feet 7 inches

19. The area of a rectangle is the same as the area of a square with a side of 8 cm. If the length of the rectangle is 16 cm, what is its width in centimeters?

(1) 4
(2) 8
(3) 16
(4) 24
(5) 64

20. How many cubes, each having an edge of 2 inches, will fit exactly inside a larger cube with an edge of 4 inches?

(1) 2
(2) 8
(3) 12
(4) 16
(5) 48

21. The sides of a triangle measure 10 yards, 12 yards, and 13 yards. What is the distance around the triangle, in feet?

(1) 35
(2) 105
(3) 420
(4) 1560
(5) Not enough information is given.

22. A rectangular frame is 8 feet long. If its width is 2 feet more than half its length, what is the perimeter of the frame, in feet?

(1) 6
(2) 8
(3) 14
(4) 28
(5) 48

Questions 23 and 24 refer to the figure below.

A kitchen and dining room have the dimensions as shown below, in feet. All corner angles are right angles.

23. How many feet of border are needed to go around the edge of the rooms?

(1) 72
(2) 70
(3) 66
(4) 60
(5) 57

24. How many square feet of tile are needed for flooring?

(1) 378
(2) 306
(3) 234
(4) 162
(5) 144

25. A computer was left on for 10 weeks in a row. For how many hours was the computer left on?

(1) 70
(2) 168
(3) 240
(4) 1680
(5) 2400

Answers start on page 407.

Mean, Median, and Mode

Finding the "center" of a group of numbers helps us to make comparisons with numbers. There are three ways to measure the center of a group of numerical data: mean, median, and mode. Each of these measures adds to our understanding of the data.

You may know the **mean** as the **average.** The average is generally thought of as typical or normal. To find the mean of a group of numbers, add the values and divide the sum by the number of items in the list. Remember: average means the mean.

Example 1   David had scores of 82, 92, 75, 82, and 84 on five tests. What was his average score?

Step 1   Add the data values. $82 + 92 + 75 + 82 + 84 = 415$
Step 2   Divide by 5, the number of scores. $415 ÷ 5 = 83$

Scientific calculators perform multiplication or division steps before addition steps. To make sure your calculator does the addition step first, press **=** before you divide.

82 + 92 + 75 + 82 + 84 = ÷ 5 = 83.

David's average test score is **83.**

The **median** is the middle value in a set of numbers. To find the median, arrange the data in order from lowest to highest or highest to lowest and find the middle number. The median value is often used when one value would dramatically affect the average of a group of values.

Example 2   Find the median of David's scores.

Step 1   Arrange the test scores in order.   92, 84, 82, 82, 75
Step 2   Find the middle value.   92, 84, **82,** 82, 75

David's median score is **82.**

If there is an even number of data items, the median is the average (mean) of the two middle numbers.

Example 3   Ami's point totals for six games of basketball were 24, 16, 19, 22, 6, and 12 points. Find the median of her point totals.

Step 1   Arrange the data in order.   24, 22, **19, 16,** 12, 6
Step 2   The two middle numbers are 19 and 16. $19 + 16 = 35$
           Average these to find the median. $35 ÷ 2 = 17.5$

Ami's median point total is **17.5 points.**

TIP

Always ask yourself whether your answer makes sense. For example, when solving for the mean, median, or mode, the answer must be between the highest and lowest values in the group of numbers.

The **mode** of a group of numbers is the number that occurs most often. In Example 1, the mode of David's test scores is 82, the only score that occurs twice in the data. In Example 3, since every item of data occurs only once, there is no mode. A set of data may have no mode, one mode, or several modes. Mode is often used in business to find out which size, price, or style is most popular. (Note: The MODE key on the GED calculator is *not* used to find the mode of data.)

Another measure that can help us understand data is **range.** To find the range, subtract the lowest number in the set from the greatest number. If the range is a small number, you know that the data values are grouped close together. If the range is large, you know the data values are spread out.

Examples: The range of David's test scores: $92 - 75 = 17$
The range of Ami's point totals: $24 - 6 = 18$

GED SKILL FOCUS

Solve. You may use a calculator for Questions 4 through 6.

1. Find the mean, median, mode, and range of Carla's test scores.

Carla's Test Scores Science—Fall Semester			
Test 1:	85	Test 5:	94
Test 2:	100	Test 6:	80
Test 3:	65	Test 7:	92
Test 4:	100		

2. The attendance figures for a community theater production for four nights were 135, 174, 128, and 215. Find the average attendance.

3. The daily video rentals for Box Office Video are shown in the table below. Find the mean, median, mode, and range of the data.

Daily Video Rentals Box Office Video—Week of May 4	
Monday	57
Tuesday	24
Wednesday	28
Thursday	57
Friday	136
Saturday	164
Sunday	38

4. Find Gordon's average weekly earnings to the nearest cent.

Weekly Earnings	
Week of Feb 2:	$315.35
Week of Feb 9:	$369.82
Week of Feb 16:	$275.58
Week of Feb 23:	$305.83
Week of Mar 2:	$289.68

5. The outdoor temperature was measured in eight locations throughout Los Angeles at 10 A.M. on April 14. The readings are shown below. Find the mean and median temperature to the nearest tenth degree and the range of the data.

61.5°F	64.8°F	69.0°F	67.3°F
65.6°F	60.8°F	61.1°F	65.4°F

6. Find the mean, median, mode, and range of Stan's bills to the nearest whole dollar.

Jan	$58	Jul	$51
Feb	$74	Aug	$55
Mar	$42	Sept	$44
Apr	$46	Oct	$36
May	$38	Nov	$68
Jun	$42	Dec	$52

Answers start on page 408.

Simple Probability

Probability is the study of chance. Probability tells how likely it is that an event will happen. For instance, you may hear on the news that there is a 10% chance of rain tomorrow. From the report, you know that it is unlikely to rain tomorrow, but there is a small chance it might. Probability doesn't tell you what will happen, only the chance that an event will happen.

Probability is often expressed as a percent from 0%, meaning the event cannot occur, to 100%, meaning the event is certain to occur.

You can also express probability as a ratio, fraction, or decimal. For example, the chance of tossing a coin and getting heads can be expressed as a

ratio: 1 out of 2, or 1:2   **fraction:** $\frac{1}{2}$
decimal: 0.5   **percent:** 50%

In any probability situation, there are two numbers to consider:

1. the number of favorable outcomes (events you want to happen)

2. the total number of possible outcomes or trials

To find probability (P), write the ratio of favorable outcomes to possible outcomes.

$$P = \frac{\text{favorable outcomes}}{\text{total possible outcomes}}$$

Example 1   Aaron bought 4 raffle tickets at a community fundraiser. If 200 tickets are sold, what is the probability that one of Aaron's tickets will be the winner?

Step 1   Use the information from the problem to write the probability ratio.

$$P = \frac{\text{favorable outcomes}}{\text{total possible outcomes}} = \frac{4}{200}$$

Step 2   The ratio has been written as a fraction. Reduce the fraction and convert it to a decimal and percent.

$$\frac{4}{200} = \frac{1}{50} = 0.02 = 2\%$$

The probability that one of Aaron's tickets will win is $\frac{1}{50}$, or **1 out of 50.** This converts to **0.02,** or **2%.**

Sometimes probability is based on the results of an experiment. The experiment is repeated a certain number of times. Each repetition is called a trial. The results of the experiment are recorded. **Experimental probability** is the ratio of favorable outcomes to the total number of trials.

TIP

To change a decimal to a percent, move the decimal point two places to the right. For example, 0.25 = 25%

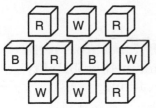

Example 2 A bag holds red, white, and blue cubes of the same size. A cube is drawn at random from the bag, the color is recorded, and the cube is replaced. The results of 10 trials are shown to the left. What is the experimental probability, expressed as a percent, of drawing a red cube?

Step 1 Write the ratio of favorable outcomes (red cubes) to the number of trials (10). $\frac{4}{10}$

Step 2 Reduce and convert to a percent. $\frac{4}{10} = \frac{2}{5} = 0.4 = 40\%$

There is a **40%** experimental probability of drawing a red cube.

GED SKILL FOCUS

A. Express each probability as a fraction, decimal, and percent.

Questions 1 through 4 refer to the spinner below.

1. The spinner has 8 equal sections. What is the probability of spinning an even number?

2. Evan spins the spinner once. What is the probability of spinning 3 or greater?

3. Jan needs either a 1 or a 2 to win the game. What is the probability that Jan will win on her next spin?

4. What is the probability of spinning a number other than 4? (*Hint:* The favorable outcomes are all numbers that are <u>not</u> 4.)

B. Solve. Express your answer as a fraction, decimal, and percent.

Questions 5 and 6 refer to the following information.

A bag contains red, white, and green marbles. A marble is drawn at random from the bag, the color is recorded, and the marble is replaced.

Results of 20 Trials				
red	white	red	green	white
white	green	white	green	red
red	white	red	red	green
white	white	green	red	white

5. Based on the results, what is the probability of selecting a white marble?

6. What is the experimental probability of <u>not</u> drawing a green marble?

Questions 7 and 8 refer to the following information.

An appliance store has identical boxes containing electric mixers on a stockroom shelf. There are 5 of Model A, 8 of Model B, 10 of Model C, and 2 of Model D, stacked randomly on the shelf. A stockroom employee takes one box from the shelf to fill an order.

7. What is the probability that the box chosen contains a Model A mixer?

8. What is the probability that the box chosen is a Model A or Model C mixer?

Answers start on page 408.

Independent and Dependent Probability

The probability of heads up when you flip a coin is $\frac{1}{2}$, but what is the probability of heads up on two coins? To find the combined probability of more than one event, make a chart or use multiplication.

Example 1   A dime and nickel are tossed in the air. What is the probability that both will land heads up?

One way to solve the problem is to make an organized list of all the possible outcomes. There are 4 possible outcomes. Only 1 outcome shows both coins as heads. In other words, $\frac{1}{4}$ of the possibilities shows two heads.

Nickel	Dime
H	**H** ←
H	T
T	H
T	T

> There are 4 possible outcomes. Only 1 outcome shows both coins as heads. In other words, $\frac{1}{4}$ of the possibilities shows two heads.

You can also find the probability that two events will both occur by multiplying the probabilities of each event occurring alone.

The probability that the nickel will land heads up: $\frac{1}{2}$

The probability that the dime will land heads up: $\frac{1}{2}$

The probability that both will land heads up: $\frac{1}{2} \times \frac{1}{2} = \frac{1}{4}$

Using either method, the probability that both coins will land heads up is $\frac{1}{4}$, **0.25, 25%,** or **1 out of 4** (which is sometimes shown as 1:4).

In Example 1, the two events are **independent.** The first event does not affect the second event. The position of the first coin does nothing to change the probability of getting heads on the second coin.

Two events are **dependent** if the result of the first event <u>does</u> affect the result of the second event.

TIP

To figure out whether events are dependent, ask yourself, "Do the conditions change after the first event?"

TIP

Problems with dependent events often involve selecting an object and not replacing it, that is, removing it from the set.

Example 2   Three white socks and two brown socks are in a drawer. Gloria removes one sock at **random,** without looking. Then, without replacing the first sock, she takes out a second sock. What is the probability that both socks are white?

Step 1   To find the probability that both socks are white, assume that the first sock Gloria selects is white. With 5 socks in the drawer, of which 3 now are white, her chance of selecting white is $\frac{3}{5}$.

Step 2   Now there are 4 socks left in the drawer, and 2 are white. Gloria's chance of selecting white the second time is $\frac{2}{4}$, or $\frac{1}{2}$.

Step 3   Multiply to find the combined probability. $\frac{3}{5} \times \frac{1}{2} = \frac{3}{10}$

The probability that both socks will be white is $\frac{3}{10}$, **0.3,** or **30%.**

These events are dependent. The first event, taking the first sock, affects the second event by changing the number of socks in the drawer.

A. Solve.

Refer to the following information to answer Questions 1 and 2.

A game is played by spinning a spinner and then, without looking, drawing a card. After each turn, the card is replaced and the cards are shuffled.

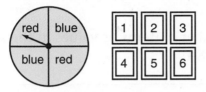

1. What is the percent chance that a player will spin red and then draw a 4 or higher?

2. Rounded to the nearest percent, what is the chance that a player will spin either red or blue and then draw a 5?

_____

3. Max rolls two standard six-sided dice. What is the chance, expressed as a fraction, that both will show a 6?

B. Solve.

Refer to the following information to answer Questions 7 and 8.

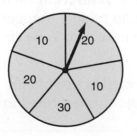

7. Kelli spins the spinner twice. What is the probability expressed as a percent that she spins 20 each time?

8. The spinner is spun twice. What is the probability expressed as a fraction, that neither spin is a 10?

4. A golf bag contains 5 white golf tees and 1 blue tee. John reaches into the bag and selects two tees at random. What is the probability, expressed as a fraction, that both are white? (*Hint:* Taking two at a time is the same as taking one, not replacing it, and then taking another.)

Refer to the following information to answer Questions 5 and 6.

A company decides to select two workers at random to attend a computer class. Stephanie and Yuki both hope to be chosen. The names of ten workers are put in a box. Two names will be drawn randomly from the box.

5. What is the probability, expressed as a decimal, that the first name drawn is either Stephanie or Yuki?

6. Suppose Stephanie's name is chosen first. What is the chance, expressed as a fraction, that Yuki's name will be chosen second?

9. Ace Manufacturing builds air-conditioning units. On Friday, 20 units were built with defective parts. The company built a total of 100 units on Friday. Before the mistake was discovered, the company shipped two air conditioners. What is the probability (to the nearest hundredth) that both air conditioners had defective parts?

10. Alex has 10 cards: 5 hearts and 5 diamonds. Sharon draws and keeps two of Alex's cards. What is the probability that both cards are hearts?

Answers start on page 408.

GED STRATEGY **Using Your Calculator**

Mean and Median

To calculate the mean (average) of a set of numbers, first add the numbers and then divide the sum by the number of values in the set.

Example 1   During the past semester, Pat's test scores in U.S. history class were 86, 76, 82, and 92. What was her mean test score?

Step 1   First add Pat's test scores. $86 + 76 + 82 + 92 = 336$
Step 2   Then divide the sum by 4, the number
of test scores. $336 \div 4 = 84$

(The number of test scores is the number of items or values in the set.) Pat's average, or mean, test score was **84.**

Check how your calculator solves this type of problem.

   86 **+** 76 **+** 82 **+** 92 **÷** 4 **=**

If your calculator is <u>not</u> programmed with the order of operations, it will give you the correct answer, 84.

However, if a calculator uses the order of operations, as the calculator used on the GED Test does, it will first perform all multiplication and division before it performs any addition and subtraction. This results in the wrong answer of 267.

In order to obtain the correct answer on a calculator that uses the order of operations, press the equals key after entering the last score to be added. This will total all the scores before dividing. Complete the problem by dividing by the number of values.

   86 **+** 76 **+** 82 **+** 92 **=** **÷** 4 **=** 84.

Remember that to find the median, list the numbers in increasing or decreasing order and then choose the middle number. If there is an even number of values in the set (and therefore no middle number in the list), find the average (mean) of the two middle numbers. You can use your calculator to find this average.

Example 2   In the last four days, Claudio earned tips of $28, $6, $30, and $20. What was the median amount he earned in tips?

Write the four amounts earned in a list of increasing or decreasing order: $6, $20, $28, $30. Since there is an even number of amounts, there is no middle amount. Therefore, find the average (mean) of the two middle amounts, $20 and $28:

   20 **+** 28 **=** **÷** 2 **=** 24.

The median amount Claudio earned in tips was **$24.**

Directions: Choose the one best answer to each item. You MAY use your calculator.

Questions 1 and 2 refer to the table below.

Game	Score
1	94
2	73
3	86
4	102
5	96
6	71

1. What was the average (mean) score for the six games listed?

   (1) 94.0

   (2) 90.0

   (3) 87.0

   (4) 86.5

   (5) 86.0

2. What was the median score for the games shown?

   (1) 94.0

   (2) 90.0

   (3) 87.0

   (4) 86.5

   (5) 86.0

3. For the past five days the high temperatures in San Francisco were 64.4°, 59.3°, 68.0°, 48.8°, and 53.6°. What was the average (mean) high temperature for those days, rounded to the nearest tenth of a degree?

   (1) 58.8°

   (2) 59.3°

   (3) 62.0°

   (4) 64.4°

   (5) 68.8°

Questions 4 and 5 refer to the table below.

Rainfall in Union City	
Month	Inches
June	6.3
July	4.5
August	3.8
September	10.2

4. What was the average (mean) rainfall in Union City during the months shown in the table, rounded to the nearest inch?

   (1) 4

   (2) 5

   (3) 6

   (4) 7

   (5) 10

5. What was the median rainfall in Union City during the months shown in the table, rounded to the nearest inch?

   (1) 4

   (2) 5

   (3) 6

   (4) 7

   (5) 10

6. Karen's electric bills for six months were $28.84, $18.96, $29.32, $16.22, $17.98, and $21.80. What was the median bill for these months, rounded to the nearest cent?

   (1) $ 6.79

   (2) $16.22

   (3) $18.96

   (4) $20.38

   (5) $21.80

Answers start on page 409.

Lesson 17 GED SKILL Tables, Charts, and Graphs

Tables and Charts

Tables and **charts** organize information or **data** in columns and rows. Specific items of data are found where columns and rows intersect, or meet. To use a table to find information, first read all **titles** and **labels** carefully. Then find the column and row that relate to the information you need.

Example 1 Greg uses **mileage tables** in his work as a driver. He needs to drive from Lamesa to Canyon and from Canyon to Guthrie. Use the table below. How many miles will he drive?

Mileage Between Cities

	Lubbock	**Lamesa**	Plainview	**Canyon**	Guthrie
Lubbock		61.4	48.0	8.0	92.8
Lamesa	61.4		108.6	67.1	140.5
Plainview	48.0	108.6		46.3	109.1
Canyon	8.0	67.1	46.3		87.6
Guthrie	92.8	140.5	109.1	87.6	

TIP

Tables usually contain more information than you need. Double-check to make sure you are using the correct items of data for your calculations.

Step 1 Find the distance from Lamesa to Canyon. Locate Lamesa in the second row and go across to the column for Canyon. Or locate Canyon in the fourth row and go across to the column for Lamesa. Both methods give the same answer.   67.1 miles

Step 2 Find the distance from Canyon to Guthrie. Locate Canyon and find where it intersects with Guthrie.   87.6 miles

Step 3 Add to find the total miles. $67.1 + 87.6 = 154.7$

The total distance of Greg's trip is **154.7 miles.**

A **frequency table** tracks how often certain events occur.

Example 2 A software company wants to know the reasons customers call customer support. Alli used a frequency table to track the calls he received. How many more callers placed orders than needed tech support?

Frequency Table: Reason for Call

Placed order	⊞⊞ ⊞⊞ ⊞⊞ ⊞⊞ ⊞⊞ ⊞⊞ II
Exchanged product	⊞⊞ III
Returned product for refund	⊞⊞ ⊞⊞ II
Needed technical support	⊞⊞ ⊞⊞ ⊞⊞ ⊞⊞ ⊞⊞ I

Step 1 Count the tally marks for "Placed order" (32). Count the tally marks for "Needed technical support" (26).

Step 2 Subtract to find the difference. $32 - 26 = 6$

There were **6 more calls** from customers placing orders than from those needing technical support.

Solve. You may use your calculator.

Refer to the following table to answer Questions 1 through 4.

Appliance Central—Refrigerators

Model	Size	Price	Annual Energy Use*
TR8	15.5 cu ft	$459	624 kwh
AD7	18.5 cu ft	$599	895 kwh
KT6	16.8 cu ft	$479	922 kwh
CV9	20.4 cu ft	$699	1108 kwh
GC2	21.6 cu ft	$699	1484 kwh

*energy use in kilowatt-hours

1. Refer to the table to find:
   a. the cost of model CV9
   b. the kilowatt-hours used by model AD7
   c. the size in cubic feet of the refrigerator that costs $479

2. Alicia plans to replace her 14.8 cu ft refrigerator with a new one. If she buys the CV9 model from Appliance Central, how many more cubic feet of storage will she have than she has now?

3. Alicia pays $0.09 for each kilowatt-hour of electricity she uses. How much more would it cost Alicia each year to operate the GC2 than the CV9 model?

4. Which model has the lower price per cubic foot of storage, TR8 or KT6?

Refer to the frequency table in Example 2 on page 192 to answer Questions 5 through 7.

5. What is the ratio of customers who returned a product for refund to those who placed an order?

6. What fraction of the calls to customer service needed technical support?

7. To the nearest percent, what percent of the callers either placed an order or exchanged a product?

Refer to the following information to answer Questions 8 and 9.

Baseball coach Tomas compiled the statistics below on five of his best hitters.

Valley Park Little League—Dodgers

Name	At Bats	Hits	Walks
Max	16	5	2
Katrina	17	6	3
David	15	7	2
Andy	18	5	3
Ruvy	16	4	6

8. A player's batting average is the number of hits divided by the number of at bats, rounded to the thousandths place. What is Katrina's batting average?

9. A player can reach first base by getting a hit or a walk. Which player has reached first base the greatest number of times?

Refer to the following frequency table to answer Questions 10 through 12.

Sixty Value Barn customers rated their shopping experience at a special sale.

Value Barn Customer Satisfaction Survey

Excellent	ɪɪɪɪ ɪɪɪɪ ɪɪɪɪ
Very good	ɪɪɪɪ ɪɪɪɪ ‖
Average	ɪɪɪɪ ɪɪɪɪ
Below average	ɪɪɪɪ ‖‖
Poor	ɪɪɪɪ ɪɪɪɪ ɪɪɪɪ

10. How many customers rated the experience as average, very good, or excellent?

11. What percent of the customers said their experience was poor?

12. What is the ratio of customers who rated their experience as excellent to those who rated their experience as poor?

Answers start on page 409.

Bar and Line Graphs

Graphs represent data visually to compare data from different sources, show change over a period of time, and make projections about the future. This **bar graph** was created to show the difference in staffing levels for each of a company's three shifts. Notice these parts of the graph:

Scale — A scale is like a ruler. It is marked with numbers that represent some unit of measure.

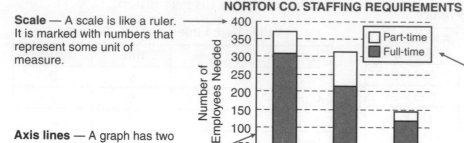

NORTON CO. STAFFING REQUIREMENTS

Title — The title tells what kind of information is found on the graph.

Key — A key, or legend, gives any additional information needed to read the graph.

Axis lines — A graph has two axis lines. The **vertical axis** runs along the side of the graph. The **horizontal axis** runs across the bottom.

Bar Labels

Often bar graph bars show two items of data: the height of the top portion is the height of the entire bar minus the bottom portion.

A graph key is needed only when data about more than one category are shown. Each axis line is labeled. Graphs may have scales on one or both axis lines. A bar graph has only one scale. Each bar has a label. These labels replace the second scale. Always read all labels carefully.

Example 1 About how many full-time and part-time employees work during the 2nd shift?

Step 1 Find the bar for the 2nd shift. The entire bar represents the total of part-time and full-time workers.

Step 2 Follow the top of the bar to the scale at the left. The bar ends between 300 and 350. A good estimate for the bar value is 320.

About 320 employees work during the 2nd shift.

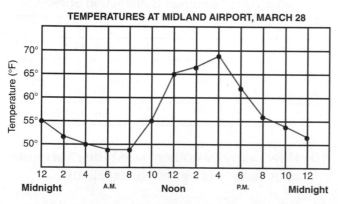

Line graphs often show changes over time with some measure on the vertical scale and time on the horizontal scale. Line graphs have two scales and often have a key as well (when the graph shows more than one line). Points plotted on the graph connect the two scales. On this graph each point represents the temperature at a specific time.

The points are then connected by a line. The line shows a **trend** or a pattern of change over time. For example, this line graph shows a warming trend from 8 A.M. until 4 P.M. Then the temperature cools steadily until midnight. We can use trends to make predictions of how data may change in the near future.

Example 2 What was the temperature at 10 A.M. on March 28?

Step 1 Find the dot directly above 10 A.M. on the horizontal scale.
Step 2 Follow across from the dot to the temperature scale.

It was **55°** at 10 A.M. on March 28.

Unit 2: Measurement and Data Analysis

Solve. You may use a calculator.

Refer to the bar graph below to answer Questions 1 through 5.

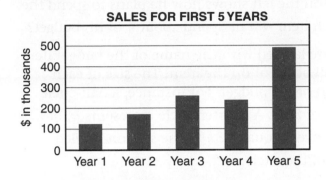

1. What was the approximate dollar amount in sales for Year 3?

2. Which year showed a decrease in sales?

3. Estimate the difference in sales from Year 4 to Year 5.

4. Approximate the ratio of sales in Year 5 to sales in Year 1.

5. Approximate the average yearly sales for the five-year period.

Refer to the bar graph in Example 1 on page 194 to answer Questions 6 through 10.

6. About how many full-time employees work during the 1st shift?

7. About how many more people work the 1st shift than work the 3rd shift?

8. What is the approximate ratio of full-time to part-time workers during the 2nd shift?

9. About how many more part-time employees work during the 2nd shift than work during the 1st shift?

10. Approximately how many employees are needed to fill all shifts at Norton Co?

Refer to the line graph in Example 2 on page 194 to answer Questions 11 and 12.

11. About how many degrees did the temperature fall between 4 P.M. and 6 P.M.?

12. In which two-hour time period did the temperature rise the most?

Refer to the following graph to answer Questions 13 through 17.

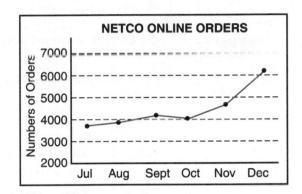

13. Netco sells its products online. The graph shows the number of orders placed during the final six months of the year. In which month did the number of orders decline from the previous month?

14. About how many more orders were there in December than in September?

15. The rate of increase from December to January is expected to equal the rate of increase from October to November. Estimate the number of orders for January.

16. The average number of orders per month during the six-month period was about 4400. Which two months were closest to the average?

17. Netco reported that the average sale during November was $35. Find November's gross sales by multiplying $35 by the number of sales.

Answers start on page 409.

Circle Graphs

Circle graphs show how parts of an amount are related to the whole amount; the entire circle equals 100%. Most circle graphs show percents, but fractions, decimals, or whole numbers can also be used.

Example 1   Cliff has a budget of $400 to plan a day trip for 50 children. The circle graph on the left shows how he plans to spend the money. On which item will he spend about $\frac{1}{3}$ of his budget?

DAY TRIP BUDGET: $400

The sections of the graph are labeled with the name of the budget item and the percentage that will be spent on the item. The size of each section represents a fraction of the budget. For instance, a half-circle represents $\frac{1}{2}$ of the budget, or 50%. A quarter-circle represents $\frac{1}{4}$, or 25%, of the total budget. Since $\frac{1}{3}$ equals $33\frac{1}{3}$%, the section labeled "Lunches 34%" is about $\frac{1}{3}$ of the circle.

Cliff will spend about $\frac{1}{3}$ of the budget on **lunches.**

You can also use the graph to find the dollar amount that is budgeted for an item.

Example 2   How much does Cliff plan to spend on the bus?

Step 1   **Read the graph.** Cliff will spend 47% of his total budget of $400 to pay for the bus.   Find 47% of $400.

Step 2   **Use a proportion.** $\frac{47}{100} = \frac{x}{\$400}$, $47 \times \$400 \div 100 = \$188$

 Using a calculator:

400 ⊠ 47 % 188.   or   400 ⊠ 4 7 SHIFT = 188.

Cliff will spend **$188** of the $400 budget to pay for the bus.

MARTINEZ FAMILY MONTHLY BUDGET

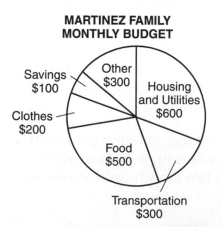

The circle graph to the left is labeled with dollar amounts. You can still use the size of the sections to understand how each part compares to the whole.

Example 3   Which item requires $\frac{1}{4}$ of the family's entire budget?

Step 1   **Find the total** value of the circle.
$600 + $300 + $500 + $200 + $100 + $300 = $2000

Step 2   **Find the fraction** closest to $\frac{1}{4}$. $\frac{\$500}{\$2000} = \frac{1}{4}$

The amount budgeted for **food** is $\frac{1}{4}$ of $2000, or $500.

TIP A circle graph represents the whole. In a circle graph using percents, the sections total 100%. In circle graphs using fractions or decimals, the sections total 1.

Solve. You may use a calculator.

Refer to the following information to answer Questions 1 through 7.

A high school has received $56,000 in donations and grants to build a new computer lab. The following graph shows how the school plans to spend the money.

COMPUTER LAB BUDGET

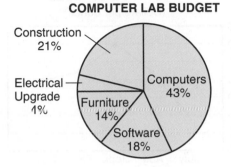

Construction 21%

Electrical Upgrade 1%

Furniture 14%

Computers 43%

Software 18%

1. What percent of the money will be spent on construction and electrical upgrade?

2. How much money is budgeted to buy computers?

3. How much money is budgeted to buy furniture?

4. What percent of the money will **not** be spent on either computers or software?

5. Which two items combined equal about $\frac{1}{3}$ of the budget?

6. For which item has the school budgeted a little more than $10,000?

7. How much money is budgeted for construction and electrical upgrading?

Refer to the Day Trip Budget in Example 1 on page 196 to answer Questions 8 and 9.

8. How much money has Cliff budgeted to pay for prizes and the park fee?

9. Which item will cost about five times the cost of the prizes?

Refer to the Martinez Family Monthly Budget on page 196 to answer Questions 10 and 11.

10. What fraction of the family's budget is spent on transportation, food, and clothes?

11. What percent of the family's budget is spent on housing and utilities?

Refer to the following information to answer Questions 12 through 16.

Mrs. Reid is an office manager. She has prepared this circle graph to show the workers in the clerk-typist pool how their time will be spent in her office.

CLERK-TYPIST TASKS

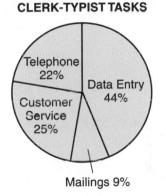

Telephone 22%

Data Entry 44%

Customer Service 25%

Mailings 9%

12. On which task will the clerk-typists spend $\frac{1}{4}$ of their time?

13. What percent of their time do clerk-typists spend on mailings and data entry?

14. What is the ratio of time spent entering data to time spent answering telephones?

15. Mark works 40 hours per week as a clerk-typist. About how many hours per week should Mark spend doing data entry?

16. Angelina works 36 hours per week. To the nearest whole hour, how many hours per week should she expect to spend on customer service and telephone tasks?

Answers start on page 410.

GED Mini-Test • Lessons 16 and 17

Directions: This is a thirty-minute practice test. After thirty minutes, mark the last question you finished. Then complete the test and check your answers. If most of your answers are correct, but you didn't finish, try to work faster next time.

Part 1

Directions: Choose the <u>one best answer</u> to each question. You <u>MAY</u> use your calculator.

<u>Questions 1 and 2</u> refer to the following information.

Five Acme employees have salaries of $27,560, $30,050, $22,750, $42,800, and $28,900.

1. What is the average (mean) salary of the employees at Acme?

   (1) $20,050
   (2) $27,560
   (3) $28,900
   (4) $29,475
   (5) $30,412

2. What is the median salary of the employees at Acme?

   (1) $20,050
   (2) $27,560
   (3) $28,900
   (4) $29,475
   (5) $30,412

---

3. A dresser drawer contains 2 red socks, 4 blue socks, and 8 black socks. What is the probability that a sock chosen at random from the drawer is <u>not</u> a black sock?

   (1) $\frac{4}{7}$
   (2) $\frac{3}{7}$
   (3) $\frac{2}{7}$
   (4) $\frac{1}{7}$
   (5) $\frac{1}{14}$

<u>Questions 4 and 5</u> refer to the graph.

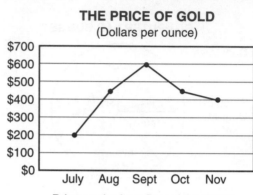

THE PRICE OF GOLD
(Dollars per ounce)

Price on the Last Day of the Month

4. By how much did the price of gold increase, in dollars per ounce, from July to September?

   (1) $100
   (2) $200
   (3) $400
   (4) $500
   (5) $600

5. What was the ratio of the price of gold in September to the price of gold in July?

   (1) 1:3
   (2) 1:2
   (3) 2:1
   (4) 3:1
   (5) 6:1

Questions 6 through 9 refer to the following graph.

RAINFALL IN INCHES

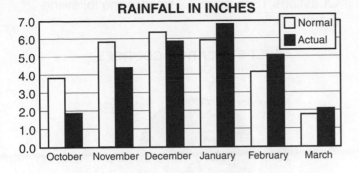

6. For which months was the actual rainfall less than normal?

   (1) October, November, and December
   (2) October, November, and January
   (3) October, December, and March
   (4) October, February, and March
   (5) January, February, and March

7. For how many months was the actual rainfall greater than 5.0 inches?

   (1) 2
   (2) 3
   (3) 4
   (4) 5
   (5) 6

8. How many more inches of rain fell in January than in March?

   (1) 2.2
   (2) 3.5
   (3) 4.0
   (4) 4.6
   (5) 5.8

9. Approximately what is the average (mean) normal rainfall for November, December, and January?

   (1) 4.5
   (2) 5.0
   (3) 5.5
   (4) 6.0
   (5) 6.5

Questions 10 and 11 refer to the following graph.

MOST POPULAR SPORTS
(Millions of participants)

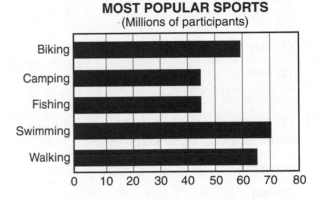

10. Approximately how many more millions of people participated in swimming than in camping?

   (1) 65
   (2) 60
   (3) 40
   (4) 35
   (5) 25

11. For the five sports listed, what was the average (mean) number of millions of participants, rounded to the nearest million?

   (1) 46
   (2) 50
   (3) 52
   (4) 57
   (5) 62

Part 2

Directions: Choose the <u>one best answer</u> to each question. You may <u>NOT</u> use your calculator.

<u>Questions 12 and 13</u> refer to the following information.

Last week, Karla exercised every day for the following number of minutes each day: 42, 54, 62, 40, 57, 50, and 38.

12. What was the average number of minutes that Karla exercised per day last week?

    (1) 45

    (2) 46

    (3) 47

    (4) 48

    (5) 49

13. What was the median number of minutes that Karla exercised last week?

    (1) 42

    (2) 50

    (3) 54

    (4) 57

    (5) 62

<u>Question 14</u> refers to the following information.

A bag contains 20 table tennis balls, each one painted with a different number from 1 to 20.

14. If a ball is chosen at random from the bag, what is the probability that it is painted with a number greater than 15?

    (1) $\frac{1}{20}$

    (2) $\frac{1}{5}$

    (3) $\frac{1}{4}$

    (4) $\frac{1}{2}$

    (5) $\frac{3}{4}$

<u>Questions 15 through 17</u> refer to the following graph.

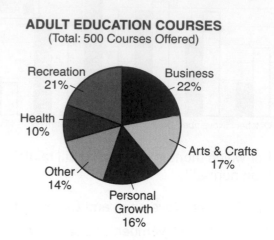

ADULT EDUCATION COURSES
(Total: 500 Courses Offered)

Recreation 21% | Business 22% | Health 10% | Arts & Crafts 17% | Other 14% | Personal Growth 16%

15. How many Personal Growth courses are offered?

    (1) 8

    (2) 16

    (3) 64

    (4) 80

    (5) 100

16. What is the ratio of Business courses offered to Health courses offered?

    (1) 5:7

    (2) 21:22

    (3) 17:10

    (4) 11:8

    (5) 11:5

17. How many more Business courses are offered than Recreation courses?

    (1) 1

    (2) 5

    (3) 10

    (4) 12

    (5) 50

Questions 18 through 20 refer to the following graph.

NUMBER OF NEW SUBSCRIBERS TO THE DAILY GAZETTE
(in thousands)

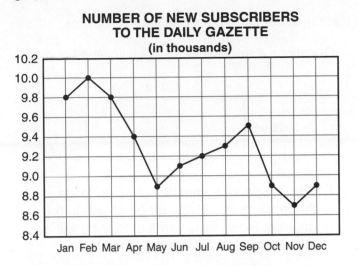

18. What is the range of new subscribers per month, from lowest to highest?

    (1) 8,400 to 10,200
    (2) 8,700 to 9,800
    (3) 8,700 to 10,000
    (4) 8,800 to 10,000
    (5) 9,800 to 10,000

19. A turn-around is a point on the graph where the direction of the line changes. How many turn-arounds are shown on this graph?

    (1) two
    (2) three
    (3) four
    (4) five
    (5) six

20. Which of the following consecutive months showed an increase in new subscribers?

    (1) February to March
    (2) March to April
    (3) September to October
    (4) October to November
    (5) November to December

Questions 21 through 23 refer to the following graph.

D & T DEPARTMENT STORE
(Net sales in thousands of dollars)

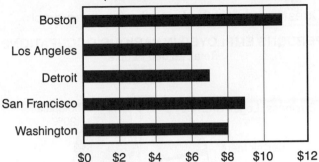

21. Approximately how much more were net sales for the Boston store than net sales for the Detroit store?

    (1) $2000
    (2) $2500
    (3) $3000
    (4) $4000
    (5) $5000

22. What is the ratio of the net sales of the Los Angeles store to the net sales of the San Francisco store?

    (1) 1:2
    (2) 2:3
    (3) 6:7
    (4) 3:2
    (5) 7:6

23. What is the average (mean) net sales of the five stores shown, in thousands of dollars?

    (1) $ 6.0
    (2) $ 7.2
    (3) $ 8.2
    (4) $10.5
    (5) $41.0

Answers start on page 411.

Unit 2 Cumulative Review **Measurement and Data Analysis**

Part 1

Directions: Choose the <u>one best answer</u> to each question. You <u>MAY</u> use your calculator.

Questions 1 and 2 refer to the following graph.

PERSONS EMPLOYED IN VARIOUS OCCUPATIONS
Total: 25,000 People

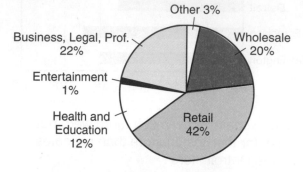

1. What was the total number of people employed in a wholesale occupation or a health and education occupation?

   (1) 2000
   (2) 3000
   (3) 5000
   (4) 7000
   (5) 8000

2. How many more people were employed in a business, legal, or professional occupation than in an entertainment occupation?

   (1) 4000
   (2) 4350
   (3) 5000
   (4) 5250
   (5) 5500

3. The length of one side of a square is 1 foot 4 inches. What is the distance around the entire square in inches?

   (1) 64
   (2) 52
   (3) 48
   (4) 28
   (5) 16

Questions 4 and 5 refer to the following figure.

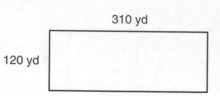

4. The city parks committee plans to fence in the rectangular driving range shown in the drawing. How many yards of fencing will it take to enclose the driving range?

   (1) 240
   (2) 430
   (3) 620
   (4) 860
   (5) 980

5. The city needs to buy grass seed to cover the driving range. If one bag of grass seed covers 75 square yards, how many bags will the city need to buy to seed the driving range?

   (1) 160
   (2) 357
   (3) 496
   (4) 653
   (5) 744

6. In a bag of candies, 12 are red, 10 are green, and 28 are yellow. What is the probability that a candy chosen at random from the bag is red?

   (1) 0.02
   (2) 0.08
   (3) 0.20
   (4) 0.24
   (5) 0.32

Question 7 refers to the figure below.

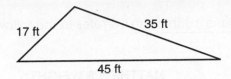

17 ft   35 ft

45 ft

7. The park district wants to use landscaping blocks to protect the edges of the flower bed shown above. Which expression can be used to find how many feet of landscaping blocks are needed?

(1) 17 + 35

(2) 17 × 45

(3) 17 + 35 + 45

(4) 17 × 35 × 45

(5) 17 × 35 − 45

8. Miguel has two pieces of pipe. One is 2 yards long, and the other is 4 feet long. How many feet longer is the first pipe?

(1) 10

(2) 9

(3) 6

(4) 4

(5) 2

9. Sarah buys 6 raffle tickets. If a total of 300 raffle tickets is sold, what is the probability that one of Sarah's tickets will win?

(1) $\frac{1}{4}$

(2) $\frac{1}{20}$

(3) $\frac{1}{25}$

(4) $\frac{1}{50}$

(5) $\frac{1}{300}$

Questions 10 and 11 refer to the table below.

UTILITY PAYMENTS	
Period	Amount
Jan–Feb	$89.36
Mar–Apr	$90.12
May–Jun	$74.47
Jul–Aug	$63.15
Sept–Oct	$59.76
Nov–Dec	$84.31

10. What is the median of the amounts in the table?

(1) $84.31

(2) $79.39

(3) $74.47

(4) $63.15

(5) Not enough information is given.

11. What is the average (mean) of the amounts in the table, rounded to the nearest cent?

(1) $ 76.86

(2) $ 79.28

(3) $ 79.39

(4) $230.58

(5) Not enough information is given.

12. A comedy club had the following ticket sales: 184, 176, 202, 178, and 190. What was the average (mean) number of tickets sold?

(1) 184.0

(2) 186.0

(3) 188.0

(4) 190.0

(5) 232.5

Directions: Choose the <u>one best answer</u> to each question. You may <u>NOT</u> use your calculator.

<u>Questions 13 and 14</u> refer to the information below.

Martin took a writing workshop and received the following grades on papers he wrote for the course: 60, 85, 95, 80, 95, 95.

13. What was the mean score for the papers, rounded to the nearest whole number?

    (1) 95
    (2) 90
    (3) 85
    (4) 80
    (5) 60

14. A student's grade in the writing workshop is either the average of the scores or the median score, whichever is greater. What was Martin's median score?

    (1) 95
    (2) 90
    (3) 85
    (4) 80
    (5) 60

15. Carrie has three projects. The first project will take 20 minutes, the second project will take the same amount of time as the first project, and the third project will take 30 minutes. What is the latest time she can start to work in order to finish all three projects by 12 o'clock noon?

    (1) 10:10 A.M.
    (2) 10:50 A.M.
    (3) 10:53 A.M.
    (4) 11:07 A.M.
    (5) 11:10 A.M.

<u>Questions 16 through 18</u> refer to the following graph.

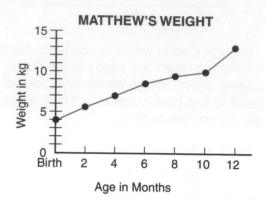

16. Over which two-month period did Matthew have the greatest weight gain?

    (1) birth to 2 months
    (2) 4 to 6 months
    (3) 6 to 8 months
    (4) 8 to 10 months
    (5) 10 to 12 months

17. The average weight for a male infant at one year of age is 10.5 kilograms. About how many <u>more</u> kilograms than average did Matthew weigh at one year?

    (1) 0.5
    (2) 0.8
    (3) 1.1
    (4) 1.3
    (5) 2.5

18. During which two-month period did Matthew have the smallest weight gain?

    (1) birth to 2 months
    (2) 2 to 4 months
    (3) 6 to 8 months
    (4) 8 to 10 months
    (5) Not enough information is given.

19. A photograph is $3\frac{3}{4}$ inches wide and $5\frac{1}{4}$ inches long. If the dimensions of the photograph are doubled, how many inches wide will the photograph be?

(1) $10\frac{1}{2}$

(2) $10\frac{1}{4}$

(3) $7\frac{3}{4}$

(4) $7\frac{1}{2}$

(5) $6\frac{3}{4}$

20. A wall in Andrea's living room is 12 feet long. She buys four bookcases to fit along this wall. If each bookcase is 35 inches wide, which of the following statements is true?

(1) They will be 8 inches too wide.

(2) They will be 4 inches too wide.

(3) They will fit exactly.

(4) They will fit with 4 inches left over.

(5) They will fit with 8 inches left over.

21. Sam uses 5 gallons of fertilizer on his lawn. How many pints of fertilizer does he use?

(1) 40

(2) 32

(3) 8

(4) 5

(5) 4

22. A rectangular box measures 5 yards long, 4 yards wide, and 2 yards high. What is the volume of the box in cubic feet?

(1) 40

(2) 120

(3) 180

(4) 360

(5) 1080

23. A cube measures 5 feet on a side. When the cube is two-fifths filled with water, how many cubic feet of water are in the cube?

(1) 15

(2) 25

(3) 50

(4) 125

(5) 250

Questions 24 and 25 refer to the figure below.

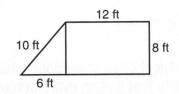

A homeowner is having a new deck built in the shape shown above. The longest side of the deck will attach to the house.

24. How many feet of railing are needed if the side attached to the house will not have a railing?

(1) 30

(2) 36

(3) 40

(4) 48

(5) 56

25. After the wood has aged and weathered, it can be stained. The surface of the rectangular section is four times the size of the triangular section. Which expression could be used to find the surface area of the deck?

(1) $12 \times 8 + 6$

(2) $(12 \times 8) + (10 \times 8)$

(3) $\frac{1}{4}(12 \times 8)$

(4) $(12 \times 8) + \frac{1}{4}(12 \times 8)$

(5) $4 \times 12 \times 8$

A box contains 15 cards, each one numbered with a different whole number from 1 to 15.

26. If a card is chosen at random from the box, what is the probability that it is less than 4?

    (1) $\frac{1}{15}$

    (2) $\frac{1}{5}$

    (3) $\frac{4}{15}$

    (4) $\frac{1}{2}$

    (5) $\frac{11}{15}$

27. If a card is chosen at random, what is the probability that it is an even number?

    (1) $\frac{1}{15}$

    (2) $\frac{7}{15}$

    (3) $\frac{1}{2}$

    (4) $\frac{7}{8}$

    (5) $\frac{14}{15}$

28. What is the ratio of even-numbered cards to odd-numbered cards?

    (1) 1:15

    (2) 7:8

    (3) 15:15

    (4) 8:7

    (5) 15:1

29. A card is chosen at random and replaced. What is the probability that the same card would be chosen twice in a row?

    (1) $\frac{1}{7}$

    (2) $\frac{2}{15}$

    (3) $\frac{1}{8}$

    (4) $\frac{1}{15}$

    (5) $\frac{1}{225}$

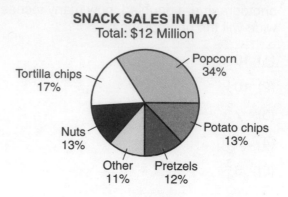

SNACK SALES IN MAY
Total: $12 Million

Tortilla chips 17%
Popcorn 34%
Potato chips 13%
Pretzels 12%
Other 11%
Nuts 13%

30. How much money, in millions of dollars, was spent on popcorn in May?

    (1) $1.32

    (2) $1.44

    (3) $1.56

    (4) $2.04

    (5) $4.08

31. What was the total amount, in millions of dollars, spent on nuts, pretzels, and tortilla chips in May?

    (1) $ 1.44

    (2) $ 1.56

    (3) $ 5.04

    (4) $10.56

    (5) $15.60

32. What was the ratio of the amount spent on popcorn to the amount spent on tortilla chips in May?

    (1) 34:13

    (2) 2:1

    (3) 17:13

    (4) 13:34

    (5) 1:2

Answers start on page 412.

Cumulative Review Performance Analysis
Unit 2 ● Measurement and Data Analysis

Use the Answers and Explanations starting on page 412 to check your answers to the Unit 2 Cumulative Review. Then use the chart to figure out the skill areas in which you need more practice.

On the chart, circle the questions that you answered correctly. Write the number correct for each skill area. Add the number of questions that you got correct on the Cumulative Review. If you feel that you need more practice, go back and review the lessons for the skill areas that were difficult for you.

Questions	Number Correct	Skill Area	Lessons for Review
3, 8, 15, **17**, 19, 20, 21	____/7	Measurement Systems	14
4, 5, 7, 22, 23, **24, 25**	____/7	Measuring Common Figures	15
6, 9, **10, 11**, 12, 13, 14, 26, 27, 28, 29	____/11	Measures of Central Tendency and Probability	16
1, 2, 16, 18, 30, 31, 32	____/7	Tables, Charts, and Graphs	17
TOTAL CORRECT	____/32		

Question numbers in **boldface** are based on graphics.

Algebra

Algebra is one of the most important areas of mathematics. It involves translating everyday situations into mathematical symbols and language. We can use algebra to solve problems and to learn to think more logically. Understanding algebra is also an important springboard into the advanced areas of mathematics that are required for jobs in science and technology.

Questions related to algebra will account for more than 25 percent of the GED Mathematics Test. Additionally, you will find that you can use many of the skills in this unit to solve problems in arithmetic and geometry.

Cartographers use the coordinate graph to plot latitude and longitude on maps they create.

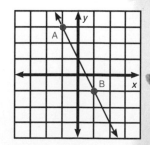

The lessons in this unit include:

Lesson 18: **Integers and Algebraic Expressions**
Integers include positive numbers, negative numbers, and zero. The number line is an important mathematical tool that uses integers. An algebraic expression involves integers, operation signs, and variables that stand for unknown numbers.

Lesson 19: **Equations**
An equation is a mathematical statement that two quantities are equal. When an equation uses a variable to stand for an unknown number or quantity, we can solve the equation for the unknown.

Lesson 20: **Exponents and Roots**
Exponents, also called powers, are used to represent repeated multiplication. The most commonly used exponents are used to "square" and "cube" numbers. A root is a number that when multiplied by itself a specified number of times gives a certain result. The most common type of root is a "square root." The square root is the base number of a squared number.

Lesson 21: **Factoring and Inequalities**
Factors are numbers and letters that are multiplied together. We may need to factor an expression to determine the numbers, terms, and variables that make up the expression. While an equation is a statement that two equations are equal, an inequality is a statement that two expressions are not equal.

Lesson 22: **The Coordinate Plane**
A coordinate plane is a type of graph that is formed from two lines that cross at a point. We can find points, graph equations, and find distances on the coordinate graph.

PROBLEM-SOLVING STRATEGIES

- Using Number Lines
- Translating Problems into Equations
- Using Distance and Cost Formulas
- Working Backwards
- Applying Patterns and Functions
- Solving Quadratic Equations
- Plotting Ordered Pairs
- Finding the Equation of a Line

Lesson 18 GED SKILL Integers and Algebraic Expressions

Understanding Integers

Integers, also called **signed numbers,** are positive whole numbers, their negatives, and zero. To show the complete set of numbers called integers, we extend the positive number line that we used earlier to the left of zero (0) to include negative numbers.

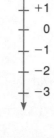

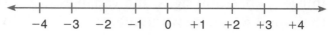

Positive numbers show an increase, a gain, or an upward movement (on a vertical number line). A positive number can be written with or without a plus sign. **Negative numbers** show the opposite: a decrease, a loss, or a downward movement. A negative number is always written with a minus sign. Note that the number zero is neither positive nor negative.

Adding and Subtracting Integers

TIP

The order of operations is always the same. But you must also apply the rules for signed numbers as you perform each operation.

We can show the addition of integers on a **number line.** Move to the right for positive numbers and to the left for negative numbers.

Example 1 Add: $(+6) + (-4)$.

Step 1 Start at 0 and move 6 units to the right.

Step 2 Start at $+6$; move 4 units left.

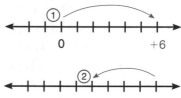

The number line shows $(+6) + (-4) = $ **+2.**

Use these rules to add integers:

RULE 1 If the integers have like signs, add the numbers and keep the same sign.

$(+3) + (+5) = +8$
$(-2) + (-6) = -8$

RULE 2 If the integers have unlike signs, find the difference between the numbers without the signs (the absolute values) and give the answer the sign of the larger number.

$(-9) + (+3) = $?
$9 - 3 = $ 6
9 is negative
$(-9) + (+3) = -6$

Since the larger number (-9) is negative, the answer is negative, **−6.**

To add more than two integers find the sum of the positive numbers and the sum of the negative numbers. Then use Rule 2 to find the total.

Example 2 $(+30) + (-8) + (-15) + (+3) + (-20) = ?$

Step 1 Add the positive numbers. Add the negative numbers. (Rule 1)

$(+30) + (+3) = +33$
$(-8) + (-15) + (-20) = -43$

Step 2 Add the unlike sums. (Rule 2)

$(+33) + (-43) = $ **−10**

Subtracting signed integers requires additional steps: **(1)** first rewrite the subtraction operation as addition, **(2)** then change the sign of the number to be subtracted, **(3)** add as usual.

Example 3   Subtract: $(+5) - (-2)$

Step 1   Change subtraction to addition.

$(+5) - (-2) = (+5) + (\ \ )$

Step 2   Change the sign of the number being subtracted.

$(+5) - (-2) = (+5) + (+2)$

Step 3   Add.

$(+5) + (+2) = +7$

The answer to $(+5) - (-2)$ is **+7.**

To subtract integers on a calculator, enter the expression without rewriting it as an addition problem. To enter negative numbers on a calculator, simply enter the number first, then press [+/−] to change the sign of the number to negative. **5** [−] **2** [+/−] **= 7.**

GED SKILL FOCUS

A. Solve. You may use your calculator for questions 11 through 15.

1. $(+7) + (+5)$

2. $(-10) + (-6)$

3. $(-6) + (+5)$

4. $(+10) - (+7)$

5. $(-3) - (+7)$

6. $(-1) - (+5)$

7. $(+6) + (-8)$

8. $(+15) - (-5)$

9. $(+10) + (-24)$

10. $(-12) - (-60)$

11. $(-118) - (-628)$

12. $(+315) - (+456)$

13. $(-1028) + (+598)$

14. $(-1482) + (-59)$

15. $(+824) + (-155)$

B. Solve each problem. You may use a calculator.

16. $(+7) + (-5) + (-4) + (+9)$

17. $(-6) - (+9) + (+10) - (+1)$

18. $(-5) - (-4) - (-8)$

19. $(+13) - (+34) + (-12)$

20. $(-12) + (-38) + (+75) - (+52)$

C. Write an expression using signed numbers. Then find the value of the expression.

21. At its lowest point, a desert is 250 feet below sea level. At its highest point, its elevation is 1000 feet above sea level. What is the difference in height between the highest and lowest points? (*Hint:* Think of sea level as 0 feet.)

22. Nita had $318 in her checking account on Monday. On Tuesday, she withdrew $60. On Wednesday, she deposited $289 and wrote a check for $50. What was her balance after writing the check?

Answers start on page 413.

Multiplying and Dividing Integers

TIP

To subtract, multiply, or divide signed numbers, two negatives become a positive:

$(+5) - (-2) = 5 + 2$

$(4)(-3)(-2) =$

$(4)(6) = 24$

$\frac{-9}{-3} = \frac{9}{3} = 3$

Multiply and divide integers as you would whole numbers. Then use the rule below to determine whether the answer is negative or positive.

Multiplication/Division Rule
If the signs are the same, the answer is positive.
If the signs are different, the answer is negative.

Examples

$(3)(5) = +15$ $-3(5) = -15$ $3(-5) = -15$ $(-3)(-5) = 15$

$\frac{24}{6} = 4$ $\frac{-24}{6} = -4$ $\frac{24}{-6} = -4$ $\frac{-24}{-6} = 4$

Applying the Order of Operations

When an algebraic expression contains several operations, you must follow the order of operations. Use parentheses to change the order in which operations are performed.

TIP

Parentheses serve two purposes: as a grouping symbol and to indicate multiplication: in $(+5) - (-2)$ and $(+5) - (6 - 2)$ parentheses mean grouping; in $(4)(-3)(-2)$ or $4(-3)(-2)$ they mean both grouping and multiplication.

Order of Operations	
Step 1	Perform all work inside grouping symbols such as parentheses or brackets: multiply and divide first; then add and subtract. The fraction bar is also a grouping symbol.
Step 2	Find the values of powers (exponents) and roots. (See Lesson 20.)
Step 3	Multiply and divide, working from left to right.
Step 4	Add and subtract, working from left to right.

Example 1 $3^2 + (-4)(2) - (4 + 6 \times 3)$

Step 1   Begin with the operations grouped $3^2 + (-4)(2) - (4 + 6 \times 3)$
in parentheses. Multiply. (6×3) $3^2 + (-4)(2) - (4 + \mathbf{18})$
Then add. $(4 + 18)$ $3^2 + (-4)(2) - \mathbf{22}$

Step 2   Find the value of the power. (3×3) $\mathbf{9} + (-4)(2) - \quad 22$

Step 3   Perform the remaining operations
in order: multiply, then add and $9 + \quad (-8) - \quad 22$
subtract from left to right. Apply $\mathbf{1} \qquad - (+22)$
the rules for signed numbers. $1 \qquad + (-22) = -21$

The answer is **−21.**

The division bar groups the top numbers and the bottom numbers as if they were in parentheses. Apply the order of operations to the numerator and denominator separately. Then do the final division.

Example 2 $\frac{3 + 5}{2 - 4}$

$\frac{3 + 5}{2 - 4} = \frac{8}{-2} = -4$

This is the same as $(3 + 5) \div (2 - 4) = 8 \div -2 = -4$.
Since the signs are different, the answer is **−4.**

Use the parentheses keys on your calculator to group certain operations. You know that the addition and subtraction operations must be performed first in Example 2, so use the parentheses keys to group these operations.

(3 + 5) ÷ (2 − 4) = −4.

Performing this calculation on a scientific calculator without using parentheses results in an incorrect answer. Without the parentheses, the calculator does the division operation first.
$3 + 5 ÷ 2 − 4 = 1.5$

GED SKILL FOCUS

A. Multiply or divide.

1. $(−2)(+3)$
2. $(−4)(−7)$
3. $(+6)(−5)$
4. $(+12)(+3)$

5. $(−6)(−1)(+2)$
6. $(+9)(−2)(−3)$
7. $(−64) ÷ (+4)$
8. $(+15) ÷ (−3)$

9. $(+20) ÷ (+5)$
10. $(−36) ÷ (−12)$
11. $\dfrac{−132}{11}$
12. $\dfrac{−4}{−1}$

B. Solve. You may use your calculator.

13. $(12)(−4)(−2)$
14. $\dfrac{54}{−27}$
15. $(2)(−112)$

16. $\dfrac{−1000}{−8}$
17. $(−8)(−9)(−1)$
18. $\dfrac{126}{−9}$

19. $(7)(350)(−5)(−2)$
20. $\dfrac{−42}{−21}$

C. Solve each expression.

21. $6 + 8 × 2^2$
22. $\dfrac{−2 − (+8)}{(6) ÷ (−6)}$
23. $(−9 × 4) − (−3 × 2)$
24. $10 + (−3 + 4 × (−2))$

25. $(−25) − 4 × 3^2$
26. $6 − (4 × 8 + (−1))$
27. $\dfrac{(−4) + (−6)}{(+4) − (−1)}$
28. $(−2 × 5)^2 + (−3 × 6)$

29. $\dfrac{−2 − 19}{−3 + −4}$
30. $2^2 + \dfrac{−25}{−4 + 9}$
31. $(2)(−7) − (3)(−4)$

TIP To use any calculator, break an expression into parts, work each part, and write down the result from each operation; then perform the final operations.

Answers start on page 413.

Variables and Algebraic Expressions

An **algebraic expression** is a group of numbers, operation signs, and variables.

Examples $2x + 3$ $4x + \frac{1}{3}$ $3x - 4$ $3(6x)$

Expressions like these are formed by translating number relationships into symbols. Analyze the following expressions carefully.

In words	In symbols
4 times a number	$4x$
6 more than a number	$x + 6$
2 less than a number	$x - 2$
one-half a number is then increased by 7	$\frac{1}{2}x + 7$ or $\frac{x}{2} + 7$
the product of 6 and a number	$6x$
the quotient of x and 5	$\frac{x}{5}$ or $x \div 5$
a number times itself or a number squared	x^2
the product of x and 8 added to the sum of 2 and x	$8x + (2 + x)$

An algebraic expression always contains **variables.** Variables are letters that are used to represent numbers. Whenever the value of x changes, the expression also changes in value.

This table shows how the value of the expression $2x + 1$ changes as the value of x changes.

x	$2x + 1$
3	$2(3) + 1 = $ **7**
0	$2(0) + 1 = $ **1**
−2	$2(-2) + 1 = $ **−3**
−4	$2(-4) + 1 = $ **−7**

An algebraic expression has a value only when all the variables are replaced by numbers. Finding the value of an expression when the variables are known is called **evaluating an expression.**

Example   Find the value of $x^2 - 3y$, when $x = -4$ and $y = 2$.

Step 1   Substitute the given values for the variables.

$x^2 - 3y$
$(-4)^2 - 3(2)$

Step 2   Follow the order of operations.
Raise −4 to the second power. $16 - 3(2)$
Multiply. $16 - \ \ 6$
Subtract. 10

After substituting the values for the variables in Step 1, you can use your calculator to find the value of the expression.

4 [+/−] [x^y] 2 [−] [(] 3 [×] 2 [)] [=] 10.

Note: The GED calculator does not require the [(] [)] keys.
The value of the expression is **10,** when $x = -4$ and $y = 2$.

A. Translate the following into algebraic expressions. Use the variable *x* to represent the unknown number in each expression unless otherwise noted.

1. the difference between a number and 2

2. twice a number, increased by 4

3. 9 less than three times a number

4. five times the sum of a number and -3

5. the product of a number and 11

6. 10 less than the product of 4 and a number

7. the quotient of a number and 3

8. 5 minus twice a number

9. twice a number increased by the product of 3 and 8

10. the quotient of 3 minus a number and 6

11. 8 minus the sum of 15 and a number

12. 5 divided by the product of *x* and *y*

13. the product of 3 and *x* divided by the sum of *x* and *y*

14. *x* multiplied by itself, then increased by the product of 12 and *y*

15. the product of 2 and the difference of *x* and *y*

B. Evaluate these expressions as directed.

16. What is the value of $3(x - 6) + 2y$
    a. when $x = -7$ and $y = 10$?
    b. when $x = 5$ and $y = -2$?
    c. when $x = 0$ and $y = 6$?
    d. when $x = 3$ and $y = 3$?

17. What is the value of $x^2 - y^2$
    a. when $x = 0$ and $y = 2$?
    b. when $x = -2$ and $y = 1$?
    c. when $x = 5$ and $y = -5$?
    d. when $x = -1$ and $y = -2$?

18. What is the value of $\frac{(x + 5)^2}{x - 5}$
    a. when $x = 0$?
    b. when $x = 1$?
    c. when $x = 3$?
    d. when $x = 4$?

19. What is the value of $8x + \frac{-2y}{-1}$
    a. when $x = 4$ and $y = 2$?
    b. when $x = 9$ and $y = -4$?
    c. when $x = -1$ and $y = 0$?
    d. when $x = 5$ and $y = -5$?

20. What is the value of $\frac{(6 + x)^2}{y}$
    a. when $x = 4$ and $y = -1$?
    b. when $x = 0$ and $y = 6$?
    c. when $x = 0$ and $y = -6$?
    d. when $x = 2$ and $y = 2$?

21. What is the value of $x^2 + 2x - 6$
    a. when $x = -3$?
    b. when $x = 2$?
    c. when $x = 4$?
    d. when $x = 8$?

22. What is the value of $-3y(y^2 + 2)$
    a. when $y = 2$?
    b. when $y = 10$?
    c. when $y = -9$?
    d. when $y = 0$?

23. What is the value of $\frac{2(x^2 + y)}{z}$
    a. when $x = 4$, $y = -2$, and $z = 7$?
    b. when $x = 3$, $y = 0$, and $z = 6$?
    c. when $x = -1$, $y = -9$, and $z = -1$?
    d. when $x = -5$, $y = -5$, and $z = -5$?

Answers start on page 414.

Simplifying Expressions

A number next to a letter means multiplication; all these mean "2 multiplied by y":
2y 2 × y
2 • y 2(y)

Simplifying an expression means combining like terms. A **term** is a number or the combination of a number and one or more variables or a variable raised to a power. The **factors** of a number are the values that, when multiplied together, result in that number.

Examples	5	x	$2x$	xy	$4x^2$
Factors	5 and 1	1 and x	2 and x	x and y	4 and x^2

In an algebraic expression, a positive or negative sign is part of the term that follows it: the term "owns" the sign that comes before it. An addition sign is understood in front of the negative sign.

Example   The expression $\underbrace{3x^2}\ \underbrace{-7x}\ \underbrace{+14}$ has three terms.

This expression can also be written as $3x^2 + (-7x) + (+14)$.

Like terms have the same variable or variables raised to the same power. Study these examples to identify like terms.

Examples $4x$ and $9x$ are like terms. Both terms contain x.
$7xy$ and $8xy$ are like terms. Both terms contain xy.
4 and $6y$ are <u>not</u> like terms. An integer and y are different.
$3x$ and $3y$ are <u>not</u> like terms. Variables x and y are different.
$5y^2$ and $6y$ are <u>not</u> like terms. The powers are different.

We combine like terms in an expression so that there is only one term containing that variable. Simplified expressions are easier to evaluate.

Example 1   Simplify $4x + 6y - 3x - 4y$.

It may be helpful to rewrite an expression grouping like terms next to each other. Remember: keep the sign that precedes each term with that term and add an addition sign.

Step 1   Group the like terms. Group the x terms and group the y terms. (The sign travels with the term.)

Step 2   Combine like terms.

$$4x + 6y - 3x - 4y =$$
$$4x + 6y + -3x + -4y =$$
$$(4x + -3x) + (6y + -4y) =$$
$$(4x - 3x) + (6y - 4y) =$$
$$x\quad +\quad 2y$$

In simplified form, $4x + 6y - 3x - 4y$ is equal to $x + 2y.$

The order of operations says to perform operations in parentheses first. However, in algebraic expressions parentheses often contain unlike terms that cannot be combined. To simplify an expression that contains parentheses, use the **distributive property** to remove the parentheses.

Distributive Property   To multiply a factor by a sum of terms, multiply the factor by each term in parentheses. Then combine the products. $5(x + y) = 5x + 5y$

Example 2   Simplify $2x(3x - 6) + 5x$.

Step 1   To remove parentheses multiply each term in the parentheses by the factor.

Step 2   Combine like terms.

$$2x(3x + -6)\qquad + 5x$$
$$2x(3x) + 2x(-6) + 5x$$

$$6x^2 -\quad 12x\ + 5x$$
$$6x^2 -\qquad 7x$$

$2x(3x - 6) + 5x$ is equal to $6x^2 - 7x.$

A. Simplify each expression.

1. $7x - 8y + 9x$

2. $5y^2 - 4y - 2y^2$

3. $4m - 9n - 3 + 6n$

4. $-5x + 16 - 8x - 14 + 10x$

5. $9x - 6 + 8x^2 + 13$

6. $25 - 3n + 16n$

7. $12(x + 3y)$

8. $5x(-y + 9)$

9. $4(2x + y) - 3(x - 5)$

10. $15 + 6(x - 4) + 8x$

11. $3m + 2(m - n) - 5(m + n)$

12. $x - 2(xy - y) + 4xy - x(3 + y)$

B. Simplify. Then evaluate each expression as directed.

13. Find the value of $3x + 5(x + 9) - 4x$, when $x = -5$.

14. Find the value of $2m - 3(m + 5) - 15$, when $m = 10$.

15. Find the value of $xy + 4x(1 - y) + 2x$, when $x = -1$ and $y = 5$.

16. Find the value of $3y(2xz + 2) - 6xyz$, when $x = -4$, $y = -3$, and $z = 7$.

17. Find the value of $4(2x - y) - 3x + 2y$, when $x = 0$ and $y = -2$.

18. Find the value of $9a - 8b(2 + a) + 16b$, when $a = -4$ and $b = -1$.

C. Choose the best answer to each question.

19. The expression $4(x + 2y) - (x + y)$ is equal to which of the following expressions?

    (1) $3x + y$

    (2) $3x + 3y$

    (3) $3x + 5y$

    (4) $3x + 7y$

    (5) $3x + 9y$

20. The expression $8n - 2(n^2 + n) + 12$ is equal to which of the following expressions?

    (1) $2n + 12$

    (2) $4n + 12$

    (3) $2n^2 + 10n + 12$

    (4) $-2n^2 + 6n + 12$

    (5) $-2n^2 + 6n + 24$

21. Which of the following expressions is equal to the expression $-m(2m + 2n) + 3mn + 2m^2$?

    (1) mn

    (2) $5mn$

    (3) $-4m^2 + mn$

    (4) $4m^2 + mn$

    (5) $4m^2 + 5mn$

22. The expression $3(-4b) - 2(a - b - c)$ is equal to which of the following expressions?

    (1) $-2a - 10b - 2c$

    (2) $2a - 10b + 2c$

    (3) $-2a - 5b + 2c$

    (4) $-2a - 4b - 2c$

    (5) $2a - 4b - 2c$

Answers start on page 415.

GED STRATEGY **Solving Word Problems**

Using Number Lines

As you have seen, number lines are useful for showing addition and subtraction operations. On the GED Mathematics Test, drawing a number line can help you solve problems that describe several increases and decreases.

Example 1 An office building has 3 floors below and 8 floors above ground level. After entering the building on the ground level, a delivery person takes the elevator to four locations, where she makes deliveries at each stop. She travels 3 floors up, 5 floors down, 9 floors up, and 6 floors down. Where does she make the final delivery?

(1) 2 floors below ground level
(2) 1 floor below ground level
(3) ground level
(4) 1 floor above ground level
(5) 2 floors above ground level

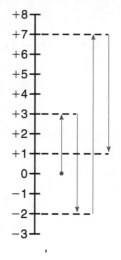

You may have realized that ground level can be represented by the integer 0. The floors above ground level can be assigned positive numbers, and the floors below ground level can be represented by negative numbers.

One way to solve the problem is to draw a vertical number line that shows the integers from -3 to $+8$. Then start at 0 (ground level) and count out each change described in the problem. Count up 3, down 5, up 9, and down 6.

You finish counting at $+1$, so the correct answer is **option (4) 1 floor above ground level.**

Note: You can also solve this problem by writing and evaluating an algebraic expression: $+3 - 5 + 9 - 6 =$, which can be written as follows: $(+3) + (-5) + (+9) + (-6)$
To solve: $(+3) + (+9) + (-5) + (-6)$
 $+12$ $+$ -11 $= +1$

Example 2 On a number line, a certain number x is 5 units greater than the number found halfway between -5 and -1. What is the value of x?

(1) -8
(2) -3
(3) 0
(4) 2
(5) 5

Remember, subtracting a positive number is the same as adding a negative number. For example,
$-3 - 5 = -3 + (-5)$ $\qquad\qquad -4 - 2 = -4 + (-2)$

Since you are not given a diagram, quickly sketch a number line, find the point halfway between −5 and −1, and count 5 spaces to the right.

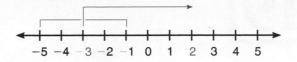
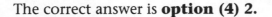

The correct answer is **option (4) 2.**

GED PRACTICE

Directions: Choose the <u>one best answer</u> for each question.

1. In a card game, Rita loses 1 point, gains 5 points, and loses 8 points. Jerry has 6 points. What is the difference in their scores?

   (1)   4
   (2)   6
   (3)   8
   (4) 10
   (5) 12

2. On a number line, Max places a mark 3 units to the left of the point halfway between 1 and −3. On what point is Max's mark?

   (1)   2
   (2)   0
   (3) −1
   (4) −3
   (5) −4

3. At 10 A.M., it is 5°F below zero. By 11 A.M., the temperature rises 6°F. If it drops 3°F by 1 P.M., what is the temperature at 1 P.M.?

   (1) −4°F
   (2) −2°F
   (3)   0°F
   (4)   2°F
   (5) 14°F

Question 4 refers to the following information.

Aaron's Dice Rolls

Round	Red Die	Green Die
3	4	6
4	2	1
5	6	4

4. In a dice game, each player rolls two dice, one red and one green. The number on the red die is added to the player's score from the previous round. The number on the green die is subtracted from the player's score. If Aaron had +4 points after the first two rounds, how many points does he have after five rounds?

   (1) −5
   (2) −3
   (3)   1
   (4)   3
   (5)   5

5. On a number line, −2 is located halfway between which of the following points?

   (1) −3 and 0
   (2) −4 and 1
   (3) −4 and −1
   (4) −4 and 0
   (5) −5 and 0

Answers start on page 416.

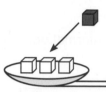

Lesson 19 GED SKILL Equations

Solving One-Step Equations

An **equation** is a mathematical statement that shows that two quantities are equal. When an equation contains a variable, we use algebra to find the value of the variable. To **solve** an equation means to find the number that makes the statement true.

Adding 1 to each side keeps the scale balanced.

Solve the equation.	$2x - 1 = 9$
When x equals 5,	$2(5) - 1 = 9$
the statement is true.	$10 - 1 = 9$
	$9 = 9$

To solve an equation, you must keep the two sides of the equation equal. Think of an equation as a balance scale. Whatever you do to one side of the scale, you must also do to the other side to keep the scale balanced.

The basic strategy in solving an equation is to **isolate the variable,** that is, get the variable alone on one side of the equation by performing **inverse,** or opposite, operations to both sides of the equation.

Remember: • Addition and subtraction are inverse operations.
• Multiplication and division are inverse operations.

Example 1 Solve: $x - 13 = 25$.

Step 1	**Think about the meaning** of the equation, the operation, and its inverse: here, the operation is subtraction; the inverse operation is addition.	$x - 13 = 25$
Step 2	**Perform the inverse operation to both sides of the equation** to isolate the variable and keep the equation balanced. Here, add 13 to both sides.	$x - 13 + 13 = 25 + 13$ $x \qquad = \quad 38$
Step 3	**Check.** Substitute your solution, 38, into the original equation for the variable x.	$38 - 13 = 25$ $25 = 25$

The value **38** makes the equation true.

Example 2 Solve: $5x = -35$.

Step 1	The operation is multiplication; the inverse of multiplication is division.	$5x = -35$
Step 2	Divide both sides by 5.	$\dfrac{5x}{5} = \dfrac{-35}{5}$
Step 3	Substitute and check.	$x = -7$ $5(-7) = -35$

The value **7** makes the equation true.

$-35 = -35$

TIP

You may be able to solve simple equations using mental math. However, writing out each step will improve your understanding of algebra and make it easier to check your work.

Study these examples to see how subtraction and multiplication can be used as inverse operations to solve equations.

Examples

Subtract 40	$x + 40 = 75$	$\frac{x}{9} = 4$	Multiply both
from both	$x + 40 - 40 = 75 - 40$		sides by 9.
sides.	$x - 35$	$_1\frac{x}{\cancel{9}} \times \cancel{9} = 4(9)$	
		$x = 36$	

(Note that cancellation applies only to the left side of the equation.)

Check. $\quad 35 + 40 = 75 \qquad\qquad \frac{36}{9} = 4$

GED SKILL FOCUS

A. Solve. Do not use a calculator.

1. $x \quad 15 - 4$

2. $x - 7 = 3$

3. $\frac{x}{2} = 12$

4. $-6x = -42$

5. $x + 9 = 22$

6. $12x = 60$

7. $x - 8 = -10$

8. $\frac{x}{-3} = 18$

9. $5x = -45$

10. $9 + x = -18$

11. $-11x = -132$

12. $\frac{7}{x} = 63$

B. Solve. You may use a calculator for these items.

13. $x - 94 = 52$

14. $6.5 + x = 12.25$

15. $0.25x = 12$

16. $200x = 25$

17. $-69 + x = 124$

18. $-3.6x = -17.28$

19. $0.38 + x = 2.5$

20. $6x = 3.3$

C. Translate each question into an algebraic equation and solve.

21. -13 added to what number equals 20?
(*Hint:* $-13 + x = 20$)

22. What number multiplied by 10 equals 900?

23. What number divided by 4 equals 60?

24. 5 subtracted from what number equals -14?

25. What number divided by 4 is 32?

26. What number multiplied by -6 equals 48?

27. 52 added to what number equals 100?

28. 4 subtracted from what number equals -17?

Answers start on page 417.

Solving Multi-Step Equations

Some equations involve more than one operation. Remember: your goal is to isolate the variable on one side of the equation. Also, when solving multi-step equations, use the reverse order of operations.

Example 1 $5x - 10 = 35$

Step 1   Perform the inverse operations for addition and subtraction first. Add 10 to both sides.

$$5x - 10 + 10 = 35 + 10$$
$$5x = 45$$

Step 2   Perform the inverse operations for multiplication and division second. Divide both sides by 5.

$$\frac{5x}{5} = \frac{45}{5}$$
$$x = 9$$

Step 3   Check. Substitute the value for x.

$$5(9) - 10 = 35$$
$$45 - 10 = 35$$
$$35 = 35$$

The solution is **$x = 9$.**

Some equations may have variable terms on both sides. If so, you need to group all of the variable terms on one side of the equation.

Example 2 $12x + 9 = 10x + 1$

Step 1   Group the variable. Subtract $10x$ from both sides.

$$12x - 10x + 9 = 10x - 10x + 1$$
$$2x + 9 = 1$$

Step 2   Subtract 9 from both sides.

$$2x + 9 - 9 = 1 - 9$$
$$2x = -8$$

Step 3   Divide both sides by 2.

$$\frac{2x}{2} = \frac{-8}{2}$$
$$x = -4$$

Step 4   Check.

$$12(-4) + 9 = 10(-4) + 1$$
$$-48 + 9 = -40 + 1$$
$$-39 = -39$$

The solution is **$x = -4$.**

Some equations contain parentheses. Remove the parentheses by multiplying each term within the parentheses by the factor.

Example 3 $3(x + 1) = -12$

Step 1   Multiply both terms inside the parentheses by 3.

$$3(x + 1) = -12$$
$$3x + 3 = -12$$

Step 2   Subtract 3 from both sides.

$$3x + 3 - 3 = -12 - 3$$
$$3x = -15$$

Step 3   Divide both sides by 3.

$$\frac{3x}{3} = \frac{-15}{3}$$
$$x = -5$$

Step 4   Check.

$$3(-5 + 1) = -12$$
$$(-15 + 3) = -12$$
$$-12 = -12$$

The solution is **$x = -5$.**

TIP

There is often more than one way to solve equations, such as first adding or subtracting the integer and then the variable. But, you must always follow the basic rules for solving equations: always add or subtract first; then multiply or divide.

The first step in solving some equations is to **combine like terms.** Always simplify each side of the equation before solving.

Example 4 $2x + 5 - 3x = 8 + 2$

Step 1   **Simplify by combining like terms.** $2x + 5 - 3x = 8 + 2$
$2x - 3x = -x$; $8 + 2 = 10$ $-x + 5 = 10$

Step 2   **Isolate the variable.** Here, subtract 5 $-x + 5 - 5 = 10 - 5$
from each side. $-x = 5$

Step 3   **Solve for x.** Multiply each side by -1 $-x(-1) = 5(-1)$
so that you solve for x, not $-x$. $x = -5$

Step 4   **Check.** $2(-5) + 5 - 3(-5) = 8 + 2$
$-10 + 5 - (-15) = 10$
$-10 + 5 + 15 = 10$
$10 = 10$

The solution is **−5.**

GED SKILL FOCUS

Solve each equation.

1. $6x + 7 = 37$

2. $4x + 5x - 10 = 35$

3. $3x - 6x + 2 = -4x$

4. $6 - x + 12 = 10x + 7$

5. $5x + 7 - 4x = 6$

6. $9x + 6x - 12x = -7x + 2x - 12 + 5x$

7. $7x + 3 = 31$

8. $3x - 8 = 28$

9. $8x + 6 = 5x + 9$

10. $11x - 10 = 8x + 5$

11. $-2x - 4 = 4x - 10$

12. $5x + 8 = x - 8$

13. $11x - 12 = 9x + 2$

14. $5(x + 1) = 75$

15. $5(x - 7) = 5$

16. $6(2 + x) = 5x + 15$

17. $4x + 5 = 21$

18. $2x - 5x + 11 = 38$

19. $3x - 8 = x + 4$

20. $7(x - 2) = 21$

21. $5x - 13x + 2x = -70 + x$

22. $8x + 12 = 44 + 4x$

23. $2(x + 4) = 14 + x$

24. $5x + 3 = 8(x - 3)$

25. $2(x + 2x) - 6 = 30$

26. $11x + 12 = 9x - 32$

27. $3(x - 9) - 2 = -35$

28. $3(4x + 3) = -9(-x + 2)$

29. $x + 11 + 3x = 20 + 7x$

30. $4(2x + 5) + 4 = 3(5x - 6)$

Answers start on page 418.

GED STRATEGY Solving Word Problems

Translating Problems into Equations

To solve word problems translate the information in the problem into algebraic symbols and write an algebraic equation relating the information. Read the problem carefully to figure out which quantities or numbers are unknown. Label all other quantities in terms of one unknown amount.

TIP

As a general rule, let x equal the quantity you know the least about; this is usually the amount to which the other amount is compared or related.

Example 1 During lunch one day, a cafe sold 8 more turkey sandwiches than ham sandwiches. If there were 32 sandwiches sold in all, how many were ham sandwiches?

Step 1 **Identify the unknown amount(s); assign the variable.** There are 2 unknown amounts: the number of ham sandwiches and the number of turkey sandwiches. Pick one to be the unknown x. Here, let x = the number of ham sandwiches.

Step 2 **Label the other quantities in terms of x.** Since there were 8 more turkey sandwiches than ham, let $x + 8$ equal the number of turkey sandwiches. If you had let x = the number of turkey sandwiches, then the number of ham sandwiches would be $x - 8$.

Step 3 **Write an equation.** You know 32 sandwiches in all were sold. Thus, the sum of the number of turkey sandwiches ($x + 8$) and the number of ham sandwiches (x) is 32: $(x + 8) + x = 32$.

The equation $(x + 8) + x = 32$ can be used to solve the problem.

Some algebra items on the GED Mathematics Test are set-up problems. Instead of solving the equation, you choose a correct method to solve the problem. To work with these items, analyze the situation and write an equation. Then compare your equation to the answer choices.

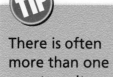

TIP

There is often more than one way to write an equation: $x + (x + 8) = 32$ and $2x + 8 = 32$ are the same as $(x + 8) + x = 32$.

Example 2 Rae's weekly income is $250 less than twice her husband's. Together they earn $890 per week. Which equation could be used to find her husband's weekly earnings (x)?

    (1) $(2x + 250) + x = 890$
    (2) $(2x - 250) + x = 890$
    (3) $(2x + 250) - x = 890$
    (4) $(2x - 250) - x = 890$
    (5) $2x + 2x - 250 = 890$

Step 1 The problem tells you to let x equal the husband's earnings.
    Let x = husband's earnings

Step 2 Rae's income is $250 less than twice x, or $2x - 250$.
    Let $2x - 250$ = Rae's earnings

Step 3 The sum of their incomes is $890.
    $x + 2x - 250 = 890$

Step 4 Since none of the choices match, rearrange your equation and compare again.
    $x + 2x - 250 = 890$ is the same as $(2x - 250) + x = 890$

Option (2) $(2x - 250) + x = 890$ is correct.

Directions: Choose the <u>one best answer</u> to each question.

1. Birnham Mills has 360 employees. The number of production employees is twelve more than three times the number of employees who work in management. Which equation could be used to find the number of management employees?

    (1) $3x + 12 = 360$

    (2) $4x = 360$

    (3) $3x - 12 + x = 360$

    (4) $(3x + 12) - x = 360$

    (5) $x + (3x + 12) = 360$

2. At a gym Frank did a certain number of pushups. Tom did 12 more than Frank. The total number both men did was 66. Which equation could be used to find the number of pushups Frank did?

    (1) $x(x + 12) = 66$

    (2) $x + 12x = 66$

    (3) $2x + 12 = 66$

    (4) $2x = 66 + 12$

    (5) $x + 12 = 66 + x$

3. Eva got two parking tickets. The fine for the second ticket was $4 less than twice the fine for the first ticket. If the fines total $65, which equation could be used to find the amount of the first fine?

    (1) $3x = 65 - 4$

    (2) $2(x - 4) = 65$

    (3) $x(x - 4) = 65$

    (4) $x + (2x - 4) = 65$

    (5) $2(2x - 4) = 65$

4. Eight times a number, divided by 4, equals two times that number. Which of the following equations could be used to find the number?

    (1) $\frac{8y}{4} = 2y$

    (2) $8\left(\frac{4}{y}\right) = 2y$

    (3) $\frac{8}{4y} = 2y$

    (4) $8y(4) = 2$

    (5) $\frac{8y}{4y} = 2y$

5. The number of girls signed up for a sports program is 12 fewer than twice the number of boys (x). If 60 children are signed up for the program, which of the following equations could be used to find the number of boys?

    (1) $2x - 12 = 60$

    (2) $2(x + x - 12) - 60$

    (3) $x + 2x = 60 - 12$

    (4) $x + 2(x - 12) = 60$

    (5) $3x = 60 + 12$

6. An adult ticket is twice the cost of a child's ticket. Angela paid $28 for two adult tickets and three children's tickets. Which of the following equations could be used to find the price of a child's ticket?

    (1) $x + 2x = 28$

    (2) $3x + 2(2x) = 28$

    (3) $2(x + 2x) = 28$

    (4) $3(2x) + 2x = 28$

    (5) $3x + 2x = 28$

Answers start on page 419.

Solving Algebraic Equations

Algebra word problems describe the relationship among the numbers in a situation. To solve an algebra problem, translate the information into algebraic symbols, write and solve an equation, and check your answer.

Example 1   The total of three **consecutive numbers** is 189. What is the greatest of the three numbers?

Step 1   **Identify the unknown amounts; assign x.** Let x represent the smallest number.

Step 2   **Label the other quantities in terms of x.** If x is the smallest number, the next two numbers are $x + 1$ and $x + 2$.

Step 3   **Write an equation.** The sum of the three numbers is 189.

$$x + (x + 1) + (x + 2) = 189$$
$$x + x + 1 + x + 2 = 189$$

Step 4   **Combine like terms and solve for x.**

$$x + x + x + 1 + 2 = 189$$
$$3x + 3 = 189$$
$$3x = 186$$
$$x = 62$$

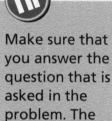

TIP

Make sure that you answer the question that is asked in the problem. The value of x may not be the answer to the question.

Step 5   **Solve the problem.** The value of x represents the smallest of three consecutive numbers: the three numbers are 62, 63, and 64.

Step 6   **Check your answer.** Read the problem again to make sure your answer is reasonable. Since $62 + 63 + 64 = 189$, the answer makes sense.

The correct answer is **64**.

In some problems, a chart is useful to clarify the information and show relationships between and among the quantities.

Example 2   Ralph is three times as old as his daughter Ella. In ten years, he will be only two times as old as Ella. How old is he now?

There are four unknowns: two present ages and two future ages.

	Ella's Age	Ralph's Age
Now	A: x	B: $3x$
In 10 years	C: $x + 10$	D: $3x + 10$

A: Let x equal Ella's age now.
B: Ralph is 3 times as old as Ella, so his age now is $3x$.
C: In ten years, Ella will be $x + 10$ years old.
D: In ten years, Ralph will be $3x + 10$ years old.

We know Ralph's age in ten years ($3x + 10$) will be 2 times Ella's age in 10 years ($x + 10$). Then solve for x.

$$3x + 10 = 2(x + 10)$$
$$3x + 10 = 2x + 20$$
$$3x - 2x + 10 - 10 = 2x - 2x + 20 - 10$$
$$x = 10$$

Use the chart to find the answer to the problem.
Substitute 10 for the variable x in each box.
Ella's age now is 10.
Ralph's age now is 30.

$$3x = 3(10) = 30$$
$$x + 10 = 10 + 10 = 20$$
$$3x + 10 = 3(10) + 10 = 40$$

As a check, note that in 10 years, Ella will be 20 and Ralph will be 40, twice as old as Ella.

Ralph is now **30 years old**.

Translate each statement into an algebraic equation. Then solve.

1. The sum of a number and twice that number is 15. What is the number?

2. The sum of 7 and twice a certain number is 10 more than the number. What is the number?

3. One number is 5 less than another. The sum of the two numbers is 181. Find the two numbers.

4. When the sum of 8 and a certain number is increased by 12, the result is the same as the product of 3 and the number. What is the number?

5. The sum of two consecutive numbers is 49. What is the lesser number?

6. George is 5 times as old as his son. In 15 years he will be only twice as old as his son. How old will his son be in 15 years?

7. The sum of three consecutive even numbers is 30. What is the greatest of the three even numbers? (*Hint:* Let x represent the first even number. Let $x + 2$ represent the second even number.)

8. Nora is 4 years older than Diana. Two years from now Nora will be twice as old as Diana. How old is Diana now?

9. A bank teller had 125 $10 and $5 bills to start a day. If the total value of the bills was $1000, how many $5 bills did the teller have? [*Hint:* If x equals the number of $5 bills, then $5x$ equals the value of the $5 bills. The number of $10 bills is $125 - x$, and the total value of the $10 bills is $10(125 - x)$.]

10. Twice a number divided by 4 is 16. What is the number?

11. The sum of three consecutive odd numbers is 315. What are the numbers? (*Hint:* If x represents the first odd number, the second number is $x + 2$.)

12. One number is two more than three times another. The sum of the numbers is 26. What is the lesser number?

13. Armando works part-time at a pet store. This week he earned $18 less than 4 times the amount he earned last week. His total earnings for the two weeks were $262. How much did he earn this week?

14. There are two consecutive numbers. The sum of the lesser number and three times the greater number is 103. Find the two numbers.

15. A shoe store sold 340 pairs of shoes in one day. The number of pairs of athletic shoes sold was 4 more than twice the number of pairs of dress shoes sold. How many pairs of athletic shoes were sold?

16. A school sold 200 tickets to a play. Ticket prices were $8 per adult and $5 per child. If the total sales for the tickets came to $1414, how many children's tickets were sold? (*Hint:* If x adult tickets were sold, then $200 - x$ children's tickets were sold.)

17. Erika's uncle is three times as old as she is now. Four years ago, he was four times as old as she was then. How old is Erika now?

Answers start on page 419.

GED STRATEGY Solving Word Problems

Using Distance and Cost Formulas

A **formula** is a special type of equation. A formula relates information to solve a certain kind of problem. When you take the GED Mathematics Test, you will be given a page of formulas to use in solving problems.

Two important formulas are the distance and cost formulas.

Distance   distance = rate × time or $d = rt$
Total Cost   total cost = (number of units) × (cost per unit) or $c = nr$

To use formulas, first choose the formula that shows how the facts in the problem are related. Then substitute the known quantities and solve.

Example 1   A plane travels at an average speed of 525 miles per hour for 4 hours. How many miles does it travel?

   (1)   60.0
   (2) 131.25
   (3) 240.0
   (4) 525.0
   (5) 2100.0

> **TIP**
>
> The variables in a formula use related units of measure: if the rate is in *miles per hour*, the distance will be in *miles*, and the time will be in *hours*.

Step 1   **Use** the distance formula where d = distance, r = rate (average speed), and t = time. $d = rt$

Step 2   **Substitute** the known quantities. $d = 525 \times 4$
Step 3   **Solve** for d. $d = 2100$

The plane traveled **2100 miles.**

You can solve for any variable in a formula if you know the values of the other variables. Substitute the values you know for the variables in the problem. Then use inverse operations to solve for the unknown variable.

Example 2   The total cost of a shipment of chairs is $2250. If each chair costs $75, how many chairs are in the shipment?

   (1)   30
   (2)   75
   (3)   225
   (4)   2,250
   (5) 168,750

> **TIP**
>
> You can use a formula to solve for any of its variables. Using $c = nr$, you can also find $n = \frac{c}{r}$ or $r = \frac{c}{n}$.

Step 1   Use the cost formula, where c = total cost, n = number of units, and r = cost per unit, to solve for n, the number of chairs. $c = nr$

Step 2   Substitute the known quantities. $\$2250 = n(\$75)$

Step 3   Solve for n. Divide both sides of the equation by $75. $\dfrac{\$2250}{\$75} = \dfrac{n(\$75)}{\$75}$
   $30 = n$

There are **option (1) 30 chairs** in the shipment.

Directions: Choose the one best answer to each question.

1. A hardware store purchased 6 dozen hammers for a total cost of $345.60. What was the cost of one dozen hammers?

   (1) $ 4.80
   (2) $ 9.60
   (3) $ 28.80
   (4) $ 57.60
   (5) $115.20

2. Marta bought 3 yards of fabric at $6.98 per yard and 4 yards of a different fabric for $4.50 per yard. Which of the following expressions could be used to find the amount of her purchase? (*Hint*: You would need to find the total cost of each type of fabric and then find the sum.)

   (1) 7($6.98)($4.50)
   (2) 7($6.98 + $4.50)
   (3) 3($6.98) + 4($4.50)
   (4) 4($6.98) + 3($4.50)
   (5) (3 + 4)($6.98 + $4.50)

3. Steve drove for 6 hours and traveled 312 miles. Which of the following expressions could be used to find his average speed during the trip?

   (1) 6 + 312
   (2) $\frac{312}{6}$
   (3) $\frac{6}{312}$
   (4) 6(312)
   (5) 6(6)(312)

4. A label on the grocery store shelf states that the store brand of shampoo sells for 14.5 cents per ounce. What is the cost of a 24-ounce bottle of the shampoo?

   (1) $0.60
   (2) $1.66
   (3) $3.48
   (4) $6.00
   (5) $7.65

5. Kate drove $2\frac{1}{2}$ hours at an average speed of 55 miles per hour and $1\frac{1}{2}$ hours at an average speed of 65 miles per hour. How many miles did she travel?

   (1) 260
   (2) 235
   (3) 220
   (4) $137\frac{1}{2}$
   (5) $97\frac{1}{2}$

Question 6 refers to the following information.

Bakery Goods Price List	
Party Tray	$ 9.99
Party Platter	$13.99
Half Sheet Cake	$26.99

6. Rodrigo is organizing a party for his office. He orders three party trays, two party platters, and a half sheet cake. How much will he spend for the order?

   (1) $ 29.07
   (2) $ 50.97
   (3) $ 80.94
   (4) $ 84.94
   (5) $305.82

Answers start on page 420.

GED Mini-Test • Lessons 18 and 19

Directions: This is a thirty-minute practice test. After thirty minutes, mark the last item you finished. Then complete the test and check your answers. If most of your answers are correct, but you didn't finish, try to work faster next time.

Part 1

Directions: Choose the <u>one best answer</u> to each question. You <u>MAY</u> use your calculator.

1. Which of the following expressions shows the product of 9 and x, subtracted from the quotient of 2 and x?

   (1) $\frac{2}{x} - 9x$

   (2) $-9x - \frac{2}{x}$

   (3) $2x(-9x)$

   (4) $9 - x - \frac{2}{x}$

   (5) $(2 + x) - 9x$

2. Which of the following expressions has the greatest value?

   (1) $(-2) + (-7)$

   (2) $(-6) + (+8)$

   (3) $(-3) - (-4)$

   (4) $(+4) - (+10)$

   (5) $(-8) + (+9)$

3. When 13 is subtracted from the sum of two consecutive numbers, the answer is 18. What are the two consecutive numbers?

   (1) 6 and 7

   (2) 9 and 10

   (3) 10 and 11

   (4) 15 and 16

   (5) 31 and 32

4. Ten less than a number is equal to the same number divided by 2. What is the number?

   (1) 8

   (2) 10

   (3) 14

   (4) 20

   (5) 28

5. Bill is one year less than twice as old as his sister Caroline. The total of their ages is 26. How old is Bill?

   (1) 9

   (2) 12

   (3) 17

   (4) 19

   (5) 24

6. Eunsook drives an average speed of 62 miles per hour for $4\frac{1}{2}$ hours. How many miles does she travel?

   (1) 67

   (2) 137

   (3) 248

   (4) 279

   (5) 725

7. Which expression does this number line show?

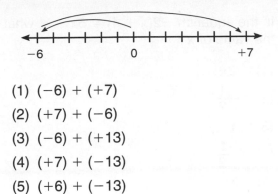

(1) $(-6) + (+7)$

(2) $(+7) + (-6)$

(3) $(-6) + (+13)$

(4) $(+7) + (-13)$

(5) $(+6) + (-13)$

8. What is the value of $-4x - \frac{3y}{2x}$, when $x = -4$ and $y = 8$?

(1) -19

(2) -13

(3) 10

(4) 13

(5) 19

9. Coop and Carni are cats. Coop is 4 months older than Carni. Three months ago, 5 times Coop's age in months was the same as 7 times Carni's age in months. Complete the chart. What is the entry for box 4?

	Coop's Age in months	Carni's Age in months
Now	1: x	2: $x - 4$
3 months ago	3:	4:

(1) $(x - 4) - 3$

(2) $5(x - 4)$

(3) $7(x - 4)$

(4) $\frac{7}{5}(x - 4)$

(5) $\frac{5}{7}(x - 4)$

10. A car travels 406 miles at an average speed of 58 miles per hour. How many hours does it take the car to travel this distance?

(1) 4

(2) 5

(3) 6

(4) 7

(5) 8

11. Brittany bought 5 plastic storage bins to help organize her closets. After adding sales tax of $2.06, the total cost of the bins was $31.51. Which of the following equations could be used to find the price of one bin (x)?

(1) $5 + x = \$31.51 - \$2.06$

(2) $5(x + \$2.06) = \$31.51$

(3) $5x = \$31.51$

(4) $5x - \$2.06 = \$31.51$

(5) $5x + \$2.06 = \$31.51$

12. The expression $-5(x - 6) - 2(x + 8)$ is equal to which of the following expressions?

(1) $7x + 14$

(2) $7x + 2$

(3) $-7x - 5$

(4) $-7x + 14$

(5) $-7x + 46$

13. In a certain game, points you win are positive numbers and points you lose are negative numbers. What is the value of this series of plays: win 8, lose 6, lose 7, win 11, lose 2?

(1) -15

(2) -4

(3) 1

(4) 12

(5) 19

Directions: Choose the <u>one best answer</u> to each question. You may <u>NOT</u> use your calculator.

14. Which of the following expressions represents the difference of 5 and -2 divided by a number multiplied by itself?

    (1) $\dfrac{5 - (-2)}{x^2}$

    (2) $\dfrac{5}{(-2) - 2x}$

    (3) $\dfrac{5 + 2}{2x}$

    (4) $\dfrac{5}{(-2) - x^2}$

    (5) $\dfrac{5 - 2}{x^2}$

15. The sum of three consecutive even numbers is 138. What is the greatest number?

    (1) 52

    (2) 50

    (3) 48

    (4) 46

    (5) 44

16. Which of the following expresses this equation?

    $$x + 4 = \dfrac{x}{5} - 6$$

    (1) Four more than x equals 6 less than the quotient of 5 and x.

    (2) The sum of 4 and x is the same as 6 less than the quotient of x and 5.

    (3) Four added to x equals the product of x and 5 decreased by 6.

    (4) The product of x and 4 is the same as x divided by the difference of 5 and 6.

    (5) Four increased by x equals the difference of x and 6 divided by 5.

17. In the equation $-2(x + 4) = 5x + 6$, what is the value of x?

    (1) -2

    (2) $-\dfrac{1}{2}$

    (3) 1

    (4) $\dfrac{1}{2}$

    (5) 2

18. Sybil is taking her Cub Scout pack to the Police Expo. Each adult ticket is $2 more than the price of a children's ticket. Sybil pays $78 to buy 12 children's tickets and 5 adult tickets. What is the price of a children's ticket?

    (1) $3.00

    (2) $3.50

    (3) $4.00

    (4) $5.00

    (5) $6.00

Question 19 refers to the following number line.

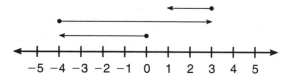

19. Which of the following expressions represents the changes shown on the number line?

    (1) $-4 + 3 + (-1)$

    (2) $-4 + 7 + (-2)$

    (3) $-4 + 7 - (-2)$

    (4) $4 + (-7) + 2$

    (5) $4 - (-7) - 2$

20. Drew and Linda each contributed to the cost of a gift for a friend. Linda spent $15 less than 4 times the amount Drew spent. If the gift cost $30, how much did Linda spend?

(1) $ 9

(2) $11

(3) $15

(4) $19

(5) $21

21. Marco is four times as old as Lindsay. In six years, he will be three times her age. How old will Marco be in six years?

(1) 54

(2) 48

(3) 24

(4) 18

(5) 12

22. Which of the following is equal to the expression $6(x + 5) - (x + 10)$?

(1) $7x + 10$

(2) $7x + 20$

(3) $5x - 4$

(4) $5x + 20$

(5) $5x + 40$

23. A store sells two brands of computer scanners. Brand B costs $40 more than twice the cost of Brand A. If Brand B costs $135 more than Brand A, what is the cost of Brand B?

(1) $ 95

(2) $125

(3) $220

(4) $230

(5) Not enough information is given.

Question 24 is based on the following diagram.

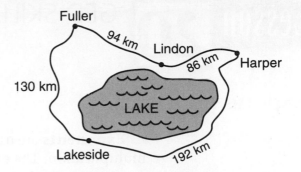

24. A trucker drives from Harper to Lakeside to Fuller and back the same way at an average speed of 88 kilometers per hour. Which of the following equations could be used to find the time (*t*) in hours the trip will take?

(1) $88t = 192 + 130$

(2) $88t = 2(192 + 130)$

(3) $88t = 192 + 130 + 94 + 86$

(4) $\dfrac{192 + 130}{2} = 88t$

(5) $\dfrac{192 + 130}{88} = 2t$

25. One number is $\frac{1}{5}$ of another number. The sum of the numbers is 78. What is the greater of the two numbers?

(1) 13

(2) 15.6

(3) 39

(4) 65

(5) 73

26. Lucia's rent is $100 less than three times her car payment. If the total of the bills is $800, how much does she pay for rent?

(1) $275

(2) $375

(3) $525

(4) $575

(5) $775

Answers start on page 421.

Exponents

Exponents are used to simplify problems that call for repeated multiplication. The expression 5^3, which is read "five to the third power" or "five cubed," has a base of 5 and an exponent of 3. The exponent tells how many times the base should appear in the multiplication problem.

Examples
$$5^3 = 5 \times 5 \times 5 = 125$$
$$12^2 = 12 \times 12 = 144$$
$$2^5 = 2 \times 2 \times 2 \times 2 \times 2 = 32$$

To raise a number to the second power, use the x^2 key.
Find the value of 13^2. **13** $\boxed{x^2}$ **169.** or **13** $\boxed{\times}$ **13** $\boxed{=}$

To raise a number to a higher power, use the x^y key.
Find the value of 5^3. **5** $\boxed{x^y}$ **4 = 125.** or **5** $\boxed{\times}$ **5** $\boxed{\times}$ **5** $\boxed{=}$

An exponent can also be 1, 0, or a negative number. Remember:

- Any number with an exponent of 1 equals itself.
- Any number (except 0) with an exponent of 0 equals 1.

Examples

$2^1 = 2$	$9^1 = 9$	$7^1 = 7$
$4^0 = 1$	$3^0 = 1$	$10^0 = 1$

TIP

The exponent for a power of 10 is the same as the number of zeros in the product.
$10^6 = 1,000,000$

Our number system is based on the idea of grouping by tens. Powers of 10 are especially important.

$$10^1 = 10$$
$$10^2 = 10 \times 10 = 100$$
$$10^3 = 10 \times 10 \times 10 = 1000$$
$$10^4 = 10 \times 10 \times 10 \times 10 = 10,000$$

Negative powers of 10 are useful for writing very small numbers. Any number to a negative power represents a fraction or decimal.

TIP

The negative exponent for a power of 10 and the number of decimal places are the same.
$10^{-4} = 0.0001$

$$10^{-1} = \frac{1}{10} = 0.1$$

$$10^{-2} = \frac{1}{10} \times 10 = 0.01$$

$$10^{-3} = \frac{1}{10} \times 10 \times 10 = 0.001$$

Scientific notation is a method that uses powers of ten to write very small and very large numbers. A number in scientific notation is expressed as a product of a number between one and ten and a power of ten.

Example 1 The distance to the sun is about 93,000,000 miles. Write the distance in scientific notation.

Step 1 Move the decimal point to the left until the last digit on the left is in the ones column.

9.3000000

Step 2 Drop the zeros and multiply by 10 raised to a power equal to the number of places the decimal point was moved, here, 7. $93,000,000 = \mathbf{9.3 \times 10^7}$

Example 2 In a scientific experiment, the mass of a sample is 2×10^{-5} kilogram. Write the mass in standard notation.

Step 1 Write the given number with a string of zeros in front of it. You haven't changed the value.

0000002.

Step 2 Move the decimal point to the left by the number of places shown in the exponent. Discard extra zeros.

00.00002.

$2 \times 10^{-5} = \mathbf{0.00002}$

If you perform operations that result in a very large or very small number, your calculator may display the solution in scientific notation. Enter this operation: $30,000 \times 5,000,000 =$

Your display may read: **1.5** ^{11} or **1.5 11** which equals $\mathbf{1.5 \times 10^{11}}$.

GED SKILL FOCUS

A. Find each value. Do not use a calculator.

1. 2^4 4. 1^6 7. 3^3 10. 8^2

2. 4^3 5. 5^0 8. 7^2 11. 5^{-3}

3. 16^1 6. 3^4 9. 3^{-2} 12. 12^0

 B. Find each value. Use a calculator for these problems.

13. 6^4 15. 3^6 17. 12^5 19. 2^{-5}

14. 9^5 16. 8^{-2} 18. 5^7 20. 7^4

C. Solve.

21. The distance across the sun (its diameter), in scientific notation, is 8.65×10^5 miles. What is this distance written in standard notation?

22. In very dense fog, a person can see about 0.019 mile. What is this distance written in scientific notation?

23. Which of these numbers is greatest: 5.4×10^2, 3.02×10^3, or 9.55×10^{-1}?

24. Fingernails grow approximately 2.8×10^{-3} inches per day. What is this distance written in standard notation?

25. Which is less: 4.2×10^3 or 42,000?

Answers start on page 422.

Square Roots

Raising a number to the second power is also called squaring the number. You have already seen that to find the area of a square, you multiply the length of one side of the square by itself. In other words, you square the length of one side to find the area.

The **square root** of a number is the number that when multiplied by itself equals the given number. The symbol for square root is $\sqrt{\ }$. To find the square root of a certain number, ask yourself: "What number times itself equals this number?"

Example 1   What is the measure of a side of a square if the area of the square is 25 square inches?

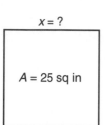
x = ?

A = 25 sq in

Step 1   The area of the square is found by multiplying the length of one side by itself. Ask: What number times itself equals 25?

Step 2   Since $5 \times 5 = 25$, the square root of 25 is 5.

Each side of the square measures **5 inches.**

Memorize the following list of squares to help you find square roots.

$1^2 = 1$	$4^2 = 16$	$7^2 = 49$	$10^2 = 100$
$2^2 = 4$	$5^2 = 25$	$8^2 = 64$	$11^2 = 121$
$3^2 = 9$	$6^2 = 36$	$9^2 = 81$	$12^2 = 144$

Example 2   What is $\sqrt{81}$?
The problem asks, "What is the square root of 81?"
Since $9^2 = 81$, $\sqrt{81} = $ **9.**

> **TIP**
>
> It is always a good idea to estimate an answer. A good estimate can help you decide whether the number in your calculator's display makes sense.

Most square roots are not whole numbers. You can use the list of common squares above to help you estimate an answer, or you can find a more exact answer using your calculator.

Example 3   What is $\sqrt{55}$?
What number times itself equals 55? You know that 7^2 equals 49 and 8^2 equals 64. Therefore, the square root of 55 must be **between 7 and 8** because 55 is between 49 and 64.

To find the square root of 55 using a calculator, use the square root key. You may need to press SHIFT or 2ndF to access the square root function.

The key sequence on your calculator may be:

55 $\boxed{\sqrt{\ }}$ 7.416198487   or   55 $\boxed{\sqrt{x}}$

55 $\boxed{\text{SHIFT}}$ $\boxed{x^2}$ 7.416198487

Some square roots are whole numbers or have a limited number of decimal digits. Some are repeating decimals. Others continue without repeating a pattern of digits. Read problems carefully to see whether you should round to a particular decimal digit.

A. Write the square roots. Do not use a calculator.

1. $\sqrt{16}$ 4. $\sqrt{9}$ 7. $\sqrt{25}$

2. $\sqrt{0}$ 5. $\sqrt{49}$ 8. $\sqrt{1}$

3. $\sqrt{100}$ 6. $\sqrt{121}$ 9. $\sqrt{144}$

B. Find the length of the side of each square.

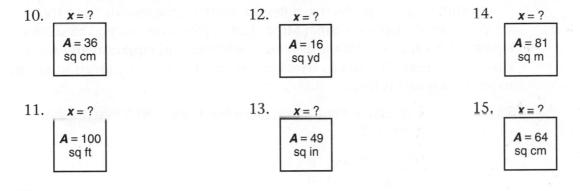

10. $x = ?$ $A = 36$ sq cm

11. $x = ?$ $A = 100$ sq ft

12. $x = ?$ $A = 16$ sq yd

13. $x = ?$ $A = 49$ sq in

14. $x = ?$ $A = 81$ sq m

15. $x = ?$ $A = 64$ sq cm

C. Use a calculator to find the square roots. Round your answers to the nearest hundredth.

16. $\sqrt{28}$ 19. $\sqrt{6}$ 22. $\sqrt{130}$

17. $\sqrt{95}$ 20. $\sqrt{324}$ 23. $\sqrt{169}$

18. $\sqrt{32}$ 21. $\sqrt{44}$ 24. $\sqrt{228}$

D. Choose the best answer to each question.

25. The square root of 22 is between which of the following pairs of numbers?

     (1)   2 and 3
     (2)   3 and 4
     (3)   4 and 5
     (4)   5 and 6
     (5) 21 and 22

26. The area of a square platform is about 72 square feet. The length in feet of each side is between which two measurements?

     (1) 4 and 5
     (2) 5 and 6
     (3) 6 and 7
     (4) 7 and 8
     (5) 8 and 9

Answers start on page 423.

GED STRATEGY Solving Word Problems

Working Backwards

Each multiple-choice question on the GED Mathematics Test has five answer options. You must choose the best answer for each question.

For most questions, it is faster to solve the problem directly. Read the problem carefully, decide what the question asks, choose the operations to use, and solve. Always make sure your answer makes sense. Then, look at the five options to see whether your answer is among them.

For some algebra problems, however, working backwards from the answer choices may save time. Most algebra problems ask you to solve for a particular variable. Ordinarily, you would write an equation and solve it. However, it may be faster to try each answer choice in the given situation to see which one is true.

Example 1 The sum of three consecutive numbers is 30. What are the numbers?

>   (1)   6, 7, and 8
>   (2)   8, 9, and 10
>   (3)   9, 10, and 11
>   (4) 11, 12, and 13
>   (5) 14, 15, and 16

TIP

Use your knowledge of averages to solve problems asking for consecutive numbers. If the sum of 3 numbers is 30, the average is 10. Look for a choice with a middle value of 10.

It is not necessary to write an equation to solve this problem. You know the numbers add up to 30, so simply add the numbers for each option. You can quickly eliminate options (4) and (5) since 10 + 10 + 10 = 30, and all the numbers in these options are greater than 10. Clearly, options (4) and (5) total more than 30. Quickly add the numbers for the first three options.

Option (1):   6 + 7 + 8 = 21
Option (2):   8 + 9 + 10 = 27
Option (3):   9 + 10 + 11 = 30

Option (3) 9, 10 , and 11 is the correct answer.

Example 2 A test has two parts. Each part is worth 50 points. When Jan took the test, she earned 10 points more on the first part than on the second part. Her total score was 86. What did she score on each part of the test?

>   (1) 46 and 50
>   (2) 38 and 48
>   (3) 36 and 46
>   (4) 44 and 42
>   (5) 32 and 54

You can narrow your choice to options (2) and (3) since these are the only answer choices with numbers 10 points apart. **Option (2) 38 and 48** is the only pair of numbers that is ten points apart and totals 86 points.

Directions: Choose the <u>one best answer</u> to each question.

1. The sum of three consecutive numbers is 45. What are the three numbers?

   (1) 10, 11, and 12
   (2) 12, 13, and 14
   (3) 13, 14, and 15
   (4) 14, 15, and 16
   (5) 15, 16, and 17

2. Jess and David took an 800-mile driving trip. Jess drove 200 miles more than David did on the trip. How many miles did David drive?

   (1) 200
   (2) 250
   (3) 300
   (4) 400
   (5) 500

3. The sum of two consecutive numbers is 95. What are the two numbers?

   (1) 40 and 41
   (2) 42 and 43
   (3) 47 and 48
   (4) 52 and 53
   (5) 57 and 58

4. Four consecutive numbers total 38. What are the four numbers?

   (1) 7, 8, 9, and 10
   (2) 8, 9, 10, and 11
   (3) 9, 10, 11, and 12
   (4) 10, 11, 12, and 13
   (5) 11, 12, 13, and 14

5. Bill works two jobs. Last week, he worked 30 hours in all. If he worked two hours more at one job than he worked at the other, how many hours did he work at each job?

   (1) 9 and 11
   (2) 13 and 15
   (3) 14 and 16
   (4) 19 and 21
   (5) 24 and 26

6. Marta scored a total of 93 points on her English test. She scored 5 points lower on the writing part of the test than on the reading part. What were her scores on each part of the test?

   (1) 43 and 48
   (2) 44 and 49
   (3) 45 and 50
   (4) 47 and 52
   (5) 54 and 59

7. Evelyn drove a total of 334 miles on Monday and Tuesday. She drove 50 miles farther on Tuesday than she did on Monday. How many miles did she drive each day?

   (1) 92 and 142
   (2) 125 and 175
   (3) 142 and 192
   (4) 234 and 284
   (5) 284 and 334

Answers start on page 423.

GED STRATEGY **Solving Word Problems**

Applying Patterns and Functions

TIP

To identify a mathematical pattern, find how one term became the one following it. That is, what function is applied to the first term to obtain the next? Then test your function on the rest of the pattern.

A mathematical **pattern** is an arrangement of numbers or terms formed by following a particular rule. If you know the rule, you can find other terms in the pattern.

Example 1   Find the eighth term in the sequence: 1, 7, 13, 19, 25, . . .

Step 1   **Identify the rule used to make the pattern.** Study the sequence. Each number in the sequence is six more than the preceding number. The rule is "add 6."

Step 2   **Apply the rule to continue the pattern.** The number 25 is the 5th term in the pattern. You need to find the 8th term.

1st	2nd	3rd	4th	5th	6th	7th	8th
1	7	13	19	25	31	37	43

$$+6 \quad +6 \quad +6 \quad +6 \quad +6 \quad +6 \quad +6$$

The correct answer is **43**.

An algebraic rule is sometimes called a **function.** You can think of a function as a machine that performs certain operations. For each number that enters the machine (x), there will be only one number that comes out (y). The function shown here multiplies a number by 3 and then subtracts 4. We can write the function as an equation: $y = 3x - 4$.

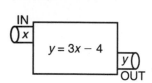

IN
x
$y = 3x - 4$
y
OUT

Example 2   For the function, $y = 3x - 4$, what numbers are needed to complete the table below?

x	−3	−2	−1	0	1	2
y	−13	−10	−7		−1	

(1) −6 and 2
(2) −5 and 2
(3) −5 and 3
(4) −4 and 2
(5) −4 and 4

Use substitution to find the value of y. Replace x with 0 and 2. Solve for y.

$y = 3x - 4$ $y = 3x - 4$
$y = 3(0) - 4$ $y = 3(2) - 4$
$y = 0 - 4$ $y = 6 - 4$
$y = -4$ $y = 2$

The missing numbers are **−4** and **2**. Check your work by testing the pattern. Each value for y is 3 more than the number before it. Continue the pattern to make sure −4 and 2 are correct.

Directions: Choose the one best answer for each question.

1. Which of the following rules can be used to form the following sequence?

    $-19, -15, -11, -7, -3, \ldots$

    (1) Add -5.
    (2) Add -4.
    (3) Subtract 4.
    (4) Subtract 6.
    (5) Add 4.

2. What is the 5th term in the sequence below?

    $64, -32, 16, -8,$ _____

    (1) 8
    (2) 4
    (3) 2
    (4) -2
    (5) -4

3. The function $y = 10x - 5$ has been used to create the following table. Which numbers are missing from the table?

x	-2	0	2	4	6
y	-25	-5			55

    (1) 5 and 25
    (2) 10 and 30
    (3) 15 and 35
    (4) 20 and 40
    (5) 25 and 45

Question 4 refers to the following diagram.

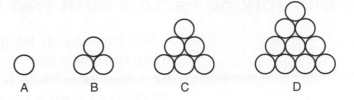

4. If you were to continue the pattern above, how many circles would be in figure E?

    (1) 12
    (2) 15
    (3) 20
    (4) 21
    (5) Not enough information is given.

5. What is the 8th term in the sequence below?

    $3, 6, 12, 24, 48, \ldots$

    (1) 96
    (2) 144
    (3) 192
    (4) 288
    (5) 384

6. For the function $y = \frac{x}{4}$, which of the following values for x results in a fractional value of y (that is, y is not a whole number)?

    (1) 42
    (2) 32
    (3) 28
    (4) 12
    (5) 8

Answers start on page 423.

GED SKILL **Factoring and Inequalities**

Multiplying Factors with Two Terms

You have already learned how to use the distributive property to multiply a single term, here 2, by a factor that has two terms, here $(x + 5)$: $2(x + 5) = 2x + 10$. Each term inside the parentheses is multiplied by the integer 2 outside the parentheses.

You can also use the distributive property to multiply two factors when each has two terms. Each term in the first factor is multiplied by each term in the second factor. To make sure you remember each step of the process, use the **FOIL method** shown in the example below.

Example 1 Multiply: $(x + 7)(x - 3)$.

Step 1 **Multiply the terms.** The letters in the word FOIL stand for First, Outer, Inner, and Last. If you multiply the terms in this order, you can be sure that you have multiplied every possible combination of terms. Remember that a term owns the operation sign that precedes it.

F	first	$(x + 7)(x - 3)$	$x(x) = x^2$
O	outer	$(x + 7)(x - 3)$	$x(-3) = -3x$
I	inner	$(x + 7)(x - 3)$	$7(x) = 7x$
L	last	$(x + 7)(x - 3)$	$7(-3) = -21$

Step 2 **Find the sum of the products from each FOIL step.** Simplify the expression.
$x^2 + (-3x) + (7x) + (-21) = x^2 + 4x - 21$

The product of $x + 7$ and $x + 3$ is $x^2 + 4x - 21$.

TIP

Remember, when simplifying an expression, you can only combine like terms.

When using the FOIL method, your answer could have two, three, or four terms. In Example 2, the solution has only two terms.

Example 2 Multiply: $(x + 4)(x - 4)$.

Step 1 Use the FOIL method to multiply the terms.

$$
\begin{array}{ll}
\textbf{F} & x(x) = x^2 \\
\textbf{O} & x(-4) = -4x \\
\textbf{I} & 4(x) = 4x \\
\textbf{L} & 4(-4) = -16
\end{array}
$$

Step 2 Find the sum of the products.
$$x^2 + (-4x) + 4x + (-16)$$
$$x^2 \qquad\qquad - 16$$

Since the sum of $-4x$ and $4x$ is 0, the answer has only two terms. The product of $x + 4$ and $x - 4$ is $x^2 - 16$.

A. Find the product of each pair of factors.

1. $(x + 1)(x + 4)$

2. $(x + 6)(x + 3)$

3. $(x - 5)(2x - 7)$

4. $(x + 2)(x - 2)$

5. $(x - 4)(y + 6)$

6. $(2x + 8)(3x + 9)$

7. $(x - 4)(x + 1)$

8. $(x - 5)(4x - 3)$

9. $(x - 1)(x + 5)$

10. $(2x - 10)(x - 6y)$

11. $(x - 8)(x - 5)$

12. $(x - 6)(x + 6)$

13. $(x + 2)(x + 3)$

14. $(3x + 8)(3x - 8)$

15. $(x - 6)(y + 9)$

16. $(4x - 1)(x - 5)$

17. $(x + 7)(x - 2)$

18. $(2x + 4)(3x + 10)$

19. $(x - 3)(x + 3)$

20. $(x + 10)(x - 12)$

B. Choose the best answer to each question.

21. Which of the following is equal to $x^2 - 14x + 48$? (*Hint*: Work backwards. Multiply the factors of each answer choice until you find the solution.)

    (1) $(x + 12)(x - 4)$
    (2) $(x - 12)(x - 4)$
    (3) $(x + 6)(x - 8)$
    (4) $(x - 6)(x - 8)$
    (5) $(x + 6)(x + 8)$

22. If $3x - 1$ is one factor of $3x^2 + 8x - 3$, which of the following is the other factor?

    (1) $x - 3$
    (2) $x + 3$
    (3) $3x - 3$
    (4) $3x + 3$
    (5) $x^2 + 3$

23. Which of the following is equal to $(x - 9)^2$? (*Hint*: The entire expression $x - 9$ is multiplied by itself.)

    (1) $x^2 + 18x - 81$
    (2) $x^2 - 18x + 81$
    (3) $x^2 - 18x - 81$
    (4) $x^2 + 18x + 81$
    (5) $x^2 - 81$

24. If $2x + 1$ is one factor of $6x^2 - x - 2$, which of the following is the other factor?

    (1) $x - 2$
    (2) $3x + 2$
    (3) $3x - 1$
    (4) $3x - 2$
    (5) $4x - 2$

Answers start on page 424.

Factoring

Factors are numbers that are multiplied together. In the algebraic term $7x$, 7 and x are factors. An expression of more than one term can sometimes be **factored.** To factor an expression, look for a number and/or a variable that divides evenly into each term in the expression.

Example 1   Factor the expression $6x + 10$.

Step 1   Find a factor that divides evenly into both terms. Both $6x$ and 10 can be divided by 2.   One of the factors is the number 2.

Step 2   Divide to find the other factor. $\dfrac{6x + 10}{2} = \dfrac{6x}{2} + \dfrac{10}{2}$

$(3x + 5)$

Step 3   Check by multiplying the factors. $2(3x + 5) = 6x + 10$

The factors of $6x + 10$ are **2** and **$3x + 5$.**

TIP

Make sure you divide both terms in the factor by 2.

$\dfrac{6x + 10}{2} =$

$\dfrac{6x}{2} + \dfrac{10}{2} = 3x + 5$

A **quadratic expression** is one that contains a variable raised to the second power, or "squared," as in $x^2 + 2x$. Both factors of quadratic expressions will always contain the variable.

Example 2   Factor $x^2 + 2x$.

Step 1   Both terms divide evenly by x.   One factor is x.

Step 2   Divide by one factor (x) to find the other factor. $\dfrac{x^2 + 2x}{x} = \dfrac{x^2}{x} + \dfrac{2x}{x}$

$(x + 2)$

Step 3   Check by multiplying the two factors. $x(x + 2) = x^2 + 2x$

The factors are **x** and **$x + 2$.**

A quadratic expression in this form, $x^2 - 3x - 4$, results when you multiply two expressions, each with a variable and an integer. To factor quadratic expressions with three terms, work backwards.

Example 3   Factor $x^2 - 3x - 4$.

Step 1   **Find all the possible factors for the third term.**
The third term in this example is -4.
The possible factors are: $(-4)(1)$, $(4)(-1)$, $(-2)(2)$, and $(2)(-2)$

Step 2   **Find the two factors from Step 1 that when added give the integer part of the middle term,** here, $-3x$.
The sum of only the factors -4 and 1 equals -3. $-4 + 1 = -3$
None of the other possible factors equal -3 when
added together: $4 + (-1) = 3$, $-2 + 2 = 0$, and $2 + -2 = 0$.

Step 3   **Write the two factors using the variable as the first term in each factor and the integers from Step 2 as the second term.**   The factors are $(x - 4)$ and $(x + 1)$.

Step 4   **Check.** Multiply using the FOIL method.

$(x - 4)\,(x + 1) = x^2 + 1x - 4x - 4 = x^2 - 3x - 4$

The factors are **$(x - 4)$** and **$(x + 1)$.**

TIP

Remember, each term "owns" the sign preceding it. The third term in the quadratic expression $x^2 - 3x - 4$ is -4, not 4.

A. Factor each expression.

1. $5x + 30$

2. $6y + 15$

3. $8x - 2$

4. $4z - 14$

5. $b^2 + 9b$

6. $y^2 + 3y$

7. $2x^2 + 4x$

8. $3x^2 + 9x$

9. $7y^2 - y$

10. $4x^2 + 2x$

11. $x^2 + 9x + 20$

12. $x^2 - 5x + 6$

13. $x^2 + 5x - 6$

14. $x^2 - 3x - 28$

15. $x^2 + 8x + 12$

16. $x^2 + 2x - 3$

17. $x^2 - 7x + 12$

18. $x^2 + 7x - 8$

19. $x^2 + 3x - 10$

20. $x^2 + 10x + 21$

21. $x^2 - 13x + 40$

22. $x^2 - x - 12$

23. $x^2 - 8x - 20$

24. $x^2 - 11x + 18$

25. $x^2 - 6x - 55$

26. $x^2 + 16x + 48$

27. $x^2 + 7x - 18$

28. $x^2 + 10x + 25$

29. $x^2 - 10x + 24$

30. $x^2 - 6x - 7$

B. Choose the best answer to each question.

31. Which of the following are the factors of $x^2 - 10x + 16$?

    (1) $(x - 4)(x - 4)$
    (2) $(x + 4)(x - 4)$
    (3) $(x - 2)(x - 8)$
    (4) $(x + 2)(x - 8)$
    (5) $(x - 2)(x + 8)$

32. What are the factors of $x^2 - 5x - 24$?

    (1) $x - 4$ and $x + 6$
    (2) $x - 4$ and $x - 6$
    (3) $x - 3$ and $x - 8$
    (4) $x + 3$ and $x - 8$
    (5) $x - 3$ and $x + 8$

Answers start on page 424.

GED STRATEGY **Solving Word Problems**

Solving Quadratic Equations

As you have learned, a quadratic expression contains a variable that is raised to the second power, or squared. When an equation contains a squared variable, it is called a **quadratic equation.** Quadratic equations usually have two different solutions. In other words, there are two values for the variable that will make the equation true. Follow these steps to solve a quadratic equation.

Example 1 If $x^2 + 3x = 10$, then what values of x make the equation true?

Step 1 **Rewrite the equation to set the quadratic expression equal to 0.** In this case, subtract 10 from both sides of the equation.

$$x^2 + 3x = 10$$
$$x^2 + 3x - 10 = 10 - 10$$
$$x^2 + 3x - 10 = 0$$

Step 2 **Factor the quadratic expression.**

$$x^2 + 3x - 10 = 0$$
$$(x + 5)(x - 2) = 0$$

Step 3 **For each factor, determine the value of x that will make that factor equal to 0.** Since any number multiplied by 0 equals 0, if either factor equals 0, the entire expression will equal 0.

If $x + 5 = 0$
and $x - 2 = 0$
then, $x = -5$ and $x = 2$

Step 4 **Check** both values by substituting them into the original equation.

$$x^2 + 3x = 10 \qquad\qquad x^2 + 3x = 10$$
$$(-5)^2 + 3(-5) = 10 \qquad (2)^2 + 3(2) = 10$$
$$25 + (-15) = 10 \qquad\qquad 4 + 6 = 10$$
$$10 = 10 \qquad\qquad\qquad 10 = 10$$

The two solutions for the equation $x^2 + 3x = 10$ are **−5** and **2.**

> **TIP**
>
> Often working backwards is a good test-taking strategy for any multiple-choice problem that involves lengthy computations.

When a quadratic equation is presented in a multiple-choice question, you may be able to solve the problem more quickly by working backwards from the answer choices.

Example 2 What are the possible values for x if $x^2 - 7x = 60$?

      (1) −20 and 3
      (2) −12 and 5
      (3) −10 and 6
      (4) −6 and 10
      (5) −5 and 12

Substitute one of the numbers from each option into the equation. You may find it easier to work with the positive number from each option.

Option 1	Option 2	Option 3	Option 4	Option 5
$x^2 - 7x = 60$	$x^2 - 7x = 60$	$x^2 - 7x = 60$	$x^2 - 7x = 60$	$x^2 - 7x = 60$
$3^2 - 7(3) = 60$	$5^2 - 7(5) = 60$	$6^2 - 7(6) = 60$	$10^2 - 7(10) = 60$	$12^2 - 7(12) = 60$
$9 - 21 = 60$	$25 - 35 = 60$	$36 - 42 = 60$	$100 - 70 = 60$	$144 - 84 = 60$
$-12 \neq 60$	$-10 \neq 60$	$-6 \neq 60$	$30 \neq 60$	$60 = 60$
false	**false**	**false**	**false**	**true**

Note: The symbol $\neq$ means "is not equal to."

Option (5) is the correct answer. If you have time, you could substitute -5, the other value from option 5, to check your work.

$$(-5)^2 - 7(-5) = 60 \qquad 25 + 35 = 60 \qquad 60 = 60 \qquad \text{true}$$

GED PRACTICE

Directions: Choose the <u>one best answer</u> for each question.

1. In the equation $x^2 + 72 = 18x$, what are the possible values for x?

    (1) -9 and -8
    (2) -9 and 8
    (3) -6 and 12
    (4) 8 and 9
    (5) 12 and 6

2. If $2x^2 - 10x + 12 = 0$, what is one possible value for x?

    (1) -4
    (2) -3
    (3) 3
    (4) 6
    (5) 12

3. In the equation $x^2 - x = 12$, what are the possible values for x?

    (1) 6 and -2
    (2) 4 and -3
    (3) 3 and -4
    (4) 2 and -6
    (5) -3 and -4

4. If $x^2 + 13x = -40$, what are the possible values for x?

    (1) 10 and 4
    (2) 8 and 5
    (3) -4 and -10
    (4) -5 and -8
    (5) -6 and -7

5. In the quadratic equation $9x^2 - 36 = 0$, which pair of solutions makes the equation true?

    (1) 9 and -4
    (2) 6 and -6
    (3) 4 and -9
    (4) 3 and -12
    (5) 2 and -2

6. In the equation $2x^2 - x = 45$, what is one possible value of x?

    (1) 9
    (2) 5
    (3) 3
    (4) -5
    (5) -9

Answers start on page 425.

Solving and Graphing Inequalities

TIP

To remember the meanings of the symbols $>$ and $<$, just remember that the symbol points to the lesser amount.

An **inequality** means two algebraic expressions are not equal. Other inequality symbols in addition to greater than and less than symbols are:

$\geq$ means "is greater than or equal to" $4 \geq 2$
$\leq$ means "is less than or equal to" $7 \leq 9$

In an inequality, a variable may have many values that make the statement true. Consider $x < 5$. The numbers 4, 3, 2, 1, and so on are all possible values for x. We can graph the possible solutions to an inequality.

Example 1   Graph the solution set of the inequality $x < 5$.

On a number line, every number to the left of 5 is a solution. Graph the solution by drawing a solid line on the number line. An empty circle at the number 5 shows that 5 itself is not included as a solution. Five is not "less than" 5.

Example 2   Graph the solution set of the inequality $x \geq -3$.

The solution set of the inequality $x \geq -3$ includes the number -3 and all numbers to the right of -3. The circle at -3 is filled in to show that -3 is included as a solution.

An inequality can be solved much like an equation. The same number can be added to or subtracted from both sides of an inequality.

Example 3   Solve $2x + 7 < x + 10$.

Step 1	Subtract x from both sides.	$x + 7 < 10$
Step 2	Subtract 7 from both sides.	$x < 3$
Step 3	Check using a number less than 3 (such as 2).	$2(2) + 7 < 2 + 10$
		$11 < 12$ is true

The solution to the inequality is **$x < 3$.**

Both sides of an inequality can also be multiplied or divided by the same number to simplify the inequality. But there is an important rule to remember: If you multiply or divide an inequality by a negative number, the inequality sign must be <u>reversed</u>.

Example 4   Solve: $3x - 4 < 5x$.

Step 1	Subtract $5x$ from both sides.	$-2x - 4 < 0$
Step 2	Add 4 to both sides.	$-2x - 4 + 4 < 0 + 4$
Step 3	Divide by -2, and reverse the inequality sign.	$\dfrac{-2x}{-2} < \dfrac{4}{-2}$
		$x > -2$
Step 4	Check using a number greater than -2.	$3(2) - 4 < 5(2)$

The solution to the inequality is **$x > -2$.**

$2 < 10$ true

A. Write the inequality for each number line.

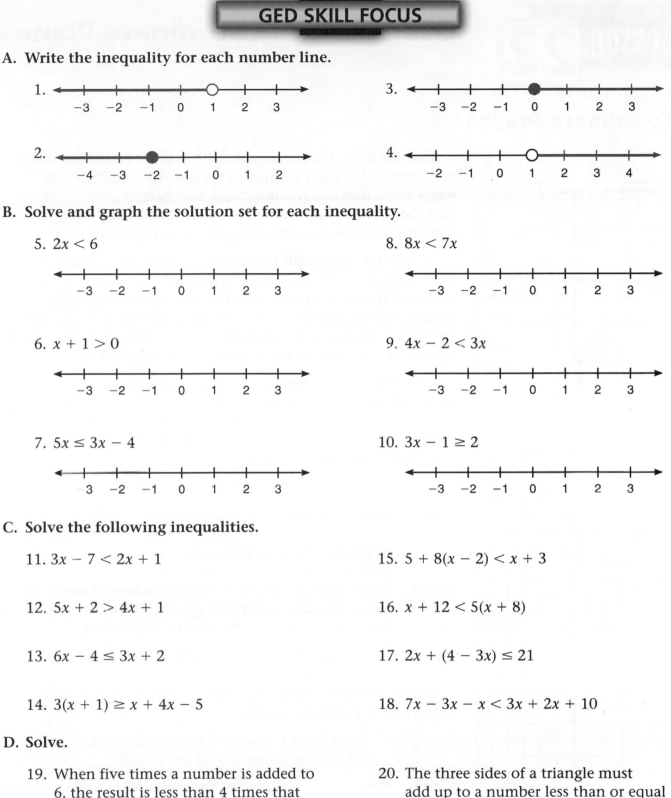

1.

-3 -2 -1 0 1 2 3

3.

-3 -2 -1 0 1 2 3

2.

-4 -3 -2 -1 0 1 2

4.

-2 -1 0 1 2 3 4

B. Solve and graph the solution set for each inequality.

5. $2x < 6$

-3 -2 -1 0 1 2 3

8. $8x < 7x$

-3 -2 -1 0 1 2 3

6. $x + 1 > 0$

-3 -2 -1 0 1 2 3

9. $4x - 2 < 3x$

-3 -2 -1 0 1 2 3

7. $5x \leq 3x - 4$

-3 -2 -1 0 1 2 3

10. $3x - 1 \geq 2$

-3 -2 -1 0 1 2 3

C. Solve the following inequalities.

11. $3x - 7 < 2x + 1$

15. $5 + 8(x - 2) < x + 3$

12. $5x + 2 > 4x + 1$

16. $x + 12 < 5(x + 8)$

13. $6x - 4 \leq 3x + 2$

17. $2x + (4 - 3x) \leq 21$

14. $3(x + 1) \geq x + 4x - 5$

18. $7x - 3x - x < 3x + 2x + 10$

D. Solve.

19. When five times a number is added to 6, the result is less than 4 times that same number added to 10. What is the solution to the inequality?

20. The three sides of a triangle must add up to a number less than or equal to 65 inches. One side is 21 inches. Another side is 18 inches. What is the longest the third side can be (in inches)?

Answers start on page 425.

Coordinate Graphs

Imagine a blank sheet of paper with one dot on it. How could you describe the exact location of the dot? You might use the edges of the paper to give directions. For example, you could say that the dot was four inches from the top edge and three inches from the left edge. A coordinate graph works the same way.

A **coordinate graph** is a system for finding the location of a point on a flat surface called a **plane.** A coordinate graph is formed from two axis lines that cross at a point called the **origin.** The horizontal line is the **x-axis** and the vertical line is the **y-axis.** Both lines are marked as number lines with the origin at zero. The axes divide the graph into four **quadrants.**

Each point on the grid is named by two numbers, an **x-coordinate** and a **y-coordinate.** The x-coordinate is always written first; the y-coordinate is always written second. Together, the coordinates are called an **ordered pair** and are enclosed in parentheses, separated by a comma.

Example 1 Plot the point (5,3) on a coordinate grid.

Step 1 **Start at the origin**—coordinates (0,0). **Move the number of units of the x-coordinate in the appropriate direction,** here 5 units to the right, the positive x direction.

Step 2 **From that point, move the number of units of the y-coordinate in the appropriate direction,** here 3 units upwards, the positive y direction.

The location of point (5,3) is shown by **the dot** on the grid.

You may be asked to use coordinates to draw a line segment or a figure on a coordinate system.

Example 2 Draw a line segment on the coordinate grid connecting points (0,−4) and (−3,2).

Step 1 Plot point (0,−4). Start at the origin. The 0 indicates that no move along the x-axis is required. Move −4 on the y-axis (down from the origin), and plot the point.

Step 2 Plot point (−3,2). Start at the origin; move 3 units to the left on the x-axis, then 2 units up; plot the point.

Step 3 Connect the points by drawing a line segment.

The location of the points and segment are shown on the grid.

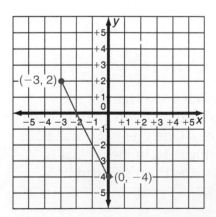

A. Use the coordinate grid to answer the following questions.

1. What are the coordinates of Point *A*?

2. Which point is found at $(-4,-2)$?

3. Which point is on the *y*-axis?

4. What are the coordinates of Point *D*?

5. Which point has a negative *x*-value and a positive *y*-value?

6. For which points are the *x*-values greater than the *y*-values?

7. Which points are found in Quadrant IV?

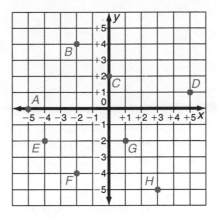

B. Graph as directed.

8. Plot the ordered pairs $(1,-4)$, $(0,5)$, and $(-2,-3)$ on the coordinate graph below.

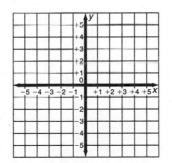

9. Draw a line segment connecting Point *A* at $(4,3)$ and Point *B* at $(2,-5)$.

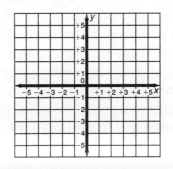

10. Graph the following points and connect them to form a square: Point *D* at $(-3,3)$, Point *E* at $(1,3)$, Point *F* at $(1,-1)$, and Point *G* at $(-3,-1)$.

11. Connect each pair of points to form two intersecting line segments.
Point *J* $(-5,-4)$ and Point *K* $(5,2)$
Point *P* $(-3,4)$ and Point *Q* $(0,-3)$

TIP The ordered pairs (5,3) and (3,5) have different locations. Remember, the location on the *x*-axis (horizontal axis) is always named first. *(x,y)*

Answers start on page 426.

GED STRATEGY **Working with Special Formats**

Plotting Ordered Pairs

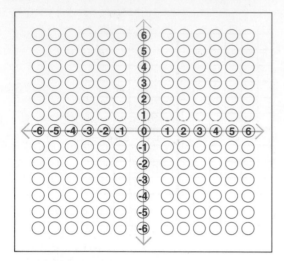

Some questions on the GED Mathematics Test ask you to show the location of a point on a coordinate grid. A special coordinate grid will be provided on the answer sheet to record your answers. This grid uses bubbles to represent each ordered pair on the coordinate plane.

The answer grid shown to the left is a sample of this GED answer format. Since positive and negative numbers are shown on the axis lines, there are no bubbles for points that lie directly on either the *x*- or *y*-axis. The origin (0,0) is not labeled, but you know that it lies at the intersection of the *x*- and *y*-axes.

To use the grid to record an answer, carefully bubble in the circle at the correct location. Be careful not to make stray marks on the grid.

Most questions that test your understanding of the coordinate grid will refer to a diagram or graph.

TIP

The *x*- and *y*-axes on a graph may not be labeled with numbers. Remember that the origin on either scale (the point where the axes cross) is always 0.

Example

Jesse has graphed three points on the coordinate grid at right. The points will become three corners of a rectangle. Where must he place the fourth point to complete the rectangle? Graph your answer on the coordinate grid.

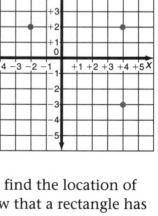

Step 1 Complete the rectangle to find the location of the fourth point. You know that a rectangle has four sides. The opposite sides must be the same length. From the three points already shown on the graph, you know the length and the width of the rectangle. The remaining point must be located at point **(−2,−3)**.

Step 2 Bubble in your answer on the coordinate grid. Starting at the origin, count two units left and three down. Fill in the circle neatly and completely.

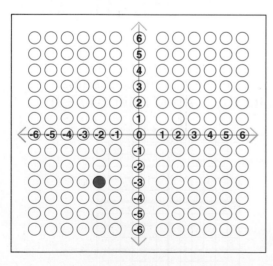

The grid to the left shows the correct location of the fourth point.

Directions: Grid in the answer to each question on the answer grid provided.

1. A point has an *x*-coordinate of 4 and a *y*-coordinate of −1. Show the location of the point on the coordinate grid.

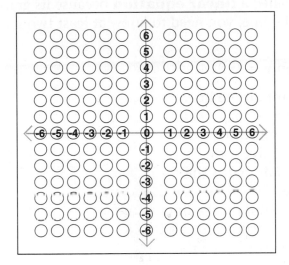

3. A point has an *x*-coordinate of −5 and a *y*-coordinate of 3. Show the location of the point on the coordinate grid.

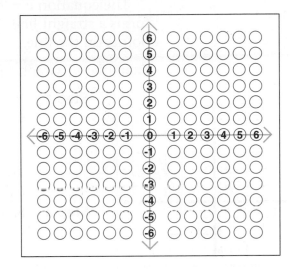

2. On the coordinate plane below, three points are drawn to mark the corners of a square. Graph the location of the fourth corner needed to complete the square.

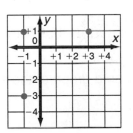

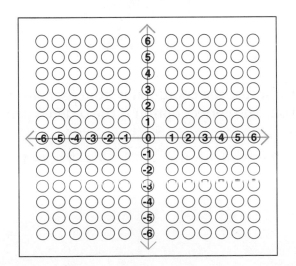

4. On the coordinate plane below, three points are drawn to mark the corners of a rectangle. Graph the location of the fourth corner needed to complete the figure.

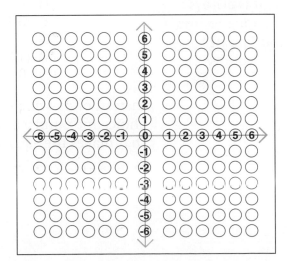

Answers start on page 427.

Graphing Equations

You know that some equations have two different variables. For example, the equation $y = 2x - 4$ has two variables, x and y. For each specific value substituted for x, there is a unique value of y. One way to show the possible solutions for such an equation is to draw the graph of the equation on a coordinate grid.

The equation $y = 2x - 4$ is called a **linear equation** because its graph forms a straight line. To draw the line, you need to know at least two points on the line.

Example 1   Graph the equation $y = 2x - 4$.

Step 1	Identify a point on the line. Choose any value for x; 0 is usually ideal. Substitute x into the equation. Solve for y. This ordered pair makes the equation true.

$$\text{Let } x = 0$$
$$y = 2(0) - 4$$
$$y = 0 - 4 = -4$$
$$(0, -4)$$

Step 2	Find another point on the line. Choose another value for x and solve for the new y. Write the coordinates.

$$\text{Let } x = 3$$
$$y = 2(3) - 4$$
$$y = 6 - 4 = 2$$
$$(3, 2)$$

Step 3   Locate both ordered pairs on a grid and draw a line through them.

The graph of the equation is shown to the left. Every point on the line satisfies, or solves, the equation.

Some questions refer to the graph of an equation, but they can be solved without drawing the graph.

Example 2   Which of the following points lies on a graph of the equation $x = 3 + y$?

(1) $(4, -1)$
(2) $(3, 1)$
(3) $(2, -1)$
(4) $(1, 2)$
(5) $(0, -4)$

Instead of drawing the graph, substitute the coordinates from each answer choice for x and y in the equation. The correct option is the ordered pair that makes the equation true.

Only **option (3) (2, −1)** makes the equation true.

$$2 = 3 + (-1)$$
$$2 = 2$$

TIP

Although you only need two points to draw the graph of a line, it is always a good idea to find a third point to check your work.

A. Graph each equation on a coordinate grid.

1. $y = 3x - 4$

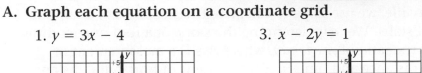

3. $x - 2y = 1$

5. $-x = y + 2$

2. $2x + y = 5$

4. $-2y = 4x$

6. $y = 6 - 3x$

B. Choose the best answer to each question.

7. The points graphed on the grid below satisfy which of the following equations?

(1) $x - y = 1$

(2) $x - y = -1$

(3) $2y - x = 0$

(4) $x = 0$

(5) $y = 0$

8. Which ordered pair is a solution of $x - y = 1$?

(1) $(-3, -4)$

(2) $(-3, -2)$

(3) $(-1, 0)$

(4) $(0, 1)$

(5) $(1, -2)$

9. Which equation of a line is shown on the graph?

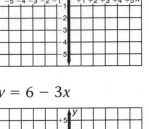

(1) $x + y = -4$

(2) $x + y = -2$

(3) $x + y = 0$

(4) $x + y = 2$

(5) $x + y = 4$

10. What is the missing x-value if $(?, 1)$ is a solution of $-4x + 7y = 15$?

(1) $\dfrac{-11}{2}$

(2) -2

(3) 2

(4) $\dfrac{19}{7}$

(5) $\dfrac{11}{2}$

Answers start on page 427.

Finding the Slope of a Line

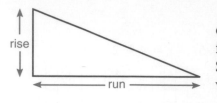

rise

run

Slope is a number that measures the steepness of a line. In everyday life, we use slope to calculate the steepness of a ramp or flight of stairs. We may determine the slope of a roof or a roadway. Slope is the ratio of *rise to run,* where rise is a measurement of vertical distance and run is a measurement of horizontal distance.

negative slope   positive slope

Slope can be positive or negative. All lines that rise as they move from left to right have a positive slope. All lines that fall as they move from left to right have a negative slope. If you have a graph of a line, you can find its slope by examining the line and counting grid units to find the rise and run.

Example 1   Find the slope of Line *A*.

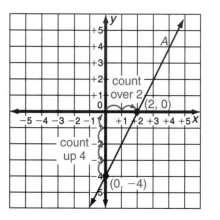

Step 1   **Select two points on the line.** Starting at either point, **count the number of units** up or down to reach the level of the second point. This is the rise of the line. Here, start at $(0,-4)$ and count up 4.

Step 2   **From this intermediate point, count the units** left or right to reach the second point. This is the run of the line. Here, count 2 to the right.

Step 3   **Write the slope as the fraction rise over run.** $\dfrac{4}{2} = 2$

Step 4   **Decide whether the slope is positive or negative.** Here, the slope is positive since the line rises as it moves from left to right.

The slope of Line *A* is **+2.**

You can also find the slope of a line by using an algebraic formula. It will be listed on the page of formulas you will be given when you take the GED Mathematics Test.

slope (*m*) of a line $= \dfrac{\textbf{rise}}{\textbf{run}} = m = \dfrac{y_2 - y_1}{x_2 - x_1}$, where (x_1,y_1) and (x_2,y_2) are two points on the line

Example 2   Find the slope of Line *B* with points $(-1,2)$ and $(1,-4)$.

Step 1   Let one point be (x_1,y_1) and the other be (x_2,y_2). In this case, let $(-1,2) = (x_1,y_1)$ and $(1,-4) = (x_2,y_2)$.

Step 2   Substitute into the formula and solve. $m = \dfrac{-4 - 2}{1 - (-1)} = \dfrac{-6}{2} = -3$

The slope of the line is **−3.**

Some unique features of slope to remember:

- The slope of any horizontal line, including the *x*-axis, is 0.
- A vertical line, including the *y*-axis, has no slope.
- All lines with the same slope are parallel.

Use the grid-unit counting method whenever you are given a graph of the line. Use the formula method when it is not practical to draw a graph of the line.

A. Find the slope of each line.

1.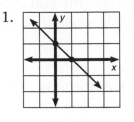

3.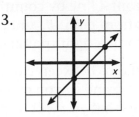

5.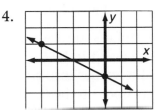

2.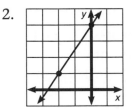

4.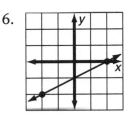

6.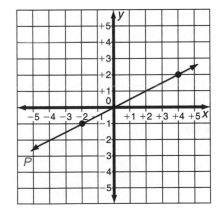

B. Find the slope of the line that passes through each pair of points.

7. (1,−3) and (0,1)

8. (2,1) and (4,2)

9. (4,5) and (3,−4)

10. (−4,2) and (5,3)

11. (−3,−3) and (−2,0)

12. (−6,−2) and (3,4)

C. Solve.

Use the following graph to answer question 13.

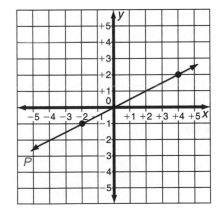

13. What is the slope of Line P?

14. The following points lie on Line R: (−4,3), (1,3), and (5,3). What is the slope of Line R?

15. Line X has a slope of 3. The line passes through Point Y at (−2,−1) and also passes through Point Z, which has an x-coordinate of 0. What are the coordinates of Point Z? (*Hint:* Substitute the given values in the slope formula.)

16. The following points lie on Line K: (−3,−3) and (5,2). What is the slope of Line K?

Answers start on page 428.

Finding the Distance Between Points

It is sometimes necessary to find the distance between two points on a coordinate grid. You can easily find the distance between points on a vertical or a horizontal line by counting. For example, on the grid at left, point A is 4 units from point B, and point B is 3 units from point C. Note that points ABC form a right triangle.

To find the distance between two points that are not on the same grid line such as points A and C, you can use a formula. This formula is on the GED formulas page that you will be given when you take the GED Mathematics Test.

$$\text{distance between points} = \sqrt{(x_2 - x_1)^2 + (y_2 - y_1)^2}$$

To use the formula, you need to know the coordinates for the two points. Assign one point to be (x_1, y_1) and the other point to be (x_2, y_2). Then substitute the values into the formula and solve. It does not matter which point you choose to be (x_1, y_1).

Example 1 In the coordinate grid at left, what is the distance between points J and K?

Step 1	**Find the coordinates of the points.**
Step 2	**Assign the variables.**

Point $J = (5,2)$; $K = (-3,-4)$

Let $J\,(5,2) = (x_1, y_1)$
Let $K\,(-3,-4) = (x_2, y_2)$

Step 3 **Substitute the coordinates into the formula and solve.**

$$\begin{aligned} d &= \sqrt{(x_2 - x_1)^2 + (y_2 - y_1)^2} \\ &= \sqrt{(-3 - 5)^2 + (-4 - 2)^2} \\ &= \sqrt{(-8)^2 + (-6)^2} \\ &= \sqrt{64 + 36} \\ &= \sqrt{100} \\ &= 10 \end{aligned}$$

The distance between points J and K is **10 units**.

The distance between points will rarely be a whole number. If you need to find the answer to a certain decimal place, use your calculator.

Example 2 Find the distance to the nearest tenth between point A at $(0,-2)$ and point B at $(1,4)$.

Step 1 **Decide which point will be (x_1, y_1).**

Let $(0,-2) = (x_1, y_1)$
Let $(1,4) = (x_2, y_2)$

Step 2 **Use the formula** for distance between points.

$$\begin{aligned} d &= \sqrt{(x_2 - x_1)^2 + (y_2 - y_1)^2} \\ &= \sqrt{(1 - 0)^2 + (4 - (-2))^2} \\ &= \sqrt{(1)^2 + (6)^2} \\ &= \sqrt{1 + 36} \\ &= \sqrt{37} \end{aligned}$$

Step 3 **Estimate the square root.**
Think: $6^2 = 36$ and $7^2 = 49$.
Since 37 is between 36 and 49,

d is between 6 and 7.

Most calculators require you to enter the number first, then press the square root key.

37 SHIFT x^2 6.08276253

Round to the nearest tenth. 6.08 rounds to 6.1.

The distance between the points is about **6.1 units.**

GED SKILL FOCUS

A. Find the distance between the following points. Round to the nearest tenth, if necessary. You may use a calculator.

Use the coordinate grid on the right to answer questions 1 through 5.

1. Points *A* and *C*

2. Points *B* and *D*

3. Points *A* and *E*

4. Points *A* and *D*

5. Points *C* and *E*

Use the coordinate grid on the right to answer questions 6 through 8.

6. A triangle is drawn by connecting points *J*, *K*, and *L*. What is the length of side *JL*?

7. What is the length of side *KL*?

8. What is the length of side *JK*?

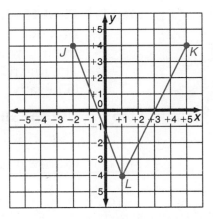

B. Solve as directed.

9. Point *X* is located at (9,3) on a coordinate grid. If a line were drawn directly to the origin, what would be the length of the line to the nearest tenth unit?

10. Two points are located at (2,5) and (−4,5). What is the distance between the points?

11. A line is drawn from point *B* at (0,6) to point *C* at (8,0). What is the length of the line to the nearest tenth unit?

12. Two points are located at (2,−1) and (2,4). What is the distance between the points?

Answers start on page 428.

GED STRATEGY Solving Word Problems

Finding the Equation of a Line

You know how to graph an equation by finding ordered pairs that make the equation true and drawing a line through those points. You may be asked to work backwards from points to determine the equation of a line.

On the GED Mathematics Test the answer choices to such questions are written in a format called the **slope-intercept form of a line.** The variable m is the slope of the line. The variable b is the **y-intercept,** the point at which the line crosses the y-axis. The sum of $mx + b$ when $y = 0$ is the x-intercept.

$$y = mx + b, \text{ where } m = \text{slope and } b = y\text{-intercept}$$

Example 1   What is the equation of the line shown on the graph?

(1) $y = -2x - 3$
(2) $y = -3x + 2$
(3) $y = -4x + 2$
(4) $y = -4x - 3$
(5) $y = -4x + 3$

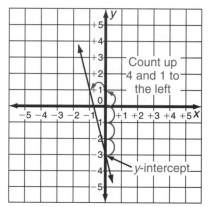

Count up 4 and 1 to the left

y-intercept

> **TIP**
>
> You can check your work by substituting the coordinates of a point on the line for x and y in the equation. If the equation is true, your answer is correct.

Step 1   **Find the y-intercept of the line.** The line shown crosses the y-axis at $(0, -3)$. Therefore:
the y-intercept is -3

Step 2   **Find the slope of the line using the grid-unit counting method.** Count from the y-intercept to another point on the line with whole numbers as the ordered pair, here, $(-1, 1)$. The line rises 4 units for every 1 unit of run to the left (a negative direction).
$$\text{slope} = \frac{\text{rise}}{\text{run}} = \frac{4}{-1} = -4$$

Step 3   **Use the slope-intercept form** to write the equation.
$$y = mx + b \qquad y = -4x + (-3) \text{ or } y = -4x - 3$$

The correct answer is **option (4) $y = -4x - 3$.**

You may need to rewrite an equation in slope-intercept form.

Example 2   Which of the lines shows the graph of the equation $2x - y = -3$?

Step 1   **Rewrite the equation** in slope-intercept form.
Isolate the variables.
Eliminate the negative variable.
Rearrange the terms.

$$2x - y = -3$$
$$y = mx + b$$
$$-y = -3 - 2x$$
$$y = 3 + 2x$$
$$y = 2x + 3$$

The slope of the line is 2 and the y-intercept is 3.

Step 2   **Examine the lines on the graph.** Only Line 2 has a slope of positive 2 and passes through point $(0,3)$.

The correct answer is **Line 2.**

Directions: Choose the one best answer to each question.

1. What are the coordinates of the y-intercept of the line $y = -3x - 2$?

   (1) $(0, -5)$

   (2) $(0, -3)$

   (3) $(0, -2)$

   (4) $(-2, 0)$

   (5) $(-3, 0)$

4. The point $(0, -5)$ is the y-intercept of which of the following lines?

   (1) $y = 2x$

   (2) $y = -x + 5$

   (3) $y = 3x - 5$

   (4) $y = -2x - 3$

   (5) Not enough information is given.

Questions 2 and 3 refer to the following graph.

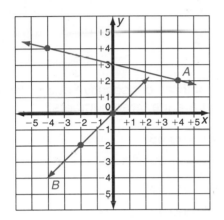

2. What is the equation of Line A?

   (1) $y - 4x = 3$

   (2) $y - \frac{1}{4}x = -2$

   (3) $y = 4x$

   (4) $y + \frac{1}{4}x = -2$

   (5) $y + \frac{1}{4}x = 3$

3. What is the equation of Line B?

   (1) $y = -x$

   (2) $y = x$

   (3) $y = 2x$

   (4) $y = -2x$

   (5) $y = x + 1$

Questions 5 and 6 refer to the following graph.

5. What would be the equation of a line drawn through points P and Q?

   (1) $y = -x + 3$

   (2) $y = -x - 3$

   (3) $y = 2x - 3$

   (4) $y = 3x + 2$

   (5) $y = 3x + 3$

6. Which of the following is the y-intercept of a line drawn through points R and Q?

   (1) $(-3, -4)$

   (2) $(0, -2)$

   (3) $(0, -3)$

   (4) $(0, -4)$

   (5) $(3, -4)$

Answers start on page 429.

Directions: This is a thirty-minute practice test. After thirty minutes, mark the last item you finished. Then complete the test and check your answers. If most of your answers are correct, but you didn't finish, try to work faster next time.

Part 1

Choose the <u>one best answer</u> to each question. You <u>MAY</u> use your calculator.

<u>Questions 1 and 2</u> refer to the following diagram.

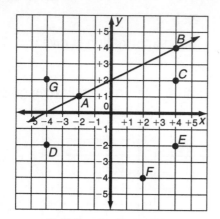

1. Which point lies at coordinates (4, −2)?

   (1) Point *C*

   (2) Point *D*

   (3) Point *E*

   (4) Point *F*

   (5) Point *G*

2. What is the slope of the line that passes through points *A* and *B* on the graph?

   (1) $-\frac{1}{2}$

   (2) $\frac{1}{3}$

   (3) $\frac{1}{2}$

   (4) $\frac{2}{3}$

   (5) 2

3. Which of the following best represents the solution set to the inequality $5x + 2 < 6x + 3x + 10$?

   (1) $x > -2$

   (2) $x < -2$

   (3) $x < 3$

   (4) $x > -3$

   (5) $x < -3$

4. The sum of three consecutive odd numbers is 135. What are the three numbers?

   (1) 41, 43, and 45

   (2) 43, 45, and 47

   (3) 44, 45, and 46

   (4) 44, 46, and 48

   (5) 45, 47, and 49

5. If the pattern continues, what is the next term in the sequence below?

   0   1   3   7   15   ____

   (1) 25

   (2) 27

   (3) 29

   (4) 31

   (5) 33

6. Which graph shows the solution of
   $x - 3 < -1$?

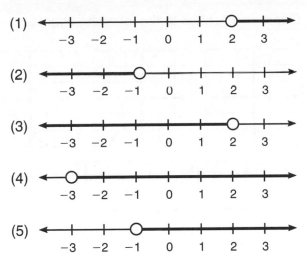

(1)
      −3 −2 −1 0 1 2 3

(2)
      −3 −2 −1 0 1 2 3

(3)
      −3 −2 −1 0 1 2 3

(4)
      −3 −2 −1 0 1 2 3

(5)
      −3 −2 −1 0 1 2 3

7. In which of the following are the numbers arranged in order from least to greatest?

(1) 2.34×10^2, 5.2×10^2, 4.7×10^{-1}

(2) 2.34×10^2, 4.7×10^{-1}, 5.2×10^2

(3) 4.7×10^{-1}, 5.2×10^2, 2.34×10^2

(4) 4.7×10^{-1}, 2.34×10^2, 5.2×10^2

(5) 5.2×10^2, 4.7×10^{-1}, 2.34×10^2

8. Which of the following shows the correct factors of the expression $x^2 - 12x + 36$?

(1) $(x + 6)(x + 6)$

(2) $(x - 6)(x - 6)$

(3) $(x - 6)(x + 6)$

(4) $(x - 3)(x - 12)$

(5) $(x + 3)(x + 12)$

9. Which ordered pair is a solution of
   $5x - y = 1$?

(1) $(1, -4)$

(2) $(0, 4)$

(3) $(1, 6)$

(4) $(-2, -11)$

(5) Not enough information is given.

Questions 10 and 11 refer to the following figure.

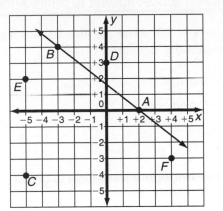

10. The graph of the equation $y = -\frac{3}{2}x + 3$ would pass through which of the following points on the coordinate grid?

(1) A and B

(2) A and C

(3) A, D, and F

(4) A and E

(5) C and D

11. What is the distance from point C to point A to the nearest whole unit?

(1) 7

(2) 8

(3) 9

(4) 10

(5) 11

12. The average human heart pumps 114,000 gallons of blood per day. Which of the following expressions represents that amount in scientific notation?

(1) 1.14×10^{-5}

(2) 1.14×10^{-4}

(3) 1.14×10^3

(4) 1.14×10^5

(5) 1.14×10^6

Part 2

Choose the <u>one best answer</u> to each question. You may <u>NOT</u> use your calculator.

13. If $x^2 + x = 20$, what are the values for x that will make the equation true?

    (1) -5 and 4

    (2) -5 and -4

    (3) 5 and 4

    (4) 5 and -4

    (5) Not enough information is given.

14. Aaron's weekly pay (p) can be represented by $p = \$200 + \$6s$, where s is the number of sales he makes in a week. How much will Aaron earn in a week if he makes 32 sales?

    (1) $192

    (2) $232

    (3) $238

    (4) $384

    (5) $392

15. Which ordered pair is a solution of $4x - y = 3$?

    (1) $(-5,2)$

    (2) $(-1,1)$

    (3) $(0,3)$

    (4) $(1,-1)$

    (5) $(2,5)$

16. A square mural has an area of about 240 square feet. What is the approximate length of one side of the mural?

    (1) between 18 and 19 feet

    (2) between 17 and 18 feet

    (3) between 16 and 17 feet

    (4) between 15 and 16 feet

    (5) between 14 and 15 feet

Question 17 refers to the following figures.

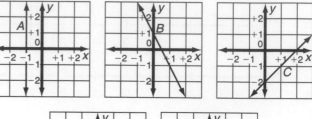

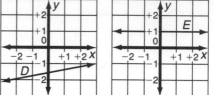

17. Which of the lines shown above has a negative slope?

    (1) A

    (2) B

    (3) C

    (4) D

    (5) E

18. Which of the following is equal to the expression $\dfrac{x + 4x}{x^2 - 2x}$?

    (1) 2

    (2) $\dfrac{5}{x - 2}$

    (3) $x + 2$

    (4) $1 + 2x$

    (5) $2x$

19. Which point is <u>not</u> on a graph of the line $2x - y = -1$?

    (1) $(-3,-5)$

    (2) $(-1,-1)$

    (3) $(1,3)$

    (4) $(2,5)$

    (5) $(3,6)$

Question 20 refers to the following figure.

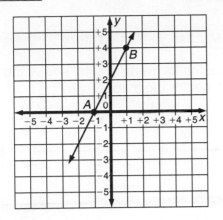

20. What is the equation of the line shown on the graph?

(1) $y = 2x + 2$

(2) $y = 2x - 1$

(3) $y = x + 2$

(4) $y = x - 1$

(5) $y = \frac{1}{2}x + 2$

21. A repair company charges a flat fee of $40 plus $30 for each hour ($h$) spent making a repair. Which of the following equations could be used to find the charge (c) for any service call?

(1) $c = \$30h$

(2) $c = \$40h$

(3) $c = \$40 + \$30h$

(4) $c = \$40h + \$30h$

(5) $c = \$30 + \$40h$

22. What is the slope of a line that passes through points at $(-2, -2)$ and $(-4, 4)$?

(1) -3

(2) -1

(3) $-\frac{1}{n}$

(4) $\frac{1}{3}$

(5) 3

23. The following amounts were deposited in a savings account each month.

| January | $20 | March | $44 |
| February | $32 | April | $56 |

If the pattern continues, how much will be deposited in December?

(1) $112

(2) $140

(3) $144

(4) $152

(5) $164

Questions 24 and 25 refer to the following graph.

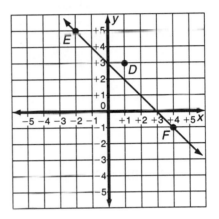

24. What is the equation of the line that passes through points E and F?

(1) $y = -3x - 3$

(2) $y = 3x + 3$

(3) $y = x + 3$

(4) $y = -x + 3$

(5) $y = -x - 3$

25. What is the distance in units from point F to point D?

(1) 3

(2) 4

(3) 5

(4) 6

(5) 7

Answers start on page 430.

Unit 3 Cumulative Review Algebra

Part 1

Directions: Choose the <u>one best answer</u> to each question. You <u>MAY</u> use your calculator.

1. What is the value of the expression $4x - 2y + xy$, when $x = -1$ and $y = 5$?

   (1) -26

   (2) -19

   (3) -9

   (4) -1

   (5) 1

2. Which of the following expressions is equal to $2 - (x + 7)$?

   (1) $x - 9$

   (2) $-x - 5$

   (3) $-x - 9$

   (4) $-x + 9$

   (5) $-x + 14$

3. If $-6(x + 1) + 4 = 8x - 9$, what is the value of x?

   (1) $\frac{1}{2}$

   (2) $-\frac{1}{2}$

   (3) -1

   (4) -3

   (5) -5

4. A certain number decreased by two is equal to seven increased by the quotient of the same number and four. What is the number?

   (1) -12

   (2) -5

   (3) 5

   (4) 7

   (5) 12

5. Which of the following graphs shows the solution set for the inequality?

   $$6 - 5x < 7x - 6$$

   (1)

   (2)

   (3)

   (4)

   (5)

6. The product of a number (x) and -4 is 8 more than 2 added to -5 times that number. Which of the following equations could be used to find the value of x?

   (1) $-4x - 8 = 2x + (-5x)$

   (2) $-4x + 8 = -5x + 2$

   (3) $-4x = -5x + 2 + 8$

   (4) $-4x = 8 + 2 + (-5)$

   (5) $-4x = 8 + x(-5 + 2)$

7. What is the slope of the line on the graph?

   (1) 2

   (2) $\frac{3}{2}$

   (3) $\frac{2}{3}$

   (4) $-\frac{2}{3}$

   (5) $-\frac{3}{2}$

8. The ordered pair $(0, -2)$ is a solution of which of the following equations?

(1) $2x - 3y = -6$

(2) $2x + 3y = 6$

(3) $-2x + 3y = -6$

(4) $-2x - 3y = 5$

(5) $x + 2y = 4$

9. For its standard checking account, Northwest Bank charges a monthly fee of $2.50 plus $0.10 per check. The function used to determine total monthly charges is $C = \$2.50 + \$0.10n$, where C = monthly charges and n = the number of checks. If a customer writes 24 checks during a month, how much will the customer be charged?

(1) $ 2.40

(2) $ 2.50

(3) $ 4.90

(4) $ 6.00

(5) $26.50

10. Which of the following expresses the product of 6,000 and 14,000 in scientific notation?

(1) 8.4×10^8

(2) 8.4×10^7

(3) 8.4×10^6

(4) 84×10^8

(5) 84×10^7

11. Which value for x makes the following inequality true: $x < 500$?

(1) 8^3

(2) 7^3

(3) 6^4

(4) 5^4

(5) 4^6

Questions 12 through 14 refer to the following graph.

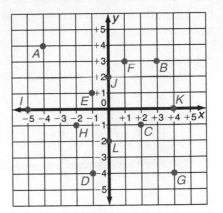

12. Which points have positive x-values and negative y-values?

(1) A, E

(2) A, E, I

(3) C, G

(4) C, G, L

(5) C, G, L, K

13. If the line for $x + 2y = -4$ were drawn on the graph, which of the following points would be on the line?

(1) D

(2) I

(3) J

(4) K

(5) L

14. What would be the slope of a line passing through points J and K?

(1) -2

(2) $-\dfrac{1}{2}$

(3) $\dfrac{1}{4}$

(4) $\dfrac{1}{2}$

(5) 2

Directions: Solve the following questions and enter your answers on the grids provided.

15. The pattern below is formed using the rule "multiply by 3, add 1." Grid in the 6th term in the pattern.

1   4   13   40 ... ...

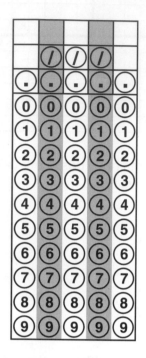

16. Grid in the value of the following expression:
$\sqrt{81} + 2^4 - \sqrt{169} + 5^2$

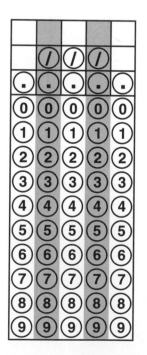

17. Show the location of the point whose coordinates are $(3, -4)$.

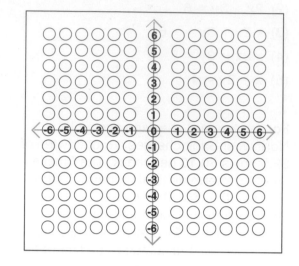

18. Show the location of the x-intercept for the line $-2x + 3y = 6$.

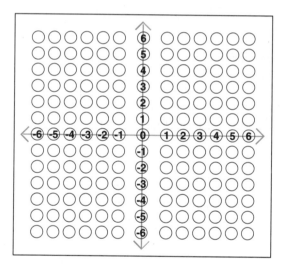

Part 2

Directions: Choose the <u>one best answer</u> to each question. You may <u>NOT</u> use your calculator.

19. The length of a rectangle is 6 times its width. The perimeter must be more than 110 feet. Which inequality can be solved to find the width (x)?

    (1) $7x > 110$

    (2) $6x^2 > 110$

    (3) $x + 6x > 110$

    (4) $2(6x) + x > 110$

    (5) $x + 6x + x + 6x > 110$

20. What is the solution set of the inequality $-5x + (-3) \leq 2x - 17$?

    (1) $x \leq -2$

    (2) $x \geq -2$

    (3) $x \leq 2$

    (4) $x \geq 2$

    (5) $x \leq 3$

21. Which of the following shows the product of -6 and x, decreased by the sum of -6 and y?

    (1) $-6x - (-6 + y)$

    (2) $-6y - (-6x)$

    (3) $(-6 + x) - (-6y)$

    (4) $(-6 + y) - (-6x)$

    (5) $(-6 + x) - (-6 + y)$

22. Twice a number, added to 3, is equal to the negative of the number. What is the number?

    (1) -3

    (2) -1

    (3) $-\dfrac{1}{3}$

    (4) 1

    (5) 3

Question 23 refers to the following graph.

-2

23. Which inequality is graphed on the number line?

    (1) $-2 > x$

    (2) $x < -2$

    (3) $-2 \leq x$

    (4) $x \leq -2$

    (5) $2 = x$

24. In the equation $x^2 - 7x = 18$, what are the possible values for x?

    (1) 2 and -9

    (2) 3 and -6

    (3) 6 and -3

    (4) 9 and -2

    (5) 9 and -9

25. What is the equation of a line that passes through points $(0,4)$ and $(-4,2)$?

    (1) $y = \dfrac{1}{2}x + 4$

    (2) $y = \dfrac{1}{2}x - 4$

    (3) $y = \dfrac{1}{2}x + 2$

    (4) $y = 2x + 4$

    (5) $y = 2x - 4$

Directions: Solve the following problems and enter your answers on the grids provided.

26. What is the value of the following expression if $x = 2$ and $y = -2$?

$$6x^2 - 5xy - 4y^2$$

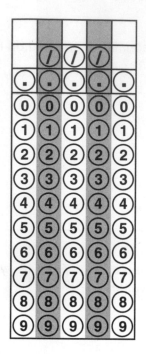

27. Albert is five times as old as Timothy. In five years, Albert will be four times as old as Timothy. How old will Timothy be in five years?

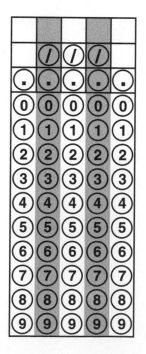

28. Show the location of the point whose coordinates are $(-3, 2)$.

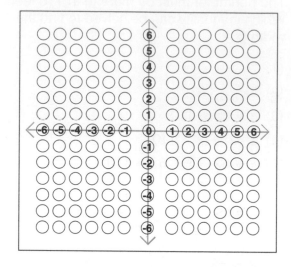

29. Show the location of the y-intercept for the line $2x - y = 4$.

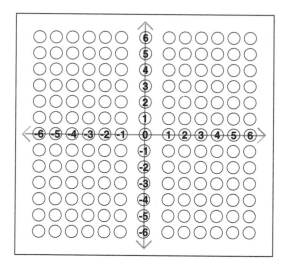

Answers start on page 431.

Cumulative Review Performance Analysis
Unit 3 • Algebra

Use the Answers and Explanations starting on page 431 to check your answers to the Unit 3 Cumulative Review. Then use the chart to figure out the skill areas in which you need more practice.

On the chart, circle the questions that you answered correctly. Write the number correct for each skill area. Add to find the total number of questions that you got correct on the Cumulative Review. If you feel that you need more practice, go back and review the lessons for the skill areas that were difficult for you.

Questions	Number Correct	Skill Area	Lessons for Review
1, 2, 21, 26	____/4	Integers and Algebraic Expressions	18
3, 4, 6, 22, 27	____/5	Equations	19
9, 10, 11, 15, 16	____/5	Exponents and Roots	20
5, 19, 20, **23**, 24	____/5	Factoring and Inequalities	21
7, 8, **12**, **13**, **14**, **17**, **18**, 25, **28**, **29**	____/10	The Coordinate Plane	22
TOTAL CORRECT	____/29		

Question numbers in **boldface** are based on graphics.

Geometry

Geometry is the area of mathematics that deals with points, lines, angles, two-dimensional shapes, and three-dimensional figures and is used to solve many common everyday problems. Geometric shapes are everywhere. You can see them indoors in rooms, furniture, clothing, and household objects and outside in buildings, streets, and bridges. One of the most important parts of geometry is learning to use formulas, such as those for perimeter, area, and volume, and the Pythagorean Relationship.

The principles of geometry show how the measurements of a shape or figure are related to its characteristics and how two-dimensional shapes and three-dimensional figures are related. Geometry is a very important topic on the GED Mathematics Test. Questions related to geometry will account for about 25 percent of the test.

Every day landscapers and other workers use geometry to do their jobs.

The lessons in this unit include:

Lesson 23: **Applying Formulas**
There is a wide variety of geometric shapes. In addition to squares and rectangles, some of the most common shapes are triangles, parallelograms, circles, pyramids, and cones. We use formulas to find the perimeter, area, and volume of these shapes.

Lesson 24: **Lines and Angles**
Many of the plane (flat) shapes that we work with are made up of lines and angles. The relationships between angles—vertical, complementary, supplementary, and congruent—are the basis for solving many common geometry problems.

Lesson 25: **Triangles and Quadrilaterals**
Some of the most common plane shapes are three-sided (triangles) and four-sided (quadrilaterals). Two plane shapes may be congruent (the same shape and size) or similar (equal angles and proportional sides).

Lesson 26: **Irregular Figures**
Not all plane figures are regular. Irregular figures—those that have unequal sides or are made up of several smaller shapes—are commonplace. Working with these figures involves using logical reasoning to determine what regular shapes make up the larger one.

Lesson 27: **Working with Right Triangles**
A right triangle is a special type of triangle involved in many problem-solving situations. You can use the Pythagorean Relationship to find the lengths of the sides of a right triangle—the legs (the two short sides) and the hypotenuse (the longest side). Sine, cosine, and tangent are important ratios that compare the lengths of specific sides of a right triangle.

PROBLEM-SOLVING STRATEGIES

- Converting Measurements
- Solving for Variables in Formulas
- Using Logical Reasoning
- Using Proportion in Geometry
- Recognizing Applications of the Pythagorean Relationship

Lesson 23   GED SKILL **Applying Formulas**

Triangles and Parallelograms

Triangles

Parallelograms

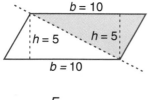

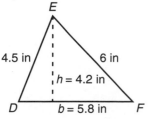

Two common shapes are triangles and parallelograms. A **triangle** has three sides and three angles. The sides of triangles can have different lengths, and their angles can have different measures.

A **parallelogram** is a four-sided figure whose opposite sides are parallel. *Parallel* means the extended lines would never intersect, or meet. Rectangles and squares are special parallelograms, although we usually think of a parallelogram as a rectangle leaning to one side.

The perimeter of geometric figure is the distance around a figure found by adding the lengths of all the sides of a figure regardless of the number or lengths of the sides.

Area is the measure of the surface of a two-dimensional shape. The area of a parallelogram is the product of the base and the height. The **base** can be any side. The **height** is the distance from a point on the opposite side straight down to the base. The height and base form a 90° angle.

Area = base × height or $A = bh$, where b = base and h = height

Example 1   Find the perimeter and area of parallelogram *ABCD*.

Step 1   Find the perimeter. Add the lengths of the sides. $10 + 10 + 8 + 8 = 36$ centimeters

Step 2   Find the area. **Choose the formula.** $A = bh$
Substitute the measures. $A = 10(5)$
Solve. $A = 50$ sq cm

The perimeter is **36 centimeters**; the area is **50 sq cm.**

A diagonal line drawn through the opposite corners divides the parallelogram into two identical triangles. Each triangle is one-half of the parallelogram. The formula for the area of a triangle is based on this fact.

Area = $\frac{1}{2}$ × base × height or $A = \frac{1}{2}bh$

Example 2   Find the perimeter and area of triangle *DEF*.

Step 1   Find the perimeter. Add the lengths of the sides. $4.5 + 6 + 5.8 = 16.3$ inches

Step 2   Find the area. Choose the formula. $A = \frac{1}{2}bh$
Substitute the measures.
Solve. $A = \frac{1}{2}(5.8)(4.2)$

$A = 12.18$ sq in

Use the decimal 0.5 for the $\frac{1}{2}$ in the area formula when using a calculator to solve problems.

area: 0.5 ✕ 5.8 ✕ 4.2 = 12.18

The perimeter of triangle *DEF* is **16.3 inches;** the area is **12.18 square inches.**

GED SKILL FOCUS

A. Find the perimeter and area of each figure. You may use your calculator.

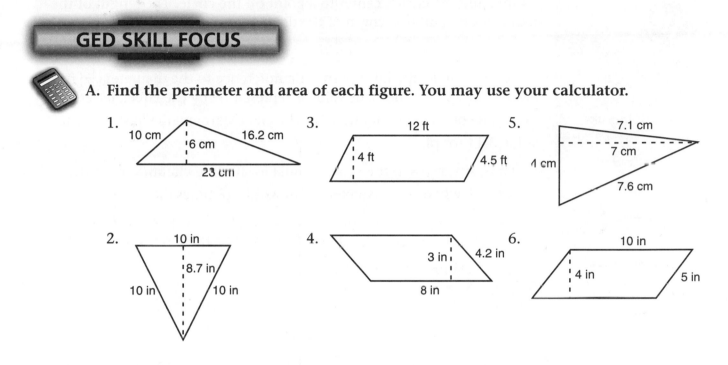

1. 10 cm 6 cm 16.2 cm 23 cm

2. 10 in 8.7 in 10 in 10 in

3. 12 ft 4 ft 4.5 ft

4. 3 in 4.2 in 8 in

5. 7.1 cm 7 cm 4 cm 7.6 cm

6. 10 in 4 in 5 in

B. Choose the best answer to the problem. Do not use a calculator.

Refer to the figure below to answer Question 7.

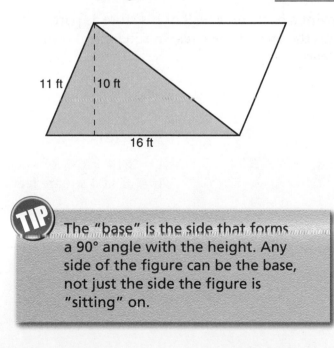

11 ft 10 ft 16 ft

7. Which of the following expressions can be used to find the area in square feet of the shaded portion of the parallelogram?

(1) 11^2

(2) 16(11)

(3) (16)(10)

(4) $\frac{1}{2}$(16)(10)

(5) $\frac{1}{2}$(16)(11)

TIP The "base" is the side that forms a 90° angle with the height. Any side of the figure can be the base, not just the side the figure is "sitting" on.

Answers start on page 434.

Circles

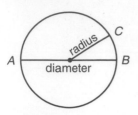

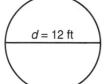

TIP

Estimate the circumference of a circle by multiplying its diameter by 3.

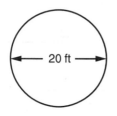

← 20 ft →

d = 12 ft

Most shapes have straight sides. A circle, on the other hand, has a curved edge. The perimeter, or the distance around a circle, is called the **circumference.** To find the circumference of a circle, you need to know either the diameter or radius of the circle.

The **diameter** of a circle is a line segment drawn through the center of the circle with endpoints on the circle. The **radius** is a line segment connecting the circle's center to a point on the circle. The length of the radius is one-half the length of the diameter.

$$r = \frac{1}{2}d = \frac{d}{2} \quad \text{or} \quad 2r = d$$

For any circle, the ratio of the circumference to the diameter $\left(\frac{C}{d}\right)$ is always the same value. This value is represented by the Greek letter π (pi). The value of π is $\frac{22}{7}$ or about 3.14. The GED Mathematics Test uses the value 3.14 for pi.

Thus, since $\frac{C}{d} = \pi$, then the formula for finding circumference (*C*) is $C = \pi \times d$, where *d* = diameter, or, in words, pi times diameter.

Example 1   Flo plans to put a railing around a circular pool. The diameter of the pool is 20 feet. What will be the length of the railing?

Step 1	Choose the formula.	$C = \pi d$
Step 2	Substitute the values.	$C = 3.14(20)$
Step 3	Solve.	$C = 62.8$ feet

The railing will be about **62.8 feet** long.

The formula for finding the area of a circle is $A = \pi r^2$, where *r* is the radius. In other words, the area of a circle is found by multiplying π (3.14) by the square of the radius.

Example 2   Paul wants to paint a circle on a wall of his store as part of a sign. What is the area of the circle in square feet if the diameter is 12 feet?

Step 1	Choose the formula.	$A = \pi r^2$
Step 2	Find the radius.	$r = \frac{1}{2}d$
		$r = \frac{1}{2}(12) = 6$ feet
Step 3	Substitute the values.	$A = 3.14 \times 6 \times 6$
Step 4	Solve.	$A = 113.04$ square feet

Even though the GED calculator has a pi key, you will probably save time by entering 3.14 for pi.

3.14 ⊠ 6 ⊠² = 113.04

The area of the circle in Paul's sign is about **113 square feet.**

A. Solve. You may use a calculator.

Refer to the diagram below to answer
Questions 1 and 2.

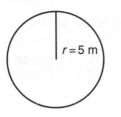

1. What is the diameter of the circle in
   meters?

2. What is the circumference of the circle
   to the nearest tenth meter?

Refer to the diagram below to answer
Questions 3 and 4.

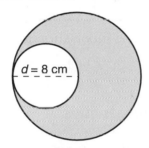

3. The diameter of the smaller circle is
   equal to the radius of the larger circle.
   What is the diameter of the larger
   circle in centimeters?

4. What is the radius of the smaller circle
   in centimeters?

5. The diameter of a circle is 7 inches.
   What is the circumference to the
   nearest inch?

6. If the radius of a circle is 2 feet, what is
   the area of the circle in square feet?

Refer to the diagram below to answer
Questions 7 and 8.

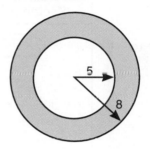

7. What is the circumference to the
   nearest inch of the larger outer circle?

8. What is the area of the shaded ring to
   the nearest square inch? (*Hint:* Subtract
   the area of the smaller circle from the
   area of the larger one.)

B. Solve.

9. The figure below shows the surface of a
   circular patio to be painted. About how
   many square feet is the surface of the
   patio? (*Hint:* Which formula gives
   square feet?)

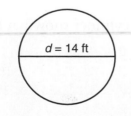

10. A circle has a radius of 3 yards. What is
    its area to the nearest square yard?

11. What is the circumference to the
    nearest centimeter of a circle with a
    radius of 7 centimeters?

Answers start on page 434.

Volume

Volume is a measure in cubic units of the amount of space inside a three-dimensional (or "solid") object. Each cubic unit is a cube made up of 6 identical square sides (called *faces*). For example, a cubic inch is a cube with 1-inch edges on each face. Imagine filling a space with neat layers of ice cubes. The volume of the space equals the number of cubes.

Three common solid shapes are a **rectangular solid**, a **cube**, and a **cylinder**. The volume (V) is the area (A) of the base (the side making a 90° angle to the height) multiplied by the height of the object. The general formula is **$V = Ah$**. This general formula is rewritten for each type of shape. Note that the base of each solid figure is a shape you already know.

TIP

Save time by memorizing the basic formulas for perimeter, area, and volume. Refer to the inside back cover of this book for the complete list of GED formulas.

Rectangular solid	Cube	Cylinder
V = (area of rectangle)h	V = (area of square)h	V = (area of circle)h
= (length × width) × height	= (edge × edge) × edge	= (pi × radius²) × height
= lwh	= s^3 (edge = side)	= $\pi r^2 h$

Example 1   What is the volume of the block shown at left?

Step 1   Choose the formula. $V = lwh$
Step 2   Substitute and solve. $V = 10 \times 6 \times 8 = 480$ cu in

The volume of the block is **480 cubic inches.**

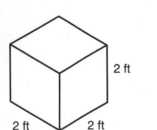

A cube is a special rectangular solid. The volume formula is still the product of length, width, and height, but the formula is written differently.

Example 2   What is the volume of a cube that is 2 feet long on each side?

Step 1   Choose the formula. $V = s^3$
Step 2   Substitute. $V = 2^3$
Step 3   Solve. $V = 2 \times 2 \times 2 = 8$ cu ft

Use the [x^y] or [x^3] key to cube a number.

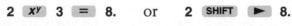

   2 **x^y** **3** **=** **8.**   or   **2** **SHIFT** **▶** **8.**

The volume of the cube is **8 cubic feet.**

The base of a cylinder is a circle. To find the volume of the cylinder, find the area of the circle (πr^2) and multiply this area by the height (h).

Example 3   What is the volume of the cylinder shown at left?

Step 1   Choose the formula. V = (area of a circle) × $h = \pi r^2 h$
Step 2   Substitute. $V = 3.14 \times 4^2 \times 10$
Step 3   Solve. $V = 3.14 \times 16 \times 10 = 502.4$ cu cm

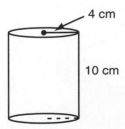

You can use either the x^2 or x^y key when solving volume problems on a calculator. Try the key strokes below to solve the cylinder problem in Example 3.

3.14 ✕ 4 ✕ 4 ✕ 10 = 502.4   or

3.14 ✕ 4 x^2 ✕ 10 = 502.4

The volume of the cylinder is about **502.4 cubic centimeters.**

GED SKILL FOCUS

A. **Find the volume of each figure to the nearest whole unit. You may use your calculator.**

1.
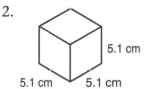
6 in
9 in
16 in

2.
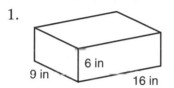
5.1 cm
5.1 cm   5.1 cm

3.

3 ft
7 ft

4.
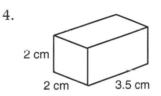
2 cm
2 cm   3.5 cm

5.
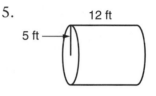
12 ft
5 ft

B. **Solve. You may use your calculator for question 9.**

6. What is the volume in cubic feet of a rectangular crate with these measurements: length = 4 feet, width = 5 feet, and height = 6 feet?

7. The rectangular trash containers at an apartment complex are 10 feet long, 6 feet wide, and 5 feet high. How many cubic feet of trash does each container hold?

8. A health club is going to build a swimming pool. The hole needs to be 100 feet long by 25 feet wide with a depth of 5 feet. How many cubic feet of dirt will be removed to dig the hole?

9. Paul needs to store a box that measures $1\frac{1}{2}$ yards on each side. What is the volume in cubic yards of the box?

Refer to the diagram below to answer Question 10.

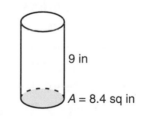
9 in
$A = 8.4$ sq in

10. Which of the following expressions can be used to find the volume in cubic inches of the vase?

(1) (8.4)9

(2) $(8.4^2)(9)$

(3) (3.14)(8.4)(9)

(4) $(3.14)(8.4^2)(9)$

(5) $(3.14)(8.4)(9^2)$

Answers start on page 435.

Pyramids and Cones

The three-dimensional solids studied so far—rectangular containers, cubes, and cylinders—all have two identical bases. You may think of these bases as the top and bottom sides of the figure. Pyramids and cones are also three-dimensional solids, but they have only one base.

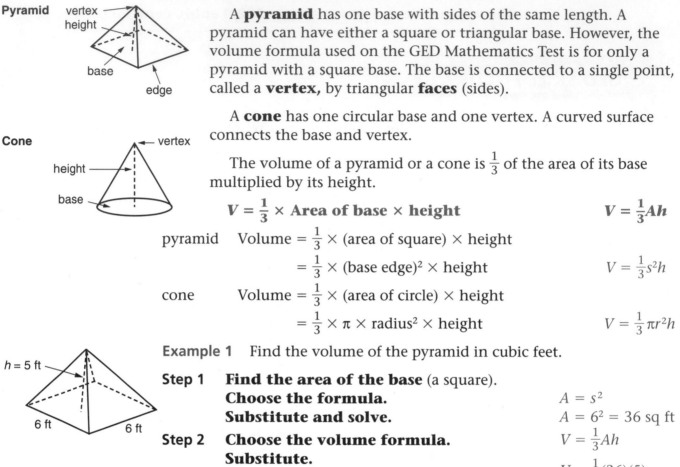

Pyramid vertex, height, base, edge

Cone vertex, height, base

A **pyramid** has one base with sides of the same length. A pyramid can have either a square or triangular base. However, the volume formula used on the GED Mathematics Test is for only a pyramid with a square base. The base is connected to a single point, called a **vertex,** by triangular **faces** (sides).

A **cone** has one circular base and one vertex. A curved surface connects the base and vertex.

The volume of a pyramid or a cone is $\frac{1}{3}$ of the area of its base multiplied by its height.

$$V = \frac{1}{3} \times \textbf{Area of base} \times \textbf{height} \qquad V = \frac{1}{3}Ah$$

pyramid   Volume $= \frac{1}{3} \times$ (area of square) $\times$ height

$= \frac{1}{3} \times$ (base edge)$^2 \times$ height $\qquad V = \frac{1}{3}s^2h$

cone   Volume $= \frac{1}{3} \times$ (area of circle) $\times$ height

$= \frac{1}{3} \times \pi \times$ radius$^2 \times$ height $\qquad V = \frac{1}{3}\pi r^2 h$

Example 1   Find the volume of the pyramid in cubic feet.

$h = 5$ ft, 6 ft, 6 ft

Step 1   **Find the area of the base** (a square).
Choose the formula. $\qquad\qquad\qquad A = s^2$
Substitute and solve. $\qquad\qquad\quad A = 6^2 = 36$ sq ft

Step 2   **Choose the volume formula.** $\qquad V = \frac{1}{3}Ah$
Substitute.
Solve. $\qquad\qquad\qquad\qquad\qquad V = \frac{1}{3}(36)(5)$
$\qquad\qquad\qquad\qquad\qquad\qquad\qquad V = 60$ cu ft

You can use the fraction key to multiply by a fraction.
Or multiply the area and height and divide by 3.

1 [a b/c] 3 [×] 36 [×] 5 [=] 60. or 36 [×] 5 [÷] 3 [=] 60.

The volume of the pyramid is **60 cubic feet.**

Example 2   Find the volume of the cone to the nearest cubic centimeter.

$h = 9$ cm, $r = 3$ cm

Step 1   Use the formula for finding the volume of a cone. $\qquad V = \frac{1}{3}\pi r^2 h$

Step 2   Substitute. $\qquad\qquad\qquad V = \frac{1}{3}(3.14)(3^2)(9)$

Step 3   Solve. $\qquad\qquad\qquad\qquad V = \frac{1}{3}(3.14)(9)(9) = 84.78,$
which rounds to 85 cu cm

The volume of the cone is about **85 cubic centimeters.**

A. Find the volume of each figure. Round your answers to the nearest whole number. You may use a calculator.

1.

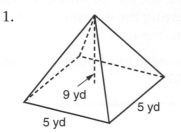

9 yd

5 yd   5 yd

3.

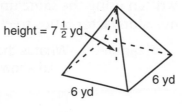

height = $7\frac{1}{2}$ yd

6 yd

6 yd

5.

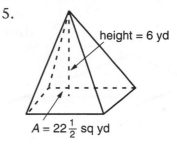

height = 6 yd

$A = 22\frac{1}{2}$ sq yd

2.

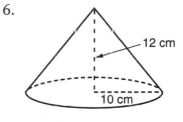

6 in

$A = 12.5$ sq in

4.

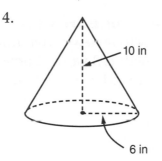

10 in

6 in

6 in

6.

12 cm

10 cm

B. Solve.

7. What is the volume in cubic centimeters of a cone with a height of 8 centimeters and a base area of 12.6 square centimeters? (*Hint:* You already know the area of the circular base. Use $V = \frac{1}{3}Ah$ instead of $V = \frac{1}{3}\pi r^2 h$.)

8. The area of the base of pyramid A is 25 square meters. The area of the base of pyramid B is 64 square meters. In cubic meters, how much greater is the volume of pyramid B than the volume of pyramid A?

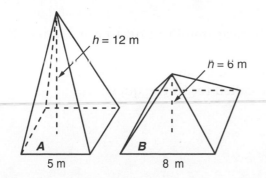

$h = 12$ m

$h = 6$ m

A   B

5 m   8 m

9. A pyramid has a square base with one edge labeled 9 centimeters and a height of 18.25 centimeters. Which of the following expressions can be used to find the volume of the pyramid in cubic centimeters?

(1) $9^2(18.25)$

(2) $9^3(18.25)$

(3) $\frac{1}{3}(9)(18.25)$

(4) $\frac{1}{3}(9^2)(18.25)$

(5) Not enough information is given.

Answers start on page 435.

GED STRATEGY Solving Word Problems

Converting Measurements

To solve perimeter, area, and volume problems, all the measurements must be written using the same units. Converting measurements involves using conversion factor ratios to change from one unit to another.

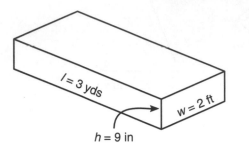

l = 3 yds
w = 2 ft
h = 9 in

Example What is the volume in <u>cubic inches</u> of the rectangular solid shown to the left?

(1)   54
(2)   648
(3) 1,944
(4) 23,328
(5) 93,312

Step 1 **Convert measurements.** Convert the length and width to inches. (To review converting measurements, see pages 158–159.) The length is 3 yards. Convert to inches using the conversion factor: 1 yard = 36 inches. Cross multiply to solve.

$$\frac{\text{yard}}{\text{inches}} \quad \frac{1}{36} = \frac{3}{l} \quad\quad l = 3(36) \quad\quad l = 108 \text{ inches}$$

The width is 2 feet. Convert to inches: 1 foot = 12 inches.

$$\frac{\text{foot}}{\text{inches}} \quad \frac{1}{12} = \frac{2}{w} \quad\quad w = 2(12) \quad\quad w = 24 \text{ inches}$$

Step 2 **Choose the appropriate formula.** $V = lwh$
Substitute and solve. $V = 108 \times 24 \times 9 = 23{,}328$ cu in

The correct option is **(4) 23,328.**

TIP

More than one unit of measure may appear in the same problem. Convert all measurements to the same unit before using formulas.

You could also have solved this problem in terms of feet or yards.

In feet:	**In yards:**
$V = lwh$	$V = lwh$
$= 3 \text{ yd} \times 2 \text{ ft} \times 9 \text{ in}$	$= 3 \text{ yd} \times 2 \text{ ft} \times 9 \text{ in}$
$= 9 \text{ ft} \times 2 \text{ ft} \times \frac{3}{4} \text{ ft}$	$= 3 \text{ yd} \times \frac{2}{3} \text{ yd} \times \frac{1}{4} \text{ yd}$
$= \mathbf{13\frac{1}{2} \text{ cu ft}}$	$= \mathbf{\frac{1}{2} \text{ cu yd}}$

Often you must decide which measurement unit to use. Generally, it is best to convert to the smallest unit so that you will not have to work with fractions. Also, read the question. You usually save time by converting all measures to the unit of measure called for in the question.

Directions: Choose the <u>one best answer</u> to each question.

<u>Questions 1 and 2</u> refer to the following figure.

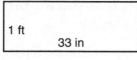

1 ft
33 in

1. What is the perimeter of the rectangle in <u>feet</u>?

   (1) $6\frac{1}{2}$

   (2) $7\frac{1}{2}$

   (3) 8

   (4) $8\frac{1}{4}$

   (5) $8\frac{1}{2}$

2. What is the area of the rectangle in <u>square inches</u>?

   (1) 364

   (2) 386

   (3) 390

   (4) 412

   (5) 432

<u>Question 3</u> refers to the following diagram.

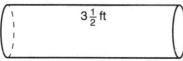

$3\frac{1}{2}$ ft

diameter of base is 12 inches

3. Which of the following expressions can be used to find the volume of the cylinder in <u>cubic inches</u>?

   (1) 42(12)

   (2) 3.14(6^2)

   (3) 3.14(6^2)(3.5)

   (4) (3.14)(6^2)(42)

   (5) (3.14)(12^2)(42)

4. What is the approximate volume in <u>cubic feet</u> of a box with a length of $2\frac{1}{2}$ ft, a width of 1 ft 6 in, and a height of 1 ft 9 in?

   (1) between 3 and 4

   (2) between 4 and 5

   (3) between 5 and 6

   (4) between 6 and 7

   (5) between 7 and 8

<u>Question 5</u> refers to the following diagram.

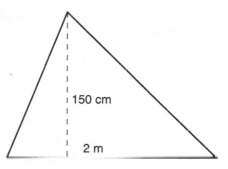

150 cm

2 m

5. What is the area in <u>square centimeters</u> of the triangle in the figure?
   (*Hint:* 1 meter = 100 centimeters)

   (1) 12,000

   (2) 12,500

   (3) 15,000

   (4) 20,000

   (5) 22,500

6. A cone has a height of 1 foot 4 inches and a base with an area of 18 square inches. What is the volume of the cone in <u>cubic inches</u>?

   (1) 84

   (2) 96

   (3) 144

   (4) 252

   (5) 288

Answers start on page 436.

GED STRATEGY Solving Word Problems

Solving for Variables in Formulas

You have already worked with various geometric formulas. Formulas are a type of equation that contains variables used to solve measurement and geometry problems. The algebraic properties that you learned in Unit 3 can be used to solve formulas for a specific variable.

Remember that an equation shows two equal mathematical statements, called *expressions*. In order to keep the expressions equal, apply the same operation to both sides of the equation.

Example 1 The volume of the rectangular container is 120 cubic feet. What is the height of the container?

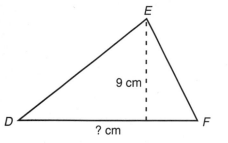

Step 1	**Choose the appropriate formula.**	$V = lwh$
Step 2	**Substitute the known values.**	$120 = 8(3)h$
Step 3	**Simplify.**	$120 = 24h$
Step 4	**Solve for the unknown variable.**	$\dfrac{120}{24} = \dfrac{24h}{24}$
		$5 = h$

The height of the container is **5 feet.**

Often, the way to answer a set-up question on the GED Mathematics Test is to rewrite the equation to solve for a certain variable. The five multiple-choice options for such questions show possible ways to solve the problem. You have to choose the correct one as shown below.

Example 2 The area of triangle *DEF* is 72 sq cm. Which of the following expressions could be used to find the length of the base of triangle *DEF*?

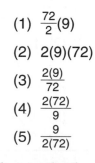

(1) $\dfrac{72}{2}(9)$

(2) $2(9)(72)$

(3) $\dfrac{2(9)}{72}$

(4) $\dfrac{2(72)}{9}$

(5) $\dfrac{9}{2(72)}$

Step 1	Choose the formula (area of a triangle).	$A = \frac{1}{2}bh$
Step 2	Rewrite the formula to solve for the base (*b*).	$2 \times A = \frac{1}{2}bh \times 2$
		$2A = bh$
		$\dfrac{2A}{h} = b$
Step 3	Substitute the known values.	$\dfrac{2(72)}{9} = b$

Option (4) $\dfrac{2(72)}{9}$ is correct.

Directions: Choose the <u>one best answer</u> to each question.

1. The area of a rectangular mural is 180 square feet. If the mural is 15 feet in length, what is its width in feet?

   (1)   6
   (2)   12
   (3)   165
   (4) 2700
   (5) Not enough information is given.

Question 2 refers to the following diagram.

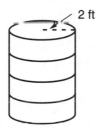

2. A storage barrel has the shape of a cylinder. The volume of the barrel is about 81.64 cubic feet. Which of the following expressions could be used to find its height in feet?

   (1) $\frac{81.64}{(3.14)(2^2)}$

   (2) $\frac{(3.14)(2^2)}{81.64}$

   (3) $\frac{81.64(2^2)}{(3.14)}$

   (4) $81.64(3.14)(2^2)$

   (5) $81.64 - (3.14)(2^2)$

3. A small section of a roof has the shape of a triangle. The total area of the section is 10.5 square feet. If the height of the section is 3.5 feet, what is the measure of the base in feet?

   (1)   0
   (2)   6
   (3)   7
   (4) 14
   (5) 36.75

Question 4 refers to the following figure.

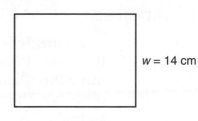

4. The perimeter of the rectangle is 64 cm. Which of the following expressions could be used to find the length of the rectangle?

   (1) $\frac{64}{14}$

   (2) $\frac{64}{2(14)}$

   (3) $64 - 14$

   (4) $\frac{64 - 2(14)}{2}$

   (5) $\frac{64 + 2(14)}{2}$

Question 5 refers to the following diagram.

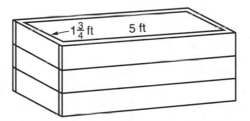

5. Mike plans to build a wooden flower box similar to the one shown in the diagram. He wants the box to have a volume of $17\frac{1}{2}$ cubic feet. If base of the box has the dimensions shown above, what should the height of the box measure in feet?

   (1)   2

   (2) $2\frac{1}{2}$

   (3) $3\frac{1}{2}$

   (4)   10

   (5) Not enough information is given.

Answers start on page 436.

Kinds of Angles

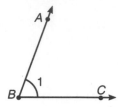

An **angle** is the space or opening between a pair of lines, called **rays,** that extend from a common point, the **vertex.** Angles can be named using three letters: a point on one ray, the vertex, and a point on the other ray. They can also be named by the letter of the vertex alone or by a number written inside the angle. The symbol for angle is ∠. This angle can be named ∠*ABC*, ∠*B*, or ∠1.

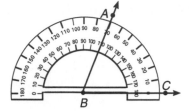

Angles are measured in degrees (°) using a protractor. When ray *BC* is placed along the bottom of the protractor, the measure of the angle is read along the scale that starts at 0. The measure (*m*) of angle *ABC* equals 70° or in symbols, *m*∠*ABC* = 70°.

Angles are classified by their measures. These measures are based on the fact that a circle contains 360°. When measuring an angle, you are actually measuring the number of degrees (or part of the circle) contained in the opening between two rays.

A **right angle** measures exactly 90°.	An **acute angle** measures less than 90°.	An **obtuse angle** measures more than 90° but less than 180°.	A **straight angle** measures exactly 180°.	A **reflex angle** measures more than 180° but less than 360°.
This symbol means the angle measures 90°.				

Angles are also related based on the sum of their measures. (Here's a memory aid: 90 comes before 180; *c* comes before *s*.)

- If the sum of the measures of two angles equals 90°, the angles are called **complementary angles.**
- If the sum of the measures of two angles equals 180°, the angles are called **supplementary angles.**

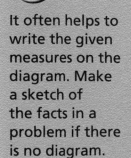

TIP

It often helps to write the given measures on the diagram. Make a sketch of the facts in a problem if there is no diagram.

Example 1 If the measure of ∠*BXC* is 25°, what is the measure of ∠*AXB*?

The angles are complementary because ∠*AXC* has a right angle symbol, and a right angle measures 90°.

Step 1 **Write an equation.**   *m*∠*AXB* + *m*∠*BXC* = 90°
Step 2 **Substitute the known measures.**   *m*∠*AXB* + 25° = 90°
Step 3 **Solve.** Subtract 25 from both sides.   *m*∠*AXB* = 65°

The measure of ∠*AXB* is **65°**.

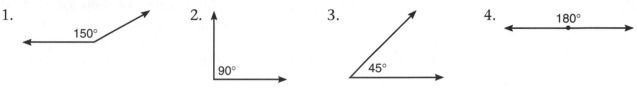

Example 2 Angles 1 and 2 are supplementary angles. If the measure of ∠1 is 35°, what is the measure of ∠2?

Step 1	**Write an equation.**	$m\angle 1 + m\angle 2 = 180°$
Step 2	**Substitute the known measures.**	$35° + m\angle 2 = 180°$
Step 3	**Solve.**	$m\angle 2 = 145°$

The measure of ∠2 is **145°**.

GED SKILL FOCUS

A. Label each angle as acute, obtuse, right, or straight.

1. 150° 2. 90° 3. 45° 4. 180°

B. Solve.

Refer to the figure below to answer Questions 5 through 8. ∠AXB and ∠BXC are complementary.

5. What is $m\angle BXC$?

6. What is $m\angle DXC$?

7. What is $m\angle BXD$?

8. Which angle forms a supplementary angle with ∠DXB?

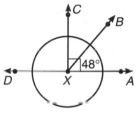

Refer to the figure below to answer Questions 9 through 12. ∠ZXY and ∠YXQ are complementary.

9. What is $m\angle ZXY$?

10. What is $m\angle ZXR$?

11. What is $m\angle QXR$?

12. What is the measure of the reflex angle marked by the curved arrow?

C. Choose the best answer to each question.

13. The measure of ∠A is 28°. The measure of ∠B is 62°. Which of the following is true?

    (1) ∠A is complementary to ∠B.

    (2) ∠A and ∠B are supplementary angles.

    (3) ∠A and ∠B are obtuse angles.

    (4) ∠A and ∠B are reflex angles.

    (5) ∠A is an acute angle; ∠B is an obtuse angle.

14. ∠M and ∠R are supplementary angles. The measure of ∠M is 40°. What is the measure of ∠R?

    (1) 40°

    (2) 50°

    (3) 90°

    (4) 140°

    (5) 180°

Answers start on page 437.

Congruent and Vertical Angles

Angles can be related in other ways. Angles that have equal measures are **congruent angles.** In the figure below, angle ABC is congruent to angle XYZ. The angles are congruent even though they are not turned in the same direction. The symbol $\cong$ means "is congruent to."

$\angle ABC \cong \angle XYZ$

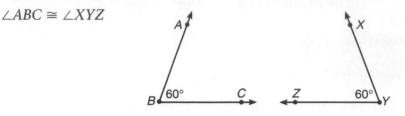

TIP

Learn the meaning of terms used in geometry. A simple problem is impossible if you don't know the vocabulary.

Some angles have a special relationship because of their location with respect to each other. When two lines intersect, or cross, four angles are formed. The angles that are across from each other are called **opposite angles,** or **vertical angles.** Each pair of vertical angles is congruent.

$\angle 5 \cong \angle 6$	$m\angle 5 = m\angle 6$
$\angle 7 \cong \angle 8$	$m\angle 7 = m\angle 8$

Angles can also be described as **adjacent** or **non-adjacent.** Adjacent angles have a common vertex and a common ray.

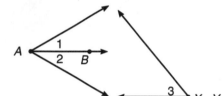

$\angle 1$ and $\angle 2$ are adjacent. They share vertex A and ray AB (also written as $\overrightarrow{AB}$).

$\angle 3$ and $\angle 4$ are non-adjacent angles.

Many geometry problems require you to apply logical reasoning to find congruent angles. Use your understanding of the properties of angles to solve geometry problems.

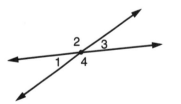

Example In the figure, angle 1 measures 30°. Find the measures of angles 2, 3, and 4.

Step 1 **Assign the known values.** $m\angle 1 = 30°$

Step 2 **Identify known relationships.**
(a) supplementary angles $m\angle 1 + m\angle 2 = 180°$
(b) vertical angles $m\angle 1 = m\angle 3;\ m\angle 2 = m\angle 4$

Step 3 **Solve for unknown values.**

(a) $m\angle 1 + m\angle 2 = 30° + m\angle 2 = 180°;\ m\angle 2 = 150°$

(b) $m\angle 3 = 30°;\ m\angle 4 = 150°$

The angle measures are $m\angle 2 = 150°$, $m\angle 3 = 30°$, and $m\angle 4 = 150°$.

A. Refer to the figure shown at the right to answer <u>Questions 1 through 9</u>.

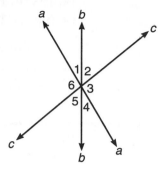

1. Name an angle adjacent to ∠3.

2. Name the angle that is the vertical angle to ∠2.

3. Name the angle that is the vertical angle to ∠6.

4. Name the angle that is the vertical angle to ∠1.

5. Name two angles that are adjacent to ∠1.

6. Name two angles that are adjacent to ∠5.

7. Name the angle congruent to ∠5.

8. Name the angle congruent to ∠4.

9. Name the angle congruent to ∠3.

B. Solve.

Refer to the following information to answer <u>Questions 10 through 15</u>.

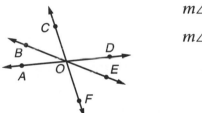

$$m\angle AOB = 30°$$
$$m\angle EOF = 50°$$

10. Since $m\angle EOF = 50°$, what other angle also has a measure equal to 50°?

11. The sum of the measures of ∠AOB, ∠BOC, and ∠COD is 180°. What is the measure of ∠COD?

12. What is the measure of ∠AOF? (*Hint:* You already found the measure of the vertical angle to ∠AOF.)

13. What is the sum of the measures of ∠DOE and ∠EOF?

14. What is the measure of the reflex angle for ∠EOF?

15. Which two angles are supplementary to ∠DOF?

16. Angle Q is congruent to its vertical angle, ∠R. Which of the following <u>must</u> be true?

(1) ∠Q and ∠R are complementary angles.

(2) ∠Q and ∠R are acute angles.

(3) ∠Q and ∠R are obtuse angles.

(4) ∠Q and ∠R are adjacent angles.

(5) ∠Q and ∠R have equal measures.

Refer to the figure below to answer <u>Question 17</u>.

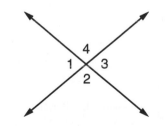

17. The measure of ∠4 = 100°. Which of the following statements is true?

(1) ∠4 and ∠2 are complementary

(2) $m\angle 2 = 100°$

(3) $m\angle 1 = 100°$

(4) $m\angle 1 + m\angle 3 = 100°$

(5) $m\angle 4 + m\angle 2 = 180°$

Answers start on page 437.

Lines and Angles

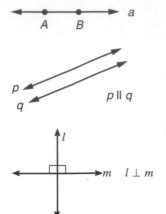

In geometry, arrows are drawn at both ends of a line to show that the line extends indefinitely in both directions. A line can be named by two points on the line. The line shown here is "line AB" ($\overline{AB}$). The line can also be named by a lower case letter (line a).

Two lines in the same plane (flat surface) either intersect (cross) or are parallel. **Parallel lines** never intersect. They have exactly the same slope. The symbol ‖ means "is parallel to."

As you have seen, intersecting lines form vertical angles. When two lines intersect to form right angles, the lines are **perpendicular.** The symbol for perpendicular lines is ⊥.

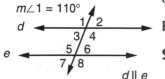

Special pairs of angles are formed when a line, called a **transversal,** crosses two or more parallel lines. In the figure at right, the transversal intersects line AB and line CD. Notice that some of the angles formed are inside the parallel lines and some are outside.

You already know that vertical angles are equal in measure ($\angle a$ and $\angle d$; $\angle b$ and $\angle c$; $\angle e$ and $\angle h$; $\angle f$ and $\angle g$). The following pairs of angles are also always equal in measure (congruent).

Corresponding angles are in the same position with respect to the transversal. That is, they are on the same side of the transversal and either both above or both below the parallel lines

$\angle a$ and $\angle e$ $\angle b$ and $\angle f$ $\angle c$ and $\angle g$ $\angle d$ and $\angle h$

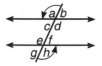

Alternate exterior angles are always outside the parallel lines and on opposite sides of the transversal.

$\angle a$ and $\angle h$ $\angle b$ and $\angle g$

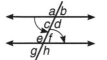

Alternate interior angles are always inside the parallel lines and on opposite sides of the transversal.

$\angle c$ and $\angle f$ $\angle d$ and $\angle e$

If you know the measure of one angle, you can find the measures of the others. There are often several ways to determine the other angles.

Example   If the measure of $\angle 1$ is 110°, what is the measure of $\angle 6$?

Step 1   **Identify an angle that is related to both the known and unknown angles.**

Angles 1 and 5 are corresponding (congruent) angles. $m\angle 1 = m\angle 5$
Angles 5 and 6 are supplementary angles. $m\angle 5 + m\angle 6 = 180°$

Step 2   **Find the measure of the angle identified in Step 1.**

Since $m\angle 1 = 110°$, and $m\angle 1 = m\angle 5$, $m\angle 5 = 110°$

Step 3   **Find the measure of the unknown angle.**

$m\angle 5 + m\angle 6 = 180°$; $m\angle 5 = 110°$ $m\angle 6 = 180° - 110° = 70°$

The measure of $\angle 6$ is **70°.**

A. Refer to the figure shown at the right to answer <u>Questions 1 through 10</u>. **Lines *p* and *m* are parallel.**

1. Name the interior angles.
2. Name the interior angle on the same side of the transversal as ∠6.
3. Name the exterior angles.
4. Name the exterior angle on the same side of the transversal as ∠4.
5. Which angle corresponds to ∠1?
6. Which angle corresponds to ∠7?
7. Which angle corresponds to ∠8?
8. Which angle corresponds to ∠2?
9. Which angle is an alternate interior angle with ∠2?
10. Which angle is an alternate exterior angle with ∠5?

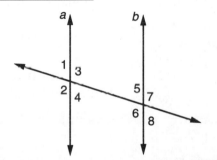

B. Choose the best answer to each question.

Refer to the diagram below to answer <u>Questions 11 and 12</u>.

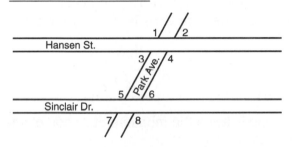

11. Hansen Street runs parallel to Sinclair Drive. Which statement is true?

    (1) $m\angle 1 = m\angle 7$

    (2) $m\angle 2 + m\angle 6 = 90°$

    (3) ∠5 is complementary to ∠6.

    (4) ∠4 is adjacent to ∠6.

    (5) $m\angle 1 + m\angle 7 = 180°$

12. The measure of ∠2 is equal to 60°. Which other angles must also measure 60°?

    (1) Only ∠3

    (2) ∠3, ∠6, and ∠7

    (3) ∠3, ∠5, and ∠8

    (4) ∠4, ∠6, and ∠8

    (5) Only ∠7

Refer to the diagram below to answer <u>Questions 13 and 14</u>.

13. Line *a* is parallel to line *b*. Which of the following statements is true?

    (1) $m\angle 2 + m\angle 5 = 180°$

    (2) ∠1 is complementary to ∠2.

    (3) ∠6 is supplementary to ∠7.

    (4) ∠2 and ∠6 are vertical angles.

    (5) ∠1 and ∠6 are corresponding angles.

14. Which of the following are <u>not</u> supplementary angles?

    (1) ∠1 and ∠2

    (2) ∠1 and ∠3

    (3) ∠3 and ∠7

    (4) ∠3 and ∠8

    (5) ∠4 and ∠6

Answers start on page 438.

GED STRATEGY **Solving Word Problems**

Using Logical Reasoning

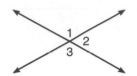

Some questions on the GED Mathematics Test are solved using logic. Based on statements called **assumptions** given in the problem and any labels on the figure, decide which of the five answer options is true.

Example 1   The sum of the measures of angles 1 and 2 is 180°. The sum of the measures of angles 2 and 3 is 180°. Based on this information, which of the following statements is true?

(1) $m\angle 1 = 120°$
(2) $m\angle 2 = 60°$
(3) $m\angle 3 = 100°$
(4) $m\angle 1 = m\angle 2$
(5) $m\angle 1 = m\angle 3$

Angles 1 and 3 are vertical angles so **option (5) $m\angle 1 = m\angle 3$** is correct.

Options (1), (2), (3), and (4) are incorrect because no information is provided about specific angle measures. Although the measure of angle 1 looks greater than the measure of angle 2 in the figure, do not base a conclusion on the appearance of a figure; you must rely only on supporting evidence. Option (4) would be correct only if the intersecting lines were perpendicular.

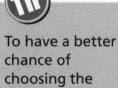

To have a better chance of choosing the correct option eliminate any answer options you know are incorrect.

You often need to apply algebraic reasoning to solve geometry problems involving complementary and supplementary angles.

Example 2   The measure of an angle is twice the measure of its complement. What is the smaller angle's measure?

(1) 20°
(2) 30°
(3) 45°
(4) 90°
(5) Not enough information is given.

Step 1   Assign the variables.

Let x = the measure of the smaller angle.
Let $2x$ = the measure of the larger angle.

Step 2   Write an equation. The sum of the measures $x + 2x = 90°$
of the two angles is 90° because the angles are complementary.

Step 3   Solve. $3x = 90°$
                                                                    $x = 30°$

The smaller angle measures 30°. **Option (2)** is correct. If the question had asked for the larger angle, the answer would be 2(30°) = 60°.

Directions: Choose the one best answer to each question.

Question 1 is based on the following figure.

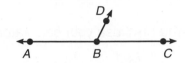

1. Angle *ABC* is a straight angle. Which of the following statements is true?

   (1) $m\angle DBC = 90°$

   (2) $\angle ABD$ and $\angle DBC$ are supplementary.

   (3) $m\angle ABD = 90°$

   (4) $\angle ADD$ and $\angle DBC$ are complementary.

   (5) $m\angle ABC = 90°$

2. Angle 1 is congruent to $\angle 5$. Which of the following pairs of angles is also congruent?

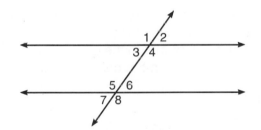

   (1) $\angle 1$ and $\angle 2$

   (2) $\angle 3$ and $\angle 4$

   (3) $\angle 3$ and $\angle 7$

   (4) $\angle 3$ and $\angle 8$

   (5) $\angle 7$ and $\angle 8$

3. One angle is 12° less than its complement. If the measure of the larger angle is *x*, which of the following statements must be true?

   (1) $x + (x - 12°) = 180°$

   (2) $x + (x - 12°) = 90°$

   (3) $x + (12° - x) = 90°$

   (4) $x + (x + 12°) = 180°$

   (5) $x - 90° = x + 12°$

4. The measure of $\angle 7$ is 116°. Which of the following is a true statement?

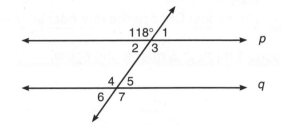

   (1) $\angle 1$ and $\angle 5$ are congruent.

   (2) $\angle 1$ and $\angle 4$ are supplementary.

   (3) $m\angle 1 + m\angle 4 = 180°$

   (4) Lines *p* and *q* are not parallel.

   (5) Lines *p* and *q* are perpendicular.

5. Which conclusion is true?

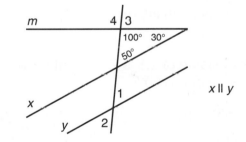

   (1) $m\angle 1 = 50°$

   (2) $m\angle 2 = 80°$

   (3) $m\angle 3 = 50°$

   (4) $m\angle 4 = 80°$

   (5) $m\angle 4 = m\angle 3$

6. What is the measure of $\angle AXB$ if it is four times the measure of its supplement, $\angle BXC$?

   (1) 36°

   (2) 45°

   (3) 72°

   (4) 135°

   (5) 144°

Answers start on page 438.

GED Mini-Test • Lessons 23 and 24

Directions: This is a thirty-minute practice test. After thirty minutes, mark the last item you finished. Then complete the test and check your answers. If most of your answers are correct, but you didn't finish, try to work faster next time.

Part 1

Directions: Choose the one best answer to each question. You MAY use your calculator.

Questions 1 through 3 refer to the figure.

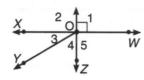

1. Which of the following angles is supplementary, but not adjacent, to ∠2?

   (1) ∠1

   (2) ∠3

   (3) ∠4

   (4) ∠5

   (5) Not enough information is given.

2. The measure of ∠3 is 25°. What is the measure of ∠WOY?

   (1) 65°

   (2) 115°

   (3) 135°

   (4) 155°

   (5) 165°

3. If an angle is supplementary to ∠XOZ, the angle must also be which of the following?

   (1) an acute angle

   (2) a right angle

   (3) an obtuse angle

   (4) a vertical angle

   (5) congruent to ∠3

4. A circular pool has a circumference of about 40 meters. Which of the following expressions could be used to find the diameter of the pool in meters?

   (1) 40π

   (2) $\frac{40}{\pi}$

   (3) $\frac{\pi}{40}$

   (4) $\frac{2(40)}{\pi}$

   (5) $\frac{\pi}{2(40)}$

5. One side of the square base of a container measures 4 inches. If the container can be filled to a height of 4 inches, how many cubic inches of liquid can the container hold?

   (1) 12

   (2) 16

   (3) 20

   (4) 32

   (5) 64

6. A rectangular frame is $2\frac{1}{2}$ feet by 18 inches. What is the frame's perimeter in <u>feet</u>?

   (1) $3\frac{3}{4}$

   (2) 4

   (3) 8

   (4) $8\frac{3}{5}$

   (5) 9

7. ∠A and ∠B are adjacent angles. If m∠A = 30°, what is the measure of ∠B?

(1) 30°

(2) 60°

(3) 90°

(4) 120°

(5) Not enough information is given.

Question 8 refers to the following information.

	length	width	height
Bin A	7.6 ft	5 ft	8 ft
Bin B	8 ft	4.5 ft	8 ft
Bin C	7 ft	5.5 ft	8 ft

8. An apartment manager is having rectangular storage bins built. Which statement about the bins is true?

(1) Bin A has the greatest volume.

(2) Bin B has the greatest volume.

(3) Bin C has the greatest volume.

(4) Bins A and C have the same volume.

(5) All three bins have the same volume.

Question 9 refers to the following figure.

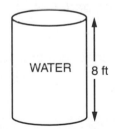

WATER   8 ft

9. The diameter of the base of the water tank shown above is 6 feet. What is the volume of the water tank to the nearest cubic foot?

(1) 28

(2) 48

(3) 72

(4) 226

(5) 904

Question 10 refers to the following diagram.

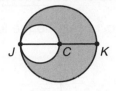

J   C   K

10. Two circles intersect at point J. If C is the center of the larger circle, and the diameter of the larger circle is 28 inches, what is the radius of the smaller circle in inches?

(1) 1.75

(2) 3.5

(3) 7

(4) 14

(5) Not enough information is given.

11. What is the volume in <u>cubic feet</u> of a rectangular crate that is $3\frac{1}{2}$ feet by 1 foot 9 inches by 24 inches?

(1) $6\frac{1}{2}$

(2) $7\frac{1}{4}$

(3) $12\frac{1}{4}$

(4) $13\frac{1}{3}$

(5) 147

Question 12 refers to the following figure.

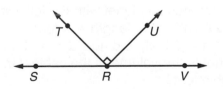

T   U

S   R   V

12. If m∠URV = 53°, what is the measure of ∠TRS?

(1) 37°

(2) 53°

(3) 106°

(4) 127°

(5) 143°

Answers start on page 438.

Part 2

Directions: Choose the <u>one best answer</u> to each question. You may <u>NOT</u> use your calculator.

<u>Questions 13 and 14</u> refer to the following figure.

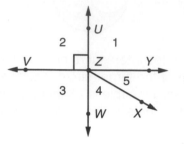

13. Line *UW* intersects line *VY* at point *Z*. The measure of ∠4 is 60°. What is the measure of ∠*UZX*?

    (1) 30°
    (2) 100°
    (3) 120°
    (4) 150°
    (5) 180°

14. If *m*∠4 = 60°, what is the measure of ∠5?

    (1) 30°
    (2) 100°
    (3) 120°
    (4) 150°
    (5) 180°

15. Susan has a cabinet with the following measurements: length = 4 feet, width = 3 feet, and height = 10 feet. What is the volume of the cabinet in cubic feet?

    (1) 60
    (2) 80
    (3) 100
    (4) 120
    (5) 160

<u>Questions 16 through 18</u> refer to the following figure.

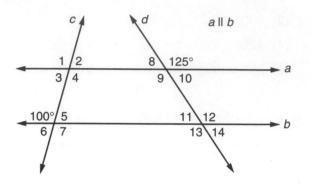

16. Which of the following statements is true?

    (1) ∠3 is complementary to ∠4.
    (2) ∠12 is supplementary to ∠13.
    (3) ∠4 and ∠10 are congruent angles.
    (4) ∠1 is a right angle.
    (5) ∠5 is supplementary to ∠1.

17. Which of these groups contains only angles that are congruent to ∠4?

    (1) ∠1, ∠2, and ∠3
    (2) ∠1 and ∠7
    (3) ∠1, ∠8, and ∠10
    (4) ∠2 and ∠7
    (5) ∠7, ∠10, and ∠14

18. What is the measure of ∠12?

    (1) 55°
    (2) 65°
    (3) 80°
    (4) 100°
    (5) 125°

TIP

Do not consider lines parallel or perpendicular unless the problem gives the information in either words or symbols.

Question 19 refers to the following figure.

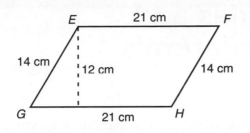

19. If $\overline{EF} \parallel \overline{GH}$ and $\overline{EG} \parallel \overline{FH}$, which expression can be used to find the area in square centimeters of figure *EFHG*?

(1) 2(21) + 2(14)
(2) 21(14 + 12)
(3) 12(14)
(4) 21(12)
(5) 21(14)

Questions 20 and 21 refer to the following figure.

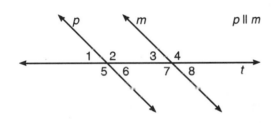

20. Which of the following angles is equal in measure to angle 4?

(1) ∠5
(2) ∠6
(3) ∠8
(4) ∠3
(5) ∠1

21. If $m\angle 8 = 45°$, which of the following statements is true?

(1) $m\angle 8 = m\angle 1$
(2) $m\angle 7 = 45°$
(3) $m\angle 6 = 135°$
(4) ∠4 and ∠8 are complementary.
(5) ∠3 ≅ ∠4

22. Which of the following expressions can be used to find the circumference of a circle with a radius of 5 centimeters?

(1) 2.5π
(2) 3π
(3) 6π
(4) 10π
(5) 25π

Question 23 refers to the following figure.

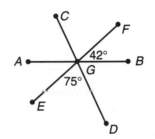

23. Which of the following explains why the measure of ∠*FGC* = 75°?

(1) ∠*FGC* and ∠*FGB* are adjacent angles.
(2) ∠*FGC* and ∠*CGA* are supplementary angles.
(3) ∠*FGC* and ∠*DGE* are vertical angles.
(4) ∠*FGC* and ∠*BGD* are corresponding angles.
(5) ∠*FGC* and ∠*FGB* are acute angles.

Question 24 refers to the following figure.

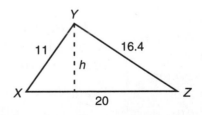

24. The area of $\triangle XYZ = 90$ square units. What is the measure of the height in units?

(1) 9
(2) 10
(3) 21
(4) 43
(5) Not enough information is given.

Answers start on page 438.

Lesson 25 — GED SKILL **Triangles and Quadrilaterals**

Triangles

A triangle has three sides and three angles and is named by its vertices (in any order). Identify a side of a triangle by the two letters that name the vertices at the ends of the side. In △ABC, the sides are $\overline{AB}$, $\overline{BC}$, and $\overline{AC}$.

A triangle is named by the lengths of its sides and the measures of its angles. The triangles below are named by the lengths of their sides.

TIP

The symbols l, ll, and lll marked on a side show which sides are congruent. Remember: *Congruent* means *equal*.

Equilateral triangle
All sides and angles are congruent; each angle measures 60°.

Isosceles triangle
Two sides and the two angles opposite these sides are congruent.

Scalene triangle
No sides and no angles are congruent.

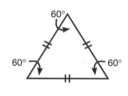

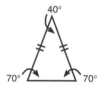

The following triangles are named by the measures of their angles.

Right triangle
One angle is a right angle (equal to 90°).

Acute triangle
All three angles are acute (less than 90°).

Obtuse triangle
One angle is obtuse (greater than 90°).

TIP

Questions on the GED Mathematics Test may include more information than you need to solve a problem. Use only the information you need based on what the question asks.

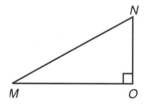

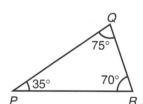

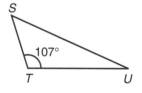

In any triangle, the sum of the measures of the angles is 180°. (Note: A triangle can have only one right or obtuse angle. The other two angles must be acute.)

Example   In a right triangle, one acute angle is twice the measure of the other acute angle. What is the measure of the larger angle?

Step 1   **Make a sketch.** A right triangle has one right angle ($m = 90°$).

Step 2   **Assign the unknowns.**

Let x = the measure of the smaller acute angle.
Let $2x$ = the measure of the larger acute angle.

Step 3   **Write an equation.** $x + 2x + 90° = 180°$

Step 4   **Solve.** $3x + 90° = 180°$

$$3x = 90°; \text{ so } x = 30° \text{ and } 2x = 60°$$

The larger acute angle measures **60°**.

A. Solve.

Refer to the figure at right to answer Questions 1 through 5. (*Hint*: The figure contains 5 triangles.)

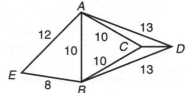

1. Name an equilateral triangle.   4. Name an acute triangle.

2. Name an isosceles triangle.   5. Name a scalene triangle.

3. Name an obtuse triangle.

Refer to the figure at right to answer Questions 6 through 14.

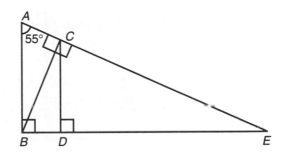

6. Name the triangle that has a right angle at *B*.

7. Name two triangles that have right angles at *D*.

8. Name two triangles that have right angles at *C*.

9. If $m\angle A = 55°$, then what is $m\angle E$?   12. What is $m\angle CBD$?

10. What is $m\angle ABC$?   13. What is $m\angle BCD$?

11. What is $m\angle DCE$?   14. How are the five triangles in the figure alike?

Refer to the figure at right to answer Question 15.

15. How many isosceles triangles are there in the figure? (*Hint*: The figure contains 8 triangles.)

_____

16. In a right triangle the measure of one acute angle is 4 times the measure of the other acute angle. What is the measure of the smaller angle?

17. In a triangle the measure of one angle is 16° more than the measure of the smallest angle, and the measure of the third angle is twice the measure of the smallest angle. What are the three angle measures?

B. Write *True* or *False* for each statement. Refer to the figure on the right to answer Questions 18 through 23.

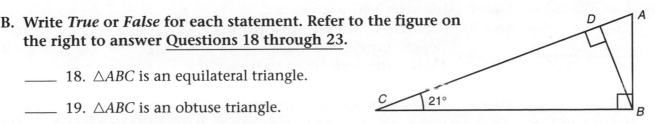

_____ 18. △*ABC* is an equilateral triangle.

_____ 19. △*ABC* is an obtuse triangle.

_____ 20. $m\angle BAC$ is equal to $m\angle CBD$.   _____ 22. △*ABC* is an acute triangle.

_____ 21. $m\angle ABD$ is less than $m\angle ACB$.   _____ 23. There are exactly three right triangles in the figure.

Answers start on page 440.

Quadrilaterals

A **quadrilateral** is any geometric figure with four (*quad*) sides (*lateral*). A figure with four sides also has four angles, and the sum of these four angle measures always equals 360°.

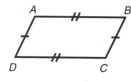

To prove this is so, draw any quadrilateral and draw a line segment called a **diagonal** between the vertices of two opposite angles. The diagonal divides the quadrilateral into two triangles. You know that the sum of the three angles in a triangle is 180°. Since there are two triangles, the sum of the angles in the quadrilateral must be 180° + 180° = 360°.

The following quadrilaterals appear on the GED Mathematics Test.

Parallelogram
opposite sides are parallel and congruent; opposite angles are of equal measure

Rectangle
special parallelogram with four right angles

Rhombus
special parallelogram with four sides of equal length

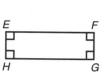

Square
special parallelogram/rhombus/rectangle with four sides of equal length and four right angles

Trapezoid
only one pair of parallel sides (called bases)

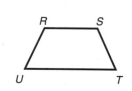

TIP

Write algebraic expressions on the drawing to remember what the variables represent.

On the GED Mathematics Test, you must combine your knowledge of algebra and geometric principles to solve problems.

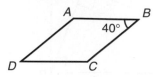

Example Angle *B* of the rhombus shown at the left measures **40°**. What is the measure of $\angle C$?

Step 1 **Identify known values.**	$m\angle B = 40°$
Step 2 **Identify known relationships.**	sum of angles = 360°
Opposite angles are equal.	$m\angle D = 40°$; $m\angle C = m\angle A$
Step 3 **Assign the unknown values.**	Let $x = m\angle C$ (and $m\angle A$)
Step 4 **Write an equation.**	$m\angle A + m\angle B + m\angle C + m\angle D = 360°$
Step 5 **Substitute known values.**	$x + 40° + x + 40° = 360°$
	$2(40°) + 2x = 360°$
Step 6 **Solve for unknown values.**	$80° + 2x = 360°$
	$2x = 280°$; $x = 140°$

The measure of $\angle C$ is **140°**.

A. Give all possibilities for the names of the following four-sided figures.

1. All sides have lengths of 10 inches.

2. All corners are right angles.

3. Opposite sides are parallel.

4. Only two sides are parallel.

5. There are no right angles.

6. Only one pair of opposite sides is equal in length.

B. Solve.

Refer to the figure below to answer Questions 7 through 9.

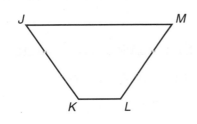

7. Side JM ‖ side KL. What is the most common name of this figure?

8. What is the sum of the four inside angle measures?

9. $m\angle K = m\angle L$ and $m\angle J = m\angle M$. If the measure of $\angle K$ is 125°, what is the measure of $\angle J$?

Refer to the figure below to answer Questions 10 through 12.

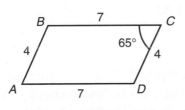

10. In the figure, $\overline{AB}$ ‖ $\overline{CD}$ and $\overline{AD}$ ‖ $\overline{BC}$. What is the most common name of this figure?

11. What is the measure of $\angle A$?

12. What is the measure of $\angle D$?

13. Quadrilateral $ABCD$ has two pairs of parallel opposite sides. Angle A measures 90°. What are the possible names of the quadrilateral?

14. In a quadrilateral, one angle is 20° less than another angle. The remaining two angles are right angles. What are the measures of the four angles?

15. The lengths of the sides of a four-sided figure, in order, are 8, 12, 8, and 12. There are no right angles, and opposite sides are parallel. What is the figure?

Refer to the figure to answer Questions 16 through 18.

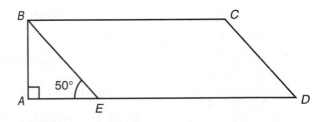

16. Quadrilateral $BCDE$ is a parallelogram. What two things must be true about sides BC and ED?

17. What is the measure of $\angle C$?

18. Quadrilateral $ABCD$ is a trapezoid. What is the measure of $\angle ABC$?

Answers start on page 441.

Congruent Figures

TIP

Always follow steps of logical reasoning to solve for the needed information.

Congruent figures are the same shape and size. One way to find out whether two figures are congruent is to place one figure on top of the other to see whether the sides and angles align perfectly. You may even be able to tell whether figures are congruent simply by looking at them. However, on the GED Mathematics Test, you need to be able to do more than identify which figures "look" congruent; you must be able to prove that the two figures are congruent.

Let's look at triangles. Congruent triangles are exactly the same shape and size. They have matching, or corresponding, vertices; sides; and angles. Marks are used to show which parts correspond.

There are three rules used to prove that two triangles are congruent. Two triangles are congruent if any one of the following rules is true:

RULE 1 Three sides (SSS) are congruent.

RULE 2 Two sides and the angle between them (SAS) are congruent.

RULE 3 Two angles and the side between them (ASA) are congruent.

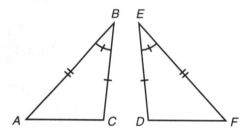

Example 1 Are triangles *ABC* and *FED* congruent?

Step 1	**Identify the given corresponding congruent parts.** $\overline{AB} \cong \overline{FE}, \overline{BC} \cong \overline{ED}$ $\angle B \cong \angle E$
Step 2	**Identify what relationships are known.** There are two pairs of corresponding congruent sides. The angles between the congruent sides are also congruent. (SAS)
Step 3	**Identify additional information needed.** None.
Step 4	**Draw a conclusion.** Rule 2 is true; the triangles are congruent.

The triangles are congruent. **△ABC ≅ △FED**

Example 2 Is △*LMN* congruent to △*ZYX*?

Step 1	**Identify the given congruent parts.** $\angle L \cong \angle Z; \overline{LN} \cong \overline{ZX}$
Step 2	**Identify known relationships.** △*LMN*: the measures of two angles and the length of the side between them (ASA) △*ZYX*: the measure of one angle and the length of the adjacent side corresponding with △*LMN*
Step 3	**Identify needed information.** measure of $\angle X$
Step 4	**Solve for needed information.** Sum of the measures of the angles of a triangle = 180°, so $m\angle X + 80° + 62° = 180°$ $m\angle X = 180° - 80° - 62° = 38°$
Step 4	**Draw a conclusion.** $m\angle X = 38°$; so $\angle X$ is congruent to $\angle N$ Rule 3 (ASA) is true; the triangles are congruent.

The triangles are congruent. **△LMN ≅ △ZYX**

A. Decide whether each pair of triangles is congruent or not. Explain your reasoning.

1.

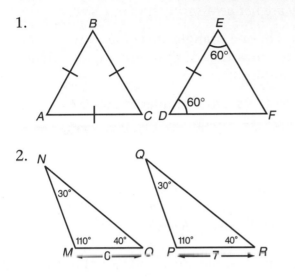

3.

2.

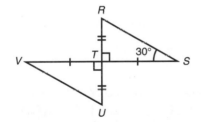

4.

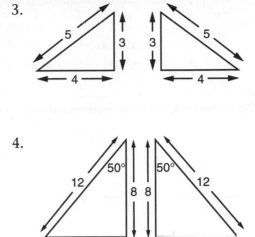

B. Answer each question. If you do not have enough information to solve a problem, write *Not enough information is given.*

Refer to the figure below to answer Questions 5 through 7.

5. Is △TRS ≅ △TUV? How do you know?

6. What is the measure of ∠V?

7. What is the measure of ∠U?

Refer to the figure below to answer Questions 8 and 9.

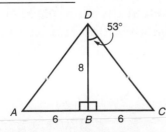

8. Is △BDA ≅ △BDC? How do you know?

9. What is the measure of ∠A?

Refer to the figure below to answer Question 10.

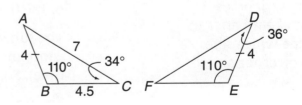

10. Is △ABC ≅ △DEF? How do you know?

Refer to the figure below to answer Questions 11 and 12.

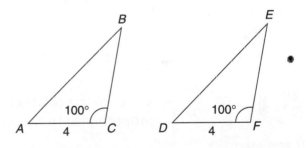

11. What is the measure of ∠A?

12. What is the length of $\overline{EF}$?

Answers start on page 441.

Similar Figures

Two figures are **similar** (~) if their corresponding angles have equal measure and the corresponding sides are in proportion. Similar figures have the same shape, but they are *not necessarily* the same size.

If the measures of two angles of one triangle are equal to two angle measures in another triangle, the measures of the third angles will also be equal (AAA) and the triangles are similar.

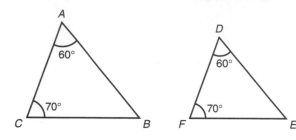

Example 1   Is △ABC similar to △DEF?

In △ABC, m∠A = 60°. In △DEF, m∠D = 60°.
In △ABC, m∠C = 70°. In △DEF, m∠F = 70°.

Since the measures of two angles of △ABC are equal to two angle measures in △DEF, the triangles are similar. **△ABC ~ △DEF**

If the lengths of the sides of one triangle are proportional to the lengths of the sides of the other triangle, the triangles are similar.

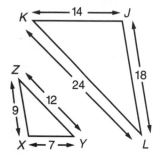

Example 2   Is △XYZ similar to △JKL?

In △XYZ, $\overline{XY}$ measures 7. In △JKL, $\overline{JK}$ measures 14.
In △XYZ, $\overline{XZ}$ measures 9. In △JKL, $\overline{JL}$ measures 18.
In △XYZ, $\overline{YZ}$ measures 12. In △JKL, $\overline{KL}$ measures 24.

Write ratios comparing a side in △XYZ to its corresponding side in △JKL. Reduce to simplest terms.
$$\frac{7}{14} = \frac{9}{18} = \frac{12}{24} \text{ Each ratio equals } \frac{1}{2}; \text{ they are equal.}$$

Since the ratios are equal, the lengths of the sides of △XYZ are proportional to the lengths of the sides of △JKL. **△XYZ ~ △JKL**

TIP

If the second triangle is turned differently than the first one, redraw one of the triangles to make it easier to see which sides correspond.

Similar triangles are often used to solve problems when it is not possible to find a distance by measuring.

Example 3   At 4 p.m., a flagpole casts a 20-foot shadow. At the same time, a person 6 feet tall casts a 4-foot shadow. What is the height of the flagpole?

The sun strikes the person and flagpole at the same angle (since measurements are taken at the same place and same time). So, the objects and shadows form similar triangles.

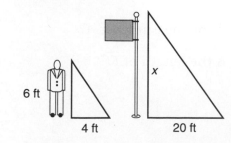

Set up a proportion. $\dfrac{\text{person's height}}{\text{flagpole's height}}\ \dfrac{6}{x} = \dfrac{4}{20}\ \dfrac{\text{person's shadow}}{\text{flagpole's shadow}}$

Solve.
$$4x = 6(20)$$
$$x = 120 \div 4$$
$$x = 30$$

The height of the flagpole is **30 feet.**

Solve.

Refer to the figure below to answer
Questions 1 and 2.

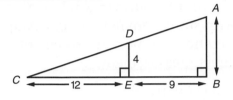

1. In the figure, $\triangle ABC \sim \triangle DEC$. Side $\overline{EC}$ is
   similar to which side of $\triangle ABC$?

2. What is the length of $\overline{AB}$?

Refer to the information and figure below to
answer Questions 3 and 4.

To determine the width of a lake, surveyors
measure off two similar isosceles triangles as
shown.

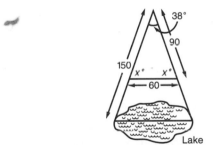

3. What is the value of x?

4. What is the distance across the longest
   part of the lake?

Refer to the figure below to answer
Questions 5 and 6.

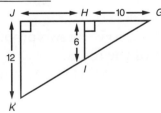

5. In the figure, $\triangle GHI$ and $\triangle GJK$ are similar.
   What is the length of $\overline{GJ}$?

6. The measure of $\angle GIH$ is equal to the
   measure of what other angle?

Refer to the figure below to answer
Questions 7 and 8.

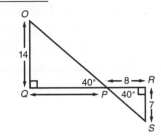

7. $\angle S$ has the same measure as what other
   angle?

8. What is the length of $\overline{PQ}$?

9. At 11 A.M., a 5-foot post casts a 3-foot
   shadow. At the same time, a tree casts a
   shadow that is 21 feet in length. What is
   the height of the tree?

10. At 6 P.M., a signpost casts a shadow that is
    4 feet in length. At the same time, a street
    lamp casts a shadow that is 16 feet in
    length. If the signpost is 6 feet tall, what is
    the height of the street lamp?

Refer to the information and figure below to
answer Questions 11 and 12.

A 42-foot tower has a diagonal brace. To reduce
the effects of the wind, an engineer wants to
add a vertical support 20 feet from the tower
and shown by the dotted line in the drawing.

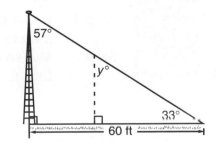

11. What is the value of $\angle y$?

12. What will be the height of the new
    support?

Answers start on page 442.

GED STRATEGY Solving Word Problems

Using Proportion in Geometry

Many measurement and geometry problems involve **indirect measurement.** Instead of making actual measurements, use proportions and knowledge of corresponding parts to find the answer. Finding a missing measurement when working with similar triangles is an example of indirect measurement. There are two other common measurement situations that can be solved using indirect measurement.

A **scale drawing** is a sketch of an object with all distances proportional to corresponding distances on the actual object. The **scale** gives the ratio of the sketch measurements to the actual measurements. A map is an example of a scale drawing.

Johnson

Taylor

8 cm

2.5 cm

Kirby
7 cm

4.5 cm

Davis

Lincoln

Scale: 1 cm = 5 km

Example 1   The distance on the map between Taylor and Davis is 4.5 cm. What is the actual distance between the two towns?

Step 1   **Read the map scale.** According to the scale 1 centimeter on the map equals 5 kilometers of actual distance.

Step 2   **Write a proportion.** $\dfrac{\text{map distance}}{\text{actual distance}}\;\dfrac{1\text{ cm}}{5\text{ km}} = \dfrac{4.5\text{ cm}}{x\text{ km}}$

Step 3   **Solve.** $x = 5(4.5) = 22.5$ km

The actual distance is **22.5 kilometers.**

A **floor plan** is another example of indirect measurement. A floor plan is a map showing the layout of the rooms in a building. A floor plan usually shows the placement of doors and windows. It may also use symbols to show the placement of furniture.

Example 2   In a floor plan of the Martin's house, the rectangular living room measures 3 inches by $4\frac{1}{2}$ inches. Every 2 inches on the floor plan represents 8 actual feet. How many square feet of carpet are needed to cover the living room floor?

Step 1   **Read the scale.** The scale is given in the problem.
2 inches = 8 feet

Step 2   **Write the proportions.** You need to write two proportions to find the actual length and width of the room.

$$\dfrac{2\text{ inches}}{8\text{ feet}} = \dfrac{4.5\text{ inches}}{l\text{ feet}} \qquad \dfrac{2\text{ inches}}{8\text{ feet}} = \dfrac{3\text{ inches}}{w\text{ feet}}$$

Step 3   **Solve.**
$2l = 8(4.5)$ $2w = 8(3)$
$2l = 36$ $2w = 24$
$l = 18$ feet $w = 12$ feet

Step 4   **Find the area.** $A = l \times w$ $12 \times 18 = 216$ square feet

The living room floor will require **216 square feet** of carpet.

TIP

With real-life situations, use experience to decide whether your answers make sense. Is it reasonable that a living room would measure 12 ft by 18 ft? Yes, it is.

Directions: Choose the one best answer to each question.

Questions 1 and 2 refer to the following drawing.

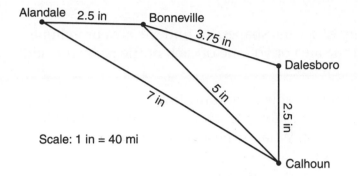

Scale: 1 in = 40 mi

1. The map distances between cities are shown on the map. What is the actual distance in miles between Bonneville and Dalesboro?

    (1) 120
    (2) 150
    (3) 160
    (4) 180
    (5) 200

2. Susan drove from Calhoun to Alandale, then from Alandale to Bonneville, and back to Calhoun. How many miles did she drive?

    (1) 460
    (2) 480
    (3) 540
    (4) 580
    (5) 620

3. Hillsboro is 50 miles from Merville. On a map these towns are 2.5 inches apart. What is the scale of this map?

    (1) 1 in $= \frac{1}{5}$ mi
    (2) 1 in = 2 mi
    (3) 1 in = 2.5 mi
    (4) 1 in = 20 mi
    (5) 1 in = 25 mi

4. In this floor plan, the scale is $\frac{3}{4}$ in = 15 ft. What are the dimensions of the actual sleeping area?

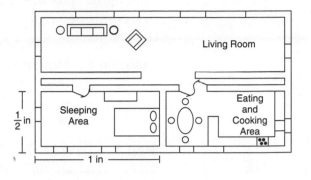

    (1) 10 feet by 20 feet
    (2) 12 feet by 24 feet
    (3) 15 feet by 30 feet
    (4) 20 feet by 40 feet
    (5) 25 feet by 50 feet

5. A floor plan is drawn to a scale of 1 in = 8 ft. On the plan, one wall is $1\frac{3}{4}$ inches long. Will a 14-foot wall unit fit on this wall?

    (1) No, the wall unit is about 2 feet too long.
    (2) No, the wall unit is about 1 foot too long.
    (3) Yes, the wall unit fits exactly.
    (4) Yes, the wall unit fits with about 1 foot of extra space remaining.
    (5) Yes, the wall unit fits with about 2 feet of extra space remaining.

6. A map scale is 1 in = 1.8 mi. How far is the actual distance in miles between two points that are 3.5 inches apart on the map?

    (1) 0.5
    (2) 1.9
    (3) 3.5
    (4) 6.3
    (5) 35.0

Answers start on page 443.

Lesson 26 GED SKILL **Irregular Figures**

Area and Volume

A figure may be made up of several shapes. To find the area or volume of a combined figure, find the area or volume of each of the parts and add the results.

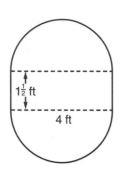

Example 1 Marcus is stripping a table for refinishing. He needs to know the area of the tabletop in order to know how much wood stripper he will need. What is the area of the tabletop to the nearest square foot?

Step 1 **Divide the figure into simple shapes.** Think of each end as a half-circle attached to a rectangle.

Step 2 **Find the area of each part.** The two half-circles can be combined to make one whole circle.

Find the area of the circle. $A = \pi \times \text{radius}^2 = \pi r^2$

Remember: $r = \frac{d}{2}$. $r = 4 \div 2 = 2$
$$A = \pi r^2$$
$$= 3.14(2^2)$$
$$= 3.14(4) = 12.56 \text{ square feet}$$

Find the area of the rectangle. $A = lw$
$$= 4\left(1\frac{1}{2}\right) = 6 \text{ square feet}$$

Step 3 **Add the areas.** $12.56 + 6 = 18.56,$
which rounds to 19 square feet

The area of the tabletop is about **19 square feet.**

Irregular figures can also be made up of common solid shapes.

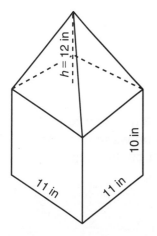

Example 2 Find the volume of the object shown at left.

Step 1 **Divide the figure into simple figures.** This figure is made up of a pyramid and a rectangular solid.

Step 2 **Find the volume of each part.**

Find the volume of the pyramid. $V = \frac{1}{3} \times A \times h$

Since the base is a square, $A = s^2$, where s = base edge.
$$V = \frac{1}{3} \times (\text{base edge})^2 \times \text{height}$$
$$= \frac{1}{3}(11^2)(12) = \frac{1}{3}(121)(12) = 484 \text{ cubic inches}$$

Find the volume of the rectangular solid. $V = l \times w \times h$
$$= 11 \times 11 \times 10 = 1210 \text{ cubic inches}$$

Step 3 **Add to find the total volume.**
$$484 + 1210 = 1694 \text{ cubic inches}$$

The volume of the object is **1694 cubic inches.**

A. Find the area of each figure. You may use a calculator.

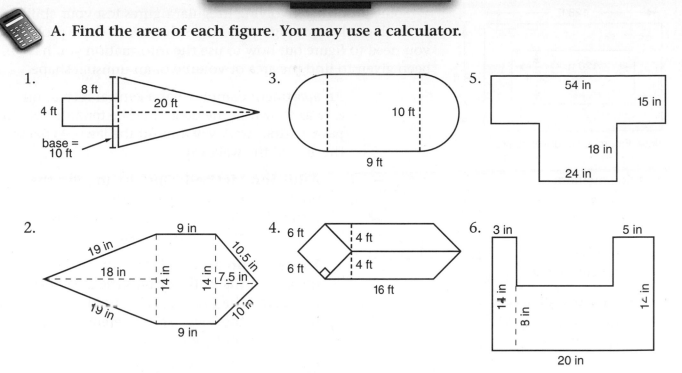

1.
8 ft
4 ft
20 ft
base = 10 ft

3.
10 ft
9 ft

5.
54 in
15 in
18 in
24 in

2.
9 in
19 in
18 in
14 in
14 in
10.5 in
7.5 in
19 in
10.9
9 in

4.
6 ft
4 ft
6 ft
4 ft
16 ft

6.
3 in
5 in
14 in
8 in
12 in
20 in

B. Each object is made of two or more solid shapes combined into one. Name the shapes and find the volume of each object. You may use a calculator.

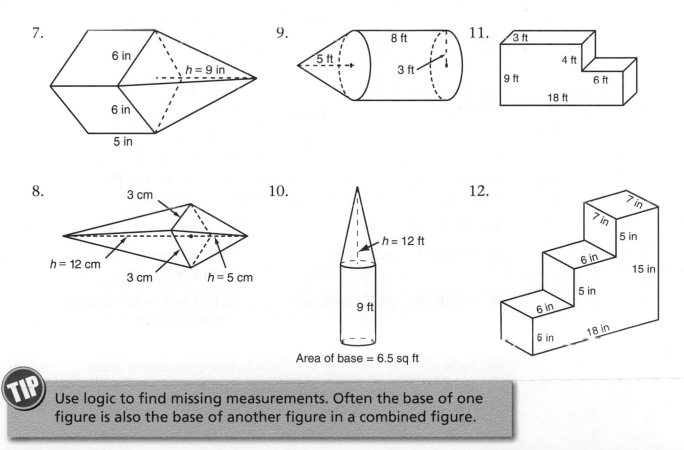

7.
6 in
6 in
5 in
h = 9 in

9.
8 ft
5 ft
3 ft

11.
3 ft
4 ft
9 ft
6 ft
18 ft

8.
3 cm
h = 12 cm
3 cm
h = 5 cm

10.
h = 12 ft
9 ft
Area of base = 6.5 sq ft

12.
7 in
7 in
5 in
6 in
15 in
5 in
6 in
6 in
18 in

TIP Use logic to find missing measurements. Often the base of one figure is also the base of another figure in a combined figure.

Answers start on page 443.

Approaching Multi-Step Problems

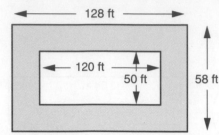

128 ft
120 ft
50 ft
58 ft

Note: Figure is not drawn to scale.

Some problems involving irregular figures test your ability to use logical reasoning to find the solution. In these problems, you need to figure out how to use the information you have been given to find the area or volume of an unusual shape.

Example   An apartment complex has a central recreation area as shown in the diagram. The tenants vote to pave a 4-foot walkway around the lawn. What is the area of the walkway?

Addition method:

Sections 2 & 4:
$A = lw = 128(4) = 512$

Sections 1 & 3:
$A = lw = 50(4) = 200$

Sections 1 + 2 + 3 + 4 =
200 + 512 + 200 + 512 =
1424 sq ft

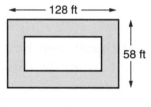

128 ft
2   4 ft
4 ft   4 ft
50 ft   1   3
4   4 ft

Addition Method: One way to solve the problem is to divide the walkway into four rectangles, find the area of each rectangle, and add to find the total area.

Subtraction Method: The total area equals the area of the walkway plus the area of the lawn. Find the total area and then subtract the area of the lawn. The difference is equal to the area of the walkway.

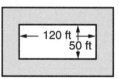

128 ft
58 ft

120 ft
50 ft

Step 1	Find the area of the larger (outer) rectangle. The outer rectangle measures 128 by 58 feet.	$A = lw$ $=128(58)$ $= 7424$ sq ft
Step 2	Find the area of the smaller rectangle. The smaller rectangle measures 120 by 50 feet.	$A = lw$ $=120(50)$ $= 6000$ sq ft
Step 3	Find the difference.	$7424 - 6000 = 1424$ sq ft

 Another method involves the use of the memory keys on your calculator. Use this key sequence on the GED calculator.

AC SHIFT MR	To clear the memory.
128 × 58 = 7424. M+	M+ means "add to memory."
120 × 50 = 6000. SHIFT M+	SHIFT M+ = M− means "subtract from memory."
MR 1424.	MR means "memory recall."

The area of the walkway is **1424 square feet.**

Solve.

1. Emily plans to tile her laundry room floor, except for the space underneath the washer and dryer. Each tile covers 1 square foot of space. How many tiles will Emily need to do the job?

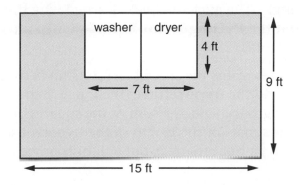

2. In the following figure, the shaded part shows the walkway around a garden. The garden measures 36 feet by 20 feet. How many square feet is the surface of the walkway?

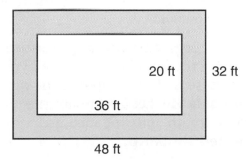

3. Construction workers will line the outside edge of a pool with tile strips, each 6 inches in length. How many strips are needed to go completely around the edge of the pool shown below?

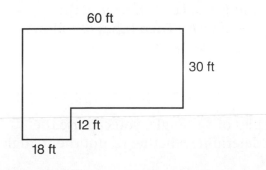

4. A toy maker is using a cylindrical container, shown below, to package a new toy. The toy is in the shape of a cube, 8 inches on a side. The remaining space inside the cylinder will be filled with protective filler. How many cubic inches of filler will be needed per package?

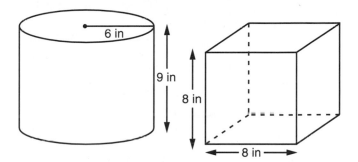

5. A circular fountain is 24 feet in diameter and has a three-foot wide gravel walkway around it. What is the area of the walkway in square feet?

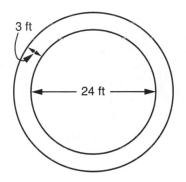

6. Jerry is ordering shingles for the roof of the storage building shown below. A bundle of shingles covers 3 square yards of roof. How many bundles of shingles should Jerry order?

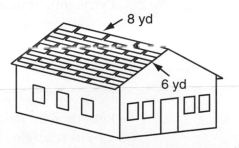

Answers start on page 444.

The Pythagorean Relationship

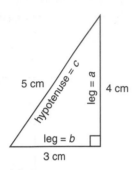

5 cm hypotenuse = c   leg = a   4 cm

leg = b

3 cm

The ancient Egyptians discovered a special property of triangles whose sides measure 3, 4, and 5 units. They learned that the angle opposite the longest side is <u>always</u> a right angle. The ancient Greeks learned why this relationship exists and named it the **Pythagorean Relationship** after the Greek mathematician Pythagoras.

The Pythagorean Relationship explains the special relationship between the **legs** (the two shorter sides) and the **hypotenuse** (the longest side) of a right triangle. It states that in a right triangle, the sum of the squares of the lengths of the legs is equal to the square of the length of the hypotenuse. Note that a 3-4-5 triangle is always a right triangle, but a right triangle is not always a 3-4-5 triangle.

Pythagorean Relationship $a^2 + b^2 = c^2$, where a and b are the legs and c is the hypotenuse of a right triangle

TIP

Watch for 3-4-5 right triangles in problems on the GED Math Test. Multiples are also commonly used: 6-8-10, 9-12-15, and 1.5-2-2.5.

You can use the Pythagorean Relationship to find a missing length of a right triangle.

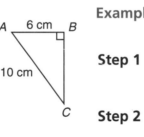

A   6 cm   B

10 cm

C

Example 1   What is the length of side BC of the triangle shown to the left?

Step 1   **Identify the legs and the hypotenuse.** Sides AB and BC are the legs. Side AC is the hypotenuse. The hypotenuse is always opposite the right angle.

Step 2   **Assign a variable.** Let b represent the measure of side BC, a leg, the missing measure.

Step 3   **Use the Pythagorean Relationship.**

$$a^2 + b^2 = c^2$$
$$6^2 + b^2 = 10^2$$
$$36 + b^2 = 100$$
$$b^2 = 64$$
$$b = \sqrt{64}$$
$$b = 8$$

To find the length of a side b using a calculator, rewrite the Pythagorean Relationship as $c^2 - a^2 = b^2$. Then input as follows:

10 x^2 ─ 6 x^2 = SHIFT x^2 8.

The length of the missing side is **8 centimeters.**

Given the lengths of the sides of a triangle, you can use the Pythagorean Relationship to determine whether or not the triangle is a right triangle.

Example 2　The lengths of the sides of a triangle are 5, 6, and 9 inches. Is the triangle a right triangle?

If the triangle is a right triangle, the longest side, 9 inches, must be the hypotenuse. Substitute the other measures for a and b. Let $a = 5$ and $b = 6$. Then solve for c. If the solution is 9, the triangle is a right triangle.

$$a^2 + b^2 = c^2$$
$$5^2 + 6^2 = c^2$$
$$25 + 36 = c^2$$
$$61 = c^2$$
$$\sqrt{61} = c \approx 7.8$$

> Use your calculator on the final step, or work backwards. If the hypotenuse, c, is 9, then $c^2 = 81$.

The triangle in the example is **not** a right triangle.

GED SKILL FOCUS

A. Each question gives the lengths of the three sides of a triangle. Write *Yes* if the triangle is a right triangle. Write *No* if it is not.

	a	*b*	*c*			*a*	*b*	*c*			*a*	*b*	*c*
1.	2	3	4		5.	11	60	61		9.	7	24	25
2.	2	6	7		6.	5	12	13		10.	25	60	65
3.	2	2	3		7.	18	24	30		11.	6.5	42	42.5
4.	3	3	5		8.	1	$1\frac{1}{3}$	$1\frac{2}{3}$		12.	8	50	51

B. Solve as directed.

Refer to the diagram to answer Questions 13 and 14.

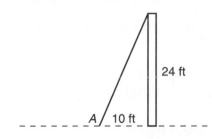

13. The pole is perpendicular to the ground. How many feet of wire are needed to reach from the top of the pole to point *A*?

14. If point *A* is moved 8 feet farther from the pole, how much more wire will be needed?

Refer to the diagram to answer Questions 15 and 16.

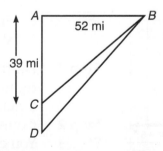

15. How far is it from point *C* to point *B*?

16. Point *D* is 11 miles from point *C*. To the nearest whole mile, how far is it from point *D* to point *B*?

Answers start on page 444.

GED STRATEGY Solving Word Problems

Recognizing Applications of the Pythagorean Relationship

Many practical problems can be solved using the Pythagorean Relationship. Since diagonal bracing is often used to make structures stronger, construction situations often involve right triangles.

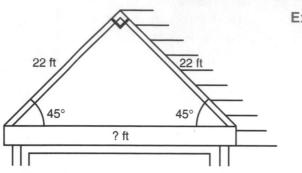

Example 1 A beam across the front of a garage needs to be replaced. Using the diagram at right, what is the length of the beam to the nearest foot?

(1) 26
(2) 31
(3) 44
(4) 968
(5) Not enough information is given.

Did you realize that the front of the garage is a right triangle? The right angle is at the peak of the roof. The other angles each measure 45°. Remember that the sum of the angles in a triangle equals 180°. Even without the right angle symbol, you can prove that the peak of the roof is a right angle because $180° - 45° - 45° = 90°$. The beam across the front is the hypotenuse.

Use the Pythagorean Relationship.

$$a^2 + b^2 = c^2$$
$$22^2 + 22^2 = c^2$$
$$484 + 484 = c^2$$
$$968 = c^2$$
$$\sqrt{968} = c \approx 31.1$$

The wooden beam is about 31 feet in length. **Option 2 is correct.**

You know the distance formula for finding the distance between points on a coordinate grid. Using the Pythagorean Relationship may be easier.

Example 2 Find the distance between points A and B on the graph shown at right.

Step 1 Let the distance between the points be the hypotenuse of a right triangle. Draw in the legs of the triangle so that they form a right angle.

Step 2 Count units to find the lengths of the legs.

Step 3 You can solve for the length of the hypotenuse using the Pythagorean Relationship; however, this triangle is the common 3-4-5 triangle. Since the legs measure 3 and 4 units, the hypotenuse is 5.

The distance between points A and B is **5 units.**

> **TIP**
>
> Don't assume that a triangle is a right triangle. Always look for evidence that the triangle <u>must be</u> a right triangle before applying the Pythagorean Relationship.

Directions: Choose the <u>one best answer</u> to each question.

Question 1 refers to the following diagram.

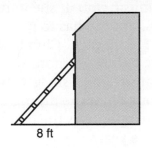

8 ft

1. The bottom of a ladder is placed 8 feet from the wall of a house. The wall and the ground form a right angle. If the ladder is 15 feet in length, how far up the wall does it reach (to the nearest foot)?

    (1) 12

    (2) 13

    (3) 17

    (4) 23

    (5) 161

Question 2 refers to the following diagram.

2. What is the distance between points J and K to the nearest tenth unit?

    (1) 6.5

    (2) 7.7

    (3) 8.1

    (4) 8.6

    (5) 11.0

Question 3 refers to the following diagram.

3. Bill wants to find the width of the pond. He places stakes at A and B and then finds C so that C is a right angle. This makes $\triangle ABC$ a right triangle. If $\overline{AC} = 60$ feet and $\overline{BC} = 80$ feet, about how far is it from A to B?

    (1) less than 85 ft

    (2) from 85 to 95 ft

    (3) from 95 to 105 ft

    (4) from 105 to 115 ft

    (5) more than 115 ft

Question 4 refers to the following diagram.

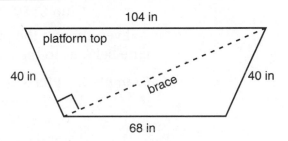

4. Jan builds a platform with a top in the shape of a trapezoid. The plans call for a diagonal brace to be added. What is the length of the brace to the nearest inch?

    (1) 64

    (2) 88

    (3) 96

    (4) 111

    (5) Not enough information is given.

Answers start on page 446.

Organizing Information

When solving problems, it is often helpful to organize a large amount of information into a chart or list. Information is often easier to understand when it is organized.

Example 1   Jane is considering joining a music club. If she joins Club A, she will receive eight free CDs, but she has to purchase four more CDs during the year at $18.95 each. Club B offers six free CDs, but Jane would have to buy six more at the club price of $14.90 each. If she joins Club C, she gets two free CDs, and she would have to buy ten more during the year for $9.50 each. Which of the three options is the best buy if she only belongs to the club for one year?

Making a table can help you save time whenever several questions are based on the same paragraph of information.

Step 1   The paragraph contains a great deal of information. As you read, find what the three clubs have in common. All three clubs offer free CDs, and all require Jane to buy more CDs at a certain price.

Step 2   Create a table with columns.

Club	Free CDs	Number to Buy	Price Per CD
A	8	4	$18.95
B	6	6	$14.90
C	2	10	$9.50

Step 3   Compare the offers. You can see that Jane would end up with 12 CDs at the end of one year, no matter which club she joins. You can find the amount she would pay at each club by multiplying the number she is required to purchase by the price per CD.

Club A: $18.95 \times 4 = $75.80
Club B: $14.90 \times 6 = $89.40
Club C: $9.50 \times 10 = $95.00

Even though the price per CD is greater, **Club A is the best offer** if Jane belongs to the club for only one year.

Example 2   Rita is shopping for a new car. She wants an automatic transmission, which costs $800, and an air conditioner for $1100. The base price is $15,789 and the transportation and handling is $979. Rita also wants an anti-theft alarm for $250. How much more will the car's total price be with the optional features added?

Step 1   Make a chart with these categories: mandatory and optional.

Mandatory		**Optional**	
Base price	$15,789	Air conditioner	$1100
Transportation/handling	979	Auto transmission	800
		Anti-theft alarm	250

Step 2   Once the prices are listed, add each column. The price of Rita's car without options is $16,768. The options will add $2,150 to the price of the car.

A. Solve. You may use your calculator. Refer to the following information to answer Questions 1 through 4.

Sheila and Paul are looking at apartments. Here are the results of what they have found.

- Apartment A rents for $545 per month. Sheila and Paul would have to pay a full month's rent as a deposit and $40 for keys.

- Apartment B requires a $1000 deposit. The rent is $525 per month. There is also a one-time $25 fee per parking space needed.

- Apartment C is $600 per month, but it requires a $450 deposit plus 10% of one month's rent for a lease fee.

- Apartment D rents for $565 per month. There is also a one-time $30 parking fee, a $580 deposit, and a $50 fee for a credit check.

1. If Sheila and Paul choose Apartment B, how much rent will they pay in one year?

_____

2. How much would it cost to rent Apartment D for a year, including initial fees?

_____

3. How much more would the most expensive apartment cost in rent per year than the least expensive?

_____

4. a. The move-in cost for an apartment includes one month's rent and any deposits or fees. How much is the move-in cost for Apartment A?

   _____

   b. How much is the move-in cost for Apartment C?

   _____

B. Solve. Refer to the following information to answer Questions 5 through 7.

Tri-Towers Office Complex has several offices for lease. Tower 1 has three available offices that face east and four that face south. Five of the offices in Tower 2 face north and three face west. In Tower 3, six offices face east, two face north, and four face south.

5. Gordon wants to lease office space that faces east or south. What are his choices?

_____

6. How many more offices are available in Tower 3 than in Tower 1?

_____

7. How many more available offices face north or south than east or west?

_____

Answers start on page 446.

Function Applications

As you may remember, a function is a rule that shows a special relationship from one set of numbers to another. We use functions in business and everyday life all the time. For example, total cost is a function of the number of items you buy. We express the function as a formula:

total cost = (number of units) × (price per unit).

Example 1   At Selton Industries, workers are paid $150 per day plus $18 per each product assembled. At Wilshire Products, workers are paid $42 per assembly. At both companies, daily pay (P) is a function of the number of products (n) assembled. The functions are shown below:

Selton Industries: $P = \$150 + \$18n$
Wilshire Products: $P = \$42n$

Jesse can complete five products in one day. How much more money would he earn per day working for Selton Industries than he would working for Wilshire Products?

Step 1   Find Jesse's pay at Selton Industries.
Step 2   Find his pay at Wilshire Products.
Step 3   Find the difference.
$240 − $210 = $30

Jesse would earn **$30 more** per day at Selton Industries.

Use your calculator to find the difference.

240 ⬛− 210 ⬛= 30

Selton Industries pays Jesse $30 more a day.

Example 2   The function $w = \frac{11(h-40)}{2}$ shows a person's recommended weight (w) in pounds as a function of his or her height (h) in inches.

Renata is 5 feet 8 inches tall. Based on the function, what is her recommended weight?

Step 1   Convert Renata's height into inches.
5 feet 8 inches = 68 inches
Step 2   Plug Renata's height into the function.

$w = \frac{11(h-40)}{2}$

$w = \frac{11(68-40)}{2}$

$w = \frac{11(28)}{2}$

$w = \frac{308}{2}$

$w = 154$ — Renata's recommended weight is 154 lbs.

Directions: Choose the <u>one best answer</u> for each question. You <u>MAY</u> use your calculator.

1. How many feet a car skids when the driver steps hard on the brakes is a function of the speed of the car in miles per hour. The graph below shows this function.

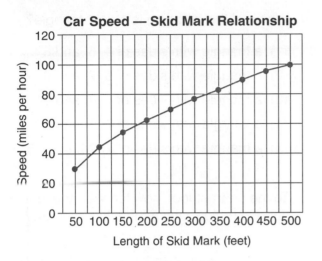

Car Speed — Skid Mark Relationship

After an accident, a police officer measures a skid mark of 310 feet. About how fast (in miles per hour) was the car traveling when the driver hit the brakes?

(1) between 55 and 70 mph

(2) between 70 and 85 mph

(3) between 85 and 100 mph

(4) between 100 and 115 mph

(5) Not enough information is given.

2. The salespeople at Weston Shoes earn $5.50 per hour (*h*) plus an 8% commission on their total sales (*s*). Which of the following formulas could be used to find the pay (*P*) for a salesperson at the shoe store?

(1) $P = \$5.50 \times 0.08 \times h \times s$

(2) $P = \$5.50 + (0.08)s$

(3) $P = \$5.50 + 0.08(s + h)$

(4) $P = \$5.50s + 0.08h$

(5) $P = \$5.50h + 0.08s$

Question 3 refers to the following information.

Details of Long Distance Calling Plans

Plan	Monthly Fee	Charge per Minute
A	$6.95	$0.07
B	None	$0.09
C	$6.50	$0.06
D	$4.95	$0.07
E	$8.50	$0.06

The following formula can be used to find the total monthly bill under any plan: $B = (c \times m) + f$, where *B* equals the total monthly bill, *c* equals the charge per minute, *m* equals the number of minutes of long distance calls, and *f* equals the monthly fee.

3. Based on prior bills, Melinda estimates that she makes about 300 minutes of long distance calls each month. Which of the calling plans would be best for her?

(1) Plan A

(2) Plan B

(3) Plan C

(4) Plan D

(5) Plan E

4. To convert Celsius to Fahrenheit, use the following function: $F = \frac{9}{5}C + 32$ where *C* equals Celsius and *F* equals Fahrenheit. Yesterday in London, England it was 15° C. What was the temperature in Fahrenheit?

(1) 32.12° F

(2) 33.4° F

(3) 59° F

(4) 71° F

(5) 84.6° F

Answers start on page 446.

Directions: This is a thirty-minute practice test. After thirty minutes, mark the last question you finished. Then complete the test and check your answers. If most of your answers are correct, but you didn't finish, try to work faster next time.

Part 1
Directions: Choose the <u>one best answer</u> to each question. You <u>MAY</u> use your calculator.

1. On a map with a scale of 1.5 cm = 60 km, 4.7 cm on the map represents how many actual kilometers?

    (1)   40
    (2) 117
    (3) 188
    (4) 282
    (5) 423

Questions 2 and 3 refer to the following diagram.

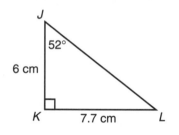

2. If △JKL is a right triangle, what is the measure of ∠L?

    (1)   26°
    (2)   38°
    (3)   52°
    (4)   90°
    (5) 128°

3. Which of the following expressions can be used to find the measure of side $\overline{JL}$?

    (1) 6 + 7.7
    (2) $(6)^2 + (7.7)^2$
    (3) 6 × 7.7
    (4) $\sqrt{6 + 7.7}$
    (5) $\sqrt{(6)^2 + (7.7)^2}$

4. Which of the following is a right triangle?

    (1) a triangle with sides of 4, 5, and 6
    (2) a triangle with sides of 5, 7, and 9
    (3) a triangle with sides of 6, 8, and 11
    (4) a triangle with sides of 7, 9, and 12
    (5) a triangle with sides of 7, 24, and 25

5. To the nearest foot, how long will the ladder need to be to reach a third floor window?

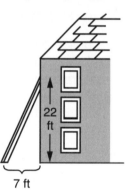

    (1) 18
    (2) 20
    (3) 22
    (4) 23
    (5) 25

6. A circular pool, 20 feet in diameter, has a 2-foot wide gravel walk around it. What is the approximate area of the walk in square feet?

    (1) 100
    (2) 138
    (3) 144
    (4) 314
    (5) 452

Question 7 refers to the following figure.

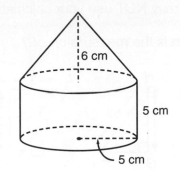

7. What is the volume to the nearest cubic centimeter of the object shown above?

(1) 79
(2) 157
(3) 393
(4) 471
(5) 550

Question 8 refers to the following figures.

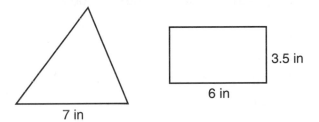

8. A rectangle and triangle have the same area. What is the height of the triangle in inches?

(1) 3
(2) 3.5
(3) 6
(4) 12
(5) 21

9. A 3-foot post casts a $4\frac{1}{2}$-foot shadow at the same time that a telephone pole casts a shadow of 33 feet. What is the length in feet of the telephone pole?

(1) 10
(2) 22
(3) 28
(4) 33
(5) 99

Question 10 refers to the following figure.

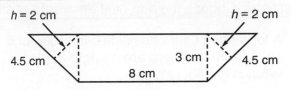

10. What is the area in square centimeters of the figure shown?

(1) 27
(2) 28.5
(3) 33
(4) 37.5
(5) 42

Questions 11 and 12 refer to the following figure.

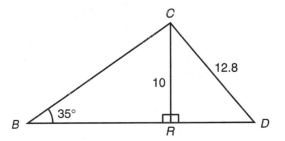

11. To the nearest unit, what is the measure of side RD?

(1) 3
(2) 5
(3) 7
(4) 8
(5) 16

12. In △BRC, what is the measure of ∠BCR?

(1) 35°
(2) 45°
(3) 55°
(4) 90°
(5) 135°

Part 2

Directions: Choose the <u>one best answer</u> to each question. You may <u>NOT</u> use your calculator.

13. A four-sided figure has sides, in order, of 6, 10, 6, and 10. There are no right angles. What is the figure?

    (1) triangle

    (2) square

    (3) trapezoid

    (4) rhombus

    (5) parallelogram

Question 14 refers to the following figure.

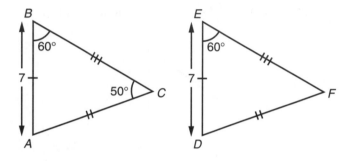

14. The two triangles are congruent. What is the measure of ∠D?

    (1) 50°

    (2) 70°

    (3) 110°

    (4) 180°

    (5) Not enough information is given.

15. The three sides of triangle *ABC* measure 12 feet, 16 feet, and 20 feet. Triangle *DEF* is similar to △*ABC*. The shortest side of △*DEF* measures 15 feet. What are the lengths in feet of the other two sides of △*DEF*?

    (1) 18 and 23

    (2) 18 and 25

    (3) 19 and 23

    (4) 20 and 24

    (5) 20 and 25

16. What is the measure of ∠L?

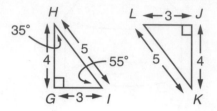

    (1) 35°

    (2) 45°

    (3) 55°

    (4) 90°

    (5) Not enough information is given.

17. Sides *AB* and *BC* of △*ABC* each measure 10 inches. If *m*∠*A* = 60° and *m*∠*B* = 60°, what is the length in inches of side *AC*?

    (1) 5

    (2) 6

    (3) 10

    (4) 14

    (5) Not enough information is given.

18. In order to prove that △*ACE* ≅ △*BCD* by *SSS*, it is necessary to know which of the following?

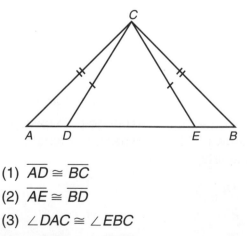

    (1) $\overline{AD} \cong \overline{BC}$

    (2) $\overline{AE} \cong \overline{BD}$

    (3) ∠*DAC* ≅ ∠*EBC*

    (4) ∠*CDE* ≅ ∠*CED*

    (5) $\overline{DE} \cong \overline{EB}$

19. A wooden rectangular frame is 6 feet by 8 feet. A diagonal brace will be added to the back of the frame. What is the length in feet of the brace?

(1) 5
(2) 7
(3) 8
(4) 10
(5) 13

20. A circle has a radius of 7 inches. Which of the following is the best estimate of the circumference of the circle in inches?

(1) 15
(2) 25
(3) 40
(4) 50
(5) 150

21. Triangle *ABC* has sides measuring 2.9, 4.6, and 4.9 cm. Its angle measures are 78°, 36°, and 66°. Triangle *ABC* can be classified as which of the following two kinds of triangles?

(1) equilateral and acute
(2) isosceles and acute
(3) isosceles and obtuse
(4) scalene and acute
(5) scalene and obtuse

22. In a right triangle, the measure of one acute angle is five times larger than the measure of the other acute angle. Which of the following equations can be used to find the measure of the smaller angle?

(1) $x + 5x + 90° = 180°$
(2) $x + (5 + x) + 90° = 180°$
(3) $x + 5x = 180°$
(4) $90x + 5x = 180°$
(5) $180° - 90° = 5x$

Question 23 refers to the following figure.

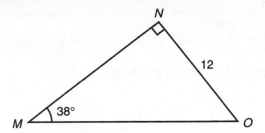

23. Which of the following expressions could be used to find angle O?

(1) $38° + 90°$
(2) $180° - 90° + 38°$
(3) $180° - (90° + 38°)$
(4) $\sqrt{38^2 + 90^2}$
(5) Not enough information is given.

Question 24 refers to the following figure.

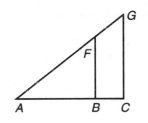

24. If $\triangle ABF \sim \triangle ACG$, then which of the following is a true proportion?

(1) $\dfrac{\overline{AF}}{\overline{AB}} = \dfrac{\overline{AB}}{\overline{AC}}$

(2) $\dfrac{\overline{AB}}{\overline{AC}} = \dfrac{\overline{FB}}{\overline{GC}}$

(3) $\dfrac{\overline{AF}}{\overline{AC}} = \dfrac{\overline{AC}}{\overline{AB}}$

(4) $\dfrac{\overline{AB}}{\overline{GC}} = \dfrac{\overline{AC}}{\overline{FB}}$

(5) $\dfrac{\overline{AG}}{\overline{AC}} = \dfrac{\overline{AB}}{\overline{AF}}$

Answers start on page 447.

Unit 4 Cumulative Review Geometry

Part 1

Directions: Choose the <u>one best answer</u> to each question. You <u>MAY</u> use your calculator.

<u>Question 1</u> refers to the following figure.

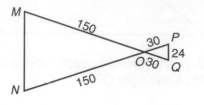

1. If $\overline{PQ}$ and $\overline{MN}$ are parallel, what is the length of $\overline{MN}$?

   (1) 48
   (2) 60
   (3) 90
   (4) 120
   (5) 150

---

2. What is the approximate area in square feet of a circular pool with a diameter of 8 feet?

   (1) 50
   (2) 48
   (3) 40
   (4) 20
   (5) 16

3. The scale on a house plan is 1 inch = 2 feet. The drawing of the kitchen is 5 inches by 7 inches. What is the area of the actual kitchen in square feet?

   (1) 12
   (2) 24
   (3) 35
   (4) 70
   (5) 140

<u>Question 4</u> refers to the following information.

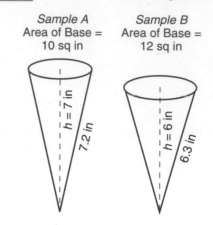

4. How many more cubic inches does Sample B hold than Sample A?

   (1) $\frac{2}{3}$
   (2) 3
   (3) 5
   (4) $6\frac{2}{3}$
   (5) 9

---

5. To the nearest tenth meter, what is the circumference of a circle with a radius of 3 meters?

   (1)   4.7
   (2)   7.1
   (3)   9.4
   (4) 18.8
   (5) 28.2

6. The inside volume of a refrigerator is 19.5 cubic feet. If the interior is 5.2 feet high and 1.5 feet deep, what is its width in feet?

   (1)   2.5
   (2)   2.9
   (3)   3.75
   (4) 13
   (5) 15.2

Question 7 refers to the following figure.

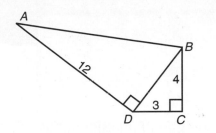

7. If ∠ADB and ∠C are right angles, what is the length of $\overline{AB}$?

(1) 5

(2) 10

(3) 13

(4) 16

(5) 17

---

8. The perimeter of a rectangle is 5 feet. The length is 6 inches longer than the width. What is the width in inches?

(1) 4

(2) 8

(3) 10

(4) 12

(5) 15

Question 9 refers to the following figure.

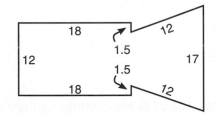

9. What is the perimeter of the figure?

(1) 72

(2) 75

(3) 90

(4) 92

(5) 101

Questions 10 and 11 refer to the following figure.

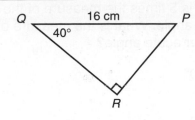

10. What is the measure of ∠RPQ?

(1) 40°

(2) 50°

(3) 60°

(4) 90°

(5) 140°

11. Which of the following statements is true about △PRQ?

(1) The lengths of $\overline{QR}$ and $\overline{PR}$ are equal.

(2) The length of $\overline{QP}$ is the shortest.

(3) The length of $\overline{PR}$ is longer than the length of $\overline{QR}$.

(4) The length of $\overline{QR}$ is longer than the length of $\overline{PR}$.

(5) The lengths of $\overline{QR}$, $\overline{PR}$, and $\overline{QP}$ are equal.

Question 12 refers to the following figure.

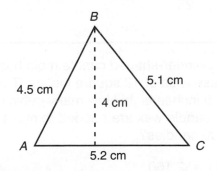

12. What is the area to the nearest square centimeter of △ABC?

(1) 10

(2) 14

(3) 17

(4) 19

(5) 21

13. In a right triangle, the measure of one acute angle is 5 times the measure of the other acute angle. What is the measure of the smaller acute angle?

   (1) 10°
   (2) 15°
   (3) 20°
   (4) 25°
   (5) 30°

Question 14 refers to the following figure.

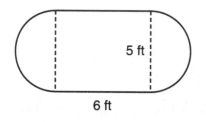

5 ft

6 ft

14. A tabletop has the measurements shown in the figure. If the ends of the table are half-circles, what is the approximate area of the tabletop in square feet?

   (1) 110
   (2) 80
   (3) 50
   (2) 40
   (1) 25

15. A cylinder-shaped candle mold has a base area of 12 square inches. The mold is 5 inches high. How many cubic inches of candle wax are needed to make 200 candles?

   (1) 452,160
   (2) 113,040
   (3) 37,680
   (4) 12,000
   (5)   3,400

Question 16 refers to the following figure.

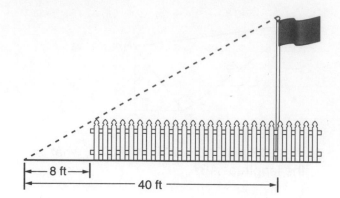

16. The shadows cast by a fence post and a flagpole are measured at the same time of day. If the fence post is 5 feet in height, what is the height in feet of the flagpole?

   (1) 22
   (2) 25
   (3) 40
   (4) 320
   (5) Not enough information is given.

17. The scale on a map is 1 inch = 1.5 miles. The actual distance from Ivey to Garrett is 4 miles. How far apart in inches are these two cities on the map?

   (1) less than 2
   (2) $2\frac{1}{3}$
   (3) $2\frac{2}{3}$
   (4) 3
   (5) 6

18. Angles M and N are complementary angles. If $\angle M$ measures 26°, what is the measure of $\angle N$?

   (1) 26°
   (2) 64°
   (3) 90°
   (4) 154°
   (5) Not enough information is given.

Directions: Solve the following questions and enter your answers on the grids provided.

19. A parallelogram has a base of 32 yards and a height of 8 yards. How many yards is the side of a square with the same area as the parallelogram?

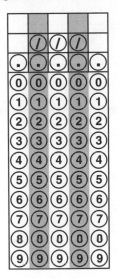

Question 20 refers to the following figure.

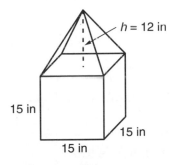

20. What is the volume of the figure in cubic inches?

Question 21 refers to the following graph.

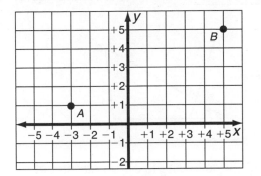

21. To the nearest whole unit, what is the distance between points A and B?

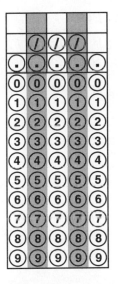

22. In a right triangle, the short leg is 9 and the hypotenuse is 15. What is the measure of the other leg?

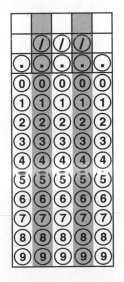

Directions: Choose the <u>one best answer</u> to each question. You may <u>NOT</u> use your calculator.

<u>Questions 23 and 24</u> refer to the following figure.   <u>Question 26</u> refers to the following figure.

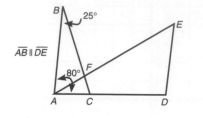

$\overline{AB} \parallel \overline{DE}$

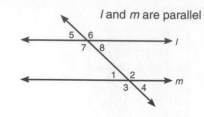

23. Which of the following is a true statement regarding the measure of $\angle D$?

    (1) $m\angle D = m\angle BAC$

    (2) $m\angle D = m\angle BCD$

    (3) $m\angle D = m\angle B + m\angle BAC$

    (4) $m\angle D + m\angle BAC = 180°$

    (5) $m\angle D + m\angle B = 90°$

26. If $\angle 8$ measures 50°, which two angles measure 130°?

    (1) $\angle 1$ and $\angle 7$

    (2) $\angle 2$ and $\angle 6$

    (3) $\angle 4$ and $\angle 6$

    (4) $\angle 4$ and $\angle 7$

    (5) $\angle 5$ and $\angle 7$

24. What is the degree measure of $\angle BCD$?

    (1) 105°

    (2) 110°

    (3) 120°

    (4) 125°

    (5) 130°

<u>Questions 27 and 28</u> refer to the following figure.

Line *a* is parallel to line *b*.
$m\angle 3 = m\angle 4$

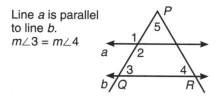

25. If C equals circumference, d = diameter, and r = radius, which of the following formulas is <u>not</u> valid?

    (1) $d = 2r$

    (2) $C = \pi d$

    (3) $C = 2\pi r$

    (4) $\dfrac{C}{d} = \pi$

    (5) $\pi = \dfrac{C}{r}$

27. Which equation is true?

    (1) $m\angle 2 = 180° - m\angle 1$

    (2) $m\angle 2 = m\angle 4$

    (3) $m\angle 2 = 180° - m\angle 3$

    (4) $m\angle 2 = 90° - m\angle 4$

    (5) $m\angle 2 = m\angle 3$

28. Which statement is true if $m\angle 3 = 60°$?

    (1) $m\angle 5 = 45°$

    (2) $m\angle 4 = 120°$

    (3) $m\angle 2 = 60°$

    (4) $m\angle 5 = 60°$

    (5) $m\angle 1 = 135°$

Question 29 refers to the following figure.

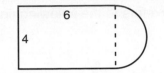

29. The figure shows a rectangle attached to a half-circle. Which of the following expressions represents the perimeter of the figure?

(1) $16 + 2\pi$

(2) $10 + 2\pi$

(3) $10 + 4\pi$

(4) $16 + 4\pi$

(5) $24 + 4\pi$

Question 30 refers to the following figure

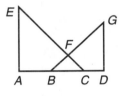

30. $\triangle AEC$ and $\triangle BDG$ are isosceles. What conclusion can be drawn?

(1) $\overline{AB} \cong \overline{BC} \cong \overline{CD}$

(2) $\overline{AC} \cong \overline{AE}$

(3) $\overline{AE} \cong \overline{DG}$

(4) $\angle E \cong \angle D$

(5) $\overline{BF} \cong \overline{FC}$

31. The hypotenuse of a right triangle measures 12 inches. If one leg measures 7 inches, which of the following expressions could be used to find the length of the other leg?

(1) $12^2 + 7^2$

(2) $\sqrt{12^2 + 7^2}$

(3) $12^2 - 7^2$

(4) $\sqrt{12^2 - 7^2}$

(5) $(12 + 7)^2$

Question 32 refers to the following figure.

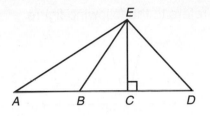

32. Triangle ECD is a right triangle. Which of the following must be an obtuse angle?

(1) $\angle ABE$

(2) $\angle ACE$

(3) $\angle BCE$

(4) $\angle DAE$

(5) Not enough information is given.

Question 33 refers to the following figure.

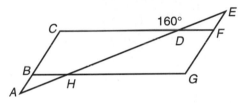

33. The measure of $\angle CDE$ is 160°. If $\overline{CF} \parallel \overline{BG}$, which other angle is congruent to $\angle CDE$?

(1) $\angle BCD$

(2) $\angle EGH$

(3) $\angle AHG$

(4) $\angle ABH$

(5) $\angle DFE$

34. The Grahams' rectangular yard measures 50 by 30 feet. They plan to plant a small square vegetable garden, measuring 12 feet per side, in one corner of the yard. The remaining area will be grass. What is the area in square feet of the grass portion of the yard?

(1) 900

(2) 1140

(3) 1356

(4) 1500

(5) 1644

Directions: Solve the following questions and enter your answers on the grids provided.

Question 35 refers to the following figure.

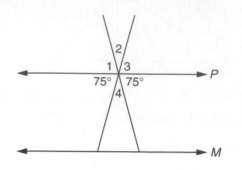

35. Lines *p* and *m* are parallel, and ∠2 and ∠4 are vertical angles. What is the measure of ∠4 in degrees?

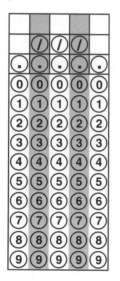

36. The height of a triangle is 40 inches. If the area of the triangle is 200 square inches, what is the length of the base in inches?

Question 37 refers to the following figure.

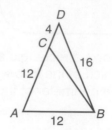

37. The measure of ∠*DAB* is 70°. What is the measure of ∠*D* in degrees?

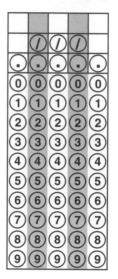

38. A sign 4 meters tall casts a shadow 5 meters long. At the same time, a tree casts a shadow 30 meters long. What is the height of the tree in meters?

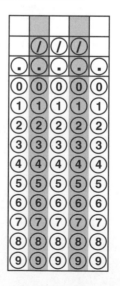

Answers start on page 449.

Cumulative Review Performance Analysis
Unit 4 • Geometry

Use the Answers and Explanations starting on page 449 to check your answers to the Unit 4 Cumulative Review. Then use the chart to figure out the skill areas in which you need more practice.

On the chart, circle the questions that you answered correctly. Write the number correct for each skill area. Add to find the total number of questions that you got correct on the Cumulative Review. If you feel that you need more practice, go back and review the lessons for the skill areas that were difficult for you.

Questions	Number Correct	Skill Area	Lessons for Review
2, **4**, 5, 6, 8, **12**, 15, 19, 25, 36	____/10	Applying Formulas	23
18, **23, 24, 26, 27, 32, 33, 35**	____/8	Lines and Angles	24
1, 3, **10**, 13, **16**, 17, **28, 30, 37**, 38	____/10	Triangles and Quadrilaterals	25
9, 14, 20, 29, 34	____/5	Irregular Figures	26
7, 11, 21, 22, 31	____/5	Working with Right Triangles	27
TOTAL CORRECT	____/38		

Question numbers in **boldface** are based on graphics.

MATHEMATICS
Part I

Directions

The Mathematics Posttest consists of multiple-choice and alternate format questions intended to measure your general mathematical skills and problem-solving ability. The questions are based on short readings that often include a graph, chart, or diagram.

You will have 90 minutes to complete the 50 questions on Parts I and II. Work carefully, but do not spend too much time on any one question. Be sure to answer every question. You will not be penalized for incorrect answers. When time is up, mark the last item you finished. This will tell you whether you can finish the real GED Test in the time allowed. Then complete the test.

Formulas you may need are given on page 335. Only some of the questions will require you to use a formula. Not all the formulas given will be needed.

Some questions contain more information than you will need to solve the problem; other questions do not give enough information. If the question does not give enough information to solve the problem, the correct answer choice is "Not enough information is given."

You may use a calculator on Part I. Calculator directions for the CASIO *fx-260SOLAR* scientific calculator can be found on page 334.

Record your answers on a copy of the separate answer sheet provided on page 473. Be sure all required information is properly recorded on the answer sheet.

To record your answers, mark the numbered space on the answer sheet that corresponds to the answer you select for each question on the test.

Example: If a grocery bill totaling $15.75 is paid with a $20.00 bill, how much change should be returned?

(1) $5.25
(2) $4.75
(3) $4.25
(4) $3.75
(5) $3.25

① ② ● ④ ⑤

The correct answer is $4.25; therefore, answer space 3 would be marked on the answer sheet.

Do not rest the point of your pencil on the answer sheet while you are considering your answer. Make no stray or unnecessary marks. If you change an answer, erase your first mark completely. Mark only one answer for each question; multiple answers will be scored as incorrect. Do not fold or crease your answer sheet.

When you finish the test, use the Performance Analysis Chart on page 349 to determine whether you are ready to take the real GED Test, and, if not, which skill areas need additional review.

Adapted with permission of the American Council on Education.

MATHEMATICS

Mixed numbers, such as $3\frac{1}{2}$, cannot be entered in the alternate format grid. Instead, represent them as decimal numbers (in this case, 3.5) or fractions (in this case, 7/2). No answer can be a negative number, such as -8.

To record your answer for an alternate format question

- begin in any column that will allow your answer to be entered;
- write your answer in the boxes on the top row;
- in the column beneath a fraction bar or decimal point (if any) and each number in your answer, fill in the bubble representing that character;
- leave blank any unused column.

Example:

The scale on a map indicates that $\frac{1}{2}$ inch represents an actual distance of 120 miles. In inches, how far apart on the map will two towns be if the actual distance between them is 180 miles?

The answer to the above example is 3/4, or 0.75, inches. The answer could be gridded using any of the methods below.

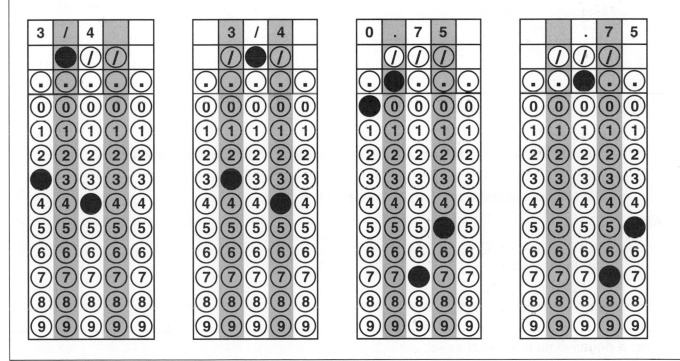

Points to remember:

- The answer sheet will be machine scored. **The circles must be filled in correctly.**
- Mark no more than one circle in any column.
- Grid only one answer even if there is more than one correct answer.
- Mixed numbers, such as $3\frac{1}{2}$, must be gridded as a decimal (3.5) or fraction (7/2).
- No answer can be a negative number.

Adapted with permission of the American Council on Education.

CALCULATOR DIRECTIONS

To prepare the calculator for use the ***first*** time, press the (ON) (upper-rightmost) key. "DEG" will appear at the top-center of the screen and "0." at the right. This indicates the calculator is in the proper format for all your calculations.

To prepare the calculator for ***another*** question, press the (ON) or the red (AC) key. This clears any entries made previously.

To do any arithmetic, enter the expression as it is written. Press (=) (equals sign) when finished.

EXAMPLE A: $8 - 3 + 9$

> First press (ON) or (AC).
> Enter the following:
>
> > 8 (−) 3 (+) 9 (=)
>
> The correct answer is 14.

If an expression in parentheses is to be multiplied by a number, press (×) (multiplication sign) between the number and the parenthesis sign.

EXAMPLE B: $6(8 + 5)$

> First press (ON) or (AC).
> Enter the following:
>
> > 6 (×) ((---) 8 (+) 5 (---)) (=)
>
> The correct answer is 78.

To find the square root of a number

> • enter the number;
> • press (SHIFT) (upper-leftmost) key ("SHIFT" appears at the top-left of the screen);
> • press (x²) (third from the left on top row) to access its second function: square root.
>   **DO NOT** press (SHIFT) and (x²) at the same time.

EXAMPLE C: $\sqrt{64}$

> First press (ON) or (AC).
> Enter the following:
>
> > 64 (SHIFT) (x²)
>
> The correct answer is 8.

To enter a negative number such as –8,

> • enter the number without the negative sign (enter 8);
> • press the "change sign" ((+/−)) key which is directly above the 7 key.

All arithmetic can be done with positive and/or negative numbers.

EXAMPLE D: $-8 - -5$

> First press (ON) or (AC).
> Enter the following:
>
> > 8 (+/−) (−) 5 (+/−) (=)
>
> The correct answer is –3.

Adapted with permission of the American Council on Education.

FORMULAS

AREA of a:

square	Area = side^2
rectangle	Area = length $\times$ width
parallelogram	Area = base $\times$ height
triangle	Area = $\frac{1}{2}$ $\times$ base $\times$ height
trapezoid	Area = $\frac{1}{2}$ $\times$ (base$_1$ + base$_2$) $\times$ height
circle	Area = π $\times$ radius^2; π is approximately equal to 3.14

PERIMETER of a:

square	Perimeter = 4 $\times$ side
rectangle	Perimeter = 2 $\times$ length + 2 $\times$ width
triangle	Perimeter = side$_1$ + side$_2$ + side$_3$

CIRCUMFERENCE of a circle   Circumference = π $\times$ diameter; π is approximately equal to 3.14

VOLUME of a:

cube	Volume = edge^3
rectangular container	Volume = length $\times$ width $\times$ height
square pyramid	Volume = $\frac{1}{3}$ $\times$ (base edge)^2 $\times$ height
cylinder	Volume = π $\times$ radius^2 $\times$ height; π is approximately equal to 3.14
cone	Volume = $\frac{1}{3}$ $\times$ π $\times$ radius^2 $\times$ height; π is approximately equal to 3.14

COORDINATE GEOMETRY

distance between points = $\sqrt{(x_2 - x_1)^2 + (y_2 - y_1)^2}$; (x_1, y_1) and (x_2, y_2) are two points in a plane.

slope of a line = $\frac{y_2 - y_1}{x_2 - x_1}$; (x_1, y_1) and (x_2, y_2) are two points on a line.

PYTHAGOREAN RELATIONSHIP

$a^2 + b^2 = c^2$; a and b are legs and c the hypotenuse of a right triangle.

MEASURES OF CENTRAL TENDENCY

mean = $\frac{x_1 + x_2 + \ldots + x_n}{n}$; where the x's are the values for which a mean is desired, and n is the total number of values for x.

median = the middle value of an odd number of *ordered* scores, and halfway between the two middle values of an even number of *ordered* scores.

SIMPLE INTEREST   interest = principal $\times$ rate $\times$ time

DISTANCE   distance = rate $\times$ time

TOTAL COST   total cost = (number of units) $\times$ (price per unit)

Adapted with permission of the American Council on Education.

Part I

Directions: Choose the one best answer to each question. You MAY use your calculator.

Questions 1 and 2 refer to the following information.

clothes.com
SALES SUMMARY

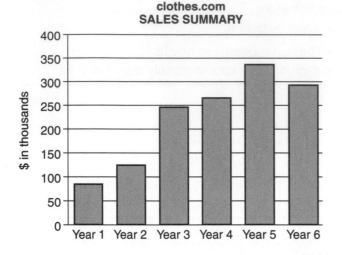

1. The graph shows the total sales for the first six years of business for clothes.com, an Internet company. About how much more did the company earn in sales in Year 5 than in Year 2?

   (1) $390,000
   (2) $340,000
   (3) $250,000
   (4) $210,000
   (5) $190,000

2. In which year did the company experience an approximately 50% increase in sales from the previous year?

   (1) Year 2
   (2) Year 3
   (3) Year 4
   (4) Year 5
   (5) Year 6

3. A school plans to buy 650 ribbons to give as prizes for a reading contest. If each ribbon cost 9.5 cents, about how much will the school pay for the ribbons?

   (1) less than $50
   (2) between $50 and $100
   (3) between $100 and $400
   (4) between $400 and $700
   (5) more than $700

Question 4 refers to the following diagram.

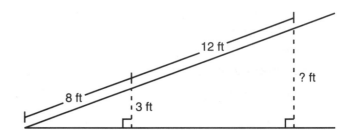

4. A worker walked 8 feet up a ramp and was 3 feet above ground level. If he walks an additional 12 feet up the ramp, how many feet will he be from the ground?

   Mark your answer in the circles in the grid on your answer sheet.

5. What is the value of the expression below?

   $15 + 5(3 + 4)^2$

   Mark your answer in the circles in the grid on your answer sheet.

Questions 6 and 7 refer to the following information.

CARDSTON'S STORE EMPLOYEES

Department	Number of Employees
Managers	16
Marketing	3
Buyers	8
Accounting	12
Sales	57

6. What percent of Cardston's employees work as either managers or buyers?

   (1) 12%

   (2) 23%

   (3) 25%

   (4) 46%

   (5) 53%

7. Cardston's is holding a contest. One employee will be chosen at random to win a trip to Hawaii. What is the probability that an employee from the accounting department will win the contest?

   (1) $\frac{1}{5}$

   (2) $\frac{1}{8}$

   (3) $\frac{1}{12}$

   (4) $\frac{1}{96}$

   (5) Not enough information is given.

8. Wayne can mow his back lawn in 45 minutes. What part of his lawn can he mow in $\frac{1}{2}$ hour?

   (1) $\frac{1}{4}$

   (2) $\frac{1}{3}$

   (3) $\frac{3}{8}$

   (4) $\frac{2}{3}$

   (5) $\frac{3}{4}$

9. Lot A and Lot B, shown below, have the same area. If Lot A is square, what is the length in yards of one of its sides?

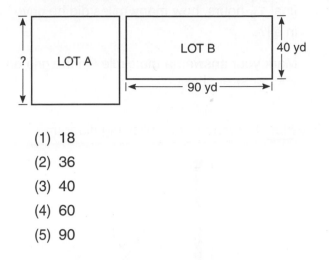

   (1) 18

   (2) 36

   (3) 40

   (4) 60

   (5) 90

10. Preston bought an antique bookcase for $90 and refinished it. He sold the bookcase for 175% of the price he paid. For what amount did he sell the bookcase?

   (1) $ 67.50

   (2) $112.50

   (3) $157.50

   (4) $265.00

   (5) Not enough information is given.

11. Melanie runs a business out of her home. She must pay a city tax according to the following formula:

   Tax = $105 + 0.01 × (Income − $10,000)

   If Melanie earned $26,000 this year, how much does she owe in city taxes?

   (1) $ 55

   (2) $160

   (3) $168

   (4) $265

   (5) $365

12. Zach completed a $3\frac{1}{2}$-hour driving trip. If he averaged 70 miles an hour for the first two hours and 60 miles per hour for the final $1\frac{1}{2}$ hours, how many miles did he drive in all?

Mark your answer in the circles in the grid on your answer sheet.

Question 13 refers to the following diagram.

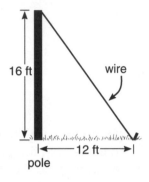

13. A 16-foot pole is perpendicular to the ground. For support, a wire is attached to the top of the pole. The other end of the wire is staked to the ground a distance of 12 feet from the base of the pole. What is the length of the wire in feet?

Mark your answer in the circles in the grid on your answer sheet.

_____

14. A city newspaper costs 50 cents per day for the Monday through Saturday editions and $1.25 for the Sunday edition. Which of the following expressions could be used to find the cost of buying the newspaper daily for 12 weeks?

(1) 12($0.50 + $1.25)

(2) 12(7)($0.50 + $1.25)

(3) 12($0.50) + 12($1.25)

(4) 6($0.50) + 12($1.25)

(5) 12(6 × $0.50 + $1.25)

Questions 15 and 16 refer to the following figure.

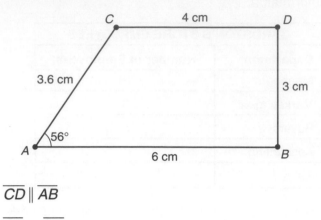

$\overline{CD} \parallel \overline{AB}$

$\overline{AB} \perp \overline{BD}$

15. What is the measure of $\angle C$?

(1) 34°

(2) 56°

(3) 124°

(4) 236°

(5) Not enough information is given.

16. Which of the following expressions can be used to find the area of quadrilateral $ABDC$ in square centimeters?

(1) $(4 \times 3) + (2 \times 3.6)$

(2) $\frac{1}{2} \times (4 \times 3 \times 3.6)$

(3) $4 \times 3 \times 6 \times 3.6$

(4) $(4 \times 3) + \frac{1}{2}(2 \times 3)$

(5) $4 + 3 + 6 + 3.6$

_____

17. The coordinates of point A are $(5, -3)$. Show the location of the point.

Mark your answer on the coordinate plane grid on your answer sheet.

18. John works at least 15 hours but no more than 25 hours each week at a part-time job. If John is paid $9 per hour, which of the following inequalities could be used to represent John's weekly earnings (represented by x)?

(1) $\$9(15) > x > \$9(25)$

(2) $\$9(15) \leq x \leq \$9(25)$

(3) $\$9(15) < x < \$9(25)$

(4) $\$9(15) \geq x \geq \$9(25)$

(5) $\$9(15) \leq x \geq \$9(25)$

Question 19 refers to the following information.

A school principal wanted to find the typical amount of time that 5th graders at her school spend on homework daily. She surveyed 15 parents (selected randomly) and gathered the following data.

TIME SPENT ON DAILY HOMEWORK	
Time	Number of Students
15 minutes	I
30 minutes	‖‖
45 minutes	‖‖
1 hour	‖‖
$1\frac{1}{2}$ hours	‖
2 hours	I

19. What is the median for the amount of time that 5th graders spend on homework at this school?

(1) $1\frac{1}{2}$ hours

(2) 1 hour

(3) 50 minutes

(4) 45 minutes

(5) 30 minutes

Question 20 refers to the following graph.

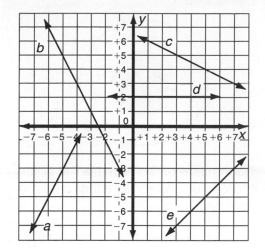

20. Which of the lines drawn on the coordinate plane above has a slope of -2?

(1) a

(2) b

(3) c

(4) d

(5) e

21. In her English class, Janet has six test scores. Her scores are as follows:

92   84   81   78   80   89

What is her average (mean) score?

Mark your answer in the circles in the grid on your answer sheet.

22. A target has two sections, an inner circle and an outer ring.

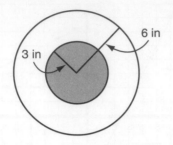

What fraction of the target is the inner circle? Record your answer as either a fraction or a decimal.

Mark your answer in the circles in the grid on your answer sheet.

Questions 23 and 24 refer to the following figure.

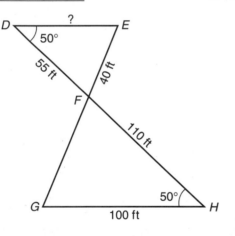

23. If triangles DEF and FGH are similar, which of the following are corresponding sides?

   (1) sides DF and FG

   (2) sides EF and FH

   (3) sides DE and DF

   (4) sides DF and GH

   (5) sides DF and FH

24. What is the length in feet of side DE in the figure?

   (1) 20

   (2) 33

   (3) 40

   (4) 50

   (5) 55

25. An early radar device (Model A) operates at a frequency of 3×10^3 megahertz. A new device (Model B) operates at 3×10^5 megahertz. Which of the following statements is true?

   (1) The frequency of Model B is less than that of Model A.

   (2) The frequency of Model B is 2 times as great as the frequency of Model A.

   (3) The frequency of Model B is 3 times as great as the frequency of Model A.

   (4) The frequency of Model B is 10 times as great as the frequency of Model A.

   (5) The frequency of Model B is 100 times as great as the frequency of Model A.

MATHEMATICS
Part II

Directions

The Mathematics Posttest consists of multiple-choice and alternate format questions intended to measure your general mathematical skills and problem-solving ability. The questions are based on short readings that often include a graph, chart, or diagram.

You will have 90 minutes to complete the 25 questions on Part II. Work carefully, but do not spend too much time on any one question. Be sure to answer every question. You will not be penalized for incorrect answers. When time is up, mark the last item you finished. This will tell you whether you can finish the real GED Test in the time allowed. Then complete the test.

Formulas you may need are given on page 343. Only some of the questions will require you to use a formula. Not all the formulas given will be needed.

Some questions contain more information than you will need to solve the problem; other questions do not give enough information. If the question does not give enough information to solve the problem, the correct answer choice is "Not enough information is given."

The use of calculators is not allowed on Part II.

Record your answers on a copy of the separate answer sheet provided on page 474. Be sure all required information is properly recorded on the answer sheet.

To record your answers, mark the numbered space on the answer sheet that corresponds to the answer you select for each question on the test.

Example: If a grocery bill totaling $15.75 is paid with a $20.00 bill, how much change should be returned?

(1) $5.25
(2) $4.75
(3) $4.25
(4) $3.75
(5) $3.25   ① ② ● ④ ⑤

The correct answer is $4.25; therefore, answer space 3 would be marked on the answer sheet.

Do not rest the point of your pencil on the answer sheet while you are considering your answer. Make no stray or unnecessary marks. If you change an answer, erase your first mark completely. Mark only one answer for each question; multiple answers will be scored as incorrect. Do not fold or crease your answer sheet.

When you finish the test, use the Performance Analysis Chart on page 349 to determine whether you are ready to take the real GED Test, and, if not, which skill areas need additional review.

Adapted with permission of the American Council on Education.

MATHEMATICS

Mixed numbers, such as $3\frac{1}{2}$, cannot be entered in the alternate format grid. Instead, represent them as decimal numbers (in this case, 3.5) or fractions (in this case, 7/2). No answer can be a negative number, such as -8.

To record your answer for an alternate format question

- begin in any column that will allow your answer to be entered;
- write your answer in the boxes on the top row;
- in the column beneath a fraction bar or decimal point (if any) and each number in your answer, fill in the bubble representing that character;
- leave blank any unused column.

Example:

The scale on a map indicates that $\frac{1}{2}$ inch represents an actual distance of 120 miles. In inches, how far apart on the map will two towns be if the actual distance between them is 180 miles?

The answer to the above example is 3/4, or 0.75, inches. The answer could be gridded using any of the methods below.

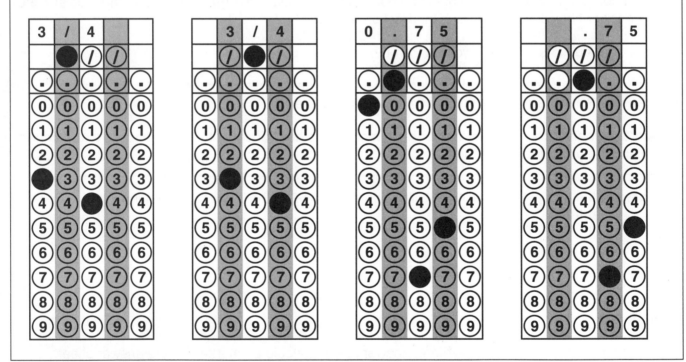

Points to remember:

- The answer sheet will be machine scored. **The circles must be filled in correctly.**
- Mark no more than one circle in any column.
- Grid only one answer even if there is more than one correct answer.
- Mixed numbers, such as $3\frac{1}{2}$, must be gridded as a decimal (3.5) or fraction (7/2).
- No answer can be a negative number.

FORMULAS

AREA of a:

square	Area = side^2
rectangle	Area = length × width
parallelogram	Area = base × height
triangle	Area = $\frac{1}{2}$ × base × height
trapezoid	Area = $\frac{1}{2}$ × (base$_1$ + base$_2$) × height
circle	Area = π × radius^2; π is approximately equal to 3.14

PERIMETER of a:

square	Perimeter = 4 × side
rectangle	Perimeter = 2 × length + 2 × width
triangle	Perimeter = side$_1$ + side$_2$ + side$_3$

CIRCUMFERENCE of a circle   Circumference = π × diameter; π is approximately equal to 3.14

VOLUME of a:

cube	Volume = edge^3
rectangular container	Volume = length × width × height
square pyramid	Volume $-$ $\frac{1}{3}$ × (base edge)^2 × height
cylinder	Volume = π × radius^2 × height; π is approximately equal to 3.14
cone	Volume = $\frac{1}{3}$ × π × radius^2 × height; π is approximately equal to 3.14

COORDINATE GEOMETRY

distance between points = $\sqrt{(x_2 - x_1)^2 + (y_2 - y_1)^2}$; (x_1, y_1) and (x_2, y_2) are two points in a plane.

slope of a line = $\frac{y_2 - y_1}{x_2 - x_1}$; (x_1, y_1) and (x_2, y_2) are two points on a line.

PYTHAGOREAN RELATIONSHIP

$a^2 + b^2 = c^2$; a and b are legs and c the hypotenuse of a right triangle.

MEASURES OF CENTRAL TENDENCY

mean = $\frac{x_1 + x_2 + \ldots + x_n}{n}$; where the x's are the values for which a mean is desired, and n is the total number of values for x.

median = the middle value of an odd number of _ordered_ scores, and halfway between the two middle values of an even number of _ordered_ scores.

SIMPLE INTEREST   interest = principal × rate × time

DISTANCE   distance = rate × time

TOTAL COST   total cost = (number of units) × (price per unit)

Adapted with permission of the American Council on Education.

Part II
Directions: Choose the one best answer to each question. You may NOT use your calculator.

1. To cover a sofa cushion, Lydia needs $4\frac{2}{3}$ yards of fabric. How many yards of fabric will she need to cover four cushions?

   (1) $18\frac{2}{3}$
   (2) $16\frac{2}{3}$
   (3) $16\frac{1}{3}$
   (4) $13\frac{1}{3}$
   (5) $8\frac{2}{3}$

2. If all adjacent sides are perpendicular, what is the perimeter of the figure?

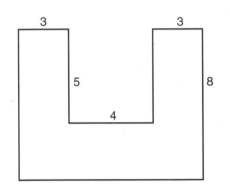

   (1) 18
   (2) 23
   (3) 36
   (4) 41
   (5) 46

3. A new computer monitor is priced 5% higher than last year's model. If last year's model cost $300, which of the following expressions could be used to find the cost of the new model?

   (1) 0.05($300)
   (2) $\frac{\$300}{0.05}$
   (3) 0.05($300) + 0.05
   (4) 0.05($300) + $300
   (5) $\frac{\$300}{0.05}$ + $300

4. Which point on the number line below represents the square root of 14?

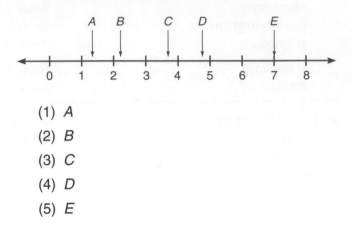

   (1) A
   (2) B
   (3) C
   (4) D
   (5) E

Questions 5 and 6 refer to the following figure.

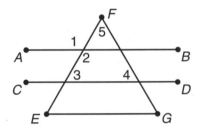

Given: $\overline{AB} \parallel \overline{CD}$ and $m\angle 3 = m\angle 4$

5. Which of the following statements is true?

   (1) $m\angle 1 = m\angle 4$
   (2) $\angle 1$ and $\angle 2$ are congruent.
   (3) $\angle 3$ and $\angle 4$ are supplementary angles.
   (4) $m\angle 2 = m\angle 3$
   (5) $\angle 1$ and $\angle 3$ are vertical angles.

6. If $m\angle 3 = 60°$, what is the measure in degrees of $\angle 5$?

   Mark your answer in the circles in the grid on your answer sheet.

Questions 7 and 8 are based on the following information.

Lake City is starting a fast-pitch softball league for girls. The circle graph below shows how the available funds for the program are budgeted.

CITY PARKS SOFTBALL BUDGET

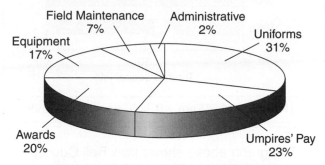

7. If Lake City's total budget is $2400, about how much money will be spent on uniforms and awards?

(1) $ 50

(2) $ 500

(3) $ 800

(4) $1000

(5) $1200

8. What fraction of the total budget is spent on equipment and umpires' pay?

(1) $\frac{3}{4}$

(2) $\frac{1}{2}$

(3) $\frac{2}{5}$

(4) $\frac{3}{8}$

(5) Not enough information is given.

9. The expression $(2x + 5)(x - 4)$ is equal to which of the following expressions?

(1) $2x^2 + 3x - 20$

(2) $2x^2 - 3x - 20$

(3) $2x^2 - x - 20$

(4) $2x^2 + 9x - 20$

(5) $2x^2 + 13x - 20$

10. Each of the walls of the rectangular living room shown below is 8 feet in height. How many square feet of carpeting is needed to cover the living room floor?

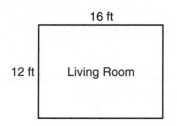

(1)   96

(2) 128

(3) 192

(4) 256

(5) 448

11. Nolan jogs 5 miles in $1\frac{1}{4}$ hours. Which of the following equations can be used to find how many miles (x) Nolan can jog in 5 hours?

(1) $1\frac{1}{4}x = 25$

(2) $5x = 6\frac{1}{4}$

(3) $6\frac{1}{4}x = 5$

(4) $5x = 25$

(5) $25x = 5$

12. A rectangle is drawn on a coordinate grid so that three vertices are located at $(-3,2)$, $(4,2)$, and $(-3,-1)$. What are the coordinates of the fourth vertex of the rectangle?

Mark your answer on the coordinate plane grid on your answer sheet.

13. A water tank is $\frac{1}{2}$ full. After 15 gallons are poured out, the tank is $\frac{1}{4}$ full. When the tank is full, how many gallons does it hold?

(1) 120

(2) 90

(3) 60

(4) 45

(5) 30

Questions 14 and 15 refer to the following graph.

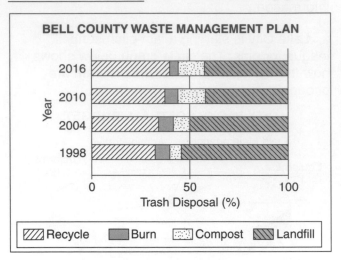

14. The graph above shows how Bell County plans to dispose of its trash over an 18-year period. In the year 2004, about what percent of the total trash will be used to make compost?

(1) 35%

(2) 30%

(3) 25%

(4) 12.5%

(5) Not enough information is given.

15. Which of the following conclusions can you draw from the data?

(1) The percent of trash placed in landfills will increase steadily through 2016.

(2) The percent of trash placed in landfills will decrease steadily through 2016.

(3) The percent of recycled trash will increase steadily through 2016.

(4) The amount of trash that is burned will increase steadily through 2016.

(5) The total amount of trash will remain about the same through 2016.

16. If the values for principal, interest, and time are known, which of the following expressions can be used to solve for the rate?

(1) $\dfrac{pt}{i}$

(2) ipt

(3) $\dfrac{ip}{t}$

(4) $\dfrac{i}{pt}$

(5) $\dfrac{p}{it}$

17. At a furniture store, the price of a dining room table is discounted by 50%. The next week, the table is discounted an additional 10%. The new sale price of the table is what percent of the original price?

(1) 40%

(2) 45%

(3) 55%

(4) 60%

(5) Not enough information is given.

18. The sum of three consecutive odd numbers is 75. What is the largest of the three numbers?

Mark your answer in the circles in the grid on your answer sheet.

19. Four decreased by a number is equal to the product of the number and -2. Let $x =$ the unknown number. Which of the following equations could be used to solve for x?

(1) $4x = -2x$

(2) $x - 4 = x + (-2)$

(3) $4 - x = x^2 + (-2)$

(4) $x - 4 = -2x$

(5) $4 - x = -2x$

20. Allison finishes a race in $5\frac{1}{4}$ minutes. Richie finishes the same race in $6\frac{2}{3}$ minutes. How many seconds after Allison crosses the finish line does Richie complete the race? (Use the conversion factor: 60 seconds = 1 minute.)

(1) 25

(2) 35

(3) 60

(4) 85

(5) 140

21. A professional basketball team has 13 players. The median height of the players is 80 inches. If the shortest player on the team is 73 inches, what is the height in inches of the tallest player on the team?

(1) 78

(2) 80

(3) 84

(4) 87

(5) Not enough information is given.

22. The line on the coordinate plane passes through point *M*. Which of the following is the equation of the line?

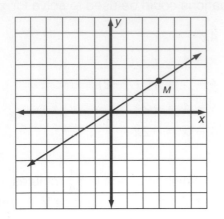

(1) $y = \frac{2}{3}x$

(2) $y = \frac{3}{2}x$

(3) $y = 2x + 3$

(4) $y = 3x + 2$

(5) $y = x + 6$

23. Janice works at a collection agency. She is paid a 5% commission on the amounts she collects. Last week, she collected the following amounts: $1800, $2400, and $4800. What is the total commission she earned for the week?

(1) $ 45

(2) $ 95

(3) $380

(4) $450

(5) $900

24. A game has a deck of 20 cards numbered as shown below. A player chooses one card at random from the deck, replaces the card, then draws another card at random. What is the probability that both cards drawn are cards numbered with a 5?

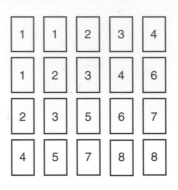

(1) $\frac{1}{5}$

(2) $\frac{1}{10}$

(3) $\frac{1}{20}$

(4) $\frac{1}{95}$

(5) $\frac{1}{100}$

25. A produce stand sells fresh-squeezed juices. Jan wants to buy 48 ounces of grapefruit juice. Which combination of sizes will cost the least amount of money?

Fresh Squeezed Grapefruit Juice		
Small	8 oz	$0.80
Medium	12 oz	$1.10
Large	16 oz	$1.50
Extra Large	20 oz	$2.20
Super Size	32 oz	$3.00

(1) 6 small bottles

(2) 4 medium bottles

(3) 3 large bottles

(4) 1 extra large bottle, 1 large bottle, and 1 medium bottle

(5) 1 super size bottle and 1 large bottle

Answers start on page 451.

Posttest Performance Analysis Charts
Mathematics

The following charts can help you determine your strengths and weaknesses on the content and skill areas of the GED Mathematics Test. Use the Answers and Explanations starting on page 451 to check your answers to the test. Then circle on the charts for Part I and Part II the numbers of the test items you answered correctly. Put the total number correct for each content area and skill area in each row and column. Look at the total items correct in each column to determine which areas are difficult for you. Use the page references to study those skills. Use a copy of the Study Planner on page 31 to guide your studying.

Part I

Content Area	Concept	Procedure	Application	Total Correct
Numbers and Operations (Pages 32–161)	5	3, 14	**6**, 10	____/5
Measurement (Pages 162–183)			8	____/1
Data Analysis (Pages 184–207)	**2**, 21	**1**, 19	**7**	____/5
Algebra (Pages 208–271)	17, 18, 25	**9**, 11	12, **20**	____/7
Geometry (Pages 272–331)	**15, 23**	**16**	**4, 13, 22, 24**	____/7
Total Correct	____/8	____/7	____/10	____/25

Part II

Content Area	Concept	Procedure	Application	Total Correct
Numbers and Operations (Pages 32–161)	17	3	1, 23, **25**	____/5
Measurement (Pages 162–183)		**2**	**10**, 20	____/3
Data Analysis (Pages 184–207)	**14**, 21		**7, 8, 15, 24**	____/6
Algebra (Pages 208–271)	**4**, 19	9, 11, 16	12, 13, 18, **22**	____/9
Geometry (Pages 272–331)	**5, 6**			____/2
Total Correct	____/7	____/5	____/13	____/25

The item numbers in **bold** are based on graphics.

MATHEMATICS
Part I

Directions

The Mathematics Simulated Test consists of multiple-choice and alternate format questions intended to measure your general mathematical skills and problem-solving ability. The questions are based on short readings that often include a graph, chart, or diagram.

You will have 90 minutes to complete the 50 questions on Parts I and II. Work carefully, but do not spend too much time on any one question. Be sure to answer every question. You will not be penalized for incorrect answers. When time is up, mark the last item you finished. This will tell you whether you can finish the real GED Test in the time allowed. Then complete the test.

Formulas you may need are given on page 353. Only some of the questions will require you to use a formula. Not all the formulas given will be needed.

Some questions contain more information than you will need to solve the problem; other questions do not give enough information. If the question does not give enough information to solve the problem, the correct answer choice is "Not enough information is given."

You may use a calculator on Part I. Calculator directions for the CASIO *fx-260SOLAR* scientific calculator can be found on page 352.

Record your answers on a copy of the separate answer sheet provided on page 473. Be sure all required information is properly recorded on the answer sheet.

To record your answers, mark the numbered space on the answer sheet that corresponds to the answer you select for each question on the test.

Example: If a grocery bill totaling $15.75 is paid with a $20.00 bill, how much change should be returned?

(1) $5.25
(2) $4.75
(3) $4.25
(4) $3.75
(5) $3.25   ① ② ● ④ ⑤

The correct answer is $4.25; therefore, answer space 3 would be marked on the answer sheet.

Do not rest the point of your pencil on the answer sheet while you are considering your answer. Make no stray or unnecessary marks. If you change an answer, erase your first mark completely. Mark only one answer for each question; multiple answers will be scored as incorrect. Do not fold or crease your answer sheet.

When you finish the test, use the Performance Analysis Chart on page 367 to determine whether you are ready to take the real GED Test, and, if not, which skill areas need additional review.

MATHEMATICS

Mixed numbers, such as $3\frac{1}{2}$, cannot be entered in the alternate format grid. Instead, represent them as decimal numbers (in this case, 3.5) or fractions (in this case, 7/2). No answer can be a negative number, such as -8.

To record your answer for an alternate format question

- begin in any column that will allow your answer to be entered;
- write your answer in the boxes on the top row;
- in the column beneath a fraction bar or decimal point (if any) and each number in your answer, fill in the bubble representing that character;
- leave blank any unused column.

Example:

The scale on a map indicates that $\frac{1}{2}$ inch represents an actual distance of 120 miles. In inches, how far apart on the map will two towns be if the actual distance between them is 180 miles?

The answer to the above example is 3/4, or 0.75, inches. The answer could be gridded using any of the methods below.

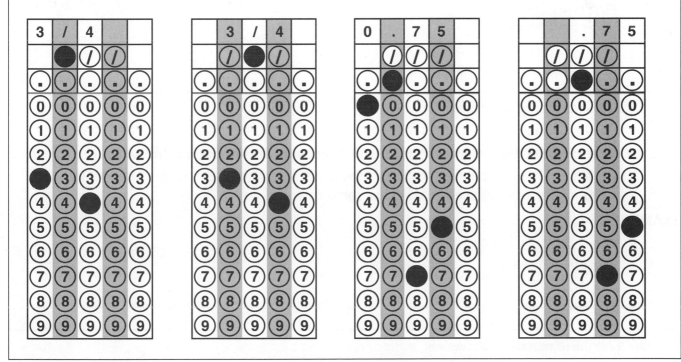

Points to remember:

- The answer sheet will be machine scored. **The circles must be filled in correctly.**
- Mark no more than one circle in any column.
- Grid only one answer even if there is more than one correct answer.
- Mixed numbers, such as $3\frac{1}{2}$, must be gridded as a decimal (3.5) or fraction (7/2).
- No answer can be a negative number.

CALCULATOR DIRECTIONS

To prepare the calculator for use the *first* time, press the ⬜ON⬜ (upper-rightmost) key. "DEG" will appear at the top-center of the screen and "0." at the right. This indicates the calculator is in the proper format for all your calculations.

To prepare the calculator for **another** question, press the ⬜ON⬜ or the red ⬜AC⬜ key. This clears any entries made previously.

To do any arithmetic, enter the expression as it is written. Press ⬜=⬜ (equals sign) when finished.

EXAMPLE A: 8 − 3 + 9

> First press ⬜ON⬜ or ⬜AC⬜.
> Enter the following:
>
> > 8 ⬜−⬜ 3 ⬜+⬜ 9 ⬜=⬜
>
> The correct answer is 14.

If an expression in parentheses is to be multiplied by a number, press ⬜×⬜ (multiplication sign) between the number and the parenthesis sign.

EXAMPLE B: 6(8 + 5)

> First press ⬜ON⬜ or ⬜AC⬜.
> Enter the following:
>
> > 6 ⬜×⬜ ⬜(⬜ 8 ⬜+⬜ 5 ⬜)⬜ ⬜=⬜
>
> The correct answer is 78.

To find the square root of a number

- enter the number;
- press ⬜SHIFT⬜ (upper-leftmost) key ("SHIFT" appears at the top-left of the screen);
- press ⬜x^2⬜ (third from the left on top row) to access its second function: square root.
  DO NOT press ⬜SHIFT⬜ and ⬜x^2⬜ at the same time.

EXAMPLE C: $\sqrt{64}$

> First press ⬜ON⬜ or ⬜AC⬜.
> Enter the following:
>
> > 64 ⬜SHIFT⬜ ⬜x^2⬜
>
> The correct answer is 8.

To enter a negative number such as −8,

- enter the number without the negative sign (enter 8);
- press the "change sign" (⬜+/−⬜) key which is directly above the 7 key.

All arithmetic can be done with positive and/or negative numbers.

EXAMPLE D: −8 − −5

> First press ⬜ON⬜ or ⬜AC⬜.
> Enter the following:
>
> > 8 ⬜+/−⬜ ⬜−⬜ 5 ⬜+/−⬜ ⬜=⬜
>
> The correct answer is −3.

Adapted with permission of the American Council on Education.

FORMULAS

AREA of a:

square	Area = side^2
rectangle	Area = length × width
parallelogram	Area = base × height
triangle	Area = $\frac{1}{2}$ × base × height
trapezoid	Area = $\frac{1}{2}$ × (base$_1$ + base$_2$) × height
circle	Area = π × radius^2; π is approximately equal to 3.14

PERIMETER of a:

square	Perimeter = 4 × side
rectangle	Perimeter = 2 × length + 2 × width
triangle	Perimeter = side$_1$ + side$_2$ + side$_3$

CIRCUMFERENCE of a circle   Circumference = π × diameter; π is approximately equal to 3.14

VOLUME of a:

cube	Volume = edge^3
rectangular container	Volume = length × width × height
square pyramid	Volume = $\frac{1}{3}$ × (base edge)^2 × height
cylinder	Volume = π × radius^2 × height; π is approximately equal to 3.14
cone	Volume = $\frac{1}{3}$ × π × radius^2 × height; π is approximately equal to 3.14

COORDINATE GEOMETRY

distance between points = $\sqrt{(x_2 - x_1)^2 + (y_2 - y_1)^2}$; (x_1, y_1) and (x_2, y_2) are two points in a plane.

slope of a line = $\frac{y_2 - y_1}{x_2 - x_1}$; (x_1, y_1) and (x_2, y_2) are two points on a line.

PYTHAGOREAN RELATIONSHIP

$a^2 + b^2 = c^2$; a and b are legs and c the hypotenuse of a right triangle.

MEASURES OF CENTRAL TENDENCY

mean = $\frac{x_1 + x_2 + \ldots + x_n}{n}$; where the x's are the values for which a mean is desired, and n is the total number of values for x.

median = the middle value of an odd number of _ordered_ scores, and halfway between the two middle values of an even number of _ordered_ scores.

SIMPLE INTEREST   interest = principal × rate × time

DISTANCE   distance = rate × time

TOTAL COST   total cost = (number of units) × (price per unit)

Adapted with permission of the American Council on Education.

Part I

Directions: Choose the <u>one best answer</u> to each question. You <u>MAY</u> use your calculator.

<u>Questions 1 and 2</u> refer to the following information.

Karen and Luis own the Sandwich Shoppe. They recently made a graph of the sandwiches sold over a two-day period.

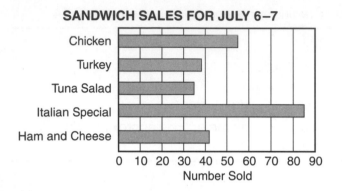

SANDWICH SALES FOR JULY 6–7

1. About how many more Italian specials were sold than chicken sandwiches?

   (1) 20
   (2) 30
   (3) 35
   (4) 40
   (5) 45

2. About what fraction of the total sandwiches sold was Italian specials?

   (1) $\frac{2}{3}$
   (2) $\frac{1}{2}$
   (3) $\frac{1}{3}$
   (4) $\frac{1}{4}$
   (5) $\frac{1}{5}$

3. A sign in the window at Keller's Hardware reads "All Tools: 20% off." A customer buys two tools regularly priced at $24.50 and $14.95. What is the total sale price of the items before tax?

   (1) $ 7.89
   (2) $29.59
   (3) $31.56
   (4) $36.63
   (5) $39.45

<u>Question 4</u> refers to the following diagram.

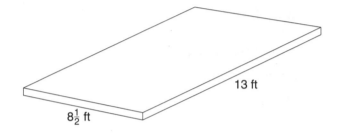

4. Jeff needs to pour a rectangular concrete slab with the dimensions shown in the diagram. If the slab is $\frac{1}{2}$ foot thick, how many cubic feet of concrete will Jeff need to do the job?

   Mark your answer in the circles in the grid on your answer sheet.

   _____

5. What is the value of the expression below?

   $25 - (7 - 3)^2 \div 2$

   Mark your answer in the circles in the grid on your answer sheet.

6. In a football game, two teams scored a total of 41 points. The winning team scored 13 more points than the losing team. How many points did the winning team score?

(1) 14

(2) 20

(3) 27

(4) 28

(5) 38

Questions 7 and 8 refer to the following information.

DISK DRIVE MAGAZINE	
Cover Price (1 issue)	$ 3.50
One-Year Subscription (12 issues)	$27.00
Two-Year Subscription (24 issues)	$42.00
Three-Year Subscription (36 issues)	$50.40

7. Adam is selling subscriptions to Disk Drive Magazine. Which of the following expressions shows how much Adam will collect if he sells 15 one-year and 12 two-year subscriptions?

(1) 15($27.00) + 12($42.00)

(2) 15($42.00) + 12($27.00)

(3) 27($42.00 + $27.00)

(4) 15(24) + 12(12)

(5) 12(24) + 15(12)

8. Anna is thinking of subscribing to Disk Drive Magazine. How much will she save per issue if she buys a three-year subscription instead of buying 36 magazines at the cover price?

(1) $0.70

(2) $1.25

(3) $1.40

(4) $1.75

(5) $2.10

9. Kira works five days a week at a shoe store. She earns a base salary plus commissions. To meet her family's expenses, Kira needs to average at least $75 per day in commissions. She has earned the following commissions for the first four days this week.

Day 1–$94
Day 2–$58
Day 3–$70
Day 4–$82

What is the least amount in commissions Kira needs to earn on Day 5 to meet her goal?

(1) $60.80

(2) $71.00

(3) $75.00

(4) $76.00

(5) Not enough information is given.

Question 10 refers to the following figure.

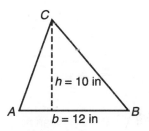

10. The triangle (shown above) and a rectangle (not shown) both have the same area. If the length of the rectangle is the same length as the base of the triangle, what is the width in inches of the rectangle?

(1) 5

(2) 10

(3) 12

(4) 15

(5) Not enough information is given.

11. A doctor prescribes medication to reduce muscle swelling. Each pill contains 500 milligrams of medicine. If the prescription bottle contains a total of 10 grams of medicine, how many pills are in the bottle?

    (1)   5
    (2) 10
    (3) 20
    (4) 50
    (5) 100

12. A map has a scale of 1 inch = 60 miles. What is the actual distance, in miles, between two cities that are $2\frac{1}{4}$ inches apart on the map?

    Mark your answer in the circles in the grid on your answer sheet.

Question 13 refers to the following drawing.

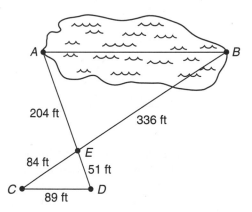

13. To find the width of a lake, a surveyor marked off two similar triangles as shown in the drawing. If $\angle A$ is congruent to $\angle D$, what is the width in feet of $\overline{AB}$ the straight-line distance across the lake?

    Mark your answer in the circles in the grid on your answer sheet.

14. Triangle *XYZ* is an isosceles triangle. Angle X measures 90°. What are the measures, in degrees, of the remaining angles?

    (1) 30 and 30
    (2) 30 and 60
    (3) 45 and 45
    (4) 60 and 60
    (5) Not enough information is given.

15. Which point on the number line below represents the value $\frac{-14}{5}$?

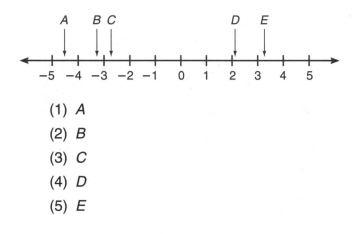

    (1) *A*
    (2) *B*
    (3) *C*
    (4) *D*
    (5) *E*

16. Working 4 hours per day, Hanna can inspect 18 computer printers. Which of the following equations could be used to represent the number of printers (*N*) Hanna could inspect if she worked 7 hours per day at the same rate?

    (1) $N = \dfrac{4(18)}{7}$

    (2) $N = \dfrac{18(7)}{4}$

    (3) $N = 18(7 + 4)$

    (4) $N = 7(18)$

    (5) $N = 7(4)(18)$

17. Two lines intersect at the point whose coordinates are $(-3, -5)$. Show the location of the point.

Mark your answer on the coordinate plane grid on your answer sheet.

Questions 18 and 19 refer to the following information.

The graph below shows what percent of the Lindsay family's income is spent on various expenses each month.

LINDSAY FAMILY EXPENSES

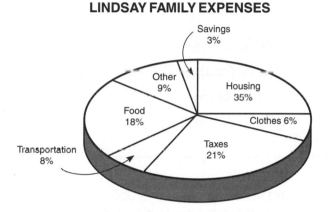

18. About how many times more money does the Lindsay family spend on housing than it spends on clothes?

    (1) 3

    (2) 5

    (3) 6

    (4) 8

    (5) Not enough information is given.

19. Which of the following conclusions can you draw from the data?

    (1) For every dollar spent on clothes, the family spends $4 on food.

    (2) The family spends more than $\frac{1}{4}$ of its income on taxes.

    (3) The family's housing costs will continue to increase each year.

    (4) The family saves approximately $300 each month.

    (5) The family spends more than half of its income on housing and food.

20. Each employee at Walker Industries will receive a cost-of-living increase and a bonus in January. The personnel department is using the following formula to determine each employee's new annual pay:

    $n = c + 0.04c + \$250$

    where n = new pay and c = current pay.

    If Sandra's annual pay is currently $19,800, how much will she be paid next year?

    (1) $ 1,042

    (2) $20,050

    (3) $20,842

    (4) $40,392

    (5) $40,642

21. A parking lot is $41\frac{1}{2}$ yards wide. What is the width of the parking lot in <u>feet</u>?

    Mark your answer in the circles in the grid on your answer sheet.

22. Su Jean is driving from Phoenix to Houston, a distance of 1185 miles. After driving for 4 hours, she calculates that she has driven 237 miles. What portion of the distance does she have left to drive?

    Mark your answer in the circles in the grid on your answer sheet.

23. When a number (x) is divided by 3, the remainder is 2. When the same number is divided by 5, the remainder is 2. Which of the following could be a possible value of x?

    (1) 11
    (2) 15
    (3) 22
    (4) 26
    (5) 32

Question 24 refers to the following figure.

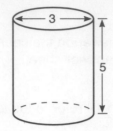

24. A cylindrical oil drum is 3 feet across and 5 feet tall. Which expression represents the approximate volume of the drum in cubic feet?

    (1) $(3.14)(1.5)^2(5)$
    (2) $(3.14)(1.5)(5)^2$
    (3) $(3.14)(3)(5)$
    (4) $(3.14)(3)^2(5)$
    (5) $(3.14)(6)^2(5)$

25. Land sonar equipment is used in construction for measuring distances and determining types of soil. Type A sonar has a range of 3.2×10^3 miles. Type B sonar has a range of 4.8×10^4 miles. Which statement is true?

    (1) The range of Type A sonar is 15 times greater than the range of Type B sonar.

    (2) The range of Type B sonar is 15 times greater than the range of Type A sonar.

    (3) The range of Type A sonar is 1.6 times greater than the range of Type B sonar.

    (4) The range of Type B sonar is 1.6 times greater than the range of Type A sonar.

    (5) The range of Type A sonar is 10 times greater than the range of Type B sonar.

MATHEMATICS
Part II

Directions

The Mathematics Simulated GED Test consists of multiple-choice and alternate format questions intended to measure your general mathematical skills and problem-solving ability. The questions are based on short readings that often include a graph, chart, or diagram.

You will have the time remaining of the total 90 minutes to complete the 50 questions on Parts I and II. Work carefully, but do not spend too much time on any one question. Be sure to answer every question. You will not be penalized for incorrect answers. When time is up, mark the last item you finished. This will tell you whether you can finish the real GED Test in the time allowed. Then complete the test.

Formulas you may need are given on page 361. Only some of the questions will require you to use a formula. Not all the formulas given will be needed.

Some questions contain more information than you will need to solve the problem; other questions do not give enough information. If the question does not give enough information to solve the problem, the correct answer choice is "Not enough information is given."

The use of calculators is not allowed on Part II.

Record your answers on a copy of the separate answer sheet provided on page 474. Be sure all required information is properly recorded on the answer sheet.

To record your answers, mark the numbered space on the answer sheet that corresponds to the answer you select for each question on the test.

Example: If a grocery bill totaling $15.75 is paid with a $20.00 bill, how much change should be returned?

(1) $5.25
(2) $4.75
(3) $4.25
(4) $3.75
(5) $3.25

① ② ● ④ ⑤

The correct answer is $4.25; therefore, answer space 3 would be marked on the answer sheet.

Do not rest the point of your pencil on the answer sheet while you are considering your answer. Make no stray or unnecessary marks. If you change an answer, erase your first mark completely. Mark only one answer for each question; multiple answers will be scored as incorrect. Do not fold or crease your answer sheet.

When you finish the test, use the Performance Analysis Chart on page 367 to determine whether you are ready to take the real GED Test, and, if not, which skill areas need additional review.

Adapted with permission of the American Council on Education.

 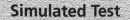

MATHEMATICS

Mixed numbers, such as $3\frac{1}{2}$, cannot be entered in the alternate format grid. Instead, represent them as decimal numbers (in this case, 3.5) or fractions (in this case, 7/2). No answer can be a negative number, such as -8.

To record your answer for an alternate format question

- begin in any column that will allow your answer to be entered;
- write your answer in the boxes on the top row;
- in the column beneath a fraction bar or decimal point (if any) and each number in your answer, fill in the bubble representing that character;
- leave blank any unused column.

Example:

The scale on a map indicates that $\frac{1}{2}$ inch represents an actual distance of 120 miles. In inches, how far apart on the map will two towns be if the actual distance between them is 180 miles?

The answer to the above example is 3/4, or 0.75, inches. The answer could be gridded using any of the methods below.

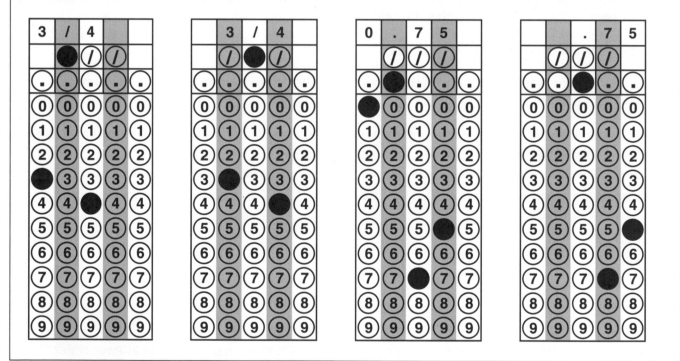

Points to remember:

- The answer sheet will be machine scored. **The circles must be filled in correctly.**
- Mark no more than one circle in any column.
- Grid only one answer even if there is more than one correct answer.
- Mixed numbers, such as $3\frac{1}{2}$, must be gridded as a decimal (3.5) or fraction (7/2).
- No answer can be a negative number.

FORMULAS

AREA of a:

square	Area = side²
rectangle	Area = length × width
parallelogram	Area – base × height
triangle	Area = $\frac{1}{2}$ × base × height
trapezoid	Area = $\frac{1}{2}$ × (base₁ + base₂) × height
circle	Area = π × radius²; π is approximately equal to 3.14

PERIMETER of a:

square	Perimeter = 4 × side
rectangle	Perimeter = 2 × length + 2 × width
triangle	Perimeter = side₁ + side₂ + side₃

CIRCUMFERENCE of a circle   Circumference = π × diameter; π is approximately equal to 3.14

VOLUME of a:

cube	Volume = edge³
rectangular container	Volume = length × width × height
square pyramid	Volume = $\frac{1}{3}$ × (base edge)² × height
cylinder	Volume = π × radius² × height; π is approximately equal to 3.14
cone	Volume = $\frac{1}{3}$ × π × radius² × height; π is approximately equal to 3.14

COORDINATE GEOMETRY

distance between points = $\sqrt{(x_2 - x_1)^2 + (y_2 - y_1)^2}$; (x_1, y_1) and (x_2, y_2) are two points in a plane.

slope of a line = $\frac{y_2 - y_1}{x_2 - x_1}$; (x_1, y_1) and (x_2, y_2) are two points on a line.

PYTHAGOREAN RELATIONSHIP

$a^2 + b^2 = c^2$; a and b are legs and c the hypotenuse of a right triangle.

MEASURES OF CENTRAL TENDENCY

mean = $\frac{x_1 + x_2 + \ldots + x_n}{n}$; where the x's are the values for which a mean is desired, and n is the total number of values for x.

median = the middle value of an odd number of *ordered* scores, and halfway between the two middle values of an even number of *ordered* scores.

SIMPLE INTEREST   interest = principal × rate × time

DISTANCE   distance = rate × time

TOTAL COST   total cost = (number of units) × (price per unit)

Adapted with permission of the American Council on Education.

Directions: Choose the one best answer to each question. You may NOT use your calculator.

1. All numbers that are evenly divisible by both 36 and 48 are also evenly divisible by which of the following numbers?

   (1) 9
   (2) 12
   (3) 18
   (4) 36
   (5) 40

Question 2 refers to the following figure.

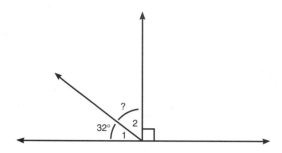

2. If ∠1 measures 32°, what is the measure of ∠2?

   (1) 32°
   (2) 45°
   (3) 58°
   (4) 90°
   (5) 148°

3. Thirty percent of the employees who work at Wells use public transportation to get to work. If 60 employees use public transportation, how many people work at Wells?

   (1) 100
   (2) 120
   (3) 180
   (4) 200
   (5) 300

4. If all adjacent sides of the figure are perpendicular to one another, what is the area of the figure in square units?

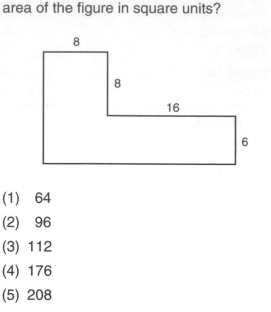

   (1) 64
   (2) 96
   (3) 112
   (4) 176
   (5) 208

5. For the equation $(x + 5)(x - 2) = 0$, there are two values of x which will make the equation true. What are these values?

   (1) 5 or 2
   (2) 5 or −2
   (3) −5 or 2
   (4) 7 or 3
   (5) −7 or 3

6. Melanie, Brad, and Robin work as clerks at Lincoln Title and Insurance. Melanie has worked 4 years longer than Brad. Brad has worked there $3\frac{1}{2}$ years less than Robin. If Robin has worked at the company for 8 years, how long has Melanie worked there?

   Mark your answer in the circles in the grid on your answer sheet.

Questions 7 and 8 are based on the following information.

AIR QUALITY OF SELECTED CITIES

Data shows number of days per year
below acceptable standards

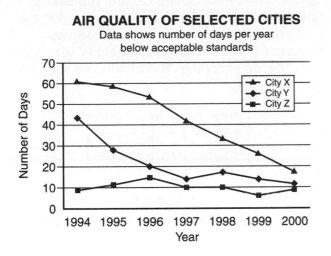

7. Of the years shown on the graph, in which year did City Z have the highest number of days below acceptable air-quality standards?

(1) 1994
(2) 1995
(3) 1996
(4) 1997
(5) 1998

8. Which of the following conclusions can you draw from the information in the graph?

(1) City X has spent the most money to improve air quality.

(2) The air quality of City X has improved each year from 1995 to 2000.

(3) The air quality of City Y has worsened during the time period shown on the graph.

(4) The air quality in City Z will always be better than the air quality in City X.

(5) Within the next five years, City X will have the best air quality of the three cities.

9. A delivery truck is loaded with boxes of shirts. Of the 200 boxes on the truck, 150 contain large shirts and 50 contain extra-large shirts. If a box is chosen at random, what is the probability that the box will contain large shirts?

(1) $\frac{1}{200}$

(2) $\frac{1}{150}$

(3) $\frac{1}{4}$

(4) $\frac{2}{3}$

(5) $\frac{3}{4}$

Question 10 refers to the following diagram.

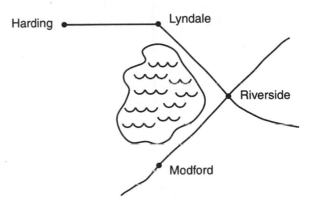

10. On the map above, the city of Harding is 12 miles due west of Lyndale. Medford is 16 miles due south of Lyndale. Which of the following equations could be used to find the straight line distance in miles (x) between Harding and Medford?

(1) $12^2 + x^2 = 16^2$
(2) $16^2 - 12^2 = x^2$
(3) $x^2 + 16^2 = 12^2$
(4) $16^2 - x^2 = 12^2$
(5) $12^2 + 16^2 = x^2$

11. The expression $-3a(b - 8)$ is equal to which of the following expressions?

   (1) $-3ab + 24a$

   (2) $-3ab + 24$

   (3) $-3ab - 24a$

   (4) $3ab + 24$

   (5) $3ab + 24a$

Question 12 refers to the following coordinate graph.

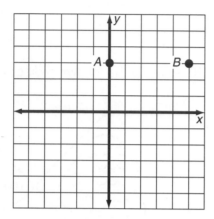

12. Points A and B are two vertices of a rectangle. If a third vertex is located at $(0, -1)$, what are the coordinates of the fourth vertex?

   Mark your answer on the coordinate plane grid on your answer sheet.

13. In a golf tournament, there are twice as many amateur golfers as professional golfers. A total of 96 golfers are in the tournament. How many of them are amateurs?

   (1) 24

   (2) 32

   (3) 43

   (4) 60

   (5) 64

Question 14 refers to the following information.

   The manager of Sports Central wants to determine the typical amount of time customers spend browsing in the store. She observes 10 customers and records the number of minutes each spends shopping. The results are shown in the table below.

75	40	32	25	30
18	25	15	45	55

14. Based on the manager's sample, what was the median amount of time spent shopping?

   (1) 25

   (2) 30

   (3) 31

   (4) 32

   (5) Not enough information is given.

15. The formula for finding the circumference (C) of a circle can be written $C = 2\pi r$, where r = radius. If the circumference of a circle is known, which of the following expressions can be used to solve for the radius?

   (1) $\dfrac{2C}{\pi}$

   (2) $\dfrac{2\pi}{C}$

   (3) $\dfrac{2}{\pi C}$

   (4) $\dfrac{C}{2\pi}$

   (5) $2\pi C$

16. At his job, Lamar is often assigned to work on more than one project at a time. He uses a spreadsheet to figure out what fraction of his time each week is spent on each project. Last week, Lamar spent 0.885 of his time on Project A. Which of the following fractions is the best estimate of the time Lamar spent on the project?

(1) $\frac{9}{10}$

(2) $\frac{4}{5}$

(3) $\frac{3}{4}$

(4) $\frac{2}{3}$

(5) $\frac{1}{2}$

17. The price of a share of stock at Monday's close was $75. The price fell $3 on Tuesday. Which of the following expressions could be used to find the percent of decrease in the price of the stock over the two-day period?

(1) $\frac{3(100)}{72}$

(2) $\frac{3(100)}{75}$

(3) $\frac{72(100)}{75}$

(4) $\frac{75(100)}{72}$

(5) $\frac{72(100)}{75 - 3}$

18. Zachary sold $\frac{1}{2}$ of a 40-acre lot. He then sold $\frac{3}{5}$ of the remaining lot. What fraction of the land did he sell in all? [Reduce the fraction to lowest terms.]

Mark your answer in the circles in the grid on your answer sheet.

19. A portion of a metal sculpture includes an isosceles triangle. The equal sides measure 15 inches each. What is the perimeter of the triangle, in inches, if all angles are acute angles?

(1) 15

(2) 30

(3) 45

(4) 60

(5) Not enough information is given.

20. The graph below shows how a foster parent program spends its funds in a given year.

FOSTER PARENT ANNUAL BUDGET

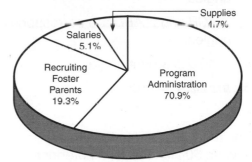

According to the graph, what percentage of the money is left after recruiting expenses?

(1)   9.8%

(2)   70.9%

(3)   80.7%

(4)   90.2%

(5)   119.3%

21. The difference between twice a number and 15 is equal to the product of −3 and the number. Let x = the unknown number. Which of the following equations could be used to find the value of x?

(1) $2x - 15 = -3 + x$

(2) $2 - 15x = -3x$

(3) $2 - 15x = -\frac{3}{x}$

(4) $2x - 15 = -3x$

(5) $2x - 15 = -\frac{3}{x}$

22. In the figure below, $\triangle ABD \cong \triangle BAC$.

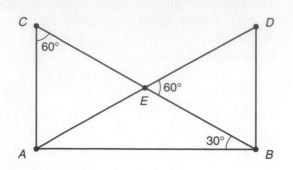

Which of the following statements about the figure must be true?

(1) $m\angle BDE = 30°$

(2) $\angle AEB$ and $\angle AEC$ are complementary angles.

(3) $\angle ACB$ and $\angle ABD$ are corresponding angles.

(4) $\angle ABD$ is a right angle.

(5) $m\angle BDA = 150°$

23. Toni and Dan need to buy an expense register, 50 file folders, 3 notebooks, and 6 adding machine tapes. The prices of the supplies are as follows:

notebooks	$4 each or 3 for $10
adding machine tapes	$1 each or 3 for $2
file folders	10 for $5
expense register	$15

What is the least amount they can spend to buy the supplies they need?

(1) $58

(2) $54

(3) $48

(4) $42

(5) $34

Questions 24 and 25 refer to the following information.

The bar graph below shows the number of people who visited First Central Bank during a recent week. The bank manager will use the data to make decisions about the number of bank tellers needed each day.

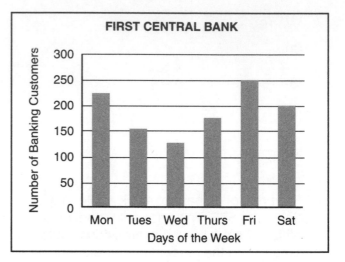

24. What was the ratio of the number of customers on Wednesday to the number of customers on Saturday?

(1) 1:2

(2) 2:5

(3) 3:5

(4) 5:8

(5) 9:10

25. On Friday, the bank was open from 10 A.M. to 6 P.M. About how many customers visited the bank per hour on Friday?

(1) 20

(2) 25

(3) 30

(4) 35

(5) 40

Answers start on page 455.

Simulated Test

Simulated Test Performance Analysis Charts
Mathematics

The following charts can help you determine your strengths and weaknesses on the content and skill areas of the GED Mathematics Test. Use the Answers and Explanations starting on page 455 to check your answers to the test. Then circle on the charts for Part I and Part II the numbers of the test items you answered correctly. Put the total number correct for each content area and skill area in each row and column. Look at the total items correct in each column to determine which areas are difficult for you. Use the page references to study those skills.

Part I

Content Area	Concept	Procedure	Application	Total Correct
Numbers and Operations (*Pages 32–161*)	5	7	3, 8, 12, 22	____/6
Measurement (*Pages 162–183*)		**24**	**4**, 11, 21	____/4
Data Analysis (*Pages 184–207*)	**18**	**1**	**2**, 9, **19**	____/5
Algebra (*Pages 208–271*)	**15**, 17, 23	**10**, 16, 20	6, 25	____/8
Geometry (*Pages 272–331*)	14		**13**	____/2
Total Correct	____/6	____/6	____/13	____/25

Part II

Content Area	Concept	Procedure	Application	Total Correct
Numbers and Operations (*Pages 32–161*)	1, 16	17	3, 18, 23	____/6
Measurement (*Pages 162–183*)			**4**	____/1
Data Analysis (*Pages 184–207*)	**7, 20**	14	**8**, 9, **24, 25**	____/7
Algebra (*Pages 208–271*)	5, **12**, 21	11, 15	6, 13	____/7
Geometry (*Pages 272–331*)	19, **22**	**10**	**2**	____/4
Total Correct	____/9	____/5	____/11	____/25

The item numbers in **bold** are based on graphics.

Answers and Explanations

Part I

1. **(2) 320** The average attendance is 300 on Mondays and about 620 on Saturdays. Subtract. 620 − 300 = 320

2. **(2) 11** The average attendance is 550 on Fridays. Set up a proportion to find the number of guards needed—think: "1 guard is to 50 visitors as how many guards are to 550 visitors?" $\frac{1}{50} = \frac{x}{550}$; 550 ÷ 50 = 11

3. **(3) between 420 and 480** 9.4 cents = $0.094 Divide. $42.30 ÷ $0.094 = 450 kilowatt-hours Note: this is actually the cost formula: $c = nr$, where $0.094 is the rate and $42.30 is the cost; you are finding the number of units.

4. **780** Find the total volume of the freight car. Volume = length × width × height. 42 × 9 × 10 = 3780 cu ft Subtract the volume of the freight to find the volume of the extra space. 3780 − 3000 = 780 cu ft

5. **15** Use the order of operations: first parentheses, then × and ÷, then + and −.
   6 + 27 ÷ (5 − 2)
   6 + 27 ÷   3
   6 +   9
       15

6. **(2) B** Find percent of increase for each style: subtract to find the difference between the two prices, then divide by the original amount (the wholesale price). You can do this quickly using your calculator. For example, to find the percent of increase for Style B, key in the following values.
   24.90 ⊟ 16.80 ⊜ 8.1 ÷ 16.80 **SHIFT** ⊜ 48.21428571 which rounds to 48%.
   The percent increase for the other options are:
   A: $45.00 − $32.00 = $13.00 ÷ $32.00 = 0.406 = 41%
   C: $41.80 − $34.00 = $7.80 ÷ $34.00 = 0.229 = 23%
   D: $28.90 − $23.00 = $5.90 ÷ $23.00 = 0.256 = 26%
   E: $74.50 − $56.50 = $18.00 ÷ $56.50 = 0.318 = 32%

7. **(4) $47.20** Substitute the known values from the chart for Style D ($n = 8$) into the given equation. $P = n(r - w) = 8(\$28.90 - \$23.00) = 8(\$5.90) = \$47.20$

8. **(3) 19** If Joel needs to average 20 sales per day, he needs 100 sales for a 5-day period (20 × 5 = 100). After 4 days, he has 15 + 22 + 18 + 26, which equals 81 sales. Subtract. 100 − 81 = 19 sales He needs at least 19 sales on the fifth day.

9. **(4) 89** Set up a proportion, cross-multiply and solve. $\frac{\text{games won}}{\text{first 40}} = \frac{\text{total games won}}{\text{total games}}$
   $$\frac{22}{40} = \frac{x}{162}$$
   $$22(162) = 40x$$
   $$3564 = 40x$$
   $$89.1 = x$$
   Ignore the decimal remainder since a team cannot win a fraction of a game.

10. **(2) 5** Divide $17\frac{1}{2}$ by $3\frac{3}{8}$. Convert the mixed numbers to improper fractions, invert and multiply.
    $$17\frac{1}{2} \div 3\frac{3}{8} = \frac{35}{2} \div \frac{27}{8} = \frac{35}{\cancel{2}_1} \times \frac{\cancel{8}^4}{27} = \frac{140}{27} = 5\frac{5}{27}$$
    Ignore the remainder (the fraction part of the mixed number). Vanya can make 5 whole vests.

11. **(3) 24** Find the area of Room A. $A = lw = 16 \times 36 = 576$ sq ft This is also the area of Room B. Room B is square, so $A = s^2 = 576$ sq ft. The length of the side of Room B is the square root of 576. Using your calculator: 576 **SHIFT** **x^2** 24

12. $1435 (Note: Enter only the numbers on the grid; there is no place for the dollar sign on the grid.) Since the used parts cost 60% less than $1400, then they actually cost 40% of $1400. $1400 × 0.4 = $560
Add the cost of the labor. $560 + $875 = $1435

13. 56 The two triangles are similar. Side *AC* corresponds to side *CE*, and side *AB* corresponds to side *DE*. Set up a proportion and solve.

$$\frac{AC}{CE} = \frac{AB}{DE}$$

$$\frac{28}{2} = \frac{x}{4}$$

$$4(28) = 2x$$
$$112 = 2x$$
$$56 = x$$

14. (5) Not enough information is given. You do not know how many employees chose the third plan or how the number who chose the third plan relates to the number who chose the other two plans.

15. (1) $\frac{5(18)}{3} = d$ Write a proportion, cross multiply, and solve. Then compare your equation to those shown in the answer choices.

$$\frac{3}{5} = \frac{18}{d}$$

$$3d = 5(18)$$

$$d = \frac{5(18)}{3}$$

This answer equals the equation in option (1).

16. (3) $\frac{3}{5}$ Subtract. Borrow 60 minutes.

$$11{:}26 = 10{:}60 + 26$$
$$-10{:}50 =$$

$$\begin{array}{r} 10{:}86 \\ -10{:}50 \\ \hline 36 \end{array}$$

Max worked 36 minutes, or $\frac{36}{60}$ of an hour.

Reduce. $\frac{36}{60} = \frac{3}{5}$ hour

17.

Starting at the origin (0,0), count four spaces to the left (−4) along the *x*-axis and 2 spaces up (+2) along the *y*-axis. The answer is in quadrant II.

18. (5) The volume of Box B is eight times the volume of Box A. Find the volume of Box A (side = 2 ft). $V = s^3 = 2 \times 2 \times 2 = 8$ cubic feet
Each side of Box B measures twice the length of each side of Box A, so each side of Box B measures $2 \times 2 = 4$ feet.
Volume of Box B = $V = s^3 = 4 \times 4 \times 4 = 64$ cu ft
Thus, the volume of Box B is 8 times the volume of Box A. $64 \div 8 = 8$
OR side of A = s, so $V = s^3$. Side of B = $2s$, so volume of Box B = $V = (2s)^2 = 2s \times 2s \times 2s = 8s^3$.

19. (3) 372 Divide the total miles by the number of days. $1860 \div 5 = 372$ miles

20. (3) −4 < x < 2 Think of the inequality symbol as an arrow that points to the smaller number. On the graph the shaded portion is *x*, −4 is less than *x* and *x* is less than 2. (The circles are open, so −4 and 2 are not included, that is, *x* is not equal to −4 or 2.)

21. 71 The scale labeled number of days tells you how many times each temperature occurred during the 14-day period. From the graph, you can make a list of temperature readings in increasing order: 67, 68, 68, 69, 69, 70, 71, 71, 71, 71, 71, 72, 72, 73. Since there is an even number of readings, the median is the mean of the two middle readings. Since both are 71, the median is 71 degrees.

22. $\frac{1}{2}$ **or 0.5 or .5** Four out of 8, or $\frac{1}{2}$, of the sections are marked with a 2. You can enter your answer as a fraction $\frac{1}{2}$ or as a decimal .5 or 0.5.

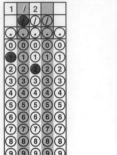 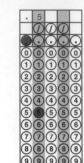

23. **(1) 53°** $\angle QCD$ measures 118° and is supplementary to $\angle QCB$. Thus, $m\angle QCB = 180° - 118° = 62°$. Since the sum of the inside angles of a triangle equals 180°, $m\angle QBC = 180° - 65° - 62° = 53°$.

24. **(3)** $\angle DCG$ $\angle QGH$ and $\angle QCD$ (option 2) are corresponding angles on transversal QR. Since corresponding angles are congruent, $m\angle QGH = m\angle QCD = 118°$. $\angle DCG$ is supplementary to $\angle QCD$ because their sum forms a straight line, or 180°. So $\angle DCG$ is also supplementary to $\angle QGH$. Note that option (1) $\angle GRP$ is not on the same parallel lines as $\angle QGH$ and options (4) and (5) $\angle BFG$ and $\angle QAB$ are on a different transversal so there is no relationship between these angles and $\angle QGH$.

25. **(2) 2.94 × 10⁶** The first factor must be a number 1 or more but less than 10 (which makes options (4) and (5) incorrect); therefore, you must move the decimal point 6 places to the left to get 2.94. Then write this number multiplied by 10 raised to the sixth power, the number of places you moved the decimal point.

Part II

1. **(5) 60** Factors can be divided into a number evenly. Of the numbers in the answer options, 6 is a factor of 24 and 60, and 15 is a factor of 15, 45, and 60. Both 6 and 15 are factors of 60. Another way to solve this question is to list the multiples of 6 and 15 until you find a multiple they have in common.
6: 6, 12, 18, 24, 30, 36, 42, 48, 54, <u>60</u>
15: 15, 30, 45, <u>60</u>

2. **(1) 10** Since there are two equal angles, there must be equal sides opposite the equal angles. So side BC, which is opposite $\angle D$, one of the two angles measuring 25°, must equal side CD, which is opposite $\angle B$, the other 25° angle. So $\overline{BC} = \overline{CD} = 10$ ft

3. **(3) 160** There are several ways to approach this problem. One way is to set up a proportion.
$\frac{75}{100} = \frac{120}{x}$ $\left(\frac{75}{100} = 75\%\right)$
$75x = 12{,}000$
$x = 160$

Another approach uses the base-rate-part formula, where 120 is the part, 75% is the rate, and you solve for the base. base $= \frac{\text{part}}{\text{rate}} = \frac{120}{.75}$.

Yet another approach involves solving an equation. Let $x =$ the total number of workers. Then, $0.75x = 120$.

4. **(4) 24** The height of the figure is 4 units (4 × 1) and the base is 8 units (4 × 2). The perimeter is the sum of all the measurements.
$2 + 1 + 2 + 1 + 2 + 1 + 2 + 1 + 8 + 4 = $ 24 units

5. **(3) C** Change $\frac{19}{8}$ to a proper fraction. $\frac{19}{8} = 2\frac{3}{8}$, which is a little less than $2\frac{1}{2}$. The best option is Point C.

6. **24** Set up a proportion, cross multiply and solve.
$\frac{\text{feet}}{\text{feet}} = \frac{\text{inches}}{\text{inches}}$ OR $\frac{w \text{ feet}}{w \text{ inches}} = \frac{l \text{ feet}}{l \text{ inches}}$
$\frac{2}{3} = \frac{16}{x}$ $\frac{2}{16} = \frac{3}{x}$
$2x = 3(16) = 48$
$x = 24$

7. **(2) 1996** The number of captive birds for each year is represented by the height of the lower part of the bar. Follow each lower portion over to the scale on the left. Only the bar for 1996 falls within the range of 90 to 100.

8. **(2) The number of wild condors increased between 1994 and 2000.** The number of wild condors for each year is represented by the upper part of each bar. Between 1994 and 2000, the size of the upper part of the bars has increased.

9. **(3)** $\frac{1}{50}$ Write the probability as a fraction and reduce. P $= \frac{\text{"desired" outcomes}}{\text{total outcomes}} = \frac{8}{400} = \frac{1}{50}$ (Note that here the "desired" outcome is a defective radio.)

Answers and Explanations

10. (1) 3.14 × 5² × 12 The formula for finding the volume of a cylinder is $V = \pi \times radius^2 \times height$. The diagram gives the measurement of the diameter. To find the radius, divide the diameter by 2. $\frac{10}{2} = 5$ Then, substitute the known values (using 3.14 for pi) and compare to the answer options.

11. (2) x − 2y + 3z The expression $x - (2y - 3z)$ is the same as $x - 1(2y - 3z)$ Multiplying both values inside the parentheses by -1 gives the result $x - 2y + 3z$.

12.

The x-coordinate of the y intercept is 0, so substitute 0 for x and solve for y.
$y = 3x + 4 = 3(0) + 4 = 0 + 4 = 4$
The y-intercept is (0,4).

13. (5) food and rent You can see that the combined sections for food and rent form a section larger than $\frac{1}{2}$ the circle. So food and rent total more than 50%. Also, 28% + 25% = 53%

14. (3) $672 The percent (part) for food and clothing is 25% + 15% = 40%. Find forty percent (rate) of $1680 (base). 0.4 × $1680 = $672. (Note: A quick way to find 40% is to find 10% and multiply by 4. 10% of $1680 is $168; $168 × 4 = $672)

15. (1) $\frac{2A}{b}$ The formula for the area of a triangle is $A = \frac{1}{2}bh$. To solve for h, use the rules of algebra to rewrite the equation so that h is alone on one side. Multiply both sides of the equation by 2 and then divide both sides by b.
$A = \frac{1}{2}bh$
$2A = 2\left(\frac{1}{2}bh\right)$
$2A = bh$
$\frac{2A}{b} = h$

16. (4) 660 There are $5\frac{1}{2}$ hours between 10 A.M. and 3:30 P.M. Multiply the number of customers per hour by the number of hours. $120 \times 5\frac{1}{2} = 120 \times 5.5 = 660$ customers
OR $120 \times 5\frac{1}{2} = \overset{60}{\cancel{120}} \times \frac{11}{\underset{1}{\cancel{2}}} = 660$

17. (2) $\frac{252}{900(2)}$ Use the simple interest formula. interest = principal × rate × time Substitute the known values. Rewrite the formula to solve for rate. $i = prt$
$252 = 900 \times r \times 2$
$\frac{252}{900(2)} = r$

18. $11.90 (Note: There is no place for $ on the answer grid. Fill in the circles for 11.90) Find the total cost of the purchase.
$12.98 + $12.98 + $2.14 = $28.10
Subtract this total from the amount given to pay.
2($20.00) − $28.10 = $40.00 − $28.10 = $11.90

19. (4) between 11 and 12 feet Use the Pythagorean Relationship. $a^2 + b^2 = c^2$ The length of the ladder is the hypotenuse, c, and the distance from the wall is one of the legs. Solve for the other leg, the height up the wall.
$4^2 + b^2 = 12^2$
$b^2 = 12^2 - 4^2 = 12(12) - 4(4) = 144 - 16 = 128$
To find the value of b, estimate the square root of 128. Since $11 \times 11 = 121$ and $12 \times 12 = 144$, the square root of 128 must be between 11 and 12.

20. (5) 2x + 3 = −x The word *sum* means to add 3 and twice a number (2x). This sum is equal to the negative of x, or −x. Thus, $2x + 3 = -x$.

21. (3) m∠2 + m∠5 = 180° Angles 2 and 6 are corresponding angles and have the same measure. Since ∠6 and ∠5 are supplementary angles, ∠2 and ∠5 are also supplementary. By definition, the sum of supplementary angles is 180°. Option (1) is incorrect because ∠6 and ∠7 are vertical angles and therefore congruent (equal), not supplementary. Option (2) is incorrect because ∠1 and ∠2 are supplementary (= 180°), not complementary (= 90°). Option (4) is incorrect because vertical angles are on a pair of intersecting lines which ∠2 and ∠6 are not. (They are corresponding angles). Option (5) is incorrect because ∠1 and ∠6 are not on the same side on the transversal (as corresponding angles are).

22. **(2)** $3x - 2y = -5$ Substitute -1 for x and 1 for y in each equation until you find the option that is true.

$$3x - 2y = -5$$
$$3(-1) - 2(1) = -5$$
$$-3 - 2 = -5$$
$$-5 = -5$$

23. **(2) 6** Let the width $= w$ and the length $= 3w$. Use the formula for the perimeter of a rectangle. Perimeter $= 2 \times$ length $+ 2 \times$ width

$$48 = 2(3w) + 2w$$
$$48 = 6w + 2w$$
$$48 = 8w$$
$$6 = w$$

24. **(5) 10:9** The number of sales for Store 1 was 400, and the number of sales for Store 2 was 360. Thus, the ratio of sales at Store 1 to those at Store 2 was 400 to 360. In simplest terms, $\frac{400}{360} = \frac{10}{9}$, or 10:9.

25. **(3) Sales are increasing at a faster rate at Store 2 than at Store 1.** Draw a line from the sales at week 5 to the sales at week 8 for both stores. The line for Store 2 is steeper. In other words, it is increasing at a faster rate.

UNIT 1: NUMBERS AND OPERATIONS

Lesson 1

GED Skill Focus (Page 35)

1. **five hundred**
2. **three million**
3. **six thousand**
4. **seven hundred thousand**
5. **fifty**
6. **zero thousand**
7. **e. eight thousand, four hundred sixteen**
8. **d. eight million, four hundred twenty thousand, one hundred six**
9. **a. eighty-four million, two hundred thousand, one hundred sixty**
10. **c. eight hundred forty-two thousand, sixteen**
11. **b. eighty-four thousand, two hundred sixteen**
12. **8,600**
13. **5,000,000**
14. **50,000**
15. **11,000**

GED Skill Focus (Page 37)

1. **1,305 < 1,503**
2. **34,000 > 29,989**
3. **102,667 > 102,657**
4. **5,690,185 < 5,690,185,100**
5. **875,438 = 875,438**
6. **75,390,000 < 75,391,540**
7. **9,500,000 < 9,500,000,000**
8. **45,100 > 45,099**
9. **7,456,795 < 7,500,000**
10. **319,002,110 > 319,002,011**
11. **Wednesday** $13,940 is greater than $13,772.
12. **Tuesday** $12,316 is less than all the other amounts.
13. **Saturday** $28,795 is greater than all the other amounts.
14. **$12,316; $13,772; $13,940; $18,756; $21,592; $28,795; or, by days: Tuesday, Thursday, Wednesday, Monday, Friday, Saturday**
15. **Bin C** 1750 is greater than 1721 and less than 2050.
16. **Bin A for Part 1488 and Bin B for Part 1491**
17. **Bin D,** which has parts numbered 2051 and higher

GED Practice (Page 39)

1. **(3) $269 × 12** You need to combine the same amount, $269, 12 times. Multiply.
2. **(1) $137 + $124** You are finding the total of two costs. Add.
3. **(5) $50 − $28** You are finding how much is left. Subtract. Be sure the total amount comes <u>before</u> the amount you subtract.
4. **(4) 348 ÷ 3** You need to break 348 pages into 3 equal parts. Divide. Be sure the amount being divided is written first.
5. **(2) $327 − $189** You are finding out how much is left. Subtract. Be sure the total amount comes <u>before</u> the amount you subtract.
6. **(5) $62 ÷ 4** You need to break an amount into equal parts. Divide. Be sure the whole amount being divided is written first.

GED Skill Focus (Page 41)

1. **4**

2. **38**

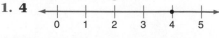

3. 0, 1, and 2 — number line 0 to 5, points at 0, 1, 2

4. 18 — number line 0 to 25+, point at 18

5. 2 — number line 0 to 5, point at 2

6. 22 — number line 0 to 25+, point at 22

7. 17 — number line 0 to 25, point at 17

8. 43 — number line 0 to 50, point at 43

Lesson 2
GED Skill Focus (Page 43)

1. 768
```
  305
 +463
  768
```

2. 8682
```
  4172
 +4510
  8682
```

3. 6927
```
    1
  6795
 + 132
  6927
```

4. 822
```
  1 1
  193
 +629
  822
```

5. 35
```
  86
 -51
  35
```

6. 327
```
   8 14
  4 9 4
 -167
  327
```

7. 412
```
   7 10
  6 8 0
 -268
  412
```

8. 1272
```
    9 16
  4 10
  5 0 6 7
 -3795
  1272
```

9. 109,593
```
    1   1
  81,427
   3,541
 +24,625
 109,593
```

10. 134
```
   1
  76
 +58
 134
```

11. 6,829
```
  9 14 9 18
  10,508
 - 3,679
   6,829
```

12. 54,271
```
    1 1
    176
 +54,095
  54,271
```

13. 3,433
```
  19 9 9 10
  20,000
 -16,567
   3,433
```

14. 1385
```
  1 1
  950
  308
   77
 + 50
 1385
```

15. 61,235
```
  1 1 1 1
  56,439
 + 4,796
  61,235
```

16. 54,961
```
  1 1 1 1
  35,075
   1,936
 +17,950
  54,961
```

17. 54,263
```
  1   1 1
  19,067
 +35,196
  54,263
```

18. 99,639
```
  1 1 1 1
  65,196
   6,725
 +27,718
  99,639
```

19. 581
```
    9 10
  7 10
  8 0 0
 -219
  581
```

20. 963
```
    11
  12 5 8
 - 295
   963
```

21. 31,313
```
  51,964
 -20,651
  31,313
```

22. 929
```
  2 11  9 15
  3 2 0 5
 -2276
   929
```

23. 188
```
   3
  36
   9
  74
  48
   6
 +15
 188
```

24. 406,985
```
      8 9 9 13
  419,003
 - 12,018
  406,985
```

25. 18,858
```
  2 16 14 9 10
  37,500
 -18,642
  18,858
```

26. 24,490
```
   9 9 9 10
  100,000
 - 75,510
   24,490
```

1. 3730

$$\begin{array}{r} \scriptstyle 2\ 3 \\ 746 \\ \times\ \ 5 \\ \hline 3730 \end{array}$$

2. 43,758

$$\begin{array}{r} \scriptstyle 7\ 5\ 1 \\ 4,862 \\ \times\ \ \ 9 \\ \hline 43,758 \end{array}$$

3. 828

$$\begin{array}{r} 36 \\ \times 23 \\ \hline 108 \\ +720 \\ \hline 828 \end{array}$$

4. 386,384

$$\begin{array}{r} 5,084 \\ \times\ \ \ 76 \\ \hline 30\ 504 \\ +355\ 880 \\ \hline 386,384 \end{array}$$

5. 458

$$\begin{array}{r} 458 \\ 7)\overline{3206} \\ -28 \\ \hline 40 \\ -35 \\ \hline 56 \\ -56 \\ \hline 0 \end{array}$$

6. 5,996

$$\begin{array}{r} 5,996 \\ 4)\overline{23,984} \\ -20 \\ \hline 3\ 9 \\ -3\ 6 \\ \hline 38 \\ -36 \\ \hline 24 \\ -24 \\ \hline 0 \end{array}$$

7. 6,366 r10

$$\begin{array}{r} 6,366\ r10 \\ 12)\overline{76,402} \\ -72 \\ \hline 4\ 4 \\ -3\ 6 \\ \hline 80 \\ -72 \\ \hline 82 \\ -72 \\ \hline 10 \end{array}$$

8. 9,138 r3

$$\begin{array}{r} 9,138\ r3 \\ 24)\overline{219,315} \\ -216 \\ \hline 3\ 3 \\ -2\ 4 \\ \hline 91 \\ -72 \\ \hline 195 \\ -192 \\ \hline 3 \end{array}$$

9. 6,976,800

$$\begin{array}{r} 2,584 \\ \times 2,700 \\ \hline 0\ 000 \\ 00\ 000 \\ 1\ 808\ 800 \\ +5\ 168\ 000 \\ \hline 6,976,800 \end{array}$$

Add zeros as placeholders.

10. 627,425

$$\begin{array}{r} 25,097 \\ \times\ \ \ \ 25 \\ \hline 125\ 485 \\ 501\ 940 \\ \hline 627,425 \end{array}$$

11. 659 r7

$$\begin{array}{r} 659\ r7 \\ 46)\overline{30,321} \\ 27\ 6 \\ \hline 2\ 72 \\ 2\ 30 \\ \hline 421 \\ 414 \\ \hline 7 \end{array}$$

12. 40,430

$$\begin{array}{r} 40,430 \\ 15)\overline{606,450} \\ 60 \\ \hline 06 \\ 0 \\ \hline 6\ 4 \\ 6\ 0 \\ \hline 45 \\ 45 \\ \hline 0 \end{array}$$

13. 415,340

$$\begin{array}{r} 2,186 \\ \times\ \ \ 190 \\ \hline 0\ 000 \\ 196\ 740 \\ 218\ 600 \\ \hline 415,340 \end{array}$$

14. 680

$$\begin{array}{r} 680 \\ 205)\overline{139,400} \\ 123\ 0 \\ \hline 16\ 40 \\ 16\ 40 \\ \hline 00 \end{array}$$

15. 8,132

$$\begin{array}{r} 8,132 \\ 16)\overline{130,112} \\ 128 \\ \hline 2\ 1 \\ 1\ 6 \\ \hline 51 \\ 48 \\ \hline 32 \\ 32 \end{array}$$

16. 4,097,450

$$\begin{array}{r} 8,050 \\ \times\ \ \ 509 \\ \hline 72\ 450 \\ 00\ 000 \\ 4\ 025\ 000 \\ \hline 4,097,450 \end{array}$$

17. 600,625

18. 7,640,000

19. 54,870

20. 3,758,458

21. 584

22. 14,121

23. 7,692

24. 1,099

25. 125,304

26. 53,685

27. 4,236

28. 28,480

29. 363,681

30. 2573

GED Practice (Page 47)

1. (5) $261

$$\begin{array}{r} \scriptstyle 1 \\ \$137 \\ +124 \\ \hline \$261 \end{array}$$

2. (5) $638

$$\begin{array}{r} \scriptstyle 7\ 11\ 17 \\ \$8\cancel{2}7 \\ -189 \\ \hline \$638 \end{array}$$

3. **(1) 322**

$$\begin{array}{r} {\scriptstyle 1\,1} \\ 168 \\ +154 \\ \hline 322 \end{array}$$

4. **(5) $3468** 1 year = 12 months; Multiply the monthly payment by 12 to find the amount for 1 year. $289 × 12 = $3468

5. **(3) $19**   114 ÷ 6 = 19.

6. **(4) $476**   68 × 7 = 476.

GED Practice (Page 49)

1. **(3) 3,577** Subtract the lower odometer reading from the higher reading.
38,874 − 35,297 = 3,577

2. **(4) $14,280** Multiply the monthly rent by the number of months in two years.
$595 × 24 = $14,280

3. **(2) 32** Divide the total sales of new stereo systems by the price of each system.
$14,688 ÷ $459 = 32

4. **(5) $1143** Add the three deposits to the initial balance. $76 + $96 + $873 + $98 = $1143

GED Mini-Test • Lessons 1 and 2
(Pages 50–51)

1. **(5) 3216**

2. **(2) 504**

3. **(4) 14** Divide the total amount needed by the amount saved per month. $3220 ÷ $230 = 14

4. **(2) $5,760** Multiply the monthly rent by 12, the number of months in a year. $480 × 12 = $5760

5. **(3) 10,967** Add the number of videotapes rented in February and March. 5,980 + 4,987 = 10,967

6. **(3) 1,978** Subtract the number of videotapes rented in April from the number rented in May.
7,985 − 6,007 = 1,978

7. **(4) 8,640** Multiply the number of tapes rented in January by 2. 4,320 × 2 = 8,640

8. **(2) 203,049** Remember, the comma between the words matches the comma between the numbers—there is no "hundreds" in the words.

9. **(1) 39,000** The digit to the right of the thousands place is 4. Since 4 is less than 5, leave the 9 as the thousands digit, and replace the digits to the right of the thousands place with zeros.

10. **(3) $387 × 12** Multiply the amount of the monthly payment by the number of months.
$387 × 12

11. **(4) $972 ÷ 3** Divide the total rent per month by the number of friends sharing the rent. $972 ÷ 3

12. **(2) $420** Multiply the price of food per person by the number of employees. $12 × 35 = $420

13. **(5) 72** Multiply the number of hours Cynthia works per day by the number of days she works per week. 4 × 6 = 24 Multiply the result by the number of weeks she works. 24 × 3 = 72

14. **(4) $1060** Subtract the amount taken out of the account from the beginning amount in the account. $1200 − $140 = $1060

15. **(1) $65** Subtract the amount Roberto saved from the cost of the computer system.
$1,050 − $985 = $65

Lesson 3
GED Skill Focus (Page 53)
NOTE: Your estimate may vary depending on the estimations or rounding you use.

1. Estimate: 1400 − 1000 = **400**
Exact: 1424 − 989 = **435**

2. Estimate: 20 × 30 = **600**
Exact: 18 × 29 = **522**

3. Estimate: 1800 ÷ 60 = **30**
Exact: 1798 ÷ 62 = **29**

4. Estimate: 40 × $10 = **$400**
Exact: 39 × $9 = **$351**

5. Estimate: $40 + $200 + $150 = **$390**
Exact: $38 + $196 + $145 = **$379**

6. Estimate: $1000 × 15 = **$15,000**
Exact: $1137 × 15 = **$17,055**

7. Estimate: 1200 − 300 = **900**
Exact: 1192 − 315 = **877**

8. Estimate: $1200 ÷ 12 = **$100**
Exact: $1152 ÷ 12 = **$96**

9. Estimate: 200 × 3 = **600**
Exact: 177 × 3 = **531**

10. Estimate: $400 − $100 = **$300**
Exact: $396 − $104 = **$292**

11. Estimate: 2400 − 700 = **1700**
Exact: 2400 − 685 = **1715**

12. Estimate: $225,000 + $20,000 = **$245,000**
Exact: $225,125 + $18,725 = **$243,850**

GED Skill Focus (Page 55)

1. The number of seats: **26,500**
The price per ticket: **$6**

2. The sale price: **$59**
The coupon discount amount: **$10**

3. Nita's earnings this week: **$456**
Her hourly wage: **$12**

4. The fund-raising goal: **$25,000**
The donated amount: **$11,450**

5. $288 Multiply the number of sweat pants sold by the sale price. 24 × $12

6. Not enough information is given. The question asks for the number of T-shirts at the start of the sale. You only know how many T-shirts were sold before the sale. You do not know the number originally in stock before the 25 were sold. You need this number to compute the number the store started the sale with: original number − 25 = number at start of sale.

7. $720 You don't need the costs for the cabinets or plumbing. Multiply the number of tiles needed by the price per tile. 240 × $3 = $720

8. 112 You don't need to know the ages of the children or the breakdown by gender. Subtract the total number of children who signed up for basketball from the total number who signed up for baseball. 432 − 320 = 112

GED Practice (Page 57)
NOTE: The placement of your answer could be left, center, or right. Just remember to leave unused columns blank.

1. 408 $615 − $172 − $35 = $408

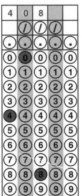

2. 1872 $78 × 24 = $1872

3. 120 $720 ÷ 6 = $120

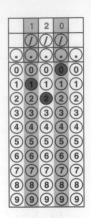

4. 566 $620 − $54 = $566

Lesson 4
GED Skill Focus (Page 59)

1. 20 25 − 20 ÷ 4 =
25 −   5   = 20

2. 42 (9 + 5) × (6 − 3) =
14   ×   3   = 42

3. 0 18 − 6 × 3 =
18 −   18   = 0

4. 3 60 ÷ (30 − 10) =
60 ÷   20   = 3

5. 23 20 + 12 ÷ 4 =
20 +   3   = 23

6. 37 13 + 7 × 2 + 10 =
13 +   14   + 10 = 37

7. 18 24 ÷ 6 × 4 + 2 =
4   × 4 + 2 =
16   + 2 = 18

8. 12 12 ÷ 2 × (8 − 6) =
12 ÷ 2 ×   2   =
6   ×   2   = 12

9. 132 11 × (4 + 2) × 2 =
11 ×   6   × 2 =
66   × 2 = 132

10. 63 7 × (3 + 6) =
7 ×   9   = 63

11. 7 $15 + 10 - 9 \times 2 =$
$15 + 10 - 18 =$
$25 - 18 = 7$

12. 6 $54 \div (4 + 5) =$
$54 \div 9 = 6$

13. 361 $(7 + 12) \times (16 + 3) =$
$19 \times 19 = 361$

14. 9 $(20 + 25) \div 5 =$
$45 \div 5 = 9$

15. 42 $4 \times 5 + 10 + 12 =$
$20 + 10 + 12 = 42$

16. (28 + 2) + (15 + 5)
$(28 + 2) = 30$ and $(15 + 5) = 20$
Combine. $30 + 20 = 50$

17. (25 × 4) × 7
$(25 \times 4) = 100$; then $(7 \times 100) = 700$

GED Skill Focus (Page 61)

1. **a. Multiply the number of medium boxes, 15, by the number in the box, 66.**
   b. Multiply the number of extra-large boxes, 24, by the number in the box, 24.
   c. subtraction
   d. 414 diapers $(15 \times 66) - (24 \times 24) =$
   $990 - 576 = 414$

2. **a. 15 + 18 + 24 = 57 boxes**
   b. multiplication
   c. 57 × $13 = $741
   d. You could multiply the number of boxes of each size by $13 and add.
   $(15 \times \$13) + (18 \times \$13) + (24 \times \$13) = \$741$

3. **a. multiplication and subtraction**
   b. $46 $(\$58 \times 12) - \$650 = ?$
   $\$696 - \$650 = \$46$

4. **a. multiplication and addition**
   b. $1,082 $(\$115 \times 8) + \$162 = ?$
   $\$920 + \$162 = \$1,082$

GED Practice (Page 63)

1. **(4) (65 × $9) + $350** Find the amount paid for food by multiplying the number of employees by the cost of the food per person ($65 \times \$9$). Then add the cost of renting the banquet room ($350).

2. **(5) $\frac{1200}{300}$** To find the number of tanks of gas needed to drive 1200 miles, divide that amount by the number of miles David can drive on one tank of gas (300 miles).

3. **(3) 70 × ($8 − $6)** To find how much more the garage owner could make by raising rates, first find the difference in the rates ($8 − $6). Then multiply by the number of parking spaces in the garage (70).

4. **(1) $\frac{(\$1800 - \$300)}{\$150}$** First subtract the $300 payment from the $1800 debt ($1800 − $300). Then divide the remaining debt by the amount to be paid each month ($150).

5. **(2) $150 − (2 × $35) − (3 × $18)** First find the costs of the textbooks. 2 for $35 (2 × $35) and 3 for $18 (3 × $18). Then subtract both amounts from $150.

6. **(4) (2 + 3) × $35** First find the number of camera sales made (2 + 3). Then multiply that amount by the commission she earns. The price of each camera is not needed.

GED Practice (Page 65)

1. **(2) addition and division** Add to find the total number of apartments. Then divide the cost of the service by the number of apartments.

2. **(3) $72** There are 43 apartments (18 + 25). Divide the yearly cost by the number of apartments. ($3096 \div 43 = \$72$)

3. **(4) 604,392** Multiply first, then add.
   $2,184 + (1,476 \times 408)$
   $1,476 \times 408 = 602,208$
   $2,184 + 602,208 = 604,392$

4. **(2) 1,693** Do the operations in the parentheses first, starting with the multiplication, then the addition. Then divide and add.
   $(908 + 23 \times 48) \div 2 + 687$
   $23 \times 48 = 1,104$
   $908 + 1,104 = 2,012$
   $2,012 \div 2 = 1,006$
   $1,006 + 687 = 1,693$

5. **(5) $14,684** For each company's shares, multiply the cost per share by the number of shares purchased, then add the two products.
   $(112 \times 58) + (89 \times 92) = 6,496 + 8,188 = 14,684$

6. **(1) $84** Multiply the cost per share by the number of shares. $68 \times 87 = 5,916$ Then subtract from the starting amount. $6,000 - 5,916 = 84$

GED Mini-Test • Lessons 3 and 4
(Pages 66–69)
Part 1

1. **(4) 345** Divide the total net sales by the cost of each laptop. $\$685,170 \div \$1,986$

2. **(1) $924,160** Multiply the number of employees by the year-end bonus. $1,216 \times \$760$

3. **(1) 650** Follow the order of operations. First divide. Then add.
   $50 + 15,000 \div 25$
   $15,000 \div 25 = 600$
   $50 + 600 = 650$

4. **(2) 1,194,036** Add the number of books sold in each of the three categories. 569,346 + 234,908 + 389,782

5. **(3) 1600** Follow the order of operations. First solve within the parentheses. Then multiply.
40 (50 − 5 × 2)
(50 − 10) = 40
40 (40) = 1600

6. **(5) 3,607,829** Subtract the difference in the votes from the number of votes received by the winner. 3,898,705 − 290,876 = 3,607,829

7. **(4) $157,717** Add the net sales of the five departments listed in the table. $20,897 + $57,941 + $31,009 + $28,987 + $18,883

8. **(2) $6,035** Add the net sales for Footwear and Sporting Goods. $20,897 + $31,009 = $51,906 Subtract the result from the net sales of Outerwear. $57,941 − $51,906 = $6,035

9. **(3) $39,058** Subtract the net sales of Skiing Equipment from the net sales of Outerwear. $57,941 − $18,883 = $39,058

10. **(3) $22,183** Subtract the expenses for magazine advertisements in February from those in January. $420,885 − $398,702 = $22,183

11. **(5) Not enough information is given.** The question asks about the first three months of the year, but the information in the table is only about the first two months. There is not enough information to answer the question.

12. **(4) $554,987** Subtract the expenses for Network TV in January from those in February. $540,987 − $526,987 = $14,000 Add the result to the expenses for Network TV in February. $540,987 + $14,000 = $554,987

Part 2

13. **(3) 2300** Add the number of new employees hired to the original number of employees. 2100 + 200

14. **(4) 250 × $3** This expression shows that you multiply the number of paving blocks (250) by the cost of each block ($3).

15. **(5) Not enough information is given.** You do not know the number of months Marcus pays for the computer.

16. **(2) 8** Follow the order of operations. First perform all multiplication and division. Then perform all additions and subtractions in the resulting expression.
3 + 4 × 2 − 6 ÷ 2
3 + 8 − 3 = 8

17. **(3) multiplication** You would multiply the amount of each monthly installment, $75, by the number of payments, 12.

18. **(2) $140** Multiply the amount of each monthly installment by the number of payments. $75 × 12 = $900 Subtract the amount you would pay in cash from the result. $900 − $760

19. **(5) 500** There are several ways to estimate by rounding and multiplying the number of boxes by the number of medium T-shirts in a box. 10 × 48 = 480 or 10 × 50 = 500 or 12 × 50 = 600

20. **(4) 200** Multiply the number of small T-shirts in a box by the number of boxes. 60 × 10 = 600 This is the number of small T-shirts ordered. Multiply the number of large T-shirts in a box by the number of boxes. 20 × 20 = 400 This is the number of large T-shirts ordered. Subtract the number of small T-shirts ordered from the number of large T-shirts ordered. 600 − 400

21. **(5) 25(3 + 2)** Multiply the amount of the commission ($25) by the number of machines sold (3 + 2).

22. **(2) $30** Subtract the daily cost for the air compressor from the cost for the chipper/shredder. $75 − $45

23. **(1) $10** Combine the rental cost for the wet/dry vacuum and the air compressor ($40 + $45 = $85). Subtract the rental cost of the chipper/shredder from that amount. $85 − $75

24. **(4) $225** Multiply the daily rental fee for the chipper/shredder by 3. $75 × 3

Lesson 5
GED Skill Focus (Page 71)

1. $\frac{5}{8}$ The figure is divided into 8 equal parts, and 5 of the parts are shaded.

2. $\frac{2}{3}$ There are 3 circles, and 2 are shaded.

3. $\frac{9}{10}$ The figure is divided into 10 equal parts, and 9 of the parts are shaded.

4. $\frac{5}{2}$ There are 3 rectangles, each divided into 2 equal parts. A total of 5 parts are shaded.

5. $\frac{1}{6}$ There are 6 figures in the group, and 1 is shaded.

6. $\frac{5}{9}$ The figure is divided into 9 equal parts, and 5 of the parts are shaded.

7. $\frac{7}{6}$ There are 2 figures, each divided into 6 equal parts, and 7 of the parts are shaded.

8. $\frac{15}{4}$ There are 4 circles, each divided into 4 equal parts, and a total of 15 parts are shaded.

9. $\frac{9}{16}$

10. $\frac{7}{10}$

11. $\frac{19}{45}$

12. $\frac{47}{50}$

13. $\frac{9}{70}$

14. $\frac{43}{500}$

GED Skill Focus (Page 73)

1. $\frac{8}{5}$, $1\frac{3}{5}$ Each figure is divided into 5 equal parts. There are 8 parts shaded among the figures. One figure is completely shaded and 3 of the 5 parts of the remaining figure are shaded.

2. $\frac{7}{2}$, $3\frac{1}{2}$ Each figure is divided into 2 equal parts. There are 7 parts shaded among the figures. Three figures are completely shaded and 1 of 2 parts of the remaining figure is shaded.

3. $\frac{8}{3}$, $2\frac{2}{3}$ Each figure is divided into 3 equal parts. There are 8 parts shaded among the figures. Two figures are completely shaded and 2 of the 3 parts of the remaining figure are shaded.

4. $\frac{17}{6}$, $2\frac{5}{6}$ Each figure is divided into 6 equal parts. There are 17 parts shaded among the figures. Two figures are completely shaded and 5 of the 6 parts of the remaining figure are shaded.

5. $\frac{11}{8}$, $1\frac{3}{8}$ Each figure is divided into 8 equal parts. There are 11 parts shaded among the figures. One figure is completely shaded and 3 of the 8 parts of the remaining figure are shaded.

6. $\frac{13}{4}$, $3\frac{1}{4}$ Each figure is divided into 4 equal parts. There are 13 parts shaded among the figures. Three figures are completely shaded and 1 out of 4 parts of the remaining figure is shaded.

7. $3\frac{1}{2}$ $7 \div 2 = 3$ r1 $= 3\frac{1}{2}$

8. $2\frac{2}{3}$ $8 \div 3 = 2$ r2 $= 2\frac{2}{3}$

9. $5\frac{7}{10}$ $57 \div 10 = 5$ r7 $= 5\frac{7}{10}$

10. 5 $15 \div 3 = 5$

11. $3\frac{1}{3}$ $10 \div 3 = 3$ r1 $= 3\frac{1}{3}$

12. $8\frac{5}{9}$ $77 \div 9 = 8$ r5 $= 8\frac{5}{9}$

13. $4\frac{3}{4}$ $19 \div 4 = 4$ r3 $= 4\frac{3}{4}$

14. $3\frac{7}{8}$ $31 \div 8 = 3$ r7 $= 3\frac{7}{8}$

15. 7 $42 \div 6 = 7$

16. $4\frac{1}{2}$ $9 \div 2 = 4$ r1 $= 4\frac{1}{2}$

17. $2\frac{5}{6}$ $17 \div 6 = 2$ r5 $= 2\frac{5}{6}$

18. $3\frac{5}{12}$ $41 \div 12 = 3$ r5 $= 3\frac{5}{12}$

19. $\frac{13}{2}$ $2 \times 6 = 12$, $12 + 1 = 13$

20. $\frac{17}{2}$ $2 \times 8 = 16$, $16 + 1 = 17$

21. $\frac{43}{8}$ $8 \times 5 = 40$, $40 + 3 = 43$

22. $\frac{23}{6}$ $6 \times 3 = 18$, $18 + 5 = 23$

23. $\frac{11}{5}$ $5 \times 2 = 10$, $10 + 1 = 11$

24. $\frac{46}{7}$ $7 \times 6 = 42$, $42 + 4 = 46$

25. $\frac{13}{8}$ $8 \times 1 = 8$, $8 + 5 = 13$

26. $\frac{47}{4}$ $4 \times 11 = 44$, $44 + 3 = 47$

27. $\frac{21}{2}$ $2 \times 10 = 20$, $20 + 1 = 21$

28. $\frac{38}{9}$ $9 \times 4 = 36$, $36 + 2 = 38$

29. $\frac{61}{12}$ $12 \times 5 = 60$, $60 + 1 = 61$

30. $\frac{47}{5}$ $5 \times 9 = 45$, $45 + 2 = 47$

GED Practice (Page 75)

1. **(2) $5\frac{3}{4} - 2\frac{3}{8}$** You are comparing two quantities and finding the difference ("how much more").

2. **(4) $6\frac{1}{4} \div 2\frac{1}{2}$** You are finding how many equal parts $\left(2\frac{1}{2}\right)$ are in the whole $\left(6\frac{1}{4}\right)$.

3. **(3) $15\frac{3}{4} \times \frac{1}{2}$** You are finding a fractional part "of" a whole amount.

4. **(4) $4\frac{1}{2} \div \frac{3}{4}$** You are finding how many equal parts $\left(\frac{3}{4}\right)$ are in the whole $\left(4\frac{1}{2}\right)$.

5. **(1) $18\frac{1}{2} + 12\frac{2}{5}$** You are finding a total.

6. **(3) $\frac{2}{5} \times \frac{5}{8}$** You are finding the fractional part of the whole. In this case, the whole is already a fraction $\left(\frac{5}{8} \text{ of the employees}\right)$. You need to find $\frac{2}{5}$ (the fraction of employees taking the express bus) of $\frac{5}{8}$ (the "whole" segment of employees that take a bus to work).

GED Skill Focus (Page 77)

1. $3\frac{3}{4}$ You should have placed a dot on **the third short line between 3 and 4.**

2. $1\frac{3}{5}$ You should have placed a dot on **the third short line between 1 and 2.**

3. $4\frac{1}{3}$ You should have placed a dot on **the first short line between 4 and 5.**

0 1 2 3 4 5

4. $\frac{4}{5}$ You should have placed a dot on **the fourth short line between 0 and 1.**

0 1 2 3 4 5

5. $\frac{2}{3}$ You should have placed a dot on **the second short line between 0 and 1.**

0 1 2 3 4 5

6. $4\frac{1}{4}$ You should have placed a dot on **the first short line between 4 and 5.**

4:15 P.M. $= 4\frac{15}{60} = 4\frac{1}{4}$

0 1 2 3 4 5

7. $3\frac{7}{8}$ You should have placed a dot on **the third short line after 3.**

0 1 2 3 4 5

Lesson 6
GED Skill Focus (Page 79)

1. $\frac{1}{2}$ Divide both the numerator (2) and denominator (4) by 2.

2. $\frac{2}{3}$ Divide both the numerator (6) and denominator (9) by 3.

3. $\frac{2}{5}$ Divide both the numerator (10) and denominator (25) by 5.

4. $\frac{3}{4}$ Divide both the numerator (6) and denominator (8) by 2.

5. $\frac{2}{5}$ Divide both the numerator (6) and denominator (15) by 3.

6. $\frac{2}{3}$ Divide both the numerator (18) and denominator (27) by 9.

7. $\frac{1}{4}$ Divide both the numerator (5) and denominator (20) by 5.

8. $\frac{1}{4}$ Divide both the numerator (12) and denominator (48) by 12.

9. $\frac{4}{5}$ Divide both the numerator (16) and denominator (20) by 4.

10. $\frac{2}{5}$ Divide both the numerator (12) and denominator (30) by 6.

11. $\frac{1}{6}$ Divide both the numerator (7) and denominator (42) by 7.

12. $\frac{2}{3}$ Divide both the numerator (24) and denominator (36) by 12.

13. $\frac{4}{6}$ **and** $\frac{8}{12}$ Both equal $\frac{2}{3}$. The other fractions reduce to $\frac{3}{5}$, $\frac{1}{2}$, and $\frac{5}{6}$.

14. $\frac{8}{16}$ **and** $\frac{3}{6}$ Both equal $\frac{1}{2}$. The other fractions do not reduce and none equals $\frac{1}{2}$.

15. $\frac{3}{12}$ **and** $\frac{2}{8}$ Both equal $\frac{1}{4}$. The other fractions reduce to $\frac{1}{2}$, $\frac{1}{5}$, and $\frac{1}{3}$.

16. $\frac{6}{10}$ **and** $\frac{3}{5}$ The fraction $\frac{6}{10}$ reduces to $\frac{3}{5}$. The other fractions equal or reduce to $\frac{5}{8}$, $\frac{3}{4}$, and $\frac{1}{4}$.

17. $\frac{1}{5}$ $\frac{8 \div 8}{40 \div 8} = \frac{1}{5}$

18. $\frac{3}{10}$ $\frac{15 \div 5}{50 \div 5} = \frac{3}{10}$

19. $\frac{1}{20}$ $\frac{50 \div 50}{1,000 \div 50} = \frac{1}{20}$

20. $\frac{3}{5}$ $\frac{\$24 \div 8}{\$40 \div 8} = \frac{3}{5}$

GED Skill Focus (Page 81)

1. $\frac{8}{12}$ Multiply the numerator of the first fraction by the same number the denominator is multiplied by to get the desired new denominator. $3 \times 4 = 12$; so $2 \times 4 = 8$

2. $\frac{6}{21}$
$7 \times 3 = 21$ so $2 \times 3 = 6$

3. $\frac{20}{25}$
$5 \times 5 = 25$ so $4 \times 5 = 20$

4. $\frac{20}{32}$
$8 \times 4 = 32$ so $5 \times 4 = 20$

5. $\frac{49}{63}$
$9 \times 7 = 63$ so $7 \times 7 = 49$

6. $\frac{36}{120}$
$10 \times 12 = 120$ so $3 \times 12 = 36$

7. $\frac{27}{36}$
$4 \times 9 = 36$ so $3 \times 9 = 27$

8. $\frac{36}{81}$
$9 \times 9 = 81$ so $4 \times 9 = 36$

9. $\frac{27}{150}$
$50 \times 3 = 150$ so $9 \times 3 = 27$

10. $\frac{1}{3} > \frac{1}{4}$ Convert each fraction to a common denominator. $\frac{1}{3} \times \frac{4}{4} = \frac{4}{12}$; $\frac{1}{4} \times \frac{3}{3} = \frac{3}{12}$
$\frac{4}{12} > \frac{3}{12}$ so $\frac{1}{3} > \frac{1}{4}$

11. $\frac{3}{4} < \frac{7}{8}$ because $\frac{6}{8} < \frac{7}{8}$

12. $\frac{3}{9} = \frac{1}{3}$ because $\frac{3}{9}$ reduces to $\frac{1}{3}$

13. $\frac{2}{3} > \frac{1}{2}$ because $\frac{4}{6} > \frac{3}{6}$

Answers and Explanations

14. $\frac{5}{6} = \frac{15}{18}$ because $\frac{15}{18}$ reduces to $\frac{5}{6}$

15. $\frac{9}{12} = \frac{3}{4}$ because $\frac{9}{12}$ reduces to $\frac{3}{4}$

16. $\frac{7}{10} > \frac{2}{3}$ because $\frac{21}{30} > \frac{20}{30}$

17. $\frac{7}{15} > \frac{2}{5}$ because $\frac{7}{15} > \frac{6}{15}$

18. $\frac{9}{10} > \frac{3}{4}$ because $\frac{18}{20} > \frac{15}{20}$

19. **Team C** The least common denominator of the 5 fractions is 20 because 2, 4, and 5 all divide evenly into 20. Change each fraction in the table to an equal fraction with this common denominator.

Team A: $\frac{8}{20}$

Team B: $\frac{10}{20}$

Team C: $\frac{5}{20}$

Team D: $\frac{12}{20}$

Team E: $\frac{15}{20}$

Team C has completed the smallest part of its goal because 5 is the lowest numerator.

20. **Team E** Team E has completed the greatest part of its goal because 15 is greater than any of the other numerators. See the explanation for question 19.

21. **Teams D and E** The fraction $\frac{10}{20}$ is equal to $\frac{1}{2}$ of the goal. Only Teams D and E have completed more than $\frac{10}{20}$ or $\frac{1}{2}$.

22. **Teams A, B, and D** Compare the original fractions to $\frac{3}{8}$ and $\frac{5}{8}$. The lowest common denominator for all of the fractions is 40.
$\frac{3}{8} = \frac{15}{40}$ and $\frac{5}{8} = \frac{25}{40}$

Team A: $\frac{16}{40}$

Team B: $\frac{20}{40}$

Team C: $\frac{10}{40}$

Team D: $\frac{24}{40}$

Team E: $\frac{30}{40}$

Compare the numerators. Only 16 (Team A), 20 (Team B), and 24 (Team D) fall between 15 and 25.

GED Skill Focus (Page 83)

1. $\frac{3}{1}$ Divide both the numerator and denominator by the same number. $\frac{18 \div 6}{6 \div 6} = \frac{3}{1}$

2. $\frac{4}{5}$ $\frac{80 \div 20}{100 \div 20} = \frac{4}{5}$

3. $\frac{4}{3}$ $\frac{16 \div 4}{12 \div 4} = \frac{4}{3}$

4. $\frac{7}{3}$ $\frac{21 \div 3}{9 \div 3} = \frac{7}{3}$

5. $\frac{23}{30}$ $\frac{69 \div 3}{90 \div 3} = \frac{23}{30}$

6. $\frac{8}{15}$ $\frac{16 \div 2}{30 \div 2} = \frac{8}{15}$

7. $\frac{17}{20}$ $\frac{85 \div 5}{100 \div 5} = \frac{17}{20}$

8. $\frac{5}{1}$ $\frac{35 \div 7}{7 \div 7} = \frac{5}{1}$

9. $\frac{1}{12}$ $\frac{10 \div 10}{120 \div 10} = \frac{1}{12}$

10. $\frac{3}{4}$ $\frac{15 \div 5}{20 \div 5} = \frac{3}{4}$

11. **80 miles per hour** A rate usually has a 1 as the denominator. Divide the numerator by the denominator. $400 \div 5 = 80$ miles per hour

12. **$12 per hour** Divide $216 by 18.

13. **9 calories per gram of fat** Divide 54 by 6.

14. **12 people per team** Divide 432 by 36.

15. **$1 per pound of grass seed** Divide $10 by 10.

16. **90 oranges per bag** Divide 5400 by 60.

17. **64 feet per second** Divide 1024 by 16.

18. **$6 per yard of fabric** Divide $150 by 25.

19. **45 pages per hour** Divide 135 by 3.

20. **230 calories per serving** Divide 460 by 2.

21. a. $\frac{5}{1}$ $\frac{\text{games won}}{\text{games lost}} = \frac{30}{6} = \frac{5}{1}$

b. $\frac{1}{6}$ $\frac{\text{games lost}}{\text{games played}} = \frac{6}{(6 + 30)} = \frac{6}{36} = \frac{1}{6}$

c. $\frac{5}{6}$ $\frac{\text{games won}}{\text{games played}} = \frac{30}{(6 + 30)} = \frac{30}{36} = \frac{5}{6}$

d. $\frac{1}{5}$ $\frac{6 \div 6}{30 \div 6} = \frac{1}{5}$

22. a. $\frac{2}{5}$ $\frac{14 \text{ non-union}}{35 \text{ union}} = \frac{2}{5}$

b. $\frac{5}{7}$ $\frac{35 \text{ union}}{(14 + 35) \text{ total}} = \frac{35}{49} = \frac{5}{7}$

c. $\frac{2}{7}$ $\frac{14 \text{ non-union}}{(14 + 35) \text{ total}} = \frac{14}{49} = \frac{2}{7}$

d. $\frac{5}{2}$ $\frac{35 \text{ union}}{14 \text{ non-union}} = \frac{5}{2}$

23. a. $\frac{4}{1}$ $\frac{16 \text{ correct}}{4 \text{ incorrect}} = \frac{4}{1}$

b. $\frac{4}{5}$ $\frac{16 \text{ correct}}{(16 + 4) \text{ total}} = \frac{16}{20} = \frac{4}{5}$

c. $\frac{1}{5}$ $\frac{4 \text{ incorrect}}{(16 + 4) \text{ total}} = \frac{4}{20} = \frac{1}{5}$

24. a. $\frac{1}{20}$ $\frac{30 \text{ defective}}{1000 \text{ total}} = \frac{1}{20}$

b. $\frac{1}{19}$ $\frac{50 \text{ defective}}{(1000 - 50) \text{ good}} = \frac{50}{950} = \frac{1}{19}$

c. $\frac{19}{20}$ $\frac{(1000 - 50) \text{ good}}{1000 \text{ total}} = \frac{19}{20}$

1. **10** Cross multiply and solve. $2 \times 15 \div 3 = 10$

2. **6** $12 \times 14 \div 28 = 6$

3. **18** $9 \times 20 \div 10 = 18$

4. **15** $5 \times 18 \div 6 = 15$

5. **12** $4 \times 9 \div 3 = 12$

6. **8** $24 \times 5 \div 15 = 8$

7. **30** $15 \times 24 \div 12 = 30$

8. **3** $6 \times 7 \div 14 = 3$

9. **23** $115 \times 6 \div 30 = 23$

10. **32** $20 \times 8 \div 5 = 32$

11. **70** $49 \times 10 \div 7 = 70$

12. **60** $32 \times 15 \div 8 = 60$

13. **1** $6 \times 3 \div 18 = 1$

14. **100** $120 \times 5 \div 6 = 100$

15. **40** $64 \times 5 \div 8 = 40$

16. **9 cups** Write a proportion; cross multiply and solve. $\frac{8}{2} = \frac{36}{?}$

$2 \times 36 \div 8 = 9$

17. **208 miles** $\frac{32}{2} = \frac{?}{13}$

$32 \times 13 \div 2 = 208$

18. **1050 calories** $\frac{315}{3} = \frac{?}{10}$

$315 \times 10 \div 3 = 1050$

19. **55 spaces** $\frac{12}{5} = \frac{132}{?}$

$5 \times 132 \div 12 = 55$

20. **10 inches** $\frac{\text{inches}}{\text{miles}} \frac{2}{150} = \frac{?}{750}$

$2 \times 750 \div 150 = 10$

21. **80 full-time workers**

$\frac{\text{full-time}}{\text{part-time}} \frac{5}{3} = \frac{?}{48}$

$5 \times 48 \div 3 = 80$

22. **$135** $\frac{\text{gallons}}{\text{dollars}} \frac{2}{\$27} = \frac{10}{\$?}$

$27 \times 10 \div 2 = 135$

23. **6 losses** $\frac{\text{wins}}{\text{losses}} \frac{7}{2} = \frac{21}{?}$

$2 \times 21 \div 7 = 6$

GED Practice (Page 87)

1. $\frac{23}{47}$

2. $\frac{15}{32}$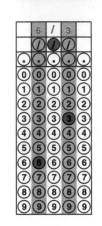

3. $\frac{6}{3}$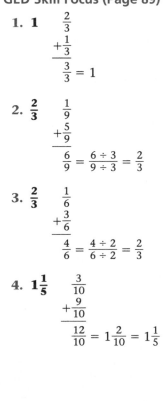

4. $\frac{3}{1}$

$\frac{21}{7} = \frac{3}{1}$

Lesson 7
GED Skill Focus (Page 89)

1. **1**

$\frac{2}{3}$

$+\frac{1}{3}$

$\frac{3}{3} = 1$

2. $\frac{2}{3}$

$\frac{1}{9}$

$+\frac{5}{9}$

$\frac{6}{9} = \frac{6 \div 3}{9 \div 3} = \frac{2}{3}$

3. $\frac{2}{3}$

$\frac{1}{6}$

$+\frac{3}{6}$

$\frac{4}{6} = \frac{4 \div 2}{6 \div 2} = \frac{2}{3}$

4. $1\frac{1}{5}$

$\frac{3}{10}$

$+\frac{9}{10}$

$\frac{12}{10} = 1\frac{2}{10} = 1\frac{1}{5}$

5. $\frac{7}{8}$

$$\frac{3}{4} = \frac{6}{8}$$
$$+\frac{1}{8} = +\frac{1}{8}$$
$$\frac{7}{8}$$

6. $1\frac{1}{12}$

$$\frac{1}{3} = \frac{4}{12}$$
$$+\frac{3}{4} = +\frac{9}{12}$$
$$\frac{13}{12} = 1\frac{1}{12}$$

7. $\frac{2}{3}$

$$\frac{1}{6} = \frac{1}{6}$$
$$+\frac{1}{2} = +\frac{3}{6}$$
$$\frac{4}{6} = \frac{4 \div 2}{6 \div 2} = \frac{2}{3}$$

8. $\frac{7}{8}$

$$\frac{5}{8} = \frac{5}{8}$$
$$+\frac{1}{4} = +\frac{2}{8}$$
$$\frac{7}{8}$$

9. $\frac{1}{2}$

$$\frac{3}{4}$$
$$-\frac{1}{4}$$
$$\frac{2 \div 2}{4 \div 2} = \frac{1}{2}$$

10. $\frac{1}{2}$

$$\frac{7}{8}$$
$$-\frac{3}{8}$$
$$\frac{4 \div 4}{8 \div 4} = \frac{1}{2}$$

11. $\frac{4}{15}$

$$\frac{13}{15}$$
$$-\frac{9}{15}$$
$$\frac{4}{15}$$

12. $\frac{1}{6}$

$$\frac{7}{12}$$
$$-\frac{5}{12}$$
$$\frac{2}{12} = \frac{2 \div 2}{12 \div 2} = \frac{1}{6}$$

13. $\frac{1}{4}$

$$\frac{3}{4} = \frac{3}{4}$$
$$-\frac{1}{2} = -\frac{2}{4}$$
$$\frac{1}{4}$$

14. $\frac{1}{2}$

$$\frac{2}{3} = \frac{4}{6}$$
$$-\frac{1}{6} = -\frac{1}{6}$$
$$\frac{3}{6} = \frac{3 \div 3}{6 \div 3} = \frac{1}{2}$$

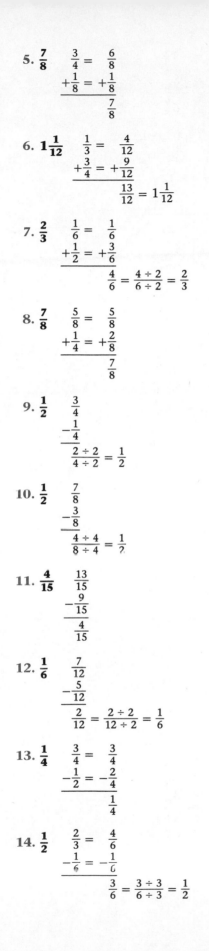

15. $\frac{1}{3}$

$$\frac{5}{6} = \frac{5}{6}$$
$$-\frac{1}{2} = -\frac{3}{6}$$
$$\frac{2}{6} = \frac{2 \div 2}{6 \div 2} = \frac{1}{3}$$

16. $\frac{7}{12}$

$$\frac{6}{9} = \frac{24}{36}$$
$$-\frac{1}{12} = -\frac{3}{36}$$
$$\frac{21}{36} = \frac{21 \div 3}{36 \div 3} = \frac{7}{12}$$

17. $\frac{11}{15}$

$$\frac{2}{5} = \frac{6}{15}$$
$$+\frac{1}{3} = +\frac{5}{15}$$
$$\frac{11}{15}$$

18. $\frac{5}{12}$

$$\frac{3}{4} = \frac{9}{12}$$
$$-\frac{1}{3} = -\frac{4}{12}$$
$$\frac{5}{12}$$

19. $\frac{2}{5}$

$$\frac{9}{10} = \frac{9}{10}$$
$$-\frac{1}{2} = -\frac{5}{10}$$
$$\frac{4}{10} = \frac{4 \div 2}{10 \div 2} = \frac{2}{5}$$

20. $\frac{9}{20}$

$$\frac{2}{8} = \frac{10}{40}$$
$$+\frac{1}{5} = +\frac{8}{40}$$
$$\frac{18}{40} = \frac{18 \div 2}{40 \div 2} = \frac{9}{20}$$

21. 1

$$\frac{1}{2} = \frac{5}{10}$$
$$\frac{3}{10} = \frac{3}{10}$$
$$+\frac{1}{5} = +\frac{2}{10}$$
$$\frac{10}{10} = 1$$

22. $\frac{3}{16}$

$$\frac{7}{16} = \frac{7}{16}$$
$$-\frac{1}{4} = -\frac{4}{16}$$
$$\frac{3}{16}$$

23. $1\frac{1}{24}$

$$\frac{5}{8} = \frac{15}{24}$$
$$\frac{1}{6} = \frac{4}{24}$$
$$+\frac{1}{4} = +\frac{6}{24}$$
$$\frac{25}{24} = 1\frac{1}{24}$$

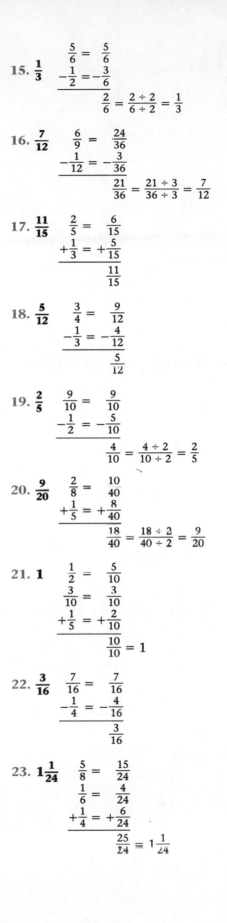

UNIT 1

24. $\dfrac{1}{12}$

$$\dfrac{5}{6} = \dfrac{10}{12}$$
$$-\dfrac{3}{4} = -\dfrac{9}{12}$$
$$\overline{\dfrac{1}{12}}$$

25. $1\dfrac{3}{8}$

$$\dfrac{1}{2} = \dfrac{4}{8}$$
$$\dfrac{5}{8} = \dfrac{5}{8}$$
$$+\dfrac{1}{4} = +\dfrac{2}{8}$$
$$\overline{\dfrac{11}{8} = 1\dfrac{3}{8}}$$

26. $\dfrac{5}{12}$ Add $\dfrac{1}{4}$ and $\dfrac{1}{6}$ to find the total fraction spent on rent and transportation.

$$\dfrac{1}{4} = \dfrac{3}{12}$$
$$+\dfrac{1}{6} = +\dfrac{2}{12}$$
$$\overline{\dfrac{5}{12}}$$

27. $\dfrac{3}{8}$ **yard** Subtract $\dfrac{3}{8}$ from $\dfrac{3}{4}$ to find the difference.

$$\dfrac{3}{4} = \dfrac{6}{8}$$
$$-\dfrac{3}{8} = -\dfrac{3}{8}$$
$$\overline{\dfrac{3}{8}}$$

28. $\dfrac{2}{9}$ **cubic yard** Subtract $\dfrac{4}{9}$ from $\dfrac{2}{3}$ to find out how many more cubic yards of concrete will be needed.

$$\dfrac{2}{3} = \dfrac{6}{9}$$
$$-\dfrac{4}{9} = -\dfrac{4}{9}$$
$$\overline{\dfrac{2}{9}}$$

29. $1\dfrac{1}{20}$ **miles** Add the fractions to find the total distance walked.

$$\dfrac{3}{10} = \dfrac{6}{20}$$
$$\dfrac{1}{2} = \dfrac{10}{20}$$
$$+\dfrac{1}{4} = +\dfrac{5}{20}$$
$$\overline{\dfrac{21}{20} = 1\dfrac{1}{20}}$$

GED Skill Focus (Page 91)

1. $8\dfrac{1}{12}$

$$3\dfrac{3}{4} = 3\dfrac{9}{12}$$
$$+4\dfrac{1}{3} = +4\dfrac{4}{12}$$
$$\overline{7\dfrac{13}{12}}$$

Simplify. $7\dfrac{13}{12} = 7 + 1\dfrac{1}{12} = 8\dfrac{1}{12}$

2. $7\dfrac{1}{8}$

$$1\dfrac{1}{2} = 1\dfrac{4}{8}$$
$$+5\dfrac{5}{8} = +5\dfrac{5}{8}$$
$$\overline{6\dfrac{9}{8}}$$

Simplify. $6\dfrac{9}{8} = 6 + 1\dfrac{1}{8} = 7\dfrac{1}{8}$

3. $21\dfrac{14}{15}$

$$12\dfrac{3}{5} = 12\dfrac{9}{15}$$
$$+ 9\dfrac{1}{3} = + 9\dfrac{5}{15}$$
$$\overline{21\dfrac{14}{15}}$$

4. $15\dfrac{13}{24}$

$$6\dfrac{7}{8} = 6\dfrac{21}{24}$$
$$+8\dfrac{2}{3} = +8\dfrac{16}{24}$$
$$\overline{14\dfrac{37}{24}}$$

Simplify. $14\dfrac{37}{24} = 14 + 1\dfrac{13}{24} = 15\dfrac{13}{24}$

5. $12\dfrac{1}{10}$

$$2\dfrac{3}{10} = 2\dfrac{3}{10}$$
$$+9\dfrac{4}{5} = +9\dfrac{8}{10}$$
$$\overline{11\dfrac{11}{10}}$$

Simplify. $11\dfrac{11}{10} = 11 + 1\dfrac{1}{10} = 12\dfrac{1}{10}$

6. $43\dfrac{7}{9}$

$$22\dfrac{1}{9} = 22\dfrac{1}{9}$$
$$+21\dfrac{2}{3} = +21\dfrac{6}{9}$$
$$\overline{43\dfrac{7}{9}}$$

7. $9\dfrac{1}{2}$

$$7\dfrac{3}{10} = 7\dfrac{3}{10}$$
$$+2\dfrac{1}{5} = +2\dfrac{2}{10}$$
$$\overline{9\dfrac{5}{10} = 9\dfrac{1}{2}}$$

8. $17\dfrac{14}{15}$

$$5\dfrac{3}{5} = 5\dfrac{9}{15}$$
$$+12\dfrac{1}{3} = +12\dfrac{5}{15}$$
$$\overline{17\dfrac{14}{15}}$$

9. $3\dfrac{1}{6}$

$$6\dfrac{1}{2} = 6\dfrac{3}{6}$$
$$-3\dfrac{1}{3} = -3\dfrac{2}{6}$$
$$\overline{3\dfrac{1}{6}}$$

10. $6\dfrac{7}{12}$

$$8\dfrac{5}{6} = 8\dfrac{10}{12}$$
$$-2\dfrac{1}{4} = -2\dfrac{3}{12}$$
$$\overline{6\dfrac{7}{12}}$$

11. $7\frac{17}{20}$

$$11\frac{1}{4} = 11\frac{5}{20} = 10\frac{25}{20}$$
$$-\;3\frac{2}{5} = -\;3\frac{8}{20} = -\;3\frac{8}{20}$$
$$\overline{\qquad\qquad\qquad\qquad\;\; 7\frac{17}{20}}$$

12. $4\frac{1}{12}$

$$16\frac{1}{4} = 16\frac{3}{12}$$
$$-12\frac{1}{6} = -12\frac{2}{12}$$
$$\overline{\qquad\qquad\quad 4\frac{1}{12}}$$

13. $11\frac{2}{3}$

$$20\frac{1}{3} = 19\frac{4}{3}$$
$$-\;8\frac{2}{3} = -\;8\frac{2}{3}$$
$$\overline{\qquad\qquad\quad 11\frac{2}{3}}$$

14. $1\frac{11}{12}$

$$5\frac{2}{3} = 5\frac{8}{12} = 4\frac{20}{12}$$
$$-3\frac{3}{4} = -3\frac{9}{12} = -3\frac{9}{12}$$
$$\overline{\qquad\qquad\qquad\qquad 1\frac{11}{12}}$$

15. $7\frac{16}{21}$

$$25\frac{1}{3} = 25\frac{7}{21} = 24\frac{28}{21}$$
$$-17\frac{4}{7} = -17\frac{12}{21} = -17\frac{12}{21}$$
$$\overline{\qquad\qquad\qquad\qquad\quad 7\frac{16}{21}}$$

16. $24\frac{7}{8}$

$$40\frac{3}{4} = 40\frac{6}{8} = 39\frac{14}{8}$$
$$15\frac{7}{8} = -15\frac{7}{8} = -15\frac{7}{8}$$
$$\overline{\qquad\qquad\qquad\qquad\; 24\frac{7}{8}}$$

17. $26\frac{1}{2}$ **gallons** Add the amounts of gasoline to find the total gallons for the month.

$$8\frac{1}{2} = 8\frac{5}{10}$$
$$9\frac{3}{10} = 9\frac{3}{10}$$
$$+8\frac{7}{10} = +8\frac{7}{10}$$
$$\overline{\qquad\qquad 25\frac{15}{10}}$$

Simplify. $25\frac{15}{10} = 25 + 1\frac{5}{10} = 26\frac{5}{10} = 26\frac{1}{2}$

18. $5\frac{1}{2}$ **days** Subtract $4\frac{1}{2}$ from 10 to find the number of vacation days Paul has left.

$$10 = 9\frac{2}{2}$$
$$-\;4\frac{1}{2} = -4\frac{1}{2}$$
$$\overline{\qquad\qquad 5\frac{1}{2}}$$

19. $1\frac{3}{4}$ **hours** Subtract to find the difference between the number of hours Maria planned to work and the number she has already worked.

$$3\frac{1}{2} = 3\frac{2}{4} = 2\frac{6}{4}$$
$$-1\frac{3}{4} = -1\frac{3}{4} = -1\frac{3}{4}$$
$$\overline{\qquad\qquad\qquad\qquad 1\frac{3}{4}}$$

20. $2\frac{7}{12}$ **feet** Subtract the length that Evan needs, $5\frac{3}{4}$ feet, from the current length of the post, $8\frac{1}{3}$ feet.

$$8\frac{1}{3} = 8\frac{4}{12} = 7\frac{16}{12}$$
$$-5\frac{3}{4} = -5\frac{9}{12} = -5\frac{9}{12}$$
$$\overline{\qquad\qquad\qquad\qquad 2\frac{7}{12}}$$

21. $2\frac{11}{12}$ **cups** Add the amounts of each kind of liquid to find the total liquid used in the recipe.

$$1\frac{2}{3} = 1\frac{8}{12}$$
$$\frac{1}{2} = \frac{6}{12}$$
$$+\frac{3}{4} = +\frac{9}{12}$$
$$\overline{\qquad\qquad 1\frac{23}{12}}$$

Simplify. $1\frac{23}{12} = 1 + 1\frac{11}{12} = 2\frac{11}{12}$

22. $4\frac{1}{4}$ **square yards** Subtract to find the difference between the estimate and the actual amount.

$$35 = 34\frac{4}{4}$$
$$-30\frac{3}{4} = -30\frac{3}{4}$$
$$\overline{\qquad\qquad 4\frac{1}{4}}$$

23. $9\frac{5}{8}$ **miles** Add the distances to find the total number of miles John walked.

$$2\frac{1}{2} = 2\frac{4}{8}$$
$$1\frac{3}{4} = 1\frac{6}{8}$$
$$2\frac{5}{8} = 2\frac{5}{8}$$
$$+2\frac{3}{4} = +2\frac{6}{8}$$
$$\overline{\qquad\qquad 7\frac{21}{8}}$$

Simplify. $7\frac{21}{8} = 7 + 2\frac{5}{8} = 9\frac{5}{8}$

24. **$3\frac{3}{4}$ hours** Subtract to find the difference between the number of hours Kyra can work, 20 hours, and the number she has already worked.

$$\begin{array}{rcl} 20 & = & 19\frac{4}{4} \\ -16\frac{1}{4} & = & -16\frac{1}{4} \\ \hline & & 3\frac{3}{4} \end{array}$$

GED Skill Focus (Page 93)

1. **$\frac{7}{10}$** $\frac{7}{\underset{2}{\cancel{8}}} \times \frac{\overset{1}{\cancel{4}}}{5} = \frac{7}{10}$

2. **$\frac{9}{28}$** $\frac{3}{4} \times \frac{3}{7} = \frac{9}{28}$

3. **$5\frac{1}{2}$**
$11 \times \frac{1}{2} = \frac{11}{1} \times \frac{1}{2} = \frac{11}{2} = 5\frac{1}{2}$

4. **$\frac{20}{27}$** $\frac{5}{\underset{3}{\cancel{6}}} \times \frac{\overset{4}{\cancel{8}}}{9} = \frac{20}{27}$

5. **$\frac{1}{20}$** $\frac{\overset{1}{\cancel{3}}}{\underset{4}{\cancel{8}}} \times \frac{\overset{1}{\cancel{2}}}{\underset{5}{\cancel{15}}} = \frac{1}{20}$

6. **48** $9 \times 5\frac{1}{3} = \frac{\overset{3}{\cancel{9}}}{1} \times \frac{16}{\underset{1}{\cancel{3}}} = 48$

7. **6** $2\frac{2}{5} \times 2\frac{1}{2} = \frac{\overset{6}{\cancel{12}}}{\underset{1}{\cancel{5}}} \times \frac{\overset{1}{\cancel{5}}}{\underset{1}{\cancel{2}}} = \frac{6}{1} = 6$

8. **$13\frac{3}{4}$** $3\frac{1}{3} \times 4\frac{1}{8} = \frac{\overset{5}{\cancel{10}}}{\underset{1}{\cancel{3}}} \times \frac{\overset{11}{\cancel{33}}}{\underset{4}{\cancel{8}}} =$
$\frac{55}{4} = 13\frac{3}{4}$

9. **$3\frac{3}{4}$**
$4\frac{1}{2} \times \frac{5}{6} = \frac{\overset{3}{\cancel{9}}}{2} \times \frac{5}{\underset{2}{\cancel{6}}} = \frac{15}{4} = 3\frac{3}{4}$

10. **$1\frac{1}{3}$** $\frac{4}{5} \times 1\frac{2}{3} = \frac{4}{\underset{1}{\cancel{5}}} \times \frac{\overset{1}{\cancel{5}}}{3} = \frac{4}{3} = 1\frac{1}{3}$

11. **$16\frac{1}{2}$**
$2\frac{3}{4} \times 6 = \frac{11}{\underset{2}{\cancel{4}}} \times \frac{\overset{3}{\cancel{6}}}{1} = \frac{33}{2} = 16\frac{1}{2}$

12. **$\frac{4}{5}$** $1\frac{2}{5} \times \frac{4}{7} = \frac{\overset{1}{\cancel{7}}}{5} \times \frac{4}{\underset{1}{\cancel{7}}} = \frac{4}{5}$

13. **$7\frac{1}{2}$**
$4 \times 1\frac{7}{8} = \frac{\overset{1}{\cancel{4}}}{1} \times \frac{15}{\underset{2}{\cancel{8}}} = \frac{15}{2} = 7\frac{1}{2}$

14. **7** $3\frac{1}{9} \times 2\frac{1}{4} = \frac{\overset{7}{\cancel{28}}}{\underset{1}{\cancel{9}}} \times \frac{\overset{1}{\cancel{9}}}{\underset{1}{\cancel{4}}} = \frac{7}{1} = 7$

15. **$5\frac{1}{3}$**
$24 \times \frac{2}{9} = \frac{\overset{8}{\cancel{24}}}{1} \times \frac{2}{\underset{3}{\cancel{9}}} = \frac{16}{3} = 5\frac{1}{3}$

16. **$27\frac{7}{8}$ pounds** Multiply to find $\frac{1}{2}$ of $55\frac{3}{4}$.
$55\frac{3}{4} \times \frac{1}{2} = \frac{223}{4} \times \frac{1}{2} =$
$\frac{223}{8} = 27\frac{7}{8}$

17. **$140\frac{5}{8}$ square feet** Multiply the dimensions of the room.
$11\frac{1}{4} \times 12\frac{1}{2} = \frac{45}{4} \times \frac{25}{2} =$
$\frac{1125}{8} = 140\frac{5}{8}$

18. **\$1,560** Multiply to find $\frac{1}{12}$ of \$18,720.
$18{,}720 \times \frac{1}{12} = \frac{18{,}720}{1} \times \frac{1}{12} =$
$\frac{18{,}720}{12} = \frac{1{,}560}{1} = 1{,}560$

19. **70 inches** Multiply $1\frac{3}{4}$ inches, the height of one tabletop, by 40, the number of tabletops in the stack.
$40 \times 1\frac{3}{4} = \frac{\overset{10}{\cancel{40}}}{1} \times \frac{7}{\underset{1}{\cancel{4}}} = \frac{70}{1} = 70$

20. **$\frac{7}{16}$** Multiply to find $\frac{1}{2}$ of $\frac{7}{8}$.
$\frac{7}{8} \times \frac{1}{2} = \frac{7}{16}$

GED Skill Focus (Page 95)

1. **$\frac{2}{5}$** $\frac{1}{3} \div \frac{5}{6} = \frac{1}{\underset{1}{\cancel{3}}} \times \frac{\overset{2}{\cancel{6}}}{5} = \frac{2}{5}$

2. **$1\frac{2}{3}$** $\frac{2}{3} \div \frac{2}{5} = \frac{\overset{1}{\cancel{2}}}{3} \times \frac{5}{\underset{1}{\cancel{2}}} = \frac{5}{3} = 1\frac{2}{3}$

3. **$\frac{7}{20}$** $\frac{7}{10} \div 2 = \frac{7}{10} \div \frac{2}{1} = \frac{7}{10} \times \frac{1}{2}$
$= \frac{7}{20}$

4. **4** $\frac{5}{6} \div \frac{5}{24} = \frac{\overset{1}{\cancel{5}}}{\underset{1}{\cancel{6}}} \times \frac{\overset{4}{\cancel{24}}}{\underset{1}{\cancel{5}}} = \frac{4}{1} = 4$

5. **$\frac{2}{7}$** $\frac{6}{7} \div 3 = \frac{6}{7} \div \frac{3}{1} = \frac{\overset{2}{\cancel{6}}}{7} \times \frac{1}{\underset{1}{\cancel{3}}} = \frac{2}{7}$

6. **$\frac{2}{3}$** $\frac{4}{9} \div \frac{2}{3} = \frac{\overset{2}{\cancel{4}}}{\underset{3}{\cancel{9}}} \times \frac{\overset{1}{\cancel{3}}}{\underset{1}{\cancel{2}}} = \frac{2}{3}$

7. **$3\frac{1}{2}$** $\frac{7}{8} \div \frac{1}{4} = \frac{7}{\underset{2}{\cancel{8}}} \times \frac{\overset{1}{\cancel{4}}}{1} = \frac{7}{2} = 3\frac{1}{2}$

8. **36** $4\frac{1}{2} \div \frac{1}{8} = \frac{9}{2} \div \frac{1}{8} =$
$\frac{9}{\underset{1}{\cancel{2}}} \times \frac{\overset{4}{\cancel{8}}}{1} = \frac{36}{1} = 36$

9. **8** $12 \div 1\frac{1}{2} = \frac{12}{1} \div \frac{3}{2} =$
$\frac{\overset{4}{\cancel{12}}}{1} \times \frac{2}{\underset{1}{\cancel{3}}} = \frac{8}{1} = 8$

10. **$2\frac{1}{4}$** $3\frac{3}{4} \div 1\frac{2}{3} = \frac{15}{4} \div \frac{5}{3} =$
$\frac{\overset{3}{\cancel{15}}}{4} \times \frac{3}{\underset{1}{\cancel{5}}} = \frac{9}{4} = 2\frac{1}{4}$

11. **26** $6\frac{1}{2} \div \frac{1}{4} = \frac{13}{2} \div \frac{1}{4} =$
$\frac{13}{\underset{1}{\cancel{2}}} \times \frac{\overset{2}{\cancel{4}}}{1} = \frac{26}{1} = 26$

12. **$1\frac{1}{2}$** $2\frac{1}{4} \div 1\frac{1}{2} = \frac{9}{4} \div \frac{3}{2} =$
$\frac{\overset{3}{\cancel{9}}}{\underset{2}{\cancel{4}}} \times \frac{\overset{1}{\cancel{2}}}{\underset{1}{\cancel{3}}} = \frac{3}{2} = 1\frac{1}{2}$

13. **27** $18 \div \frac{2}{3} = \frac{18}{1} \div \frac{2}{3} =$
$\frac{\overset{9}{\cancel{18}}}{1} \times \frac{3}{\underset{1}{\cancel{2}}} = \frac{27}{1} = 27$

14. **10** $2\frac{2}{5} \div \frac{6}{25} = \frac{12}{5} \div \frac{6}{25} =$
$\frac{\overset{2}{\cancel{12}}}{\underset{1}{\cancel{5}}} \times \frac{\overset{5}{\cancel{25}}}{\underset{1}{\cancel{6}}} = \frac{10}{1} = 10$

15. **$4\frac{1}{5}$** $4\frac{9}{10} \div 1\frac{1}{6} = \frac{49}{10} \div \frac{7}{6} =$
$\frac{\overset{7}{\cancel{49}}}{\underset{5}{\cancel{10}}} \times \frac{\overset{3}{\cancel{6}}}{\underset{1}{\cancel{7}}} = \frac{21}{5} = 4\frac{1}{5}$

16. **$3\frac{1}{3}$** $6\frac{1}{9} \div 1\frac{5}{6} = \frac{55}{9} \div \frac{11}{6} =$
$\frac{\overset{5}{\cancel{55}}}{\underset{3}{\cancel{9}}} \times \frac{\overset{2}{\cancel{6}}}{\underset{1}{\cancel{11}}} = \frac{10}{3} = 3\frac{1}{3}$

17. **8** $2\frac{2}{3} \div \frac{1}{3} = \frac{8}{\underset{1}{\cancel{3}}} \times \frac{\overset{1}{\cancel{3}}}{1} = \frac{8}{1} = 8$

18. **$3\frac{1}{5}$** $4 \div 1\frac{1}{4} = \frac{4}{1} \div \frac{5}{4} = \frac{4}{1} \times \frac{4}{5} =$
$\frac{16}{5} = 3\frac{1}{5}$

19. **$5\frac{19}{40}$** $9\frac{1}{8} \div 1\frac{2}{3} = \frac{73}{8} \div \frac{5}{3} =$
$\frac{73}{8} \times \frac{3}{5} = \frac{219}{40} = 5\frac{19}{40}$

20. **$8\frac{1}{3}$** $10 \div 1\frac{1}{5} = \frac{10}{1} \div \frac{6}{5} =$
$\frac{\overset{5}{\cancel{10}}}{1} \times \frac{5}{\underset{3}{\cancel{6}}} = \frac{25}{3} = 8\frac{1}{3}$

21. **35** $8\frac{3}{4} \div \frac{1}{4} = \frac{35}{4} \div \frac{1}{4} =$
$\frac{35}{\underset{1}{\cancel{4}}} \times \frac{\overset{1}{\cancel{4}}}{1} = \frac{35}{1} = 35$

22. **27** $12 \div \frac{4}{9} = \frac{12}{1} \div \frac{4}{9} =$
$\frac{\overset{3}{\cancel{12}}}{1} \times \frac{9}{\underset{1}{\cancel{4}}} = \frac{27}{1} = 27$

23. **20** $16 \div \frac{4}{5} = \frac{16}{1} \div \frac{4}{5} =$
$\frac{\overset{4}{\cancel{16}}}{1} \times \frac{5}{\underset{1}{\cancel{4}}} = \frac{20}{1} = 20$

24. $1\frac{9}{11}$ $4 \div 2\frac{1}{5} = \frac{4}{1} \div \frac{11}{5} = \frac{4}{1} \times \frac{5}{11} = \frac{20}{11} = 1\frac{9}{11}$

25. 16 pieces Divide the length of the board, 12 feet, by the length of the pieces, $\frac{3}{4}$ foot.

$$12 \div \frac{3}{4} = \frac{12}{1} \div \frac{3}{4} = \frac{\overset{4}{\cancel{12}}}{1} \times \frac{4}{\underset{1}{\cancel{3}}} = \frac{16}{1} = 16$$

26. 45 specials Divide the total number of pounds, 15, by the amount used in each special, $\frac{1}{3}$ pound.

$$15 \div \frac{1}{3} = \frac{15}{1} \div \frac{1}{3} = \frac{15}{1} \times \frac{3}{1} = \frac{45}{1} = 45$$

27. 32 books Divide the height of the stack, 24 inches, by the thickness of one book, $\frac{3}{4}$ inch.

$$24 \div \frac{3}{4} = \frac{24}{1} \div \frac{3}{4} = \frac{\overset{8}{\cancel{24}}}{1} \times \frac{4}{\underset{1}{\cancel{3}}} = \frac{32}{1} = 32$$

28. 10 bicycles Divide the number of hours, 25, by the time it takes Carina to build one bicycle, $2\frac{1}{2}$ hours.

$$25 \div 2\frac{1}{2} = \frac{25}{1} \div \frac{5}{2} = \frac{\overset{5}{\cancel{25}}}{1} \times \frac{2}{\underset{1}{\cancel{5}}} = \frac{10}{1} = 10$$

29. 8 batches Divide the amount of sugar on hand, 10 cups, by the amount needed for 1 batch, $1\frac{1}{4}$ cups.

$$10 \div 1\frac{1}{4} = \frac{10}{1} \div \frac{5}{4} = \frac{\overset{2}{\cancel{10}}}{1} \times \frac{4}{\underset{1}{\cancel{5}}} = \frac{8}{1} = 8$$

GED Practice (Page 97)

1. (3) 30 Round the amounts. $14\frac{1}{3}$ rounds to 14

$6\frac{3}{4}$ rounds to 7

$9\frac{1}{4}$ rounds to 9

Add the rounded amounts. $14 + 7 + 9 = 30$

2. (4) 78 Round the amounts. $9\frac{5}{8}$ rounds to 10

$27\frac{1}{4}$ rounds to 27

$4\frac{2}{3}$ rounds to 5

$36\frac{3}{8}$ rounds to 36

Add the rounded amounts.
$10 + 27 + 5 + 36 = 78$

3. (2) 22 Round the amounts. $10\frac{2}{5}$ rounds to 10

$12\frac{1}{6}$ rounds to 12

Add the rounded amounts. $10 + 12 = 22$

4. (1) 2 Round the amounts.
peanuts in Mix B: $4\frac{1}{5}$ rounds to 4

peanuts in Mix A: $2\frac{3}{0}$ rounds to 2
Subtract the amounts. $4 - 2 = 2$

5. (4) 5 Round the amounts.
cashews: $2\frac{2}{3}$ rounds to 3
Brazil nuts: $2\frac{1}{8}$ rounds to 2
Add the rounded amounts. $3 + 2 = 5$

6. (4) 4 Round the amounts in Mix A.

$2\frac{2}{3}$ rounds to 3

$2\frac{3}{8}$ rounds to 2

$3\frac{1}{2}$ rounds to 4

$2\frac{1}{8}$ rounds to 2

Add the rounded amounts. $3 + 2 + 4 + 2 = 11$
Round the amounts in Mix B.

$6\frac{1}{2}$ rounds to 7

$3\frac{7}{8}$ rounds to 4

$4\frac{1}{5}$ rounds to 4

Add the rounded amounts. $7 + 4 + 4 = 15$
Subtract to find the difference. $15 - 11 = 4$

GED Practice (Page 99)

1. $\frac{9}{8}$

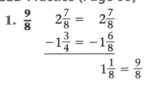

$2\frac{7}{8} = 2\frac{7}{8}$
$-1\frac{3}{4} = -1\frac{6}{8}$
$\phantom{-1\frac{3}{4} =} 1\frac{1}{8} = \frac{9}{8}$

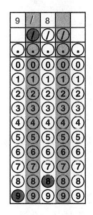

2. $\frac{11}{12}$ $2\frac{3}{4} \div 3 = \frac{11}{4} \div \frac{3}{1} = \frac{11}{4} \times \frac{1}{3} = \frac{11}{12}$

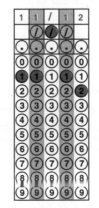

3. $\frac{4}{3}$ If Rachel uses $\frac{2}{3}$ of the flour, $\frac{1}{3}$ is left. Find $\frac{1}{3}$ of 4 cups. $\frac{1}{3} \times 4 = \frac{1}{3} \times \frac{4}{1} = \frac{4}{3}$

4. $\frac{27}{4}$ Set up a proportion and solve.

$$\frac{\text{inches}}{\text{miles}} \quad \frac{\frac{1}{3}}{3} \quad \frac{\frac{3}{4}}{x}$$

$$\left(3 \times \frac{3}{4}\right) \div \frac{1}{3} = \left(\frac{3}{1} \times \frac{3}{4}\right) \times \frac{3}{1} = \frac{9}{4} \times \frac{3}{1} = \frac{27}{4}$$

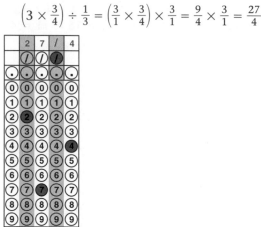

GED Mini-Test • Lessons 5–7
(Pages 100–103)

Part 1

1. **(3)** $\frac{1}{480}$ Form a fraction with 50 in the numerator and 24,000 in the denominator. $\frac{50}{24,000}$ Reduce the fraction to lowest terms by dividing the numerator and denominator by the common divisor, 50.

2. **(1) 472** Set up a proportion using the ratio of the number of miles driven to the number of gallons of gasoline used. Solve for the unknown number of miles. $\frac{354}{15} = \frac{?}{20}$

   $354 \times 20 \div 15 = 7080 \div 15 = 472$

3. **(4)** $9\frac{5}{8}$ Rewrite the fractions with a common denominator and add the mixed numbers. $7\frac{3}{4} + 1\frac{7}{8} = 7\frac{6}{8} + 1\frac{7}{8} = 8\frac{13}{8} = 9\frac{5}{8}$

4. **(1)** $\frac{2}{5}$ **mile** The trip from Ramon's to Joe's to work is $\frac{3}{5}$ mile $+ \frac{4}{5}$ mile $= 1\frac{2}{5}$ miles. The direct route is 1 mile and the difference is $\frac{2}{5}$ mile.

5. **(2) 74 × 60 × 7** This expression shows 74 words multiplied by 60 minutes (1 hour) multiplied by 7 hours.

6. **(2) 812** Divide the total volume of the tank by the volume of each container. $5,075 \div 6\frac{1}{4} = \frac{5,075}{1} \times \frac{4}{25} = 812$

7. **(3) 5280 × $\frac{1}{4}$** This expression shows multiplying to find "$\frac{1}{4}$ of" a mile.

8. **(3) $2,000** Round $39,000 to $40,000, and then multiply. $40,000 \times \frac{1}{20} = \$2,000$

9. **(3)** $14\frac{4}{15}$ Rewrite the fractions with a common denominator and add the mixed numbers. $7\frac{2}{3} + 6\frac{3}{5} = 7\frac{10}{15} + 6\frac{9}{15} = 13\frac{19}{15} = 14\frac{4}{15}$

10. **(3)** $6\frac{1}{4}$ Set up a proportion using the ratio of the number of inches on the map to the actual number of feet on the highway. Solve for the unknown number of inches on the map.

    $$\frac{2\frac{1}{2}}{2200} = \frac{?}{5500}$$

    $2\frac{1}{2} \times 5500 \div 2200 = \frac{5}{2} \times 5500 \div 2200 =$

    $13,750 \div 2,200 = 6\frac{1}{4}$

11. **(5) Central** Change all of the fractions to like fractions.

    Northeast: $\frac{1}{8} = \frac{5}{40}$

    Southeast: $\frac{1}{4} = \frac{10}{40}$

    Northwest: $\frac{1}{8} = \frac{5}{40}$

    Southwest: $\frac{1}{5} = \frac{8}{40}$

    Central: $\frac{3}{10} = \frac{12}{40}$

    The fraction $\frac{3}{10}$ is the largest.

12. **(1)** $\frac{1}{20}$ Add the fractions of profit from the Northeast and Northwest regions, and then subtract the fraction from the Southwest region. $\frac{5}{40} + \frac{5}{40} - \frac{8}{40} = \frac{10}{40} - \frac{8}{40} = \frac{2}{40} = \frac{1}{20}$

13. **(2) $397,573** Multiply the total company profit by the fraction that came from the Southwest region. $\$1,987,865 \times \frac{1}{5} = \$397,573$

Part 2

14. **(2)** $\frac{1}{8}$ Form a fraction with 4 as the numerator and 32 as the denominator. $\frac{4}{32}$ Reduce the fraction to lowest terms by dividing the numerator and denominator by 4.

15. **(2) $3\frac{1}{8} - 2\frac{4}{5}$** Subtract the number of hours of the flight from New York City to Chicago $\left(2\frac{4}{5}\right)$ from the number of hours of the return flight $\left(3\frac{1}{8}\right)$.

16. **(4) $14\frac{13}{16}$** You need to subtract.

$$
\begin{array}{r}
18\tfrac{1}{4} = 18\tfrac{4}{16} = 17\tfrac{20}{16} \\
- 3\tfrac{7}{16} = -3\tfrac{7}{16} = -3\tfrac{7}{16} \\
\hline
14\tfrac{13}{16}
\end{array}
$$

17. **(1) 3** Round the mixed numbers to the nearest whole number. $6\frac{1}{3}$ rounds to 6, and $2\frac{7}{8}$ rounds to 3. Subtract. $6 - 3 = 3$

18. **(3) $2\frac{1}{2} \times 5\frac{1}{2}$** Multiply the number of inches per week by the number of weeks.

19. **(5) Not enough information is given.** You don't know how much Kim earns per hour.

20. **(2) 15 $6\frac{1}{4}$** This expression shows 15 total days minus $6\frac{1}{4}$ days.

21. **(4) $\frac{1}{4}$** Since 75 out of 100 renters do not carry renter's insurance, 25 do $(100 - 75)$. So the ratio is $\frac{25}{100}$, which reduces to $\frac{1}{4}$.

22. **(5) 36** Divide the total amount of gravy by the amount used per serving.
$12 \div \frac{1}{3} = \frac{12}{1} \times \frac{3}{1} = \frac{36}{1} = 36$

23. **(2) 4** Multiply the fraction of a mile jogged per minute by the total number of minutes.
$\frac{2}{15} \times 30 = \frac{2}{15} \times \frac{30}{1} = 4$

24. **(1) $6\frac{3}{4}$** Set up a proportion using the ratio of the number of inches on the map to the number of miles. Solve for the unknown number of miles.

$$\frac{\frac{3}{4}}{5} = \frac{?}{45}$$

$$\frac{3}{4} \times 45 \div 5 = \frac{3}{4} \times \frac{45}{1} \div \frac{5}{1} =$$

$$\frac{3}{4} \times \frac{\overset{9}{\cancel{45}}}{1} \times \frac{1}{\underset{1}{\cancel{5}}} = \frac{27}{4} = 6\frac{3}{4}$$

25. **(1) Rent** To compare the fractions, convert them to like fractions.

Rent:	$\frac{3}{8}$	$= \frac{15}{40}$
Salaries:	$\frac{1}{4}$	$= \frac{10}{40}$
Advertising:	$\frac{1}{5}$	$= \frac{8}{40}$
Supplies:	$\frac{1}{8}$	$= \frac{5}{40}$
Miscellaneous:	$\frac{1}{20}$	$= \frac{2}{40}$

The fraction $\frac{3}{8}$ is the largest of the fractions.

26. **(3) $6,000** Add the fractions for Salaries and Supplies, and multiply the result by the total amount of the budget for March.

$$\left(\frac{1}{4} + \frac{1}{8}\right) \times \$16,000 =$$

$$\left(\frac{10}{40} + \frac{5}{40}\right) \times \$16,000 =$$

$$\frac{15}{40} \times \$16,000 =$$

$$\frac{3}{8} \times \$16,000 = \$6,000$$

Lesson 8
GED Skill Focus (Page 105)

1. **five thousandths** The 5 is in the thousandths place.

2. **eight tenths** The 8 is in the tenths place.

3. **seven hundredths** The 7 is in the hundredths place.

4. **nine ten-thousandths** The 9 is in the ten-thousandths place.

5. **one tenth** The 1 is in the tenths place.

6. **nine hundredths** The 9 is in the hundredths place.

7. **c. one and thirty-five hundredths**

8. **b. one and thirty-five thousandths**

9. **a. one and three hundred five thousandths**

10. **d. one and three hundred five ten-thousandths**

11. **d. one and two tenths**

12. **a. twelve hundredths**

13. **c. twelve ten-thousandths**

14. **b. twelve thousandths**

15. **five and twenty-five hundredths**

16. **six and eight thousandths**

17. **thirty-seven hundredths**

18. **one and one hundredth**

19. **two and five thousandths**

20. **four and five hundredths**

21. **three and nine tenths**

22. **eight hundredths**

23. **three and four thousandths**

24. **twelve and six tenths**

GED Skill Focus (Page 107)

1. **3.6** The number to the right of the tenths place is 5 or more. 3.5719 Add 1 to the tenths place and drop the remaining digits to the right.

2. **5.13** The number to the right of the hundredths place is less than 5. 5.13̲2 Drop the remaining digit to the right.

3. **1** The number to the right of the ones place is 5 or more. 0.5̲43 Add 1 to the ones place and drop the remaining digits to the right.

4. **7.1** The number to the right of the tenths place is 5 or more. 7.0̲813 Add 1 to the tenths place and drop the remaining digits to the right.

5. **1.070** or **1.07** The number to the right of the thousandths place is 5 or more. 1.069̲9 Add 1 to the thousandths place. This affects the hundredths place. (69 + 1 = 70). Drop the remaining digits.

6. **0.32 > 0.3109** Add zeros, then compare. Since 3200 is greater than 3109, then 0.3200 > 0.3109.

7. **0.98 < 1.9** The first number, 0.98, does not have a whole number part; the second number, 1.9, has a whole number part of 1, so it is greater.

8. **0.5 = 0.50** The 0 after the 5 in 0.50 does not change the value of the number. Both have the same value: five tenths.

9. **0.006 < 0.06** Add zero to the second number. 0.060 The first number, 0.006, is less because 6 is less than 60.

10. **1.075 < 1.57** Both have the same whole number part. Add a zero to the second number. 1.570 The first number, 1.075, is smaller because 75 is less than 570.

11. **0.18 > 0.108** Add a zero to the first number. 0.180 The first number, 0.18, is greater because 180 is greater than 108.

12. **2.38 < 2.83** Both have the same whole number part. The first number is less because 38 is less than 83.

13. **3.60 = 3.600** Both have the same whole number part. The zeros after the 6 in both numbers do not change the value. Both have the same value.

14. Transistor A.   0.3619 rounds to **0.4 g**
    Transistor B.   0.7082 rounds to **0.7 g**
    Transistor C.   0.0561 rounds to **0.1 g**
    Transistor D.   0.9357 rounds to **0.9 g**

15. **4, 1, 3, 2** Only the weight of Package #4 has a whole number part, so it must be the greatest. To compare the remaining packages, list the weights in a column, aligning the decimal points. Add a zero to the weight of Package #1 so that all decimals have the same number of places and compare. Package #1: 0.50; Package #2: 0.05; Package #3: 0.15 From greatest to least, the weights are 0.50, 0.15, and 0.05, because 50 is greater than 15, which is greater than 5.

16. **It weighs more.** Compare 0.55 and 0.50. The decimal 0.55 is greater than 0.5 because 55 is greater than 50.

GED Practice (Page 109)

1. **(4) between $25 and $35** Estimate the cost of the three games on sale:

	Sale Price	Estimate
Fast Pitch	$8.99	$9
Crown of Power	10.09	10
Dugout Derby	12.78	13
Total estimate		32

2. **(5) Par 4** Estimate the sale price of Dugout Derby. $12.78 rounds to $13. Subtract the estimate from the amount Ana has to spend. $20 − $13 = $7 Since Ana would have about $7 left to spend, Par 4 is the only game she can afford.

3. **(2) $8** Different approaches can be used to solve this problem. Estimate the difference between the regular and sale prices:

	Actual	Rounded
Dugout Derby	$17.25 − $12.78	$17 − $13 = $4
Crown of Power	$13.72 − $10.09	$14 − $10 = $4
		$8

4. **(4) $48** Estimate the cost of one smoke detector. $12.39 rounds to $12. Multiply the estimate by 4. $12 × 4 = $48

5. **(1) $3** Estimate the cost of the carton of nails. $17.85 rounds to $18. Divide by 6 to find the estimated cost per box. $18 ÷ 6 = $3

6. **(5) $700** Estimate the amount deducted for health insurance per paycheck. $27.50 rounds to $30 Since the amount is deducted twice a month, multiply the estimate by 2 to find the monthly deduction. 2 × $30 = $60 Multiply by 12 to find the estimated yearly amount. $60 × 12 = $720 The best estimate listed in the choices is $700.

GED Skill Focus (Page 111)

The number lines below show sample answers. Note that since the number line between 0 and 1 is divided into 10 equal spaces, each hash mark on the number line represents an increase of 0.1.

1. **0.5** $\frac{5}{10} = \frac{1}{2} = 0.5$

2. **0.55** Five-tenths = .5; six-tenths = .6 Halfway between 0.50 and 0.60 is 0.55

3. 0.8 0.825 rounds to 0.8

4. 0.25 0.245 rounds to 0.25

5. 1.3 One and three-tenths = $1\frac{3}{10}$ = 1.3

6. 1.6 1.625 rounds to 1.6

7. 1.3 $1\frac{1}{4}$ = 1.25 rounds to 1.3

8. 1.0 1.025 rounds to 1.0

Lesson 9
GED Skill Focus (Page 113)

1. 2.63

```
  0.03
+2.60
 2.63
```

2. 5.4
```
    1
  1.35
+4.05
 5.40
```

3. 5.547
```
   9 10
  8 10
6.9000
-1.353
 5.547
```

4. 2.925
```
 4 10
5.075
-2.150
 2.925
```

5. 15.103
```
 7.100
+8.003
15.103
```

6. 4.175
```
      9 10
    2 10
10.3000
- 6.125
  4.175
```

7. 4.81
```
  3.61
+1.20
 4.81
```

8. 11.78
```
    9 15
  5 10
16.05
- 4.27
 11.78
```

9. 82.887
```
  1.850
 10.030
 19.007
+62.000
 82.887
```

10. 44.155
```
  1 1  1
 12.400
 11.080
 16.100
+ 4.575
 44.155
```

11. 9,032
```
     9 10
   13 10
16,004.1
- 6,972.1
  9,032.0
```

12. 2.794
```
   9 10
 7 10
3.800
-1.006
 2.794
```

13. 2.947
```
  11 18
    6 10
12.870
- 9.923
  2.947
```

14. 17.105
```
 1 12 10
     6 10
23.070
- 5.965
 17.105
```

15. 22.668
```
     1
 14.010
  8.600
+ 0.058
 22.668
```

16. 31.85
```
  5 17
  7 10
56.80
-24.95
 31.85
```

17. 6.701

18. 0.2593

19. 10.316

20. 23.35

21. 5.295

22. 12.75

GED Skill Focus (Page 115)

1. 3.40 or 3.4 8.5 × 0.4 = 3.40 There are 2 decimal places in the problem. Once the decimal point is placed, you can drop the zero in the hundredths place.

2. 0.024 0.04 × 0.6 = 0.024 There are 3 decimal places in the problem. You need to write a zero in the tenths place as a placeholder.

3. 0.0112 5.6 × 0.002 = 0.0112 There are 4 decimal places in the problem. You need to write a zero in the tenths place as a placeholder.

4. 36.72 12 × 3.06 = 36.72 There are 2 decimal places in the problem.

5. 310.17 21.1 × 14.7 = 310.17 There are 2 decimal places in the problem.

6. 0.096 0.008 × 12 = 0.096 There are 3 decimal places in the problem. You need to write a zero in the tenths place as a placeholder.

7. 12.84
```
  1.07
×  12        There are 2 decimal places
 214         in the problem.
1070
12.84
```

8. 0.549
```
 0.09
× 6.1        There are 3 decimal places
 009         in the problem.
 540
0.549
```

9. 2.56
```
      2.56
  8)20.48
      16
       4 4
       4 0
         48
         48
```

10. 1.0972
```
       1.0972
  3)3.2916
     3
     2
     0
     29
     27
      21
      21
       06
        6
```

UNIT 1

11. 4.086

$$
\begin{array}{r}
2.27 \\
\times\ 1.8 \\
\hline
1\,816 \\
2\,270 \\
\hline
4.086
\end{array}
$$
There are 3 decimal places in the problem.

12. 75.6

$$
\begin{array}{r}
5.04 \\
\times\ 15 \\
\hline
25\,20 \\
50\,40 \\
\hline
75.60
\end{array}
$$
There are 2 decimal places in the problem.

13. 2.14

$$
\begin{array}{r}
2.14 \\
3.6.)\overline{7.7.04} \\
7\,2 \\
\hline
5\,0 \\
3\,6 \\
\hline
1\,44 \\
1\,44
\end{array}
$$

14. 6.094

$$
\begin{array}{r}
6.094 \\
1.05.)\overline{6.39.870} \\
6\,30 \\
\hline
9\,8 \\
0 \\
\hline
9\,87 \\
9\,45 \\
\hline
420 \\
420
\end{array}
$$

15. 0.02

$$
\begin{array}{r}
0.008 \\
\times\ 2.5 \\
\hline
0040 \\
0\,0160 \\
\hline
0.0200
\end{array}
$$
There are 4 decimal places in the problem.

16. 0.1155

$$
\begin{array}{r}
1.05 \\
\times 0.11 \\
\hline
105 \\
1050 \\
00000 \\
\hline
0.1155
\end{array}
$$
There are 4 decimal places in the problem.

17. 0.0035

$$
\begin{array}{r}
0.0035 \\
6)\overline{0.0210} \\
18 \\
\hline
30 \\
30
\end{array}
$$

18. 62

$$
\begin{array}{r}
62. \\
0.07.)\overline{4.34.} \\
4\,2 \\
\hline
14 \\
14
\end{array}
$$

19. 0.14 0.144 rounds to 0.14

20. 0.29 0.285 rounds to 0.29

21. 0.21 0.2145 rounds to 0.21

22. 0.27 0.272 rounds to 0.27

23. 18.38 18.375 rounds to 18.38

24. 0.83 0.8333 rounds to 0.83

GED Practice (Page 117)

1. **(2) $35 − ($12.98 + $10.67 + $5.98)** You need to add the prices for the three items together and then subtract the total from $35. The parentheses around the three prices in option (2) tell you to do that step first, then subtract.

2. **(1) $3.00** Carry out the operations:
$35 − ($12.98 + $10.67 + $5.98 + $2.37) =
$35 − $32.00   = $3.00

3. **(1) 25 ($1.05 − $0.89)** One way to work the problem is to find the difference between the two prices for one recordable CD. Then multiply the difference by 25 to find the total savings. (You can also get the same answer by multiplying each price by 25 and finding the difference [25($1.05) − 25($0.89)], but this is not one of the answer options.)

4. **(3) 2($45.79) + $18.25** Multiply the cost of one tire by 2 and add the amount for the oil change.

5. **(2) $8.42** Find the difference between the cost of one tire at each place, then multiply by 2, the number of tires. $50 − $45.79 = $4.21
$4.21 × 2 = $8.42

6. **(5) $202** Subtract to find the annual increase. Divide the annual increase by 12, the number of months in a year.
$21,000 − $18,575 = $2,425
$2,425 ÷ 12 = $202.083, which rounds to $202.

GED Practice (Page 119)

1. **15.75** Add to find the total miles.
4.5 + 5.25 + 6 = 15.75

Answers and Explanations

2. 0.065 Subtract to find the difference.
.340 − .275 = .065

3. 50 Divide to find the number of equally sized pieces.
60 ÷ 1.2 = 50

4. $41.86 Multiply the number of parts by the cost per part.
$2.99 × 14 = $41.86

Lesson 10
GED Skill Focus (Page 121)

1. $\frac{1}{4}$ Write 25 over 100 and reduce to lowest terms.
$$\frac{25 \div 25 = 1}{100 \div 25 = 4}$$

2. $\frac{2}{5}$ Write 4 over 10 and reduce to lowest terms.
$$\frac{4 \div 2 = 2}{10 \div 2 = 5}$$

3. $\frac{7}{20}$ Write 35 over 100 and reduce to lowest terms.
$$\frac{35 \div 5 = 7}{100 \div 5 = 20}$$

4. $\frac{7}{8}$ Write 875 over 1000 and reduce to lowest terms.
$$\frac{875 \div 125 = 7}{1000 \div 125 = 8}$$

5. $\frac{4}{5}$ Write 8 over 10 and reduce to lowest terms.
$$\frac{8 \div 2 = 4}{10 \div 2 = 5}$$

6. $\frac{19}{25}$ Write 76 over 100 and reduce to lowest terms.
$$\frac{76 \div 4 = 19}{100 \div 4 = 25}$$

7. $\frac{16}{125}$ Write 128 over 1000 and reduce to lowest terms.
$$\frac{128 \div 8 = 16}{1000 \div 8 = 125}$$

8. $\frac{1}{20}$ Write 5 over 100 and reduce to lowest terms.
$$\frac{5 \div 5 = 1}{100 \div 5 = 20}$$

9. $\frac{5}{16}$ $\dfrac{31\frac{1}{4}}{100} = 31\frac{1}{4} \div 100 = \dfrac{\overset{5}{\cancel{125}}}{4} \times \dfrac{1}{\underset{4}{\cancel{100}}} = \dfrac{5}{16}$

10. $\frac{1}{12}$ $\dfrac{8\frac{1}{3}}{100} = 8\frac{1}{3} \div 100 = \dfrac{\overset{1}{\cancel{25}}}{3} \times \dfrac{1}{\underset{4}{\cancel{100}}} = \dfrac{1}{12}$

11. $\frac{7}{15}$ $\dfrac{46\frac{2}{3}}{100} = 46\frac{2}{3} \div 100 = \dfrac{\overset{7}{\cancel{140}}}{3} \times \dfrac{1}{\underset{5}{\cancel{100}}} = \dfrac{7}{15}$

12. $\frac{15}{16}$ $\dfrac{93\frac{3}{4}}{100} = 93\frac{3}{4} \div 100 = \dfrac{\overset{15}{\cancel{375}}}{4} \times \dfrac{1}{\underset{4}{\cancel{100}}} = \dfrac{15}{16}$

13. $\frac{4}{15}$ $\dfrac{26\frac{2}{3}}{100} = 26\frac{2}{3} \div 100 = \dfrac{\overset{4}{\cancel{80}}}{3} \times \dfrac{1}{\underset{5}{\cancel{100}}} = \dfrac{4}{15}$

14. $\frac{1}{15}$ $\dfrac{6\frac{2}{3}}{100} = 6\frac{2}{3} \div 100 = \dfrac{\overset{1}{\cancel{20}}}{3} \times \dfrac{1}{\underset{5}{\cancel{100}}} = \dfrac{1}{15}$

15. $\frac{19}{80}$ $\dfrac{23\frac{3}{4}}{100} = 23\frac{3}{4} \div 100 = \dfrac{\overset{19}{\cancel{95}}}{4} \times \dfrac{1}{\underset{20}{\cancel{100}}} = \dfrac{19}{80}$

16. $\frac{49}{600}$ $\dfrac{8\frac{1}{6}}{100} = 8\frac{1}{6} \div 100 = \dfrac{49}{6} \times \dfrac{1}{100} = \dfrac{49}{600}$

17. $\frac{13}{120}$ $\dfrac{10\frac{5}{6}}{100} = 10\frac{5}{6} \div 100 = \dfrac{\overset{13}{\cancel{65}}}{6} \times \dfrac{1}{\underset{20}{\cancel{100}}} = \dfrac{13}{120}$

18. $\frac{51}{400}$ $\dfrac{12\frac{3}{4}}{100} = 12\frac{3}{4} \div 100 = \dfrac{51}{4} \times \dfrac{1}{100} = \dfrac{51}{400}$

19. $\frac{9}{10}$ Write 9 over the 10. The fraction is reduced to lowest terms.

20. $\frac{5}{8}$ Write 625 over 1000 and reduce to lowest terms.
$$\frac{625 \div 125}{1000 \div 125} = \frac{5}{8}$$

21. $\frac{7}{25}$ Write 28 over 100 and reduce to lowest terms.

$$\frac{28 \div 4}{100 \div 4} = \frac{7}{25}$$

22. $\frac{1}{8}$ Write 125 over 1000 and reduce to lowest terms.

$$\frac{125 \div 125}{1000 \div 125} = \frac{1}{8}$$

23. $\frac{11}{20}$ Write 55 over 100 and reduce to lowest terms.

$$\frac{55 \div 5}{100 \div 5} = \frac{11}{20}$$

24. $\frac{5}{16}$ Write 3,125 over 10,000 and reduce to lowest terms.

$$\frac{3,125 \div 625}{10,000 \div 625} = \frac{5}{16}$$

25. $\frac{7}{16}$ $43\frac{3}{4} \div 100 = \frac{175}{4} \div \frac{100}{1} = \frac{\overset{7}{\cancel{175}}}{4} \times \frac{1}{\underset{4}{\cancel{100}}} = \frac{7}{16}$

26. $\frac{1}{6}$ $16\frac{2}{3} \div 100 = \frac{50}{3} \div \frac{100}{1} = \frac{\overset{1}{\cancel{50}}}{3} \times \frac{1}{\underset{2}{\cancel{100}}} = \frac{1}{6}$

27. $\frac{3}{8}$ $37\frac{1}{2} \div 100 = \frac{75}{2} \div \frac{100}{1} = \frac{\overset{3}{\cancel{75}}}{2} \times \frac{1}{\underset{4}{\cancel{100}}} = \frac{3}{8}$

28. $\frac{1}{40}$ $2\frac{1}{2} \div 100 = \frac{5}{2} \div \frac{100}{1} = \frac{\overset{1}{\cancel{5}}}{2} \times \frac{1}{\underset{20}{\cancel{100}}} = \frac{1}{40}$

GED Skill Focus (Page 123)

1. **0.8** Divide 4 by 5.

```
   0.8
5)4.0
   4 0
```

2. **0.375** Divide 3 by 8.

```
   0.375
8)3.000
   2 4
    60
    56
    40
    40
```

3. **0.667** Divide 2 by 3. Divide to four decimal places and round to the thousandths place.

```
   0.6666
3)2.0000
   1 8
    20
    18
    20
    18
    20
```

4. **0.417** Divide 5 by 12 to four decimal places and round to the thousandths place.

```
    0.4166
12)5.0000
    4 8
     20
     12
     80
     72
     80
```

5. **0.55** Divide 11 by 20.

```
    0.55
20)11.00
    10 0
     1 00
     1 00
```

6. **0.625** Divide 5 by 8.

```
   0.625
8)5.000
   4 8
    20
    16
    40
    40
```

7. **0.425** Divide 17 by 40.

```
    0.425
40)17.000
    16 0
     1 00
       80
      200
      200
```

8. **0.75** Divide 3 by 4.

```
   0.75
4)3.00
   2 8
    20
    20
```

9. **0.6** Divide 3 by 5.

```
   0.6
5)3.0
   3 0
```

10. **0.28** Divide 7 by 25.

```
    0.28
25)7.00
    5 0
    2 00
    2 00
```

11. **0.7** Divide 7 by 10.

```
    0.7
10)7.0
    7 0
```

12. 0.125 Divide 1 by 8.

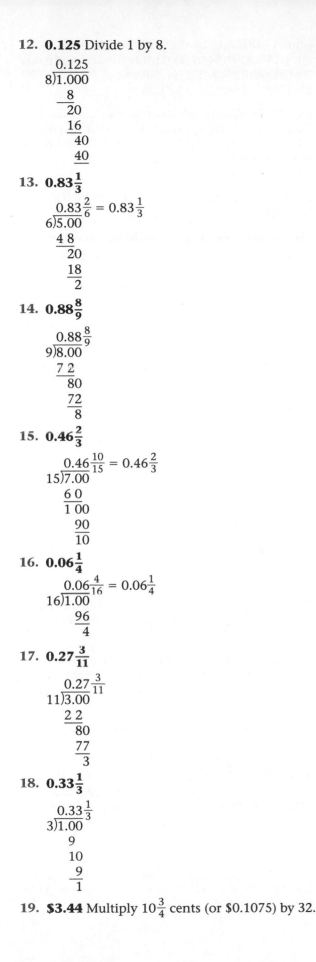

$$8\overline{)1.000}$$
$$\underline{8}$$
$$20$$
$$\underline{16}$$
$$40$$
$$\underline{40}$$

13. $0.83\frac{1}{3}$

$6\overline{)5.00}$ $0.83\frac{2}{6} = 0.83\frac{1}{3}$
$\underline{4\,8}$
20
$\underline{18}$
2

14. $0.88\frac{8}{9}$

$9\overline{)8.00}$ $0.88\frac{8}{9}$
$\underline{7\,2}$
80
$\underline{72}$
8

15. $0.46\frac{2}{3}$

$15\overline{)7.00}$ $0.46\frac{10}{15} = 0.46\frac{2}{3}$
$\underline{6\,0}$
$1\,00$
$\underline{90}$
10

16. $0.06\frac{1}{4}$

$16\overline{)1.00}$ $0.06\frac{4}{16} = 0.06\frac{1}{4}$
$\underline{96}$
4

17. $0.27\frac{3}{11}$

$11\overline{)3.00}$ $0.27\frac{3}{11}$
$\underline{2\,2}$
80
$\underline{77}$
3

18. $0.33\frac{1}{3}$

$3\overline{)1.00}$ $0.33\frac{1}{3}$
$\underline{9}$
10
$\underline{9}$
1

19. $3.44 Multiply $10\frac{3}{4}$ cents (or $0.1075) by 32.

20. $0.23\frac{1}{2}$ Divide $4.23 by 18 to two decimal places and write the remainder as a fraction.

21. Brand B Find the unit price for both brands by dividing the price by the number of yards. Convert to like fractions.

Brand A: $2.70 ÷ 50 = $5\frac{2}{5}$ cents = $5\frac{4}{10}$ cents

Brand B: $3.18 ÷ 60 = $5\frac{3}{10}$ cents

The unit price for Brand B is less than the unit price for Brand A. Brand B is the better buy.
$5\frac{3}{10} < 5\frac{4}{10}$ so $5\frac{3}{10} < 5\frac{2}{5}$

22. $1.56 Multiply $6\frac{1}{2}$ cents (or $0.065) by 24.

23. Zesty Find the unit price for both brands by dividing the price by the number of ounces. Convert to like fractions.

Zesty: $2.59 ÷ 28 = $9\frac{1}{4}$ cents

Store brand: $2.47 ÷ 26 = $9\frac{1}{2}$ cents = $9\frac{2}{4}$ cents

The unit price for Zesty sauce is less than the unit price for the store brand. Zesty is the better buy.
$9\frac{1}{4} < 9\frac{2}{4}$ so $9\frac{1}{4} < 9\frac{1}{2}$

24. $2.12 Multiply $13\frac{1}{4}$ cents (or $0.1325) by 16.

GED Practice (Page 125)
NOTE: The answers below were entered in the grid as decimals. Each could also be entered as an improper fraction. You cannot enter a mixed number in the grid.

1. **7.5** Change all the fractions to decimals and add the miles.
2.25 + 1.5 + 3.75 = 7.5
(Fraction = $\frac{15}{2}$)

2. **$4.50** Multiply the cost per gallon of gasoline by the number of gallons of gasoline.
$1.25 × 3.6 = $4.50

3. **10.8** Divide the total weight of the can of green beans by the weight per serving.
40.5 ÷ 3.75 = 10.8

4. **6.25** Subtract the length of the piece from the total length of the wooden board.
9.375 − 3.125 = 6.25

GED Practice (Page 127)
1. **(4) 68.925** Change the fractions to decimals and add the miles ridden. 26.8 + 14.375 + 27.75
2. **(5) $7\frac{3}{4}$** Multiply the rate at which snow fell by the number of hours. 1.24 × 6.25 = 7.75, or $7\frac{3}{4}$

UNIT 1

3. **(3) $554.56** Multiply the regular rate per hour by 40 hours. $9.50 × 40 = $380 Subtract 40 from the actual time worked to find the number of overtime hours. 52.25 − 40 = 12.25 Multiply the overtime hours by the rate per hour by 1.5. 12.25 × $9.50 × 1.5 = $174.5625, or $174.56 rounded to the nearest cent. Add the two amounts earned. $380 + $174.56

4. **(3) $22.41** Multiply the price per gallon by the number of gallons.
   $1.39 × 16$\frac{1}{8}$ = $1.39 × 16.125 = $22.41375, or $22.41 rounded to the nearest cent.

5. **(1) 1.275** Subtract the number of miles jogged by Brett from the number of miles jogged by Alicia.
   4.875 − 3$\frac{3}{5}$ = 4.875 − 3.6

6. **(4) 13.225** Add the number of miles jogged by the three people.
   4.875 + 3$\frac{3}{5}$ + 4$\frac{3}{4}$ = 4.875 + 3.6 + 4.75

GED Mini-Test • Lessons 8–10
(Pages 128–131)
Part 1
1. **(3) 0.43** Divide 3 by 7. 3 ÷ 7 = 0.428 or 0.43, rounded to the nearest hundredth.

2. **(4) $300.06** Add the five electric bills.
   $64.16 + $78.92 + $63.94 + $50.17 + $42.87 = $300.06

3. **(1) $17.07** Add the cost of the three items and the total tax.
   $17.60 + $9.25 + $3.68 + $2.40 = $32.93
   Subtract the result from the amount given in payment. $50 − $32.93 = $17.07

4. **(2) $192.88** Add the three deposits to the initial balance.
   $528.60 + $45.24 + $17.50 + $67.45 = $658.79
   Subtract the two checks from the result.
   $658.79 − $412.72 − $53.19 = $192.88

5. **(3) 18.6** Divide the number of miles driven by the number of gallons of gasoline used.
   28,606.8 ÷ 1,538 = 18.6

6. **(2) $115** Use a proportion and cross multiply.
   $\frac{6.87}{1,500} = \frac{?}{25,000}$ Another way of looking at this problem is to divide the amount of the policy by the amount the policy could increase.
   $25,000 ÷ $1,500 = 16.67 Multiply by $6.87, the cost for each $1,500 increase.
   16.67 × $6.87 = $114.52, which rounds to $115.

7. **(2) $93.75** Multiply the number of reams of paper by the price per ream. 25 × $3.75 = $93.75

8. **(5) $71.25** Multiply the number of boxes of computer disks by the price per box.
   65 × $7.95 = $516.75 This is the amount paid for the computer disks. Multiply the number of

printer cartridges by the price per cartridge.
30 × $14.85 = $445.50 This is the amount paid for the printer cartridges. Subtract.
$516.75 − $445.50 = $71.25

9. **(1) 10.025** Change all the fractions to decimals. Add the miles Millie hiked on the first two days.
   10.6 + 11.875 = 22.475 Subtract the result from the total length of the hike.
   32.5 − 22.475 = 10.025

10. **(2) 5.0** Divide the amount of growth by the number of inches per week. 16.25 ÷ 3.25

11. **(3) $4,250** Change $\frac{3}{8}$ to the decimal 0.375 Subtract the fraction budgeted for food from the fraction budgeted for taxes. 0.375 − 0.25 = 0.125 Multiply the result by the gross annual salary.
    0.125 × $34,000 = $4,250

12. **(2) $\frac{3}{8}$** Add the fractions budgeted for taxes and food. $\frac{3}{8} + \frac{1}{4} = \frac{3}{8} + \frac{2}{8} = \frac{5}{8}$ Subtract the result from 1 to find the remaining fraction of William's gross annual salary. $1 − \frac{5}{8} = \frac{3}{8}$

Part 2
13. **(2) 23.037** Since the decimal is "thousandths," there must be three digits to the right of the decimal point.

14. **(3) 2.14** Since the 7 in the thousandths place is greater than 5, increase the digit in the hundredths place by 1 and drop all the remaining digits to its right.

15. **(4) $100** Round the amount paid back to $1200, a number easily divided by 12.
    $1200 ÷ 12 = $100

16. **(2) $175 − ($54.25 + $30.50)** You would add the amounts of the purchases and subtract the total from $175.

17. **(3) 5** Divide $10 by the price of one 3-inch potted plant. $10 ÷ $1.79 = 5.59 Therefore, the greatest number of plants that Mohammed can buy is 5.

18. **(2) 3** Multiply the price of a 5-inch potted plant by 2, and add the price of one watering can.
    2 × $3.69 + $1.89 = $9.27 Subtract the result from $20. $20 − $9.27 = $10.73 Divide the result by the cost of one 4-inch potted plant.
    $10.73 ÷ $2.89 = 3.7 Therefore, the greatest number of plants that Anya can buy is 3.

19. **(3) $5** Round the prices to the nearest dollar. Multiply the price of a bag of potting soil by 2, and add the price of one 5-inch potted plant.
    2 × $3 + $4 = $10 Subtract the result from $15.
    $15 − $10 = $5

20. **(4) 14 ($1.29 − $1.25)** You would subtract the price per gallon of gas at Atlas Gas from the price per gallon at Bradley Gas to get the difference in price per gallon and then multiply the result by 14 gallons.

21. **(3) $12.61** Multiply the price per pound by the number of pounds. $4.85 × 2.6 = $12.61

22. **(2) 2.4** Divide the total cost of the ground sirloin by the price per pound. $8.24 ÷ $3.45 = 2.38, or 2.4 rounded to the nearest tenth.

23. **(4) $480** Round the gross monthly salary to a close number easily divisible by 5. $2,400 ÷ 5 Dividing by 5 is the same as multiplying by $\frac{1}{5}$.

24. **(5) Not enough information is given.** The problem doesn't state how many hours a week Fabrice works.

25. **(2) $4\frac{1}{8}$** Subtract the low value from the high value. $28\frac{3}{8} - 24\frac{2}{8} = 4\frac{1}{8}$

26. **(3) $30\left(24\frac{1}{4}\right) + 40\left(36\frac{1}{2}\right)$** Multiply the number of shares of each stock by the stock's high price, and then add the two products together.

Lesson 11
GED Skill Focus (Page 133)

1. **0.6** 60% = .60. = 0.6

2. **0.38** 38% = .38. = 0.38

3. **0.108** 10.8% = .10.8 = 0.108

4. **0.04** 4% = .04. = 0.04

5. **2** 200% = 2.00. = 2

6. **$0.05\frac{1}{2}$ or 0.055** $5\frac{1}{2}\% = .05.\frac{1}{2} = 0.05\frac{1}{2}$

7. **1.3** 130% = 1.30. = 1.3

8. **$0.09\frac{1}{4}$ or 0.0925** $9\frac{1}{4}\% = .09.\frac{1}{4} = 0.09\frac{1}{4}$

9. **3.25** 325% = 3.25. = 3.25

10. **85%** 0.85 = 0.85. = 85%

11. **36%** 0.36 = 0.36. = 36%

12. **14.4%** 0.144 = 0.14.4 = 14.4%

13. **40%** 0.4 = 0.40. = 40%

14. **450%** 4.5 = 4.50. = 450%

15. **$16\frac{2}{3}\%$** $0.16\frac{2}{3} = 0.16.\frac{2}{3} = 16\frac{2}{3}\%$

16. **875%** 8.75 = 8.75. = 875%

17. **37.5%** 0.375 = 0.37.5 = 37.5%

18. **$7\frac{1}{3}\%$** $0.07\frac{1}{3} = 0.07.\frac{1}{3} = 7\frac{1}{3}\%$

19. **2.25** Divide. 225 ÷ 100 = 2.25

20. **150%** Multiply. 1.5 × 100 = 150%

21. **0.8** Divide. 80 ÷ 100 = 0.8

22. **24%** Multiply. 0.24 × 100 = 24%

23. **60%** Multiply. 0.6 × 100 = 60%

24. **0.03** Divide. 3 ÷ 100 = 0.03

25. **12.5% or $12\frac{1}{2}\%$** Multiply. 0.125 × 100 = 12.5%

26. **5.5** Divide. 550 ÷ 100 = 5.5

GED Skill Focus (Page 135)

1. $\frac{13}{20}$ $\frac{65 \div 5}{100 \div 5} = \frac{13}{20}$

2. $\frac{21}{25}$ $\frac{84 \div 4}{100 \div 4} = \frac{21}{25}$

3. $1\frac{2}{5}$ $\frac{140 \div 20}{100 \div 20} = \frac{7}{5} = 1\frac{2}{5}$

4. $2\frac{3}{4}$ $\frac{275 \div 25}{100 \div 25} = \frac{11}{4} = 2\frac{3}{4}$

5. $\frac{39}{100}$ $\frac{39}{100}$ This fraction cannot be reduced.

6. $4\frac{1}{2}$ $\frac{450 \div 50}{100 \div 50} = \frac{9}{2} = 4\frac{1}{2}$

7. **37.5%** Calculator. 3 [÷] 8 [SHIFT] [=] 37.5

8. **93.75%** Calculator. 15 [÷] 16 [SHIFT] [=] 93.75

9. **1.25** Calculator. 125 [÷] 100 [=] 1.25

10. **0.875** Calculator. 87.5 [÷] 100 [=] 0.875

11.	**0.2**	$\frac{1}{5}$	20%
12.	**0.25**	$\frac{1}{4}$	**25%**
13.	0.3	$\frac{3}{10}$	**30%**
14.	**$0.33\frac{1}{3}$**	$\frac{1}{3}$	**$33\frac{1}{3}\%$**
15.	**0.4**	$\frac{2}{5}$	40%
16.	**0.6**	$\frac{3}{5}$	60%
17.	$0.66\frac{2}{3}$	$\frac{2}{3}$	**$66\frac{2}{3}\%$**
18.	**0.75**	$\frac{3}{4}$	**75%**
19.	**0.8**	$\frac{4}{5}$	80%
20.	0.9	$\frac{9}{10}$	**90%**

GED Practice (Page 137)

1. **(1) $7** Write a proportion. $\frac{?}{\$35} = \frac{20}{100}$
Cross multiply and solve. $35 × 20 ÷ 100 = $7

2. **(4) $562.50** $\frac{?}{\$625} = \frac{90}{100}$
$625 × 90 ÷ 100 = $562.50

3. **(3) $33.60** $\frac{?}{\$1,344} = \frac{2.5}{100}$
$1,344 × 2.5 ÷ 100 = $33.60

4. (2) 70 $\frac{56}{?} = \frac{80}{100}$

$56 \times 100 \div 80 = 70$

5. (1) 40% $\frac{18}{45} = \frac{?}{100}$

$18 \times 100 \div 45 = 40$

6. (5) 375 $\frac{300}{?} = \frac{80}{100}$

$300 \times 100 \div 80 = 375$

Lesson 12
GED Skill Focus (Page 139)

1. **15** $0.03 \times 500 = 15$

2. **$142.50** $0.15 \times \$950 = \$142.50$

3. **64.8** $0.90 \times 72 = 64.8$

4. **119** $0.85 \times 140 = 119$

5. **$275** $1.25 \times \$220 = \$275$

6. **276** $1.50 \times 184 = 276$

7. **60** $0.75 \times 80 = 60$

8. **$10** $0.05 \times \$200 = \$10$

9. **$128** $0.08 \times \$1600 = \$128$

10. **$11** $0.55 \times \$20 = \$11$

11. **16.5** $0.055 \times 300 = 16.5$

12. **$200** $33\frac{1}{3}\% = \frac{1}{3}$ Multiply. $\frac{1}{3} \times \$600 = \$200$

13. **$5.07** $0.06 \times \$84.50 = \$5.07$

14. **51.12** $0.04 \times 1278 = 51.12$

15. **$333.38** $2.10 \times \$158.75 = \$333.375$, which rounds to $333.38

16. **$4.86** $0.45 \times \$10.80 = \$4.86$

17. **$50.31** $0.0875 \times \$575.00 = \$50.3125$, rounds to $50.31

18. **$0.75** $0.015 \times \$50.00 = \$0.75$

19. **3.47** $0.07 \times 49.5 = 3.465$, rounds to 3.47

20. **$23.63** $1.35 \times \$17.50 = \$23.625$, rounds to $23.63

21. **180** Find 15% of 1200.
$0.15 \times 1200 = 180$

22. **$457.60** Find 22% of $2080.
$0.22 \times \$2080 = \$457.60$

23. **$1622.40** Find 78% of $2080, or subtract the amount deducted, $457.60, from $2080.
$0.78 \times \$2080 = \$1622.40$ OR
$\$2080 - \$457.60 = \$1622.40$

24. **$745.20** Find the amount of the sales tax by finding 8% of $690. $0.08 \times \$690 = \$55.20$ Add the sales tax to the cost of the sofa.
$\$55.20 + \$690 = \$745.20$

25. **$27.95** Find 15% of $186.35.
$0.15 \times \$186.35 = \$27.9525$, which rounds to $27.95

26. **$111.33** Find 150% of $74.22.
$1.50 \times \$74.22 = \$111.33$
Note: You should expect the result to be greater than $74.22 since the percent is greater than 100%.

GED Skill Focus (Page 141)

1. **15%** $123 \div 820 = 0.15 = 15\%$

2. **75%** $\$4.50 \div \$6.00 = 0.75 = 75\%$

3. **80%** $\$18.00 \div \$22.50 = 0.8 = 80\%$

4. **17.5% or $17\frac{1}{2}$%** $350 \div 2,000 = 0.175 = 17.5\%$

5. **400%** The base is 60. The word *of* usually comes before the base. $240 \div 60 = 4 = 400\%$

6. **3%** $120 \div 4,000 = 0.03 = 3\%$

7. **3.125% or $3\frac{1}{8}$%**
$\$5 \div \$160 = 0.03125 = 3.125\%$

8. **180%** Since the part ($72.00) is greater than the base ($40.00), you know the rate (percent) will be greater than 100%.
$\$72.00 \div \$40.00 = 1.8 = 180\%$

9. **2%** $\$3.50 \div \$175.00 = 0.02 = 2\%$

10. **25%** $326 \div 1304 = 0.25 = 25\%$

11. **4.5% or $4\frac{1}{2}$%** $225 \div 5000 = 0.045 = 4.5\%$

12. **96%** $\$144 \div \$150 = 0.96 = 96\%$

13. **75%** $\$82.50 \div \$110.00 = 0.75 = 75\%$

14. **250%** Since the part (40) is greater than the base (16), you know the rate will be greater than 100%. $40 \div 16 = 2.5 = 250\%$

15. **15%** Subtract. $1725 - 1500 = 225$ Divide by the original amount. $225 \div 1500 = 0.15 = 15\%$

16. **12%** Subtract. $\$582.40 - \$520.00 = \$62.40$ Divide by the original amount.
$\$62.40 \div \$520.00 = 0.12 = 12\%$

17. **75%** Subtract. $280 - 70 = 210$ Divide by the original amount. $210 \div 280 = 0.75 = 75\%$

18. **5%** Subtract. $\$1,200 - \$1,140 = \$60$ Divide by the original amount. $\$60 \div \$1,200 = 0.05 = 5\%$

19. **85%** You need to find what percent 119 is of 140. Divide. $119 \div 140 = 0.85 = 85\%$

20. **40%** You need to find what percent 10 is of 25. Divide. $10 \div 25 = 0.4 = 40\%$

21. **4%** You need to find percent of increase. Subtract. $\$1508 - \$1450 = \$58$ Divide by the original amount. $\$58 \div \$1450 = 0.04 = 4\%$

22. **88%** You need to find what percent 44 is of 50. Divide. $44 \div 50 = 0.88 = 88\%$

23. 30% You need to find percent of decrease. Subtract. $790.00 − $550.00 = $240.00 Divide by the original amount. $240.00 ÷ $790.00 is about 0.303, which rounds to 30%

24. 8% You need to find what percent $44 is of $550. Divide. $44 ÷ $550 = 0.08 = 8%

GED Practice (Page 143)

1. (3) 852 Find 10% of 8520 by moving the decimal point one place to the left. 8520. → 852. This is the same as dividing by 10 or multiplying by 0.1.

2. (4) $3.90 Find 10% by moving the decimal point one place to the left. $26.00 → $2.60 Divide $2.60 by 2 to find 5%.
$2.60 ÷ 2 = $1.30
Add to find 15%. $2.60 + $1.30 = $3.90
This is the same as multiplying by 0.15.
0.15 × $26 = $3.90

3. (5) $7.50 Find 10% by moving the decimal point one place to the left. $150.00 → $15 Divide by 2 to find 5%.
$15.00 ÷ 2 = $7.50
Or multiply. 0.05 × $150 = $7.50

4. (2) $14.00 Find 10% by moving the decimal point one place to the left. $70.00 → $7 Multiply by 2 to find 20%.
$7.00 × 2 = $14.00

5. (4) $375 Find 10% by moving the decimal point one place to the left. $1,500. = $150
Multiply $150 by 2 to find 20%. $150 × 2 = $300
Divide $150 by 2 to find 5%. $150 ÷ 2 = $75
Add 20% + 5% = 25%. $300 + $75 = $375

6. (2) 540 Find 10% by moving the decimal point one place to the left. 1800. = 180.
Multiply 180 by 3 to find 30%. 180 × 3 = 540

Lesson 13
GED Skill Focus (Page 145)

1. $90 $54 ÷ 0.6 = $90

2. 8000 720 ÷ 0.09 = 8000

3. $32 $1.92 ÷ 0.06 = $32

4. 500 85 ÷ 0.17 = 500

5. $550 $495 ÷ 0.90 = $550

6. 300 810 ÷ 2.7 = 300

7. $180 $207 ÷ 1.15 = $180

8. $1200 $1020 ÷ 0.85 = $1200

9. $3.00 $0.21 ÷ 0.07 = $3.00

10. 528 660 ÷ 1.25 = 528

11. $42 $6.30 ÷ 0.15 = $42

12. 9000 $66\frac{2}{3}\% = \frac{2}{3}$ It is easier to use the fraction.
$6000 ÷ \frac{2}{3} = 6000 × \frac{3}{2} = 9000$

13. $5.00 $3.75 ÷ 0.75 = $5.00

14. 64 9.6 ÷ 0.15 = 64

15. $450.00 $157.50 ÷ 0.35 = $450.00

16. $112.00 $26.88 ÷ 0.24 = $112.00

17. $60.00 $62.40 ÷ 1.04 = $60.00

18. $20.00 $0.76 ÷ 0.038 = $20.00

19. $12,940 $679.35 ÷ 0.0525 = $12,940

20. $36.00 $1.26 ÷ 0.035 = $36.00

21. $9375 Divide the part ($7500) by the rate (80%) to find the base. $7500 ÷ 0.8 = $9375

22. $23,700 Divide the part ($3,555) by the rate (15%) to find the base. $3,555 ÷ 0.15 = $23,700

23. 22 Divide the part (178) by the rate (89%) to find the base. 178 ÷ 0.89 = 200 Then subtract to find the number of members who did not vote for Elena. 200 − 178 = 22
Another way to solve this problem: If 89% voted for Elena, then 11% of the total voting did not vote for her (100% − 89%). Find 11% (.11) of 200. 200 × .11 = 22

24. 828 Divide the part (207) by the rate (25%) to find the base. 207 ÷ 0.25 = 828

25. $140 Divide the part ($98) by the rate (70%) to find the base. $98 ÷ 0.7 = $140

26. 15 The number of glass tables returns, 3, is 20% of the total sales. To find the total sales, divide the part (3) by the rate (20%). 3 ÷ 0.20 = 15

27. 105 This problem has two steps. First, find the total number of rolling tables sold by dividing the number of returns by the rate.
15 ÷ 0.125 = 120 Then subtract the number of tables returned to find the number that were not returned. 120 − 15 = 105

28. 96% Read carefully. The problem asks simply what percent of the folding step chairs were not returned. You know that 4% were returned. Subtract to find the percent not returned.
100% − 4% = 96%

GED Skill Focus (Page 147)

1. $300 $1250 × 0.12 × 2 = $300

2. $228 $2400 × 0.095 × 1 = $228

3. $36 $900 × 0.08 × 0.5 = $36
(6 months = $\frac{6}{12} = \frac{1}{2}$ or 0.5 year)

4. $50 $4000 × 0.05 × 0.25 = $50
(3 months = $\frac{3}{12} = \frac{1}{4}$ or 0.25 year)

UNIT 1

5. **$113.40** $840 × 0.09 × 1.5 = $113.40
(18 months = $\frac{18}{12}$ = 1.5 years)

6. **$330** $1100 × 0.075 × 4 = $330

7. **$176** $5\frac{1}{2}$% = 5.5% = 0.055
$3200 × 0.055 × 1 = $176

8. **$260** $500 × 0.08 × 6.5 = $260

9. **$46** $2300 × 0.04 × 0.5 = $46
(6 months = $\frac{6}{12}$ = $\frac{1}{2}$ or 0.5 year)

10. **$15** $800 × 0.075 × 0.25 = $15
(3 months = $\frac{3}{12}$ = $\frac{1}{4}$ or 0.25 year)

11. **$45** $600 × 0.0375 × 2 = $45
($3\frac{3}{4}$% = 3.75% = 0.0375)

12. **$630** First find the interest. (6 months = $\frac{6}{12}$ = $\frac{1}{2}$ or 0.5 year) $600 × 0.1 × 0.5 = $30 Then add the principal and interest. $600 + $30 = $630

13. **$5724** First find the interest. (9 months = $\frac{9}{12}$ = $\frac{3}{4}$ or 0.75 year) $5400 × 0.08 × 0.75 = $324 Then add the principal and interest. $5400 + $324 = $5724

14. **$12,800** First find the interest. $8,000 × 0.12 × 5 = $4,800 Then add the principal and interest. $8,000 + $4,800 = $12,800

15. **$306** First find the interest. (4 months = $\frac{4}{12}$ = $\frac{1}{3}$ year) $300 × 0.06 × $\frac{1}{3}$ = $6 Then add the principal and interest. $300 + $6 = $306

16. **$6,600** $20,000 × 0.0825 × 4 = $6,600
($8\frac{1}{4}$% = 8.25% = 0.0825)

17. **$1567.50** First find the interest. (18 months = $\frac{18}{12}$ = $1\frac{6}{12}$ = $1\frac{1}{2}$ or 1.5 years) $1500 × 0.03 × 1.5 = $67.50 Then add the principal and the interest. $1500 + $67.50 = $1567.50

18. **$936** First find the interest. (12 months = $\frac{12}{12}$ = 1 year) $900 × 0.04 × 1 = $36 Then add the principal and the interest. $900 + $36 = $936

19. **$1805** $9500 × 0.095 × 2 = $1805
($9\frac{1}{2}$% = 9.5% = 0.095)

20. **$5512.50** First find the interest. $4500 × 0.075 × 3 = $1012.50 Then add the principal and the interest. $4500 + $1012.50 = $5512.50

21. **$125** $2500 × 0.05 × 1 = $125

22. **$112.50** (9 months = $\frac{9}{12}$ = $\frac{3}{4}$ or 0.75 year) $2500 × 0.06 × 0.75 = $112.50

GED Practice (Page 149)

1. **(4) $17.00** Find the amount of the discount. $20 × 0.15 = $3 Subtract to find the sale price. $20 − $3 = $17

2. **(2) $9 + 0.06 × $9** Find the raise (0.06 × $9), and then add that amount to her current wage to find her new hourly wage. $9 + 0.06 × $9

3. **(3) 200%** Find the difference in the two amounts. $4500 − $1500 = $3000 Divide by the original amount. $3000 ÷ $1500 = 2.00 = 200%

4. **(2) 0.4(30) + 30** You need to find the increase by multiplying 0.4 by 30. Then add the increase to the original amount.

5. **(1)** $\frac{\$160 − (\$160 × 0.1)}{6}$ Subtract the amount of the down payment from the cost of the coat. $160 − ($160 × 0.1) Then divide that amount by the number of monthly payments, 6.

6. **(2) 336** Find the number of workers to be laid off first. 1400 × 0.05 = 70 Subtract from the original. 1400 − 70 = 1330 Find the number of workers in the second layoff. 1330 × 0.20 = 266 Add the number of workers in both layoffs. 70 + 266 = 336

GED Practice (Page 151)

1. **(3) 414** Multiply the total number of employees at the end of the first quarter by the percent of increase in the second quarter. 3450 × 0.12 = 414

2. **(4) 18%** Divide the amount of the tip by the total bill. $21.60 ÷ $120 = 0.18 = 18%

3. **(4) $50,000** Divide the amount of the contribution by the percent of the salary. $4,375 ÷ 0.0875 = $50,000

4. **(2) 12.5%** Subtract the office expenses for this month from the office expenses for last month. $1400 − $1225 = $175 Divide the result by the amount of expenses for last month. $175 ÷ $1400 = 0.125 = 12.5%

5. **(3) $236.40** Multiply the regular price of the microwave oven by the percent of discount. $394 × 0.4 = $157.60 Subtract the result from the regular price. $394 − $157.60 = $236.40 Another approach: Since the discount is 40% off, the sale price is 60% of the original price (100% − 40%). 0.6 × $394 = $236.40

6. **(4) 18%** Subtract the sales of toothpaste in April from the sales of toothpaste in May. $4,956 − $4,200 = $756 Divide the result by the sales of toothpaste in April. $756 ÷ $4,200 = 0.18, or 18%

GED Mini-Test • Lessons 11–13

(Pages 152–155)

Part 1

1. **(5) $42,500** Divide the amount paid for taxes by the percent paid for taxes. $13,600 ÷ 0.32 = $42,500

2. **(4) $45.47** Multiply the list price of the stapler by the percent of discount. $69.95 × 0.35 = $24.48, rounded to the nearest cent. Subtract the result from the list price. $69.95 − $24.48 = $45.47

3. **(3) 12.5%** Subtract the original value of the inventory from the value at the end of the first quarter to get the increase. $52,200 − $46,400 = $5,800 Divide the result by the original value. $5,800 ÷ $46,400 = 0.125 = 12.5% increase

4. **(4) $68** The decrease in price was 23%. So, the closing price of the stock on Friday was 77% of the closing price on Thursday. Divide the closing price on Friday by this percent. $52.36 ÷ 0.77 = $68 Another way to solve this problem is to use the equation $\frac{(\text{original amount} - \text{new amount})}{\text{original amount}} =$ percent of change. $\frac{(x - \$52.36)}{x} = 0.23$

5. **(3) 22%** Divide the amount of the down payment by the list price. $209 ÷ $950 = 0.22 = 22%

6. **(5) Not enough information is given.** You need to know the amount of the gross sales to find how much he earned in commission.

7. **(2) 11%** Add the sales for the 6 months listed. $2 + $6 + $8 + $8 + $14 + $18 = $56 Divide the sales in February by this total. $6 ÷ $56 = 0.107 = 11%, rounded to the nearest whole percent

8. **(1) January to February** The percent of increase for each pair of consecutive months is the increase in sales from one month to the next divided by the sales in the first month in the pair. From January to February the percent of increase is ($6 − $2) ÷ $2 = $4 ÷ $2 = 200%. For each of the other pairs of consecutive months the percent of increase is less than 100%.

9. **(5) $7,000** Multiply the amount borrowed by the annual interest rate by the number of years of the loan. $12,500 × 0.16 × 3.5

10. **(3) 8%** Divide the amount of the raise by the current annual salary. $3,280 ÷ $38,650 = 0.084 = 8%, rounded to the nearest whole percent.

11. **(3) ($136 × 0.0825) + $136** Multiply the price of the coat by the sales tax percent, and add the result (the amount of sales tax) to the price of the coat. ($136 × .0825) + $136

12. **(1) 15%** Subtract the attendance for this year from the attendance for last year. 1420 − 1209 = 211 Divide the result by the attendance for last year. 211 ÷ 1420 = 0.148 = 15%, rounded to the nearest whole percent.

13. **(3) increase of 4%** Subtract the circulation in September ("original") from the circulation in October ("new"). 247,624 − 238,100 = 9,524 Then divide the difference by the circulation in September. 9,524 ÷ 238,100 = 0.04 = 4% Since the circulation in October is greater than that in September, the change is an increase. $\frac{247,624 - 238,100}{238,100} \times 100\% = 4\%$

Part 2

14. **(5) (180 − 150) ÷ 150** Subtract the sales in July from the sales in August, and divide the result by the sales in July.

15. **(4) 2470** Since 5% of the telephones inspected are defective, 95% of them are not defective. Multiply the number of telephones inspected by this percent. 2600 × 0.95

16. **(4) 8%** Divide the amount of the raise by the current annual salary. $2,080 ÷ $26,000 = 0.08 = 8%

17. **(2) $20,400** Divide the amount of the commission by the percent of commission. $1,020 ÷ 0.05

18. **(3) $400** The price of the CD/DVD player after the sales tax is 105% of the price before the sales tax. Divide the price after the sales tax by this percent. $420 ÷ 1.05 Another way to look at this problem: 105% = rate and $420 = part. base $= \frac{\text{part}}{\text{rate}} = \frac{\$420}{1.05}$

19. **(1) $2625** Use the formula. $i = prt$. Find the interest. $2500 × 0.025 × 2 = $125 Add interest to principal. $125 + $2500 = $2625

20. **(4) $16,782** Multiply February's net sales by 120%. $13,985 × 1.2

21. **(3) $126** Multiply the regular price of the chair by the percent of mark down. $180 × 0.3 = $54 Subtract the result from the regular price of the chair. $180 − $54

22. (2) $5400 Subtract the percent budgeted for advertising from the percent budgeted for supplies. 25% − 16% = 9% Multiply the total amount of the budget by the resulting percent. $60,000 × 0.09

23. (5) $6200 Multiply the amount of the investment by the annual interest rate by the number of years. $5000 × 0.08 × 3 = $1200 Add the resulting interest earned to the original amount invested. $5000 + $1,200

24. (2) 200% Find the change in price. $3 − $1 = $2 Find the percent of increase. $2 ÷ $1 = 2 = 200%

25. (2) $44 After paying 20% as a down payment, 80% remains. Multiply the original price of the television by 80%. $440 × 0.8 = $352 Divide the result by 8. $352 ÷ 8

Unit 1 Cumulative Review
(Pages 156–160)
Part 1

1. (4) $89.16 Set up a proportion using the ratio of the cost of insurance to the amount of insurance. Cross multiply and solve. $\frac{\$7.43}{\$2,500} = \frac{?}{\$30,000}$
$7.43 × $30,000 ÷ $2,500 = $89.16

2. (3) $14,000 × 0.0975 × 3.5 Change the rate of interest to a decimal. $9\frac{3}{4}\% = 0.0975$ Change the amount of time to a decimal. $3\frac{1}{2} = 3.5$ Use the interest formula. $i = prt = \$14,000 × .0975 × 3.5$

3. (1) $980 Find the part (7% of $14,000) by multiplying.
base × rate = $14,000 × 0.07 = $980

4. (3) $14,300 Add all the deposits to the current balance; then subtract both checks from the result.
$15,000 + $1,800 + $3,000 + $900 = $20,700
$20,700 − $3,600 − $2,800 = $14,300

5. (5) $98.50 Find the difference between the regular and sale price for pants.
$87.50 − $62.00 = $25.50 Multiply to find the savings on 3 pairs of pants. $25.50 × 3 = $76.50
Find the difference between the regular and sale price for shirts. $38.95 − $27.95 = $11 Multiply to find the savings on 2 shirts. $11 × 2 = $22
Add to find the total savings.
$76.50 + $22 = $98.50 OR
3($87.50 − $62) + 2($38.95 − $27.95) =
3 × $25.50 + 2 × $11 = $76.50 + $22 = $98.50

6. (3) 28% Subtract the sale price for shirts from the regular price for shirts $38.95 − $27.95 = $11 Divide the result by the regular price of the shirts. $11 ÷ $38.95 = 0.282, or 28%, rounded to the nearest percent.

7. (1) $\frac{16}{\$15.92} = \frac{20}{?}$ Choose the proportion with ratios that compare the number of pounds of turkey to the cost. $\frac{\text{pounds}}{\$\text{cost}} = \frac{\text{pounds}}{\$ \text{cost}}$

8. (3) $38.25 Multiply the price of the lamp by the percent of discount. $45 × 0.15 = $6.75 Subtract the result from the original price. $45 − $6.75 = $38.25

9. (3) $10\frac{1}{2}$ Add the three amounts of paint.
$$4\frac{1}{2} = \quad 4\frac{4}{8}$$
$$2\frac{7}{8} = \quad 2\frac{7}{8}$$
$$+3\frac{1}{8} = +3\frac{1}{8}$$
$$9\frac{12}{8} = 10\frac{4}{8} = 10\frac{1}{2}$$

10. (4) 300% Subtract the original amount from the new amount and divide by the original amount. ($8 − $2) ÷ $2 = 3 Change the result to a percent by multiplying by 100. 3 × 100 = 300%

11. (4) $320.00 The price of the stereo system after the discount is 85% of the original price (100% − 15%). Divide the discounted price of the stereo system by this percent. $272 ÷ .85 = $320

12. (5) Not enough information is given. The problem gives the number of miles Mateo jogged this week, but it does not give the number of miles he jogged the week before. You do not have enough information to solve the problem.

13. (1) 749.8 Subtract the number of miles driven by Anne from the number of miles driven by Barbara. 2,098.4 − 1,348.6 = 749.8

14. 3.4 Divide the price of the piece of salmon by the cost per pound. $31.28 ÷ $9.20 = 3.4

15. 6 Add the amounts.
3 + 2 + 4 + 2 + 3 = 14
Subtract the sum from the usual total. 20 − 14 = 6

16. 226.1 Multiply Peter's original weight by the percent of weight loss. 238 × 0.05 = 11.9 Subtract the result from his original weight. 238 − 11.9 = 226.1

17. $80.43 Add the two amounts that Areta borrowed.
$42.48 + $64.76 = $107.24
After she paid back $\frac{1}{4}$ of this amount, she still owed $\frac{3}{4}$ of this amount. Change $\frac{3}{4}$ to a decimal and multiply by the total amount.
$107.24 × .75 = $80.43

Part 2

18. **(1) 3** Subtract the amount Jonathan has already saved from the cost of the vacation. $720 − $480 = $240 Divide the result by the amount he saves each month. $240 ÷ $80 = 3

19. **(3) $13\frac{1}{8}$** Change the fractions to fractions with common denominators. Then add the hours worked on the three days.
$2\frac{3}{4} + 4\frac{1}{2} + 5\frac{7}{8} = 2\frac{6}{8} + 4\frac{4}{8} + 5\frac{7}{8} = 11\frac{17}{8} = 13\frac{1}{8}$

20. **(5) 150** The question asks for an approximate answer. Round 14.82 to 15. Multiply by 2 to find the mileage going to and from work. 15 × 2 = 30 Multiply the mileage by 5 days per week. 30 × 5 = 150

21. **(4) $7100** Multiply the amount borrowed by the interest rate, and then multiply the result by the number of years. $5000 × 0.14 × 3 = $2100 Add the interest to the amount borrowed. $5000 + $2100 = $7100

22. **(3) 1,132.7** Subtract the starting odometer reading from 10,000. 10,000 − 8,867.3 = 1,132.7

23. **(5) $44.52** Multiply the number of boxes in a case by the number of cases. 8 × 3.5 = 28 Multiply the result by the price of each box. $1.59 × 28 = $44.52

24. **(3) $79\frac{3}{4}$** Change $5\frac{1}{2}$ to 5.5 Multiply the number of baskets picked per hour by the number of hours. 14.5 × 5.5 = 79.75 Since answer choices are fractions, change 79.75 to $79\frac{3}{4}$.

25. **$\frac{9}{20}$** Find a fraction of a fraction. Multiply the fraction of employees that drive to work by the fraction of employees that drive in a carpool.
$\frac{3}{4} \times \frac{3}{5} = \frac{9}{20}$

26. **4.9** Divide the total length of the board by 4. 19.6 ÷ 4 = 4.9

27. **130** Change the mixed number to a decimal. $1\frac{1}{2} = 1.5$
Set up a proportion using the ratio of the number of miles to the number of hours. Solve for the unknown number of miles.
$\frac{78}{1.5} = \frac{?}{2.5}$; 78 × 2.5 ÷ 1.5 = 130

28. **$96** Find the price of insurance for two months. $33 × 2 = $66 Find the amount paid for doctor visits. $5 × 6 = $30 Add the two amounts. $66 + $30 = $96

UNIT 2: MEASUREMENT AND DATA ANALYSIS
Lesson 14
GED Skill Focus (Page 165)

1. **240 seconds** $\frac{\text{seconds}}{\text{minutes}}$ $\frac{60}{1} = \frac{x}{4}$
60 × 4 ÷ 1 = 240 sec

2. **9 pints** $\frac{\text{pints}}{\text{cups}}$ $\frac{1}{2} = \frac{x}{18}$; 1 × 18 ÷ 2 = 9 pints

3. **10 feet 6 inches** $\frac{\text{yards}}{\text{feet}}$ $\frac{1}{3} = \frac{3\frac{1}{2}}{x}$
$3 \times 3\frac{1}{2} \div 1 = \frac{3}{1} \times \frac{7}{2} \div 1 = \frac{21}{2} = 10\frac{1}{2}$ or 10.5 ft
1 foot = 12 inches, so $\frac{1}{2}$ ft = 6 in; therefore, 10.5 ft = 10 ft 6 in

4. **140 minutes** $\frac{\text{hours}}{\text{minutes}}$ $\frac{1}{60} = \frac{2\frac{1}{3}}{x}$
$60 \times 2\frac{1}{3} \div 1 = \frac{60}{1} \times \frac{7}{3} \div 1 = \frac{140}{1} = 140$ minutes

5. **9 cups** $\frac{\text{cups}}{\text{fl oz}}$ $\frac{1}{8} = \frac{x}{72}$
1 × 72 ÷ 8 = 9 cups

6. **54 inches** Use the conversion factors you know to find out how many inches are in one yard.
1 ft = 12 in and 1 yd = 3 ft; therefore, 1 yd =
$3 \text{ ft} = 36 \text{ in } \frac{\text{yards}}{\text{inches}} \frac{1}{36} = \frac{1\frac{1}{2}}{x}$; $36 \div 1\frac{1}{2} \div 1 = 54$ in

7. **68 ounces** $\frac{\text{pounds}}{\text{ounces}}$ $\frac{1}{16} = \frac{4\frac{1}{4}}{x}$
$16 \times 4\frac{1}{4} \div 1 = 68$ ounces

8. **23 quarts** $\frac{\text{gallons}}{\text{quarts}}$ $\frac{1}{4} = \frac{5\frac{3}{4}}{x}$
$4 \times 5\frac{3}{4} \div 1 = 23$ quarts

9. **$2\frac{1}{4}$ yards**
1 ft = 12 in; 6 ft 9 in = $6\frac{9}{12}$ ft, or $6\frac{3}{4}$ ft
$\frac{\text{yards}}{\text{feet}}$ $\frac{1}{3} = \frac{x}{6\frac{3}{4}}$
$1 \times 6\frac{3}{4} \div 3 = 2\frac{1}{4}$ yards

10. **$4\frac{5}{8}$ pounds** $\frac{\text{pounds}}{\text{ounces}}$ $\frac{1}{16} = \frac{x}{74}$
$1 \times 74 \div 16 = 4\frac{5}{8}$ pounds

11. **26,400 feet** $\frac{\text{miles}}{\text{feet}}$ $\frac{1}{5,280} = \frac{5}{x}$
5,280 × 5 ÷ 1 = 26,400 ft

12. **32 cups** Find a conversion factor that relates cups and gallons. 1 gal = 4 qt; 1 qt = 2 pt; so, 1 gal = 8 pt Since 1 pt = 2 c and 8 pt = 1 gal, 1 gal = 16 c. $\frac{\text{gallons}}{\text{cups}}$ $\frac{1}{16} = \frac{2}{x}$; 16 × 2 ÷ 1 = 32 cups

13. **$3\frac{1}{4}$ hours** Change $3\frac{1}{4}$ hours to minutes and

compare. $\frac{\text{hours}}{\text{minutes}}$ $\frac{1}{60} = \frac{3\frac{1}{4}}{x}$

$60 \times 3\frac{1}{4} \div 1 = 195$ minutes

195 minutes $<$ 200 minutes

14. **$4\frac{1}{2}$ pounds** Change $4\frac{1}{2}$ pounds to ounces and

compare. $\frac{\text{pounds}}{\text{ounces}}$ $\frac{1}{16} = \frac{4\frac{1}{2}}{x}$

$16 \times 4\frac{1}{2} \div 1 = 72$ ounces

72 ounces $<$ 75 ounces

15. **No, 3 feet is greater than 30 inches.**

$\frac{\text{feet}}{\text{inches}}$ $\frac{1}{12} = \frac{3}{x}$

$12 \times 3 \div 1 = 36$ inches

16. **Yes** You need to know how many pints equal $1\frac{1}{2}$ gallons. 1 gallon = 4 quarts and 1 quart =

2 pints, so 1 gallon = 8 pints. $\frac{\text{gallon}}{\text{pints}}$ $\frac{1}{8} = \frac{1\frac{1}{2}}{x}$

$8 \times 1\frac{1}{2} \div 1 = 12$ pints

17. **77 ounces** Find the number of ounces in

4 pounds. $\frac{\text{pounds}}{\text{ounces}}$ $\frac{1}{16} = \frac{4}{x}$

$16 \times 4 \div 1 = 64$ oz

Add 13 ounces to this amount. $64 + 13 = 77$ oz

18. **Package A** Find the weight of each package in ounces, using the conversion factor that 1 lb = 16 oz. Package A weighs 75 oz, package B weighs 76 oz, and package C weighs 77 ounces. Package A weighs the least amount.

GED Skill Focus (Page 167)

1. **16 feet 10 inches**

```
   8 ft   8 in
   3 ft   5 in
 + 4 ft   9 in
 ─────────────
  15 ft  22 in = 15 ft + 12 in + 10 in
              = 15 ft + 1 ft + 10 in = 16 ft 10 in
```

2. **9 minutes 15 seconds** Since 1 hr = 60 min, then $\frac{1}{2}$ hr = 30 min. Regroup 1 min to 60 sec, and subtract.

```
   30 min          =   29 min 60 sec
 −20 min 45 sec =  −20 min 45 sec
 ─────────────────────────────────
                      9 min 15 sec
```

3. **7 inches**
```
   2 ft 2 in =    1 ft 14 in
 −1 ft 7 in =  −1 ft   7 in
 ──────────────────────────
                     7 in
```

4. **17 quarts** Use the conversion factor 1 gal = 4 qt to find the number of quarts in 3 gallons.

$\frac{\text{gallons}}{\text{quarts}}$ $\frac{1}{4} = \frac{3}{x}$

$4 \times 3 \div 1 = 12$ quarts

Add. 12 qt + 5 qt = 17 quarts

5. **11 pounds 14 ounces**

```
    3 lb  8 oz
    5 lb 13 oz
 +  2 lb  9 oz
 ──────────────
   10 lb 30 oz = 10 lb + 16 oz + 14 oz
              = 10 lb +  1 lb  + 14 oz =
                11 lb 14 oz
```

6. **1 foot** 18 inches = 1 ft 6 in Subtract.

```
   2 ft 6 in
 −1 ft 6 in
 ───────────
   1 ft 0 in = 1 ft
```

7. **16 pounds 4 ounces**

```
    3 lb 4 oz
 ×          5
 ──────────────
  15 lb 20 oz = 15 lb + 16 oz + 4 oz
             = 15 lb +  1 lb  + 4 oz = 16 lb 4 oz
```

8. **8 inches** Since 1 yd = 3 ft and 1 ft = 12 in, then 1 yd = 3 ft = 36 in Convert 1 yd 4 in to inches. 1 yd 4 in = 36 in + 4 in = 40 in; 40 in ÷ 5 = 8 in

9. **18 yards 2 feet**

```
    2 yd 1 ft
 ×          8
 ──────────────
  16 yd 8 ft            1 yd = 3 ft, so
  16 yd + 2 yd + 2 ft = 18 yd 2 ft
```

10. **3 quarts** Convert 3 gallons to quarts. Use the conversion factor: 1 gal = 4 qt 3 gal = 12 qt; 12 qt ÷ 4 = 3 qt

11. **6 pieces** You can work the problem using either feet or inches.

1 ft 9 in = $1\frac{3}{4}$ ft

$12 \div 1\frac{3}{4} = 12 \div \frac{7}{4} = 12 \times \frac{4}{7} = \frac{48}{7} = 6\frac{6}{7}$

Or, 12 ft = 144 in and 1 ft 9 in = 21 in

144 ÷ 21 = 6 r18

Using either method, you can cut 6 whole pieces from the length of tubing with some tubing left over (as the remainder or fraction of a piece).

12. **10 pints** Use the conversion factors: 1 gal = 4 qt and 1 qt = 2 pt So, 2 gal = 8 qt = 16 pt; 16 − 6 = 10 pt

13. **12 inches** Since the answer must be in inches, work the problem in inches. Use the conversion factors: 1 yd = 3 ft = 36 in and 1 ft = 12 in

$3\frac{1}{4}$ yd $3\frac{1}{4} \times 36$ in $= \frac{13}{4} \times \frac{36}{1} = 117$ in

−2 yd 2 ft 9 in $(2 \times 36) + (2 \times 12) + 9 = \frac{-105\ \text{in}}{12\ \text{in}}$

14. **$41\frac{1}{4}$ feet** Multiply 15 by 2 ft 9 in. Since your answer must be in feet, work in feet: express 2 ft 9 in as $2\frac{9}{12}$, or $2\frac{3}{4}$ ft

$2\frac{3}{4}$ ft $\times$ 15 $= \frac{11}{4} \times \frac{15}{1} = \frac{165}{4} = 41\frac{1}{4}$ ft

If you work with feet and inches, you will need to convert inches to feet after multiplying. 2 ft 9 in $\times$ 15 = 30 ft 135 in = 30 ft + 11 ft 3 in = 41 ft 3 in = $41\frac{3}{12}$ ft = $41\frac{1}{4}$ ft

15. **9 cabinets** Divide $3\frac{3}{4}$ hours by 25 minutes. First, convert $3\frac{3}{4}$ hours to minutes using the conversion factor: 1 hour = 60 minutes. $3\frac{3}{4}$ hr $\times \frac{60}{1} = \frac{15}{4} \times \frac{60}{1} = 225$ min 225 min $\div$ 25 min per cabinet = 9 cabinets

16. **3 cups** Use the conversion factor 8 oz = 1 cup. Divide. 24 oz $\div$ 8 oz per cup = 3 cups

17. **12 oz** Each serving $= 1\frac{1}{2}$ cups. Use the conversion factor 8 oz = 1 cup. $1\frac{1}{2}$ cups $\times$ 8 oz per cup = 12 oz

18. **10** Each package makes 24 fl oz. First, find the number of fluid ounces 5 packages will make. 24 fl oz $\times$ 5 = 120 fl oz Convert the serving size of $1\frac{1}{2}$ cups to fluid ounces. Use the conversion factor: 1 cup = 8 fl oz. So, $1\frac{1}{2}$ cups = 12 fl oz. Divide. 120 fl oz $\div \frac{12 \text{ fl oz}}{\text{serving}} = 10$ servings

GED Skill Focus (Page 169)

1. **5 meters** Move the decimal point 3 places to the left. 5000 mm = 5.000 m

2. **3400 milligrams** Move the decimal point 3 places to the right. 3.400 g = 3400. mg

3. **3000 grams** Move the decimal point 3 places to the right. 3.000 kg = 3000. g

4. **29.5 meters** Move the decimal point 2 places to the left. 2950. cm = 29.5 m

5. **3 liters** Move the decimal point 3 places to the left. 3000 mL = 3.000 L

6. **240 centimeters** Move the decimal point 2 places to the right. 2.40 m = 240. cm

7. **661** Convert 4.6 m to 460 cm Add. 75 cm + 126 cm + 460 cm = 661 cm

8. **16.8** 1,200 g $\times$ 14 = 16,800 g To convert to kilograms, move the decimal point 3 places to the left. 16,800 g = 16.800 kg

9. **5,700** 3.8 km + 1.9 km = 5.7 km To convert to meters, move the decimal point 3 places to the right. 5.700 km = 5700. m

Lesson 15
GED Skill Focus (Page 171)
1. **34.8 cm** (11.6 $\times$ 2) + (5.8 $\times$ 2) = 34.8 cm

2. **60 in** 15 $\times$ 4 = 60 in

3. **39 m** 16 + 13 + 10 = 39 m

4. **5 in** Subtract to find the length of the unlabeled side. 1 − 0.25 = 0.75 in Then add to find the perimeter. 1 + 1 + 0.75 + 0.5 + 0.25 + 1.5 = 5 in

5. **52 ft** (14 $\times$ 2) + (12 $\times$ 2) = 52 ft

6. **68.0 cm** (14.3 $\times$ 2) + (13.5 $\times$ 2) + 12.4 = 68.0 cm

7. **154 ft** 33 + 60.5 + 33 + 27.5 = 154 ft

8. **66 ft** 16.5 $\times$ 4 = 66 ft

GED Skill Focus (Page 173)
1. **54 square meters** 4.5 $\times$ 12 = 54 square meters

2. **576 square inches** 24 $\times$ 24 = 576 square inches

3. **630 square feet** 35 $\times$ 18 = 630 square feet

4. **21 square centimeters** 4.6 $\times$ 4.6 = 21.16, which rounds to 21 square centimeters

5. **168 square feet** 28 $\times$ 6 = 168 square feet

6. **5 quarts** 32 $\times$ 15 = 480 sq ft Divide to find the number of quarts needed. 480 $\div$ 100 = 4.8 qt The city would need to buy full quarts of protective coating, so round up. 4.8 rounds to 5.

7. **7020 square feet** 78 $\times$ 90 = 7020 square feet

8. **3600 square feet**
Think of the new wing as two rectangles: an upper and lower.
Area of lower rectangle: 28 $\times$ 36 = 1008 sq ft
Subtract to find the missing measurements of the upper rectangle. 162 − 90 = 72 ft;
64 − 28 = 36 ft
Area of upper rectangle: 72 $\times$ 36 = 2592 sq ft
Add to find the total area.
1008 + 2592 = 3600 sq ft
(162 − 90) $\times$ (64 − 28) + (28 $\times$ 36) = 3600 sq ft

9. **9600 square feet** 120 $\times$ 80 = 9600 square feet

10. **27,900 square feet** (250 $\times$ 150) − (120 $\times$ 80) = 37,500 − 9,600 = 27,900 square feet

GED Skill Focus (Page 175)
1. **720 cubic inches** 15 $\times$ 8 $\times$ 6 = 720 cubic inches

2. **132.651 cubic inches** 5.1 $\times$ 5.1 $\times$ 5.1 = 132.651 cubic inches

3. **21 cubic inches** 4.2 $\times$ 2 $\times$ 2.5 = 21 cubic inches

4. **96 cubic centimeters** 8 $\times$ 6 $\times$ 2 = 96 cubic centimeters

5. **1440 cubic inches** 15 $\times$ 24 $\times$ 4 = 1440 cubic inches

6. **27 cubic yards** $3 \times 3 \times 3 = 27$ cubic yards

7. **576 cubic feet** $12 \times 8 \times 6 = 576$ cubic feet

8. **6 cubic yards** $(6 \times 3 \times 9) \div 27 = 6$ cubic yards
   OR convert from feet to yards.
   $2 \times 1 \times 3 = 6$ cubic yards

9. **157.5 cubic feet**
   $7.5 \times 6 \times 3.5 = 157.5$ cubic feet

10. **1728 cubic inches**
    $12 \times 12 \times 12 = 12^3 = 1728$ cubic inches

GED Practice (Page 177)

1. **(4) 7** Convert the width to feet.
   1 ft = 12 in so 1 ft 6 in = $1\frac{1}{2}$ ft
   $P = l + l + w + w = 2 + 2 + 1\frac{1}{2} + 1\frac{1}{2} = 7$ ft

2. **(3) 432** Work in inches. 1 ft = 12 in;
   1 ft 6 in = 18 in and 2 ft = 24 in Find the area to
   find the number of square inches of glass needed
   to cover the painting.
   $A = L \times W = 18 \times 24 = 432$ sq in OR
   $1.5 \times 2 = 3$ sq ft; 1 sq ft = $12 \times 12 = 144$ sq in
   $3 \times 144 = 432$ sq in

3. **(5) 10 × 8 × 7** The space inside the room is the
   volume. Volume = length × width × height

4. **(2) 37** Find the perimeter of the top of the
   carton. The measurements of the top are the
   same as those of the bottom, so the top is 8.5 cm
   by 10 cm. Add the sides.
   $8.5 + 8.5 + 10 + 10 = 37$ cm

5. **(4) 8.5 × 12** To find the area of the rectangular
   front of the carton, multiply the rectangle
   length × width.

6. **(5) 1020** Volume is the measure of how much a
   container holds.
   Volume = length × width × height
   $V = 8.5 \times 12 \times 10 = 1020$ cubic centimeters

GED Practice (Page 179)

1. **(4) 5900** The area of the rectangular playground
   is $100 \times 75 = 7500$ sq m. The area of the square
   blacktop: $40 \times 40 = 1600$ sq m Subtract the area
   of the blacktop from the area of the playground
   to find the area of the grassy portion.
   $7500 - 1600 = 5900$ sq m

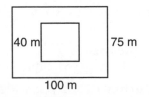

2. **(2) 128** Since the base is
   square, the length and width
   both measure 4 inches. The
   height is 8 inches. Volume =
   length × width × height
   $V = 4 \times 4 \times 8 = 128$ cu in

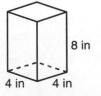

3. **(2) 15** Sketch the quilt and count the points
   where four squares meet.

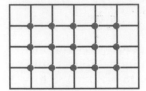

4. **(5) 2.2** Make a sketch and label the distance
   from the start to checkpoint 1 (1.8 km) and
   the distance from checkpoint 3 to the finish
   (1.2 km). Subtract the distances you know
   (1.8 + 1.2 = 3 km) from the total length of the
   race to find the distance from checkpoint 1 to
   checkpoint 3 (5 km − 3 km = 2 km). Since
   checkpoint 2 is at the midpoint of this distance,
   checkpoint 2 is 1 km from checkpoint 1 and
   1 km from checkpoint 3. Add to find the
   distance from checkpoint 2 to the finish line.
   $1.0 + 1.2 = 2.2$

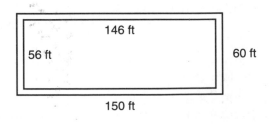

5. **(3) 3** Janice has gone north 4 blocks and south
   4 blocks so she is back in line with the place
   where she began. She walked 5 blocks east and
   only 2 blocks west, so she is 3 blocks east of the
   place where she started.

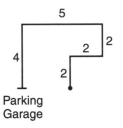

6. **(5) 404** The chalk line forms a rectangle two feet
   inside the other rectangle in all directions. Thus,
   the measurements of the new rectangle are 146
   feet by 56 feet. (Subtract 2 feet from both ends of
   each side, or 4 feet from each measurement.)
   The perimeter of the chalk rectangle is the sum
   of the sides. $146 + 146 + 56 + 56 = 404$ ft

Part 1

1. **(5) Not enough information is given.** Without knowing the width of the rectangle, its area cannot be computed.

2. **(5) 1130** Add the lengths of all the sides. $278 + 234 + 301 + 174 + 143 = 1130$ cm

3. **(3) 2 pounds 13 ounces** Subtract the weight of the puppy in January from its weight in April. Regroup 1 pound from 11 pounds, convert to ounces (1 lb = 16 oz), and add to 12 ounces. Finally, subtract the lesser amount.

   $$\begin{array}{r} 11 \text{ lb } 12 \text{ oz} = 10 \text{ lb } 28 \text{ oz} \\ - 8 \text{ lb } 15 \text{ oz} \quad - 8 \text{ lb } 15 \text{ oz} \\ \hline 2 \text{ lb } 13 \text{ oz} \end{array}$$

4. **(2) 200** Find the area of the larger rectangle. Area = length × width $A = 32 \times 22 = 704$ sq ft
   Find the area of the smaller rectangle.
   $A = 28 \times 18 = 504$ sq ft
   Subtract the area of the smaller rectangle from the area of the larger rectangle.
   $704 - 504 = 200$ sq ft

5. **(2) 16** Perimeter is the sum of the lengths of the four sides.
   Larger rectangle: $P = 32 + 32 + 22 + 22 = 108$ ft
   Smaller rectangle: $P = 28 + 28 + 18 + 18 = 92$ ft
   Subtract the perimeter of the smaller rectangle from the perimeter of the larger rectangle.
   $108 - 92 = 16$ ft

6. **(1) 12** Area of the floor = length × width
   $A = 60 \times 40 = 2400$ sq ft Divide the area of the floor by the area covered by one gallon of paint.
   $2400 \div 200 = 12$ gallons

7. **(3) 14 yards 2 feet** Multiply the length of one board by the number of boards.
   3 yd 2 ft × 4 = 12 yd 8 ft
   Reduce the answer. 1 yd = 3 ft
   12 yd 8 ft = 12 yd + 2 yd + 2 ft = 14 yd 2 ft

8. **(5) 55.95** Add the three sides of the figure to find the perimeter. $16.52 + 17.24 + 22.19 = 55.95$

9. **(3) 54 feet** Add all the sides of the figure.
   12 ft 2 in + 11 ft 8 in + 12 ft 4 in + 8 ft 7 in + 9 ft 2 in = 52 ft 23 in
   Reduce; round to the nearest foot.
   52 ft 23 in = 52 ft + 1 ft + 11 in = 53 ft 11 in, which rounds to 54 ft

10. **(5) 42.875** All sides of a cube are equal.
    Volume = length × width × height
    $V = 3.5 \times 3.5 \times 3.5 = 42.875$ cu ft

11. **(4) 19,200** Volume = length × width × height
    $V = 100 \times 32 \times 8 = 25,600$ cu ft
    Multiply the volume by $\frac{3}{4}$, or 0.75.
    $25,600 \times 0.75 = 19,200$ cu ft

12. **(5) 1458** Multiply the length of the coffee table by its width to find the area of its surface.
    $54 \times 27 = 1458$ sq in

Part 2

13. **(2) 21 + 21 + 18 + 18** Add the four sides of the figure to find the perimeter. $21 + 21 + 18 + 18$

14. **(1) 56** Add the two lengths and the two widths.
    $25 + 25 + 3 + 3 = 56$ ft

15. **(4) 108** To find the area, multiply the length by the width. $18 \times 6 = 108$ sq m

16. **(4) 36** Add the three sides of the triangle to find the perimeter. $10 + 12 + 14 = 36$

17. **(4) 11 feet 3 inches** Add the lengths of the two pieces. 6 ft 8 in + 4 ft 7 in = 10 ft 15 in Reduce.
    10 ft 15 in = 10 ft + 1 ft + 3 in = 11 ft 3 in

18. **(5) 2 feet 7 inches** Change the length of the piece of rope from feet to inches. 1 ft = 12 in
    $7 \text{ ft} \times \frac{12 \text{ in}}{\text{ft}} + 9 \text{ in} = 93 \text{ in}$
    Divide the result by 3 to find the length of each piece. 93 ÷ 3 = 31 in Change the result back to feet and inches. 31 ÷ 12 = 2 ft 7 in

19. **(1) 4** Find the area of the square by multiplying the side of the square by itself. $8 \times 8 = 64$ sq cm Divide the resulting area by the length of the rectangle to find the width. $64 \div 16 = 4$ cm

20. **(2) 8** Find the volume of the larger cube: cube the length of its edge. $4 \times 4 \times 4 = 64$ cu in Find the volume of the smaller cube by cubing the length of its edge. $2 \times 2 \times 2 = 8$ cu in Divide the volume of the larger cube by the volume of the smaller cube.
    $64 \div 8 = 8$ cubes

21. **(2) 105** Add the lengths of the sides to find the perimeter. $10 + 12 + 13 = 35$ yd
    The answer must be in feet. Since 1 yd = 3 ft, multiply the perimeter measured in yards by 3.
    $35 \times 3 = 105$ ft

22. **(4) 28** Find the width of the rectangle by taking half its length and adding 2. $\frac{1}{2} \times 8 + 2 = 6$ ft
    Add the two lengths and the two widths.
    $8 + 8 + 6 + 6 = 28$ ft

23. **(2) 70** There are two missing measurements in the figure. To find the left side, add the two opposite lengths. $5 + 12 = 17$ ft
    To find the short missing side, subtract the two lengths at opposite ends of the figure.
    $18 - 12 = 6$ ft
    Fill in the missing sides of the figure and add to find the perimeter.
    $18 + 5 + 6 + 12 + 12 + 17 = 70$ ft

UNIT 2

24. **(3) 234** Divide the figure into two rectangles. Find the area of the top rectangle by multiplying its length by its width. $18 \times 5 = 90$ sq ft
Find the area of the bottom rectangle by multiplying its length by its width.
$12 \times 12 = 144$ sq ft
Add the two areas. $90 + 144 = 234$ sq ft

25. **(4) 1680** Multiply the number of weeks times the number of days in a week, 7, times the number of hours in a day, 24.
$10 \times 7 \times 24 = 1680$ hr

Lesson 16
GED Skill Focus (Page 185)

1. **mean: 88** $\dfrac{85 + 100 + 65 + 100 + 94 + 80 + 92}{7} = 88$
   median: 92 Arrange the data in order.
   65, 80, 85, 92, 94, 100, 100
   The middle value is 92
   mode: 100 The value 100 appears twice.
   range: 35 high − low = 100 − 65 = 35

2. **mean: 163** $\dfrac{135 + 174 + 128 + 215}{4} = 163$

3. **mean: 72** $\dfrac{57 + 24 + 28 + 57 + 136 + 164 + 38}{7} = 72$
   median: 57 24, 28, 38, 57, 57, 136, 164
   mode: 57 The value 57 appears twice.
   range: 140 high − low = 164 − 24 = 140

4. **$311.25** $311.252 rounds to $311.25
   $\dfrac{\$315.35 + \$369.82 + \$275.58 + \$305.83 + \$289.68}{5} =$
   311.252

5. **mean: 64.4°**
   $\dfrac{61.5° + 65.6° + 64.8° + 60.8° + 69.0° + 61.1° + 67.3° + 65.4°}{8}$
   $= \dfrac{515.5°}{8} = 64.4375$, which rounds to 64.4°
   median: 65.1°
   60.8°, 61.1°, 61.5°, 64.8°, 65.4°, 65.6°, 67.3°, 69.0°
   Average the two middle values.
   $(64.8 + 65.4) \div 2 = 65.1$
   range: 8.2° high − low = 69.0° − 60.8° = 8.2°

6. **mean: $51** Add the amounts and divide by 12.
   $606 \div 12 = $50.50
   median: $49 ($51 + $46) \div 2 = $48.50
   mode: $42 This value appears twice.
   range: $38 high − low = $74 − $36 = $38

GED Skill Focus (Page 187)

1. $\frac{1}{2}$, **0.5, 50%** There are 4 even numbers out of 8 total numbers. $P = \dfrac{\text{favorable outcomes}}{\text{total outcomes}} = \dfrac{4}{8} = \dfrac{1}{2}$

2. $\frac{5}{8}$, **0.625, 62$\frac{1}{2}$% or 62.5%** Five numbers are 3 or greater out of 8 total numbers. $\frac{5}{8} = 0.625$

3. $\frac{3}{8}$, **0.375, 37$\frac{1}{2}$% or 37.5%** There are 3 sections marked 1 or 2 out of 8 total sections. $\frac{3}{8} = 0.375$

4. $\frac{3}{4}$, **0.75, 75%** 6 sections marked with a number other than 4, out of a total of 8 sections $\frac{6}{8} = \frac{3}{4}$

5. $\frac{2}{5}$, **0.4, 40%** Of 20 total trials 8 were white.
   $\frac{8}{20} = \frac{2}{5}$

6. $\frac{3}{4}$, **0.75, 75%** Of 20 total trials 15 were <u>not</u> green.
   $\frac{15}{20} = \frac{3}{4}$

7. $\frac{1}{5}$, **0.2, 20%** There are 25 mixers on the stockroom shelf (5 + 8 + 10 + 2 = 25). Of these, 5 are Model A. $\frac{5}{25} = \frac{1}{5} = 0.2$

8. $\frac{3}{5}$, **0.6, 60%** Out of the 25, 5 are Model A and 10 are Model C. $5 + 10 = 15$ and $\frac{15}{25} = \frac{3}{5} = 0.6$

GED Skill Focus (Page 189)

1. **25%** Chance of spinning red $= \frac{2}{4} = \frac{1}{2}$
   Chance of drawing 4 or higher $= \frac{3}{6} = \frac{1}{2}$
   Chance of both $= \frac{1}{2} \times \frac{1}{2} = \frac{1}{4} = 25\%$

2. **17%** There are 4 sections and all four are either red or blue. There is one 5 in the six cards.
   Chance of spinning either red or blue $= \frac{4}{4}$
   Chance of drawing a 5 $= \frac{1}{6}$
   Chance of both $= \frac{4}{4} \times \frac{1}{6} = \frac{4}{24} = \frac{1}{6} = 0.166 =$ 16.6%, which rounds to 17%

3. $\frac{1}{36}$ The events are independent.
   Chance Max will roll a 6 on the first die $= \frac{1}{6}$
   Chance he will roll a 6 on the second die $= \frac{1}{6}$
   Chance of both $= \frac{1}{6} \times \frac{1}{6} = \frac{1}{36}$

4. $\frac{2}{3}$ The second choice is dependent upon the first.
   Chance John will choose a white tee first $= \frac{5}{6}$
   Chance John will choose white second (note: there are only 5 tees left, 4 of which are white) $= \frac{4}{5}$ Chance of both $= \frac{5}{6} \times \frac{4}{5} = \frac{20}{30} = \frac{2}{3}$

5. **0.2** Two out of ten names are favorable outcomes. $P = \frac{2}{10} = 0.2$

6. $\frac{1}{9}$ The events are dependent. After the first name is drawn, only nine names remain in the box.
   Probability = 1 out of 9 $= \frac{1}{9}$

7. **16%** The two events are independent.
   Chance of spinning the number 20 on one spin $= \frac{2}{5}$
   Chance of spinning 20 twice $= \frac{2}{5} \times \frac{2}{5} = \frac{4}{25} = 0.16 = 16\%$

8. $\frac{9}{25}$ The events are independent. Probability of spinning a number other than 10 = 3 out of 5 $= \frac{3}{5}$ The probability of spinning a number other than 10 twice $= \frac{3}{5} \times \frac{3}{5} = \frac{9}{25}$

Answers and Explanations

9. **0.04** The second event is dependent on the first. Chance 1st unit was defective = $\frac{20}{100}$, or $\frac{1}{5}$

Chance 2nd unit was defective = $\frac{19}{99}$

Chance both were defective = $\frac{1}{5} \times \frac{19}{99} = \frac{19}{495} = 0.038$, which rounds to 0.04

10. $\frac{2}{9}$ These events are dependent. Chance Sharon will draw a heart on the first pick = $\frac{5}{10} = \frac{1}{2}$
Chance she will draw a heart on the 2nd pick = $\frac{4}{9}$
Chance of both = $\frac{1}{2} \times \frac{4}{9} = \frac{4}{18} = \frac{2}{9}$

GED Practice (Page 191)

1. **(3) 87.0** On your calculator:
94 **+** 73 **+** 86 **+** 102 **+** 96 **+**
71 **=** 522 **÷** 6 **=** 87

2. **(2) 90.0** Write the 6 scores in increasing or decreasing order. 71, 73, 86, 94, 96, 102
Since there is an even number of games, there is no middle number. Find the average (**mean**) of the two middle numbers, 86 and 94.
$(86 + 94) \div 2 = 90$

3. **(1) 58.8°** Add the temperatures and divide by five. $\frac{64.4° + 59.3° + 68.0° + 48.8° + 53.6°}{5} = \frac{294.1°}{5} = 58.82°$, or $58.8°$, rounded to the nearest tenth

4. **(3) 6** Add the rainfall for the four months. Divide the result by the number of months. On your calculator: 6.3 **+** 4.5 **+** 3.8 **+** 10.2 **=** 24.8 **÷** 4 **=** 6.2, or 6 rounded to the nearest inch.

5. **(2) 5** Write the values in order. 3.8, 4.5, 6.3, 10.2 Find the mean of the two middle values.
$(4.5 + 6.3) \div 2 = 10.8 \div 2 = 5.4$, or 5 rounded to the nearest inch

6. **(4) $20.38** Write the values in order. $16.22, $17.98, $18.96, $21.80, $28.84, $29.32
Find the mean of the two middle values.
$($18.96 + $21.80) \div 2 = $40.76 \div 2 = 20.38

Lesson 17
GED Skill Focus (Page 193)

1. a. **$699**
   b. **895 kwh**
   c. **16.8 cu ft**

Appliance Central—Refrigerators

Model	Size	Price	Annual Energy Use*
TR8	4. 15.5 cu ft	$459	624 kwh
AD7	18.5 cu ft	$599	895 kwh 1b.
KT6	1c. 4. 16.8 cu ft	$479	922 kwh
CV9	2. 20.4 cu ft	$699 1a.	1108 kwh 3.
GC2	21.6 cu ft	$699	1484 kwh

*energy use in kilowatt-hours

2. **5.6** Subtract the current capacity from the capacity of the CV9. $20.4 - 14.8 = 5.6$ cubic feet

3. **$33.84** There are two ways to work the problem. Method 1: Find the annual cost for each of the two models. Then subtract.

GC2: $1484 \times \$0.09 = \$133.56$
CV9: $1108 \times \$0.09 = \$99.72$
$\$133.56 - \$99.72 = \$33.84$

Method 2: Find the difference in kilowatt-hours and multiply by $0.09. $1484 - 1108 = 376$
$376 \times \$0.09 = \$33.84$

4. **KT6** For each model, divide the price by the number of cubic feet.

TR8: $\$459 \div 15.5$ is approximately $29.61
KT6: $\$479 \div 16.8$ is approximately $28.51

5. **3 to 8** The number of customers returning a product for refund is 12 and the number placing an order is 32. Write the ratio and reduce. $\frac{12}{32} = \frac{3}{8}$

6. $\frac{1}{3}$ 26 of 78 calls were for technical support.
$\frac{26}{78} = \frac{1}{3}$

7. **51%** 32 callers placed an order, and 8 callers exchanged a product, for a total of 40. Set up a proportion to find what percent 40 is of 78.
$\frac{40}{78} = \frac{x}{100}$ $40 \times 100 \div 78 = 51.2$, rounds to 51%

8. **.353** Find Katrina's statistics in the chart. Divide. $6 \div 17 = 0.3529$, which rounds to 0.353

9. **Ruvy** For each player, add the hits and walks. Ruvy, with a total of 10, has reached first base more times than any other player.

10. **37** Add the numbers. $15 + 12 + 10 = 37$

11. **25%** 15 out of 60 = $\frac{1}{4}$, or 25%.

12. **1:1 or $\frac{1}{1}$** The numbers in each category are the same. $\frac{15}{15}$ reduces to $\frac{1}{1}$

GED Skill Focus (Page 195)

1. **$260,000** Read the label on the vertical scale for the middle bar. Your answer should be between $200,000 and $300,000. The scale markings are in thousands of dollars.

2. **Year 4** Compare each bar to the one that comes before it. Only the bar for Year 4 is lower than the previous year's bar.

3. **between $230,000 and $260,000**
A good estimate for Year 5 is $490,000
A good estimate for Year 1 is $250,000
Subtract to find the difference. $240,000

4. **4:1, or $\frac{4}{1}$** Compare the bar for Year 5 (about $490,000) to the bar for Year 1 (about $125,000).
$\frac{\$490,000}{\$125,000}$ is about 4

5. **between $250,000 to $270,000** Add estimates for the sales (height of the bars) and divide by 5, the number of years (number of bars). One possible estimate is: $120,000 + $170,000 + $260,000 + $250,000 + $490,000 = $1,290,000; $1,290,000 ÷ 5 = $258,000

6. **between 300 and 325** Find where the height of the shaded portion of the first bar aligns with the scale on the vertical axis. The number 310 is a close estimate.

7. **between 200 and 250** The 1st shift has about 375 workers and the 3rd shift has close to 150 workers. Subtract to find the difference. 375 − 150 = 225 Even if you used different estimates, the difference between the bars should fall between 200 and 250.

8. **2:1, or $\frac{2}{1}$** The shaded portion of the bar for the second shift (about 220) is about twice the size of the unshaded portion of the bar (about 100).

9. **between 30 and 40 workers** Estimate the number of part-time workers on the 1st shift. 375 − 310 = 65 Estimate the number on the 2nd shift. 320 − 220 = 100 Subtract to find the difference. 100 − 65 = 35

10. **between 825 and 875** Estimate the number of workers for each shift and add. 375 + 320 + 145 = 840

11. **between 6° and 8°** The times between noon and midnight are P.M. Estimate the temperature at 4 P.M. and at 6 P.M. and subtract to find the difference. It was about 68° at 4 P.M. and about 62° at 6 P.M. 68° − 62° = 6°

12. **10 A.M. to 12 noon** The temperature increased from 8 A.M. until 4 P.M. Each line segment represents the change over a two-hour period. The steepest line represents the greatest change. The temperature increased by 10° from 10 A.M. to noon, which is the greatest increase shown on the graph.

13. **October** The number of orders in October is lower, or less, than the number in September. All other months show an increase from the previous month.

14. **about 2000** The number of orders in December was about 6200; the number in September was about 4200. Subtract. 6200 − 4200 = 2000

15. **about 7130** Your answer is correct if it falls between 6900 and 7500. Subtract to find the difference in sales for October and November. 4600 − 4000 = 600 Then find the rate of increase. $\frac{600}{4000}$ = 0.15 = 15% Therefore the rate of increase from December to January is also 15%, and 15% of 6200 (December's orders) is 930. Add 930 to 6200 to predict January's orders. 6200 + 930 = 7130

16. **September and November** Locate a point on the scale for 4400. Then mentally draw a horizontal line across the graph. The points for September and November are closest to the line.

17. **between $150,000 and $166,000** November had approximately 4,600 orders. 4,600 × $35 = $161,000

GED Skill Focus (Page 197)

1. **25%** Add the percents for construction and electrical upgrades. 21% + 4% = 25%

2. **$24,080** Find 43% of $56,000. $\frac{x}{\$56,000} = \frac{43}{100}$ $56,000 × 43 ÷ 100 = $24,080

3. **$7,840** Find 14% of $56,000. $\frac{x}{\$56,000} = \frac{14}{100}$ $56,000 × 14 ÷ 100 = $7,840

4. **39%** Add the percents to be spent on computers and software and subtract from 100%. Computers 43% + Software 18% = 61% 100% − 61% = 39%

5. **furniture and software** Remember, $\frac{1}{3} = 33\frac{1}{3}$%. Add to find the two amounts with a sum that is nearest $33\frac{1}{3}$%. Furniture 14% + Software 18% = 32%, which is nearly $\frac{1}{3}$ of the total budget. (Note: Furniture and construction total 35%, which is also about $\frac{1}{3}$ of the total budget.)

6. **software** Find what percent $10,000 is of $56,000. Then compare the percentage to the graph. $\frac{\$10,000}{\$56,000} = \frac{x}{100}$ $10,000 × 100 ÷ $56,000 is about 17.9%. The item closest to 17.9% is software with a budget of 18%.

7. **$14,000** You know that 21% and 4% will be spent on construction and electrical upgrading. 21% + 4% = 25%, or $\frac{1}{4}$ 25% of $56,000, or $\frac{1}{4}$ of $56,000, is $14,000

8. **$76** Combine the percents for the two items. 13% + 6% = 19% Find 19% of $400. $\frac{19}{100} = \frac{x}{\$400}$ 19 × $400 ÷ 100 = $76

9. **lunches** The percent for prizes is 6%, and 5 × 6% = 30%. The item on the graph nearest to 30% is lunches at 34%.

10. **$\frac{1}{2}$** Observe that the sections for clothes, food, and transportation together make a half circle, which equals 50%, or $\frac{1}{2}$. You can also solve the problem by adding all the amounts to find the total value of the circle, $2000. Then add the amounts for clothes, food, and transportation. $200 + $500 + $300 = $1000 Then write a fraction and reduce. $\frac{\$1000}{\$2000} = \frac{1}{2}$

11. **30%** Add all amounts to find the total budget. The sum is $2000. The amount spent on housing and utilities is $600. Find what percent $600 is of $2000. $\frac{\$600}{\$2000} = \frac{x}{100}$; $\$600 \times 100 \div \$2000 = 30\%$

12. **customer service** Since $\frac{1}{4}$ is equal to 25%, look for this percent on the graph.

13. **53%** Add the percents for data entry and mailings. 44% + 9% = 53%

14. **2:1** Use the percents to write a ratio. 44%:22% = 2:1

15. **between 17 and 18 hours** Find 44% of 40. $\frac{x}{40} = \frac{44}{100}$; $40 \times 44 \div 100 = 17.6$ hr

16. **17 hours** Add the percents for customer service and telephone. 25% + 22% = 47%. Find 47% of 36. $\frac{x}{36} = \frac{47}{100}$; $36 \times 47 \div 100 = 16.92$, rounds to 17

GED Mini-Test • Lessons 16 and 17
(Pages 198–201)
Part 1

1. **(5) $30,412** Add the five annual salaries. Divide the result by the number of salaries. $27,560 + $30,050 + $22,750 + $42,800 + $28,900 = $152,060 ÷ 5 = $30,412

2. **(3) $28,900** List the salaries in order. $22,750, $27,560, $28,900, $30,050, $42,800 The median is the middle number in the list.

3. **(2) $\frac{3}{7}$** Find the total number of possibilities which are not a black sock by adding the number of red socks and the number of blue socks. 2 + 4 = 6 Write a fraction by placing the result over the total number of outcomes, 14. Reduce the fraction to lowest terms. $\frac{6}{14} = \frac{3}{7}$

4. **(3) $400** Subtract the price of gold in July from the price in September. $600 − $200 = $400

5. **(4) 3:1** Form a ratio of the price of gold in September to the price of gold in July. Reduce. $600:$200 = 3:1

6. **(1) October, November, and December** In October, November, and December, the shaded bars, representing the actual rainfall amounts, are lower than the unshaded bars, representing the normal rainfall amounts.

7. **(2) 3** The shaded bars representing December, January, and February are all above 5.0 inches.

8. **(4) 4.6** Subtract the actual rainfall in March from the actual rainfall in January. 6.8 − 2.2 = 4.6 in

9. **(4) 6.0** Add the normal rainfalls for November, December, and January. 5.8 + 6.5 + 6.0 = 18.3 Divide the result by the number of months, 3. 18.3 ÷ 3 = 6.1, which is approximately 6.0 inches

10. **(5) 25** Subtract the number of millions of participants in camping from the number of millions of participants in swimming. 70 − 45 = 25

11. **(4) 57** Add the number of millions of participants in all five sports. Divide by the number of sports, $\frac{58 + 45 + 45 + 70 + 65}{5} = \frac{283}{5} = 56.6$, which rounds to 57 (million)

Part 2

12. **(5) 49** Add the number of minutes for all the days. Divide the result by the number of days, 7. $\frac{42 + 54 + 62 + 40 + 57 + 50 + 38}{7} = 343 ÷ 7 = 49$

13. **(2) 50** List the numbers in order. 38, 40, 42, 50, 54, 57, 62. The median is the middle number in the list.

14. **(3) $\frac{1}{4}$** The total number of possible outcomes is 20. The total number of favorable outcomes (the numbers 16, 17, 18, 19, or 20) is 5. Write a fraction with the total number of favorable outcomes over the total number of outcomes. $\frac{5}{20}$ Reduce the fraction to lowest terms. $\frac{5}{20} = \frac{1}{4}$

15. **(4) 80** Multiply the total number of courses offered by the percent of Personal Growth courses. 500 × 0.16 = 80

16. **(5) 11:5** Compare the percent of Business courses offered to Health courses offered: 22%:10%. Reduce. 22%:10% = 11:5

17. **(2) 5** Subtract the percent of Recreation courses from the percent of Business courses. 22% − 21% = 1% Multiply the result by the total number of courses. 500 × 0.01 = 5

18. **(3) 8,700 to 10,000** The lowest value is in November (8,700) and the highest value is in February (10,000).

19. **(3) four** The graph makes a turnaround in February, May, September, and November.

20. **(5) November to December** Of the consecutive months listed, only from November to December was there an increase in new subscribers.

21. **(4) $4000** Subtract the net sales of the Detroit store from the net sales of the Boston store. $11.0 − $7.0 = $4.0 The scale lists sales in thousands of dollars, so $4.0 represents $4000.

22. **(2) 2:3** Write a ratio of the net sales of the Los Angeles store to the net sales of the San Francisco store. 6:9 Reduce the ratio. 6:9 = 2:3

23. **(3) $8.2** Add the five net sales in the graph. $11 + $6 + $7 + $9 + $8 = $41 Divide the result by the number of stores, 5. $41 ÷ 5 = $8.2

Unit 2 Cumulative Review (Pages 202–206)
Part 1

1. **(5) 8000** Add the percent employed in a wholesale occupation to the percent employed in a health or education occupation.
20% + 12% = 32%
Multiply the result by the total number of people. 25,000 × 0.32 = 8000

2. **(4) 5250** Subtract the percent employed in an entertainment occupation from the percent employed in a business, legal, or professional occupation. 22% − 1% = 21%
Multiply the result by the total number of people. 25,000 × 21% = 25,000 × 0.21 = 5250

3. **(1) 64** Change the length of one side of the square to inches. 1 ft 4 in = 12 in + 4 in = 16 in
Since a square has four equal sides, multiply the length of one side by 4. 16 in × 4 = 64 inches

4. **(4) 860** Find the perimeter of the figure. Add the two lengths and the two widths.
310 + 310 + 120 + 120 = 860 yd

5. **(3) 496** Find the area. Multiply the length of the driving range by its width. 310 × 120 = 37,200
Divide the resulting area by the area covered by one bag of grass seed. 37,200 ÷ 75 = 496

6. **(4) 0.24** Add to find the total number of possible outcomes. 12 + 10 + 28 = 50 The total number of favorable outcomes is 12. Write a fraction with the total number of favorable outcomes over the total number of possible outcomes.
$\frac{12}{50} = \frac{24}{100} = 0.24$

7. **(3) 17 + 35 + 45** To find the perimeter of a figure, add the lengths of the sides.

8. **(5) 2** Convert the length of the longer pipe to feet. 1 yard = 3 feet; 2 yd = 6 ft
Subtract the length of the shorter pipe from the longer pipe. 6 ft – 4 ft = 2 ft

9. **(4) $\frac{1}{50}$** Write a fraction with the total number of successful outcomes over the total number of possible outcomes. Reduce the fraction. $\frac{4}{200} = \frac{1}{50}$

10. **(2) $79.39** List the amounts in the table in increasing or decreasing order.
$59.76, $63.15, $74.47, $84.31, $89.36, $90.12.
Since there are 6 amounts, find the average (mean) of the two middle numbers.
($74.47 + $84.31) ÷ 2 = $158.78 ÷ 2 = $79.39

11. **(1) $76.86** Add the amounts in the table.
$89.36 + $90.12 + $74.47 + $63.15 + $59.76 + $84.31 = $461.17
Divide the result by the number of amounts, 6.
$461.17 ÷ 6 = $76.861 = $76.86, rounded to the nearest cent

12. **(2) 186.0** Add the five scores. Divide the result by the number of scores, 5.
184 + 176 + 202 + 178 + 190 = 930 ÷ 5 = 186

Part 2

13. **(3) 85** Add all the grades. Divide the result by the number of grades.
$\frac{60 + 85 + 95 + 80 + 95 + 95}{6}$ = 510 ÷ 6 = 85

14. **(2) 90** List the grades in increasing or decreasing order: 95, 95, 95, 85, 80, 60. Since there are six grades, average the two middle grades.
(95 + 85) ÷ 2 = 180 ÷ 2 = 90

15. **(2) 10:50 A.M.** Add the times of the three projects. 20 + 20 + 30 = 70 min, or 1 hr 10 min
Subtract the result from 12 noon, or 12 hr.

```
  12 hr          =    11 hr 60 min
−  1 hr 10 min   = −   1 hr 60 min
                     10 hr 50 min
```

16. **(5) 10 to 12 months** The line is the steepest (increases the most) from 10 months to 12 months.

17. **(5) 2.5** Matthew's weight after 1 year, or 12 months, is approximately 13 kg. Subtract the average weight of 10.5 kg from this amount.
13 − 10.5 = 2.5

18. **(4) 8 to 10 months** The line appears to be flattest (increases the least) from 8 months to 10 months.

19. **(4) $7\frac{1}{2}$** One method is to change the fraction to a decimal. $3\frac{3}{4}$ = 3.75 To double the width, multiply by 2. 3.75 × 2 = 7.5 Change the decimal to a fraction. 7.5 = $7\frac{5}{10}$ = $7\frac{1}{2}$ inches

20. **(4) They will fit with 4 inches left over.** Change the length of the wall to inches by multiplying by the number of inches in a foot, 12. 12 × 12 = 144 in
Find the length of the four bookcases in inches.
35 in × 4 = 140 in
Subtract to compare. 144 in − 140 in = 4 in

21. **(1) 40** Use the following conversion factors.
1 gal = 4 qt; 1 qt = 2 pt; thus, 1 gal = 8 pts
5 × 8 = 40 pints

22. **(5) 1080** Change each measurement to feet.
5 yards = 15 feet; 4 yd = 12 ft; 2 yd = 6 ft
Volume = length × width × height
V = 15 × 12 × 6 = 1080 cubic feet

23. **(3) 50** Volume of the cube is the length of the side cubed. V = 5 × 5 × 5 = 125 cu ft
Multiply the result by $\frac{2}{5}$ or its decimal equivalent 0.4.
125 × 0.4 = 50 cu ft

24. **(1) 30** Add the three outer edges that do not attach to the house. 10 + 12 + 8 = 30 ft

Answers and Explanations

25. **(4)** $(12 \times 8) + \frac{1}{4}(12 \times 8)$ To find the area of the rectangle, multiply length by width (12×8). Since the area of the rectangle is four times the area of the triangle, the triangle is $\frac{1}{4}$ the area of the rectangle: $\frac{1}{4}(12 \times 8)$. Add the two areas.

26. **(2)** $\frac{1}{5}$ Three of the 15 cards are less than 4: 3, 2, 1. The probability of drawing one of those three cards is $\frac{3}{15}$. Reduce. $\frac{3}{15} = \frac{1}{5}$

27. **(2)** $\frac{7}{15}$ There are 7 cards numbered with an even number: 2, 4, 6, 8, 10, 12, and 14. Write a fraction with the total number of favorable outcomes, 7, over the total number of possible outcomes, 15. $\frac{7}{15}$

28. **(2) 7:8** There are seven even-numbered cards: 2, 4, 6, 8, 10, 12, and 14. There are eight odd-numbered cards: 1, 3, 5, 7, 9, 11, 13, and 15. The ratio should compare even to odd. Remember that the order in which the ratio is written is important. The number of even-numbered cards should be written first.

29. **(5)** $\frac{1}{225}$ The probability of choosing any one of the cards is $\frac{1}{15}$. By replacing the card, the probability of drawing the same card the next time is also $\frac{1}{15}$. The probability of drawing the same card twice in a row is the product of the two independent probabilities. $\frac{1}{15} \times \frac{1}{15} = \frac{1}{225}$

30. **(5) $4.08** Multiply the percent spent on popcorn by the total amount spent. $0.34 \times \$12 = \$4.08$ million

31. **(3) $5.04** Add the three percents spent on nuts, pretzels, and chips. $13\% + 12\% + 17\% = 42\%$ Multiply the resulting percent by the total amount spent. $0.42 \times \$12$ million $= \$5.04$ million

32. **(2) 2:1** Write a ratio of the percent spent on popcorn to the percent spent on tortilla chips. 34:17 Reduce the ratio. $34:17 = 2:1$

UNIT 3: ALGEBRA
Lesson 18
GED Skill Focus (Page 211)
1. **12** $(+7) + (+5) = +12$
2. **−16** $(-10) + (-6) = -16$
3. **−1** $(-6) + (+5) = -1$
4. **3** $(+10) - (+7) = +3$
5. **−10** $(-3) - (+7) = -10$
6. **−6** $(-1) - (+5) = -6$
7. **−2** $(+6) + (-8) = -2$
8. **20** $(+15) - (-5) = +20$

9. **−14** $(+10) + (-24) = -14$
10. **48** $(-12) - (-60) = +48$
11. **510** $(-118) - (-628) = +510$
12. **−141** $(+315) - (+456) = -141$
13. **−430** $(-1028) + (+598) = -430$
14. **−1541** $(-1482) + (-59) = -1541$
15. **669** $(+824) + (-155) = +669$
16. **7** $(+7) + (-5) + (-4) + (+9) =$
        $(+7) + (+9) + (-5) + (-4) =$
        $\quad(+16) \quad + \quad (-9) \quad = 7$
17. **−6** $(-6) - (+9) + (+10) - (+1) =$
        $(-6) + (-9) + (+10) + (-1) =$
        $(-6) + (-9) + (-1) + (+10) =$
        $\quad(-16) \quad\quad + (+10) = -6$
18. **7** $(-5) - (-4) - (-8) =$
        $(-5) + (+4) + (+8) =$
        $(-5) + \quad (+12) \quad = 7$
19. **−33** $(+13) - (+34) + (-12) =$
        $(+13) + (-34) + (-12) =$
        $(+13) + \quad (-46) \quad = -33$
20. **−27** $(-12) + (-38) + (+75) - (+52) =$
        $(-12) + (-38) + (+75) + (-52) =$
        $(-12) + (-38) + (-52) + (+75) =$
        $\quad(-102) \quad\quad + (+75) = -27$
21. **1250 ft** $(+1000) - (-250) =$
        $(+1000) + (+250) = 1250$
22. **$497**
        $(+\$318) + (-\$60) + (+\$289) + (-\$50) =$
        $(+\$318) + (+\$289) + (-\$60) + (-\$50) =$
        $\quad(+\$607) \quad\quad + (-\$110) \quad\quad = \$497$

GED Skill Focus (Page 213)
1. **−6** $(-2)(+3) = -6$
2. **28** $(-4)(-7) = +28$
3. **−30** $(+6)(-5) = -30$
4. **36** $(+12)(+3) = +36$
5. **12** $(-6)(-1)(+2) = (+6)(+2) = +12$
6. **54** $(+9)(-2)(-3) = (-18)(-3) = +54$
7. **−16** $(-64) \div (+4) = -16$
8. **−5** $(+15) \div (-3) = -5$
9. **4** $(+20) \div (+5) = +4$
10. **3** $(-36) \div (-12) = +3$
11. **−12** $\frac{-132}{11} = -12$
12. **4** $\frac{-4}{-1} = +4$
13. **96** $(12)(-4)(-2) = (-48)(-2) = +96$

14. **−2** $\frac{54}{-27} = -2$

15. **−224** $(2)(-112) = -224$

16. **125** $\frac{-1000}{-8} = 125$

17. **−72** $(-8)(-9)(-1) = (+72)(-1) = -72$

18. **−14** $\frac{126}{-9} = -14$

19. **24,500** $(7)(350)(-5)(-2) = (2450)(-5)(-2) =$
$(-12,250)(-2) = 24,500$

20. **2** $\frac{-42}{-21} = +2$

21. **38** $6 + 8 \times 2^2 = 6 + 8 \times 4 = 6 + 32 = 38$

22. **10** $\frac{-2 - (+8)}{(6) \div (-6)} = \frac{-10}{-1} = 10$

23. **−30** $(-9 \times 4) - (-3 \times 2) =$
$-36 \quad - \quad (-6) \ = -36 + 6 = -30$

24. **−1** $10 + (-3 + 4 \times (-2)) =$
$10 + (-3 + \quad (-8)) \quad =$
$10 + \quad (-11) \qquad = -1$

25. **−61** $(-25) - 4 \times 3^2 =$
$(-25) - 4 \times 9 =$
$(-25) \quad - \quad 36 \ = -61$

26. **−25** $6 - (4 \times 8 + (-1)) =$
$6 - (\quad 32 \ + (-1)) =$
$6 - \qquad 31 \qquad = -25$

27. **−2** $\frac{(-4) + (-6)}{(+4) - (-1)} = \frac{-10}{5} = -2$

28. **82** $(-2 \times 5)^2 + (-3 \times 6) =$
$(-10)^2 + \quad (-18) =$
$100 \ + \quad (-18) = 82$

29. **3** $\frac{-2 - 19}{-3 + -4} = \frac{-21}{-7} = 3$

30. **−1** $2^2 + \frac{-25}{-4 + 9} = 4 + \frac{-25}{5} = 4 + (-5) = -1$

31. **−2** $(2)(-7) - (3)(-4) =$
$-14 \ - \ (-12) = -14 + 12 = -2$

GED Skill Focus (Page 215)

1. $x - 2$

2. $2x + 4$

3. $3x - 9$

4. $5(x + (-3))$

5. $11x$

6. $4x - 10$

7. $\frac{x}{3}$

8. $5 - 2x$

9. $2x + (3)(8)$

10. $\frac{3 - x}{6}$

11. $8 - (15 + x)$

12. $\frac{5}{xy}$

13. $\frac{3x}{x + y}$

14. $x^2 + 12y$

15. $2(x - y)$

16. **a. −19** $3(-7 - 6) + 2(10) =$
$3 \ (-13) + \quad 20 =$
$-39 + \quad 20 = -19$

   b. −7 $3(5 - 6) + 2(-2) =$
$3 \ (-1) \ + \ (-4) =$
$-3 \quad + \ (-4) = -7$

   c. −6 $3(0 - 6) + 2(6) =$
$3 \ (-6) \ + \quad 12 =$
$-18 \ + \quad 12 = -6$

   d. −3 $3(3 - 6) + 2(3) =$
$3 \ (-3) \ + \quad 6 =$
$-9 \ + \quad 6 = -3$

17. **a. −4** $0^2 - 2^2 = 0 - 4 = -4$
   b. 3 $(-2)^2 - 1^2 = 4 - 1 = 3$
   c. 0 $5^2 - (-5)^2 = 25 - 25 = 0$
   d. −3 $(-1)^2 - (-2)^2 =$
$1 - 4 = -3$

18. **a. −5** $\frac{(0 + 5)^2}{0 - 5} =$
$\frac{5^2}{-5} =$
$\frac{25}{-5} = -5$

   b. −9 $\frac{(1 + 5)^2}{1 - 5} =$
$\frac{6^2}{-4} =$
$\frac{36}{-4} = -9$

   c. −32 $\frac{(3 + 5)^2}{3 - 5} =$
$\frac{8^2}{-2} =$
$\frac{64}{-2} = -32$

   d. −81 $\frac{(4 + 5)^2}{4 - 5} =$
$\frac{9^2}{-1} =$
$\frac{81}{-1} = -81$

19. a. 36 $8(4) + \dfrac{-2(2)}{-1} =$

$32 + \dfrac{-4}{-1} =$

$32 + 4 = 36$

b. 64 $8(9) + \dfrac{-2(-4)}{-1} =$

$72 + \dfrac{8}{-1} =$

$72 + (-8) = 64$

c. −8 $8(-1) + \dfrac{-2(0)}{-1} =$

$-8 + \dfrac{0}{-1} =$

$-8 + 0 = -8$

d. 30 $8(5) + \dfrac{-2(-5)}{-1} =$

$40 + \dfrac{10}{-1} =$

$40 + (-10) = 30$

20. a. −100 $\dfrac{(6 + 4)^2}{-1} =$

$\dfrac{10^2}{-1} =$

$\dfrac{100}{-1} = -100$

b. 6 $\dfrac{(6 + 0)^2}{6} =$

$\dfrac{6^2}{6} =$

$\dfrac{36}{6} = 6$

c. −6 $\dfrac{(6 + 0)^2}{-6} =$

$\dfrac{6^2}{-6} =$

$\dfrac{36}{-6} = -6$

d. 32 $\dfrac{(6 + 2)^2}{2} =$

$\dfrac{8^2}{2} =$

$\dfrac{64}{2} = 32$

21. a. −3 $(-3)^2 + 2(-3) - 6 =$

$9 + (-6) - 6 =$

$3 \qquad - 6 = -3$

b. 2 $2^2 + 2(2) - 6 =$

$4 + 4 - 6 =$

$8 \quad - 6 = 2$

c. 10 $4^2 + 2(4) - 6 =$

$16 + 8 - 6 =$

$24 \quad - 6 = 18$

d. 74 $8^2 + 2(8) - 6 =$

$64 + 16 - 6 =$

$80 \quad - 6 = 74$

22. a. −36 $-3(2)(2^2 + 2) =$

$-6 \ (4 + 2) =$

$-6 \quad (6) = -36$

b. −3060 $-3(10)(10^2 + 2) =$

$-30 \ (100 + 2) =$

$-30 \quad (102) = -3060$

c. 2241 $-3(-9)(-9^2 + 2) =$

$27 \quad (81 + 2) =$

$27 \qquad (83) = 2241$

d. 0 $-3(0)(0^2 + 2) =$

$0 \ (0 + 2) =$

$0 \quad (2) = 0$

23. a. 4 $\dfrac{2(4^2 + (-2))}{7} =$

$\dfrac{2(16 + (-2))}{7} =$

$\dfrac{2 \ (14)}{7} =$

$\dfrac{28}{7} = 4$

b. 3 $\dfrac{2(3^2 + 0)}{6} =$

$\dfrac{2(9 + 0)}{6} =$

$\dfrac{2 \ (9)}{6} =$

$\dfrac{18}{6} = 3$

c. 16 $\dfrac{2(-1^2 + (-9))}{-1} =$

$\dfrac{2(\ 1 + (-9))}{-1} =$

$\dfrac{2 \ (-8)}{-1} =$

$\dfrac{-16}{-1} = 16$

d. −8 $\dfrac{2(-5^2 + (-5))}{-5} =$

$\dfrac{2(25 + (-5))}{-5} =$

$\dfrac{2 \ (20)}{-5} =$

$\dfrac{40}{-5} = -8$

GED Skill Focus (Page 217)
NOTE: You may have written terms in a different order. Your answer is correct if all terms are included and each has the correct sign. Remember, the term owns the sign that comes before it.

1. **16x − 8y** $7x - 8y + 9x$
$16x \quad 8y$

2. **3y² − 4y** $5y^2 - 4y - 2y^2$
$3y^2 - 4y$

3. **4m − 3n − 3** $4m - 9n - 3 + 6n$
$4m - 3n - 3$

4. −3x + 2 $-5x + 16 - 8x - 14 + 10x$
$-13x + 2 + 10x$
$-3x + 2$

5. 8x² + 9x + 7 $9x - 6 + 8x^2 + 13$
$8x^2 + 9x + 7$

6. 13n + 25 $25 - 3n + 16n$
$13n + 25$

7. 12x + 36y $12(x + 3y)$
$12x + 36y$

8. −5xy + 45x $5x(-y + 9)$
$-5xy + 45x$

9. 5x + 4y + 15 $4(2x + y) - 3(x - 5)$
$8x + 4y - 3x + 15$
$5x + 4y + 15$

10. 14x − 9 $15 + 6(x - 4) + 8x$
$15 + 6x - 24 + 8x$
$14x - 9$

11. −7n $3m + 2(m - n) - 5(m + n)$
$3m + 2m - 2n - 5m - 5n$
$- 7n$

12. −2x + xy + 2y $x - 2(xy - y) + 4xy - x(3 + y)$
$x - 2xy + 2y + 4xy - 3x - xy$
$-2x + xy + 2y$

13. 25 $3x + 5(x + 9) - 4x$
$3x + 5x + 45 - 4x$
$4x + 45$
$4(-5) + 45 = -20 + 45 = 25$

14. −40 $2m - 3(m + 5) - 15$
$2m - 3m - 15 - 15$
$-m - 30$
$-10 - 30 = -40$

15. 9 $xy + 4x(1 - y) + 2x$
$xy + 4x - 4xy + 2x$
$6x - 3xy$
$6(-1) - 3(-1)(5) = -6 + 15 = 9$

16. −18 $3y(2xz + 2) - 6xyz$
$6xyz + 6y - 6xyz$
$6y$
$6(-3) = -18$

17. 4 $4(2x - y) - 3x + 2y$
$8x - 4y - 3x + 2y$
$5x - 2y$
$5(0) - 2(-2) = 0 + 4 = 4$

18. −68 $9a - 8b(2 + a) + 16b$
$9a - 16b - 8ab + 16b$
$9a - 8ab$
$9(-4) - 8(-4)(-1) =$
$-36 - 32 = -68$

19. (4) 3x + 7y $4(x + 2y) - (x + y)$
$4x + 8y - x - y$
$3x + 7y$

20. (4) −2n² + 6n + 12 $8n - 2(n^2 + n) + 12$
$8n - 2n^2 - 2n + 12$
$-2n^2 + 6n + 12$

21. (1) mn $-m(2m + 2n) + 3mn + 2m^2$
$-2m^2 - 2mn + 3mn + 2m^2$
mn

22. (2) −2a − 10b + 2c $3(-4b) - 2(a - b - c)$
$-12b - 2a + 2b + 2c$
$-2a - 10b + 2c$

GED Practice (Page 219)

1. (4) 10 Start at zero, add −1, add 5, and add −8.
$0 + (-1) + 5 + (-8) = -4$ Rita has −4 points,
which is 10 points less than Jerry's score of +6.

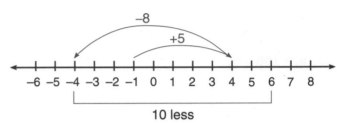

2. (5) −4 The point halfway between 1 and −3 is
−1. Counting 3 units to the left is the same as
adding −3. $-1 + (-3) = -4$.

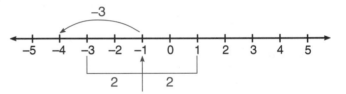

3. (2) −2°F Start at −5; then go up 6 and down 3.
The temperature at 1 P.M. is −2°F.

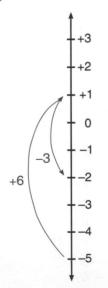

4. (5) 5 To solve the problem on a number line, start at + 4. Move right for the red die scores and left for the green die scores.

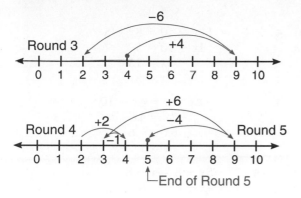

-6

Round 3

0 1 2 3 4 5 6 7 8 9 10

+6

+2

-4

Round 4

-1

Round 5

0 1 2 3 4 5 6 7 8 9 10

End of Round 5

You can also add integers to find the answer.
$(+4) + (+4) + (+2) + (+6) + (-6) + (-1) + (-4) = +5$

5. (4) −4 and 0 Find each pair of points on a number line and locate the midpoint.

2   2

−5 −4 −3 −2 −1 0 1 2 3 4 5

Lesson 19
GED Skill Focus (Page 221)

1. 19
$$x - 15 = 4$$
$$x - 15 + 15 = 4 + 15$$
$$x = 19$$

2. 10
$$x - 7 = 3$$
$$x - 7 + 7 = 3 + 7$$
$$x = 10$$

3. 24
$$\frac{x}{2} = 12$$
$$\frac{2x}{2} = 12(2)$$
$$x = 24$$

4. 7
$$-6x = -42$$
$$\frac{-6x}{-6} = \frac{-42}{-6}$$
$$x = 7$$

5. 13
$$x + 9 = 22$$
$$x + 9 - 9 = 22 - 9$$
$$x = 13$$

6. −5
$$-12x = 60$$
$$\frac{-12x}{-12} = \frac{60}{-12}$$
$$x = -5$$

7. −2
$$x - 8 = -10$$
$$x - 8 + 8 = -10 + 8$$
$$x = -2$$

8. −54
$$\frac{x}{-3} = 18$$
$$\frac{-3x}{-3} = 18(-3)$$
$$x = -54$$

9. −9
$$5x = -45$$
$$\frac{5x}{5} = \frac{-45}{5}$$
$$x = -9$$

10. −27
$$9 + x = -18$$
$$9 - 9 + x = -18 - 9$$
$$x = -27$$

11. 12
$$-11x = -132$$
$$\frac{-11x}{-11} = \frac{-132}{-11}$$
$$x = 12$$

12. 9
$$7x = 63$$
$$\frac{7x}{7} = \frac{63}{7}$$
$$x = 9$$

13. 146
$$x - 94 = 52$$
$$x - 94 + 94 = 52 + 94$$
$$x = 146$$

14. 5.75
$$6.5 + x = 12.25$$
$$6.5 - 6.5 + x = 12.25 - 6.5$$
$$x = 5.75$$

15. 48
$$0.25x = 12$$
$$\frac{0.25x}{0.25} = \frac{12}{0.25}$$
$$x = 48$$

16. $\frac{1}{8}$ or 0.125
$$200x = 25$$
$$\frac{200x}{200} = \frac{25}{200}$$
$$x = \frac{1}{8} \text{ or } 0.125$$

17. 193
$$-69 + x = 124$$
$$-69 + 69 + x = 124 + 69$$
$$x = 193$$

18. 4.8
$$-3.6x = -17.28$$
$$\frac{-3.6x}{-3.6} = \frac{-17.28}{-3.6}$$
$$x = 4.8$$

19. 2.12
$$0.38 + x = 2.5$$
$$0.38 - 0.38 + x = 2.5 - 0.38$$
$$x = 2.12$$

20. 0.55
$$6x = 3.3$$
$$\frac{6x}{6} = \frac{3.3}{6}$$
$$x = 0.55$$

21. 33
$$-13 + x = 20$$
$$-13 + 13 + x = 20 + 13$$
$$x = 33$$

22. 90
$$10x = 900$$
$$\frac{10x}{10} = \frac{900}{10}$$
$$x = 90$$

23. 240

$$\frac{x}{4} = 60$$

$$\frac{4x}{4} = 60(4)$$

$$x = 240$$

24. −9

$$x - 5 = -14$$
$$x - 5 + 5 = -14 + 5$$
$$x = -9$$

25. 128

$$\frac{x}{4} = 32$$

$$\frac{4x}{4} = 32(4)$$

$$x = 128$$

26. −8

$$-6x = 48$$

$$\frac{-6x}{-6} = \frac{48}{-6}$$

$$x = -8$$

27. 48

$$52 + x = 100$$
$$52 - 52 + x = 100 - 52$$
$$x = 48$$

28. −13

$$x - 4 = -17$$
$$x - 4 + 4 = -17 + 4$$
$$x = -13$$

GED Skill Focus (Page 223)

1. 5

$$6x + 7 = 37$$
$$6x = 30$$
$$x = 5$$

2. 5

$$4x + 5x - 10 = 35$$
$$9x - 10 = 35$$
$$9x = 45$$
$$x = 5$$

3. −2

$$3x - 6x + 2 = -4x$$
$$-3x + 2 = -4x$$
$$2 = -x$$
$$-2 = x$$

4. 1

$$6 - x + 12 = 10x + 7$$
$$18 - x = 10x + 7$$
$$18 = 11x + 7$$
$$11 = 11x$$
$$1 = x$$

5. −1

$$5x + 7 - 4x = 6$$
$$x + 7 = 6$$
$$x = -1$$

6. −4

$$9x + 6x - 12x = -7x + 2x - 12 + 5x$$
$$3x = -12$$
$$x = -4$$

7. 4

$$7x + 3 = 31$$
$$7x = 28$$
$$x = 4$$

8. 12

$$3x - 8 = 28$$
$$3x = 36$$
$$x = 12$$

9. 1

$$8x + 6 = 5x + 9$$
$$3x + 6 = 9$$
$$3x = 3$$
$$x = 1$$

10. 5

$$11x - 10 = 8x + 5$$
$$3x - 10 = 5$$
$$3x = 15$$
$$x = 5$$

11. 1

$$-2x - 4 = 4x - 10$$
$$-2x = 4x - 6$$
$$-6x = -6$$
$$x = 1$$

12. −4

$$5x + 8 = x - 8$$
$$4x + 8 = -8$$
$$4x = -16$$
$$x = -4$$

13. 7

$$11x - 12 = 9x + 2$$
$$2x - 12 = 2$$
$$2x = 14$$
$$x = 7$$

14. 14

$$5(x + 1) = 75$$
$$5x + 5 = 75$$
$$5x = 70$$
$$x = 14$$

15. 8

$$5(x - 7) = 5$$
$$5x - 35 = 5$$
$$5x = 40$$
$$x = 8$$

16. 3

$$6(2 + x) = 5x + 15$$
$$12 + 6x = 5x + 15$$
$$12 + x = 15$$
$$x = 3$$

17. 4

$$4x + 5 = 21$$
$$4x = 16$$
$$x = 4$$

18. −9

$$2x - 5x + 11 = 38$$
$$-3x + 11 = 38$$
$$-3x = 27$$
$$x = -9$$

19. 6

$$3x - 8 = x + 4$$
$$2x - 8 = 4$$
$$2x = 12$$
$$x = 6$$

20. 5

$$7(x - 2) = 21$$
$$7x - 14 = 21$$
$$7x = 35$$
$$x = 5$$

21. 10

$$5x - 13x + 2x = -70 + x$$
$$-6x = -70 + x$$
$$-7x = -70$$
$$x = 10$$

22. **8**
$$8x + 12 = 44 + 4x$$
$$4x + 12 = 44$$
$$4x = 32$$
$$x = 8$$

23. **6**
$$2(x + 4) = 14 + x$$
$$2x + 8 = 14 + x$$
$$x + 8 = 14$$
$$x = 6$$

24. **9**
$$5x + 3 = 8(x - 3)$$
$$5x + 3 = 8x - 24$$
$$3 = 3x - 24$$
$$27 = 3x$$
$$9 = x$$

25. **6**
$$2(x + 2x) - 6 = 30$$
$$2x + 4x - 6 = 30$$
$$6x - 6 = 30$$
$$6x = 36$$
$$x = 6$$

26. **−22**
$$11x + 12 = 9x - 32$$
$$2x + 12 = -32$$
$$2x = -44$$
$$x = -22$$

27. **−2**
$$3(x - 9) - 2 = -35$$
$$3x - 27 - 2 = -35$$
$$3x - 29 = -35$$
$$3x = -6$$
$$x = -2$$

28. **−9**
$$3(4x + 3) = -9(-x + 2)$$
$$12x + 9 = 9x - 18$$
$$3x + 9 = -18$$
$$3x = -27$$
$$x = -9$$

29. **−3**
$$x + 11 + 3x = 20 + 7x$$
$$4x + 11 = 20 + 7x$$
$$-3x + 11 = 20$$
$$-3x = 9$$
$$x = -3$$

30. **6**
$$4(2x + 5) + 4 = 3(5x - 6)$$
$$8x + 20 + 4 = 15x - 18$$
$$8x + 24 = 15x - 18$$
$$-7x + 24 = -18$$
$$-7x = -42$$
$$x = 6$$

GED Practice (Page 225)

1. **(5) $x + (3x + 12) = 360$** Let x = the number of employees in management. Let $3x + 12$ = the number of employees in production. The sum of these expressions is equal to the total number of workers, so $x + (3x + 12) = 360$

2. **(3) $2x + 12 = 66$** Let x equal the number of pushups Frank did and $x + 12$ equal the number of pushups Tom did. The sum of these expressions is equal to 66. So $x + (x + 12) = 66$ or $2x + 12 = 66$.

3. **(4) $x + (2x - 4) = 65$** Let x = the fine for the first ticket. The second fine is $4 less than twice the first fine: $2x - 4$. The sum of the fines is equal to $65, so $x + (2x - 4) = 65$.

4. **(1) $\frac{8y}{4} = 2y$** Eight times a number, y, is divided by 4: $\frac{8y}{4}$ This expression equals two times the number, or $2y$. Only option (1) shows that these expressions are equal.

5. **(5) $3x = 60 + 12$** Let x = the number of boys. Let $2x - 12$ = the number of girls. Add the expressions and set them equal to 60.
$$x + (2x - 12) = 60$$
Combine like terms. $3x - 12 = 60$
Simplify. $3x = 60 + 12$

6. **(2) $3x + 2(2x) = 28$** Let x = the cost of a children's ticket. Let $2x$ = the cost of an adult ticket. Angela bought 2 adult tickets and 3 children's tickets: $2(2x)$ and $3x$. The total cost (sum of the expressions) is $28; the equation is $3x + 2(2x) = 28$

GED Skill Focus (Page 227)

1. **5**
$$x + 2x = 15$$
$$3x = 15$$
$$x = 5$$

2. **3**
$$7 + 2x = x + 10$$
$$7 + x = 10$$
$$x = 3$$

3. **93 and 88** The numbers are represented by x and $x - 5$.
$$x + (x - 5) = 181$$
$$2x - 5 = 181$$
$$2x = 186$$
$$x = 93 \text{ and } x - 5 = 88$$

4. **10**
$$8 + x + 12 = 3x$$
$$x + 20 = 3x$$
$$20 = 2x$$
$$10 = x$$

5. **24** The consecutive numbers are represented by x and $x + 1$.
$$x + (x + 1) = 49$$
$$2x = 48$$
$$x = 24$$

6. **20** Let x = George's son's age now.
   Let $5x$ = George's age now.
In 15 years, George's son will be $x + 15$ and George will be $5x + 15$, which will be twice the son's age.
$$5x + 15 = 2(x + 15)$$
$$5x + 15 = 2x + 30$$
$$3x = 15$$
$$x = 5$$
The son is now 5 years old; in fifteen years, he will be 20 years old.

7. **12** Consecutive even numbers are x, $x + 2$, and $x + 4$.

$$x + (x + 2) + (x + 4) = 30$$
$$3x + 6 = 30$$
$$3x = 24$$
$$x = 8$$

The numbers are 8, 10, and 12.

8. **2** Let x equal Diana's age now and $x + 4$ equal Nora's age now. In 2 years, Diana will be $x + 2$ and Nora will be $(x + 4) + 2$, which will be twice Diana's age.

$$2(x + 2) = (x + 4) + 2$$
$$2x + 4 = x + 6$$
$$x + 4 = 6$$
$$x = 2$$

9. **50** Let x = number of bills
The value of $5 bills = $5x$.
The value of $10 bills = $[10 (125 - x)]$.
Sum = total value of $1000

$$5x + 10(125 - x) = 1000$$
$$5x + 1250 - 10x = 1000$$
$$-5x + 1250 = 1000$$
$$-5x = -250$$
$$x = 50$$

There are 50 $5 bills and 75 $10 bills.

10. **32**
$$\frac{2x}{4} = 16$$
$$2x = 64$$
$$x = 32$$

11. **103, 105, and 107**
$$x + (x + 2) + (x + 4) = 315$$
$$3x + 6 = 315$$
$$3x = 309$$
$$x = 103$$

The variable x is the smallest number. The other numbers are 105 and 107.

12. **6** Let x = the first number. The second number is equal to $2 + 3x$.

$$x + (2 + 3x) = 26$$
$$4x + 2 = 26$$
$$4x = 24$$
$$x = 6$$

The first number is 6; the second number is $2 + 3(6)$, or 20. Therefore, the lesser of the two numbers is 6.

13. **$206** Let x = last week's earnings
Let $4x - 18$ = this week's earnings

$$x + (4x - 18) = 262$$
$$5x - 18 = 262$$
$$5x = 280$$
$$x = 56$$

Armando earned $56 last week; this week he earned $4($56$) - $18 = $206

14. **25 and 26**
Let x and $x + 1$ represent the two numbers.
$$x + 3(x + 1) = 103$$
$$x + 3x + 3 = 103$$
$$4x + 3 = 103$$
$$4x = 100$$
$$x = 25 \text{ and } x + 1 = 26$$

15. **228 pairs**
Let x = the number of pairs of dress shoes. Let $2x + 4$ = the number of pairs of athletic shoes.
$$x + (2x + 4) = 340$$
$$3x + 4 = 340$$
$$3x = 336$$
$$x = 112$$
Substitute 112 for x in the expression for athletic shoes. $2(112) + 4 = 228$

16. **62** Multiply the number of adult tickets, x, by the cost per ticket, $8. Multiply the number of children's tickets, $200 - x$, by the cost per ticket, $5. Set the sum of these two terms equal to the total sales, $1414.
$$8x + 5(200 - x) = 1414$$
$$8x + 1000 - 5x = 1414$$
$$3x + 1000 = 1414$$
$$3x = 414$$
$$x = 138$$
There were 138 adult tickets sold, and $200 - 138$, or 62 children's tickets sold.

17. **12** Let x equal Erika's age now.
Let $3x$ equal her uncle's age now.
Let $x - 4$ equal Erika's age four years ago.
Let $3x - 4$ equal her uncle's age four years ago, which was four times Erika's age then.
$$4(x - 4) = 3x - 4$$
$$4x - 16 = 3x - 4$$
$$x - 16 = -4$$
$$x = 12$$

GED Practice (Page 229)
1. **(4) $57.60** Use the cost formula.
$$c = nr$$
$$\$345.60 = 6r$$
$$\frac{\$345.60}{6} = \frac{6r}{6}$$
$$\$57.60 = r$$

2. **(3) 3($6.98) + 4($4.50)** For each type of fabric, the total cost can be found using $c = nr$. The total cost of the first fabric is 3($6.98). The total cost of the second fabric is 4($4.50). Only option (3) shows the sum of these expressions.

3. **(2) $\frac{312}{6}$** Substitute the distance and time and solve for the rate, r.
$$d = rt$$
$$312 = 6r$$
$$\frac{312}{6} = r$$

Answers and Explanations

4. (3) $3.48 Remember, 14.5 cents = \$0.145.
$$c = nr$$
$$c = 24(0.145)$$
$$c = 3.48$$

5. (2) 235 Find the distance for each part of the journey and add. $d = rt$
Part one: $d = 55(2.5) = 137.5$ miles
Part two: $d = 65(1.5) = 97.5$ miles
$$137.5 + 97.5 = 235 \text{ miles}$$

6. (4) \$84.94 For each item, use $c = nr$. The number of items multiplied by the unit price or rate (r) is the cost for that item. Add the costs.
$$3(\$9.99) + 2(\$13.99) + \$26.99 =$$
$$\$29.97 + \$27.98 + \$26.99 = \$84.94$$

GED Mini-Test • Lessons 18 and 19
(Pages 230–233)
Part 1

1. (1) $\frac{2}{x} - 9x$ The product of 9 and x is 9 times x or $9x$. The quotient of 2 and x means $2 \div x$ or $\frac{2}{x}$. Only option (1) shows $9x$ subtracted from $\frac{2}{x}$.

2. (2) $(-6) + (+8)$ Evaluate each expression.
$$(-2) + (-7) = -9$$
$$(-6) + (+8) = +2$$
$$(-3) - (-4) = -3 + 4 = +1$$
$$(14) - (+10) = -6$$
$$(-8) + (+9) = +1$$
Of the results, $+2$ is greatest.

3. (4) 15 and 16 Let x and $x + 1$ represent the consecutive numbers. Write an equation and solve.
$$x + (x + 1) - 13 = 18$$
$$2x - 12 = 18$$
$$2x = 30$$
$$x = 15 \text{ and } x + 1 = 16$$

4. (4) 20 Write an equation and solve.
$$x - 10 = \frac{x}{2}$$
$$2(x - 10) = \frac{2x}{2}$$
$$2x - 20 = x$$
$$-20 = -x$$
$$(-1)(-20) = (-1)(-x)$$
$$20 = x$$

5. (3) 17 Let x equal Caroline's age. Bill's age is $2x - 1$. Write an equation and solve.
$$x + (2x - 1) = 26$$
$$3x - 1 = 26$$
$$3x = 27$$
$$x = 9$$
Caroline is 9 years old, and Bill is $2(9) - 1$, or 17.

6. (4) 279 Use the formula $distance = rate \times time$.
$$d = rt$$
$$d = 62 \times 4.5$$
$$d = 279 \text{ miles}$$

7. (3) $(-6) + (+13)$ The addition starts at 0 and moves 6 spaces to the left to -6. Then the arrow moves 13 spaces to the right, in the positive direction.

8. (5) 19 Substitute the values for x and y and solve.
$$-4(-4) - \frac{3(8)}{2(-4)} =$$
$$16 - \frac{24}{-8} = 16 - (-3) = 16 + 3 = 19$$

9. (1) $(x - 4) - 3$ Box 1 is x, Coop's age now. Box 2 is $x - 4$ because Carni is 4 months younger than Coop. To determine their ages 3 months ago, subtract 3 from each expression. Therefore, Carni's age 3 months ago was $(x - 4) - 3$.

10. (4) 7 Use the formula $distance = rate \times time$.
$$d = rt$$
$$406 = 58t$$
$$\frac{406}{58} = t$$
$$7 \text{ hours} = t$$

11. (5) $5x + \$2.06 = \$31.51$ Using the formula $total \ cost = number \ of \ units \times cost \ per \ unit$, or $c = nr$, you know that 5 times the cost per one bin is the total cost of the bins before tax. The problem states that \$2.06 in sales tax has been added for a total bill of \$31.51. If x represents the cost of one bin, only option (5) shows the correct sequence of operations.

12. (4) $-7x + 14$ Simplify the expression.
$$-5(x - 6) - 2(x + 8)$$
$$-5x + 30 - 2x - 16$$
$$-7x + 14$$

13. (3) 4 Write integers and find their sum.
$$(+8) + (-6) + (-7) + (+11) + (-2) = +4$$

Part 2

14. (1) $\frac{5 - (-2)}{x^2}$
The difference of 5 and -2 is $5 - (-2)$. A number multiplied by itself is x^2. Only option (1) shows the correct difference divided by x^2.

15. (3) 48 Let x, $x + 2$, and $x + 4$ represent the consecutive even numbers. Write an equation and solve.
$$x + (x + 2) + (x + 4) = 138$$
$$3x + 6 = 138$$
$$3x = 132$$
$$x = 44$$
The numbers are 44, 46, and 48.

16. (2) The sum of 4 and x is the same as 6 less than the quotient of x and 5. The equation shows the sum of 4 and x (or 4 added to x) set equal to 6 subtracted from the quotient of x and 5 (or 6 less than the quotient of x and 5). Remember that when division is expressed as a fraction, the numerator is divided by the denominator. Only option (2) expresses each operation as shown in the equation.

17. **(1) −2** Solve the equation.
$$-2(x + 4) = 5x + 6$$
$$-2x - 8 = 5x + 6$$
$$-7x - 8 = 6$$
$$-7x = 14$$
$$x = -2$$

18. **(3) $4.00** Let x equal the cost of a children's ticket and $x + 2$ equal the cost of an adult's ticket. Write an equation and solve.
$$5(x + 2) + 12x = 78$$
$$5x + 10 + 12x = 78$$
$$17x + 10 = 78$$
$$17x = 68$$
$$x = 4$$

19. **(2) −4 + 7 + (−2)** The series of operations begins at 0 and moves 4 in a negative direction. Then the arrow moves 7 in a positive direction, followed by 2 in a negative direction. Only option (2) shows this series of changes.

20. **(5) $21** Let x equal the amount Drew spent and $4x - 15$ equal the amount Linda spent. Write an equation and solve. $x + (4x - 15) = 30$
$$5x - 15 = 30$$
$$5x = 45$$
$$x = 9$$
If Drew spent $9, Linda spent $4(9) - 15$, or $21.

21. **(1) 54** Lindsay's age now is x, and Marco's age now is $4x$. In six years, Lindsay will be $x + 6$ and Marco will be $4x + 6$. Marco's age in 6 years will be 3 times Lindsay's age in 6 years. Write an equation and solve.
$$4x + 6 = 3(x + 6)$$
$$4x + 6 = 3x + 18$$
$$x + 6 = 18$$
$$x = 12$$
Lindsay is 12 years old now; she will be 18 in six years. Marco is 4(12), or 48 years old now; he will be 54 in six years.

22. **(4) 5x + 20** Simplify the expression.
$$6(x + 5) - (x + 10)$$
$$6x + 30 - x - 10$$
$$5x + 20$$

23. **(4) $230** Let x equal the price of Brand A. The price of Brand B is $2x + 40. If you subtract the price of Brand A from the price of Brand B, the difference is $135. Write an equation and solve.
$$(2x + \$40) - x = \$135$$
$$x + \$40 = \$135$$
$$x = \$95$$
If Brand A costs $95, then Brand B costs $2(\$95) + \$40$, or $230.

24. **(2) 88t = 2(192 + 130)** Use the formula *distance = rate × time*. The distance is twice the number of kilometers from Harper to Lakeside to Fuller: 2(192 + 130). The rate is 88 kilometers per hour. Multiply the rate times t for time and set it equal to distance. Only option (2) shows this relationship.

25. **(4) 65** Let x and $\frac{1}{5}x$ represent the two numbers. The sum of the numbers is 78. Write and solve the equation.
$$x + \frac{1}{5}x = 78$$
$$1\frac{1}{5}x = 78$$
$$x = 78 \div 1\frac{1}{5}$$
$$x = 78 \div \frac{6}{5}$$
$$x = 78 \times \frac{5}{6} = 65$$

26. **(4) $575** Let x represent Lucia's car payment and $3x - \$100$ represent her rent. Write an equation and solve.
$$(3x - \$100) + x = \$800$$
$$4x - \$100 = \$800$$
$$4x = \$900$$
$$x = \$225$$
If the car payment is $225, then $800 − $225, or $575, is the rent payment.

Lesson 20
GED Skill Focus (Page 235)

1. **16** $2^4 = 2 \times 2 \times 2 \times 2 = 16$

2. **64** $4^3 = 4 \times 4 \times 4 = 64$

3. **16** A number to the first power is equal to itself.

4. **1** $1^6 = 1 \times 1 \times 1 \times 1 \times 1 \times 1 = 1$

5. **1** Any number (except 0) to the zero power is equal to 1.

6. **81** $3^4 = 3 \times 3 \times 3 \times 3 = 81$

7. **27** $3^3 = 3 \times 3 \times 3 = 27$

8. **49** $7^2 = 7 \times 7 = 49$

9. **$\frac{1}{9}$** $3^{-2} = \frac{1}{3 \times 3} = \frac{1}{9}$

10. **64** $8^2 = 8 \times 8 = 64$

11. **$\frac{1}{125}$ or 0.008** $5^{-3} = \frac{1}{5 \times 5 \times 5} = \frac{1}{125}$

12. **1** Any number (except 0) to the zero power is equal to 1.

13. **1296**

14. **59,049**

15. **729**

16. **0.015625 or $\frac{1}{64}$**

17. **248,832**

18. **78,125**

19. **0.03125 or $\frac{1}{32}$**

20. **2401**

21. **865,000 miles** Move the decimal point 5 places to the right adding zeros as needed. 8.65000

UNIT 3

22. 1.9×10^{-2} mile Move the decimal point 2 places to the right so that there is a digit only in the ones place. 0.019 Since you moved the decimal point 2 places to the right, multiply by 10^{-2}.

23. 3.02×10^3 One way to solve the problem is to change each to standard form and compare the results.

$$5.4 \times 10^2 = 540.$$
$$3.02 \times 10^3 = 3020.$$
$$9.55 \times 10^{-1} = 0.955$$

24. 0.0028 inch Move the decimal point 3 places to the left, adding placeholder zeros as needed. 0002.8

25. 4.2×10^3 $4.2 \times 10^3 = 4.200 = 4200$
4,200 is less than 42,000.

GED Skill Focus (Page 237)

1. **4** $4 \times 4 = 16$

2. **0** $0 \times 0 = 0$

3. **10** $10 \times 10 = 100$

4. **3** $3 \times 3 = 9$

5. **7** $7 \times 7 = 49$

6. **11** $11 \times 11 = 121$

7. **5** $5 \times 5 = 25$

8. **1** $1 \times 1 = 1$

9. **12** $12 \times 12 = 144$

10. **6 cm**
Since $6^2 = 36$, the length of each side is 6 cm.

11. **10 ft**
Since $10^2 = 100$, the length of each side is 10 ft.

12. **4 yd**
Since $4^2 = 16$, the length of each side is 4 yd.

13. **7 in** Since $7^2 = 49$, the length of each side is 7 in.

14. **9 m** Since $9^2 = 81$, the length of each side is 9 m.

15. **8 cm**
Since $8^2 = 64$, the length of each side is 8 cm.

16. **5.29**

17. **9.75**

18. **5.66**

19. **2.45**

20. **18**

21. **6.63**

22. **11.40** Since you are rounding to the hundredths place, show the 0 in the hundredths column.

23. **13**

24. **15.10**

25. **(3) 4 and 5** $4^2 = 16$ and $5^2 = 25$; Since 22 is between 16 and 25, the square root of 22 is between 4 and 5.

26. **(5) 8 and 9** $8^2 = 64$ and $9^2 = 81$; Since 72 is between 64 and 81, the square root of 72 is between 8 and 9.

GED Practice (Page 239)

1. **(4) 14, 15, and 16** Quickly add the numbers in each option. Only option (4) has a sum of 45.

2. **(3) 300** You know that Jess's mileage is 200 miles more than David's. Add 200 to each answer choice (to get Jess's mileage), then add the answer choice to that sum (to get the total mileage). Look for a total sum of 800 miles. If David drove 300 miles, Jess drove 500. $300 + 500 = 800$ miles
OR subtract 200 from 800 and divide by 2. $\frac{(800 - 200)}{2} = 300$

3. **(3) 47 and 48** Add the numbers for each option. $47 + 48 = 95$

4. **(2) 8, 9, 10, and 11** Add the numbers for each option. You may be able to add more quickly if you pair up the numbers. $8 + 10 = 18$ and $9 + 11 = 20$; $18 + 20 = 38$

5. **(3) 14 and 16** All the choices show a difference of 2 hours. Add the numbers in each option to find a sum of 30 hours. $14 + 16 = 30$ hours

6. **(2) 44 and 49** All the choices show a difference of 5 points. Add the numbers in each option to find a sum of 93 points. $44 + 49 = 93$

7. **(3) 142 and 192** All the choices show a difference of 50 miles. Add the numbers in each option to find a sum of 334 miles. $142 + 192 = 334$

GED Practice (Page 241)

1. **(5) Add 4.** Each number in the sequence is 4 more than the number preceding it.

2. **(2) 4** Each term in the sequence is found by dividing the term before it by -2. $-8 \div -2 = 4$

3. **(3) 15 and 35** Substitute 2 and 4 into the function to find the two values for y.
$$y = 10(2) - 5 \qquad y = 10(4) - 5$$
$$y = 20 - 5 = 15 \qquad y = 40 - 5 = 35$$

4. **(2) 15** Each new figure adds a row consisting of the number of circles in the bottom row of the preceding figure plus 1. There are 4 circles in the bottom row of figure D, and 10 circles in all. Figure E should look like figure D with an additional bottom row of 5 circles for a total of 15 circles.

5. **(5) 384** Each term is two times the number before it. This is a good problem to solve with a calculator.

  The 6th term is $48 \times 2 = 96$.
  The 7th term is $96 \times 2 = 192$.
  The 8th term is $192 \times 2 = 384$.

6. **(1) 42** In order for y to be a whole number, x must be evenly divisible by 4. The numbers 8, 12, 28, and 32 are multiples of 4. If 42 is equal to x, y will not be a whole number; therefore, option (1) is the correct choice.

Lesson 21
GED Skill Focus (Page 243)

1. $x^2 + 5x + 4$ $x^2 + 4x + x + 4 = x^2 + 5x + 4$

2. $x^2 + 9x + 18$
  $x^2 + 3x + 6x + 18 = x^2 + 9x + 18$

3. $2x^2 - 17x + 35$
  $2x^2 - 7x - 10x + 35 = 2x^2 - 17x + 35$

4. $x^2 - 4$ $x^2 - 2x + 2x - 4 = x^2 - 4$

5. $xy + 6x - 4y - 24$ This expression cannot be simplified. Note: The terms in expressions are generally written so that the variables are in alphabetical order. Your answer is still correct if the terms are in a different order; however, you must make sure that each term has the correct sign.

6. $6x^2 + 42x + 72$
  $6x^2 + 18x + 24x + 72 = 6x^2 + 42x + 72$

7. $x^2 - 3x - 4$ $x^2 + x - 4x - 4 = x^2 - 3x - 4$

8. $4x^2 - 23x + 15$
  $4x^2 - 3x - 20x + 15 = 4x^2 - 23x + 15$

9. $x^2 + 4x - 5$ $x^2 + 5x - x - 5 = x^2 + 4x - 5$

10. $2x^2 - 12xy - 10x + 60y$ This expression cannot be simplified.

11. $x^2 - 13x + 40$
  $x^2 - 5x - 8x + 40 = x^2 - 13x + 40$

12. $x^2 - 36$ $x^2 + 6x - 6x - 36 = x^2 - 36$

13. $x^2 + 5x + 6$ $x^2 + 3x + 2x + 6 = x^2 + 5x + 6$

14. $9x^2 - 64$
  $9x^2 - 24x + 24x - 64 = 9x^2 - 64$

15. $xy + 9x - 6y - 54$ This expression cannot be simplified.

16. $4x^2 - 21x + 5$
  $4x^2 - 20x - x + 5 = 4x^2 - 21x + 5$

17. $x^2 + 5x - 14$
  $x^2 - 2x + 7x - 14 = x^2 + 5x - 14$

18. $6x^2 + 32x + 40$
  $6x^2 + 20x + 12x + 40 = 6x^2 + 32x + 40$

19. $x^2 - 9$ $x^2 + 3x - 3x - 9 = x^2 - 9$

20. $x^2 - 2x - 120$
  $x^2 - 12x + 10x - 120 = x^2 - 2x - 120$

21. **(4) $(x - 6)(x - 8)$** Multiply. $x^2 - 8x - 6x + 48$
  $x^2 - 14x + 48$
  You may have realized that both whole number terms in the factor must have the same sign in order for 48 to be positive. In addition, the sum of the two whole numbers must be -14. So, both terms had to be negative.

22. **(2) $x + 3$** If $3x - 1$ is one factor of $3x^2 + 8x - 3$, the first term of the second factor must be x, since $3x(x) = 3x^2$. In order to get -3 as the third term in the final expression, the second term in the second factor must be 3 since $-1(3) = -3$. You could also multiply $3x - 1$ by each factor in the choices to find the answer.

23. **(2) $x^2 - 18x + 81$** $(x - 9)^2$ means $(x - 9)(x - 9)$, which equals $x^2 - 9x - 9x + 81 = x^2 - 18x + 81$.

24. **(4) $3x - 2$** Use logical reasoning. To arrive at a result of $6x^2 - x - 2$, you know that the first term of the second factor must be $3x$ since $3x(2x) = 6x^2$. The second term of the second factor must be -2 since $1(-2) = -2$.

GED Skill Focus (Page 245)

1. **$5(x + 6)$** Divide both terms by 5, which is the first term. The result is the second term.
  $$\frac{5x}{5} + \frac{30}{5} = x + 6$$

2. **$3(2y + 5)$**   Divide both terms by 3.

3. **$2(4x - 1)$**   Divide both terms by 2.

4. **$2(2z - 7)$**   Divide both terms by 2.

5. **$b(b + 9)$**   Divide both terms by b.

6. **$y(y + 3)$**   Divide both terms by y.

7. **$2x(x + 2)$**   Divide both terms by $2x$.

8. **$3x(x + 3)$**   Divide both terms by $3x$.

9. **$y(7y - 1)$**   Divide both terms by y.

10. **$2x(2x + 1)$** Divide both terms by $2x$.

11. **$(x + 4)(x + 5)$** Check: $(x + 4)(x + 5)$
  $= x^2 + 5x + 4x + 20$
  $= x^2 + 9x + 20$

12. **$(x - 2)(x - 3)$** Check: $(x - 2)(x - 3)$
  $= x^2 - 3x - 2x + 6$
  $= x^2 - 5x + 6$

13. **$(x + 6)(x - 1)$** Check: $(x + 6)(x - 1)$
  $= x^2 - x + 6x - 6$
  $= x^2 + 5x - 6$

14. **$(x + 4)(x - 7)$** Check: $(x + 4)(x - 7)$
  $= x^2 - 7x + 4x - 28$
  $= x^2 - 3x - 28$

Answers and Explanations

15. (x + 2)(x + 6) Check: $(x + 2)(x + 6)$
$$= x^2 + 6x + 2x + 12$$
$$= x^2 + 8x + 12$$

16. (x + 3)(x − 1) Check: $(x + 3)(x − 1)$
$$= x^2 − x + 3x − 3$$
$$= x^2 + 2x − 3$$

17. (x − 3)(x − 4) Check: $(x − 3)(x − 4)$
$$= x^2 − 4x − 3x + 12$$
$$= x^2 − 7x + 12$$

18. (x + 8)(x − 1) Check: $(x + 8)(x − 1)$
$$= x^2 − x + 8x − 8$$
$$= x^2 + 7x − 8$$

19. (x − 2)(x + 5) Check: $(x − 2)(x + 5)$
$$= x^2 + 5x − 2x − 10$$
$$= x^2 + 3x − 10$$

20. (x + 3)(x + 7) Check: $(x + 3)(x + 7)$
$$= x^2 + 7x + 3x + 21$$
$$= x^2 + 10x + 21$$

21. (x − 5)(x − 8) Check: $(x − 5)(x − 8)$
$$= x^2 − 8x − 5x + 40$$
$$= x^2 − 13x + 40$$

22. (x + 3)(x − 4) Check: $(x + 3)(x − 4)$
$$= x^2 − 4x + 3x − 12$$
$$= x^2 − x − 12$$

23. (x + 2)(x − 10) Check: $(x + 2)(x − 10)$
$$= x^2 − 10x + 2x − 20$$
$$= x^2 − 8x − 20$$

24. (x − 2)(x − 9) Check: $(x − 2)(x − 9)$
$$= x^2 − 9x − 2x + 18$$
$$= x^2 − 11x + 18$$

25. (x + 5)(x − 11) Check: $(x + 5)(x − 11)$
$$= x^2 − 11x + 5x − 55$$
$$= x^2 − 6x − 55$$

26. (x + 4)(x + 12) Check: $(x + 4)(x + 12)$
$$= x^2 + 12x + 4x + 48$$
$$= x^2 + 16x + 48$$

27. (x + 9)(x − 2) Check: $(x + 9)(x − 2)$
$$= x^2 − 2x + 9x − 18$$
$$= x^2 + 7x − 18$$

28. (x + 5)² or (x + 5)(x + 5) Check: $(x + 5)(x + 5)$
$$= x^2 + 5x + 5x + 25$$
$$= x^2 + 10x + 25$$

29. (x − 4)(x − 6) Check: $(x − 4)(x − 6)$
$$= x^2 − 6x − 4x + 24$$
$$= x^2 − 10x + 24$$

30. (x + 1)(x − 7) Check: $(x + 1)(x − 7)$
$$= x^2 − 7x + x − 7$$
$$= x^2 − 6x − 7$$

31. (3) (x − 2)(x − 8) Check: $(x − 2)(x − 8)$
$$= x^2 − 8x − 2x + 16$$
$$= x^2 − 10x + 16$$

32. (4) x + 3 and x − 8 Check: $(x + 3)(x − 8)$
$$= x^2 − 8x + 3x − 24$$
$$= x^2 − 5x − 24$$

GED Practice (Page 247)

1. (5) 12 and 6 Rewrite the equation in standard quadratic form so that the quadratic expression is equal to 0. $x^2 − 18x + 72 = 0$
Factor the equation. $(x − 12)(x − 6) = 0$
Determine the value for x for each factor that will make the factor equal to 0:

$x − 12 = 0$ $x − 6 = 0$
$x = 12$ $x = 6$

Check:

$x^2 + 72 = 18x$ $x^2 + 72 = 18x$
$12^2 + 72 = 18(12)$ $6^2 + 72 = 18(6)$
$144 + 72 = 216$ $36 + 72 = 108$
$216 = 216$ $108 = 108$

2. (3) 3 When the squared variable is multiplied by a number (such as $2x^2$), it is often faster and easier to test the answer choices rather than to factor the equation. Only option (3) makes the equation true.
$$2x^2 − 10x + 12 = 0$$
$$2(3^2) − 10(3) + 12 = 0$$
$$2(9) − 30 + 12 = 0$$
$$18 − 30 + 12 = 0$$
$$0 = 0$$

3. (2) 4 and −3 Rewrite: $x^2 − x − 12 = 0$
Factor: $(x − 4)(x + 3) = 0$
The values for x must be 4 and −3.

4. (4) −5 and −8 Rewrite: $x^2 + 13x + 40 = 0$
Factor: $(x + 5)(x + 8) = 0$
The values for x must be −5 and −8.

5. (5) 2 and −2 Substitute the numbers from each option into the equation. To save time, start with the first number in each pair. Only option (5) makes the equation true.

$x = 2$ $x = −2$
$9x^2 − 36 = 0$ $9x^2 − 36 = 0$
$9(2^2) − 36 = 0$ $9(−2^2) − 36 = 0$
$9(4) − 36 = 0$ $9(4) − 36 = 0$
$36 − 36 = 0$ $36 − 36 = 0$
$0 = 0$ $0 = 0$

6. (2) 5 Substitute the answer choices. Only option (2) makes the equation true.
$$2x^2 − x = 45$$
$$2(5^2) − 5 = 45$$
$$2(25) − 5 = 45$$
$$50 − 5 = 45$$
$$45 = 45$$

GED Skill Focus (Page 249)

1. $x < 1$

2. $x ≤ −2$

3. $x ≥ 0$

4. $x > 1$

5. $x < 3$　　$2x < 6$, so $x < 3$

6. $x > -1$　　$x + 1 > 0$, so $x > -1$

7. $x \leq -2$　　$5x \leq 3x - 4$
　　　　　　　　$2x \leq -4$
　　　　　　　　$x \leq -2$

8. $x < 0$　　$8x < 7x$, so $x < 0$

9. $x < 2$　　$4x - 2 < 3x$
　　　　　　　$4x < 3x + 2$
　　　　　　　$x < 2$

10. $x \geq 1$　　$3x - 1 \geq 2$
　　　　　　　$3x \geq 3$
　　　　　　　$x \geq 1$

11. $x < 8$　　$3x - 7 < 2x + 1$
　　　　　　　$x - 7 < 1$
　　　　　　　$x < 8$

12. $x > -1$　　$5x + 2 > 4x + 1$
　　　　　　　$x + 2 > 1$
　　　　　　　$x > -1$

13. $x \leq 2$　　$6x - 4 \leq 3x + 2$
　　　　　　　$3x - 4 \leq 2$
　　　　　　　$3x \leq 6$
　　　　　　　$x \leq 2$

14. $x \leq 4$　　$3(x + 1) \geq x + 4x - 5$
　　　　　　　$3x + 3 \geq 5x - 5$
　　　　　　　$-2x + 3 \geq -5$
　　　　　　　$-2x \geq -8$
　　　　　　　$x \leq 4$

Notice that the inequality sign reverses when both sides are divided by -2.

15. $x < 2$　　$5 + 8(x - 2) < x + 3$
　　　　　　　$5 + 8x - 16 < x + 3$
　　　　　　　$8x - 11 < x + 3$
　　　　　　　$7x - 11 < 3$
　　　　　　　$7x < 14$
　　　　　　　$x < 2$

16. $x > -7$　　$x + 12 < 5(x + 8)$
　　　　　　　$x + 12 < 5x + 40$
　　　　　　$-4x + 12 < 40$
　　　　　　　$-4x < 28$
　　　　　　　$x > -7$

Notice that the inequality sign reverses when both sides are divided by -4.

17. $x \geq -17$　　$2x + (4 - 3x) \leq 21$
　　　　　　　$2x + 4 - 3x \leq 21$
　　　　　　　$-x + 4 \leq 21$
　　　　　　　$-x \leq 17$

Divide both sides by -1 and reverse the inequality sign. $x \geq -17$

18. $x > -5$　　$7x - 3x - x < 3x + 2x + 10$
　　　　　　　$3x < 5x + 10$
　　　　　　　$-2x < 10$
　　　　　　　$x > -5$

Notice that the inequality sign reverses when both sides are divided by -2.

19. $x < 4$　　Set up an inequality and solve.
　　　　　　　$5x + 6 < 4x + 10$
　　　　　　　$x + 6 < 10$
　　　　　　　$x < 4$

20. $x \leq 26$　　Set up an inequality and solve.
　　　　　　　$21 + 18 + x \leq 65$
　　　　　　　$39 + x \leq 65$
　　　　　　　$x \leq 26$

Lesson 22
GED Skill Focus (Page 251)

1. **(−5,0)** Remember to read the *x*-axis first.

2. **Point *E***

3. **Point *C***

4. **(5,1)**

5. **Point *B***

6. ***D* (5,1), *F* (−2,−4), *G* (1,−2),** and ***H* (3,−5)**

7. ***G* and *H***

8.

9.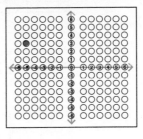

10.

11.

GED Practice (Page 253)

1. Count 4 to the right along the *x*-axis (horizontal line) and 1 down along the *y*-axis (vertical line).

2. A square has 4 sides of equal lengths. From the graph in the problem, you can see that each side of the square is 4 units long. By counting, you can see that the missing corner must be placed at (3, −3).

3. Count 5 to the left along the *x*-axis and 3 up along the *y*-axis.

4. A rectangle has four sides, with opposite sides of equal length. From the graph in the problem, you can see that the missing corner must be located at (−5, −3).

GED Skill Focus (Page 255)
For questions 1–6, two ordered pairs on the line are given. You may have found other ordered pairs in order to draw your line. Your answer is correct if it passes through the points given here.

1. **(0, −4), (1, −1)**

2. **(1, 3), (2, 1)**

3. **(1, 0), (3, 1)**

4. (0,0), (1,−2)

5. (2,−4), (1,−3)

6. (1,3), (2,0)

7. (2) $x - y = -1$ Choose an ordered pair from the graph and substitute the x- and y-values into each equation in the answer choices. If the ordered pair makes more than one equation true, use another ordered pair from the graph. Remember, each point on the line is a solution for the equation of the line.

8. (1) (−3,−4) Substitute the ordered pairs in the answer choices in the given equation. Only option (1) makes the equation true.
$$x - y = -1$$
$$-3 - (-4) = 1$$
$$-3 + 4 = 1$$
$$1 = 1$$

9. (4) $x + y = 2$ Find the ordered pair from a point on the graph: (2,0) or (0,2). Try the values for one of the points in each equation. If the point lies on the line, it will make the equation true.

10. (2) −2 Although you could graph the equation in order to solve the problem, the easiest way is to substitute the value 1 for y in the equation and solve for x.
$$-4x + 7y = 15$$
$$-4x + 7(1) = 15$$
$$-4x + 7 = 15$$
$$-4x = 8$$
$$x = 22$$

GED Skill Focus (Page 257)

1. **−1** The line goes downward 1 unit as it moves 1 unit to the right. $\frac{-1}{1} = -1$

2. $\frac{3}{2}$ The line rises 3 units as it moves 2 units to the right. $\frac{3}{2}$

3. **1** The line rises 2 units as it moves 2 units to the right. $\frac{2}{2} = 1$

4. $\frac{-1}{2}$ The line goes downward 2 units as it moves 4 units to the right. $\frac{-2}{4} = \frac{-1}{2}$

5. **0** A horizontal line has a slope of 0.

6. $\frac{1}{2}$ The line rises 2 units as it moves 4 units to the right. $\frac{2}{4} = \frac{1}{2}$

For questions 7–12, use the slope formula: $m = \frac{y_2 - y_1}{x_2 - x_1}$

7. **−4** $m = \frac{1 - (-3)}{0 - 1} = \frac{4}{-1} = -4$

8. $\frac{1}{2}$ $m = \frac{2 - 1}{4 - 2} = \frac{1}{2}$

9. **9** $m = \frac{-4 - 5}{3 - 4} = \frac{-9}{-1} = 9$

10. $\frac{1}{9}$ $m = \frac{3 - 2}{5 - (-4)} = \frac{1}{9}$

11. **3** $m = \frac{0 - (-3)}{-2 - (-3)} = \frac{3}{1} = 3$

12. $\frac{2}{3}$ $m = \frac{4 - (-2)}{3 - (-6)} = \frac{6}{9} = \frac{2}{3}$

13. $\frac{1}{2}$ The line rises 3 units for every 6 units it moves to the right: $\frac{3}{6} = \frac{1}{2}$.

14. **0** You can use the slope formula to find an answer. However, you may have noticed that the y-coordinates in the ordered pairs are the same number. This means the line must be parallel to the x-axis and have a slope of 0.

15. **(0,5)** Substitute the given values in the slope formula.
$$3 = \frac{-1 - y}{-2 - 0} = \frac{-1 - y}{-2}$$
$$-2(3) = -1 - y$$
$$-6 = -1 - y$$
$$-5 = -y$$
$$5 = y$$

16. $\frac{5}{8}$ Substitute the ordered pairs in the slope formula.
$$\frac{2 - (-3)}{5 - (-3)} = \frac{2 + 3}{5 + 3} = \frac{5}{8}$$

GED Skill Focus (Page 259)

1. **8** Since the points lie on a vertical line, count spaces to find the distance. Point C is 8 spaces above Point A.

2. **6.3** Point B is at (−4,1) and point D is at (2,3). Use the formula to find the distance.
$$\text{distance} = \sqrt{(x_2 - x_1)^2 + (y_2 - y_1)^2}$$
$$= \sqrt{(2 - (-4))^2 + (3 - 1)^2}$$
$$= \sqrt{6^2 + 2^2}$$
$$= \sqrt{36 + 4}$$
$$= \sqrt{40} \approx 6.32, \text{ which rounds to } 6.3$$
(If you could not use a calculator, you would know that $\sqrt{40}$ is between 6 ($\sqrt{36}$) and 7 ($\sqrt{49}$).)

Answers and Explanations

3. **6** Since the points lie on a horizontal line, count spaces to find the distance. Point E is 6 spaces to the right of Point A.

4. **7.6** Point A is at $(-1,-4)$ and point D is at $(2,3)$. Use the formula to find the distance.

$$\text{distance} = \sqrt{(x_2 - x_{+1})^2 + (y_2 - y_1)^2}$$
$$= \sqrt{(2 - (-1))^2 + (3 - (-4))^2}$$
$$= \sqrt{3^2 + 7^2}$$
$$= \sqrt{9 + 49}$$
$$= \sqrt{58} \approx 7.61, \text{ which rounds to } 7.6$$

(If you could not use a calculator, you would know that $\sqrt{58}$ is between 7 ($\sqrt{49}$) and 8 ($\sqrt{64}$).)

5. **10** Point C is at $(-1,4)$ and point E is at $(5,-4)$. Use the formula to find the distance.

$$\text{distance} = \sqrt{(x_2 - x_1)^2 + (y_2 - y_1)^2}$$
$$= \sqrt{(5 - (-1))^2 + (-4 - 4)^2}$$
$$= \sqrt{6^2 + (-8)^2}$$
$$= \sqrt{36 + 64}$$
$$= \sqrt{100} = 10$$

6. **8.5** Point J is at $(-2,4)$ and point L is at $(1,-4)$. Use the formula to find the distance.

$$\text{distance} = \sqrt{(x_2 - x_1)^2 + (y_2 - y_1)^2}$$
$$= \sqrt{(1 - (-2))^2 + (-4 - 4)^2}$$
$$= \sqrt{3^2 + (-8)^2}$$
$$= \sqrt{9 + 64}$$
$$= \sqrt{73} \approx 8.54, \text{ which rounds to } 8.5$$

(If you could not use a calculator, you would know that $\sqrt{73}$ is between 8 ($\sqrt{64}$) and 9 ($\sqrt{81}$).)

7. **8.9** Point K is at $(5,4)$ and point L is at $(1,-4)$. Use the formula to find the distance.

$$\text{distance} = \sqrt{(x_2 - x_1)^2 + (y_2 - y_1)^2}$$
$$= \sqrt{(1 - 5)^2 + (-4 - 4)^2}$$
$$= \sqrt{(-4)^2 + (-8)^2}$$
$$= \sqrt{16 + 64}$$
$$= \sqrt{80} \approx 8.94, \text{ which rounds to } 8.9$$

(If you could not use a calculator, you would know that $\sqrt{80}$ is between 8 ($\sqrt{64}$) and 9 ($\sqrt{81}$).)

8. **7** Since the points lie on a horizontal line, count spaces to find the distance. Point K is 7 spaces to the right of Point J.

9. **9.5** Point X is at $(9,3)$ and the origin is at $(0,0)$. Use the formula to find the distance.

$$\text{distance} = \sqrt{(x_2 - x_1)^2 + (y_2 - y_1)^2}$$
$$= \sqrt{(0 - 9)^2 + (0 - 3)^2}$$
$$= \sqrt{(-9)^2 + (-3)^2}$$
$$= \sqrt{81 + 9}$$
$$= \sqrt{90} \approx 9.48, \text{ which rounds to } 9.5$$

(If you could not use a calculator, you would know that $\sqrt{90}$ is between 9 ($\sqrt{81}$) and 10 ($\sqrt{100}$).)

10. **6** The points have the same y-coordinate which means they lie on the same horizontal grid line. You could solve the problem by plotting the points and counting the spaces. You can also use the formula.

$$\text{distance} = \sqrt{(x_2 - x_1)^2 + (y_2 - y_1)^2}$$
$$= \sqrt{(-4 - 2)^2 + (5 - 5)^2}$$
$$= \sqrt{(-6)^2 + 0^2}$$
$$= \sqrt{36 + 0}$$
$$= \sqrt{36} = 6$$

11. **10** Use the formula to find the distance.

$$\text{distance} = \sqrt{(x_2 - x_1)^2 + (y_2 - y_1)^2}$$
$$= \sqrt{(8 - 0)^2 + (0 - 6)^2}$$
$$= \sqrt{8^2 + (-6)^2}$$
$$= \sqrt{64 + 36}$$
$$= \sqrt{100} = 10$$

12. **5** The points have the same x-coordinate which means they lie on the same vertical grid line. You could solve the problem by plotting the points and counting the spaces. You can also use the formula.

$$\text{distance} = \sqrt{(x_2 - x_1)^2 + (y_2 - y_1)^2}$$
$$= \sqrt{(2 - 2)^2 + (4 - (-1))^2}$$
$$= \sqrt{0^2 + 5^2}$$
$$= \sqrt{0 + 25}$$
$$= \sqrt{25} = 5$$

GED Practice (Page 261)

1. **(3) $(0,-2)$** In the slope-intercept form of a line, the y-intercept is added to or subtracted from the product of the slope (m) and x. The x-coordinate of the y-intercept is always 0.

2. **(5) $y + \frac{1}{4}x = 3$** Line A rises 1 unit for every 4 units it moves to the left (a negative direction), so the slope is $-\frac{1}{4}$. The y-intercept is 3. In slope-intercept form, the equation of Line A is $y = -\frac{1}{4}x + 3$. Only option (5) is equal to this equation.

3. **(2) $y = x$** Line B rises 2 units for every 2 units it moves to the right, so the slope is $\frac{2}{2} = 1$. The line crosses the y-axis at the origin $(0,0)$, so its y-intercept is 0. In slope-intercept form, the equation is $y = 1x + 0$, which equals $y = x$.

4. **(3) $y = 3x - 5$** Only option (3) subtracts 5 from the product of x and a number.

5. **(1) $y = -x + 3$** Find the slope using the coordinates of points P and Q. The line must rise 2 units for every 2 units it moves to the left: $\frac{2}{-2} = -1$. If you continue the line at a slope of -1, it will cross the y-axis at point $(0,3)$. Using the slope-intercept form, the equation must be $y = x + 3$.

6. **(2) (0,–2)** The line described must have a slope of $\frac{2}{3}$, meaning it rises 2 units for every 3 units it moves to the right. From Point R, count up 2 units and 3 to the right. You are at coordinates $(0,-2)$, the y-intercept of the line.

GED Mini-Test • Lessons 20–22
(Pages 262–265)
Part 1

1. **(3) Point E** To find $(4,-2)$, count 4 units to the right of the origin and then down 2 units.

2. **(3) $\frac{1}{2}$** The line rises at it goes from left to right so the slope is positive. The line rises 3 units for every 6 units it runs to the right. Write the ratio and simplify. $\frac{3}{6} = \frac{1}{2}$

3. **(1) $x > -2$** Solve the inequality.
$$5x + 2 < 6x + 3x + 10$$
$$5x + 2 < 9x + 10$$
$$-4x + 2 < 10$$
$$-4x < 8$$
$$x > -2$$
You must reverse the inequality sign when you divide both sides of the equation by -4.

4. **(2) 43, 45, and 47** You can eliminate options (3) and (4) since they do not list consecutive odd numbers. Use your calculator to add the numbers in the remaining options. Only the numbers in option (2) add up to 135.

5. **(4) 31** Find the differences between the terms in the sequence:

0	1	increase of 1
1	3	increase of 2
3	7	increase of 4
7	15	increase of 8

Look at the list of increases. Each increase is double the one before it. The next increase must be $2 \times 8 = 16$. Add 16 to the last term in the sequence. $15 + 16 = 31$

6. **(3)**
Solve the inequality.
$$x - 3 < -1$$
$$x < 2$$
In option (3) the portion of the number line to the left of 2 is shaded to show that all values less than 2 are solutions to the inequality. The number 2 has an open circle to show that 2 is not a solution.

7. **(4) 4.7×10^{-1}, 2.34×10^2, 5.2×10^2** Find the value of each expression.
$4.7 \times 10^{-1} = 0.47$ Move decimal 1 place left.
$2.34 \times 10^2 = 234$ Move decimal 2 places right.
$5.2 \times 10^2 = 520$ Move decimal 2 places right.
Compare the resulting values and put the original expressions in order from least to greatest.

8. **(2) $(x - 6)(x - 6)$** Use the FOIL method to multiply each factor pair. Only option (2) equals the original expression.
$$(x - 6)(x - 6) = x^2 - 6x - 6x + 36 =$$
$$x^2 - 12x + 36$$

9. **(4) $(-2,-11)$** Substitute the answer choices into the equation. Only option (4) makes the equation true.
$$5x - y = 1$$
$$5(-2) - (-11) = 1$$
$$-10 + 11 = 1$$
$$1 = 1$$

10. **(3) A, D, and F** One way to solve the problem is to find the coordinates of some of the points on the graph and substitute them in the given equation. If you choose this method, remember that it isn't necessary to try every point. Choose points that appear in only one or two choices in order to eliminate as many choices as possible.
   Another way to solve the problem is to graph the equation on the grid. Notice that the equation is written in slope-intercept form, or $y = mx + b$, where $m = $ slope and $b = y$-intercept. The y-intercept is $(0,3)$, the location of point D. The slope is $\frac{-3}{2}$. To find another point on the line, start at point D and count down 3 and 2 to the right. You are now at point A. The correct option passes through points A, D, and F.

11. **(2) 8** Use the distance formula.
$$\text{distance} = \sqrt{(x_2 - x_1)^2 + (y_2 - y_1)^2}$$
Remember, it doesn't matter which point you choose to be (x_1,y_1) and (x_2,y_2). The solution below uses A $(2,0)$ as (x_1,y_1) and C $(-5,-4)$ as (x_2,y_2).
$$\text{distance} = \sqrt{(x_2 - x_1)^2 + (y_2 - y_1)^2}$$
$$= \sqrt{(-5 - 2)^2 + (-4 - 0)^2}$$
$$= \sqrt{(-7)^2 + (-4)^2}$$
$$= \sqrt{49 + 16}$$
$$= \sqrt{65} \approx 8$$
(If you could not use a calculator, you would know that $\sqrt{65}$ is close to 8 ($\sqrt{64}$).)

12. **(4) 1.14×10^5** To write a number in scientific notation, move the decimal point until only one digit is to the left of the decimal point. In this case, you have to move the decimal point 5 places to the left, so the power of ten is 10^5.

Part 2

13. **(1) −5 and 4** This is a quadratic equation. Either use factoring or simply substitute each answer choice into the equation until you find the correct one.

   To use the factoring method, rewrite the equation so that the quadratic expression equals 0. Then factor.
$$x^2 + x = 20$$
$$x^2 + x - 20 = 0$$
$$(x + 5)(x - 4) = 0$$

   Then find the value of x for each factor that will make that factor equal to 0.
$$x + 5 = 0 \qquad x - 4 = 0$$
$$x = -5 \qquad x = 4$$

14. **(5) $392** Substitute 32 for s in the function and solve for p.
$$p = \$200 + \$6(32)$$
$$p = \$200 + \$192$$
$$p = \$392$$

15. **(5) (2, 5)** Substitute the answer choices into the equation. Only option (5) makes the equation true.
$$4x - y = 3$$
$$4(2) - 5 = 3$$
$$8 - 5 = 3$$
$$3 = 3$$

16. **(4) between 15 and 16 feet**
   Since the area of a square equals the side squared, the side of a square equals the square root of the area. Try squaring the numbers in the answer choices to find the approximate square root of 240.
   You know $12 \times 12 = 144$ and $20 \times 20 = 400$, so start with values between these two.
   $14 \times 14 = 196 \quad 15 \times 15 = 225 \quad 16 \times 16 = 256$
   $\sqrt{240}$ is between 15 and 16.

17. **(2) B** A line with a negative slope moves downward as it goes from left to right. The slope of Line A is undefined. Lines C and D have positive slopes, and the slope of Line E is 0.

18. **(2) $\dfrac{5}{x - 2}$** Factor each expression. Then simplify.
$$\frac{x + 4x}{x^2 - 2x} = \frac{x(1 + 4)}{x(x - 2)} = \frac{5}{x - 2}$$

   Note: You can cancel x from the numerator and the denominator in the second step since $\dfrac{x}{x} = 1$.

19. **(5) (3,6)** Substitute the ordered pairs in the answer options until you find the one that does not make the equation true.
$$2x - y = -1$$
$$2(3) - 6 \neq -1$$

20. **(1) $y = 2x + 2$** The answer choices are written in slope-intercept form $y = mx + b$, where m = slope and b = y-intercept. Remember, slope

is the ratio of *rise over run*. Notice that the line rises 4 units and runs 2 units as it goes from Point A to Point B; therefore, the slope is $\frac{4}{2} = +2$. The y-intercept of the line, the point where the line crosses the y-axis, is +2. Therefore, the correct equation of the line is $y = 2x + 2$.

   You could also solve the problem by finding the coordinates of two points on the line and substituting to find the correct equation. Always use two points since more than one line could pass through only one point.

21. **(3) $c = \$40 + \$30h$** The charge for a service call is the sum of $40 (the flat fee) and the number of hours multiplied by $30. Only option (3) shows this sequence of operations.

22. **(1) −3** Use the slope formula. Let $(-2,-2) = (x_1,y_1)$ and $(-4,4) = (x_2,y_2)$
$$m = \frac{y_2 - y_1}{x_2 - x_1}$$
$$m = \frac{4 - (-2)}{-4 - (-2)}$$
$$m = \frac{6}{-2} = -3$$

23. **(4) $152** Each month an additional $12 is deposited. Continue adding $12 until you reach December, the 12th month. You can also solve the problem by multiplying $12 by 11, the number of increases, and adding $20, the beginning deposit. $11(\$12) + \$20 = \$152$

24. **(4) $y = -x + 3$** The line moves downward 1 unit each time it goes to the right 1 unit for a slope of $\frac{-1}{1} = -1$. The y-intercept is +3. Use the slope-intercept form to write the equation of the line. $y = mx + b$, where m = slope and b = y-intercept.
$$y = -1x + 3, \text{ or } y = x + 3$$

25. **(3) 5** Use the formula for finding the distance between two points. Let $D (1,3) = (x_1,y_1)$ and $F (4,-1) = (x_2,y_2)$.
$$\text{distance} = \sqrt{(x_2 - x_1)^2 + (y_2 - y_1)^2}$$
$$= \sqrt{(4 - 1)^2 + (-1 - 3)^2}$$
$$= \sqrt{3^2 + (-4)^2}$$
$$= \sqrt{9 + 16}$$
$$= \sqrt{25} = 5$$

Unit 3 Cumulative Review (Pages 266–270)

Part 1

1. **(2) −19** Substitute the values for x and y and solve.
$$4x - 2y + xy$$
$$4(-1) - 2(5) + (-1)(5)$$
$$-4 \ - \ 10 \qquad - 5 = -19$$

2. **(2) $-x - 5$** Think of the subtraction operation as multiplying the contents of the parentheses by -1. $2 - (x + 7) = 2 + (-1)(x + 7) = 2 - x - 7 = -x - 5$

3. (1) $\frac{1}{2}$ Solve for x as shown.

$$-6(x + 1) + 4 = 8x - 9$$

Remove parentheses.	$-6x - 6 + 4 = 8x - 9$
Combine like terms.	$-6x - 2 = 8x - 9$
Subtract $8x$ from both sides.	$-14x - 2 = \quad\quad -9$
Add 2 to both sides.	$-14x = \quad -7$
Divide both sides by -14.	$x = \frac{-7}{-14} = \quad \frac{1}{2}$

4. (5) 12 Write an equation and solve.

$$x - 2 = 7 + \frac{x}{4}$$

Multiply both sides by 4.	$4(x - 2) = 4(7 + \frac{x}{4})$
	$4x - 8 = 28 + x$
Subtract x from both sides.	$3x - 8 = 28$
Add 8 to both sides.	$3x = 36$
Divide both sides by 3.	$x = 12$

5. (5)

A number line from -3 to 3 with point at 1 circled and values greater than 1 shaded.

Solve the inequality for x.	$6 - 5x < 7x - 6$
Add 6 to both sides.	$12 - 5x < 7x$
Add $5x$ to both sides.	$12 < 12x$
Divide both sides by 12.	$1 < x$ or $x > 1$

Only option (5) shows the integer 1 circled and all values greater than 1 shaded.

6. (3) $-4x = -5x + 2 + 8$ The product of a number and -4 can be written $-4x$. Two added to -5 times the number is $2 + (-5x)$. The problems states that $-4x$ is 8 more than $2 + (-5x)$. In order to create an equation with two equal expressions, 8 must either be subtracted from $-4x$ or added to $2 + (-5x)$. The only correct equation is option (3).

7. (4) $\frac{-2}{3}$ The line rises 2 units as it moves 3 units to the left (a negative direction). The slope is $\frac{-2}{3}$.

8. (3) $-2x + 3y = 26$ Substitute the ordered pair for x and y in each equation. Only option (3) can be solved using the ordered pair $(0, -2)$.
$$-2x + 3y = -6$$
$$-2(0) + 3(-2) = -6$$
$$-6 = -6$$

9. (3) \$4.90 Substitute 24 for n and solve for C.
$$C = \$2.50 + \$0.10(24)$$
$$C = \$2.50 + \$2.40$$
$$C = \$4.90$$

10. (2) 8.4×10^7 You may want to use your calculator to perform the multiplication.
$$6{,}000 \times 14{,}000 = 84{,}000{,}000$$
To write the number in scientific notation, you must place the decimal point after the first digit. To do so, you will move the decimal point 7 places to the left. The product is 8.4×10^7.

11. (2) 7^3 Use your calculator to evaluate the expressions.
$$8^3 = 512 \quad\quad 7^3 = 343$$
$$6^4 = 1296 \quad 5^4 = 625 \quad 4^6 = 4096$$
Of these expressions, only 7^3 has a value less than 500.

12. (3) C, G Ordered pairs with positive x-values and negative y-values are found in quadrant IV, the lower-right quadrant.

13. (5) L You can either try the ordered pairs of the points in the answer options by substituting their x- and y-values into the equation, or you can rewrite the equation in slope-intercept form in order to graph it on the coordinate grid. The equation $x + 2y = -4$ can be rewritten as $y = \frac{-1}{2}x - 2$; therefore, $(0, -2)$ must be the y-intercept. Since $(0, -2)$ are the coordinates for point L, you know that option (5) is correct.

14. (2) $-\frac{1}{2}$ Moving from point K to point J, the line rises 2 units as it moves 4 units to the left (a negative direction): $\frac{2}{-4} = \frac{-1}{2}$. You can also use the slope formula and the coordinates for J and K: $(0,2)$ and $(4,0)$.
$$m = \frac{y_2 - y_1}{x_2 - x_1} \quad\quad m = \frac{0 - 2}{4 - 0} = \frac{-2}{4} = -\frac{1}{2}$$

15. 364 Continue applying the rule until you find the sixth term. You may wish to use your calculator.

$$40 \times 3 + 1 = 121$$
$$121 \times 3 + 1 = 364$$

16. 37 Use your calculator.
$$\sqrt{81} = 9 \quad 2^4 = 16 \quad \sqrt{169} = 13 \quad 5^2 = 25$$
$$9 + 16 - 13 + 25 = 37$$

17. $(3, -4)$ Start at the origin $(0,0)$. Move 3 units to the right and 4 units down. The point is in quadrant IV.

A coordinate grid bubble sheet with a point plotted at $(3, -4)$.

18. (−3, 0) Substitute $y = 0$ for the x-intercept. Solve.

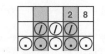

$$-2x + 3y = 6$$
$$-2x + 3(0) = 6$$
$$-2x + 0 = 6$$
$$-2x = 6$$
$$x = \frac{6}{-2} = -3$$

Part 2

19. (5) $x + 6x + x + 6x > 110$ Make a sketch of a rectangle. Let $x =$ the width and $6x =$ the length. The perimeter is equal to the sum of the lengths of the four sides: $x + 6x + x + 6x$. Only option (5) sets this sum as greater than 110.

20. (4) $x \geq 2$ Solve the inequality.
$$-5x + (-3) \leq 2x - 17$$
Subtract $2x$ from both sides. $-7x + (-3) \leq -17$
Add 3 to both sides. $\quad\quad -7x \leq -14$
Divide both sides by -7. $\quad\quad x \geq 2$
Remember to reverse the inequality symbol.

21. (1) $-6x - (-6 + y)$ The product of -6 and x can be expressed as $-6x$. The sum of -6 and y can be written $(-6 + y)$. Only option (1) subtracts the sum from the product.

22. (2) -1 Write an equation and solve.

$\quad\quad\quad\quad\quad\quad\quad\quad\quad\quad 2x + 3 = -x$
Add x to both sides. $\quad\quad\quad 3x + 3 = 0$
Subtract 3 from both sides. $\quad\quad 3x = -3$
Divide both sides by 3. $\quad\quad\quad x = -1$

23. (4) $x \leq -2$ The closed dot on -2 indicates that -2 is part of the solution set. The line is darkened to the left of -2 indicating that all values less than -2 are included in the solution set.

24. (4) 9 and -2 You can try the values from the answer options in the equation or you can solve the quadratic equation by factoring.
$$x^2 - 7x = 18$$
$$x^2 - 7x - 18 = 0$$
$$(x - 9)(x + 2) = 0$$
$$x = 9 \text{ or } x = -2$$

25. (1) $y = \frac{1}{2}x + 4$ The answer options are written in slope-intercept form $(y = mx + b)$. You may have noticed that the point $(0,4)$ is the y-intercept; therefore, b is equal to 4. Only options (1) and

(4) are possible choices. Now use the slope formula to find m.
$$m = \frac{y_2 - y_1}{x_2 - x_2} \quad\quad m = \frac{2 - 4}{-4 - 0} = \frac{-2}{-4} = \frac{1}{2}$$
The slope is $\frac{1}{2}$, and the equation must be $y = \frac{1}{2}x + 4$.

26. 28 Substitute the given values and evaluate the expression.

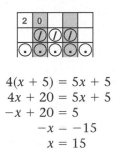

$$6x^2 \quad - \quad 5xy \quad - \quad 4y^2$$
$$6(2)(2) - 5(2)(-2) - 4(-2)(-2)$$
$$24 \quad + \quad 20 \quad - \quad 16 \quad = 28$$

27. 20 Let Timothy's age now $= x$ and Albert's age now $= 5x$. In 5 years, Timothy will be $x + 5$ and Albert will be $5x + 5$. At that time, Albert's age will be 4 times Timothy's age. Write an equation and solve.

$$4(x + 5) = 5x + 5$$
$$4x + 20 = 5x + 5$$
$$-x + 20 = 5$$
$$-x = -15$$
$$x = 15$$

Timothy is 15 now. In five years, he will be 20 years old.

28. (−3,2) Start at the origin $(0,0)$. Move 3 units to the left and 2 units up. The point is in Quadrant II.

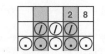

29. (0,−4) Substitute $x = 0$ for the y-intercept. Solve.
$$2x - y = 4$$
$$2(0) - y = 4$$
$$-y = 4$$
$$y = -4$$

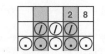

UNIT 4: GEOMETRY
Lesson 23
GED Skill Focus (Page 275)

1. **P = 49.2 cm; A = 69 sq cm**
   To find perimeter, add the lengths of the sides.
   $$10 + 23 + 16.2 = 49.2 \text{ cm}$$
   To find area, use the formula for the area of a triangle. $\quad A = \frac{1}{2}bh$
   $$A = \frac{1}{2}(23)(6) = 69 \text{ sq cm}$$

2. **P = 30 in; A = 43.5 sq in or $43\frac{1}{2}$ sq in** The base is the side that forms a 90° angle with the dotted line indicating the height. In this case, the base is 10 in, since all sides have the same measure. To find perimeter, add the lengths of the sides. $10 + 10 + 10 = 30$ in
   To find area, use the formula, for the area of a triangle. $\quad A = \frac{1}{2}bh$
   $$A = \frac{1}{2}(10)(8.7) = 43.5 \text{ sq in}$$

3. **P = 33 ft; A = 48 sq ft** Opposite sides of a parallelogram are equal. Therefore, the top and bottom sides both measure 12 ft and the left and right sides each measure 4.5 ft. The height is 4 ft. To find perimeter, add the lengths of the sides. $12 + 12 + 4.5 + 4.5 = 33$ ft
   To find area, use the formula for the area of a parallelogram. $\quad A = bh$
   $$A = 12(4) = 48 \text{ sq ft}$$

4. **P = 24.4 in; A = 24 sq in** Remember that the opposite sides of a parallelogram are equal. Therefore, the top and bottom sides both measure 8 in and the sides on the left and right each measure 4.2 in. The height is 3 in. To find perimeter, add the lengths of the sides.
   $$8 + 8 + 4.2 + 4.2 = 24.4 \text{ in}$$
   Then use the area formula.
   $$A = bh$$
   $$A = 8(3) = 24 \text{ sq in}$$

5. **P = 18.7 cm; A = 14 sq cm**
   To find perimeter, add the lengths of the sides.
   $$7.1 + 7.6 + 4 = 18.7 \text{ cm}$$
   Then use the area formula.
   $$A = \frac{1}{2}bh$$
   $$A = \frac{1}{2}(4)(7) = 14 \text{ sq cm}$$

6. **P = 30 in; A = 40 sq in**
   To find perimeter, add the lengths of the sides.
   $$10 + 10 + 5 + 5 = 30 \text{ in}$$
   Then use the area formula.
   $$A = bh$$
   $$A = 10(4) = 40 \text{ sq in}$$

7. **(4) $\frac{1}{2}(16)(10)$** The line segment that divides the parallelogram forms two triangles. Use the formula for area of a triangle.
   Area = $\frac{1}{2}$ × base × height, or $A = \frac{1}{2}bh$
   $$A = \frac{1}{2}(16)(10)$$

GED Skill Focus (Page 277)

1. **10 meters** The diameter is twice the radius.
   $d = 2r$
   $d = 2(5)$
   $d = 10$ m

2. **31.4 meters** $C = \pi d$
   $\quad C = 3.14(10)$
   $\quad C = 31.4$ m

3. **16 centimeters** $d = 2r$
   $\quad d = 2(8)$
   $\quad d = 16$ cm

4. **4 centimeters** The radius is half the diameter. Divide the diameter by 2. $8 \div 2 = 4$ cm

5. **22 inches** $C = \pi d = 3.14(7) = 21.98$, round to 22 in

6. **12.56 square feet** $A = \pi r^2$
   $\quad A = 3.14(2^2)$
   $\quad A = 3.14(4)$
   $\quad A = 12.56$ sq ft

7. **50 inches** The diameter of the outer circle is twice the diameter of the inner circle, which is the radius of the outer circle. $8 \times 2 = 16$ inches
   $C = \pi d = 3.14(16) = 50.24$, round to 50 in

8. **122 square inches** Find the area of the smaller circle and the area of the larger circle. Then subtract the area of the smaller circle from the area of the larger one. Finally, round your answer to the nearest square inch.

   Smaller circle: $\quad A = \pi r^2$
   $\quad\quad\quad\quad\quad\quad A = 3.14(5^2)$
   $\quad\quad\quad\quad\quad\quad A = 3.14(25)$
   $\quad\quad\quad\quad\quad\quad A = 78.5$ square inches

   Larger circle: $\quad A = \pi r^2$
   $\quad\quad\quad\quad\quad\quad A = 3.14(8^2)$
   $\quad\quad\quad\quad\quad\quad A = 3.14(64)$
   $\quad\quad\quad\quad\quad\quad A = 200.96$ square inches

   Find the difference. $220.96 - 78.5 = 122.46$, round to 122 sq in

9. **153.86 square feet** Square feet is a measure of area. The radius $\frac{1}{2}$ the diameter, or $14 \div 2 = 7$.
   $\quad A = \pi r^2$
   $\quad A = 3.14(7^2)$
   $\quad A = 3.14(49)$
   $\quad A = 153.86$ sq ft

10. **28 square yards** $A = \pi r^2$
$$A = 3.14(3^2)$$
$$A = 3.14(9)$$
$$A = 28.26, \text{ round to 28 sq yd}$$

11. **44 centimeters** The radius of the circle is 7 cm; the diameter is twice the radius, or $7 \times 2 = 14$ cm.
$$C = \pi d$$
$$C = 3.14(14)$$
$$C = 43.96, \text{ round to 44 cm}$$

GED Skill Focus (Page 279)

1. **864 cubic inches** Use the formula. $V = lwh$. *Note*: You may not be able to tell which measurement is the length, which is the width, and which is the height. This does not matter since the order in which you multiply numbers does not affect the result.
$V = 16(9)(6) = 864$ cu in

2. **133 cubic centimeters** The figure is a cube.
$V = s^3 = 5.1^3 = 5.1(5.1)(5.1) = 132.651$ cubic centimeters, round to 133 cu cm

3. **198 cubic feet** The figure is a cylinder.
$V = \pi r^2 h$
$V = 3.14(3^2)(7) = 3.14(9)(7) = 197.82$ cubic feet, round to 198 cu ft

4. **14 cubic centimeters** The figure is a rectangular solid. $V = lwh$
$V = 2(2)(3.5) = 14$ cu cm

5. **942 cubic feet** The figure is a cylinder.
$V = \pi r^2 h$
$V = 3.14(5^2)(12) = 3.14(25)(12) = 942$ cu ft

6. **120 cubic feet** The figure is a rectangular solid.
$V = lwh = 4(5)(6) = 120$ cu ft

7. **300 cubic feet** The figure is a rectangular solid.
$V = lwh = 10(6)(5) = 300$ cu ft

8. **12,500 cubic feet** The figure is a rectangular solid.
$V = lwh = 100(25)(5) = 12{,}500$ cu ft

9. **3.375 cubic yards** To use a calculator, use 1.5 for $1\frac{1}{2}$. The figure is a cube.
$V = s^3 = 1.5^3 = 1.5(1.5)(1.5) = 3.375$ cu yd

10. **(1) (8.4)(9)** The volume of a cylinder is the area of the base times the height. The problem gives the area of the base. Therefore, you already know that $\pi \times \text{radius}^2 = 8.4$ sq in. Choose the expression that multiplies this area by the height. (8.4)(9)

GED Skill Focus (Page 281)

1. **75 cubic yards** Area of base $= 5^2 = 25$ sq yd
Volume of pyramid $= \frac{1}{3}(25)(9) = 75$ cu yd

2. **25 cubic inches** You are given the area of the circular base. Solve for volume.
$V = \frac{1}{3}Ah$
$V = \frac{1}{3}(12.5)(6)$
$V = 25$ cu in

3. **90 cubic yards**
Area of base $= 6^2 = 36$ sq yd
Volume of pyramid $= \frac{1}{3}(36)\left(7\frac{1}{2}\right) = 90$ cu yd

4. **377 cubic inches**
Area of circular base. $A = \pi r^2$
$$A = (3.14)(6^2)$$
$$A = 3.14(36)$$
$$A = 113.04 \text{ sq in}$$
Volume of cone. $V = \frac{1}{3}(113.04)(10)$
$V = 376.8$ cu in, round to 377 cu in

5. **45 cubic yards** You have already been given the area of the base. Solve for volume.
$V = \frac{1}{3}Ah$
$V = \frac{1}{3}\left(22\frac{1}{2}\right)(6)$
$V = 45$ cu yd

6. **1256 cubic centimeters**
Area of circular base. $A = \pi r^2$
$$A = (3.14)(10^2)$$
$$A = 3.14(100)$$
$$A = 314 \text{ sq cm}$$
Volume of cone. $V = \frac{1}{3}(314)(12)$
$V = 1256$ cu cm

7. **33.6 cubic centimeters** Solve for volume.
$V = \frac{1}{3}Ah$
$V = \frac{1}{3}(12.6)(8)$
$V = 33.6$ cu cm

8. **28 cubic meters** Use the formula $V = \frac{1}{3}Ah$ for both pyramids.
pyramid A $V = \frac{1}{3}Ah = \frac{1}{3}(25)(12) = 100$ cu m
pyramid B $V = \frac{1}{3}Ah = \frac{1}{3}(64)(6) = 128$ cu m
Find the difference in volumes by subtracting.
$128 - 100 = 28$ cu m

9. **(4) $\frac{1}{3}(9^2)(18.25)$** To find the volume of a square pyramid, multiply the area of the base by the height by $\frac{1}{3}$. Since the base of the pyramid is a square, the area of the base is the square of the length of one side (9^2). $\frac{1}{3}(9^2)(18.25)$

1. **(2) $7\frac{1}{2}$** Convert inches to feet. Solve for length.

$$\frac{\text{inches}}{\text{foot}} \qquad \frac{12}{1} = \frac{33}{l}$$

$$12l = 33$$

$$l = \frac{33}{12} = 2\frac{9}{12} = 2\frac{3}{4} \text{ ft}$$

$$P = 2l + 2w$$

$$P = 2\left(2\frac{3}{4}\right) + 2(1)$$

$$P = 5\frac{1}{2} + 2$$

$$P = 7\frac{1}{2} \text{ ft}$$

2. **(3) 396** Convert 1 foot to inches. $1 \times 12 = 12$ in Use the formula for finding the area of a rectangle.

$$A = lw$$
$$A = 33(12)$$
$$A = 396 \text{ sq in}$$

3. **(4) $(3.14)(6^2)(42)$** Convert $3\frac{1}{2}$ feet to inches.

$$\frac{\text{foot}}{\text{inches}} \qquad \frac{1}{12} = \frac{3.5}{x}$$

$$x = 12(3.5) = 42 \text{ inches}$$

The first step in finding the volume is to find the area of the base. Remember, the radius is $\frac{1}{2}$ the diameter. Substitute the known values in the formula for finding the volume of a cylinder.

$$A = \pi r^2 \qquad\qquad V = Ah$$
$$A = 3.14\left(\frac{12^2}{2}\right) \qquad V = 3.14(6^2)(42)$$
$$A = 3.14(6^2)$$

4. **(4) between 6 and 7** Convert the width and height to feet.

$$1\text{ft } 6\text{ in} = 1\frac{6}{12} = 1\frac{1}{2} \text{ ft} \qquad 1\text{ft } 9\text{ in} = 1\frac{9}{12} = 1\frac{3}{4} \text{ ft}$$

Find the volume of the box.

$$V = lwh$$
$$V = 2\frac{1}{2}\left(1\frac{1}{2}\right)\left(1\frac{3}{4}\right)$$
$$V = \frac{5}{2} \times \frac{3}{2} \times \frac{7}{4}$$
$$V = \frac{105}{16}$$
$$V = 6\frac{9}{16} \text{ cu ft, which is between 6 and 7 cu ft}$$

5. **(3) 15,000** Convert the base measurement to centimeters. $\frac{\text{meter}}{\text{centimeters}} \quad \frac{1}{100} = \frac{2}{x}$

$$x = 100(2) = 200 \text{ centimeters}$$

$$A = \frac{1}{2}bh$$
$$A = \frac{1}{2}(200)(150)$$
$$A = 15{,}000 \text{ sq cm}$$

6. **(2) 96** Convert the height to inches. Use this conversion factor. 1 ft = 12 in.

$$1\text{ ft } 4\text{ in} = 12\text{ in} + 4\text{ in} = 16\text{ in}$$

Find the volume of the cone.

$$V = \frac{1}{3}Ah$$
$$V = \frac{1}{3}(18)(16)$$
$$V = 96 \text{ cu in}$$

1. **(2) 12** Use the formula. $A = lw$

Substitute. $\qquad\qquad 180 = 15w$

Solve. $\qquad\qquad \frac{180}{15} = \frac{15w}{15}$

$$12 = w$$

2. **(1) $\frac{81.64}{3.14(2^2)}$** Use the formula. $V = \pi r^2 h$, where r = the radius of the base of the cylinder and h = height. Rewrite the formula to solve for height. Divide both sides of the formula by πr^2 and substitute the known measurements into the equation.

$$\frac{V}{\pi r^2} = h$$

$$\frac{81.64}{3.14(2^2)} = h$$

Only option 1 matches this setup.

3. **(2) 6** Use the formula. $A = \frac{1}{2}bh$, where b = base and h = height.

$$A = \frac{1}{2}bh$$

Substitute. $\qquad 10.5 = \frac{1}{2}(b)(3.5)$

Multiply both sides by 2. $\quad 21 = 3.5b$

Divide both sides by 3.5. $\quad \frac{21}{3.5} = \frac{3.5b}{3.5}$

$$6 = b$$

4. **(4) $\frac{64 - 2(14)}{2}$** Use the formula. $P = 2l + 2w$, where l = length and w = width. Rewrite the formula to solve for length. Begin by subtracting $2w$ from both sides. Then divide both sides by 2. Substitute the known measurements.

$$P = 2l + 2w$$

$$P - 2w = 2l$$

$$\frac{P - 2w}{2} = l$$

$$\frac{64 - 2(14)}{2} = l$$

5. **(1) 2** Use the formula. $V = lwh$, where l = length, w = width, and h = height. Substitute, changing fractions to decimals.

$$V = lwh$$
$$17.5 = 5(1.75)h$$

Solve for h. $\qquad 17.5 = 8.75h$

$$\frac{17.5}{8.75} = \frac{8.75h}{8.75}$$

$$2 = h$$

Lesson 24

GED Skill Focus (Page 287)

1. **obtuse** Angles that measure between 90° and 180° are obtuse angles, so an angle of measure 150° is obtuse.

2. **right** An angle that measures exactly 90° is a right angle.

3. **acute** An angle that measures between 0° and 90° is an acute angle, so an angle of measure 45° is acute.

4. **straight** An angle that measures exactly 180° is a straight angle.

5. **42°** $\angle BXC$ and $\angle AXB$ are complementary. That is, their sum is 90°. $90° - 48° = 42° = m\angle BXC$

6. **90°** $\angle AXB$ and $\angle BXC$ are complementary. These two angles form $\angle AXC$. Therefore, $m\angle AXC$ is 90°. $\angle AXD$ is a straight angle of 180° Since $m\angle AXC + m\angle DXC = m\angle AXD$, then $90° + m\angle DXC = 180°$ and $m\angle DXC = 90°$

7. **132°** $m\angle BXD = m\angle BXC + m\angle DXC$; therefore, $m\angle BXD = 42° + 90° = 132°$

8. **$\angle AXB$ or $\angle BXA$** Supplementary angles have a sum of 180°, which is a straight angle. Therefore, $\angle DXB$ and $\angle AXB$ are supplementary.

9. **35°** $m\angle ZXY + m\angle YXQ = 90°$ Since $m\angle YXQ = 55°$, $m\angle ZXY = 90° - 55° = 35°$

10. **145°** $\angle ZXR$ and $\angle ZXY$ are supplementary. In question 9, you found that the measure of $\angle ZXY$ is 35°. Therefore, $m\angle ZXR = 180° - 35° = 145°$

11. **125°** $\angle QXR$ and $\angle QXY$ are supplementary. Since $m\angle QXY = 55°$, $= m\angle QXR = 180° - 55° = 125°$

12. **270°** The sum of the reflex angle and $\angle QXZ$ is 360°. Since $m\angle QXZ = 90°$, the measure of the reflex angle is $360° - 90° = 270°$.

13. **(1) $\angle A$ is complementary to $\angle B$.** The sum of the measures of $\angle A$ and $\angle B$ is $28° + 62°$, or 90°. Angles with a sum of 90° are complementary.

14. **(4) 140°** When two angles are supplementary, their measures total 180°. $m\angle M = 40°$; therefore, $m\angle R = 180° - 40° = 140°$

GED Skill Focus (Page 289)

1. **$\angle 2$ or $\angle 4$** Adjacent angles share a common vertex and a common ray. There are two angles adjacent to, or touching, $\angle 3$. Those angles are $\angle 2$ and $\angle 4$.

2. **$\angle 5$** Vertical angles are two angles formed by two intersecting lines that are opposite each other. Even though there are three intersecting lines in this diagram, select the two lines that form $\angle 2$—

lines b and c—to find the angle on the other side of the vertex. Angle 5 is the vertical angle to $\angle 2$.

3. **$\angle 3$** On lines a and c, $\angle 3$ is the vertical angle to $\angle 6$.

4. **$\angle 4$** On lines a and b, $\angle 4$ is the vertical angle to $\angle 1$.

5. **$\angle 6$ and $\angle 2$** Both $\angle 6$ and $\angle 2$ share a common vertex and a common ray with $\angle 1$.

6. **$\angle 6$ and $\angle 4$** Both $\angle 6$ and $\angle 4$ share a common vertex and a common ray with $\angle 5$.

7. **$\angle 2$** Vertical angles are congruent.

8. **$\angle 1$** Vertical angles are congruent.

9. **$\angle 6$** Vertical angles are congruent.

10. **$\angle BOC$** $m\angle EOF = 50°$. Since $\angle BOC$ is a vertical angle to $\angle EOF$, its measure is also 50°.

11. **100°** Angles EOF and BOC are vertical angles; therefore, $m\angle BOC = 50°$.
    Fact: $m\angle AOB + m\angle BOC + m\angle COD = 180°$
    Substitute: $30° + 50° + m\angle COD = 180°$
    Isolate the unknown: $m\angle COD = 180° - (30° + 50°)$
    Solve: $m\angle COD = 180° - 80° = 100°$

12. **100°** This problem has several steps in the reasoning process to arrive at the answer:
    Identify given data: $m\angle AOB = 30°$; $\angle BOC$ and $\angle EOF$ are vertical angles, so $m\angle EOF = m\angle BOC = 50°$
    Identify fact about $m\angle AOF$: $\angle AOF$ and $\angle COD$ are vertical angles and therefore congruent.
    Find: $m\angle COD$ (computed in #11) = 100°
    Find $m\angle AOF$: $m\angle AOF = m\angle COD = 100°$

13. **80°** Angles AOB and DOE are vertical angles; therefore, $m\angle AOB = m\angle DOE = 30°$ $m\angle DOE + m\angle EOF = 30° + 50° = 80°$

14. **310°** The reflex angle is the measure of the outside angle. Since the sum of all the angles equals 360°, and the measure $\angle EOF$ equals 50°, subtract to find the measure of the reflex angle. $360° - 50° = 310°$

15. **$\angle COD$ and $\angle FOA$** Supplementary angles total 180°, or form a straight line. $\angle COD$ and $\angle FOA$ are both supplementary to $\angle DOF$.

16. **(5) $\angle Q$ and $\angle R$ have equal measures.** Vertical angles are congruent. When angles are congruent, their measures are equal. No information is given about the specific measures of $\angle Q$ and $\angle R$, so it is impossible to know if options (1), (2), (3), (4) are true.

17. **(2) $m\angle 2 = 100°$** Since $\angle 4$ and $\angle 2$ are vertical angles, they are congruent and have equal measures. Since both $\angle 4$ and $\angle 2$ measure 100°, they cannot be complementary (sum to 90°) or sum to 180°, so options (1) and (5) are incorrect. Since $\angle 4$ and $\angle 1$ and also $\angle 4$ and $\angle 3$ are supplementary (sum to 180°) and $m\angle 4 = 100°$, $m\angle 1$ and $m\angle 3$ both equal 80°, making options (3) and (4) incorrect.

GED Skill Focus (Page 291)

1. $\angle 2$, $\angle 3$, $\angle 6$, $\angle 7$

2. $\angle 7$

3. $\angle 1$, $\angle 4$, $\angle 5$, $\angle 8$

4. $\angle 1$

5. $\angle 3$

6. $\angle 5$

7. $\angle 6$

8. $\angle 4$

9. $\angle 7$

10. $\angle 4$

11. **(5) $m\angle 1 + \angle 7 = 180°$** $\angle 1$ and $\angle 8$ are alternate exterior angles; therefore, $m\angle 1 = m\angle 8$. $\angle 8$ and $\angle 7$ are supplementary angles; therefore, $m\angle 8 + m\angle 7 = 180°$ $m\angle 1 = m\angle 8$, therefore, $m\angle 1 + m\angle 7 = 180°$

12. **(2) $\angle 3$, $\angle 6$, and $\angle 7$** Angles 2 and 3 are vertical angles and have the same measure. Angles 2 and 6 are corresponding angles, and angles 3 and 7 are corresponding. Therefore, each of these four angles measures 60°.

13. **(1) $m\angle 2 + m\angle 5 = 180°$** Angles 2 and 6 are corresponding angles; therefore, $m\angle 2 = m\angle 6$. Angles 6 and 5 are supplementary angles; therefore, $m\angle 6 + m\angle 5 = 180°$ $m\angle 2 = m\angle 6$, therefore, $m\angle 2 + m\angle 5 = 180°$

14. **(3) $\angle 3$ and $\angle 7$** Angles 3 and 7 are corresponding angles and have the same measure. They are not right angles, so the sum of their measures is not 180°.

GED Practice (Page 293)

1. **(2) $\angle ABD$ and $\angle DBC$ are supplementary.** $m\angle ABD + m\angle DBC = m\angle ABC$; $\angle ABC$ is a straight angle, which measures 180°. When the sum of the measures of two angles is 180°, they are supplementary.

2. **(3) $\angle 3$ and $\angle 7$** Since $\angle 1$ is congruent to $\angle 5$, the figure shows two parallel lines crossed by a transversal. Angles 3 and 7 are congruent because

they are corresponding angles. In other words, they are both in the same position with regard to the transversal.

3. **(2) $x + (x - 12°) = 90°$** The larger angle is represented by x. The measure of the smaller angle must be 12° less than x, or $x - 12°$. Since they are complementary, their sum is 90°. Only option (2) correctly sets the sum of the expressions equal to 90°.

4. **(4) Lines p and q are not parallel.** Although the lines look parallel, neither the figure nor the text gives this information. If the lines were parallel, the measure of $\angle 7$ would equal 118° because $\angle 7$ corresponds to $\angle 3$, which is a vertical angle to the angle measuring 118°.

5. **(1) $m\angle 1 = 50°$** Angle 1 corresponds to the angle that measures 50°. Since corresponding angles are congruent, angle 1 also measures 50°.

6. **(5) 144°** Let the measure of $\angle BXC = x$ and the measure of $\angle AXB = 4x$. Since the angles are supplementary, their sum is equal to 180°. Write an equation and solve.
$$x + 4x = 180°$$
$$5x = 180°$$
$$x = 36°$$
The measure of $\angle BXC$ is 36° and the measure of $\angle AXB$ is $4(36) = 144°$.

GED Mini-Test • Lessons 23 and 24
(Pages 294–297)
Part 1

1. **(4) $\angle 5$** $\angle 1$ is a right angle, and $\angle 1$ is supplementary to both $\angle 2$ and $\angle 5$. $\angle 1$ is supplementary, but also adjacent, to $\angle 2$. Only $\angle 5$ is supplementary to $\angle 2$, but not adjacent.

2. **(4) 155°** $\angle WOY$ and $\angle 3$ are supplementary. $m\angle 3 = 25°$, thus, $m\angle WOY = 180° - 25° = 155°$

3. **(2) a right angle** $\angle XOZ$ is a vertical angle to $\angle 1$, which is a right angle; therefore, $\angle XOZ$ must be a right angle. Since the sum of two supplementary angles is 180°, any angle supplementary to $\angle XOZ$ must measure $180° - 90° = 90°$, a right angle.

4. **(2) $\dfrac{40}{\pi}$** Use the formula for finding the circumference of a circle: $\qquad C = \pi d$
Substitute known value for C: $\qquad 40 = \pi d$
Solve for d: $\qquad \dfrac{40}{\pi} = d$

5. **(5) 64** The container has a square base, with each side measuring 4 inches. If the container is filled to a depth of 4 inches, the liquid fills a cube shape 4 inches on each side. Use the formula for finding the volume of a cube.
$V = s^3 = 4^3 = 64$ cu in

6. (3) 8 Since you need to express the answer in feet, convert 18 inches to feet. Use the conversion factor 12 inches = 1 foot.
$\frac{1}{12} = \frac{x}{18}$ $x = 1\frac{1}{2}$ feet To find the perimeter of a rectangle, either add the measures of the four sides or use the formula.

$P = 2l + 2w$

$= 2\left(2\frac{1}{2}\right) + 2\left(1\frac{1}{2}\right)$

$= 2\left(\frac{5}{2}\right) + 2\left(\frac{3}{2}\right)$ OR $= 2(2.5) + 2(1.5)$

$= 5 + 3 = 8$ ft

7. (5) Not enough information is given. Without knowing the sum of the measures of $\angle A$ and $\angle B$ or some other relationship between the angles, there is no way to determine the measure of $\angle B$.

8. (3) Bin C has the greatest volume. To find the volume of each bin, multiply length × width × height. However, you may have noticed that the height of each bin is the same; therefore, you can save time by multiplying only the length and width. You don't need to know the actual volume to solve the problem. You simply need to compare the areas of the bases. $A = lw$
A: 7.6(5) = 38   B: 8(4.5) = 36   C: 7(5.5) = 38.5

9. (4) 226 To use the formula for finding the volume of a cylinder, $V = \pi r^2 h$, you need to know the radius of the base. Since the diameter of the base is 6 ft, the radius is half the diameter, or 3 ft.
$V = \pi r^2 h = 3.14(3^2)(8) = 3.14(9)(8) = 226.08$, round to 226 cu ft

10. (3) 7 The radius of the larger circle is equal to the diameter of the smaller circle. Since the diameter of the larger circle is 28 inches, its radius is 14 inches. The radius of the smaller circle is half its diameter. Since the diameter of the smaller circle is 14 inches, its radius is 7 inches.

11. (3) $12\frac{1}{4}$ Since your answer must be expressed in feet, begin by converting all measurements to feet. Use the fact 12 inches = 1 foot. The dimensions of the crate are $3\frac{1}{2}$ ft, $1\frac{3}{4}$ ft, and 2 ft. Use the formula for the volume of a rectangular solid. $V = lwh$

$= \left(3\frac{1}{2}\right)\left(1\frac{3}{4}\right)(2)$ OR $= (3.5)(1.75)(2)$

$= \left(\frac{3}{1}\right)\left(\frac{7}{4}\right)(2)$

$= 12\frac{1}{4}$ cu ft   OR $= 12.25 = 12\frac{1}{4}$

Although the answer options are all expressed as mixed numbers, sometimes it is easier to do your calculations with decimals and convert your answer to the mixed number.

12. (1) 37° The sum of the measures of angles TRS, TRU, and URV is 180°. $m\angle TRU = 90°$ Since $m\angle URV = 53°$, find the measure of the missing angle by subtracting. $180° - 90° - 53° = 37°$

Part 2

13. (3) 120° $\angle UZX$ is supplementary to $\angle 4$. Subtract to find its measure. $m\angle UZX$ $180° - 60° = 120°$

14. (1) 30° The symbol in $\angle 2$ indicates that $\angle 2$ is a right angle and that lines UW and VY are perpendicular. So, $m\angle WZY$ is also = 90° since it is a vertical angle to $\angle 2$. Thus, $\angle 4$ and $\angle 5$ are complementary, so the sum of their measures is 90°. Find the measure of $\angle 5$ by subtracting the given measure of $\angle 4$. $90° - 60° = 30°$

15. (4) 120 The cabinet is a rectangular solid. $V = lwh = 4(3)(10) = 120$ cu ft

16. (5) $\angle 5$ is supplementary to $\angle 1$. The figure shows two sets of angles formed by parallel lines and a transversal. Each set must be addressed independently; they are not related to each other. Use logical reasoning to eliminate incorrect answer choices. Option (1) is false. Angles 3 and 4 are supplementary, not complementary. Option (2) is false because angles 12 and 13 are vertical angles, each measuring 125°. They are not supplementary since their sum does not equal 180°. Option (3) is false because $\angle 4$ and $\angle 10$ are not corresponding angles. They are not in the same position in relation to the *same* transversal. Option (4) is false because $\angle 1$ corresponds to an angle measuring 100°; therefore, its measure is also 100°, not 90°. Option (5) is true because $\angle 5$ is supplementary to an angle measuring 100°; therefore, its measure is $180° - 100° = 80°$. Since $\angle 1$ measures 100°, the sum of the measures of $\angle 5$ and $\angle 1$ is 180°, and the angles are supplementary.

17. (2) $\angle 1$ and $\angle 7$ Angles 1 and 4 are vertical angles and are congruent. Angles 4 and 7 are corresponding angles and are congruent. Angles 2 and 3 are each supplementary to angle 4; supplementary angles are not congruent unless they are each right angles, so options (1) and (4) are incorrect. Angles 8, 10, and 14 are on a different transversal from angle 4 and thus cannot be compared. So options (3) and (5) can be eliminated as incorrect.

18. (5) 125° Angle 12 and the angle marked as measuring 125° are corresponding angles. Both are in the same position in relation to the transversal *a*; therefore, their measures are equal.

19. (4) 21(12) The figure has two sets of parallel lines and so is a parallelogram. To find the area of a parallelogram, multiply the base (21 cm) by the height (12 cm). You do not need the other measures. $V = bh = 21(12)$

20. **(1) ∠5** Three angles in the figure are equal to ∠4: ∠7 (vertical angle), ∠2 (corresponding angle), and ∠5 (alternate exterior angle). Only ∠5 is an answer option.

21. **(1) $m\angle 8 = m\angle 1$** Angles 1 and 8 are alternate exterior angles (on the outside of the parallel lines and on opposite sides of the transversal). Alternate exterior angles have the same measure. Options (2) and (3) are incorrect because the figure gives no information about specific measures of the angles. Option (4) is incorrect because the measures of angles 4 and 8 total 180°, making these angles supplementary, not complementary (totaling 90°). Option (5) is incorrect because the measures of angles 3 and 4 total 180°, making these angles supplementary, not congruent which is the meaning of the symbol ≅. (Supplementary angles that are congruent would be two right angles, which the figure does not indicate.)

22. **(4) 10π** The circumference of a circle is equal to pi (π) × diameter. The radius of the circle is 5 cm; therefore, the diameter must be 2(5), or 10 cm. Substituting 10 for diameter, gives $C = \pi(10)$, or 10π. Remember, the order in which terms are multiplied does not affect the result.

23. **(3) ∠FGC and ∠DGE are vertical angles.** Option (1) is true, but it does not help you know the measure of ∠FGC. Option (2) is not true. You know the sum of the angles mentioned is not 180° because ∠FGA is not a straight angle. Option (4) is not true because the angles are not positioned in relation to a transversal. Option (5) is true, but this fact has no bearing on the measure of ∠FGC. Only option (3) provides proof that ∠FGC measures 75°. Since ∠DGE measures 75° and vertical angles are equal, $m\angle FGC = 75°$.

24. **(1) 9** Find the height of the triangle that has an area = 90 and base = 20. Use the area formula.

Formula:	$A = \frac{1}{2} \times \text{base} \times \text{height}$
Substitute values:	$90 = \frac{1}{2}(20)h$
Solve for h:	$90 = 10h$
	$9 = h$

Lesson 25
GED Skill Focus (Page 299)

1. **△ABC (or △ACB or △CBA)** Each side has the same length, 10. Note: The order of the letters in the name of the triangle does not matter.

2. **△ABD** Two of its sides have the same length, 13. (The equilateral triangle, △ABC, is a special case of an isosceles triangle.)

3. **△ACD and △BCD** In each triangle, there is one angle that is obtuse, that is, greater than 90°.

4. **△ABE, △ABC, and △ABD** All the angles are acute angles, that is, less than 90°.

5. **△ABE, △ACD, and △BCD** No sides are equal.

6. **△ABE**

7. **△BDC and △CDE**

8. **△ACB and △BCE**

9. **35°** The sum of the measures of all three angles of △ABE must be equal to 180°.
$$m\angle A + m\angle ABE + m\angle E = 180°$$
Since $m\angle A = 55°$ and $m\angle ABE = 90°$, then
$$m\angle E = 180° - 55° - 90° = 35°$$

10. **35°** In △ABC it is given that $m\angle ACB = 90°$ and $m\angle A = 55°$. The measures total 145°. Then, $m\angle ABC = 180° - 145° = 35°$

11. **55°** In △DCE, $m\angle CDE = 90°$ and $m\angle E = 35°$ (see question 9), which totals 125°. Then, $m\angle DCE = 180° - 125° = 55°$

12. **55°** In △BCE, $m\angle BCE = 90°$ and $m\angle E = 35°$ (see question 9), which totals 125°. Then, $m\angle CBD = 180° - 125° = 55°$. Also, since $m\angle ABE = 90°$ and $m\angle ABC = 35°$ (from question 10), then $m\angle CBD = 90° - 35° = 55°$

13. **35°** In △BCD, $m\angle BDC = 90°$ and $m\angle CBD = 55°$ (see question 12), which totals 145°. Then, $m\angle BCD = 180° - 145° = 35°$. Also, since $m\angle BCE = 90°$ and $m\angle DCE = 55°$ (see question 11), $m\angle BCD = 90° - 55° = 35°$

14. **5** All five triangles are right triangles. They also have the same angle measures: 35°, 55°, and 90°.

15. **4** A triangle with two sides of the same length is isosceles. △AEB has two sides of length 6. △CED has two sides of length 3. △ACD has two sides of length 5. △CDB has two sides of length 5.

16. **18°** Since the triangle is a right triangle, one angle measures 90°. The measures of the other angles can be represented by x and $4x$. Write an equation and solve. $x + 4x + 90° = 180°$
$$5x + 90° = 180°$$
$$5x = 90°$$
$$x = 18°$$

17. **41°, 57°, and 82°** Let $x =$ the smallest angle measure. The other angle measures can be represented by $x + 16°$ and $2x$. Write an equation and solve. $x + x + 16° + 2x = 180°$
$$16° + 4x = 180°$$
$$4x = 164°$$
$$x = 41°$$
Substitute to find the other measures.
$$x + 16° = 41° + 16° = 57°$$
$$2x = 2(41°) = 82°$$

18. **False** Each angle in an equilateral triangle measures 60°. Since ∠B is a right angle, it must measure 90°.

19. **False** One angle in an obtuse triangle must be greater than 90°. In this triangle, the largest angle is $\angle B$, which measures 90°.

20. **True** Triangles ABC and BCD both have one right angle and an angle equal to 21°. In both triangles, the measure of the third angle must be $180° - 90° - 21° = 69°$.

21. **False** $\triangle ABD$ is smaller than the other triangles in the figure, but its angle measures are the same. $\angle BDA$ must measure 90° since it is a supplement to $\angle BDC$, which measures 90°. Since $m\angle ABC = 90°$ and $m\angle C = 21°$, and the sum of the three angles in $\triangle ABC = 180°$, then $180° - 90° - 21° = 69° = m\angle A$. If $m\angle BDA = 90°$ and $m\angle BAD = 69°$, then $m\angle DBA = 21°$

22. **False** An acute triangle has three angles with measures less than 90°. $\triangle ABC$ has a right angle, so it is a right triangle, not an acute triangle.

23. **True** Angles ABC and BDC are right angles as indicated by the right angle symbol (the small square in the angle) on the figure. Since $\angle BDC$ is a right angle and is supplementary to $\angle BDC$ (that is their measures total 180°) $\angle BDC$ must also be a right angle.

GED Skill Focus (Page 301)

1. **rhombus, square, parallelogram, or rectangle** Remember, a rhombus is a special parallelogram and a square is a special rectangle.

2. **square, rectangle, rhombus, or parallelogram** Remember, a square is a kind of rhombus and a rectangle is a kind of parallelogram.

3. **parallelogram, square, rectangle, or rhombus** A trapezoid has only one pair of parallel opposite sides.

4. **trapezoid**

5. **parallelogram, rhombus, or trapezoid**

6. **trapezoid**

7. **trapezoid**

8. **360°** The sum of the inside angle measures of any quadrilateral is 360°.

9. **55°** Angles K and L each measure 125° for a total of 250°. The remaining angles must measure $360° - 250° = 110°$. Let x stand for the measure of angle J. Since the remaining angles are equal, $2x = 110°$ and $x = 55°$; therefore, $m\angle J = 55°$.

10. **parallelogram**

11. **65°** In a parallelogram, the opposite angles are equal; therefore, the measure of $\angle A$ is 65°, the same as the measure of $\angle C$.

12. **115°** If angles A and C each measure 65°, their sum is $2(65°) = 130°$. The sum of the remaining angles must be $360° - 130° = 230°$. Since the remaining angles have an equal measure, each measure is half of 230°, or 115°, $m\angle D = 115°$.

13. **square, rectangle, rhombus, parallelogram** The figure is either a square or a rectangle, but you should remember that a square is a kind of rhombus and a rectangle is a kind of parallelogram.

14. **90°, 90°, 100°, and 80°** You know that the sum of the four angles is 360°. Two angles are right angles, each measuring 90°. Let x = the measure of the larger unknown angle and $x - 20°$ = the measure of the smaller unknown angle. Write an equation and solve.
$$x + (x - 20°) + 90° + 90° = 360°$$
$$2x - 20° = 180°$$
$$2x = 200°$$
$$x = 100°$$
$$x - 20° = 100° - 20° = 80°$$
The angles are 90°, 90°, 100°, and 80°.

15. **parallelogram** The figure cannot be a rectangle because there are no right angles. It cannot be a rhombus or square because all sides are not equal in length. It cannot be a trapezoid because there are two pairs of opposite parallel sides.

16. **They are parallel, and they are the same length.** In a parallelogram, opposite sides are always parallel. (Note that the definition of a parallelogram gives no information about the measures of the angles. However, a parallelogram can be looked at as parallel lines cut by a transversal, so given the measure of one angle, the measures of the other angles can be determined.)

17. **130°** Angle AEB of the triangle and $\angle DEB$ of the parallelogram are supplementary; that is, their sum is 180°.
Since $m\angle AEB = 50°$, $m\angle DEB = 180° - 50° = 130°$.
In a parallelogram, the opposite angles are equal in measure, so $m\angle C = 130°$.

18. **90°** Since lines $\overline{AD}$ and $\overline{BC}$ are parallel and the transversal, line $\overline{AB}$, is perpendicular to $\overline{AB}$ (because $m\angle A = 90°$), $\overline{AB}$ is also perpendicular to $\overline{BC}$. Thus, $m\angle ABE = 90°$.

GED Skill Focus (Page 303)

1. **Yes** The triangles are equilateral and congruent. Since $\angle D$ and $\angle E$ each measure 60°, $\angle F$ must also measure 60°, making $\triangle DEF$ equilateral. You know that the three sides of $\triangle ABC$ are equal and that the sides are equal to the measure of side. If a triangle has three sides with equal measures, it is equilateral. Therefore, both are equilateral and congruent.

2. **No** The triangles have equal angle measures, but this is *not* proof that the triangles are congruent. Since $\overline{MO}$ does not *equal* the measure of its corresponding side $\overline{PR}$, the triangles cannot be congruent. They are the same *shape* but not the same *size*.

3. **Yes** The lengths of the corresponding sides are equal; therefore, the triangles are congruent according to the SSS rule.

4. **Yes** The lengths of two sides and the measure of the angle between them are equal for both triangles; therefore, the triangles are congruent according to the SAS rule.

5. **Yes** $\overline{TV}$ and $\overline{TS}$ have the same measure, $\overline{TR}$ and $\overline{TU}$, and the angles between each pair of sides have the same measures (90°). Thus, the triangles are congruent according to Rule SAS.

6. **30°** $\angle V$ corresponds to $\angle S$

7. **60°** If $m\angle V = 30°$ and $m\angle T = 90°$, then $m\angle U = 180° - 30° - 90° = 60°$

8. **Yes** $\overline{BD}$ is a side in both triangles. $\overline{AB}$ and $\overline{BC}$ have the same measure. In each triangle, the sides mentioned have a right angle between them. Therefore, the triangles are congruent according to the SAS rule.

9. **37°** $m\angle BDC = 53°$, so $m\angle C = 180° - 90° - 53° = 37°$ $\angle A$ corresponds to $\angle C$ and the triangles are congruent, so $m\angle A = 37°$

10. **Not enough information is given.** The triangles may or may not be congruent. You need either the measures of $\angle A$ and $\angle D$ or the measures of sides $\overline{CB}$ and $\overline{FE}$ to determine whether the triangles are congruent.

11. **36°** The sum of the angles of a triangle equals 180°. $180° - 110° - 34° = 36°$

12. **4.5** The triangles are congruent since $m\angle A = 36°$. (See question 11.) Since the triangles are congruent, side $\overline{EF}$ must equal 4.5.

GED Skill Focus (Page 305)

1. $\overline{BC}$

2. **7** Write a proportion and solve. Note that the length of side $\overline{BC} = 12 + 9 = 21$
$$\frac{12}{21} = \frac{4}{x}$$
$$12x = 4(21)$$
$$12x = 84$$
$$x = 7$$

3. **71°** An isosceles triangle has two angles with the same angle measures (x). Write an equation.
$$38° + 2x = 180°$$
$$2x = 142°$$
$$x = 71°$$

4. **100** Write a proportion and solve.
$$\frac{150}{90} = \frac{x}{60}$$
$$90x = 150(60)$$
$$90x = 9000$$
$$x = 100$$

5. **20** Write a proportion and solve.
$$\frac{6}{12} = \frac{10}{x}$$
$$6x = 12(10)$$
$$6x = 120$$
$$x = 20$$

6. **$\angle GKJ$** Side GI corresponds to $\overline{GK}$, and $\overline{IH}$ corresponds to $\overline{KJ}$. The angles between these sides are congruent.

7. **$\angle O$**

8. **16** Write a proportion and solve.
$$\frac{7}{14} = \frac{8}{x}$$
$$7x = 14(8)$$
$$7x = 112$$
$$x = 16$$

9. **35 feet** Write a proportion and solve.
$$\frac{\text{post's height}}{\text{tree's height}} = \frac{\text{post's shadow}}{\text{tree's shadow}}$$
$$\frac{5}{x} = \frac{3}{21}$$
$$21(5) = 3x$$
$$105 = 3x$$
$$35 = x$$

10. **24 feet** Write a proportion and solve.
$$\frac{\text{signpost's height}}{\text{street lamp's height}} = \frac{\text{signpost's shadow}}{\text{street lamp's shadow}}$$
$$\frac{6}{x} = \frac{4}{16}$$
$$96 = 4x$$
$$24 = x$$

11. **57°** The ground, tower, and brace form a triangle. The new support will create another similar triangle inside the larger one. The angle from the new support to the brace corresponds to the angle from the tower to the brace.

12. 28 feet The support is 20 ft from the tower. Thus, the base of the smaller triangle is $60 - 20 = 40$. Write a proportion and solve.

$$\frac{42}{x} = \frac{60}{40}$$
$$42(40) = 60x$$
$$1680 = 60x$$
$$28 = x$$

GED Practice (Page 307)

NOTE: Throughout this section, decimal values have been used for fractions. However, you can solve the same proportions using fractions. When using a calculator to solve problems, use decimals for common fractions such as

$$\frac{1}{4} = 0.25 \quad \frac{1}{2} = 0.5 \quad \frac{3}{4} = 0.75$$

1. (2) 150 Write a proportion and solve.

$$\frac{1 \text{ in}}{40 \text{ mi}} = \frac{3.75 \text{ in}}{x \text{ mi}}$$
$$1x = 40(3.75)$$
$$x = 150 \text{ mi}$$

2. (4) 580 Add the distances on the map between the cities. $7 \text{ in} + 2.5 \text{ in} + 5 \text{ in} = 14.5 \text{ in}$. Write a proportion and solve.

$$\frac{1 \text{ in}}{40 \text{ mi}} = \frac{14.5 \text{ in}}{x \text{ mi}}$$
$$1x = 40(14.5)$$
$$x = 580 \text{ mi}$$

3. (4) 1 in = 20 mi Write a proportion and solve.

$$\frac{2.5 \text{ in}}{50 \text{ mi}} = \frac{1 \text{ in}}{x \text{ mi}}$$
$$2.5x = 50(1)$$
$$x = 20 \text{ mi}$$

4. (1) 10 feet by 20 feet Write proportions to find both

$$\frac{0.75 \text{ in}}{15 \text{ ft}} = \frac{0.5 \text{ in}}{x \text{ ft}}$$
$$0.75x = 15(0.5)$$
$$0.75x = 7.5$$
$$x = 10 \text{ ft}$$

$$\frac{0.75 \text{ in}}{15 \text{ ft}} = \frac{1 \text{ in}}{x \text{ ft}}$$
$$0.75x = 15(1)$$
$$0.75x = 15$$
$$x = 20 \text{ ft}$$

5. (3) Yes, the wall unit fits exactly. Write the ratios in the form of inches to feet and solve the proportion.

$$\frac{1 \text{ in}}{8 \text{ ft}} = \frac{1.75 \text{ in}}{x \text{ ft}}$$
$$1x = 8(1.75)$$
$$x = 14 \text{ ft}$$

6. (1) 6.3 Write the ratios in the form of inches to miles. Then solve the proportion.

$$\frac{1 \text{ in}}{1.8 \text{ mi}} = \frac{3.5 \text{ in}}{x \text{ mi}}$$
$$1x = 1.8(3.5)$$
$$x = 6.3 \text{ mi}$$

Lesson 26
GED Skill Focus (Page 309)

1. 132 square feet Think of the figure as a rectangle and a triangle. Find the area of each

Rectangle: $A = lw$
$= 8(4)$
$= 32 \text{ sq ft}$

Triangle: $A = \frac{1}{2}bh$
$= \frac{1}{2}(10)(20)$
$= 100 \text{ sq ft}$

Add the two areas. $32 + 100 = 132 \text{ sq ft}$

2. 304.5 square inches Think of the figure as two triangles and a rectangle. Find the area of each element and add the areas.

Left triangle: $A = \frac{1}{2}bh = \frac{1}{2}(14)(18) = 126 \text{ sq in}$

Rectangle: $A = lw = 14(9) = 126 \text{ sq in}$

Right triangle: $A = \frac{1}{2}bh = \frac{1}{2}(14)(7.5) = 52.5 \text{ sq in}$

Add. $126 + 126 + 52.5 = 304.5 \text{ sq in}$

3. 168.5 square inches Think of the figure as a circle and a rectangle since the two half-circles can be combined to form a circle. Find the area of each element and add the results.

Circle: The diameter $= 10$ in; so, the radius $= 5$ in
$A = \pi r^2 = 3.14(5^2) = 3.14(25) = 78.5 \text{ sq in}$
Rectangle: $A = lw = 10(9) = 90 \text{ sq in}$
Add. $78.5 + 90 = 168.5 \text{ sq in}$

4. 164 square feet Think of the figure as two equal parallelograms and a square.

Parallelograms: $A = bh = 16(4) = 64 \text{ sq ft}$
Square: $A = s^2 = 6^2 = 36 \text{ sq ft}$
Add. $64 + 64 + 36 = 164 \text{ sq ft}$

5. 1242 square inches Think of the figure as two rectangles. Find the area of each and add.

Top rectangle: $A = lw = 54(15) = 810 \text{ sq in}$
Bottom rectangle: $A = lw = 24(18) = 432 \text{ sq in}$
Add. $810 + 432 = 1242 \text{ sq in}$

6. 208 square inches Think of the figure as three rectangles. Find the area of each element and add the results. Note that you must subtract the widths of the left and right rectangles from the total width of the figure to find the unknown dimension of the middle rectangle.

$20 - 3 - 5 = 12 \text{ in}$
Left rectangle: $A = lw = 14(3) = 42 \text{ sq in}$
Middle rectangle: $A = lw = 12(8) = 96 \text{ sq in}$
Right rectangle: $A = lw = 14(5) = 70 \text{ sq in}$
Add. $42 + 96 + 70 = 208 \text{ sq in}$

7. **288 cubic inches** Think of the figure as a rectangular solid and a pyramid with a square base. Find the volume of each and add to find the total volume.

Rectangular solid: $V = lwh = 6(6)(5) = 180$ cu ft

Square pyramid: $V = \frac{1}{3}Ah = \frac{1}{3}s^2h$

$= \frac{1}{3}(6^2)(9) = 108$ cu in

Add. $180 + 108 = 288$ cu in

8. **51 cubic centimeters** Think of the figure as two square pyramids.

Left pyramid: $V = \frac{1}{3}s^2h = \frac{1}{3}(3^2)(12) = 36$ cu cm

Right pyramid: $V = \frac{1}{3}s^2h = \frac{1}{3}(3^2)(5) = 15$ cu cm

Add. $36 + 15 = 51$ cu cm

9. **273.18 cubic feet** Think of the figure as a cylinder and a cone. Add the volumes to find the total volume.

Cylinder:
$V = Ah = \pi r^2h = 3.14(3^2)(8) = 226.08$ cu ft

Cone: $V = \frac{1}{3}\pi r^2h = \frac{1}{3}(3.14)(3^2)(5) = 47.1$ cu ft

Add. $226.08 + 47.1 = 273.18$ cu ft

10. **84.5 cubic feet** Think of the figure as a cylinder and a cone. Find the volume of each and add to find the total volume.
Cylinder: The figure gives the area of the base instead of the radius. Remember: volume equals area of base × height for cylinders, cubes, and rectangular solids. $V = Ah = (6.5)(9) = 58.5$ cu ft
Cone: volume equals $\frac{1}{3}$ × area of base × height

$V = \frac{1}{3}Ah = \frac{1}{3}(6.5)(12) = 26$ cu ft

Add. $58.5 + 26 = 84.5$ cu ft

11. **414 cubic feet** Think of the figure as two rectangular solids. Find the volume of each and add the results. The missing height for the lower solid is $18 - 6$, or 12 ft. The missing length for the upper solid is $9 - 4$, or 5 ft.
Lower solid: $V = lwh = 9(3)(12) = 324$ cu ft
Upper solid: $V = lwh = 6(5)(3) = 90$ cu ft
Add. $324 + 90 = 414$ cu ft

12. **1260 cubic inches** Think of the figure as three rectangular solids.
The lower has a height of $18 - 6 - 6$, or 6 inches.
The middle solid has a length of $15 - 5$, or 10 in.
The upper solid has a length of $15 - 5 - 5$, or 5 in.
Lower solid: $V = lwh = 15(7)(6) = 630$ cu in
Middle solid: $V = lwh = 10(7)(6) = 420$ cu in
Upper solid: $V = lwh = 5(7)(6) = 210$ cu in
Add. $630 + 420 + 210 = 1260$ cu in

GED Skill Focus (Page 311)
1. **107 tiles** Since each tile equals 1 square foot, the area in square feet equals the number of tiles

needed. Find the area of the entire room and subtract the area occupied by the washer and dryer.
Area of room: $A = lw = 15(9) = 135$ sq ft
Washer-dryer area: $A = lw = 7(4) = 28$ sq ft
Subtract. $135 - 28 = 107$ sq ft or tiles

2. **816 square feet** The area of the walkway is the difference between the area of the larger rectangle and the area of the garden.
Larger rectangle: $A = lw = 48(32) = 1536$ sq ft
Garden: $A = lw = 36(20) = 720$ sq ft
Subtract. $1536 - 720 = 816$ sq ft

3. **408 strips** First find the missing measures.
The left side of the pool is 42 ft.
The missing bottom dimension is 42 ft.
Add the lengths of the sides to find the perimeter.
$60 + 30 + 42 + 12 + 18 + 42 = 204$ ft
Convert from feet to inches. $204 \times 12 = 2448$ in
Divide the number of inches in the perimeter by 6, the number of inches in one strip.
$2448 \div 6 = 408$

4. **505.36 cubic inches** Find the volume of each figure in cubic inches. Then subtract the volume of the toy from the volume of the cylinder to find the volume of the protective filler.
Cylinder: $V = \pi r^2h = 3.14(6^2)(9) = 1017.36$ cu ft
Toy Cube: $V = s^2 = (8^2) = 512$ cu ft
Subtract. $1017.36 - 512 = 505.36$ cu in

5. **254.34 square feet** Find the area of the larger circle (walkway and fountain combined) and subtract the area of the fountain. The difference is the area of the walkway.
Larger circle: The diameter of the fountain plus the walkway is $24 + 3 + 3 = 30$ ft, so the radius is $\frac{30}{2} = 15$ ft.
$A = \pi r^2 = 3.14(15^2) = 3.14(225) = 706.5$ cu ft
Fountain: The radius of the fountain is $\frac{24}{2} = 12$ ft.
$A = \pi r^2 = 3.14(12^2) = 3.14(144) = 452.16$ cu ft
Subtract. $706.5 - 452.16 = 254.34$ sq ft

6. **32 bundles** Find the area of the roof in square yards. Divide by 3 to find the number of bundles needed.
Area of half the roof: $A = lw = 8(6) = 48$ sq yd
Area of the whole roof: $2 \times 48 = 96$ sq yd
Number of bundles. $96 \div 3 = 32$ bundles

Lesson 27
GED Skill Focus (Page 313)
For questions 1–12, solve the Pythagorean Relationship using a and b. Then compare your answer to the value for c listed in the problem.
1. **No** $c^2 = a^2 + b^2$
$c^2 = 2^2 + 3^2$
$c^2 = 4 + 9$
$c^2 = 13$
$c = \sqrt{13} \approx 3.6$

Answers and Explanations

2. **No** $c^2 = a^2 + b^2$
$c^2 = 2^2 + 6^2$
$c^2 = 4 + 36$
$c^2 = 40$
$c = \sqrt{40} \approx 6.3$

3. **No** $c^2 = a^2 + b^2$
$c^2 = 2^2 + 2^2$
$c^2 = 4 + 4$
$c^2 = 8$
$c = \sqrt{8} \approx 2.8$

4. **No** $c^2 = a^2 + b^2$
$c^2 = 3^2 + 3^2$
$c^2 = 9 + 9$
$c^2 = 18$
$c = \sqrt{18} \approx 4.2$

5. **Yes** $c^2 = a^2 + b^2$
$c^2 = 11^2 + 60^2$
$c^2 = 121 + 3600$
$c^2 = 3721$
$c = 3721 \approx 61$

6. **Yes** $c^2 = a^2 + b^2$
$c^2 = 5^2 + 12^2$
$c^2 = 25 + 141$
$c^2 = 169$
$c = \sqrt{169} = 13$

7. **Yes** An easy way to solve this problem is to look at the lengths of the sides: $18 - 24 - 30$. These values reduce to $3 - 4 - 5$. A triangle with sides in this relationship is always a right triangle. This can be proven using the Pythagorean Relationship.
$c^2 = a^2 + b^2$
$c^2 = 18^2 + 24^2$
$c^2 = 324 + 576$
$c^2 = 900$
$c = \sqrt{900} = 30$

8. **Yes** $c^2 = a^2 + b^2$
$c^2 = 1^2 + \left(1\frac{1}{3}\right)^2$
$c^2 = 1^2 + \left(\frac{4}{3}\right)^2$
$c^2 = 1 + \frac{16}{9}$
$c^2 = \frac{25}{9}$
$c = \sqrt{\frac{25}{9}} = \frac{5}{3} = 1\frac{2}{3}$

9. **Yes** $c^2 = a^2 + b^2$
$c^2 = 7^2 + 24^2$
$c^2 = 49 + 576$
$c^2 = 625$
$c = \sqrt{625} = 25$

10. **Yes** $c^2 = a^2 + b^2$
$c^2 = 25^2 + 60^2$
$c^2 = 625 + 3600$
$c^2 = 4225$
$c = \sqrt{4225} = 65$

11. **Yes** $c^2 = a^2 + b^2$
$c^2 = 6.5^2 + 42^2$
$c^2 = 42.25 + 1764$
$c^2 = 1806.25$
$c = \sqrt{1806.25} = 42.5$

12. **No** $c^2 = a^2 + b^2$
$c^2 = 8^2 + 50^2$
$c^2 = 64 + 2500$
$c^2 = 2564$
$c = \sqrt{2564} \approx 50.6$

13. **26 feet** The wire, the ground, and the pole form a right triangle. Let $a = 10$ ft and $b = 24$ ft. Solve for the hypotenuse, the length of the wire.
$c^2 = a^2 + b^2$
$c^2 = 10^2 + 24^2$
$c^2 = 100 + 576$
$c^2 = 676$
$c = \sqrt{676} = 26$

14. **4 feet** Moving point A away from the pole changes the length of a. Let $a = 10$ ft $+ 8$ ft, or 18 ft and $b = 24$ ft. Solve for the hypotenuse, the length of the wire. Then find the difference between the new length of the wire and the length of the wire before point A was moved.
$c^2 = a^2 + b^2$
$c^2 = 18^2 + 24^2$
$c^2 = 324 + 576$
$c^2 = 900$
$c = \sqrt{900} = 30$
30 feet − 26 feet (see question 13) = 4 feet

15. **18 centimeters** Let $a = 24$ cm and $c = 30$ cm. Solve for b.
$a^2 + b^2 = c^2$
$24^2 + b^2 = 30^2$
$576 + b^2 = 900$
$b^2 = 324$
$b = \sqrt{324} = 18$

16. **65 miles** Points A, B, and C form a right triangle. Let $a = 39$ mi and $b = 52$ mi. Solve for the hypotenuse, the distance between Point C and Point B.
$c^2 = a^2 + b^2$
$c^2 = 39^2 + 52^2$
$c^2 = 1521 + 2704$
$c^2 = 4225$
$c = \sqrt{4225} = 65$

17. **72 miles** The distance from Point A to Point D equals the sum of the distance from Point A to Point C and the distance from Point C to Point D. Let $a = 39$ mi $+ 11$ mi $= 50$ mi and $b = 52$ mi. Solve for the hypotenuse, the distance from Point D to Point B.
$c^2 = a^2 + b^2$
$c^2 = 50^2 + 52^2$
$c^2 = 2500 + 2704$
$c^2 = 5204$
$c = \sqrt{5204} \approx 72$

1. **(2) 13** The ladder is the hypotenuse. Let the distance from the wall (8 ft) equal a. Solve for b.

$$a^2 + b^2 = c^2$$
$$8^2 + b^2 = 15^2$$
$$64 + b^2 = 225$$
$$b^2 = 161$$
$$b = \sqrt{161} \approx 12.7, \text{ round to } 13$$

2. **(3) 8.1** Draw a right triangle so that the distance from J to K forms the hypotenuse. The legs of the triangle measure 7 and 4 units. Solve for the hypotenuse.

$$c^2 = a^2 + b^2$$
$$c^2 = 7^2 + 4^2$$
$$c^2 = 49 + 16$$
$$c^2 = 65$$
$$c = 65 \approx 8.1$$

3. **(3) from 95 to 105 ft** The distance from A to B is the hypotenuse of a right triangle. Solve for the hypotenuse.

$$a^2 + b^2 = c^2$$
$$60^2 + 80^2 = c^2$$
$$3,600 + 6,400 = c^2$$
$$10,000 = c^2$$
$$c = \sqrt{10,000} = 100$$

Also: This is a multiple of the 3-4-5 right triangle. Since $3 \times 20 = 60$ and $4 \times 20 = 80$, the hypotenuse must be $5 \times 20 = 100$.

4. **(3) 96** The brace is one of the legs of a right triangle. The side measuring 104 inches is actually the hypotenuse. Don't be distracted by the orientation of the triangle. Always look for the right angle, locate the hypotenuse, and then determine which sides are the legs. Solve for b, the second leg.

$$a^2 + b^2 = c^2$$
$$40^2 + b^2 = 104^2$$
$$1,600 + b^2 = 10,816$$
$$b^2 = 9,216$$
$$b = \sqrt{9,216} = 96$$

GED Skill Focus (Page 317)

1. **$6300** Multiply the monthly rent by 12: $\$525 \times 12 = \$6300$ Ignore the information about deposits and fees for this question.

2. **$7440** Multiply the monthly rent by 12 to find the yearly rent. Then add the parking fee ($30), the deposit ($580), and the credit check fee ($50). $(\$565 \times 12) + \$30 + \$580 + \$50 = \$7440$

3. **$900** The most expensive rent listed is $600 per month, and the least expensive is $525 per month. Multiply each rent by 12 to find the yearly rent cost. Then subtract to find the difference:
$(\$600 \times 12) - (\$525 \times 12) = \$7200 - \$6300$
$= \$900$

4. a. **$1130** The move-in cost for Apartment A is found by adding the rent, the deposit, and the key fee. $\$545 + \$545 + \$40 = \$1130$

   b. **$1110** The move-in cost for Apartment C includes a lease fee equal to 10% of $600, or $60. Add. $\$600 + \$450 + \$60 = \$1110$

5. **17** Make a table and add the offices facing east or south. South (8) + East (9) = 17

Tower	N	S	E	W
1		4	3	
2	5			3
3	2	4	6	

6. **5** There are 12 offices in Tower 3 and 7 in Tower 1. Subtract. $12 - 7 = 5$

7. **3** Add the number of offices that face north or south: $7 + 8 = 15$
Add the number of offices that face east or west: $9 + 3 = 12$
Find the difference: $15 - 12 = 3$

GED Practice (Page 319)

1. **(2) between 70 and 85 mph** The horizontal axis has grid lines every 25 feet and labeled in increments of 50 feet. Find the location that would best represent 310 feet. Move upward to the line on the graph and check the corresponding value on the speed scale on the vertical axis. A skid mark of 310 feet would occur at a little less than 80 mph.

2. **(5) $P = \$5.50h + 0.08s$** To find a salesperson's pay, you need to multiply his or her hours (h) by $5.50, which can be written $\$5.50h$, and multiply his or her sales by 8%, which can be written $0.08s$. Add the two products. Only option (5) performs the three operations correctly.

3. **(3) Plan C** Since both Plan A and Plan D charge 7 cents a minute, Plan D must be less expensive because its monthly fee is less. Eliminate Plan A. Since both Plan C and Plan E charge 6 cents a minute, Plan C must be less expensive because its monthly fee is less. Eliminate Plan E. Use the formula and your calculator to find the cost of plans B, C, and D.
Plan B: $(\$0.09 \times 300) + \$0 = \$27.00$
Plan C: $(\$0.06 \times 300) + \$6.50 = \$24.50$
Plan D: $(\$0.07 \times 300) + \$4.95 = \$25.95$
Plan C is the least expensive.

4. **(3) 59° F** Substitute 15 for C in the formula and use your calculator to solve.

$$F = \left(\frac{9}{5}\right)(15) + 32$$
$$F = 27 + 32$$
$$F = 59$$

15° C equals 59° F

GED Mini-Test • Lessons 25–27

(Pages 320–323)

Part 1

1. **(3) 188** Write a proportion and solve.

$$\frac{1.5 \text{ cm}}{60 \text{ km}} = \frac{4.7 \text{ cm}}{x \text{ km}}$$

$$1.5x = 4.7(60)$$
$$1.5x = 282$$
$$x = 188 \text{ km}$$

2. **(2) 38°** The sum of the angles in a triangle equals 180°. To find the missing measure, subtract.
$180° - 90° - 52° = 38°$

3. **(5) $\sqrt{(6) + (7.7)}$** Since the lengths of the two legs of a right triangle are given, use the Pythagorean relationship.
$a^2 + b^2 = c^2$, so $c^2 = \sqrt{a^2 + b^2} = \sqrt{(6)^2 + (7.7)^2}$

4. **(5) a triangle with sides 7, 24, and 25** Use the Pythagorean Relationship to evaluate each of the answer choices. Only the sides listed in option (5) make the equation true.

$$c^2 = a^2 + b^2$$
$$c^2 = 7^2 + 24^2$$
$$c^2 = 49 + 576$$
$$c^2 = 625$$
$$c = \sqrt{625} = 25$$

5. **(4) 23** Solve for the hypotenuse.

$$c^2 = a^2 + b^2$$
$$c^2 = 7^2 + 22^2$$
$$c^2 = 49 + 484$$
$$c^2 = 533$$
$$c = \sqrt{533} \approx 23.08, \text{ round to 23 feet}$$

6. **(2) 138** First find the area of the pool. The diameter of the pool is 20 feet, so the radius is half of 20, or 10 feet.

$$A = \pi r^2$$
$$= 3.14(10^2)$$
$$= 3.14(100)$$
$$= 314 \text{ sq ft}$$

Next find the area of the pool and walkway combined. The walkway adds 4 feet to the diameter, or 2 feet to the radius. $10 + 2 = 12$ ft

$$A = \pi r^2$$
$$= 3.14(12^2)$$
$$= 3.14(144)$$
$$= 452.16 \text{ sq ft}$$

Finally, subtract the area of the pool from the area of the pool and walkway combined.
$452.16 - 314 = 138.16$, round to 138 sq ft

7. **(5) 550** This irregular figure combines a cylinder and a cone. Find separate volumes and combine.
Cylinder: $V = \pi r^2 h = 3.14(5^2)(5) = 392.5$ cu cm

Cone: $V = \frac{1}{3}\pi r^2 h = \frac{1}{3}(3.14)(5^2)(6) = 157$ cu cm

Add. $392.5 + 157 = 549.5$, round to 550 cu cm

8. **(3) 6** Find the area of the rectangle.
$A = lw = 6(3.5) = 21$ sq in
Use the formula for finding the area of a triangle to solve for h (the height).

$$A = \frac{1}{2}bh$$
$$21 = \frac{1}{2}(7)h; \quad h = 6 \text{ in}$$

9. **(2) 22**

$$\frac{3 \text{ ft}}{x} = \frac{4.5 \text{ ft}}{33 \text{ ft}}$$
$$4.5x = 3(33)$$
$$4.5x = 99$$
$$x = 22 \text{ ft}$$

10. **(3) 33** Find the area of the rectangle and triangles separately. Then add to find total area. Note. The triangles are congruent. Find the area of one and multiply by 2.

Triangle: $A = \frac{1}{2}bh$

$$= \frac{1}{2} \times 4.5 \times 2$$
$$= 4.5 \text{ sq cm}$$

Multiply by 2. $4.5 \times 2 = 9$ sq cm

Rectangle: $A = lw$

$$= 8 \times 3$$
$$= 24 \text{ sq cm}$$

Add. $24 + 9 = 33$ sq cm

11. **(4) 8** $a^2 + b^2 = c^2$

$$10^2 + b^2 = 12.8^2$$
$$100 + b^2 = 163.84$$
$$b^2 = 63.84$$
$$b = \sqrt{63.84} \approx 7.9, \text{ round to 8 units}$$

12. **(3) 55°** Since the sum of the angles in a triangle equal 180°, add the two known angles and subtract from 180°.
$35° + 90° = 125°$ and $180° - 125° = 55°$

Part 2

13. **(5) parallelogram** Although the problem does not state that the opposite sides are parallel, they must be so in order for the side measures to appear in the order given. There is no other possible option.

14. **(2) 70°** The triangles are congruent, so angles A and D must be congruent. You can find the measure of $\angle A$ by subtracting.
$180° - 60° - 50° = 70°$ Angle D must have the same measure.

15. **(5) 20 and 25** There are several ways to solve this problem. One way is to write proportions to solve for each of the missing sides. Or notice that the 12–16–20 triangle is a multiple of the common 3–4–5 triangle. Therefore, $\triangle DEF$ must also be similar to a 3–4–5 triangle, which means that the remaining sides must be 20 and 25 feet.

UNIT 4

16. (3) 55° Since the corresponding sides of the triangles are equal, the triangles are congruent. Mentally rotate the second triangle so that the corresponding sides are oriented the same way. You may find it helpful to redraw the second triangle. Since $\angle L$ is congruent to $\angle I$, the measure of $\angle L$ is 55°.

17. (3) 10 Since the measures of $\angle A$ and $\angle B$ are each 60°, then the measure of $\angle C$ must also measure 60°. Therefore, the triangle is an equilateral triangle. By definition, an equilateral triangle has three sides of the same length; therefore, side AC must measure 10 inches.

18. (2) $\overline{AE} \cong \overline{BD}$ You know that sides AC and CB are congruent; you also know that sides CE and CD are congruent. To know that the triangles have three pairs of congruent sides, you need to know that the measure of side AE equals the measure of side BD.

19. (4) 10
$$c^2 = a^2 + b^2$$
$$c^2 = 6^2 + 8^2$$
$$c^2 = 36 + 64$$
$$c^2 = 100$$
$$c = \sqrt{100} = 10 \text{ feet}$$

20. (3) 40 The formula for finding the circumference of a circle is $C = \pi d$, where $d =$ diameter. The diameter is twice the length of the radius. $2(7) = 14$ inches. To estimate the circumference, use 3 for the value of pi. $C = 3(14) = 42$ in. The best estimate is option (3).

21. (4) scalene and acute A triangle with three sides of different lengths is a scalene triangle. A triangle with three acute angles is an acute triangle.

22. (1) $x + 5x + 90° = 180°$ The sum of the measures of the three angles is 180°. If you let x equal the measure of the smaller acute angle, then $5x$ equals the measure of the larger angle. The third angle is the right angle measuring 90°. To write the equation, set the sum of the three angle measures equal to 180°.

23. (3) $180° - (90° + 38°)$ Since the sum of the angles in a triangle equal 180°, add the two known angles and subtract from 180°. Option (2) is incorrect because both known values need to be subtracted.

24. (2) $\overline{AB}/\overline{AC} = \overline{FB}/\overline{GC}$ Two pairs of corresponding sides in these triangles are $\overline{AB}$ and $\overline{AC}$ and $\overline{FB}$ and $\overline{GC}$. Since corresponding sides of similar triangles have equal ratios, this is a true proportion.

Unit 4 Cumulative Review
(Pages 324–330)
Part 1

1. (4) 120 $\triangle MON$ and $\triangle POQ$ are similar isosceles triangles. Therefore, the corresponding sides are proportional.
$$\frac{x}{24} = \frac{150}{30}$$
$$30x = 3600$$
$$x = 120$$

2. (1) 50
$$A = \pi r^2$$
$$A = 3.14(4^2)$$
$$A = 50.24 \text{ sq ft}$$

3. (5) 140 Find the dimensions of the room using the map scale of 1 inch = 2 feet.
$$\frac{1 \text{ in}}{2 \text{ ft}} = \frac{5 \text{ in}}{w} \qquad w = 10 \text{ ft}$$
$$\frac{1 \text{ in}}{2 \text{ ft}} = \frac{7 \text{ in}}{l} \qquad l = 14 \text{ ft}$$
The area is 10×14, or 140 square feet.

4. (1) $\frac{2}{3}$ Find the volume of each cone using the formula $V = \frac{1}{3} \times$ area of base $\times$ height. Sample B is 24 cubic inches, and Sample A is $23\frac{1}{3}$ cubic inches. (The information about the length of the side is not needed.) Subtract to find the difference. $24 - 23\frac{1}{3} = \frac{2}{3}$ cubic inch. Sample B holds $\frac{2}{3}$ cubic inch more volume than Sample A.

5. (4) 18.8 The formula for finding the circumference of a circle is $C = \pi d$. Remember: diameter (d) = 2 × radius (r). Since the radius of the circle is 3 meters, the diameter is 6 meters. The circumference is 3.14×6, which equals 18.84 meters. 18.84 rounds to 18.8 meters.

6. (1) 2.5 Use the volume formula $V = lwh$, and solve for w.
$$19.5 = 5.2 \times w \times 1.5$$
$$19.5 = 7.8 \times w$$
$$2.5 \text{ feet} = w$$

7. (3) 13 Use the Pythagorean Relationship twice. First find the measure of $\overline{BD}$; then find the measure of $\overline{AB}$.

$c^2 = a^2 + b^2$	$c^2 = a^2 + b^2$
$c^2 = 3^2 + 4^2$	$c^2 = 12^2 + 5^2$
$c^2 = 9 + 16$	$c^2 = 144 + 25$
$c^2 = 25$	$c^2 = 169$
$c = \sqrt{25} = 5$ feet	$c = \sqrt{169} = 13$ feet

8. **(4) 12** Use the conversion factor 1 ft = 12 in to convert the perimeter from feet to inches.

$5 \times 12 = 60$ in

Let w stand for width. The length is $w + 6$. Use the formula for perimeter of a rectangle to write an equation.

$$P = 2l + 2w$$
$$60 = 2(w + 6) + 2w$$
$$60 = 2w + 12 + 2w$$
$$60 = 4w + 12$$
$$48 = 4w$$
$$12 \text{ in} = w$$

9. **(4) 92** Find the sum of all the sides.
$12 + 18 + 1.5 + 12 + 17 + 12 + 1.5 + 18 = 92$

10. **(2) 50°** The sum of the angles in a triangle is 180°, so $m\angle RPQ = 180° - 90° - 40° = 50°$

11. **(4) The length of $\overline{QR}$ is longer than length of $\overline{PR}$.** Since angle P is greater than angle Q, the side opposite angle P is longer than the side opposite angle Q.

12. **(1) 10** Find the area of a triangle.
$A = \frac{1}{2}bh = \frac{1}{2}(5.2)(4) = 10.4$, round to 10 sq cm

13. **(2) 15°** The sum of the angles in a triangle is 180°, and one of the angles in a right triangle must measure 90°. The remaining angles are the acute angles described in the problem. Let x = the measure of the smaller angle and $5x$ = the measure of the larger angle.
$$x + 5x + 90° = 180°$$
$$6x = 90°$$
$$x = 15°$$

14. **(3) 50** Think of the figure as a rectangle and two half-circles. The two half-circles make one whole circle. Find the area of the rectangle and the area of the circle and add the results.

Rectangle: $A = lw$
$A = 6 \times 5$
$A = 30$ sq ft

Circle: $A = \pi r^2$
$A = 3.14 \times 2.5^2$
$A = 19.625$ sq ft

Add. $30 + 19.625 = 49.625$, round to 50 sq ft

15. **(4) 12,000** The formula for finding the volume of a cylinder is $V = \pi r^2 h$. However, in this problem you are given the area of the base. You only need to multiply the area of the base by the height to find the volume. Then multiply the volume by 200. $12 \times 5 = 60$ cu in and $60 \times 200 = 12,000$ cu in.

16. **(2) 25** At any given time, the ratio of all objects to their shadows is the same. Write the ratios in the same order and solve the proportion.
$$\frac{5}{x} = \frac{8}{40}$$
$$8x = 200$$
$$x = 25 \text{ ft}$$

17. **(3) $2\frac{2}{3}$** Use the proportion.
$$\frac{1}{1.5} = \frac{x}{4}$$
$$1.5x = 4$$
$$x = 2\frac{2}{3} \text{ in}$$

18. **(2) 64°** The sum of complementary angles is 90°, so $m\angle N = 90° - 26° = 64°$

19. **16** The area of a parallelogram is equal to base $\times$ height, so $A = 32 \times 8$, or 256 sq yd. The area of a square is equal to a side squared. If the area of the square is 256 sq yd, you can find the measure of the side by finding the square root of 256, which is 16 yards.

20. **4275** Think of the figure as a cube and a pyramid. Find the volumes separately and add the results.

Cube: $V = s^3$
$V = 15^3 = 3375$ cubic inches

Square pyramid: $V = \frac{1}{3} \times$ (base edge)$^2 \times$ height
$V = \frac{1}{3} \times 15^2 \times 12 = 900$ cu in

Add. $3375 + 900 = 4275$ cu in

21. **8** Draw a right triangle so that side AB is the hypotenuse. The legs of the triangle are 8 and 4 units.
$$c^2 = a^2 + b^2$$
$$c^2 = 8^2 + 4^2$$
$$c^2 = 64 + 16$$
$$c^2 = 80$$
$$c = \sqrt{80} \approx 8.9, \text{ round to 9 units}$$

22. **12** Use the Pythagorean Relationship to solve for b.
$$a^2 + b^2 = c^2$$
$$9^2 + b^2 = 15^2$$
$$81 + b^2 = 225$$
$$b^2 = 144$$
$$b = \sqrt{144} = 12$$
You may have recognized that 9 and 15 are multiples of 3 and 5. This triangle is related to the common 3-4-5 triangle. Since $3 \times 3 = 9$ and $3 \times 5 = 15$, the missing leg is $3 \times 4 = 12$.

Part 2

23. **(4) $m\angle D + m\angle BAC = 180°$** $\overline{AB}$ is parallel to $\overline{DE}$. $\overline{AD}$ is a transversal of $\overline{AB}$ and $\overline{DE}$. Interior angles on the same side of a transversal are supplementary, and the sum of supplementary angles is 180°.

24. **(1) 105°** The sum of the angles in a triangle is 180°, so $\angle ACB$ must equal $180° - 80° - 25° = 75°$. $\angle ACB$ and $\angle BCD$ are supplementary and the sum of supplementary angles is 180°; therefore, $\angle BCD = 180° - 75° = 105°$.

25. **(5) $\pi = C/r$** This formula gives $C = \pi r$ which is false. The correct formula is $C = \pi d$.

UNIT 4

26. **(2) ∠2 and ∠6** If $m\angle 8 = 50°$, then $m\angle 6 = 130°$ because ∠6 and ∠8 are supplementary angles. The measure of ∠7 is also 130° because ∠6 and ∠7 are vertical angles. Since ∠2 corresponds to ∠6 and ∠3 corresponds to ∠7, these must also measure 130°. Only option (1) names two angles from those that measure 130°.

27. **(3) $m\angle 2 = 180° - m\angle 3$** Since lines a and b are parallel, ∠3 and the supplementary angle for ∠2 are congruent. Therefore, angles 2 and 3 are supplementary. Subtract $m\angle 3$ from 180° to find $m\angle 2$.

28. **(4) $m\angle 5 = 60°$** The problem gives the information $m\angle 3 = m\angle 4$. If $m\angle 3 = 60°$, then $m\angle 4 = 60°$. Since the sum of the angles in a triangle equals 180°, $m\angle 5$ must be 60° also. $180° - 60° - 60° = 60°$

29. **(1) $16 + 2\pi$** The sum of the three straight sides is $6 + 4 + 6 = 16$. The circumference of the half-circle is $\frac{1}{2}\pi(4)$, which equals 2π. The perimeter of the whole figure is $16 + 2\pi$.

30. **(2) $\overline{AC} \cong \overline{AE}$** Sides $\overline{AC}$ and $\overline{AE}$ are the congruent sides of an isosceles triangle. However, the figure does not give any information that would make option (1) or (5) correct. Option (3) is incorrect because corresponding sides of similar triangles are in proportion but not congruent. Option (4) is incorrect because ∠D appears to be a right angle and ∠E is clearly less than 90°.

31. **(4) $\sqrt{12^2 - 7^2}$**
Since $c^2 - a^2 = b^2$, then $12^2 - 7^2 = b^2$. To set the left side of the equation equal to b, find the square root of both sides of the equation. $\sqrt{12^2 - 7^2} = b$

32. **(1) ∠ABE** If ∠ECD is a right angle, then its supplement, ∠ECB, must also be a right angle. If ∠ECB measures 90°, then △ECB is a right triangle and ∠CBE and ∠BEC must be acute angles. If ∠EBC is acute (less than 90°), then its supplement, ∠ABE, must be obtuse (greater than 90°).

33. **(3) ∠AHG** Line segments CF and BG are parallel and line segment AE is a transversal. Therefore, ∠CDE and ∠AHG are alternate exterior angles and must be congruent.

34. **(3) 1356** Find the area of the rectangle and the area of the square. Then subtract the area of the square.
Rectangle: $A = lw$
$A = 50 \times 30$
$A = 1500$ sq ft
Square: $A = s^2$
$A = 12^2$
$A = 144$ sq ft
Subtract. $1500 - 144 = 1356$ square feet

35. **30** You don't need to know that angles 2 and 4 are vertical angles. You know that the sum of the two angles measuring 75° and ∠4 must be 180° because the sum of these three angles is a straight line. $180° - 75° - 75° = 30°$

36. **10** Use the formula for finding the area of a triangle.
$$A = \frac{1}{2}bh, \text{ where } b = \text{base and } h = \text{height.}$$
$$200 = \frac{1}{2} \times b \times 40$$
$$200 = 20 \times b$$
$$\frac{200}{20} = b$$
$$10 = b$$

37. **40** By adding the lengths of $\overline{AC}$ and $\overline{CD}$, you can see that △ABD is an isosceles triangle. By definition, an isosceles triangle has two equal sides and two equal angles. The equal angles are opposite the equal sides. Since ∠DAB measures 70°, ∠ABD must have the same measure. Since the sum of the angles in a triangle must equal 180°, $m\angle D = 180° - 70° - 70° = 40°$

38. **24** At any given time, the ratio of all objects to their shadows is the same. Write the ratios in the same order and solve the proportion.
$$\frac{4}{5} = \frac{x}{30}$$
$$5x = 120$$
$$x = 24 \text{ meters}$$

POSTTEST (Pages 336–348)
Part I

1. **(4) $210,000** The scale on the vertical axis represents thousands of dollars. The bar for Year 5 is about $340,000; the bar for Year 2 is about $130,000. Subtract to find the increase in sales. $340,000 - $130,000 = $210,000

2. **(1) Year 2** A 50% increase means about one-half more. So, mentally add one-half the length of a bar to the end of the bar. Year 1 reaches a height of about 80 on the scale to the left. One-half of 80 is 40, and $80 + 40 = 120$, which is about the height of the bar for Year 2. The bar for Year 3 shows nearly a 100% increase from the year before (to almost 250 from 120 in Year 2). Year 4 shows only a very slight increase over Year 3. Years 4 and 5 show increases of less than 50%, and Year 6 shows a decrease.

3. **(2) between $50 and $100** Use rounding and estimate this answer. Round 9.5 cents for each ribbon to 10 cents, or $.10. Multiply to find the total cost. $650 \times \$.10 = \$65$ So, the ribbons cost about $65. Or use your calculator. $650 \times \$0.095 = \$61.75$, which is between $50 and $100.

4. $\frac{15}{2}$ or **7.5** The two triangles shown are similar because they are both right triangles and share the angle at the bottom of the ramp. Similarity means their corresponding sides are proportionate.

The hypotenuse of the small triangle (S) is 8 ft and corresponds to the hypotenuse of the large triangle (L) which measures 8 + 12 = 20 ft. The height (leg) of the smaller triangle is 3 feet and corresponds to the unknown height of the larger triangle. Write a proportion.

$$\frac{\text{hypotenuse S}}{\text{hypotenuse L}} = \frac{\text{leg S}}{\text{leg L}}$$

Substitute. $\frac{8}{20} = \frac{3}{x}$

Solve. $8x = 3(20)$

$8x = 60$

$x = \frac{60}{8} = \frac{15}{2} = 7.5$ ft

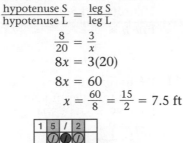

5. **260** Use the order of operations.

$15 + 5\,(3 + 4)^2$
$15 + 5 \quad (7)^2$
$15 + 5 \quad (7)(7)$
$15 + 5 \quad (49)$
$15 + 245$
260

6. **(3) 25%** Use the percent formula.
base × rate = part
Add to find the total number of employees (the base). 16 + 3 + 8 + 12 + 57 = 96
Add to find the total number of managers and buyers (the part). 16 + 8 = 24
Find (the rate): what percent 24 is of 96.

rate = $\frac{\text{part}}{\text{base}}$

rate = $\frac{24}{96}$ = .25 = 25%

OR reduce the ratio $\frac{24}{96} = \frac{1}{4} = 25\%$

7. **(2)** $\frac{1}{8}$ Probability = $\frac{\text{desired outcome (accounting)}}{\text{total outcomes (all employees)}}$

There are 96 employees and 12 work in accounting, so the probability that someone in accounting will win is $\frac{12}{96}$, which reduces to $\frac{1}{8}$.

8. **(4)** $\frac{2}{3}$ There are several ways to approach this problem. Change $\frac{1}{2}$ hour to 30 minutes. Then find what fraction 30 minutes is of 45 minutes. $\frac{30}{45} = \frac{2}{3}$ So, Wayne can mow $\frac{2}{3}$ of the lawn in 30 minutes.

OR write a proportion.

$$\frac{1 \text{ lawn}}{\frac{3}{4} \text{ hour}} = \frac{x \text{ lawn}}{\frac{1}{2} \text{ hour}}$$

$1 \times \frac{1}{2} \div \frac{3}{4} = 1 \times \frac{1}{2} \times \frac{\overset{2}{\cancel{4}}}{3} = \frac{2}{3}$ of a lawn

9. **(4) 60** Use the area formula.
Area = length × width
Find the area of Lot B:
$A = lw = 90(40) = 3600$ sq yd
The area of Lot A (a square):
$A = lw = s^2 = 3600$ sq yd
To find the length of a side of Lot A find the square root of 3600. $\sqrt{3600} = \sqrt{36(100)}$
$\sqrt{36} = 6$ and $\sqrt{100} = 10$, so $\sqrt{3600} = 6(10) = 60$
Or use your calculator. 3600 **SHIFT** **x²** 60

10. **(3) $157.50** Find 175% of $90. Use the percent formula, base × rate = part: rate is 175% or 1.75 and base is $90. Multiply using your calculator.
90 **×** 1.75 **=** 157.5

11. **(4) $265** Substitute $26,000 for *Income* and solve using the order of operations.
Tax = $105 + 0.01 × ($26,000 − $10,000)
     = $105 + 0.01 × $16,000
     = $105 + $160
     = $265

12. **230** Use the distance formula for each part of the trip. rate (miles per hour) × time (hours) = distance (miles) First 2 hours: 70 × 2 = 140
Remaining time:
60 × 1.5 = 90
Add. 140 + 90 = 230 miles

13. 20 A perpendicular pole forms a right angle with the ground. Use the Pythagorean Relationship.
$$a^2 + b^2 = c^2$$
$$12^2 + 16^2 = c^2$$
$$144 + 256 = c^2$$
$$400 = c^2$$
$$\sqrt{400} = c = 20 \text{ ft}$$

14. (5) 12(6 × \$0.50 + \$1.25) Find the cost for one week as the sum of 6 days at \$0.50 and 1 day at \$1.25, which can be represented by the expression (6 × \$0.50 + \$1.25). To find the cost for 12 weeks, multiply the entire expression by 12. Only option (5) shows the correct combination of operations.

15. (3) 124° Sides *AB* and *BD* are perpendicular, so ∠*B* is a right angle: *m*∠*B* = 90°. Sides *CD* and *AB* are parallel, so $\overline{BD}$ is also perpendicular to $\overline{CD}$. This means ∠*D* also measures 90°. The sum of the four inside angles of a quadrilateral is 360°. Therefore, 56° + 90° + 90° + *m*∠*C* = 360°, and *m*∠*C* = 124°

16. (4) (4 × 3) + $\frac{1}{2}$ (2 × 3) Divide the quadrilateral into a triangle and a rectangle by drawing a vertical line parallel to side *BD* from point *C*. Notice that the height of the triangle is 3 cm, the length of side *BD*. The base of the triangle is 2 cm (the difference in length between $\overline{AB}$ and $\overline{CD}$.) Find the two areas and add.
Area of rectangle = *lw* = 4 × 3
Area of triangle = $\frac{1}{2}$ *bh* = $\frac{1}{2}$ (2 × 3)
Total area = (4 × 3) + $\frac{1}{2}$ (2 × 3)

17.

Starting at the origin (0,0), count 5 units to the right along the *x*-axis and 3 units down along the *y*-axis. The point is in quadrant IV.

18. (2) \$9(15) ≤ *x* ≤ \$9(25) Let *x* = John's earnings. He works at least 15 hours so John's earnings must be greater than or equal to \$9(15) ≤ *x* and he works no more than 25 hours so his earnings must be less than or equal to *x* ≤ \$9(25). The only choice that shows this relationship is option (2).

19. (4) 45 minutes To find the median list the values in order and find the middle value. List each time in the chart once for each student— for example, 5 students took 30 minutes so list 30 minutes 5 times. Since there are 15 values, the middle value is the 8th one. 15 min, 30, 30, 30, 30, 30, 45, **45**, 45, 1 hr, 1, 1, $1\frac{1}{2}$, $1\frac{1}{2}$, 2

20. (2) *b* A line with a negative slope slants toward the left (downward as it goes from left to right). Only lines *b* and *c* have a negative slope. Slope is the ratio of *rise* over *run*. Line *b* moves down 10 units and 5 units to the right. Slope of line *b* = $\frac{-10}{5} = \frac{-2}{1} = -2$ (The slope of line *c* is $\frac{-3}{6} = \frac{-1}{2}$.)

21. 84 To find the mean add the values and divide by the number of values. 92 + 84 + 81 + 78 + 80 + 89 = 504   504 ÷ 6 = 84

22. $\frac{1}{4}$ or 0.25 Use the formula for the area of a circle. $A = \pi \times r^2$
$$\frac{\text{area inner circle}}{\text{area entire target}} = \frac{\pi r^2}{\pi r^2} = \frac{\pi(3^2)}{\pi(6^2)} = \frac{9}{36} = \frac{1}{4} = 0.25$$
(Notice that you can cancel π because $\frac{\pi}{\pi} = 1$.)
You could also find the area of both circles.
$$\frac{3.14(3^2)}{3.14(6^2)} = \frac{28.26}{113.04} = 0.25$$

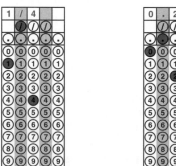

23. (5) sides *DF* and *FH* Mentally rotate △*DEF* so that angles *D* and *H* are in the same position (lower right). The corresponding sides are $\overline{DF}$ and $\overline{FH}$, $\overline{DE}$ and $\overline{GH}$, and $\overline{EF}$ and $\overline{FG}$.

POSTTEST

24. (4) 50 Write a proportion using the two known corresponding sides, DF and FH.

$$\frac{\overline{DF}}{\overline{FH}} = \frac{\overline{DE}}{\overline{GH}}$$

$$\frac{55}{110} = \frac{x}{100}$$

$$x = 50 \text{ feet}$$

25. (5) The frequency of Model B is 100 times as great as the frequency of Model A.
Model A: $10^3 = 1,000$ and Model B: $10^5 = 100,000$ Since 100,000 is 100 times greater than 1,000, you know that 3×10^5 is 100 times greater than 3×10^3. OR subtract the exponents.
$10^5 - 10^3 = 10^2 = 100$

Part II

1. (1) $18\frac{2}{3}$ Multiply.

$$4\frac{2}{3} \times 4 = \frac{14}{3} \times 4 = \frac{56}{3} = 18\frac{2}{3} \text{ yards}$$

2. (5) 46 First find the unknown sides. The base of the figure measures $3 + 4 + 3 = 10$ units. The outer left side measures 8 units. The inner right side measures 5 units. Add all the sides to find the perimeter. $3 + 5 + 4 + 5 + 3 + 8 + 10 + 8 = 46$ units

3. (4) 0.05($300) + $300 To find 5% (rate) of $300 (base), multiply $300 by 0.05—but this is only the amount of the increase in price (part). The new price is the sum of the increase and last year's price or 5% of $300 and $300. Only option (4) shows this sum.

4. (3) C Since $3^2 = 9$ and $4^2 = 16$, the square root of 14 must fall between 3 and 4. Only point C is between 3 and 4 on the number line.

5. (2) $\angle 1$ and $\angle 2$ are congruent. Angles 1 and 2 are vertical angles, and by definition, vertical angles are congruent. Option (1) is incorrect because angles 1 and 4 are on different transversals and cannot be compared. Option (3) is incorrect because angles 3 and 4 are both acute angles (less than 90°) so cannot be supplementary (total 180°). Option (4) is incorrect because angles 2 and 3 are supplementary, not congruent (equal). Option (5) is incorrect because angles 1 and 3 are not on the same pair of intersecting lines (as vertical angles are). Also, one of each pair of angles in options (4) and (5) is acute and one is obtuse, so the pair cannot be equal.

6. 60 Start with the facts given in the problem.
Given: $m\angle 3$ is 60° and $m\angle 3 = m\angle 4$, so $m\angle 4 = 60°$
Fact: The sum of the measures of the angles of any triangle must equal 180°. Look at the triangle made by angles 3, 4, and F: $m\angle 3 = m\angle 4 = 60°$, so $180° - 60° - 60° = 60°$
Thus, $\angle F$, or $\angle EFG$, must also measure 60°.

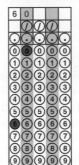

7. (5) $1200 The total percentage spent on uniforms (31%) and awards (20%) is 51%, about $\frac{1}{2}$ of the budget. One-half of the total budget of $2400 is $1200.

8. (3) $\frac{2}{5}$ Add the percentages for equipment and umpires' pay. $17\% + 23\% = 40\%$ Convert 40% to a fraction. $40\% = \frac{40}{100}$, which reduces to $\frac{2}{5}$.

9. (2) $2x^2 - 3x - 20$ Use the FOIL method. Multiply each term in the second factor by each term in the first factor and simplify.

$$(2x + 5)(x - 4) = 2x(x) + 2x(-4) + 5(x) +$$
$$5(-4) = 2x^2 - 8x + 5x - 20 = 2x^2 - 3x - 20$$

10. (3) 192 The question asks for square feet, or the *area*, or the floor. The formula for finding the area of a rectangle is Area = length × width. The height of the walls is extra information and is not needed. $A = lw = 16 \times 12 = 192$ sq ft

11. (1) $1\frac{1}{4}x = 25$ Write a proportion and begin to solve. Compare each step of your solution with the equations in the answer choices.

$$\frac{5 \text{ mi}}{1\frac{1}{4} \text{ hr}} = \frac{x \text{ mi}}{5 \text{ hr}}$$

$$5(5) = 1\frac{1}{4}(x)$$

$$25 = 1\frac{1}{4}x$$

12. (4, −1) Make a quick sketch of a coordinate grid and locate the three given vertices. Use the sketch to determine the coordinates of the fourth vertex.

13. (3) 60 There are several ways to approach this problem. When 15 gallons are removed from the tank, the tank is only $\frac{1}{4}$ full. Since $\frac{1}{2} - \frac{1}{4} = \frac{1}{4}$, 15 gallons is equal to $\frac{1}{4}$ of the tank. The volume of the full tank $\left(\frac{4}{4}\right) = 15 \times 4 = 60$ gallons OR write an equation. Let x equal the volume of the full tank.

$$\frac{1}{2}x - 15 = \frac{1}{4}x$$
$$\frac{1}{4}x - 15 = 0$$
$$\frac{1}{4}x = 15$$
$$x = 60 \text{ gallons}$$

14. (4) 12.5% According to the key, compost is represented by black dots on a white background. For year 2004, this area is a little over one-fifth the length between 0 and 50, or 12.5%.

15. (3) The percent of recycled trash will increase steadily through 2016. The entire bar for each year represents the total amount of trash to be processed during that year. Compare the totals for the four years shown. The four bars are nearly equal in length. None of the other options is true.

16. (4) $\frac{i}{pt}$ Use the rules of algebra to isolate r on one side of the interest equation. $i = prt$. Divide both sides by p and t.

$$i = prt \qquad \frac{i}{pt} = \frac{prt}{pt} \qquad \frac{i}{pt} = r$$

17. (2) 45% Suppose the table originally cost $100. At 50% off, the first sale price would be $50. The amount of the second discount is 10% of $50 or $5. After the second discount, the table costs $50 − $5 = $45. Find what percent this sale price is of the original price. $\frac{\$45}{\$100} = 0.45 = 45\%$

18. 27 Let x = the smallest number, $x + 2$ = the middle number, and $x + 4$ = the largest number. Write an equation.

$$x + (x + 2) + (x + 4) = 75$$
Solve.
$$3x + 6 = 75$$
$$3x = 69$$
$$x = 23$$

The numbers are 23, 25, and 27. Since the problem asks for the largest number, enter 27 in the grid.

19. (5) 4 − x = −2x "Four decreased by a number" (the number is designated as x) is written as $4 - x$. A *product* is the answer to a multiplication problem, so "the product of a number and −2" is $-2x$. The correct equation sets these two expressions as equal.

20. (4) 85 Convert each fraction from minutes to seconds. $\frac{1}{4}$ min $= \frac{1}{4} \times 60$ sec $= 15$ seconds
$\frac{2}{3}$ minute $= \frac{2}{3} \times 60$ seconds $= 40$ seconds

Subtract.
$$\begin{array}{r} 6\frac{2}{3} \text{ min} = 6 \text{ min } 40 \text{ sec} \\ -5\frac{1}{4} \text{ min} = -5 \text{ min } 15 \text{ sec} \\ \hline 1 \text{ min } 25 \text{ sec} \end{array}$$

Convert the answer to seconds.
1 min 25 sec = 60 sec + 25 sec = 85 sec

21. (5) Not enough information is given. The *median* height is the middle height. It does not tell you anything about the upper and lower ends of the data. You know that half the values are equal to or greater than 73 inches, but you cannot know what they are.

22. (1) $y = \frac{2}{3}x$ Find the slope-intercept equation of the line: $y = mx + b$, where m = slope and b = y-intercept, or the point where the line crosses the y-axis $(0,b)$. Using point M $(3,2)$, you find that the line rises 2 units as it moves 3 units to the right, so the slope of the line (*rise* over *run*) is $\frac{2}{3}$. The line passes through the origin $(0,0)$, so $b = 0$. The equation of the line is $y = \frac{2}{3}x + 0$, or $y = \frac{2}{3}x$. Another approach is to substitute the coordinates of point M, $(3,2)$, as the x and y values into each equation to see which equation is true.

23. (4) $450 Commission = 5% × total collections Add the amounts to find total collections. $1800 + $2400 + $4800 = $9000 Then find 5% of $9000. 0.05 × $9000 = $450 OR find 5% by first finding 10% by moving the decimal point one place to the left, then dividing by 2. 10% of $9000 is $900, so 5% is $450.

24. (5) $\frac{1}{100}$ There are 2 cards numbered 5. The probability of drawing one 5 is $\frac{2}{20} = \frac{1}{10}$. Repeat the experiment and the probability is $\frac{1}{10}$. Multiply these fractions. $\frac{1}{10} \times \frac{1}{10} = \frac{1}{100}$

25. (2) 4 medium bottles Use multiplication and addition to evaluate each of the answer options.
(1) 6 small bottles: $0.80 × 6 = $4.80
(2) 4 medium bottles: $1.10 × 4 = $4.40
(3) 3 large bottles: $1.50 × 3 = $4.50
(4) 1 extra large, 1 large, and 1 medium bottle:
        $2.20 + $1.50 + $1.10 = $4.80
(5) 1 super size bottle and 1 large bottle:
        $3.00 + $1.50 = $4.50
Compare the five prices. The lowest cost is $4.40 for 4 medium bottles.

SIMULATED TEST (Pages 354–365)
Part I

1. **2 (30)** Compare the bars for the two sandwiches with the scale at the bottom of the graph. The store sold about 85 Italian specials and about 55 chicken sandwiches. Subtract. 85 − 55 = 30 sandwiches

2. **(3) $\frac{1}{3}$** Find the total number of sandwiches sold: estimate the value for each bar and add. 55 + 38 + 35 + 85 + 42 = 255 Since 85 Italian specials were sold, the fraction that was Italian specials is $\frac{85}{255}$ = about 0.33, or about $\frac{1}{3}$.

3. **(3) $31.56** Add the regular prices of the items purchased. $24.50 + $14.95 = $39.45
Find 20% (multiply by 0.2). $39.45 × 0.2 = $7.89
Subtract the discount from the regular price total. $39.45 − $7.89 = $31.56
OR find 80% of the total regular price. Since 20% is the amount of the discount, the sale price is 80% of the original price. $39.45 × 0.8 = $31.56

4. **55.25** Use the formula for finding the volume of a rectangular container. ("Thickness" is the height.)
$V = lwh = 13 × 8\frac{1}{2} × \frac{1}{2} = 55.25$ cubic feet

5. **17** Use the order of operations.
$25 − (7 − 3)^2 ÷ 2$
$25 − \quad (4)^2 \quad ÷ 2$
$25 − \quad 16 \quad ÷ 2$
$25 − \qquad 8$
$\qquad 17$

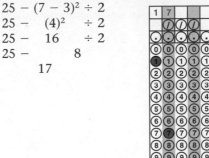

6. **(3) 27** Let x = the points scored by the losing team and $x + 13$ = the points scored by the winning team. Write and solve an equation.
$x + (x + 13) = 41$
$2x + 13 = 41$
$2x = 28$
$x = 14$
The losing team scored 14 points, so the winning team scored 14 + 13 = 27 points.

7. **(1) 15($27.00) + 12($42.00)** The total amount collected is the sum of 15 times the price for a one-year subscription and 12 times the price for a two-year subscription.

8. **(5) $2.10** Find the cost per magazine for the three-year subscription: divide the 3-yr cost by 36 issues. $50.40 ÷ 36 = $1.40 Subtract this price from the cover price. $3.50 − $1.40 = $2.10

9. **(2) $71.00** If Kira averages $75 for 5 days, she will earn $75 × 5 = $375 during the five-day period. Add to find her commissions for the first 4 days. $94 + $58 + $70 + $82 = $304. Subtract to find the amount she must earn on day 5. $375 − $304 = $71

10. **(1) 5** Find the area of the triangle.
$A = \frac{1}{2} × base × height = \frac{1}{2}(12)(10) = 60$ sq in
The area of the rectangle is also 60 sq in and its length equals 12 in. Use the formula for finding the area of a rectangle to solve for the width.
Area = length × width
$60 = 12w$
$w = 5$ inches

11. **(3) 20** You are given 500 mg/pill and 10 g/bottle and asked to find pills/bottle. You must first convert to the same units.
1 g = 1000 mg, so 10 g = 10,000 mg
Divide. 10,000 mg/bottle ÷ 500 mg/pill = 10,000 mg/bottle × pill/500 mg = 20 pills/bottle

12. **135** Write a proportion, cross multiply, and solve.

$$\frac{1 \text{ inch}}{60 \text{ miles}} = \frac{2.25 \text{ inches}}{x \text{ miles}}$$

$$1x = 60(2.25)$$

$$x = 135 \text{ miles}$$

13. **356** Side AB corresponds to side CD. Use any other pair of corresponding sides to write a proportion. Then solve for the length of side AB using corresponding sides DE and AE.

$$\frac{DE}{AE} = \frac{CD}{AB}$$

$$\frac{51}{204} = \frac{89}{x}$$

$$51x = 204(89)$$

$$51x = 18{,}156$$

$$x = 356 \text{ feet}$$

14. **(3) 45 and 45** Given: $\triangle XYZ$ is an isosceles triangle. Fact: An isosceles triangle has two angles with equal measures. Given: $m\angle X = 90°$; Since a triangle cannot have 2 right angles, $m\angle Y = m\angle Z$. Let $x = m\angle Y = m\angle Z$

Fact: $m\angle X + m\angle Y + m\angle Z = 180°$
Substitute: $90° + x + x = 180°$
Solve: $2x = 90°$
                    $x = 45° = m\angle Y = m\angle Z$

15. **(3) C** $\frac{-14}{5} = -2\frac{4}{5}$, which is between -3 and -2 on the number line. Only Point C is in this range.

16. **(2) $N = \frac{18(7)}{4}$** Write the proportion. Then use the rules of algebra to isolate the variable.

$$\frac{18 \text{ printers}}{4 \text{ hours}} = \frac{N \text{ printers}}{7 \text{ hours}}$$

$$4N = 18(7)$$

$$N = \frac{18(7)}{4}$$

17.

Count 3 to the left along the x-axis and 5 down along the y-axis; $(-3,-5)$ is in quadrant III.

18. **(3) 6** Compare the percentages for the sections: Housing is 35%, Clothes is 6%. 35% is about 36%, which is 6 times greater than 6%.

19. **(5) The family spends more than half of its income on housing and food.** Read each statement and compare it to the information on the graph. Option (1) is false: $3 is spent on food for every $1 spent on clothes $\left(\frac{\$18}{\$6}\right)$. Option (2) is false: taxes = 21% which is less than $\frac{1}{4}$ (25%). Options (3) and (4) may be true, but they cannot be proved true from the information stated in the graph. Only option (5) is true; the family spends 35% on housing and 18% on food. 35% + 18% = 53%, which is more than 50%, or half, of the family's income.

20. **(3) $20,842** Use the formula given.

$n =$ c $+ 0.04\,(c)$ $+ \$250$
Substitute. $n = \$19{,}800 + 0.04(\$19{,}800) + \$250$
Solve. $n = \$19{,}800 +$ 792 $+ \$250$
        $n = \$20{,}842$

21. **124.5 or $\frac{249}{2}$** 1 yd = 3 ft So 3 × the number of yards = ft

$$41\frac{1}{2} = \frac{83}{2} \times 3 = \frac{249}{2} = 124\frac{1}{2} = 124.5 \text{ ft}$$

22. 0.80 The total distance is 1185 miles (base). Of this distance she has driven 237 miles (the part). Find the portion (percent or rate) left.
base × rate = part   237 ÷ 1185 = .20 already driven Subtract to find the portion left to drive.
(100% − 20%) = 80% = 0.80

23. (5) 32 Divide each answer choice, first by 3 and then by 5. Only option (5) fits the criteria stated in the problem. 32 ÷ 3 = 10 r2 and 32 ÷ 5 = 6 r2

24. (1) (3.14)(1.5)²(5) Use the formula for finding the volume of a cylinder. $V = \pi \times radius^2 \times height$ The diagram gives the diameter as 3 feet, so the radius is one-half the diameter or 3 ÷ 2 = 1.5. Substitute into the formula. $V = \pi r^2 h = (3.14)(1.5)^2(5)$

25. (2) The range of Type B sonar is 15 times greater than the range of Type A sonar. The range of Type A sonar is $3.2 \times 10^3 = 3,200$ miles, the range of Type B is $4.8 \times 10^4 = 48,000$ miles. Divide. 48,000 ÷ 3,200 = 15

Part II

1. (2) 12 Find a number evenly divisible by 3 and 20, such as, 60. To do this, list multiples of 3 and 20:
   3: 30, <u>60</u>, 90;   20: 40, <u>60</u>, 80, 100
Divide 60 by each of the answer options. Only option (2) divides evenly into 60.

2. (3) 58° The sum of the measures of angles 1 and 2 is 90°. Subtract to find the measure of ∠2.
90° − 32° = 58°

3. (4) 200 Write and solve a proportion.

$$\frac{30\%}{60 \text{ workers}} = \frac{100\%}{x \text{ workers}}$$

$$30x = 60(100)$$
$$30x = 6000$$
$$x = 200$$

OR use the percentage formula, base × rate = part, substituting 30% as the rate and 60 as the part, and solving for the base.

$$\text{base} = \frac{\text{part}}{\text{rate}} = \frac{60}{.3} = 200$$

4. (5) 208 Think of the figure as two rectangles and find the area of each. Area = length × width
<u>Right rectangle.</u> $A = lw = 16(6) = 96$ sq units
<u>Left rectangle.</u> Add to find the length of the left

side of the other rectangle. 8 + 6 = 14
Then find the area. $A = lw = 14(8) = 112$ sq units
Add the two areas. 96 + 112 = 208 sq units
The figure is also a square 8 units on each side
($A = s^2 = 8^2 = 64$) and a rectangle 8 + 16 = 24
units long and 6 units wide ($A = 24(6) = 144$).
Total area = 64 + 144 = 208 sq units

5. (3) − 5 or 2 In the equation, the product of the two factors is 0. For this to be true, one of the factors must equal 0. If $x + 5 = 0$, then $x = -5$. If $x - 2 = 0$, then x = 2. Therefore, x must equal either −5 or 2.

6. 8.5 or $\frac{17}{2}$ You can work backwards to solve this problem. You know that Robin has worked at the company for 8 years. Thus, Brad has worked there $8 - 3\frac{1}{2} = 7\frac{2}{2} - 3\frac{1}{2} = 4\frac{1}{2}$ years, and Melanie has worked there $4\frac{1}{2} + 4 = 8\frac{1}{2}$ yr. Enter 8.5 or $\frac{17}{2}$ in grid.

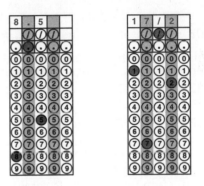

7. (3) 1996 City Z is the lowest line on the graph. The highest point on this line is above the year 1996.

8. (2) The air quality of City X has improved each year from 1995 to 2000. This graph shows the number of days per year below acceptable standards. Therefore, a downward movement of the line shows improvement. Since the line for City X has moved steadily in a downward direction, option (2) is true. Options (1), (4), or (5) may be true, but they cannot be proved using the information on the graph. Option (3) is false; air quality in City Y has improved (moved downward).

9. (5) $\frac{3}{4}$ The probability that a box of large shirts will be chosen is $\frac{150}{200}$, which reduces to $\frac{3}{4}$.

10. (5) $12^2 + 16^2 = x^2$ Since Lyndate is "due east" and "due north" of the other two cities, the angle at Lyndale to the other two is a right angle. Thus, use the Pythagorean Relationship $a^2 + b^2 = c^2$ The distance between Harding and Medford becomes the hypotenuse (c) of a right triangle. The distances given in the problem are the lengths of the legs of the triangle.

11. (1) −3ab + 24a Use the distributive property to multiply the factors.
$$-3a(b - 8) = -3a(b) + (-3a)(-8) = -3ab + 24a$$

12.

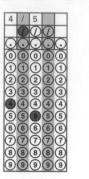

(5,−1) Point A is 5 units from Point B. Locate the third vertex at $(0,-1)$. Since the figure is a rectangle, the remaining vertex must be located 5 units to the right of $(0,-1)$ at $(5,-1)$ (in quadrant IV).

13. (5) 64 Let x = the number of professional golfers and $2x$ = the number of amateurs. The total is 96. Write an equation. $\qquad x + 2x = 96$
Solve. $\qquad\qquad\qquad\qquad 3x = 96$
$$x = 32$$
Therefore, the number of amateurs is $2(32) = 64$.

14. (3) 31 Arrange the numbers in order 15, 18, 25, 25, 30, 32, 40, 45, 55, 75. The two middle values are 30 and 32 minutes. Find the mean of these values to find the median.
$$30 + 32 = 62 \text{ and } \tfrac{62}{2} = 31 \text{ minutes}$$

15. (4) $\frac{C}{2\pi}$ Begin with the formula for the circumference of a circle. $C = 2\pi r$ Divide both sides of the formula by 2π to isolate the unknown variable r.

16. (1) $\frac{9}{10}$ The percent 88.5% = 0.885 which rounds to 0.9. This decimal equals the fraction $\frac{9}{10}$. The decimal equivalents of the other fractions in the options are not close to 0.885:
$\frac{4}{5} = 0.8$, $\frac{3}{4} = 0.75$, $\frac{2}{3} \approx 0.667$, and $\frac{1}{2} = 0.5$

17. (2) $\frac{3(100)}{75}$ Write a proportion to find percent of change x. The amount of change is $3, and the original amount is $75. Substitute and solve for x.

% change = $\frac{\text{amount of change}}{\text{original amount}}$ $\qquad \frac{3}{75} = \frac{x}{100}$
$$75x = 3(100)$$
$$x = \frac{3(100)}{75}$$

18. $\frac{4}{5}$ or .8 During the first sale, Zachary sold $\frac{1}{2}$ of the land. During the second sale, he sold $\frac{3}{5}$ of $\frac{1}{2}$ or $\frac{3}{5} \times \frac{1}{2} = \frac{3}{10}$. Add to find the total. $\frac{1}{2} + \frac{3}{10} = \frac{5}{10} + \frac{3}{10} = \frac{8}{10} = \frac{4}{5} = 0.8$

19. (5) Not enough information is given. The perimeter of a triangle is the sum of the lengths of the three sides. Even knowing 2 of these lengths is not enough information. You must know either the third length or the measure of at least one angle.

20. (3) 80.7% Subtract the percentage for recruiting (19.3%) from the total budget (100%).
$$100\% - 19.3\% = 80.7\%$$

21. (4) $2x - 15 = -3x$ Let x be the unknown number. "Twice a number" is expressed as $2x$. "The difference" means subtract so "the difference of twice a number and 15" is written $2x - 15$. The word *product* indicates multiplication; therefore, the product of -3 and the number is written $-3x$. These two expressions are equal.

22. (4) $\angle ABD$ is a right angle. Triangles ABD and BAC are congruent ($\cong$), so the measures of their corresponding angles and sides are equal. The triangles share the same base (AB), so the angles opposite the base, $\angle C$ and $\angle D$ are corresponding angles (are equal) (so option (3) is incorrect). Given: $m\angle C = 60°$, so $m\angle D = 60°$ (so options (1) and (5), both of which refer to $\angle D$ are incorrect). Given: $m\angle DEB = 60°$ Look at $\triangle DEB$. The sum of the measures of the angles of a triangle is 180°, co 180° $- m\angle D - m\angle DEB = 180° - 60° - 60° = 60°$ So, $m\angle DBE$ (the third angle of $\triangle DBE$) = 60° Given: $m\angle ABE = 30°$. Look at $\angle DBA$. Since $m\angle DBE = 60°$, the measure of $\angle ABD$ is 60° + 30° = 90°; therefore, $\angle ABD$ is a right angle, making option (4) true. Option (2) is incorrect because the two angles are supplementary (totalling 180°) not complementary (totalling 90°).

23. **(2) $54** Find the best price for each item and add.

The weekly expense register	$15
Fifty file folders at 10 for $5 = 5 × $5	$25
Three notebooks	$10
(which is cheaper than $4 × 3 = $12)	
Six adding machine tapes at 3 for $2 cost	$ 4
(cheaper than $1 × 6 = $6).	
Total cost =	$54

24. **(4) 5:8** Estimate the values for Wednesday and Saturday by comparing the bars to the scale on the left of the graph. There were approximately 125 customers on Wednesday and about 200 customers on Saturday. Write a ratio and reduce it to simplest terms. $\frac{125}{200} = \frac{5}{8} = 5:8$

25. **(3) 30** To find the average number of customers per hour divide the total customers by the number of hours. There are 8 hours from 10 A.M. to 6 P.M. The total number of customers, according to the graph, was 250. Divide. $250 ÷ 8 = 31\frac{1}{4}$, or about 30 customers per hour.

Glossary

acute angle an angle that measures less than 90°

acute triangle a triangle with three acute angles

add/addition numerical operation used to combine quantities; find a total (sum)

adjacent angles angles that have a common vertex and a common ray

algebraic expression a mathematical expression that contains one or more variables; a group of numbers, variables, and operation signs

alternate exterior angles a pair of congruent angles formed by two parallel lines cut by a transversal, located outside the parallel lines and on opposite sides of the transversal

alternate interior angles a pair of congruent angles formed by two parallel lines cut by a transversal, located inside the parallel lines and on opposite sides of the transversal

angle a pair of rays extending from a common point

area the measure of the surface inside a flat (plane or 2-dimensional) figure expressed in square units

associative [grouping] property a mathematical rule stating that when more than two numbers are added or multiplied, the result will be the same no matter how the numbers are grouped: $(a + b) + c = a + (b + c)$; $(a \times b) \times c = a \times (b \times c)$
Subtraction and division do not have this property.

assumption a statement that is taken to be true until it is proved false

average the sum of the data in a list divided by the number of items in that list; the mean of the list

axis horizontal and vertical scales on a graph or coordinate plane, referred to as the x- and y-axis

bar graph visual presentation of data from different sources as the height or length of bars against the same scale

base the whole amount in a percent problem; in geometry, the side (face) on which a figure sits

borrow to regroup from a greater place value to a lesser place value (e.g., one ten to ten ones) in order to subtract

canceling the process of reducing to multiply and divide fractions; dividing out common factors

from the numerator and denominator of a fraction before multiplying or dividing

carry to regroup from a lesser place value to a greater place value (e.g., ten ones to one ten) in order to add

chart visual organization and presentation of data in rows and columns

circle the curve formed by all the points in a plane that are the same distance (radius) from a given point (center)

circle graph visual presentation of data showing parts of a whole (the circle) using percents, decimals, or fractions

circumference the distance around a circle; the perimeter of a circle

common denominator a number that two or more denominators will divide into evenly; any common multiple of the denominators of two or more fractions

commutative [order] property a mathematical rule stating that the order in which numbers are added (or multiplied) does not change the sum (or product): $a + b = b + a$; $a \times b = b \times a$
Subtraction and division do not have this property.

comparing determining which number is greater; arranging numbers in order; using equality and inequality symbols $(=, >, <, \geq, \leq)$

compatible numbers numbers that are easy to work with in problem solving; numbers that form a basic division fact

complementary angles two angles for which the sum of their measures is 90°

cone a solid (3-dimentional) figure with a circular base and sides that meet at a point

congruent angles angles that have equal measures

congruent figures figures that have the same shape and size

consecutive numbers numbers in counting order

conversion factor equivalency to change from one unit of measurement to another (e.g., 1 hr = 60 min)

coordinate graph a set of points formed by a grid with a horizontal (*x*-) and a vertical (*y*-) axis; sometimes called a coordinate plane or grid

corresponding angles angles that are in the same position in relation to a transversal that cuts across two parallel lines; the angles are either both above or both below the two parallel lines and on the same side of the transversal; always equal in measure

cross product in a pair of equivalent fractions, the product of the numerator of one fraction and the denominator of the other fraction; the products of cross multiplying; when two fractions are equal, the cross products are equal

cube a rectangular solid with six square sides (faces; all edges of equal length); raise to the third power (exponent of 3)—multiply a number times itself 3 times: $x \times x \times x = x^3$

cubic units units in the shape of a cube with the length of each side equal to the linear unit (e.g., a cubic inch) used to measure the volume of a three-dimensional figure; units needed to fill the space inside a 3-dimensional figure

customary (U.S.) system of measurement the measurement system commonly used in the United States; some examples of standard units are feet, miles, pounds, and ounces

cylinder a solid (3-dimensional) figure with two congruent circular bases and straight sides

data a collection of numbers and information

decimal a fraction expressed in the place value system to the right of the decimal point

denominator the bottom number in a fraction that tells the number of equal parts in the whole object or group

dependent in probability, an event whose outcome (occurring later) is affected by the outcome of an earlier event

diagonal a line segment drawn between the vertices of two non-adjacent sides of a figure that has four or more straight sides

diameter a line segment drawn through the center of a circle connecting two points on the circle; twice the length of the radius

diameter

difference the answer to a subtraction problem

digit one of the numerals 0, 1, 2, 3, 4, 5, 6, 7, 8, and 9 used to represent numbers in a place-value system

distributive property a mathematical rule stating that the product (or quotient) of a number and a sum (or difference) is equal to the sum (or difference) of the products (or quotients) of the number and the individual terms within the parentheses:

$$a(b + c) = ab + ac; \quad a(b - c) = ab - ac;$$
$$\frac{(b + c)}{a} = \frac{b}{a} + \frac{c}{a} \quad \frac{(b - c)}{a} = \frac{b}{a} - \frac{c}{a}$$

divide/division numerical operation used to split a quantity (the dividend) into equal parts (the divisor); find a quotient

dividend the number (the whole) being divided by the divisor

divisor the number being divided into the dividend; the number of parts

equation a mathematical statement that says two expressions are equal

equilateral triangle a triangle with three congruent sides; an equilateral triangle also has three congruent angles, each measuring 60°

equivalent (equal) fractions fractions that have the same value

estimate to find an approximate solution when an exact answer is not needed

evaluate an expression substitute known or given values for the variables into an algebraic expression and perform the operations (in the order of operations) to obtain the solution

experimental probability chance of a specific outcome determined by performing a number of trials; the ratio of the number of favorable outcomes obtained to total number of trials

exponent a raised number at the right of another number that tells how many times the number is to be used as a factor e.g., a number cubed = x^3, the 3 is the exponent or "power" (e.g., $4^3 = 4 \times 4 \times 4 = 64$)

face one flat 2-dimensional surface (face) of a solid figure

factors numbers or algebraic expressions that are multiplied together (e.g., 3 and 4 are factors of 12; 2 and *x* are factors of 2*x*)

factoring an expression finding the algebraic terms or expressions (called factors) that when multiplied will result in a certain product (e.g., factors of 2*x* are 2 and *x*; factors of $x^2 + 6x + 8$ are (*x* + 2) and (*x* + 4)

FOIL method a system for multiplying algebraic factors with more than one term; FOIL stands for first-outer-inner-last:

$$(a + b)(c + d) = ac + ad + bc + bd$$

formula an equation showing a mathematical relationship in which the letters stand for specific kinds of quantities

fraction a way to show part (the numerator or top number) of a whole (the denominator or bottom number); digits grouped above and below a division bar; a ratio

frequency table a chart used to summarize data that shows the number of times certain events occur

function an algebraic rule involving two variables in which for every value of the first variable (x) there is a unique value of the second variable (y)

graph visual representation comparing data from different sources or over time

height the measure of the vertical distance of a plane (2-D) shape or solid (3-D) figure from the base to the opposite side (parallelogram) or face (rectangular container or cylinder) or vertex (triangle, pyramid, or cone); an imaginary line perpendicular to the base

horizontal axis scale that runs along the bottom or left to right on a graph or coordinate grid; the x-axis

hypotenuse in a right triangle, the side opposite the right angle; the longest side in a right triangle

improper fraction a fraction that shows a quantity equal to or greater than 1; a fraction in which the numerator is equal to or greater than the denominator

independent in probability, an event whose outcome (occurring later) is *not* affected by the outcome of an earlier event

indirect measurement a method used to find measures when there is no actual way to perform the measurement

inequality a mathematical statement that two expressions are not always equal; one expression may be *greater than* (>), *greater than or equal to* (≥), *less than* (<) or *less than or equal to* (≤) the other expression

integers all whole numbers, positive and negative, and zero

interest a fee charged for using someone else's money; usually expressed as a rate—a percent of the amount being used (the principal) over a unit of time

intervals equal segments on a number line

inverse opposite: addition and subtraction are inverse operations as are multiplication and division

irregular figure a figure made of several common shapes

isolate the variable perform operations to get the variable alone on one side of an equation

isosceles triangle a triangle that has two congruent sides (of the same length); the angles opposite the congruent sides have equal measures

key the part of a graph that indicates how to interpret symbols or colors

leg in a right triangle, one of the two sides that form the right angle

like fractions fractions that have the same denominator

like terms algebraic terms that contain exactly the same variables and exponents

linear equation an equation that does not contain a variable to any power (exponent) greater than 1; an equation whose graph is a straight line

line graph visual presentation of data as a line on a grid, often showing change over time (a trend)

lowest (or least) common denominator the smallest number that is a common multiple of the denominators of two or more fractions

lowest terms used to describe a fraction in which there is no number other than 1 that will divide evenly into both the numerator and the denominator

mean the sum of the data in a list divided by the number of items on that list; the average

median the middle number in a list of data arranged in order; for an even number of data items, the mean of the two numbers in the middle

metric system of measurement a measurement system used throughout most of the world that is based on the powers of ten; common units are meters, grams, liters

mixed number an quantity expressed as a whole number and a proper fraction

mode in a list of data, the number occurring most often

multiple the result of multiplying a given number by the counting numbers (0, 1, 2, 3, and so on)

multiply/multiplication numerical operation used to combine the same quantity many times; find a product

negative number a number to the left of zero on a number line; a number less than zero in value; used to show a decrease, a loss, or downward direction; always preceded by a minus sign

non-adjacent angles angles that do not share a common ray; they may or may not share a common vertex

number line a line divided into equal segments (intervals) by points corresponding to integers, fractions, or decimals; points to the right of 0 are positive; those to the left are negative

numerator the top number in a fraction; it tells the number of equal parts to which you are referring

obtuse angle an angle that measures more than 90° but less than 180°

obtuse triangle a triangle with one obtuse angle (a triangle can have only one obtuse angle)

operation something done to one or more numbers to produce an answer: addition, subtraction, multiplication, division, exponents, roots

opposite angles the angles that are across from each other when two lines intersect or cross; in a geometric shape, opposite angles are directly across from each other; in the examples below, ∠1 and ∠3 are opposite, and ∠2 and ∠4 are opposite angles; also called vertical angles

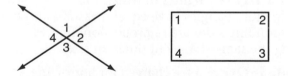

ordered pair a pair of numbers that names a point on a coordinate graph; presented in parentheses as (the x-coordinate, the y-coordinate)

order of operations a sequence, agreed upon by mathematicians, for performing mathematical operations: 1. operations in grouping symbols, 2. exponents and roots, 3. multiplication and division from left to right, 4. addition and subtraction from left to right

origin the point at which the x-axis and y-axis in a coordinate graph intersect; the point represented by the ordered pair (0,0)

parallel lines two lines on the same plane that do not intersect

parallelogram a quadrilateral with both pairs of opposite sides parallel; opposite sides are of equal length and opposite angles are of equal measure

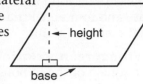

part a portion of the whole or base in a percent problem

partial product when multiplying numbers with more than one digit, the result of multiplying the number on top by one of the digits in the bottom number

pattern a list of numbers that is ordered according to a special rule or combination of rules

percent a way to show a part of a whole by setting the whole equal to 100; a number per hundred followed by a percent sign (%): 5% is 5 out of 100

perimeter the distance around a flat (2-D) figure; the sum of the lengths of all the sides of a flat figure

period each group of from 1 to 3 digits separated from other digits in a number by a comma

perpendicular lines two lines that intersect, forming adjacent right angles

pi (π) the constant ratio of the circumference of a circle to the diameter; approximately 3.14

placeholder the digit 0 when used to fill a place-value column

place value the value of a digit determined by its position in a number; examples: the 5 in 589 has a value of 500; the 5 in 0.05 has a value of $\frac{5}{100}$

plane a set of points that forms a flat surface

point a single, exact location often represented by a dot

positive number a number to the right of zero on a number line; a number greater than zero in value; used to show an increase, a gain, or upward direction; may be preceded by a plus sign

principal an amount of money borrowed or invested

probability a number (whole, fraction, decimal, or ratio) that shows how likely it is that an event will happen; chance

product the answer to a multiplication problem

proper fraction a quantity less than 1; the numerator is always less than the denominator

proportion an equation that states that two ratios (fractions) are equal

pyramid a solid figure with a square base and four equal triangular sides that meet at a point

Pythagorean Relationship in a right triangle, the square of the hypotenuse is equal to the sum of the squares of the other two sides (legs): $a^2 + b^2 = c^2$

quadrant one-fourth of a coordinate grid, formed by the intersecting axes

quadratic equation an equation that contains a variable raised to the second power; there may be two solutions to a quadratic equation

quadratic expression an algebraic expression containing a variable raised to the second power

quadrilateral any flat (plane) figure with four sides

quotient the answer to a division problem; the amount in each part of the whole

radius a line segment connecting the center of a circle to a point on the circle; $\frac{1}{2}$ the length of the diameter

random selected by chance, with no outcome more likely than any other

range in a list of data, the spread between the lowest number and the highest number

rate a ratio of two different kinds of units used to show a relationship: $\frac{\text{miles}}{\text{gallon}}$, miles per hour; the percent relationship of the part to the base in a percent problem

ratio a way of comparing two numbers using division; can be written as a fraction, using the word "to", or using a colon; examples: $\frac{3}{4}$, 3 to 4, 3:4

ray a part of a line having only one endpoint; one side of an angle

rectangle a parallelogram having four right angles

rectangular solid a three-dimensional figure in which all sides are rectangles and all corners are square

reducing finding an equal fraction with a smaller numerator and denominator

reflex angle an angle that measures more than 180° but less than 360°

regroup moving an amount from one place-value column to another; the common processes of carrying and borrowing are examples of regrouping

remainder the amount left over in a division problem

repeating decimal a decimal number that continues infinitely, repeating a pattern of digits

rhombus a parallelogram with four sides of equal length

right angle an angle that makes a "square corner" that measures exactly 90°

This symbol means the angle measures 90°.

right triangle a triangle in which one angle is a right angle

rounding using an approximation for a number

scale the units on the axis of a graph; the equivalency (ratio) of drawn measurements to the corresponding actual measurements (e.g., on a map or scale drawing)

scale drawing a diagram of an object with all distances in proportion to corresponding distances on the actual object; a drawing of the same shape as but a smaller size than the actual

scalene triangle a triangle in which no two sides (or angles) are congruent (of the same length)

scientific notation a way of writing very large numbers and very small decimals in which the numbers are expressed as the product of a number between 1 and 10 and a power of 10

signed numbers positive and negative numbers; often used to show quantity, distance, or direction

similar figures figures in which the corresponding angles have equal measures and the corresponding sides are in proportion; figures having the same shape but different sizes

simple interest a fee charged for borrowing money (or earned for investing money) for a particular period of time; simple interest = principal × rate × time

simplifying an expression performing all the operations you can within an algebraic expression

slope the ratio of rise to run that results in a number that measures the steepness of a line

slope-intercept form of a line an equation of a line that takes the following form: $y = mx + b$, where m is the slope and b is the y-intercept

solve find the number that makes a statement, algebraic expression or equation true

square a figure with 4 right angles (a type of rectangle) and 4 sides of equal length (a special rhombus); numerical operation in which a number is multiplied by itself, represented by the exponent 2: x^2

square root a number that when multiplied times itself equals a given number

square unit unit used to measure the area of a two-dimensional figure; units needed to cover a surface

standard grid new GED answer format in which the answer is written in the top row, one digit per column, with blackening of the corresponding bubble below (in the same column containing that digit)

straight angle an angle that measures exactly 180°

subtract/subtraction numerical operation used to take away a quantity from another quantity; find a difference; find "how many(much) more(left)"

sum the answer to an addition problem; total

supplementary angles two angles for which the sum of their measures is 180°

terms a number or a number and one or more variables or a variable raised to a power; parts of a fraction (the numerator and denominator) or algebraic expression

transversal a line crossing two or more parallel lines

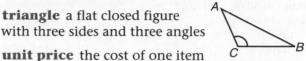

trapezoid a quadrilateral with only one pair of parallel sides

trend a pattern of change; used to make predictions based upon current data

triangle a flat closed figure with three sides and three angles

unit price the cost of one item

unit rate a ratio with a denominator of 1

unlike fractions fractions with different denominators

variable any letter used to stand for a number

vertex the point at which two or more line segments or sides of a figure meet; the point at which the two rays that form an angle meet

vertical angles the angles that are across from each other when two lines intersect, or cross; also called opposite angles

vertical axis scale that runs along the side or top to bottom on a graph or coordinate grid; the y-axis

volume the measure of the amount of space inside a three-dimensional figure; measured in cubic units

x-axis the horizontal axis in a coordinate graph

x-coordinate the first number in an ordered pair, the distance from the origin along the x-axis

x-intercept the point at which a line crosses the x-axis on a coordinate graph; the ordered pair $(x,0)$

y-axis the vertical axis in a coordinate graph

y-coordinate the second number in an ordered pair, the distance from the origin along the y-axis

y-intercept the point at which a line crosses the y-axis on a coordinate graph; the ordered pair $(0,y)$

Index

Addition, 32, 36–38, 82–85,
    106–107, 204–205
Algebra (unit 3), 202–265
    coordinate plane, 203, 244–255
    cumulative review, 260–265
    equations, 203, 214–227
    exponents and roots, 203,
        228–235
    factoring and inequalities,
        203–204, 236–243
    integers and algebraic
        expressions, 203–213
    mini-tests, 224–227, 256–259
Algebraic equations, 214–227
Algebraic expressions, 208–211
Alternate answer formats
    coordinate grid, 246–247
    standard grid, 50–51, 80–81,
        92–93, 112–113, 118–119
Angles, 280–291
    acute, 280
    adjacent and non-adjacent, 282
    alternate exterior, 284
    alternate interior, 284
    complementary, 280
    congruent and vertical, 282–283
    corresponding, 284
    kinds of, 280–281
    lines and, 284–285
    mini-test, 288–291
    obtuse, 280
    opposite, 282
    reflex, 280
    right, 280 (*See also* right angle)
    straight, 280
    supplementary, 280–281
    vertical, 282
    word problems involving, 286
Area
    of circles, 270
    of irregular figures, 302–305
    of squares and rectangles,
        166–167, 170–171
    of triangles and parallelograms,
        268–269
Associative property, 53
Assumptions, 286
Average, 178–179, 184–185
Axes, 188, 244

Bar graphs, 188–189
Base, 130, 268, 274
Borrow, 38

Calculator, using a, 439–442
    basic functions of, 42–43
    fractions and decimals, 120–121
    mean and median, 184–185
    order of operations and, 58–59
    parentheses keys, 207

    percent key, 144
    sine, cosine, and tangent, 310
    square root key, 230
Canceling, 86
Central tendencies and probability,
    157, 178–185
    independent and dependent
        probability, 182–183
    mean, median, mode and range,
        178–179, 184–185
    simple probability, 180–181
Charts and tables, 186–197
Choosing the operation, 32, 68
Circle graphs, 190–191
Circles, 270–271
Circumference, 270
Common denominator, 74–75
Commutative property, 53
Comparing, 30–31, 74–75, 100–101
Compatible numbers, 47
Cones, 274–275
Congruent figures, 292, 294,
    296–297
Consecutive numbers, 220–221,
    232–233
Conversion factors, 158–159
Converting measurements,
    158–163, 276–277
Coordinate grid, alternate answer
    format, 246–247
Coordinate plane, 203, 244–255
    coordinate graphs, 244–245
    distance between 2 points,
        252–253
    finding equation of a line,
        254–255
    finding slope of a line, 250–251
    graphing equations, 248–249
    ordered pairs, 246
    plotting points, 246–247
Corresponding parts, 284, 296
Cost formula, 222–223
Cross multiply, 72, 78
Cross-product rule, 78
Cross products, 72
Cube, 272–273
Cubic units, 168
Cumulative review
    unit 1, 150–155
    unit 2, 196–201
    unit 3, 260–265
    unit 4, 318–325
Customary measurement system,
    158–159
Cylinder, 272–273

Data, 48, 156–201
Decimals, 98–127, 180
    adding and subtracting, 106–107

    fractions and, 114–121
    introduction to, 98–105
    mini-test, 122–125
    money, 102–103
    multiplying and dividing,
        108–109
    on alternate answer format,
        92–93, 118–119
    on grids, 112–113, 118–119
    on number lines, 104–105
    operations with, 106–113
    percents and, 126–127
    repeating, 116
    rounding, 100–101
    word problems, 102–103,
        110–111
Dependent probability, 182
Denominator, 64
Diagonal (of a quadrilateral), 294
Diameter, 270
Difference, 36
Distance between two points,
    252–253
Distance formula, 222–223
Distributive property, 210
Division, 32, 38–39, 68, 88–89,
    108–109, 206–207
Drawing a picture, 172

Equations, algebraic, 203, 214–227
    graphing, 248–255
    linear, graphing of, 248–249
    multi-step, 216–217
    of a line, 254–255
    one-step, 214–215
    solving, 220–221
    translating problems into,
        218–219
Equivalent fractions, 72–73
Estimating to solve problems, 46–47
Estimating with fractions, 90–91
Estimation and money, 102–103
Evaluating an expression, 208
Experimental probability, 180–181
Exponents, 166, 203, 228–235
Expressions, algebraic, 208–209

Factoring and inequalities, 203,
    236–243
    factoring, 238–239
    factors with 2 terms, 236–239
    multiplying factors with
        two terms, 236–237
    solving inequalities, 242–243
    solving quadratic equations,
        240–241
Floor plans, 300
FOIL method, 236
Formulas
    cost, 222–223

distance, 222–223
interest, 140–141
Formulas in geometry, 164–168,
    170–171, 268–279, 302–305
    area, 166–167, 170–171,
        268–271, 302–305
    circles, 270–271
    converting measurements, 158,
        276
    perimeter, 166–167, 170–171
    pyramids and cones, 274–275
    solving for variables in, 278–279
    triangles and parallelograms,
        268–269
    volume, 166–167, 170–171,
        272–275, 302–305
Fractions, 64–97, 180
    adding and subtracting, 82–85
    common denominators, 74–75
    comparing, 74–75
    decimals and, 114–121
    dividing, 88–89
    equivalent, 72–73
    estimating with, 90–91
    improper fractions and mixed
        numbers, 64–67
    introduction to, 64–71
    in word problems, 68–69
    like, 74–75, 82
    mini-test, 94–97
    multiplying, 86–87, 122–125
    on alternate answer format,
        80–81, 92–93, 118–119
    on number lines, 70–71
    percents and, 128–129
    proper, 64
    raising to higher terms, 74
    ratios and proportions, 76–79
    reducing, 72–73
    unlike, 74
Frequency tables, 186
Functions (algebraic rules), 234–235

Geometry (unit 4), 266–325
    cumulative review, 318–325
    formulas, 267, 268–279
    irregular figures, 267, 302–305
    lines and angles, 267, 280–291
    mini-tests, 288–291, 314–317
    right triangles, 267, 292, 306–313
    triangles and quadrilaterals,
        292–301
Graphing equations, 248–249
Greater than symbol (>), 30
Gridding in answers
    basic pointers, 50–51
    decimals on standard grid,
        112–113, 118–119
    fractions on standard grid,
        80–81, 92–93, 118–119

Height, 168, 268
Higher terms, 74–75
Hypotenuse, 306

Improper fractions, 64, 66–67
Indirect measurement, 300
Inequalities, 30, 242–243
Integers
    adding and subtracting, 204–205
    algebraic expressions and, 203,
        213
    multiplying and dividing,
        206–207
    on number lines, 212–213
    understanding, 204–205
Interest, simple 140
Intervals, 34
Inverse operations, 88
Irregular figures, 302–305

Key, 188

Legs of a right triangle, 306
Length, 164–172
Less than symbol (<), 30
Like fractions, 74, 82
Like terms, 210, 217
Line graphs, 188–189
Lines, 267, 284–285
Logical reasoning, 286–287
Lowest common denominator,
    74–75
Lowest terms, 72

Mean, 178–179, 184–185
Measurement and data analysis
    (unit 2), 156–201
    central tendencies and
        probability, 157, 178–185
    cumulative review, 196–201
    measurement systems, 157–163
    measuring common figures, 157,
        164–173
    mini-tests, 174–177, 192–195
    tables, charts, and graphs, 157,
        186–191
Measurement systems, 157–163
    customary system, 158–159
    metric system, 162–163
    operations with, 160–161
Measuring common figures,
    157–178
    area of squares and rectangles,
        166–167, 170–171
    perimeter, 164–165, 170–171
    volume, 168–170
    word problems and, 170–173
Measurements, converting,
    158–159, 276–277
Median, 178, 179, 181, 185
Metric system, 162–163
Mini-tests for algebra (unit 3)
    coordinate plane, factoring and
        inequalities, 256–259
    integers, algebraic expressions,
        and equations, 224–227
Mini-tests for geometry (unit 4)
    formulas and lines and angles,
        288–291

triangles and quadrilaterals and
    irregular figures, 314–317
Mini-tests for measurement and
    data analysis (unit 2)
    measurements, 174–177
    measures of central tendency
        and probability, and tables,
        charts, and graphs, 192–195
Mini-tests for numbers and
    operations (unit 1)
    decimals and fractions, 122–125
    fractions, 94–97
    number and operation sense and
        operations with whole
        numbers, 44–45
    percent problems, 146–149
    word problems, 60–63
Mixed numbers, 66–67, 84–85,
    88–89
Mode, 179
Multiplying, 32, 38, 39, 68, 74,
    86–87, 108–109, 206–207
Multistep problems, 52–58,
    110–111, 142–143, 304–305

Negative numbers, 204
Number lines
    decimals on, 104–105
    defined, 34–35
    fractions on, 70–71
    integers on, 212–213
Number patterns, 30–31
Numbers and operations
    (unit 1), 26–155
    cumulative review, 150–155
    decimals, 98–113
    decimals and fractions, 114–125
    fractions, 64–97
    mini-tests, 44–45, 60–63,
        94–97, 122–125, 146–149
    multi-step problems, 52–59
    number and operation sense,
        28–35
    percent and percent problems,
        126–149
    whole number operations, 36–45
    word problems, 46–63
Numerator, 64

Operations
    choosing, 32–33, 68–69
    order of, 52–53, 58, 206
    with decimals, 106–113
    with fractions, 68–69, 86–87
    with whole numbers, 36–45
Ordered pair, 244, 246
Ordering, 30–31, 100–101
Order of operations, 52–53, 58, 206
Origin, 244

Parallel lines, 284
Parallelograms, 268–269
Parentheses keys on calculator, 207
Part, 130
Partial product, 38

Patterns, mathematical, 234–235
Percent problems, 132–145
    calculators and, 144–145
    elements of, 132
    finding the base, 138–139
    finding the part, 132–133
    finding the rate, 134–135
    interest problems, 140–141
    mental math for, 136–137
    multistep problems, 142–143
Percents, 126–131, 180
    decimals to percents, 127
    fractions to percents, 128
    meaning of, 126
    percents to decimals, 126
    percents to fractions, 128
    rate of change, 134, 141
    word problems, 130–131,
        142–143
Perimeter, 164–165, 170–171
Period (place value), 28
Perpendicular lines, 284
Placeholder, 98
Place value, 28–29
Plotting points, 246–247
Positive numbers, 204
Principal, 140
Probability
    experimental, 180–181
    independent and dependent,
        182–183
    simple, 180–181
Problem solving (See also Word
    problems.)
    setting up, 56–57
    steps , 40–41
Product, 38
Proper fractions, 64
Proportions, solving, 78, 158, 180
    and congruent figures, 296–297
    and similar figures, 298–299
    in geometry problems, 300–301
    in percent problems, 131–132
Protractor, 280
Pyramids and cones, 274–275
Pythagorean Relationship, 252,
        306–309, 312–313

Quadrants, 244
Quadratic equations, 240–241
Quadratic expressions, 238
Quadrilaterals, 294–301
    congruent figures, 296–297
    proportion in geometry, 300–301
    similar figures, 298–299
Quotient, 38

Radius, 270
Raising to higher terms, 74–75
Range, 179
Rate, 67, 130, 140
Ratios, 76–79, 158, 180, 310
Rectangles, 164, 166–167, 272, 294

Rectangular solid, 168, 272
Reducing fractions, 72–73
Regroup (carry), 36
Remainders, 38
Repeating decimals, 116
Review, cumulative
    unit 1, 150–155
    unit 2, 196–201
    unit 3, 260–265
    unit 4, 318–325
Rhombus, 294
Right triangles, 292
    Pythagorean Relationship, 252,
        306–309, 312–313
    sine, cosine, and tangent,
        310–311
    solving problems with, 312–313
Rise and run, 250
Roots, 203, 228–235
Rounding, 90–91, 100–101
Rounding whole numbers, 29

Scale, on graph, 188
Scale drawings, 300
Scientific notation, 228–229
Set-up problems, 56–57
Signed numbers, 204
Similar figures, 298–299
Simple interest, formula, 140
Simplifying expressions, 210–211
Slope, 250–251, 254
Slope-intercept form of a line,
        254–255
Solving for variables in formulas,
        278–279
Square roots, 230–231
Squares, 164, 166, 170, 294
Square units, 166
Standard grid, alternate answer
        format
    decimals, 112–113, 118–119
    fractions, 80–81, 92–93,
        118–119
    whole numbers, 50–51
Subtraction, 32, 36–37, 82–85,
        106–107, 204–205
Sum, 36

Tables, charts, and graphs, 157,
        186–195
    bar and line graphs, 188–189
    circle graphs, 190–191
    tables and charts, 186–187
Terms of a fraction, 64
Title, 188
Transversal, 284
Trapezoids, 294
Trends, 188
Triangles, 268–269, 292–293
    acute, 292
    and parallelograms, 268–269
    and quadrilaterals, 267
    congruent figures, 296–297

equilateral, 292
formulas, 268–269
isosceles, 292
obtuse, 292
proportion in geometry, 300–301
right, 292. See right triangles.
scalene, 292
similar figures, 298–299

Unit price, 114–117
Unit rate, 76–77
Unlike fractions, 74, 82

Variables
    and algebraic expressions,
        208–211, 289
    in formulas, 178–179, 278–279
Vertex, 274
Vertical axis, 188
Volume
    defined, 168, 272
    formulas for, 272–273, 302
    of common figures, 168–171
    of irregular figures, 302–305
    of pyramids and cones, 274–275

Whole numbers, 28–63
Width, 164–173
Word problems
    choosing the operation for,
        32–33
    drawing a picture, 172–173
    finding the equation of a line,
        254–255
    formulas and, 278
    mental math, 136
    solving quadratic equations,
        240–241
    step-by-step approach to, 40–41
    steps for solving, 46–51
    steps for solving multi-step
        problems, 52–63, 110–111,
        142–143, 304–305
    translating problems into
        algebraic equations, 218–219
    using logical reasoning, 286–287
    with angles, 222–223, 286
    with consecutive numbers,
        220–221, 232–233
    with decimals, 102–103, 110–111
    with fractions, 68–69, 90–91
    with number lines, 212–213
    with patterns, 234–235
    with percents, 130–145
    with perimeter, area, volume,
        170–173
    with right triangles, 312–313
    working backwards, 232–233

X and y-axis, 244
X and y-coordinate, 244
X and y-intercept, 254

CASIO *fx-260SOLAR* Calculator Reference Handbook

When you take the GED Mathematics Test, you will be allowed to use a calculator on Part One of the test. This calculator, which will be provided by the testing center, is the CASIO *fx-260SOLAR*. The information in this handbook is provided to help you use this calculator effectively.

The CASIO *fx-260SOLAR* is a scientific calculator. It has many more keys and functions than you need for the test. The keys that will be most helpful to you are labeled in the diagram below. Throughout this book you have learned basic operations that you can perform with most calculators. This handbook focuses on special features of the GED calculator.

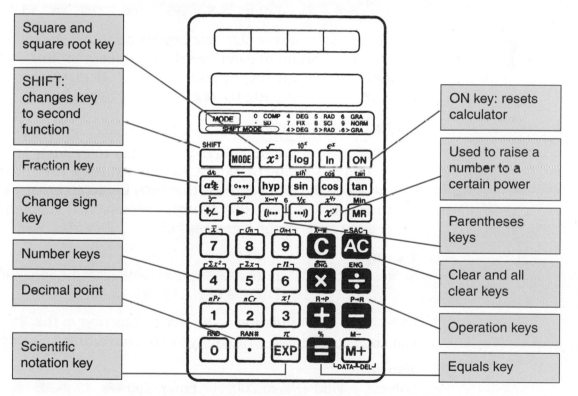

Square and square root key

SHIFT: changes key to second function

Fraction key

Change sign key

Number keys

Decimal point

Scientific notation key

ON key: resets calculator

Used to raise a number to a certain power

Parentheses keys

Clear and all clear keys

Operation keys

Equals key

Getting Started

ON Press the ON key to begin using the calculator. The ON key clears the memory and sets the display to 0. You will see the letters "DEG" at the top of the display window.

AC The "all clear" key clears all numbers and operations from the display. Always press AC or ON when you are ready to start a new problem.

C The "clear" key erases only the last number or operation that you entered. Use this key when you know that you have entered a number incorrectly. Press C, then enter the correct number.

Working with Signed Numbers

Use the ⊞⁺⁄₋ key to change the sign of a number. To enter a negative number, enter the digits of the number first, then press ⊞⁺⁄₋.

Examples

Solve: $6 + (-9)$ Enter: 6 ➕ 9 ⁺⁄₋ 🟰 -3.

Solve: $-5 \times 4 \div (-2)$ Enter: 5 ⁺⁄₋ ✖ 4 ➗ 2 ⁺⁄₋ 🟰 10.

Working with Parentheses

Use the parentheses keys 【⁻⁻ and ⁻⁻】 to enter grouping symbols when an expression contains more than one operation. Put grouping symbols around the operation that must be performed first. Without parentheses, the calculator will always perform the multiplication and division steps first (following the order of operations).

Examples

Solve: $\dfrac{-4 + 6}{-2}$ Enter: 【⁻⁻ 4 ⁺⁄₋ ➕ 6 ⁻⁻】 ➗ 2 ⁺⁄₋ 🟰 -1.

Solve: $5(4 + 7)$ Enter: 5 ✖ 【⁻⁻ 4 ➕ 7 ⁻⁻】 🟰 55.

In the last example, the algebraic expression shows the number 5 next to an operation in parentheses. Remember that this means multiply. To evaluate the expression using a calculator, you must press ✖ before entering the operation in parentheses.

Other Features

π   Use the second function of the **EXP** key to evaluate an expression containing pi. Notice that the symbol π is printed in yellow above the EXP key. Press the **SHIFT** key to access any of the functions printed above the calculator keys. Note that entering 3.14 for pi also results in the correct answer.

Example

Solve: Find 4π.   Enter: 4 ✖ **SHIFT** **EXP** 🟰 12.56637061

Enter: 4 ✖ 3.14 🟰 12.56

%   The percent function is the second function of the 🟰 key. You can enter a percent as written instead of converting it to a decimal.

Example

Solve: Find 45% of 200.   Enter: 200 ✖ 45 **SHIFT** 🟰 90.

Squares and Square Roots

To find the square of a number, you multiply the number by itself. For example, $6^2 = 6 \times 6 = 36$. You can square numbers quickly using the x^2 key on your calculator. You can also perform operations using squares. You will find this feature useful when solving problems involving the Pythagorean Relationship.

Examples

Solve: $8^2 = ?$ Enter: 8 x^2 64.

Solve: $12^2 - 7^2 = ?$ Enter: 12 x^2 $-$ 7 x^2 $=$ 95.

The square root function is the second operation assigned to the square key x^2. To find the square root of a number, enter the number, then press SHIFT and the square key.

Examples

Solve: What is the square root of 225?   Enter: 225 SHIFT x^2 15.

Solve: $\sqrt{256} + \sqrt{81} = ?$

     Enter: 256 SHIFT x^2 $+$ 81 SHIFT x^2 $=$ 25.

Exponents and Scientific Notation

To raise a number to a power other than 2, use the x^y key, where x is the base and y is the exponent. Enter the base, press the x^y key, and enter the exponent.

Examples

Solve: $5^4 = ?$ Enter: 5 x^y 4 $=$ 625.

Solve: $6^3 + 3^5 = ?$ Enter: 6 x^y 3 $+$ 3 x^y 5 $=$ 459.

In scientific notation, a number greater than or equal to one and less than ten is multiplied by a power of ten. Use the EXP key to enter a number written in scientific notation.

Examples

Solve: Express 3.2×10^6 in standard notation.

          Enter: 3.2 EXP 6 $=$ 3200000.

Solve: Express 4.89×10^5 in standard notation.

          Enter: 4.89 EXP 5 $=$ 489000.

To prepare the calculator for use the *first* time, press the ⓞ (upper-rightmost) key. "DEG" will appear at the top-center of the screen and "0." at the right. This indicates the calculator is in the proper format for all your calculations.

To prepare the calculator for **another** question, press the ⓞ or the red (AC) key. This clears any entries made previously.

To do any arithmetic, enter the expression as it is written. Press (=) (equals sign) when finished.

EXAMPLE A: 8 − 3 + 9

> First press (ON) or (AC).
> Enter the following:
> > 8 (−) 3 (+) 9 (=)
> The correct answer is 14.

If an expression in parentheses is to be multiplied by a number, press (×) (multiplication sign) between the number and the parenthesis sign.

EXAMPLE B: 6(8 + 5)

> First press (ON) or (AC).
> Enter the following:
> > 6 (×) [(---) 8 (+) 5 (---)] (=)
> The correct answer is 78.

To find the square root of a number

- • enter the number;
- • press (SHIFT) (upper-leftmost) key ("SHIFT" appears at the top-left of the screen);
- • press (x^2) (third from the left on top row) to access its second function: square root.
  DO NOT press (SHIFT) and (x^2) at the same time.

EXAMPLE C: $\sqrt{64}$

> First press (ON) or (AC).
> Enter the following:
> > 64 (SHIFT) (x^2)
> The correct answer is 8.

To enter a negative number such as −8,

- • enter the number without the negative sign (enter 8);
- • press the "change sign" ((+/−)) key which is directly above the 7 key.

All arithmetic can be done with positive and/or negative numbers.

EXAMPLE D: −8 − −5

> First press (ON) or (AC).
> Enter the following:
> > 8 (+/−) (−) 5 (+/−) (=)
> The correct answer is −3.

Adapted with permission of the American Council on Education.

Answer Sheet

GED Mathematics Test, Part I

Name: _____ Class: _____ Date: _____

○ Pretest   ○ Posttest   ○ Simulated Test

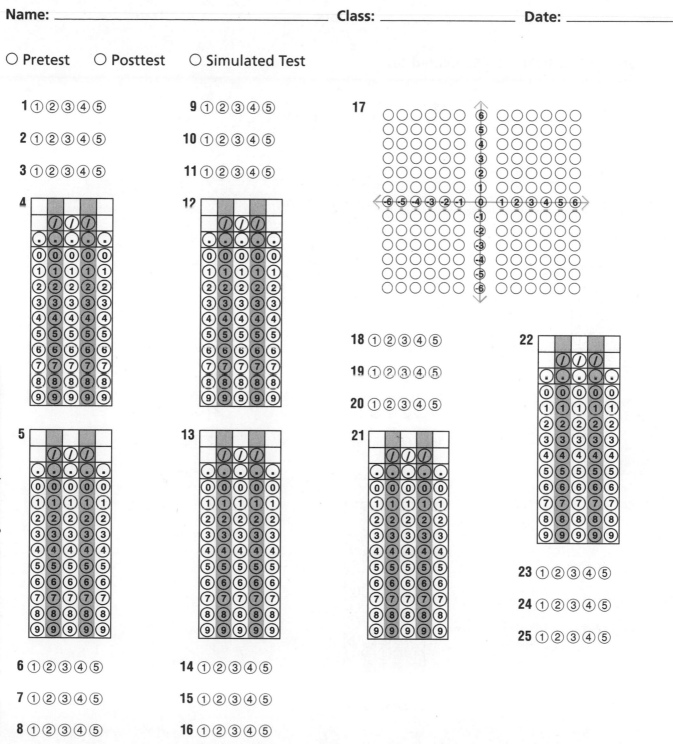

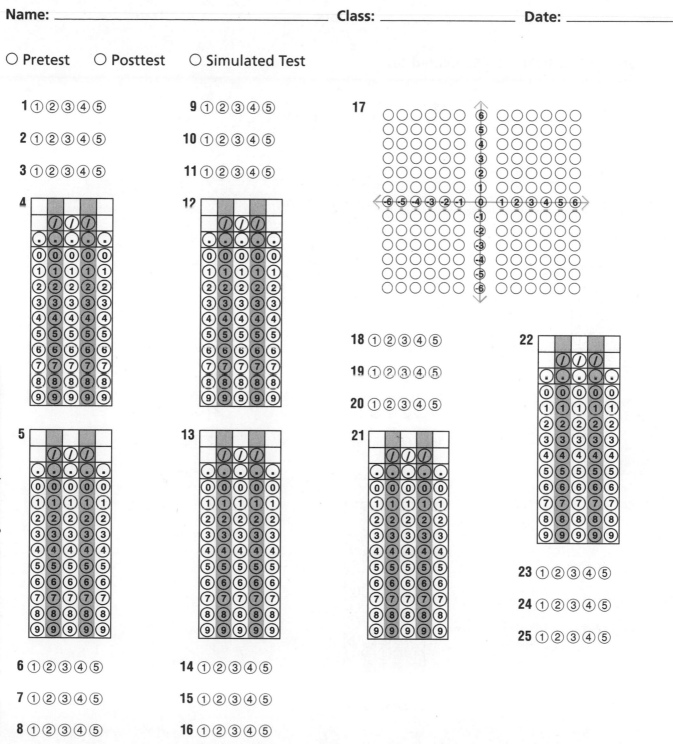

GED Mathematics Test, Part II

Name: _____ Class: _____ Date: _____

○ Pretest   ○ Posttest   ○ Simulated Test

1 ① ② ③ ④ ⑤

2 ① ② ③ ④ ⑤

3 ① ② ③ ④ ⑤

4 ① ② ③ ④ ⑤

5 ① ② ③ ④ ⑤

6

7 ① ② ③ ④ ⑤

8 ① ② ③ ④ ⑤

9 ① ② ③ ④ ⑤

10 ① ② ③ ④ ⑤

11 ① ② ③ ④ ⑤

12

13 ① ② ③ ④ ⑤

14 ① ② ③ ④ ⑤

15 ① ② ③ ④ ⑤

16 ① ② ③ ④ ⑤

17 ① ② ③ ④ ⑤

18

19 ① ② ③ ④ ⑤

20 ① ② ③ ④ ⑤

21 ① ② ③ ④ ⑤

22 ① ② ③ ④ ⑤

23 ① ② ③ ④ ⑤

24 ① ② ③ ④ ⑤

25 ① ② ③ ④ ⑤

Answer Sheet